Accounting Education Research
Prize-winning Contributions

T0383880

An annual prize is awarded for the best paper appearing in *Accounting Education: an international journal,* and this book contains the prize-winning papers for every year from 1992 to 2012.

The journal's primary mission since the first issue was published in March 1992 has been to enhance the educational base of accounting practice, and all the papers in this book relate to that mission. These papers, reporting on research studies undertaken by accounting education scholars from around the world, build on research findings from the broader domain of education scholarship and embrace a wide array of topics including: curriculum development, pedagogic innovation, improving the quality of learning, and assessing learning outcomes. Of particular interest are three themes, each of which runs through several of the papers:

- students' approaches to learning and learning style preferences;
- ethics and moral intensity; and
- innovation within the accounting curriculum.

Accounting educators will find many ideas in the book to help them in enriching their work, and accounting education researchers will be able to identify many points of departure for extending the studies on which the papers report – whether comparatively or longitudinally.

This book is a compilation of papers originally published in *Accounting Education: an international journal.*

Professor Richard M. S. Wilson has devoted his career to boundary-spanning (e.g. as practitioner and professor, across disciplines, and in different locations). For 40 years he has been active nationally and internationally in educational policy-making on the interface of accounting education and training; has worked in more than a dozen countries; has published widely; is the founding editor (and currently Editor-in-Chief) of *Accounting Education: an international journal*; holds two Lifetime Achievement Awards (one specifically for his work in the field of accounting education); and is an Academician of the Academy of Social Sciences.

Accounting Education Research
Prize-winning Contributions

Edited by
Richard M. S. Wilson

LONDON AND NEW YORK

First published 2014
by Routledge
2 Park Square, Milton Park, Abingdon, Oxfordshire OX14 4RN

Simultaneously published in the USA and Canada
by Routledge
711 Third Avenue, New York, NY 10017

First issued in paperback 2015

Routledge is an imprint of the Taylor & Francis Group, an informa business

British Library Cataloguing in Publication Data
A catalogue record for this book is available from the British Library

ISBN 13: 978-1-138-94947-8 (pbk)
ISBN 13: 978-0-415-71146-3 (hbk)

Typeset in Times New Roman
by Taylor & Francis Books

Publisher's Note
The publisher accepts responsibility for any inconsistencies that may have arisen during the conversion of this book from journal articles to book chapters, namely the possible inclusion of journal terminology.

Disclaimer
Every effort has been made to contact copyright holders for their permission to reprint material in this book. The publishers would be grateful to hear from any copyright holder who is not here acknowledged and will undertake to rectify any errors or omissions in future editions of this book.

Dedication

In the setting up and sustained publication of a research-based journal, such as *Accounting Education: an international journal*, any founding editor requires support in the form of a lot of effort on the part of:

- Authors who are willing to submit their papers.
- Referees who have the expertise to review those papers.
- Associate Editors who are able to offer advice on accept/revise/reject decisions.
- Editorial Advisors who have the experience to comment on the journal's progress in pursuing its mission and achieving its aims.
- Staff in the journal's publishing company who work hard to put ideas into print.

This book is dedicated to all those participants in the *College Without Walls* who have helped in ensuring the journal's success in its first 21 years, as reflected in this collection of prize-winning papers.

Contents

CONTENTS

CONTENTS

Citation Information

The chapters in this book were originally published in various issues of *Accounting Education: an international journal*. When citing this material, please use the original page numbering for each article, as follows:

Chapter 1
Purposes and paradigms of management accounting: beyond economic reductionism
Martin Kelly and Michael Pratt
Accounting Education: an international journal, volume 1, issue 3 (September 1992)
pp. 225-246

Chapter 2
From fresher to finalist: a three year analysis of student performance on an accounting degree programme
Susan Bartlett, Michael J. Peel and Maurice Pendlebury
Accounting Education: an international journal, volume 2, issue 2 (June 1993) pp. 111-122

Chapter 3
Teaching ethics in accounting and the ethics of accounting teaching: educating for immorality and a possible case for social and environmental accounting education
Rob Gray, Jan Bebbington and Ken McPhail
Accounting Education: an international journal, volume 3, issue 1 (March 1994) pp. 51-74

Chapter 4
Competence is not enough: meta-competence and accounting education
Reva Berman Brown and Sean McCartney
Accounting Education: an international journal, volume 4, issue 1 (March 1995) pp. 43-53

Chapter 5
Fostering deep and active learning through assessment
Len Hand, Peter Sanderson and Mike O'Neil
Accounting Education: an international journal, volume 5, issue 2 (June 1996) pp. 103-119

Chapter 6

Improving the quality of accounting students' learning through action-oriented learning tasks
Ralph W. Adler and Markus J. Milne
Accounting Education: an international journal, volume 6, issue 3 (September 1997) pp. 191-215

Chapter 7

Exporting accounting education to East Africa – squaring the circle
Patrick J. Devlin and Alan D. Godfrey
Accounting Education: an international journal, volume 7, issue 4 (December 1998) pp. 269-285

Chapter 8

The quality of learning in accounting education: the impact of approaches to learning on academic performance
Peter Booth, Peter Luckett and Rosina Mladenovic
Accounting Education: an international journal, volume 8, issue 4 (December 1999) pp. 277-300

Chapter 9

Identifying and overcoming obstacles to learner centred approaches in tertiary accounting education: a field study and survey of accounting educators' perceptions
Ralph W. Adler, Markus J. Milne and Carolyn P. Stringer
Accounting Education: an international journal, volume 9, issue 2 (June 2000) pp. 113-134

Chapter 10

A study of students' perceptions of the usefulness of case studies for the development of finance and accounting-related skills and knowledge
Sidney Weil, Peter Oyelere, Joanna Yeoh and Colin Firer
Accounting Education: an international journal, volume 10 issue 2 (June 2001) pp. 123-146

Chapter 11

Accountability of accounting educators and the rhythm of the university: resistance strategies for postmodern blues
Russell Craig and Joel Amernic
Accounting Education: an international journal, volume 11, issue 2 (June 2002) pp. 121-171

Chapter 12

A comparison of the dominant meta programme patterns in accounting undergraduate students and accounting lecturers at a UK business school
Nigel Brown
Accounting Education: an international journal, volume 12, issue 2 (June 2003) pp. 159-175

Editor's Introduction

As the founding Editor of *Accounting Education: an international journal* (henceforth *AE*), when setting up the journal in 1991 I was in the fortunate position of being able to specify that its primary aim should be **to enhance the educational base of accounting practice**.

Two years later, as the founding Convenor of the British Accounting Association's first Special Interest Group – on Accounting Education, I suggested that the same mission be adopted for that enterprise, and this was approved.

Over the years which have followed, the common interests of *AE* and the BAA-SIG (which subsequently became the British Accounting & Finance Association's SIG, hence BAFA-SIG) have happily run in parallel in promoting accounting education scholarship and research. This has been evident in, for example:

(a) *AE*'s joint sponsorship of the BAFA-SIG's annual conferences (which have become increasingly international over the years).
(b) The publication of edited papers from BAFA-SIG conferences in dedicated issues of *AE* [including: 4.1 (1995); 5.2 (1996); 7 Supplement (1998); 11.1 (2002); 12.2 (2003); 13 Supplement (2004); 14.4 (2005); 15.3 (2006); 20.3 (2011); 21.6 (2012)].
(c) The BAFA-SIG's sponsorship of a prize for the best paper published in each volume of *AE*.

The electors for (c) have been the members of *AE*'s distinguished Editorial Advisory Board, comprising senior figures from around the world who have expert knowledge of accounting education as a field of intellectual enquiry and of its relevance to improving accounting practice. Neither *AE*'s Editor nor the Associate Editors have had a voice in choosing the best paper each year. The process operates wholly at arm's length from those who undertake reviews and make editorial decisions on submitted manuscripts (regarding accept/revise/reject), and it seems to function very effectively.

There are three specific criteria to guide the electors in making their choices. These are that a paper should have:

- a focus on enhancing the educational base of accounting practice;
- a transferable message which goes beyond institutional or national boundaries; and
- empirical content.

During my 21 years of editing *AE* (1992-2012), there have been 22 BAFA-SIG Best Paper Prizes awarded: in 2006 there was a dead heat and two prizes were awarded. All these papers are included in this book.

Clearly the winning papers have been through several hoops (typically involving a number of reviews – both prior to and following submission, and evaluation by *AE*'s Editorial Advisory Board), so they exhibit scholarly merit. Indeed, whilst the idea for this book was under discussion, and then when the book was under development, the working title for the project was '*AE*'s **Greatest Hits**' !

The geographic distribution of the authors of the prize-winning papers (based on their institutional affiliations at the time of publication of those papers) is as follows:

Australia	12*
New Zealand	9**
Scotland	9
England	6
Wales	4
Ireland	2
Canada	1
Japan	1
South Africa	1
U.S.A.	1
TOTAL	46

*After eliminating the duplication of two authors (Ralph W. Adler and Markus J. Milne) who jointly won the prize twice – in 1997 and again in 2000.

**After eliminating the duplication of one author (Rosina Mladenovic) who won the prize twice – in 1999 and again in 2004.

This distribution shows a concentration of prize winners in Australasia (Australia and New Zealand) on the one hand, and in the British Isles (Scotland+England+Wales and the Republic of Ireland) on the other, but no prize winners have yet emerged from countries in Africa, the Middle East, or South America. Maybe next year?

What about the themes on which the prize-winning papers focus? Using very broad categories, the following pattern emerges:

A. CURRICULUM   6

   Ethics and moral intensity (3)
   Curriculum development and content (3)

B. LEARNING   5

   Approaches to learning (2)
   Learning style preferences (1)
   Active-learning (1)
   Learner-centred approaches (1)

C. PEDAGOGY   4

Use of case studies (1)
Textbooks as cultural artifacts (1)
Concept mapping (1)
Learning portfolios (1)

D. OUTCOMES   4

Students' performance (1)
Competences (1)
Learning outcomes (1)
Plagiarism (1)

E. OTHER   3

Accountability of accounting educators (1)
Meta-programme patters (1)
Exporting accounting education (1)

We can see a broad array of themes across these papers, with some concentration of emphasis on papers dealing with curriculum and learning issues. The key aspects (i.e. inputs, process, outputs, feedback) of a systems model of accounting education are clearly in evidence.

It cannot be assumed with any validity that the papers in this collection, whilst a population in itself, are in any way a representative sample of the contents of *AE* Volumes 1 to 21, but they all contribute towards the challenging aspiration of enhancing the educational base of accounting practice. This is no less important today than it was when Martin Kelly and Mike Pratt won the first BAA-SIG Prize in 1992.

Onwards and forwards!

Emeritus Professor Richard M S Wilson
Loughborough University, U.K.
April, 2013

Purposes and paradigms of management accounting: beyond economic reductionism

MARTIN KELLY and MICHAEL PRATT

University of Waikato, New Zealand

Abstract

Neo-classical economics does not of itself provide an adequate explanation of current management accounting practice and research. Ideas from several other disciplines have been used in an attempt to facilitate a more complete understanding of management accounting. There now exists a multiplicity of 'ways of seeing' management accounting which adds richness to the literature. This paper first describes a number of the current theoretical-paradigmatic approaches, and then offers a typology for understanding them. It is suggested that each of these schools has different insights to offer the study of management accounting and that attempts to privilege one school over another should be avoided. Management accounting is seen as fulfilling a multiplicity of purposes which can only be understood by analysing the actions of the management accounting actors involved.

Introduction

This paper describes alternative schools of management accounting thought and provides a typology for understanding them. It is hoped that it will be of value as an introductory paper in graduate or senior undergraduate courses in management accounting, and to educators who seek an introduction to alternative and emergent perspectives on management accounting. The paper demonstrates that the dominant rational models deriving from neo-classical economics, which have colonized management accounting over many decades, are coming under increasing attack from researchers who ground their theories in political and sociological literatures. It adopts the view that each of these schools has different insights to offer in the study of management accounting. It suggests that management accounting fulfils a range of purposes which can only be understood by analysing the actions of the management accounting actors involved. The proliferation of alternative 'ways of seeing' management accounting suggests that it is both a vibrant and problematic field of study.

Background

Scapens (1988) tells of when, in the early 1970s, a senior professor of accounting advised him against becoming involved in management accounting research. The professor believed that all the interesting problems had been solved. In retrospect it is now clear just how wrong the professor was. Management accounting practitioners cannot even agree on the purpose(s) of management accounting, nor can theorists. Therefore it is impossible to identify and define any problem in a universally acceptable way. However, there is no doubt that there are plenty of problems to be defined and solved; they are witnessed by the plethora of approaches to studying management accounting which has evolved over the recent past (as discussed later).

One can guess at the reasoning underlying the professor's comment. The term 'management accounting' came into common usage about 1950 (Sizer, 1969). Management accounting grew out of cost accounting, but was potentially more widely applicable and more influential than cost accounting. It was grounded in the 'theory of the firm', and thereby in neo-classical economics. This theory argued that if each firm acts to maximize its profitability, then the profitability of the total economy will be maximized. Some economic schools, notably the Cambridge School (Harcourt, 1972), have developed theories which recognize the difference between individual firm behaviour and the aggregate effect on the economy, but their work appears to go unrecognized by 'mainstream' management accounting academics and practitioners. The traditional neo-classical perspective is seductive in that a large measure of self interest is identified with the public good. From that perspective management accountants are perceived as staff members responsible for advising line managers on profit maximization.

Academics who accept this view of the function of management accounting see the problems largely as ones involving mathematical modelling. They have developed stock control models, discounted cash flow models, linear programming models, and decision support techniques, such as monte-carlo simulation. In 1982 a new management accounting textbook, written 'to teach students how to apply analytical reasoning and use formal models when designing and evaluating management accounting systems' (Kaplan, 1982, p. xi), was criticized as 'a cornucopia of techniques, of answers seeking problems' (Choudry, 1983). From the traditional perspective it appeared that, as Scapens' professor had anticipated, the solutions had overrun the problems.

Traditional management accounting theory has accepted that there is a concrete world full of resources. This world can be viewed objectively by anyone (and everyone) who cares to observe it. The role of the management accountant in this world is to aid 'rational' economic decision making. Popular textbooks (for example, Horngren and Foster, 1987; Drury, 1992; Kaplan, 1982) have accepted this perspective and set about describing how to achieve economic, efficient and effective decision making in this 'given' world.

Underlying the traditional, technical approach to management accounting appears to be a premise that, over time, technical progress will bring perfection to rational decision making. However, a belief in inevitable historical progress has now been abandoned by some traditionalists. Notably Johnson and Kaplan (1987) argue that management accounting has not progressed (as a rational decision making tool) for fifty years or more. Furthermore, they argue that recent 'sloppy' application of accounting principles is resulting in 'incorrect' decisions being made based on poor representations of the 'facts' surrounding those decisions. Kaplan and his followers argue that basic management accounting practices must be revisited and (new) procedures must be (re)invented in order that the inexorable progress towards 'true' reporting and 'correct' decision making can (re)commence. Thus Johnson and Kaplan maintain traditional beliefs in a concrete world and the role of accounting in rational decision making. They argue that recent setbacks for management accounting practices in the business environment have been caused by a fall from grace by practitioners. What is now required, they argue, is a return to pure applications of basic principles in order for management accounting practitioners to regain the high ground.

Neo-classical economic theory continues to provide the major element of Kaplan's and most other current management accounting theories, despite numerous critiques concerning its partial and simplistic nature (e.g. Robinson 1961, 1964; Arrington and Francis 1989; Macintosh 1989). Cooper (1980) proffers:

> Within a business context, it is perhaps unsurprising that the techniques that have been developed from neo-classical marginal theory are rarely implemented. Many managers recognise the simplistic and partial nature of the models and therefore have little confidence in the level of their prescriptions (p. 162).

Academics (non-accountants) who were involved in studies of how decisions were being made in organizations in the 1950s noted that the economic model of the firm was inadequate. As early as 1959 Simon reported that the behavioural scientists had identified many of the problems inherent in attempting to explain the organizational decision making process purely in economic terms. He observed that 'The normative micro-economist "obviously" doesn't need a theory of human behavior: he wants to know how people *ought* to behave, not how they *do* behave' (p. 254). He thus chides economists for deductive reasoning which they pursue with no regard as to how the derived theories explain real practices. His plea is for more empirical research. He explains that:

> The growing separation between ownership and management has directed attention to the motivations of managers and the adequacy of the profit maximization assumption. So-called human relations research has raised a variety of issues about the motivation of both executives and employees.... New definitions had to be constructed, by no means as 'obviously' intuitive as simple maximization, to extend the theory of rational behavior to bilateral monopoly and to other bargaining and outguessing situations.... [Often] the equity owners and active managers of an enterprise are separate and distinct groups of people, so that the latter may not be motivated to maximize profits (pp. 256–62).

Simon goes on to attack one of the most fundamental assumptions of neo-classical economics; that is that people are rational profit-maximizing decision makers. He questions several further assumptions. Should the maximization be over the short term or the long term? Must maximization be economic only, or can 'psychic income' be considered (that is where profits are forgone by choice, but not necessarily irrationally)? Note that if 'psychic income' is allowed, then any semblance of objective measurement of maximization is lost. Might it be that the typical manager aims to earn 'satisfactory' profits rather than to maximize profits? If we accept this suggestion it would be more appropriate to speak of satisfying than of maximizing. However, it may be that people are more interested in minimizing 'regret' than in satisfying. Simon defines 'regret' as 'the difference between the reward obtained and that which could have been obtained with perfect foresight' (p. 267). However in some situations, where objectives, inputs and outputs can be well defined, rational profit maximization models may well provide useful insights.

Simon also introduces the concept of 'bounded rationality'. He argues that the business environment is too complex to be understood in its entirety. Business people, when making decisions, are therefore forced to draw artificial boundaries around the decision models. This ploy allows decisions to be made, and justified, provided the nature of the decisions and the boundaries of the decision models are agreed upon. However, individuals may be incapable of identifying all possible options even within their restricted decision models. This inability of individuals to understand the world fully, to identify all possible options and to process all available data, stands in contrast to the all-knowing economic person.

Argyris (1990) takes this notion a step further when he suggests that information is not only complex but may also purposely be distorted by individuals who believe that lack of clarity is necessary for their personal and corporate survival:

> The distortion of the information is taken for granted because it is seen as necessary for the survival of the players as well as the organization (p. 506).

Approaches to the study of management accounting

Despite the considerable number of critiques of neo-classical economics based models, these models still permeate management accounting teaching and text books. There follows a brief summary of various alternative approaches to the study of management accounting which can be identified from the literature.

Decision making approach

This approach follows the work of Simon (1959) and others who see organizations as decision making bodies and attempt to discover how people actually do make decisions within them. It recognizes that people are not necessarily rational (in the sense of rational profit-maximizers), nor do they always have clearly defined goals or complete knowledge and control of their environment. In considering the environment in which organizational decisions are made, it overlaps with the 'markets and hierarchies approach' (see later) and the work of academics such as Williamson (for example see Williamson and Write, 1991).

March and Olsen (1976) introduce the 'garbage can' model of organizational decision making which they believe offers a way of understanding organizations which do not have clearly defined goals, for example universities. They suggest that decisions are made largely by chance meetings of four independent factors: problems, solutions, participants and choice opportunities. They suggest that problems and solutions often arise independently from each other and this results in solutions looking for problems as well as the more normal view of problems seeking solutions. Participators come and go and only chance attaches them to any particular decision opportunity. A decision will be made when the four streams of garbage come together within the organization in the right mix.

Systems/Cybernetic approach

This approach was developed originally in the engineering sciences. A system is 'an entity consisting of two or more components or subsystems that interact to achieve a goal' (Cushing, 1982, p. 13).

> ... Systems are wholes which lose their essential properties when taken apart. Therefore, they are wholes which cannot be understood by analysis. This realization, in turn, gave rise to synthetic or systems thinking. Three steps are involved in this process. First, a thing to be understood is conceptualized as a part of one or more larger wholes, not as a whole to be taken apart. Then understanding of the larger containing system is sought. Finally, the system to be understood is explained in terms of its role or function in the containing system. Analysis

of a system reveals its structure and how it works; it yields know-how, not understanding. It does not explain why a system works the way it does. Systems thinking is required for this. . . . (Churchman and Ackoff, 1957, p. 8, reproduced in Holzer, 1980).

Wiener (1948), an early champion of the cybernetic approach, defined cybernetics as 'the science of control and communication in the animal and the machine'. Cushing describes it as 'the theoretical study of feedback control systems' (1982, p. 79). Tocher (1970, 1976) developed a cybernetic control model. Probably the currently most influential writer in this area is Stafford Beer who has published extensively.

Feedback allows systems to regulate themselves provided that they have a defined goal. A simple example often used to illustrate the application of a cybernetic system is a thermostat. Scholars of the behaviouralist school would assert that people do not act like thermostats.

Although the systems approach is interesting it is a difficult approach to pin down. The following quotation from Otley is apposite:

> A wide variety of approaches can be included under this heading [systems view], ranging from relatively classical foundations of responsibility accounting (McNally, 1980; Parker, 1977; Buckley and McKenna, 1972) to the application of cybernetics (Otley and Berry, 1980) or general system theoretic models (Amey, 1979; Ansari, 1979; Lowe and Tinker, 1977). Nevertheless, the area is a theoretical minefield, with accounting being viewed as anything from the major means by which managers achieve organizational control to a minor irrelevance used only to rationalize decisions taken for other reasons (in Scapens *et al.*, 1984, pp. 128–129).

Contingency theory approach

At its simplest, contingency theory states that there is no one best way to structure organizations in order to achieve optimum results. The theory was pioneered by Woodward (1965) working on organization theory. Contingency theory was developed at a time when the classical management theorists were attempting to discover an organizational panacea. 'Students and managers were taught how to design formal structures by applying principles of Scientific Management, derived from the work of people like Fayol, Urwick, Follett and Taylor' (Dawson and Wedderburn 1980, p. xiv).

The theory, which denies universal solutions, has been applied widely to explain the diversity of organizational phenomena. However, the theory has not been very successful in determining which factors are contingent on which others, or showing how the evolution of organizations will affect their optimal structures (Wood, 1979).

The theory entered the accounting literature in the late 1970s (see for example Hayes, 1977). It provided a popular framework for management accounting researchers in the early 1980s, but interest in it appears to have declined, probably for the reasons given above.

Agency theory approach

Agency theory evolved during the 1970s, was very influential in the 1980s, and still has a large following. The strongest support for the theory has come from the Rochester School (Jensen and Meckling, 1976). It is based on the premise that individuals operate within a system of competitive markets but that they attempt to maximize their own utility rather than that of the firm. The theory addresses the problem that managers in the 1950s and 1960s were observed not to be attempting to maximize their firms' profits in the way that the conventional theory of the firm suggested. It still attempts to explain organizational behaviour in terms of maximization, and therefore it is open to many of the same criticisms as the traditional approach to management accounting (e.g. psychic rewards, satisfying only). However, it does directly address the problem of conflicts of interest which can arise. It explores conflicts between the providers and managers of capital. It provides convincing explanations for some observed behaviour, for example the search for 'public interest' arguments to support preconceived positions. Nevertheless, it is only selectively convincing and denies the possibility of economically irrational or altruistic behaviour. Jensen and Meckling (see for example, 1976) and Watts and Zimmerman (see for example, 1986) have been influential on the establishment of this school of accounting thought.

Markets and hierarchies, or organizations failures framework, or transactions cost approach

This approach takes the basic unit of analysis as a transaction, whereas in agency theory all transactions are governed by contracts. Under this approach hierarchies supplant markets as a means of arranging transactions when the costs of writing and enforcing contracts in a market setting become too high. The object of developing organizations is to minimize contracting costs. Labour costs are internalized, thereby reducing transaction costs and encouraging co-operation.

Individuals are assumed to be selfish maximizers, and ready to contract dishonestly (opportunistically) if it benefits them to do so. They are assumed to have only bounded rationality. This approach has been used to provide an explanation for the evolution and present working of our modern economies. Johnson (1983) describes how it can provide an explanation for the emergence of management accounting systems. The approach grew from work completed by Coase (1937) which has been developed by many academics over the years, but notably by Chandler (1977) and Williamson (1964).

Information–economics approach

This approach maintains that the major task for management accountants is 'the designing of efficient information systems serving certain managerial needs among which *performance control* and the *simulation* of alternative scenarios predominate' (Mattessich, 1980, pp. 217–18). It recognizes that information itself is a 'good' with an economic value, and suggests that cost-benefit analysis can be used to determine whether it is worth producing additional information. The impact of computers from the 1960s onwards has been a driving force behind the increased interest in cost efficient information systems. Generally the assumption is made that the purpose of producing additional information for managers is to enable them to employ rational decision models and to maximize profitability.

Societal approach

The societal approach to accounting takes in a broad spectrum of thinkers. The common thread of their writings is that accounting is both socially created, and helps to create (reinforce) societal values. The development of accounting is therefore too important to be left to the vagaries of the market place. Thought must be given to how accounting information is used in society, and how it should be used. This approach therefore demands a statement of normative values on which suggested accounting models can be built. Societal accounting is concerned with why accounting information is generated, disclosure models (Mathews, 1988), and how accounting information is used. It does not take the purpose of accounting as given, but it tends to accept the need for accounting as given.

Ramanathan (1976) suggests that the approach rests on two basic premises: (1) the solutions to many of the current social problems require the active and willing involvement of private business organizations, (2) to the extent that measured corporate profits are an inadequate guide to policy, a broader scheme of corporate performance is necessary.

Followers of the societal approach (for example, Gray *et al.*, 1988) believe accountants must ensure that there is adequate disclosure of information to enable individuals outside the firm to take part in informed debates about what the firm's social goals should be. Subsequently the disclosed information must be sufficient to allow outsiders to measure how well the agreed goals are being achieved. Basically those adopting this approach to accounting believe that accounting has the potential to be a socially useful discipline and thought must be given as to how it can best be developed to this end.

Critical approach

The critical school contains several different approaches to the study of accounting, the common theme of which is criticism of the conventional wisdom of accounting. While the societal accounts tend to argue for a 'better' use of accounting within society in order that society can be 'improved', the critical theorists see accounting as one of the causes of many of the problems we experience within society and question the need for accounting in its current (or indeed any) form.

Political economy or Marxist studies such as those of Tinker (1985) target their criticisms at the role of accounting preserving capitalist and class based systems of domination. Foucauldian based critical theory, by contrast, calls for historical research that would negate the bases of meta-theories such as capitalism or Marxism, (for example Hoskin and Macve, 1988; Hopwood, 1987). Macintosh (1989) explains that:

> Foucauldian inspired studies trace accounting practices to specific historical archaeological sites and reconstruct them in terms of the social and academic, political discursive practices of that era (p. 41).

Deconstructionists who follow Derrida, such as Arrington and Francis (1989) and Macintosh (1989), dismiss metaphysics in general and meta-theories such as capitalism and neo-classical economics in particular. They attack the current privileging of positivism and empiricism. Other critical theorists have adopted the radical humanism of Habermas (e.g. Chua, 1986; Laughlin, 1987) or symbolic interactionism (e.g. Roberts and Scapens, 1985; Hines, 1988).

At the root of each approach lies a belief in a different set of value judgements which provide differing opinions as to what the purpose of accounting research should be and what the purpose of accounting should be. The debate on these matters is basically an ethical one and is outside the scope of this paper.

Current management accounting theory and practice

Hopper and Powell (1985) adopt Burrell and Morgan's (1979) multiple paradigm model in an attempt to explain the diversity of theoretical perspectives. They follow Kuhn in suggesting that at any point in time there is likely to be a dominant paradigm. Market based positivism can be regarded as that paradigm as at this time, but its dominance is coming under more frequent attack in the academic literature. The emergence of several new journals in recent years evidences this trend; *Accounting, Organizations and Society* (1976); *Journal of Accounting and Public Policy* (1982); *Accounting, Auditing and Account-*

ability (1988); *Behavioural Accounting* (1989); *Critical Perspectives in Accounting* (1990); *Management Accounting Research* (1990); *Accounting Education* (1992).

An holistic understanding of the current state of management accounting theory and practice is difficult to achieve, partly because of the multiplicity of approaches which overlap and interweave with each other. Currently there are two major strands in management accounting thought, economic theory and organization theory (the latter of which is taken to encompass social and human relations approaches). Since looking outside economics, management accounting theory has embraced ideas from organization theory. Many of these ideas were, in turn, imported into organization theory from such diverse disciplines as psychology, politics, sociology, history, anthropology, linguistics, philosophy, and mathematics. More recently attempts have been made to import ideas directly from other social sciences into accounting, for example Tomkins and Groves (1983) who follow Burrell and Morgan (1979). These approaches reflect the emphases which their followers place on various aspects of management accounting, but they are not mutually exclusive. Many publications make use of more than one approach:

> This paper has attempted to supplement contingency theory by drawing on the related disciplines of agency theory and the markets and hierarchies literature, (Tiessen and Waterhouse, 1983, p. 265).

But there is some rivalry between supporters of the various approaches for example:

> Viewing management accounting as an organizational rather than an economic phenomenon provides an alternative explanation of management accounting, richer than that of agency theory (Hayes, 1983, p. 242).

The insights provided by the various approaches are, in our opinion, best thought of as complementary, rather than in rivalry. Each group may have an approach which best fits its purpose, but what is the purpose of management accounting?

It is suggested that management accounting is used for multiple purposes, and that this may help to explain the multiplicity of approaches to studying it. A problem encountered in pursuing the question is that professed purposes may differ from actual purposes, which in turn may differ from what 'ought' to be the purpose. Management accountants may state that their purpose is to maximize the profits of their firms, whereas actually they may limit their everyday activity to satisfying the perceived information needs of managers. Perhaps they 'ought' to be ensuring that the maximum benefits to society are being procured from the use of the assets entrusted to their firms. We follow Mattessich in believing that

> Such notions as cost, efficiency, improvement, and so forth, can be defined and measured correctly only when comprehending the norms and goals of the larger social system in which management and its accounting frame is embedded, (1980, p. 211).

Boland (1989) uses Morgan's 'metaphors of organizations' to demonstrate the way in which the claim to rational pre-eminence of neoclassical economics is shown to be insufficient to understand the organizational purposes of accounting. He challenges the pre-eminence of any one way of 'seeing':

> Morgan (1986) explores his images of organization in a way that leaves each intact, important and believable. He carefully avoids denigrating or idolizing any of them, for he recognizes that each image is ideologically informed and none alone is adequate for representing organizations.

Organizations are all these things and more simultaneously. Morgan's message is to break from our slumber of absolutist, singular theories of organization and to become skilled at more subtle reading than any 'school' or 'contingency' model currently provides us (p. 600).

Chua (1988) lists eight 'roles' or 'purposes' for accounting which are identified in Burchell *et al.* (1980):

a. a rational/instrumental role	e. a political/bargaining role
b. a symbolic role	f. a legitimate/retrospective rationalizing role
c. a ritualistic role	g. a disciplinary role
d. a mythical role	h. a repressive/dominating/ideological role.

Chua follows Burchell *et al.* in writing about the 'role' of accounting. The concept of role is grounded firmly in the Weberian structuralist tradition and embodies the idea that 'roles' have an existence separate to and apart from the actors who fulfil them (Biddle, 1986). This paper takes the view that actions need to be construed in the light of the intentions of the actors. The term 'purpose' is therefore preferred, implying purposeful action, and is adopted hereafter.

Some personal observations

We believe that the economic perspective has wrongly been allowed to dominate in explaining the purpose of management accounting. We provide below two narratives from our personal experiences which support the claim that neoclassical economic theory is inadequate to provide a holistic understanding of management accounting practice.

The first narrative concerns the workings of a stock model in a company which carried out engineering work throughout Scotland. The engineers had traditionally had most power within the organization but numerous efficiency drives had the effect of transferring significant power over to the accounting function. A new head of supplies was appointed. He introduced a stock control model based on Pareto distributions of historical usages. Traditionally the engineers had been able to carry stocks consistent with no possibilities of production difficulties. The stock control model indicated that large cuts in stock holding levels were possible with minimal adverse effect on the engineers' operating efficiency. These were carried out over many months and the new head of supplies earned himself a good reputation. Having shaved off the 'fat' easily, he then attempted to refine his model and identify the rational need for further cuts in stock holdings. His model began to indicate that one area stock centre should be closed and its users sourced from the adjacent area store. This was too much for the engineers who felt that their status was being undermined. They began to oppose the head of supplies in any way that they could although they never attacked the logic of his model which was generally perceived as sound. The head of supplies realized that he had pushed the engineers too far and revised the parameters of his model to show that slightly higher stock levels were justified and all stores should remain open. He was conscious that without a certain amount of goodwill from the engineers he would not be able to push through a number of other changes which he perceived as necessary. By not pursuing the logic of his model the head of supplies was able to (1) retain a reasonable working relationship with the engineers, (2) keep the credit for the considerable good work in stock cutting which he had already achieved, (3) keep the controls which were already in place operating smoothly, (4) gain a widespread reputation as a 'man who was willing to listen to reason' and (5) obtain the thanks of the chairman who avoided the task of having to act as mediator in an unpleasant dispute. This example illustrates that accounting information where objectives are 'certain' – in this case to minimize stock costs, consistent with overall operating efficiency (alternatively one might conclude that objectives are never certain) – can still succumb to political pressure when the greater system in which the model is operating is considered. Thus a neoclassical economic interpretation of the situation is inappropriate.

The second narrative relates to our experiences in capital budgeting, which lead us to conclude that discounted cash flow techniques are often used to justify decisions that have already been made. When minimum internal rates of returns on projects are required it is a simple matter to change the starting assumptions so that the desired rate can be exceeded. We have been personally associated with several organizations where such practices were common, in some cases the manipulations were for the benefit of the subsidiaries' parent companies, in others they were for the benefit of the external lenders. Once a project has been accepted there is a need for all concerned to show that it is successful. Head office management does not want to admit that it was deceived or that its investment criteria are rationally simplistic. We are not alone in observing this phenomenon; Bower (1970) suggests that the practice of using capital budgeting procedures to justify decisions, rather than aid decision making, is commonplace. Similarly a study by Wildavsky (1976) found that data collected during a pollution control study were used to rationalize intended actions rather than to help in the choice of the best pollution control strategy.

Purposes of management accounting

If one accepts that the purpose for which management accounting is used may not be to maximize profits, then it is appropriate to consider what purposes management accountants may perceive themselves to be fulfilling. The possible purposes for management accounting listed in Chua (1988) will be considered in turn.

A rational/instrumental purpose

Adherents to the decision making approach to management accounting recognize that managers are capable of pursuing objectives with only bounded rationality (Simon, 1957). However, it was Simon et al. (1954) who suggested three purposes for management accounting, i.e. scorecard, problem solving, and attention directing. These were taken up by Horngren (1962) in his, now classic, management accounting textbook which has given a rational/instrumental introduction to several generations of management accounting students. The systems approach, contingency theory approach and information economics approach to management accounting are all relevant in a rational/instrumental environment.

The rational/instrumental literature assumes that managers have a defined objective (usually profit maximization) and it offers rational approaches to consider how best to achieve the objective. However, the rational/instrumentalist approach to accounting based on profit-maximization which is put forward in most textbooks, does not appropriately reflect the practice of accounting within organizations. Kelly and Pratt (1988) provide a literature survey which identifies ten areas where gaps have been recorded between practice and textbook representation of management accounting. These areas include; the given decision making environment; the influence of qualitative factors on decision outcomes versus the use of quantitative models; behavioural considerations of accounting use; the use of computer systems; and a general appreciation of the 'role' of the management accountant within organizations.

The realization that the rational/instrumental approach to accounting, based on profit-maximization which informs our textbooks does not appropriately reflect the practice of accounting within organizations, is important; if areas of practice are not, or may not be, based on economically rational profit maximization, then studies of accounting practice should attempt to understand and explain what does happen, rather than assume complete economic rationality. Some suggested alternative purposes for management accounting are considered below.

A symbolic purpose

Feldman and March (1981) describe symbolic purpose as involving the use of accounting as a signalling device to others in society. Accepting this purpose will often produce different perceptions from those which arise when one accepts accounting as the provider of 'face value' input to the control or decision making process. To understand 'signalling' it is necessary to be clear about the distinction which can exist between actual motivations and perceived motivations. For example, office juniors may decide to go to college and study in the evenings in order that their employers perceive them as individuals who are keen to better themselves, thus increasing their chances of promotion. Many observers may believe the office juniors are going to college to learn about bookkeeping or office administration. Whilst such skills may be acquired they are not the immediate purpose of the studying.

The symbolic purpose of accounting is to signal to others inside and outside the organization that decisions are being taken rationally and that managers in the organization are accountable (to whom and for what are other much larger questions). It is accepted that individuals possess only bounded rationality, and that because of risk and uncertainty things will not always turn out as envisaged. However, it is recognized that western culture demands the exercise of free choice in an overtly rational manner. Those who fail to comply with this norm are transgressing societal expectations. At the extreme it is more important to be perceived as being rational, than actually to be rational. Accounting can be used as a symbolic 'proof' of rationality. For an in depth study of rationality, see Northcott (1991).

Feldman and March suggest that some seemingly strange human behaviour may contain a coding of intelligence that is not adequately reflected in engineering models. They suspect that decision makers are not systematically stupid. They believe that:

> A static analysis of information use, however, is likely to be misleading. The symbolic significance of any activity depends on the social norms within which it is undertaken. Information is significant symbolically because of a particular set of cultures. These beliefs include broad commitments to reason and to rational discourse (p. 184).

Thus decision makers who use accounting for symbolic purposes may be pursuing the most rational options they believe available within their environment. Other decision makers may construct 'optimum' decision making systems which allow them to make the 'best' decisions with the lowest information gathering costs, but if their colleagues perceive them as liable to make decisions without undertaking sufficient ground work, their standing and influence in the organization may wane. Furthermore symbolism has its own dynamic. The office juniors who go to college do learn skills which allow them to progress and perhaps perform further symbolic acts which will further benefit them in the long run. The decision maker who continually demands more information may, through serendipity, discover appropriate information for the required purpose; brute logic may not disclose this information.

The premise that management accounting has a symbolic purpose acknowledges the use of accounting in regulating relationships between various interested parties. Both the agency theory and the transaction cost approaches attempt to explain why individuals in organizations behave, and use accounting information, in the way that they do. Although these approaches have grown out of a rational/instrumental approach to understanding, it is possible that supporters of both will find it useful to consider the symbolic purpose of management accounting. Symbolic misrepresentation of information, and the recognition of such misrepresentations, are necessary skills for successful maximizers:

> Most information that is generated and processed in an organization is subject to misrepresent-ation. Information is gathered and communicated in a context of conflict of interest and with consciousness of potential decision consequences. Often information is produced in order to persuade someone to do something. It is obvious that information can be an instrument of power, and substantial recent efforts to refine the economics of information and the economics of agency focus on managing the problems of strategic unreliablity of information . . . a decision maker would be curiously unwise to consider information as if it were innocent (Feldman and March, 1981, pp. 176–7).

The symbolic purpose of accounting is recognized by radicals, but criticized, and used to help to explain why society is not functioning as it should.

A ritualistic purpose

Gambling (1987) tells of a primitive African people, the Azande. Many of them have been converted to Christianity but beliefs in witchcraft still flourish: 'It seems as if the Azande have no trouble in saying something to the effect: "Maybe that's how things work in other parts of the world, but with us, there is witchcraft to consider as well"' (p. 320). Such ingenuous reasoning may make us smile, but if a totally rational Vulcan were to comment on the sophistication of our own mental agility, s/he may find us equally ingenuous. Gambling believes that many problems we encounter defy rational solutions; thus absolute truth lies beyond human comprehension. At the limits of rational thought there is religion and attendant rituals. Western society has created a 'sort of secular religion' (p. 319) out of accounting, which has its associated rituals.

There are many logical contradictions in the way that western societies manage their resources. Gambling suggests that such contradictions have to be ritualized in order for them to be allowed within society. The ritual of passing tax laws serves to show the people that, at face value, the rich are being asked to pay considerably more tax than the poor. This helps to maintain the perception of an egalitarian society. If the matter rested there it would result in wealthy people leaving the country, or evading taxes and breaking the law. Instead the accountants are consulted by the rich. They perform a series of rituals, which may lead to court rituals, in the process of negotiating with the revenue services. The result is lesser taxes for the rich. However, the rich are generally not allowed to avoid taxation altogether as the rituals do not allow this. The whole 'game' depends on the players knowing the rules and performing within the parameters fixed by the rituals. The rituals may appear logically unnecessary, but they obscure what is happening and they make it more difficult to change what is happening. Because of this they protect the current fabric of society.

Use of accounting for such purposes is an anathema to those who have a radical approach to accounting. Radicals may regard rituals as being a current purpose of management accounting whereby 'bad' practices are legitimized, and attack it on those grounds (Tinker, 1985). Societal accountants, like Gambling, see a need to study and understand such rituals so that the changes in society which they perceive are necessary, can be facilitated. Those employing an open system approach, contingency theory, or a decision making approach, may find it useful to consider the possible effect of the rituals on their models, but consideration of accounting as ritual does not normally find its way into the literature of these approaches. Those approaching accounting via agency theory or information economics will probably consider the possible use of accounting for ritualistic purposes irrelevant to their work, as they assume rationality (in the profit-maximizing sense) both of individuals, and in markets.

A mythical purpose

Myths may, and do in the sense used here, help to construct an illusion of reality. If one is prepared to accept some myths unquestioningly, it can become possible to understand and explain much of 'reality'. Marx believed accounting 'provided a means of mystifying rather than revealing the true nature of the social relationships which constitute productive endeavour' (Burchell *et al.*, 1980). This purpose is one which those using the radical approach to accounting are keen to demonstrate. Those who adopt a systems approach to the study of accounting recognize that it may help their understanding if they impose artificial (mythical) boundaries on the system being studied. Accounting itself works within such mythical boundaries. What is a company, where does it start and end? (Williamson and Write, 1991). Can organizations have *an* objective when they are made up of numerous subsidiary units and individuals? Hines (1988) gives an interesting insight into how accounting is used to construct reality by paralleling Castenda's (1970) anthropological study of his search for reality through the drug influenced culture of the Yaqui Indians. This purpose of accounting serves to reduce some complex inter-relationships within society to dimensions which are comprehensible to decision makers. It recognizes, and offers some solution to, the bounded rationality of decision makers.

Often the cost of appearing to be rational is not worth the effort. However, modern managers, accountants and academics are expected to display rationality. Given the problematic nature of the notion of rationality, they may be forced (or find it convenient) to resort to myths to demonstrate 'truly logical' decisions. The pressure for this overt rationality, comes not only from other individuals in society, but also from the individuals themselves; they too are culturally conditioned. Meyer (1983) describes the problem well:

> The point is that legitimating rationality is necessary for survival, but so is coming to terms with reality. For proper functioning, it is often useful to keep the two partly separate, so that the legitimating rules do not constrain practical activity and so that the exigencies of partial activity do not expose the ongoing anarchy (March and Olson, 1976) and lead to loss of legitimacy. Much organizational administration, therefore, consists of keeping one's head in the sand (p. 237).

'Keeping one's head in the sand', involves such ploys as (1) issuing tight budgets with clear accounting rules, but not policing them too closely so that flexibility is made possible within a framework of rationality, (2) discarding accounting information which appears to conflict with desired strategies and seeking 'better' accounting information, (3) 'allowing' unofficial contingency funds to be secreted away so that when rationality fails, practicalities can be dealt with.

The mythical purpose is similar to the ritualistic purpose. The difference lies in that the ritualistic approach appears to imply the manipulation of the system by those who control the rituals, whereas the mythical purposes serves those who have to 'make sense', and be seen to 'make sense', of the resultant environment. To a certain extent it is the rituals which, as they evolve, provide the myths or make it necessary that new myths are invented. An extreme example is where those with power perform rituals to 'justify' a war, although it may possibly not be a 'rational' war. It may be that the common soldier's lot is unlikely to improve much whatever the outcome of the war, but officers will create myths with which to motivate themselves and the common soldiers. As with the ritualistic approach, it is unlikely that those who approach accounting from an economic perspective would recognize the significance of this purpose of accounting.

A political/bargaining purpose

There have been numerous references to the political/bargaining role of accounting, for examples see Chua (1988). Many ways may be chosen to achieve political power or a bargaining advantage and some will involve the use of account information. Burchell *et al.* suggest, more cautiously:

> Rather than creating a basis for dialogue and interchange in situations where objectives are uncertain or in dispute, accounting systems are often used to articulate and promote particular interest positions and values ... [Organizations] are arenas in which people and groups participate with a diversity of interests with political processes being an endemic feature of organizational life. ... The design of information and accounting systems are also implicated in the management of these political processes. ... The powerful are helped to observe the less powerful but not vice versa (p. 17).

Note that Burchell *et al.* require that uncertain objectives are a prerequisite for the use of accounting for political purposes. Where objectives are certain they believe that accounting can be used to produce answers (for example using a stock control model) or learning assistance (the use of 'what if' models). We cannot accept this distinction; it is inconsistent, for example, with our experience of the stock model in Scotland (see earlier).

Those who follow a traditional economic approach to accounting will not seek to study the political purpose of accounting because, 'Neoclassical theory appeared to take economics out of the political arena by denying value judgements and by avoiding questions of income distribution' (Scapens, 1988, p. 14). However, the theories of agency and transaction costs which have developed out of economics have much to say on conflicts of interest. Researchers using these approaches may be able to offer explanations of observed political usage of accounting information, which has largely escaped study until recently. Those approaching accounting from a societal or radical perspective will be interested in studying its political usage, as will those who approach accounting from perspectives such as decision making, contingency theory and systems theory.

A legitimating/retrospective rationalizing purpose

Burchell *et al.* give several examples of this use of accounting which are contained in the literature:

Much of the irrationality of life in modern organizations arises because the organization itself must maintain a rational corporate persona: We find planners and economists who will waste their time legitimizing plans that have already been made, accountants to justify our prices, and human relations professionals to deflect blame from our conflicts. Life in modern organizations is a constant interplay between the activities that we need to carry on and the organization accounts we need to give (Meyer and Rowan, 1978).

A second example is taken from Pringle (1978) who describes how the pioneering work on cost-benefit analysis by British officials in mid-nineteenth century India was oriented towards mystifying rather than deciding what was to be done. It is interesting to note that these early cost-benefit studies took into account not only the direct benefits which investments returned to the British, but also the benefits of the projects to the infrastructure of Indian society; they represent an early attempt at societal accounting.

The behaviour described in these two examples may not be as irrational as it at first appears. If we accept bounded rationality and an inability of individuals to fully understand complex decision situations then we must move away from the economists' rational decision models. It is doubtful that the normal decision making approach in reality is the formulation of goals, identification of problems, listing of possible solutions and the exercise of rational choice of solutions based on clearly defined criteria. When faced with overpowering complexity, some individuals may take no action, whereas others may adopt the ploy of taking some (any) action and then awaiting feedback; they may adopt a heuristic (trial and error) approach to the problem. The feedback may help to identify all the variables and if properly analysed – which involves looking backward – may allow the formulation of parameters within which future attempts to solve similar problems may be made. Such an approach may be made less rational if, for political reasons, the overriding purpose of analysing the feedback becomes the justification of the original decision. Indeed the need to defend the first decision may lead to the framing of inferior rules for making future decisions, because the rules must then be seen to accommodate the first 'blind' attempt at solving such problems. Nevertheless, the risks of stepping into the unknown may well be less than the risks of not doing so, and there is a body of literature which attempts to explain why some organizations are seen to operate in terms of action preceding rationalization.

Cooper *et al.* (1981), in an attempt at understanding many real life situations, criticize the traditional economic and organizational theories and instead suggest that many organizations should be perceived as organized anarchies which house a 'technology of foolishness'. Weick (1969) suggests that it is impossible to obtain consensus in an organization unless there is something tangible around which consensus can occur. Thus actions may take place as a means of attempting to reach a consensus. In this way actions may precede the setting of goals – the goals supplying the retrospective framework for justifying past actions. It may be that budgeting is a way of discovering goals rather than a way of achieving them because the exercise often involves looking backwards prior to extrapolation into the future

The budget process may be interpreted as a means for justifying past actions and making them appear sensible to both the actor and others (Cooper *et al.*, 1981, p. 181).

As suggested earlier our society demands that rationality is exhibited when choice is exercised, although widely accepted notions of rationality will often not stand up to rigorous logical analysis. The demand for exhibited rationality places accounting in a central position, because the ritual of auditing, and the myth of 'true and fair' give it rational credibility. Such is the power of accounting within our society that, 'Organizations without formal accounting systems are vulnerable to claims that they are negligent, irrational, illegitimate and even unnecessary', (Cooper et al., 1981, p. 184). However, the use made of accounting systems may not always be what it is perceived to be by many lay people:

> Sophisticated accounting systems may, rather than aiding efficiency itself, instead provide a dramatization of efficiency, maintaining a rational facade and thus providing a respectable identity for an organization (Cooper et al., 1981, p. 181).

Are organizations generally perceived as demonstrating rational behaviour? Here is an area ripe for research. What perceptions of business efficiency do the general public hold, how do they obtain these perceptions and how important is the public in moulding the development of management accounting? Does the need to rationalize actions inhibit the development of 'better'[1] management accounting techniques? How much decoupling of ideas about how business works, and news reports of what is going wrong with the relationship between business and society is necessary, and possible, if current beliefs (and society) are not to be destabilized?

Those who approach accounting from a societal or radical perspective have much interest in the above questions. Authors from the agency theory and transaction cost theory schools have not written widely on retrospective rationalization, except to note that agents will control accounting information flows to ensure that all reporting is consistent with their best economic interests. Authors from the information economics approach do not concern themselves with the past rationalization uses for accounting. Those interested in understanding how organizations work, who use the systems, contingency and decision making approaches to accounting, are likely to be concerned with how the need for retrospective rationalizing is to be incorporated into their models.

A disciplinary purpose

'Discipline' is used here in the manner suggested by Foucault (1977). Discipline is embedded in routine social practices within modern power-knowledge regimes and serves to constrain individuals by generally subtle means. Knights and Collinson (1987) state that '[Accounting] has the effect of disciplining workers in such a way that they voluntarily extend the power of their own subjection' (p. 459). This purpose of accounting is part of a greater political purpose '[One must be prepared] to understand accounting not simply as a set of neutral techniques but as a *political process*, one effect of which is to lend support to management's control over labour', (Knights and Collinson, 1987, p. 457, emphasis added).

Cooper et al. (1981) are also aware of the disciplinary power which accounting has within organizations:

> The structure and elements of an accounting system help to create the appropriate and acceptable ways of acting, organizing and talking about issues in organizations. Accounting systems are a significant component of the power system in an organization. . . . Power is

---

[1] And how do we know what is 'better' anyway?

not just overt behaviour forcing or coercing others to comply with a particular individual or way of doing things. It also has a latent or unobservable aspect, such as the ability to control agendas and issues (p. 182).

Anyone studying how organizations work ought to be aware of such a potential use of accounting information. For those adopting the social and radical approaches such a purpose of management accounting will be a principal focus of study.

A repressive/dominating/ideological purpose

This suggested purpose for accounting is couched in such terms that it will have appeal only to those approaching accounting from a radical, or possibly a societal, perspective. However, it should be noted that others (notably the transaction cost theorists) are likely to be interested in understanding the relationship between shareholders, managers, capital and labour. In non-radical literature the words 'repression', 'domination', and 'ideology' may give way to such terms as 'control', 'management' and 'objectives' and allow for discussion in the same areas. The words chosen above, however, are in common usage in the critical literature, wherein scholars are critical of the present uses of accounting systems (for example see Neimark and Tinker, 1986). Let us then explore their arguments. A key theme in this literature is 'alienation'. It is a sociological term that describes the differentiation and separation of individuals from society. They are alienated in that they are perceived as not sharing a common humanity with other groups within society; they are isolated. The process of giving soldiers' and prisoners' numbers to identify themselves is alienating. It separates the individual from his/her past personality and cultural roots; 'It simultaneously renders him [sic] accessible to accounting procedures – a *thing* to be reckoned rather than a *person* to be reckoned with', (Cherns, 1978, p. 105). Marxists believe that the stratification of society based on the capitalist system results in widespread alienation. The demise of feudalism and the emergence of capitalism resulted in bonded labour being released from the land and becoming a commodity that is freely bought and sold in the market. Labour is worthless unless it is mixed with capital in the correct proportions. In order to allow such mixing it is necessary to organize jobs so that they can be done by transitory labour with limited skills. This labour can easily be 'moved on' when not required but can equally easily be reunited with capital if marginal demand increases. Such an objective does away with the need for craft and skilled work people, who consequently are devalued in society and become more dependent on the managers of capital. Managers of capital are assessed, not in terms of how well they serve the labour 'entrusted' to them, but now well they protect the interests of the absentee owners of the capital. In order to serve this end it is necessary for managers to initiate a surveillance system to monitor the performance of the de-skilled labour. The accounting discipline evolved quickly to fill this purpose as the overseer's tool. In organizations people will be given payroll numbers or other numerical identifiers and these will often be used in the construction of accounting systems and feature in accounting reports. Thus accounting itself tends to dehumanize and alienate individuals.

Conclusion

Accounting is part of the political process within society (Harris and Spannier, 1987). The economically rational models of profit maximization which have greatly influenced the development of western society are not of themselves adequate to explain the place of accounting within society, because they ignore the socio-political forces which also have helped shape both society and accounting practices. Alternative approaches to understanding management accounting in its political and organizational contexts have been presented. Any attempt to privilege one approach above another is problematical, and can be grounded only in value judgements. Nevertheless, neo-classical economic theories will prove to be robust because of the pervasive web of neo-classical economic thought which is rooted in western society.

If academics accept that their economic environments and inherited value systems as given, they may well have some success at explaining the purpose of accounting, and developments in accounting, in those terms. It must be realized, however, that they are attempting to understand the workings of a system which does not conform entirely to the principles of economic rationality enunciated in textbooks. It is not surprising that the behaviour of pragmatic business people sometimes fails to conform with the narrowly defined characteristics of rational economic people.

To add to the confusion, Simon's concept of bounded rationality suggests that even if the system itself were rational, the ability of individuals to make rational decisions within the system would be less than perfect. The economic approach to management accounting now appears to have shifted to agency theory and transaction costs. These newer theories attempt to explain the breaches of neo-classical theory by recognizing that individual motivations will not aggregate to accord with organizational goals as suggested by neo-classical analysts.

The literature surveyed made no mention of any empirical studies of public perceptions of the purpose of accounting and economic thought, but we suspect that most western citizens expect firms to maximize profits and believe that it is in the public interest for firms to do so. It appears to be a culturally accepted axiom that the best way of ensuring that the capital in society is used most productively, is to demand that it generates maximum 'profits'. The meaning of the word 'profit' and the way that it is measured are poorly understood, but accountants are generally trusted to ensure that 'profits' are truly and fairly reported. We suggest that the average citizen does not bother too much with the actual profits reports which are made available within society, but believes that press and politicians, with help from accountants, will ensure fair play. However, as Mattessich (1980) points out, profit can only be defined once the norms and goals of the larger social system, and an accounting framework, have been defined. Current models of profit ignore in large measure, for example, the effect of entity activities on human capital, and the effects of the entity on the environment.

Accounting has a plurality of observable purposes and approaches, some of which have been illustrated in this paper. It is argued that each approach can offer insights into what accounting does, but that each will lead its protagonists towards the assumption of differing purpose(s) for management accounting. Furthermore, if the purposes of management accounting are 'known' to an individual then this knowledge will lead the individual to favour certain approaches to understanding the activity. Thus combinations of purposes and approaches are mutually supportive. Different approaches and purpose will be used at different times by different people. Several purposes may be present at the same time and each will become apparent if all available approaches are utilized. Actual purposes are best studied in their organizational contexts.

Acknowledgements

Our thanks go to Dr M. H. B. Perera for his comments on an earlier draft, and to the anonymous reviewers of *Accounting Education* for their insightful guidance.

References

Amernic, J. H. (1985) The roles of accounting bargaining, *Accounting, Organizations and Society*, **10**, (2), 227–53.

Amey, L. R. (1979) Towards a new perspective on accounting control, *Accounting, Organizations and Society*, **4** (4), 247–58.

Ansari, S. L. (1979) Behavioral factors in variance control: Report on a laboratory experiment, *Journal of Accounting Research*, **4** (3), 189–221.

Arrington, C. E. and Francis, J. R. (1989) Letting the chat out of the bag, *Accounting, Organizations and Society*, **14** (1/2), 1–28.

Argyris, C. (1990) The dilemma of implementing controls: The case of management accounting, *Accounting, Organizations and Society*, **15** (6), 503–11.

Baiman, S. (1988) *Agency Research in Managerial Accounting: A Second Look*, Management Accounting Research Conference: The University of New South Wales.

Bell, P. W. (1988) *Accounting as a Discipline for Study and Practice: What Content? . . . In Whose Interest?* Canberra: AAANZ Conference Paper.

Biddle, B. J. (1986) Recent developments in role theory, *Annual Review of Sociology*, (**12**), 67–92.

Boland, R. J. and Pondy, L. R. (1983) Accounting in organizations: A Union of Natural and Rational Perspectives, *Accounting, Organizations and Society*, **8** (2/3), 223–34.

Boland, R. J. (1989) Beyond the objectivist and the subjectivist: Learning to read accounting text, *Accounting, Organizations and Society*, **14** (5/6), 591–604.

Bower, J. L. (1970) *Managing the Resource Allocation Process*, Homewood: Irwin.

Buckley, A. and McKenna, E. (1972) Budgetary control and business behaviour, *Accounting and Business Research*, Spring, pp. 137–50.

Burchell, S., Clubb, C., Hopwood, A., Hughes, J. and Nahapiet, J. (1980) The roles of accounting in organizations and society, *Accounting, Organizations and Society*, **5** (1), 5–27.

Burrell, G. and Morgan, G. (1979) *Social Paradigms and Organizational Analysis*, London: Heinemann.

Castaneda, C. (1970) *The Teachings of Don Juan: A Yaqui Way of Knowledge*, Harmondsworth: Penguin.

Chambers, R. J. (1980) The myths and science of accounting, *Accounting, Organizations and Society*, **5** (1), 167–80.

Chandler, A. D. (1977) *The Visible Hand: The managerial revolution in American business*, Boston, Mass.: Harvard University Press.

Cherns, A. B. (1978) Alienation and accountancy, *Accounting, Organizations and Society*, **3** (2), 105–14.

Choudry, N. (1983) Book review, *Accounting and Business Research*, Autumn, pp. 92–3.

Chua, W. F. (1986) Radical developments in accounting thought, *Accounting Review*, LXI (4), 601–32.

Chua, W. F. (1988) *Accounting as a Social Practice in Organizations – A Critical Review*, Management Accounting Research Conference: The University of New South Wales.

Churchman, C. W. and Ackoff, R. L. (1957) *Introduction to Operations Research*, New York: Wiley.

Coase, R. H. (1937) The nature of the firm. *Economica*, November, pp. 386–405.

Cooper, D. (1980) Discussion of towards a political economy of accounting, *Accounting, Organizations and Society*, **5** (1), 161–6.

Cooper, D. J., Hayes, D. and Wolf, F. (1981) Accounting in organized anarchies: Understanding and designing accounting systems in ambiguous situations, *Accounting, Organizations and Society*, **6** (3), 175–91.

Cushing, B. E. (1982) *Accounting Information Systems and Business Organizations*, Massachusetts: Addison-Wesley.

Dawson, S. and Wedderburn, D. (1980) *Introduction, Industrial Organization* (2nd edn), Oxford University Press.

Drury, J. C. (1992) *Management and Cost Accounting* (3rd edn), London: Chapman & Hall.

Fayol, H. (1949) *General and Industrial Management*, London: Pitman.

Feldman, M. S. and March, J. G. (1981) Information in organizations as signal and symbol, *Administrative Science Quarterly*, **26**, 171–86.

Foucault, M. (1977) *Discipline and Punish: The Birth of the Prison*, London: Allen Lane.

Friedman, M. (1953) *Essays in Positive Economics*, University of Chicago.

Gambling, T. (1987) Accounting for rituals, *Accounting, Organizations and Society*, **12** (4), 319–29.

Gray, R. H., Owen, D. L. and Maunders, K. T. (1988) Corporate social reporting: Emerging trends in Accountability and the Social Contract, *Accounting, Auditing and Accountability Journal*, **1** (1), 6–20.

Harris, I. and Spannier, R. (1987) Accountability: Answerability and liability, *Journal for the Theory of Social Behaviour*, **6** (3), 253–9.

Hayes, D. C. (1983) Accounting for accounting, *Accounting, Organizations and Society*, **8** (2/3), 235–40.

Hayes, D. C. (1977) The contingency theory of management accounting, *The Accounting Review*, **52** (1), 22–39.

Harcourt, G. C. (1972) *Some Cambridge Controversies in the Theory of Capital*, Cambridge University Press.

Hills, F. S. and Mahoney, T. A. (1978) University budgets and organizational decision making, *Administrative Science Quarterly*, **23**, 454–6.

Hines, R. (1988) Financial accounting: In communicating reality, we construct reality, *Accounting, Organizations and Society*, **13** (3), 251–62.

Hopper, T. and Powell, A. (1985) Making some research into the organizational and social aspects of management accounting: A review of its underlying assumptions, *Journal of Management Studies*, vol. 22, no. 5, pp. 429–65.

Hopper, T., Story, J. and Wilmott, H. (1987) Accounting for accounting: Towards the development of a dialectic view, *Accounting, Organizations and Society*, **12** (5), 437–56.

Holzer, H. P. (Ed) (1980) Management accounting 1980. *Proceedings of the University of Illinois Management Accounting Symposium*, Department of Accountancy, University of Illinois.

Hopwood, A. G. (1987) The archaeology of accounting systems, *Accounting, Organizations and Society*, **12** (3), 207–34.

Norngren, C. T. (1962) *Cost Accounting: A Managerial Emphasis*, Englewood Cliffs, New Jersey: Prentice-Hall.

Horngren, C. T. (1987) *Cost Accounting: A Managerial Emphasis*, 6th edn, Englewood Cliffs, New Jersey: Prentice-Hall.

Hoskins, K. W. and Macve, R. H. (1988) The genesis of accountability: The West Point connections, *Accounting, Organizations and Society*, **13** (1), 37–73.

Jensen, M. and Meckling, W. H. (1976) Theory of the firm: Managerial behavior, agency costs and ownership structure, *Journal of Financial Economics*, October, pp. 305–60.

Johnson, H. T. (1983) The search for gain in markets and firms: A review of the historical emergence of management accounting systems, *Accounting, Organizations and Society*, **8** (2/3), 139–46.

Johnson, H. T. and Kaplan, R. S. (1987) *Relevance Lost*, Boston: Harvard Business School Press.

Kaplan, R. S. (1982) *Advanced Management Accounting*, Englewood Cliffs, New Jersey: Prentice-Hall.

Knights, D. and Collinson, D. (1987) Disciplining the shopfloor: A comparison of the disciplinary effects of managerial psychology and financial accounting, *Accounting, Organizations and Society*, **12** (5), 457–77.

Kelly, M. and Pratt, M. J. (1988) *The Gaps Between Theory, Current Practice and Best Practice in Management Accounting*, Canberra: AAANZ Conference Paper.

Kuhn, T. S. (1970) *The Structure of Scientific Revolutions* (2nd edn), Chicago University Press.

Laughlin, R. C. (1981) On the nature of accounting methodology, *Journal of Business Finance and Accounting*, **8** (3), 329–51.

Laughlin, R. C. (1987) Insights into the nature and application of a critical theoretic methodological approach for understanding and changing accounting systems and their organizational contents, *Accounting, Organizations and Society*, **12** (5), 479–502.

Lowe, E. A. and Tinker, T. (1977) *New Directions for Management Accounting*, Omega, pp. 173–83.

McGregor, D. (1960) *The Human Side of Enterprise*. New York: McGraw-Hill.

Macintosh, N. B. (1989) *Accounting and Deconstruction: A Postmodern Strategy for 'Reading' Accounting*, Working Paper Queen's University, Kingston.

McNally, G. M. (1980) Responsibility accounting and organizational control: Some perspective and prospects, *Journal of Business Finance and Accounting*, **7** (2), 165–82.

March, J. G. and Olsen, J. P. (1976) *Ambiguity and Choice in Organizations*, Bergen: Universitetsforlaget.

Mathews, M. R. (1988) *Social Accounting Models – Potential Applications of Reformist Proposals*, Massey University Discussion Paper, No. 64.

Mattessich, R. V. (1980). Management accounting, past, present and future. In Holzer, H. P. (Ed), *Management Accounting 1980*, pp. 209–40. University of Illinois.

Mayo, E. (1945). *The Social Problems of An Industrial Civilization*. Boston: Harvard University Press.

Meyer, J. W. (1983) On the celebration of rationality, *Accounting, Organizations and Society*, **8** (2/3), 235–40.

Meyer, J. and Rowan, B. (1978) *The Structure of Educational Organizations*, in M. W. Meyer *et al.* (eds). *Environments and Organizations*, San Francisco: Jossey-Bass.

Morgan, G. (1986) *Images of Organization*, Beverly Hills: Sage.

Neimark, M. and Tinker, T. (1986) The social construction of management control systems, *Accounting, Organizations and Society*, **11** (4/5), 369–95.

Northcott, D. N. (1991) Rationality and decision making in capital budgeting. *British Accounting Review*, **23**, 219–233.

Otley, D. T. and Berry, A. J. (1980) Control, organization and accounting. *Accounting, Organizations and Society*, **5** (2), 231–44.

Parker, L. (1977) A reassessment of the role of control in corporate budgeting. *Accounting and Business Research*, Spring, pp. 135–43.

Perera, M. B. H. and Mathews, M. R. (1987). *The Interrelationship of Culture and Accounting with Particular Reference to Social Accounting*, Massey University Discussion Paper, No. 59.

Pfeffer, J. and Salanick, G. R. (1974) Organizational decision making as a political process, *Administrative Science Quarterly*, 131–51.

Porter, B. (1988) *The Social Role of the External Auditor – A Conceptual Framework*. Massey University working paper.

Ramanathan, K. V. (1976) Toward a theory of corporate social accounting, *The Accounting Review*, **51** (3), 516–28.

Roberts, J. and Scapens, R. (1985) Accounting systems and systems of accountability – understanding accounting practices in their organizational contents, *Accounting, Organizations and Society*, **10** (4), 443–56.

Robinson, J. (1961) Prelude to a critique of economic theory, *Oxford Economic Papers*, pp. 7–14.

Robinson, J. (1964) *Economic Philosophy*, Harmondsworth: Penguin.

Scapens, R. W., Otley, D. T. and Lister, R. J. (1984) *Management Accounting, Organizational Theory and Capital Budgeting*, London: Macmillan.

Scapens, R. W. (1988) *Management Accounting – Research Practice. A Review of the Practice of Research*, Canberra: AAANZ Conference Paper.

Sennett, R. and Cobb, J. (1977) *The Hidden Injuries of Class*. Cambridge University Press.

Simon, H. A., Guetzkow, H., Kozmetsky, G. and Tyndall, G. (1954) *Centralization v. Decentralization in Organizing the Controller's Department*, New York: Controllership Foundation.

Simon, H. A. (1957) *Administrative Behavior* (2nd edn), New York: Macmillan.

Simon, H. A. (1959) Theories of decision making in economics and behavioral science, *The American Economic Review*, June, 233–83.

Sizer, J. (1969) *An Insight into Management Accounting*, Harmondsworth: Penguin.

Spicer, B. H. (1978) Accounting for Corporate Social Performance: Some Problems and Issues, *Journal of Contemporary Business*, **7** (1), 151–170.

Taylor, F. W. (1911) *The Principles of Scientific Management*, New York: Harper & Row.

Tinker, A. M., Marino, B. D. and Neimark, M. D. (1982) The normative origins of positive theories: Ideology and accounting thought, *Accounting, Organizations and Society*, **7** (2), 167–200.

Tinker, T. (1980) An empirical illustration of the Cambridge controversies, *Accounting, Organizations and Society*, **5** (1), 147–60.

Tinker, T. (1985) *Paper Prophets*, New York: Praeger.

Tinker, T. (1988) Panglossian accounting theories: The science of apologising in style, *Accounting, Organizations and Society*, **13** (2), 165–89.

Tiessen, P. and Waterhouse, J. H. (1983) Towards a descriptive theory of management accounting, *Accounting, Organizations and Society*, **8** (2/3), 251–67.

Tocher, K. (1970) Control, *Operations Research Quarterly*, June, vol. 21, no. 1, pp. 159 80.

Tocher, K. (1976) Notes for discussion on control, *Operations Research Quarterly*, June, vol. 27, no. 1, pp. 231–9.

Tomkins, C. and Groves, R. E. C. (1983) The everyday accountant and researching his reality, *Accounting, Organizations and Society*, **8** (4), 361–74.

Vimer, J. (1927) *Adam Smith and Laissez Faire. Adam Smith, 1776–1826: Lectures to Commemorate the Sesquicentennial of 'The Wealth of Nations'*. Reprinted 1966. New York/Augustus M. Kelley.

Watts, R. L. and Zimmerman, J. L. (1986) *Positive Accounting Theory*, Englewood Cliffs, New Jersey: Prentice-Hall.

Weber, M. (1942) *The Theory of Social and Economic Organization*, New York: Free Press.

Weick, K. E. (1969) *The Social Psychology of Organizing*, Reading: Addison Wesley.

Wiener, N. (1948) *Cybernetics*, Cambridge Mass: MIT Press.

Wildavsky, A. (1976) Economy and environment/rationality and ritual: A review essay, *Accounting, Organizations and Society*, **1** (1), 117–29.

Williamson, O. E. (1964) *The Economics of Discretionary Behavior: Managerial Objectives in a Theory of the Firm*, Englewood Cliffs N.J.: Prentice-Hall.

Williamson, O. E. and Write, S. G. (1991) *The Nature of the Firm's Origins, Evolution and Development*, New York: OUP.

Wood, J. (1979) A reappraisal of the contingency theory of organizations, *Journal of Management Studies*, 334–54.

Woodward, J. (1965) *Industrial Organization*, Oxford University Press.

From fresher to finalist[1]: a three year analysis of student performance on an accounting degree programme

SUSAN BARTLETT, MICHAEL J. PEEL
and MAURICE PENDLEBURY

Cardiff Business School

Abstract

This paper reports the results of a longitudinal study of the determinants of student performance on undergraduate accounting degree examinations. The educational background, demographic characteristics and financial/investment characteristics of a group of undergraduate students were determined in an attempt to explain differences in student performance in both first year and third year examinations. The results indicate that few of these background variables had a significant impact on examination performance and that the best predictor of third year performance was in fact performance in the first year examinations.

Introduction

Given the pressures on universities to attempt to maintain the quality of teaching in the face of increasing student numbers and a declining level of funding per student, it is likely that there will be less opportunity for faculty to know the strengths and weaknesses of students on an individual basis. Small group tutorials or seminars which enabled differences in student ability to be identified at an early stage are already a thing of the past on most university accounting courses. In consequence, therefore, perhaps the only way to explain variations in current student performance and predict future performance will be to rely on the statistical analysis of overall student data.

This study extends earlier work by Peel *et al.* (1991) and Bartlett *et al.* (1992) and attempts to analyse the performance of students specializing in accounting throughout the three year period of an undergraduate degree programme. The students used for the study were drawn from those who enrolled for either single or joint honours accounting degree programmes at the University of Wales College of Cardiff in October 1989. At the very beginning of their first year these students (together with students enrolled for economics

---

[1] On a UK university degree programme, a 'fresher' is a first year student and a 'finalist' is a final year student.

and management studies degree programmes) undertook a short multiple choice test of basic accounting and financial understanding and at the same time completed a question-naire about their educational and personal background.[1]

Of the 212 students who took part in this test a total of 69 intended to specialize in accountancy and of these, 46 (67%) were identified for analysis over the first year of the degree programme.[2] The performance of this group of 46 students in first year assessed tests and examinations was analysed by Bartlett *et al.* (1992). In this paper the results of a subsequent analysis of the third (final) year examination performance of this group of students is reported. The main purpose of this paper is to examine whether a range of variables (attributes) pertaining to: students' education; gender; demographic factors; prior study of accounting/business studies; and students' financial/investment character-istics, influenced student performance in undergraduate accounting examinations. More specifically, we examine the intertemporal consistency of the potential explanatory variables on student examination performance over the three years of the undergraduate accounting degree programme.

Of the 46 accounting specialists that are identified in the first year only 39 remained by the third year.[3] The results of this group of 39 students in the initial basic test of financial understanding, the first year end-year examinations and the third year examinations form the basis of the analysis. The university examinations used for the purpose of this study were the core subjects of financial accounting and management accounting that were taken at the end of both the first and third years.

The paper also shows the relationship between performance in the initial test and the subsequent university examinations during the three years of the undergraduate programme. In the empirical results section of this paper the first year financial accounting and management accounting examinations are referred to as FAEX1 and MAEX1 respectively, the third year financial accounting and management accounting examinations are referred to as FAEX3 and MAEX3 respectively, and the initial test is referred to as TEST. Details of the background variables that were obtained from the initial test and included in the analysis as potential explanatory variables are provided in Appendix 1.[4]

Evidence from previous research

There have been a number of studies which have attempted to explain relative performance in university (undergraduate) accountancy examinations.

Studies in the US by Baldwin and Howe (1982) and Bergin (1983), found that university students who had studied accountancy at high school had a superior performance initially

[1] See Peel *et al.* (1991) and Bartlett *et al.* (1992) for details of the questions contained in the multiple choice test (TEST), the scoring method used and the background variables included in the questionnaire.
[2] At the time the students completed the multiple choice test of basic financial understanding and the questionnaire about their educational and personal background, no attempt was made to identify the individual respondents. It was felt that the anonymity of the exercise would help to minimize any 'anxiety' that the student may have had about taking part. The steps that were then taken to identify those individual students used for further analysis throughout the three years of the degree programme are reported in Bartlett *et al.* (1992).
[3] The reason only 39 of the 46 students could be included in this analysis is because 2 students withdrew before the final year and there were 5 cases of students missing one or more of the university examinations.
[4] Of the wide range of background variables used in this study, only those for which 5 or more observations were recorded are reported in Appendix 1.

in university accounting courses, but this early superiority diminished over time and had been completely eroded by the end of the first year.

Schroeder (1986), in a further study based on US data, found that students with one year or less of prior tuition in accounting performed at a superior level in the first college examination only, there were no significant differences in subsequent examinations. However, students with more than one year of accounting study prior to attending university were found to be performing at a significantly higher level in all stages of the course.

A somewhat contradictory study by Eskew and Faley (1988), also based on US data, found that the study of accounting at high school had a significant impact throughout the first college year. In addition, they found that a student's academic ability, past and present academic performance, previous exposure to related subjects (*eg*, mathematics and statistics) and variables proxying effort/motivation all had a significant and positive impact on examination performance.

A UK study by Mitchell (1985) found that students with a school accounting qualification only performed at a superior level in the *computational* aspects of university examinations in accountancy. Mitchell (1988) extended his earlier study to examine the effects of students' numerical skills (based on a student's high school mathematics grade) on examination performance. A statistically significant positive relationship was found between students' high school grades and performance in the quantitative aspects of their first year examinations.

Keef (1988), in a New Zealand study, examined the effects of the prior study of accounting, mathematics, economics and English. An advantage appeared to be gained on the first level accounting course by having undertaken previous study in economics, though this was most marked in respect of the management accounting section of the course. The previous study of mathematics also had a significant positive impact on the management accounting section of the course, but for the course as a whole, its effect was negligible. Prior tuition in accounting had no significant impact on course performance, nor did the previous study of English. In a later study, Keef (1992) examined whether the *amount* of prior study of accountancy conferred any advantage on first level university performance in accounting, and found that there was no advantage to be gained from having one *or* two years of prior study, results inconsistent with those of Schroeder (1986).

Peel *et al.* (1991), in a UK study, compared the performance of a group of first and third year students in a multiple choice test of basic financial understanding. The test was taken by first year BSc econ. students and third year accounting specialists in their first lecture of the academic year. In addition to the test, both groups of students completed a questionnaire which elicited details of a wide range of background and educational variables and these were used in a multivariate analysis to establish the determinants of student performance in the test. It was found that possession of an 'A' level[5] accounting

---

[5] The terms 'A' and 'O' level refer respectively to the advanced level and ordinary level stages of the General Certificate of Education (GCE). GCE 'O' level (replaced now by the General Certificate of Secondary Education [GCSE]), and GCE 'A' level are the principal tests of pre-university educational attainment in the British educational system. GCE 'O' level (now GCSE) is typically taken after two years of secondary school/high school study at the age of about 16, and GCE 'A' level is typically taken after a further two years of study at the age of about 18. However, both 'O' and 'A' level qualifications are often taken by much older individuals by attending further education courses, evening classes, or through distance learning programmes etc. The 'O' level and 'A' level qualifications are usually an important requirement for entry onto a degree programme at a British university.

qualification and previous residence in the south eastern part of the UK had a significant positive impact, and overseas student status a significant negative impact, on first year performance, but none of these variables had a detectable impact on third year student performance.

However, in Bartlett *et al.*'s (1992) extension of the Peel *et al.* (1991) study, it was found that both the first and third year students who had an 'A' level accounting qualification achieved a superior performance in the test of basic financial understanding. This study also analysed the subsequent performance of the first year students in assessed tests and examinations in accounting subjects and found that performance in the initial test of financial understanding was a poor predictor of students' first year performance. Their results suggested that the best predictor of performance in first year university examinations in accountancy was the relative performance in the earlier end of term assessed tests.

Although the results of the extant literature are not wholly consistent, the evidence would, on balance, seem to point to the prior study of accounting conferring only a temporary advantage on performance in accounting examinations at university.

A number of other studies on undergraduate performance in accountancy examinations have tested the impact of gender. However, these studies have produced conflicting results. For example, Fraser *et al.* (1978); Hanks and Shivaswamy (1985); Mutchler *et al.* (1987); and Tyson (1989) all found that female students outperformed their male counterparts. On the other hand, studies by Lipe (1989) and Doran *et al.* (1991) failed to detect any evidence of a gender effect.

Empirical results

In this section we outline the results of our empirical analysis. The first section reports the results of a univariate analysis of the impact of the various potential explanatory variables (see Appendix 1) on student performance in the test and in university accounting examinations. The second section provides additional empirical evidence in a multivariate context. The final section presents empirical results on the degree of association between student performance in accountancy exams throughout their period of study.

Univariate results

Table 1 presents an analysis of the binary explanatory variables, whereas Table 2 reports the correlation coefficients of the non-binary explanatory variables with student performance.

So far as educational factors are concerned, Table 1 reveals that there are few significant relationships between student performance and students' educational attributes. Except in respect of the initial test, where students who possessed an 'A' level or an 'O' level in accountancy, on average, outperformed those without these qualifications, the prior study of accountancy (at 'A' or 'O' level) did not appear to confer any significant advantage on students in either their first year examinations (MAEX1, FAEX1), or their final examinations (MAEX3, FAEX3).[6]

---

[6] As previous studies (*eg*, Mitchell 1985 and 1988) have shown that the quantitative and qualitative nature of an examination paper can be important, it might be helpful to indicate the structure of the third year financial accounting (FAEX3) and management accounting (MAEX3) examinations. FAEX3 contained 2 computational and 1 essay type question in section A, and 1 computational and 2 essay type questions in section B. Students were required to answer 2 questions from each section. MAEX3 contained 5 computational questions and 4 essay type questions, and students were required to answer 2 computational and 2 essay type questions.

Table 1. Test and first and third year examination performance average score of students analysed by the variables specified

Variables	FAEX3 %	MAEX3 %	FAEX1 %	MAEX1 %	TEST %
Educational					
SELECT = 1	56.6	62.1	64.0	56.1	49.5
SELECT = 0	58.3	63.9	65.7	58.2	47.2
ACCOUNT-O = 0	62.6	63.4	64.9	57.7	45.1
ACCOUNT-A = 1	56.0	62.6	69.0	59.6	64.9*
ECON-O = 1	58.8	62.4	62.9	51.3**	52.4
ECON-O = 0	57.7	63.9	66.1	59.7	46.3
ECON-A = 1	60.8***	65.3	68.1***	61.3**	51.8
ECON-A = 0	55.1	61.8	62.5	54.1	43.4
BUSINESS-O = 1	65.8**	69.6*	68.4	63.2	62.4
BUSINESS-O = 0	56.8	62.7	64.9	57.0	45.5
MATHS-A = 0	59.0	64.1	66.7	59.1	44.9**
MATHS-A = 0	57.4	65.0	61.4	56.0	68.0
Fin./Invest.					
SHR EVER = 1	58.7	67.2**	65.6	52.9	52.9
SHR EVER = 0	57.8	62.5	65.3	59.2	46.1
SHR NOW = 1	56.6	66.6***	64.0	51.3***	51.4
SHR NOW = 0	58.3	62.9	65.7	59.2	46.9
BLD SOC = 1	56.7	62.8	64.3	56.5	48.2
BLD SOC = 0	59.5	64.4	66.7	59.2	47.1
POST = 1	57.8	63.2	65.9	59.1	55.6**
POST = 0	58.2	64.0	64.9	56.6	40.2
BANK = 1	58.2	64.9	67.6	58.6	46.4
BANK = 0	57.8	62.2	63.1	56.9	49.1
INV-OTHER = 1	53.2	60.2	60.0	53.3***	56.0
INV-OTHER = 0	58.8	64.2	66.4	58.6	46.2
CHEQUE = 1	56.3	65.3	64.5	58.3	45.5
CHEQUE = 0	59.5	61.9	66.2	57.3	49.8
CASH CARD = 1	59.4	64.9	64.9	58.8	45.9
CASH CARD = 0	55.5	61.1	66.3	56.0	50.9
CREDIT CARD = 1	51.0*	63.0	66.4	57.0	60.8
CREDIT CARD = 0	59.0	63.6	65.2	57.9	45.8
General					
GENDER = 1	56.6	63.3	65.4	57.1	49.6
GENDER = 0	61.4	63.5	63.5	58.9	36.5
CAREER = 1	57.4	62.8**	65.2	56.9	51.3**
CAREER = 0	61.0	67.7	66.5	62.3	29.3

(Continued)

Table 1. (*Continued*)

Variables	FAEX3 %	MAEX3 %	FAEX1 %	MAEX1 %	TEST %
CAREER-ACC = 1	57.8	63.1	65.2	57.2	50.4
CAREER-ACC = 0	58.7	65.6	66.1	60.4	35.4
ACCOUNTS-EXP = 1	60.5	64.3	66.1	56.5	44.7
ACCOUNTS-EXP = 0	57.0	63.3	65.1	58.3	48.9
REGION = 1	58.7	65.1	63.4	55.2	40.0
REGION = 0	57.8	63.1	66.0	58.5	50.0

*, **, ***, Indicates significant difference between means at the 1%, 5% and 10% statistical significance levels respectively (two-tailed Student's t-test).

Table 2. Pearson's correlation coefficient: explanatory variables with performance measures

	AGE	SCORE-O	SCORE-A	INV-NUMBER	FIN-NUMBER
TEST	0.17	−0.20	−0.05	0.23	−0.04
FAEX1	−0.09	0.05	0.07	−0.04	−0.04
MAEX1	−0.17	0.18	0.15	−0.23	0.07
FAEX3	−0.27***	0.12	0.29***	−0.18	−0.07
MAEX3	−0.26***	0.06	0.10	0.05	0.22

***, Indicate's Pearson's correlation coefficient [R] is significant at the 10% statistical significance level (two-tailed test).

In contrast, students who possessed an 'A' level in economics, outperformed their fellow students, on average, in all examinations (and in the test), and significantly so in respect of MAEX1, FAEX1, and FAEX3. However, the prior study of economics at (the lower) 'O' level, does not exhibit a similar influence on examination performance. Indeed, students who possessed an 'O' level in economics appeared on average to significantly underperform in the first year management accounting examination (MAEX1).

It is also interesting to note that those students who held an 'O' level in business studies outperformed those students without this qualification in the test and in all examinations – but only significantly so in respect of their third year financial accounting examination (FAEX3).

A point of further interest is that students who had obtained an 'A' level in Mathematics, did not, on average, significantly outperform students without this qualification in any of the accounting examinations – although they appeared to underperform in the test. In addition, the type of secondary school attended by a student (SELECT) did not appear to impact significantly on student performance in any examinations or the test.

Turning to the investment and financial variables, Table 1 reveals that, in general, few variables appeared to have a significant impact on student performance. In respect of the shareholding variables, students who had ever owned shares (SHR EVER), or who currently owned shares (SHR NOW), performed at a significantly higher level, on average, in the third year management accounting examination (MAEX3). In contrast, however, students currently holding shares (SHR NOW) appeared to significantly underperform in the first year management accounting examination (MAEX1) – as did students holding some other form of financial investment (INV-OTHER).

The only other significant explanatory variable in Table 1 is CAREER. Students who had indicated they had a firm idea on the career they wished to pursue on completing their degree (CAREER), performed at a significantly higher level in the test, but (perhaps surprisingly) at a significantly lower level in MAEX3.

Table 2 also reveals few significant correlations between the remaining (non-binary) explanatory variables and the various performance measures. We do note, however, that older students (AGE), on average, achieved lower marks in all their examinations – and significantly so in respect of FAEX3 and MAEX3, but higher marks in the initial test. One reason for this might be that their maturity had equipped them to deal with the initial test of basic understanding, but disadvantaged them when it came to settling down to the routine of undergraduate study and examination. In addition, Table 2 reveals that the 'A' level points score variable (SCORE-A) is also positively correlated with all examination results – though only significantly so in respect of FAEX3.

Overall the univariate results reported in Tables 1 and 2 reveal few significant relationships between examination (and test) performance, and the range of educational, financial and general variables used in this study. The most consistent result is in respect ECON-A and BUSINESS-O. Students who held these qualifications, on average, outperformed their fellow students in the test and university examinations – and significantly so in a number of them.

Multivariate models

Using multivariate regression analysis, this section reports a number of models where the incremental impact of a particular explanatory variable on student performance can be assessed (simultaneously), whilst controlling for the effects of other independent variables.

Given the relatively small sample size (n = 39), which restricts the statistical degrees of freedom, a selection of key variables (by reference to previous studies) were included in the models (other variables such as MATHS-A and ACCOUNT-O proved insignificant in all estimated models and are therefore not reported).

Table 3 reports five Ordinary Least Squares regression (OLS) models, where the dependent variables are TEST, MAEX1, FAEX1, MAEX3 and FAEX3 (equations 1–5, respectively). Overall, the models are poorly determined (by reference to R^2 and F-values), with few variables exhibiting significant coefficients. This may be (at least) partly attributable to the relatively small sample size. However, the analysis does tend to support the univariate analysis – in that few explanatory variables appear to impact significantly on student performance.

We do note, however, that three variables appear to significantly explain student performance in the initial test (EQ1). These results suggest that males (GENDER), were outperforming females, and that students who possessed an 'O' level in business studies and/or an 'A' level in accounting were outperforming their fellow students who did not hold these qualifications. However, in respect of all university examinations, it is interesting to note that these qualifications, in a multivariate context, were insignificant predictors of examination performance.

Consistent with the univariate analysis, Table 3 shows that those students who held an economics 'A' level, on average, outperformed students without this qualification – in the

Table 3. OLS multivariate models (student performance)

Variables	EQ1 DEP = TEST (Coefficients)	EQ2 DEP = MAEX1 (Coefficients)	EQ3 DEP = FAEX1 (Coefficients)	EQ4 DEP = MAEX3 (Coefficients)	EQ5 DEP = FAEX3 (Coefficients)
AGE	0.908	−0.522	−0.708	−0.811	−0.659
	(0.63)	(0.74)	(0.94)	(1.35)	(1.09)
GENDER	15.51***	1.53	−1.64	1.11	−3.71
	(1.77)	(0.36)	(0.36)	(0.31	(0.32)
SELECT	14.31	0.434	−0.340	−0.878	−1.52
	(1.57)	(0.09)	(0.72)	(0.23)	(0.40)
SCORE-A	−0.674	−0.158	0.516	−0.231	0.613
	(0.40)	(0.19)	(0.59)	(0.33)	(0.88)
ECON-A	2.96	4.87	7.06***	3.14	6.17**
	(0.41)	(1.36)	(1.86)	(1.04)	(2.02)
BUSINESS-O	20.73***	−0.66	0.982	5.69	3.08
	(1.70)	(0.12)	(0.15)	(1.13)	(0.61)
ACCOUNT-A	18.03***	3.24	1.39	−2.63	−4.11
	(1.90)	(0.69)	(0.28)	(0.67)	(1.04)
CONST.	14.69	68.88*	62.41*	79.59*	63.65*
	(0.37)	(3.55)	(3.02)	(4.87)	(3.83)
R²	0.30	0.10	0.16	0.16	0.28
F =	1.80	0.49	0.81	0.83	1.67
	(p = 0.12)	(p = 0.83)	(p = 0.58)	(p = 0.56)	(p = 0.15)

Key: DEP = Dependent variables; p = probability
*, **, *** Indicates t-values of coefficients (in parenthesis) are significant at the 1%, 5% and 10% levels of statistical significance respectively (two-tailed test).

test and in all examinations – but only significantly so in the two financial accounting examinations (FAEX1, FAEX3). In summary, the multivariate analysis tends to confirm the univariate analysis which preceded it.

Correlation of exam and test performance

Table 4 reports a correlation matrix of the performance of students in the initial basic test and subsequent university examinations. Perhaps as may have been expected, it reveals that, in general, the best predictor of the variance in student performance in university accountancy examinations is the relative level of student performance in previous university examinations.

The results show that the strongest levels of association are in respect of those examinations most closely related in time to each other. Hence, there is a very strong positive correlation between student performance in MAEX3 and FAEX3 (R = 0.65) and between FAEX1 and MAEX1 (R = 0.72). However, weaker (though still positive and significant) levels of association are evident in respect of the first and third year examination results. We also note that the initial test (TEST) is a poor predictor of future examination performance – and is not significantly correlated with any of the first or third year examination results.

Table 4. Pearson's correlation matrix: test and examinations performance

	FAEX3	MAEX3	FAEX1	MAEX1
MAEX3	0.65*			
FAEX1	0.48*	0.36**		
MAEX1	0.51*	0.38**	0.72*	
TEST	0.04	−0.01	0.15	0.01

*, ** Indicates Pearson's Correlation Coefficient [R] is significant at the 1% and 5% statistical significance levels respectively (two-tailed test).

Conclusions

A somewhat surprising conclusion that can be drawn from the empirical findings of this study is that very few of the educational, demographic or financial characteristics variables appear to have a significant influence on student performance in university accounting examinations. More specifically, the prior study of accountancy at 'O' or 'A' level, although showing a significant relationship with performance in the initial test, was not a significant determinant of performance in either the first year or final year university examinations. This quick erosion of any advantage that the pre-university study of accountancy might confer is consistent with a number of previous studies.

Further specific findings were that the overall 'A' level points score of students and the study of mathematics at 'A' level, which are widely perceived to be indicators of general academic ability and the ability to cope with the numerical aspects of accountancy respectively, did not have a significant impact on examination performance. The lack of a significant relationship between overall 'A' level score and subsequent university examination performance might be explained by the very low variation in the 'A' level scores of the sample group. It might also reflect that differences in the 'quality' of the 'A' level examinations of different examining boards are not accurately reflected in the composite variable used for the purposes of this study.

The empirical findings do, in fact, show that the most consistent explanatory variable of first and third year examination performance was the prior study of economics at 'A' level. One possible explanation for this is that the study of theories and concepts that underpin economics does facilitate the understanding of the theories and concepts of accounting.

This study made use of a wide and comprehensive range of background variables. These were selected by reference to both the specific literature on accountancy examination performance and the more general literature on overall academic performance. The study was also, to the best of our knowledge, the first attempt to undertake a longitudinal analysis of performance over the three years of an undergraduate accounting degree programme. Of this wide range of background variables only the possession of 'A' level Economics had a consistent significant impact on university examination performance. What our results do in fact show quite clearly is that the best predictor of university examination performance is the performance of students in earlier university examinations.

All of this suggests that the determinants of student performance in accounting degree examinations cannot be found in the background characteristics (that were tested in this study) that the students exhibited when entering university. It might be that there are other characteristics not identified in this study that affected performance but we feel that the most likely determinants are the intervening variables that are acquired or developed during the three years of the degree programme. These intervening variables might include: student motivation; changes in attitude and maturity; ability to make the transition from the more structured and disciplined regime of 'A' level study to the relative independence of university study; the awareness of career opportunities and requirements; and, of course, the quality of the lecturing and tutorial inputs. Intervening variables of this nature will clearly be difficult to measure with any precision, and yet without such measures the results of this study suggest that any attempts to analyse and understand variations in the examination performance of undergraduate accountancy students are unlikely to be completely successful.

References

Baldwin, B. A. and Howe, K. R. (1982) Secondary-level study of accounting and subsequent performance in the first college course, *The Accounting Review*, LVII (3), July, 619–26.

Bartlett, S., Peel, M., Pendlebury, M. and Groves, R. (1992) *An Analysis of Student Performance in Undergraduate Accountancy Courses*, ACCA Occasional Research Paper No. 13, The Chartered Association of Certified Accountants, London.

Bergin, J. L. (1983) The effect of previous accounting study on student performance in the first college-level financial accounting course, *Issues in Accounting Education*, Fall, 19–28.

Doran, B. M., Bouillon, M. L. and Smith, C. G. (1991) Determinants of student performance in accounting principles 1 and 11, *Issues in Accounting Education*, 6 (1), Spring, 74–84.

Eskew, R. K. and Faley, R. H. (1988) Some determinants of student performance in the first college-level financial accounting course, *The Accounting Review*, January, LXIII (I), 137–47.

Fraser, A. A., Lyttle, R. and Stolle, C. (1978) Profile of female accounting majors: academic performance and behavioural characteristics, *The Woman CPA*, October, 18–21.

Hanks, G. and Shivaswamy, M. (1985) Academic performance in accounting: is there a gender gap?, *Journal of Business Education*, January, 154–6.

Keef, S. P. (1988) Preparation for a first level university accounting course: the experience in New Zealand, *Journal of Accounting Education*, 6 (2), 293–307.

Keef, S. P. (1992) The effect of prior accounting education: some evidence from New Zealand, *Accounting Education*, 1 (1), March, 63–68.

Lipe, M. G. (1989) Further evidence on the performance of female versus male accounting students, *Issues in Accounting Education*, 4 (1), Spring, 144–52.

Mitchell, F. (1985) School accounting qualifications and student performance in a first level university accounting examination *Accounting and Business Research*, 15 (58), Spring, 81–86.

Mitchell, F. (1988) High school accounting and student performance in the first level university accounting course: a UK study, *Journal of Accounting Education*, 6 (2), 279–91.

Mutchler, J. F., Turner, J. H. and Williams, D. D. (1987) The performance of female versus male accounting students, *Issues in Accounting Education*, 2 (1), Spring, 103–11.

Peel, M. J., Pendlebury, M. W. and Groves, R. E. V. (1991) The determinants of students' financial awareness – some UK evidence, *The British Accounting Review*, 23 (1), 23–49.

Schroeder, N. W. (1986) Previous accounting education and college-level accounting examination performance, *Issues in Accounting Education*, 1 (1), Spring, 37–47.

Tyson, T. (1989) Grade performance in introductory accounting courses: why female students outperform males, *Issues in Accounting Education*, 4 (1), Spring, 153–60.

Appendix 1

Variable definitions		Frequencies ($\bar{x}$ = mean)
General background[7]		
1. AGE:	= age in years and months	$\bar{x} = 19.4$
2. GENDER:	1 = male;	79%
	0 = female	
3. REGION:	1 = from southern region;	23%
	0 = otherwise	
Educational[8]		
4. SELECT:	1 = grammar or fee-paying;	21%
	0 = otherwise	
5. ECON-O:	1 = economics 'O' level;	23%
	0 = otherwise	
6. ECON-A:	1 = economics 'A' level;	51%
	0 = otherwise	
7. MATHS-A	1 = mathematics 'A' level;	84%
	0 = otherwise	
8. SCORE-O:	= total 'O' level points score [A = 3, B = 2, C = 1]	$\bar{x} = 17.2$
9. SCORE-A:	= total 'A' level points score [A = 5, ..., E = 1]	$\bar{x} = 12.2$
Accounting/Business Studies Quals		
10. ACCOUNT-O:	1 = accounting 'O' level;	13%
	0 = otherwise	
11. ACCOUNT-A:	1 = accounting 'A' level;	23%
	0 = otherwise	
12. ACCOUNT-OTH:	1 = some other accounting qualification (e.g. ONC/D, BTECH, HNC/D);	3%
	0 = otherwise	
13. BUSINESS-O:	1 = business studies/commerce 'O' level;	13%
	0 = otherwise	
14. ACCOUNTS-EXP:	1 = accounting/bookkeeping experience;	28%
	0 = otherwise	

[7] The age and gender variables are self-explanatory. The Southern region variable (REGION) was included in an attempt to ascertain whether the difference in the economic fortunes of the south-eastern part of the UK, which underpins much of the popularized notion of 'a North-South divide', had a detectable impact on the test and examination performance of undergraduate accountancy students. Students were asked to indicate their county of residence prior to entering university and if this fell within the area included in the South East Economic Planning Region, then the student was classified as coming from the 'southern region'. The South East Economic Planning Region consists of: all inner and outer London boroughs and the counties of Bedfordshire, Berkshire, Buckinghamshire, East Sussex, Essex, Hampshire, Hertfordshire, Kent, Oxfordshire, Surrey and West Sussex.

[8] The variable SELECT relates to the type of school the students attended before coming to university. Fee paying and grammar schools tend to have some selection process for admitting students and students from these schools were categorized as having attended a selective entry school (SELECT).

Appendix 1 (*Continued*)

		Frequencies ($\bar{x}$ = mean)
Variable definitions		
15. CAREER:	1 = have decided on career area; 0 = otherwise	85%
16. CAREER-ACC:	1 = have decided on career in accountancy/accountancy related area; 0 = otherwise	82%
Time		
17. TIME	= time taken to complete finance quiz (mins)	$\bar{x}$ = 5.5
Investments[9]		
18. SHR EVER:	1 = if ever owned shares; 0 = otherwise	23%
19. SHR NOW:	1 = if currently hold shares; 0 = otherwise	18%
20. BLD SOC:	1 = have building society account; 0 = otherwise	54%
21. POST:	1 = have post office account; 0 = otherwise	49%
22. BANK:	1 = have bank deposit account; 0 = otherwise	51%
23. INV-OTHER:	1 = some other form of invest.; 0 = otherwise	15%
24. INV-NUMBER:	= number of different types of investment held	$\bar{x}$ = 2.2

Financial Transactions[9]

Students were requested to indicate whether they used/held any of the following prior to coming to university:

25. CHEQUE:	1 = used a cheque book; 0 = otherwise	49%
26. CASH CARD:	1 = used a cash card; 0 = otherwise	64%
27. CREDIT CARD:	1 = used a general credit card; 0 = otherwise	13%
28. FIN-NUMBER:	= number of different financial transactions methods used/held	$\bar{x}$ = 1.3

Note: The frequencies shown represent the percentage of students who exhibited the particular characteristic. For example, for the variable GENDER, 79% of the students were male, for the variable REGION, 23% of the students came from the 'southern' region of the UK (see note 7), and so on.

[9] The categories referred to as 'investments' and 'financial transactions' included variables such as share ownership (SHR EVER), use of cheque book (CHEQUE) etc., in an attempt to isolate differences in the financial maturity and 'financial awareness' of students and the impact, if any, on the test and examination performance of undergraduate accountancy students.

Teaching ethics in accounting and the ethics of accounting teaching: educating for immorality and a possible case for social and environmental accounting education

ROB GRAY, JAN BEBBINGTON and KEN McPHAIL

University of Dundee, Dundee, UK

Abstract

A number of the ethical issues associated with university accounting education are explored. The argument has three principal themes. Although there is much to admire about current accounting practice there is also considerable evidence of ethical and intellectual failure among accounting practitioners. At least some responsibility for these failures can be laid at the door of accounting education. There is evidence that accounting education fails to develop students' intellectual and, relatedly, ethical maturity. This, it can be argued, may be seen as a moral failure on the part of accounting educators. The content of much of what currently passes for core accounting knowledge has characteristics which can be associated with both superficial learning strategies and ethically immature moral positions. Thus, it may be that 'current accounting knowledge' implicitly reinforces intellectual and ethical atrophy and this may go some way towards helping explain the evidence on accounting education. There are many possible solutions to this problem. One possible, and partial, solution may lie with social and environmental accounting, which challenges much of the traditional approach to accounting education in universities, offers a vehicle within which many of the implicit assumptions of accounting and accounting education can be explored and provides a potential opportunity to enhance the ethical and intellectual development of accounting students.

Introduction

University accounting education in the English-speaking world continues to hold – and seems incapable of resolving – a range of conflicting objectives. These conflicting objectives appear to include preparation of accounting graduates for the syllabuses of the professional examinations (techniques acquisition); preparation of accounting graduates for employment as accounting trainees (training); and development of the intellectual abilities of the student in the widest sense (education). There is, clearly, some degree of overlap between these three aspects of accounting teaching but the considerable literature discussing them suggests that conflict exists and that the three are far from congruent objectives (see, for example, Shute, 1979; Lee, 1989; Zeff, 1989; Accounting Education Change Commission (AECC), 1990; Gill, 1993).

Of the three objectives, evidence (and personal experience) seems to suggest that university teaching practice tends to be dominated by techniques acquisition (see, for example, Sterling, 1973; Gynther, 1983; Marsh and Henning, 1987; Sikka, 1987; Lehman, 1988; AECC, 1990). If this is so, then it carries a price: accounting graduates, as Gill (1993) observes, are neither practically trained individuals who can 'be immediately useful in the office' nor educationally developed individuals with a sophisticated capacity to enquire, reason, conceptualize and evaluate. Neither the 'training' nor the 'education' of accounting students is satisfactory. This failure, at least of the 'educational' component of university accounting teaching, has been widely remarked upon (Baxter, 1981; Standish, 1983; Lyall, 1985; Laughlin et al., 1986; Hopwood, 1990) and has been consistently and persuasively linked with the behaviour of accountants in practice (see, for example, Sterling, 1973; Lehman, 1988, 1992; Zeff, 1989; Cousins, 1991b; Power, 1991, 1992; Bebbington et al., 1992).

One central element in this discussion of the failure of accounting education and, relatedly, accounting practice concerns the level of ethical maturity and reasoning experienced by accounting students and exhibited by accounting practitioners. Educational experience seems to be an important factor in both intellectual development and ethical maturity (see, for example, Armstrong, 1987; Cohen and Pant, 1991; French et al., 1992) and accounting education, in addition to providing a significant proportion of new recruits to the profession, provides the intellectual framework within which practice – and the dialogues of practice – operate (see, for example, Lehman, 1988, 1992; Napier and Power, 1992). If there are ethical failures in accounting practice it is therefore probable that at least some of the responsibility must be laid at the door of the educators.

On the face of it, high ethical standards might seem a *sine qua non* for an accountancy profession with an explicit commitment to the 'public interest' (Briloff, 1988; Gavin and Klinefelter, 1989; Karnes et al., 1989; Gaa, 1990; Cohen and Pant, 1991; Hauptman and Hill, 1991; Mitchell et al., 1991; Waples and Shaub, 1991; Huss and Patterson, 1993) and whilst this may still be *perceived* to be the case by non-accountants (Brokowski and Ugras, 1992) the evidence of practice does not substantiate it (McCabe et al., 1991).[1] Many 'operational' ethical issues within the organizational setting – for example, treatment of expense claims, overtime hours claimed, secrecy and so on – are receiving considerable attention (see, for example, the articles by Leech reproduced in Denham, 1991; see also Beets and Killough, 1990; Schlachter, 1990; Stanga and Turpen, 1991), but it is in the widening recognition that the *important* ethical dilemmas obtain at a much broader level

---

[1] In part the problem seems to stem from a lack of clarity over what is the appropriate level of ethical domain. Views appear to vary. At one end of the spectrum there appear to be major groups of practitioners who are either unaware of the ethical dilemmas that they face (see, for example, Belkaoui and Chan, 1988; Claypool *et al.*, 1990; Tyson, 1992; Huss and Patterson, 1993) or who appear able to assume that their ethical standards are high – or at least as high as other groups (see, for example, Brenner and Molander, 1977; Ferrel and Weaver, 1978; Pitt and Abratt, 1986; McDonald and Zepp, 1988; Elm and Nicolas, 1990; Modic (1987) in Davis and Welton, 1991; Tyson, 1992). To the extent that ethical dilemmas are recognized the 'holier-than-thou' view appears to be related to either a sense of helplessness about change (see, for example, Mintzberg, 1983; Forisha and Forisha (1986) in Davis and Welton, 1991; Trevino, 1992), an ignorance of what ethical codes are expected (Shertzer and Morris, 1972; Baldick, 1980; Hughson and Kohn, 1980; Davis, 1984; Martin et al., 1991) or a focus on codes of conduct to the exclusion of independent moral reasoning (Brooks, 1989; Schweikart, 1992).

that has the most important potential ramifications for education. Schweikart (1992), for example, identifies ethical dilemmas in the disclosure of information to financial participants; Gunz and McCutcheon (1991) are concerned with the ethical elements of independence and Karnes *et al.* (1989) argue that accountants need to identify the cultural basis of ethical choices. Mahoney (1990) and Ruland and Lindblom (1992) take the issues wider still and recognize that it is not possible to identify the ethical standing of acts without an understanding of the political, social and economic context within which the action takes place. Ultimately, this leads to a recognition that a whole range of systemic matters – power, ethnocentricity, exploitation, justice, culture, etc. – are essential elements of the accountants' ethical domain (see, for example, Arlow, 1991; Davis and Welton, 1991; Power, 1991b; Schwartz *et al.*, 1991; Cohen *et al.*, 1992; Roslender, 1992, p. 92). Yet accountants seem ill equipped to handle such matters (see, for example, Gavin and Klinefelter, 1989; Ponemon, 1990, 1992). Although it is not clear whether accountants are more or less ethical than other business professionals (Patten and Williams, 1990; Paradice and Dejoie, 1991) there is evidence that:

- the promotion to manager or partner of an accountant is associated with a decline in ethical reasoning (Ponemon, 1990);
- acountants' ethical development is arrested (Ponemon, 1992); and
- accountants' moral maturity is, when controlled for age and education levels, less than that for the population as a whole (Armstrong, 1987, but see also Jeffrey, 1993).[2]

The education that accountants receive may well contribute to this situation and is, at a minimum, an important element in the problem. It is this that we seek to explore in this paper and, drawing from the educational and cognitive development literature, the substantial literature on business ethics and the literature from both 'conventional' and 'critical' accounting commentators we attempt to make a case for a radical change in what passes for undergraduate accounting education. An essential theme in what follows is that, although the focus is upon 'ethics' in accounting teaching, this focus is largely inseparable from (1) the ethical responsibility of the teacher to seek maximum educational development in the student; and (2) the apparent relationship between ethical and educational development. This will, we hope, become clear as the paper progresses.

As a final introductory remark we should stress that we are not directly concerned with what constitutes 'right' and 'wrong' action by reference to some black and white moral code. Our emphasis, rather, is on the ethical development and maturity (at least as it is understood in the substantive literature, see below) of accounting students and accounting professionals; and the ethical responsibility of the teacher to develop the intellectual capacities of the student and to avoid what we shall shortly identify as 'indoctrination' in particular moral philosophies.

The paper is organized as follows. The next section introduces some educational and learning theory and relates this to experience of accounting education; some approaches

---

[2] The evidence reported in Jeffrey (1993) is potentially important as it is the first evidence (of which we are aware) which has suggested that accounting students may exhibit *higher* levels of moral reasoning than other groups. Although this goes against the tenor of the other evidence and argument to date, Jeffrey does not directly address this potential contradiction. Possible explanations include the possibility that previous research is unsound – although we must state that we find this counterintuitive – or that the Jeffrey study was performed after influence from AECC was being felt in undergraduate programmes. The study by Jeffrey is undated so this possibility remains speculative.

to ethical theory and ethical reasoning with particular reference to business and accounting education are then reviewed. An analysis of the ethical and intellectual emphasis which is (usually implicitly) provided in accounting education follows. This comes to the conclusion that accounting educators implicitly encourage students, at an intellectually and ethically vulnerable age, to restrict their ethical development. Rather than simply leaving the criticism of accounting education, we discuss the possible solutions to this problem and suggest social and environmental accounting education as one element in a strategy to help develop the intellectual and ethical maturity of accounting students. The final section contains the conclusions.

Some educational theory and accounting education

While accounting educators have paid considerable attention to teaching method, especially in relation to the use of computing (see, for example, Kaye, 1988; Curtis, 1989; Sangster and Wilson, 1991; Williams, 1991), the mainstream accounting literature does not appear to have given the same emphasis to learning theory in accounting education (see, for example, Shute, 1979; AECC, 1990; Ainsworth and Plumlee, 1992; Albrecht, 1992). One major theme that is gaining notice in accounting relates to learning and cognitive maturity and sophistication. Shute (1979) and Ainsworth and Plumlee (1992) have both employed Bloom's taxonomy of learning (Bloom, 1956) to good effect to illustrate the levels of intellectual maturity that are sought in the education process (see Table 1).

While not all students can necessarily attain the 'highest level' in all elements of a degree, the taxonomy focuses attention on the stages of intellectual development a university education should seek to inculcate. Although the taxonomy is open to a wide variety of interpretations (see, for example, Ainsworth and Plumlee, 1992), there is a significant amount of evidence that can be interpreted as suggesting that accounting education, typically, does not encourage progress through the levels of the taxonomy and may, indeed, reinforce the lower levels of cognition (see, for example, Zeff, 1989; AECC, 1990; Power, 1991a; French *et al.*, 1992; Gill, 1993).

Table 1. Bloom's taxonomy of learning/cognitive objectives*

1. Knowledge: this is the lowest level of learning. It includes recall and memory.
2. Comprehension: this is the lowest level of understanding. The student uses facts or ideas without relating them.
3. Application: this is the intellectual skill that entails the use of information in specific situations. Information may be in the form of general ideas, concepts, principles or theories which must be remembered and applied.
4. Analysis: this skill involves taking information apart and making relationships in order to discover hidden meaning and the basic structure of an idea or fact. The student is able to distinguish between fact and opinion and to assess consistency.
5. Synthesis: the student is able to re-assemble the component parts of an idea in order to develop new or creative ideas.
6. Evaluation: this is the highest level of cognition. It involves making judgements on materials, information or method. In problem solving, it involves selecting from among competing alternative solutions by systematic evaluation of the alternatives.

*Adapted from Ainsworth and Plumlee (1992) and Bloom (1956).

Table 2. Defining features of approaches to learning[a]

Surface approach/shallow-reiterative/reproducing/concrete-operational
- Intention simply to reproduce parts of the content
- Accepting ideas and information passively
- Concentrating only on assessment requirements
- Not reflecting on purpose or strategies in learning
- Memorizing facts and procedures routinely
- Failing to recognize guiding principles or patterns

Deep approach/deep-elaborative/transforming/formal-operational
- Intention to understand material for oneself
- Interacting vigorously and critically with content
- Relating ideas to previous knowledge and experience
- Using organizing principles to integrate ideas
- Relating evidence to conclusions
- Examining the logic of the argument

[a]Adapted from Entwistle *et al.*, 1992, p. 4.

Bloom's taxonomy has been widely employed and, it seems to us, has considerable intuitive appeal in aiding initial conceptualization of educational objectives. However, more recent (though related; Shute, 1979) learning theory has tended to emphasize the more focused approach associated with the analysis of shallow and deep approaches to learning. These two approaches are developed and contrasted in Table 2.

Education is normally assumed to be aiming to achieve deep learning. Deep learning involves some change in the student – in conceptions, perceptions, understanding and reactions (see, for example, Harvey *et al.*, 1961; Schmeck, 1983). Deep learning is defined by Tan and Choo (1990) as being 'intentional, interpretative, critical and analytical' and involving the ability to 'compare and contrast concepts for the purpose of critically evaluating the merits of each' (p. 68). This is to be contrasted with 'literal memorization' which would characterize the shallow learner (for more detail see Tan and Choo, 1990; Entwistle, 1991).

Many educational writers have elaborated upon these categorizations. One of the more important characteristics which has emerged is that of the learner's motivation (Zook, 1982; Willis and Clift, 1988; Entwistle *et al.*, 1992). Deep learning appears to be related to, and is actually dependent upon, the learner experiencing *intrinsic* motivation for the study of the subject, i.e. interest and learning for its own sake. By contrast, *extrinsic* motivation exists where the purpose of the activity is the achievement of some external goal such as a qualification or career opportunities. Other elements of a possible categorization are shown in Table 3 (see also Marton and Saljo, 1984).

In summary, deep learning – and the related intrinsic motivation – is associated with good academic performance, involvement, enjoyment and satisfaction of the student, better intellectual development and longer-term effects. It is of considerable concern, therefore, to discover that much (if not most) accounting education is not of this sort (see, for example, Shute, 1979; Willis and Clift, 1988; Gill, 1993; and, by implication, Gambling, 1983; Lee, 1989; Zeff, 1989; AECC, 1990; Power, 1991b; French *et al.*, 1992; and, especially, Gul *et al.*, 1989). Such evidence as there is appears to point to accounting education's tendency to

Table 3. General learning orientations[a]

General orientation	Major characteristics	Brief explanation
Meaning orientation	Deep approach	Looks for meaning; interacts actively; links with real life
	Use of evidence	Examines evidence critically and uses it cautiously
	Relating ideas	Actively relates new information to previous knowledge
	Intrinsic motivation	Interested in learning for its own sake
Reproducing orientation	Surface approach	Relies on rote learning; conscious of exam demands
	Syllabus boundness	Prefers to restrict learning to defined syllabus and specified tasks
	Fear of failure	Anxiously aware of assessment requirements; lacking in self-confidence
	Improvidence	Not prepared to look for relationships between ideas; fact bound
Achieving orientation	Strategic approach	Actively seeks information about assessment requirements; tries to impress staff
	Extrinsic motivation	Qualifications as main source of motivation for learning
	Achievement motivation	Competitive and self-confident; motivated by hope of success
Non-academic orientation	Disorganized study methods	Organizes time ineffectively; fails to plan ahead; not prompt in submitting work
	Negative attitudes	Little involvement in work set; cynical and disenchanted about higher education
	Globe trotting	Over-readiness to generalize and jump to conclusions without evidence

[a]Adapted from Ramsden, 1984, p. 159; Willis and Clift, 1988, p. 2.

emphasize shallow-reiterative learning (see also Laughlin *et al.*, 1986; Blundell and Booth, 1988; Lewis *et al.*, 1992).[3] Indeed, the recent view expressed by French *et al.* (1992), who use words like 'dull', 'unexciting', 'repetitious', 'non-creative' as adjectives for much of what passes for accounting education, may well be widespread (see, for example, Sterling, 1973; Zeff, 1989; Power, 1991b). Sadly, much personal experience reinforces this view; yet few educators will talk in terms of the boredom they impose on students and their reasons (if any) for doing so. As we have seen, a failure to engage deeper learning strategies encourages shallow reactions from students.

[3] Of perhaps even greater concern, Willis and Clift claim that while shallow learning was exhibited by students in their accounting and commerce course, they did not necessarily exhibit this characteristic in other courses 'selected for interest'. This suggests that students may be capable of deep learning but either are discouraged from pursuing it or (as Ramsden, 1984, suggests) employ a range of strategies during their education.

One major link between the foregoing and ethical reasoning is that development of ethical reasoning requires deeper and developmental learning patterns to facilitate the release of more sophisticated ethical responses to dilemmas. The evidence suggests that accounting (and to an extent business education in general) is largely guilty of a failure to develop the students' intellectual and moral abilities and may actually encourage its atrophy and reverse. This is well expressed by Lehman (1988) when she says:

> It seems unlikely that accounting students who receive only an occasional random chapter devoted to integrating business and ethics, within a four-year university education, are receiving any long-lasting, meaningful, or rich understanding of the complexities regarding ethics in our society.

> Accounting students are trained in how to do ... why [is] either unarticulated or not scrutinised. This is tantamount to establishing that the first task of teachers is to serve the economy by turning out 'skilled robots and uncritical consumers for the hi-tech age' rather than regard the classroom as a place to question rules and standards, a place to direct, formulate and cultivate character and the ethos of life.

> Education should, by definition, be a human advance, something we can morally approve of, denoting an increase in human achievement. Can we say that the emphasis in accounting education ... entail[s] a qualitative human advance?

Ethics, business and accounting education

> Ethics is concerned with the goods worth seeking in life, and with the rules that ought to govern human behaviour and social interaction. Business is basic to human society and it would be nice to show that moral action is always best for business. But this seems not to be true, especially in the short run: lying, fraud, deception and theft sometimes lead to greater profits than their opposites, hence moral judgements sometimes differ from business judgements. (Donaldson, 1988, p. 20, adapted from De George and Pilcher, 1978, pp. 3–4)[4]

At its simplest, ethics relates to how we determine the 'rightness' or 'wrongness' of an action, attitude or decision (see, for example, Donaldson, 1988). Although a tautological statement, it must be the case that all human action can be evaluated as 'right' or 'wrong' by reference to some set of moral values or ethical code (see, for example, McKee, 1986; Donaldson, 1988; Jacobson, 1991).[5] Further, the decision to choose not to evaluate action in this way or, more pertinently, to choose to treat action as morally 'neutral' – as removed from the moral domain – is itself a moral decision (McKee, 1986; Raines and Jung, 1986; Reilly and Kyj, 1990; Jacobson, 1991).

[4] We recognize that one interpretation of this quotation is that the systemic forces and structure of business, the structures in which business operates and which, to a degree at least, they also control and create are treated as non-problematic. If so, then we would not share such a view.
[5] There are two points that should be added here. First, there may well be human actions which are of a nature which makes any moral content effectively trivial (e.g. the giving of a name or the blowing of one's nose) or, indeed, it may be that there is a class of actions which, in fact, are outside the moral dimension. Such actions do not appear to be relevant here. Secondly, while we are attempting to avoid the 'relativist-absolutist' debates and do not deny (in Keats's 'negative capability' sense) the possibility of absolute 'rightness' or 'wrongness', it will be obvious that our arguments are predominantly relativist..

Table 4. Kohlberg's levels of ethical development

1. Heteronomous morality: the avoidance of punishment
2. Individualism, instrumental purpose and exchange: immediate self-interest
3. Mutual interpersonal expectations, relationships and interpersonal conformity: conform to what is expected by others; concern for others is evident; desire to be a good person
4. Social system and conscience: duty driven, upholding the law and rules becomes very important; cooperation beyond immediate self-interest
5. Social contract or utility and individual rights: recognition of the variety of views held and that values are relative to one's social group; recognition of equity and fairness
6. Universal ethical principles: self-chosen principles on a non-irrational basis derived from general principles (actually very rare)

This then leads to the idea that an individual is capable of developing his or her moral reasoning. This may involve not just a recognition of the moral elements of a situation and the (potentially) conflicting ways of assessing that moral dimension but also of refining and developing the complexity and maturity of the ethical reasoning process ('wisdom' as Paradice and Dejoie (1991) suggest). The most widely employed articulation of this developmental process is Kohlberg's levels of ethical development (see, for example, Kohlberg, 1969, 1981; Rest, 1979; Ponemon, 1990, 1992; and Paradice and Dejoie, 1991, for useful reviews of this). A summary of Kohlberg's 'ladder' is presented in Table 4.

Kohlberg further divides up the ladder into three levels which focus upon the self (stages 1 and 2), focus upon relationships (stages 3 and 4) and focus upon principles (stages 5 and 6). These three levels have important implications for accounting education, as we shall see shortly.

The evidence is not perfectly clear on the apparent determinants of ethical maturity but age, gender, childhood, background and years in education are amongst the most favoured (see, for example, Rest, 1974, 1987; Rohatyn, 1987). Arguments in favour of ethical education do, however, appear to have both the educational and the political will behind them (see, for example, AECC, 1990). The essence of the argument is that exposure to ethical issues sensitizes students to moral dilemmas and solutions, and that this sensitivity is a major determinant of ethical response (McCabe *et al.*, 1991; Huss and Patterson, 1993; Mahoney, 1993; Smith, 1993).[6] Students – as young adults – would appear to be at an important and vulnerable stage in their intellectual and ethical development (Rest, 1987; Galbraith, 1991; Brokowski and Ugras, 1992), and educational experience at undergraduate

---

[6] One problem that arises, however, is how this should be achieved. The central arguments appear to be about the value of a stand-alone course which permits detailed analysis of the issues or the integration of ethical matters into the core of the curriculum (see, for example, George, 1987, 1988; Mai-Dalton, 1987; Gandz and Hayes, 1988; Stead and Miller, 1988; Furman, 1990; Loeb, 1991; Kraft and Singhapakdi, 1991; McCabe *et al.*, 1991; Mahoney, 1993). The dominant view appears to favour the treatment of ethics within the core curriculum – otherwise there is a danger that the matters discussed do not overflow into other courses (Hiltebeitel and Jones, 1991) and there is no counter to the 'ethical indoctrination' (Loeb, 1991) present in the rest of the course (see below). There currently appears to be no resolution to the question of whether professional codes of ethics strengthen or weaken ethical maturity. The sensitizing effect of the introduction of an ethical code may well be more than offset by the tendency to rely upon that code as a complete specification of ethical standards and thereby avoid personal ethical development..

level plays an important role in forming the intellectual frameworks and ethical maturity of the student[7] (see, for example, Martin, 1981; Schwartz *et al.*, 1991; Weber and Green, 1991; but see also Boyd, 1981; Brokowski and Ugras, 1992).

As a result, the tenor of research findings that suggest that accounting and business education have a *negative* influence on ethical reasoning is disturbing. The studies by Lewis (1989), Ponemon and Glazer (1990), Hiltebeitel and Jones (1992) and McCabe *et al.* (1991) plus, by implication, that by Armstrong (1987) all suggest that, while ethical reasoning does rise during business and accounting education, it does so to a noticeably lesser degree than is typical in other subjects (but see Arlow, 1991, and Jeffrey, 1993). As we shall see below, results that suggest that accounting (and business) education stultifies moral development should really come as no surprise to professional business educators given the orientation and emphasis that is offered (see, for example, Hawley, 1991). However, such results must be a source of concern to educators and others with the best interests of the accounting profession at heart.

Consider, for example, Stewart (1991), who, as part of his review of debate on financial disclosure in UK financial statements, concludes that ethical development is slight and:

> Educators therefore need to rediscover the ethics of character or virtue, a type of ethics that places primacy on the formation of the moral self.

That is, some explicit analysis of the ethical foundations of accounting and accounting education is necessary. As researchers have found, however, little explicit examination of accounting and business ethics occurs in undergraduate courses (Lehman, 1988; Loeb, 1991; McCabe *et al.*, 1991; Hiltebeitel and Jones, 1992) and the explicit introduction of ethics education, although growing, is still marginal in most cases (Chua *et al.*, 1991). In part, this seems to be due to the ambivalence of the educators (see, for example, Belkaoui and Chan, 1988) and in part due to the educational experience to which accounting students are subject (see, for example, Power, 1991b; Hiltebeitel and Jones, 1991).

Loeb (1988) sets out a series of educational goals for accounting ethics education (see Table 5). Although widely quoted (see, for example, Huss and Patterson, 1993), Loeb's goals raise a fundamental problem in that they assume that current accounting education

Table 5. Loeb's goals of accounting ethics education[a]

- Relate accounting education to moral issues
- Recognize issues in accounting that have ethical implications
- Develop a sense of moral obligation or responsibility
- Develop abilities to deal with ethical conflicts
- Learn to deal with the uncertainties of the accounting profession
- Set the stage for change in ethical behaviour
- Appreciate and understand the history and the composition of all aspects of accounting ethics and their relationship with the general field of ethics

Adapted from Loeb, 1988, p. 322.

[7] It should be stressed that this does not mean that students learn what is right and what is wrong. Indeed, not only is there a view that this should not be taught but that it cannot be taught. Students' ethical maturity starts with a recognition of the ethical content of situations and develops to involve more sophisticated postures in response to ethical situations. For more detail see Mischel and Mischel (1976) and Trevino (1992).

Table 6. Ways of assessing the rightness or wrongness or action

There are, broadly, three bases upon which people can assess whether an action is ethically right or wrong:

- Consequentialism: the rightness or wrongness of an action is assessed by reference to the consequences of the action – are they good or bad? Consequentialist reasoning has a subset, utilitarianism, by which we assess actions by reference to the utility they generate. This is further narrowed down by financial utilitarianism whereby those actions which generate greater financial utility (e.g. profit) are considered better actions that those which generate less financial utility (e.g. losses). *Most accounting thought implicitly applies this form of ethical reasoning.*
- Motivism: the rightness or wrongness of an act is determined by reference to the motivation of the actor. A well intentioned act with bad consequences could still be judged to be an ethically sound act. Motivism will usually also involve reference to duty – I did something because it was my duty to do so – the 'Brutus' syndrome.
- Deontological: the rightness or wrongness of an act is judged by reference to the intrinsic nature of the act itself regardless of its consequences or the motive of the actor. Environmental demonstrators may know that their acts will achieve no change (for example) in government policy and may recognize that they do not really know their own motivation (who ever does?) or, indeed, may suspect that the acts are selfishly motivated; but they may be, to environmentalists, intrinsically good.

NB There is *no* implication that these three approaches to ethical reasoning form any kind of progression or hierarchy.

---

is – or can be – orientated towards encouraging the student's use of personal referents and encouraging him or her to seek out and resolve intellectual conflicts. Loeb's goals for accounting ethics education seem to us to require the same sorts of intellectual characteristics as are suggested for deep learning in Tables 2 and 3. Achievement of the higher Loeb goals requires that intellectual progress has been made through Bloom's taxonomy and for the student to be exhibiting deep-learning orientation. If this holds – and the literature appears to be silent on this connection – then it should come as no surprise that lack of ethical development goes hand in hand with a lack of intellectual development.

Before proceeding to look more closely at accounting education itself, there is one further aspect of ethical reasoning that we believe it is necessary to introduce. Although largely alien to the student of economics and accounting (of which more later) there are, broadly, three ways in which we can evaluate 'rightness' and 'wrongness': by reference to consequentialist, motivist or deontological reasoning. These three approaches are briefly summarized in Table 6.

Consequentialist reasoning – and, in particular, that subset of consequential reasoning, utilitarianism – predominates in formal analysis in accounting, finance and business, and (as we shall see) is indeed an essential component of economic and accounting reasoning. There is, however, no absolute reason why such reasoning must be considered essentially superior to the other forms. Indeed, it seems that individuals, in general, use all three styles of reasoning. At times, all three may be in harmony. Thus, for illustration, we might choose to produce and disclose a set of financial statements because:

- Consequentially, we believe the consequences of so doing are 'good' and the consequences of not doing so are 'bad'.
- Motivist reasoning leads us to believe that it is our duty to do so because (say) our professional code requires us to, the client requires us to and the Companies' Act which we are sworn to uphold requires us to.
- Deontologically, we currently believe that it is an intrinsically 'good' thing to account and there is something intrinsically 'right' about producing a financial account in line with current practice.

It is, however, unlikely that all three modes of reasoning will produce the same answer and recognition of moral conflict within our choices is a first step towards the development of ethical reasoning. In accounting, as we shall attempt to demonstrate, a three-way analysis will often suggest that what we take for granted is, in fact, moral in only a very limited sense of the word.[8]

At this point, the potential implications for accounting education should begin to become apparent. The principle we take for granted and inculcate into our students – short-term self-interest – represents a low level of moral development and depends upon only one subset (financial utilitarianism) of all possible ethical reasoning systems (see also Shepard and Hartenian, 1991). It is this apparently systematic restriction of our students' ethical growth with which we deal in the next section.

The ethics of accounting teaching

Although a degree of equivocation seems appropriate, the evidence we have reviewed above suggests that accounting education emphasizes shallow rather than deep learning and thus fails to develop students' intellectual potential and is associated with a lack of ethical development. If this is so, and the tentative connection between intellectual and ethical development is plausible (see Nelson and Obremski, 1990, and Weber, 1990; but see also Burton et al., 1991, and Serwinek, 1992), it seems reasonable to infer that there is something in the form of accounting education which is failing to produce students who possess qualities suitable for the role of 'professional' accountant.[9] While this may be in part related to a self-selection bias in students choosing to study accounting, the evidence seems to suggest that the educational process itself is significantly at fault (Armstrong and Vincent, 1988; Lehman, 1988; Lee, 1989; Zeff, 1989; AECC, 1990; Cohen and Pant, 1991; Power, 1991a; French et al., 1992).

Loeb (1991), adapting from Rosen and Caplan (1980) and Maklin (1980), says that

---

[8] Although we should note that accountants, it would seem, however, do not like to think of themselves as immoral (see, for example, Patten, 1990; Bebbington et al., 1992).

[9] The debate on what constitutes appropriate education for a prospective accountant is extensive but far from resolved (see, for example, Shute, 1979; Flanagan and Juchau, 1982; Gynther, 1983; Standish, 1983; ICAEW, 1986, 1987; Laughlin et al., 1986; Sikka, 1987; Zeff, 1989; Armstrong and Vincent, 1988; AECC, 1990; Cousins, 1991; Gray, 1990a; Lessem, 1991a; Power, 1991b). There does, however, appear to be a measure of agreement that such education requires inculcation in core skills and knowledge but that this must be matched and placed in context by a demanding education experience that develops intellectual capacity and produces an accounting student with a sense of the public interest and the social role of 'profession' (see, for example, Greenwood, 1957; Millerson, 1964; Lindblom, 1984; Gerboth, 1988; Sikka et al., 1989; Hopwood, 1990; Willmott, 1990; Allen, 1991; Power, 1991b). There is no evidence to suggest that these are incompatible. There is a lot of evidence to suggest that the former is happening, but unsatisfactorily, and the latter rarely happens at all..

indoctrination is what occurs when a teacher tries to indicate a view without allowing the intended learner to exercise his or her own reasoning ability – when a view is inculcated without critical analysis and the use of 'rational' methods. McCabe *et al.* (1991) demonstrate, successfully in our view, that this is exactly what happens in accounting education. Students absorb the current (often implicit) values of the industrial system and the accounting profession – *without being aware that this is happening and that some matters are contestable* (Mahoney, 1990; Lehman, 1992). The point at issue is not whether or not the values impressed on the student are 'right' or 'wrong' but that the educational process itself discourages the student from examining them and making a thoughtful choice about their adoption.

This criticism is especially relevant in the way accounting education tends to treat the discipline as a neutral, technical, value-free activity (Hopwood, 1990; Lewis *et al.*, 1992). Not only are matters such as industrial structure, unemployment, stock market activity, profit, growth, control over employees and corporate power treated as unproblematic (which, of course, they are not – see Tinker, 1984, 1985) but accounting education also implicitly adopts, *inter alia*, the rationalizations of neoclassical economics and especially the pursuit of self-interest as though, they too, were uncontentious. We should recall that the emphasis on self-interest is identified by Kohlberg as a lower level of ethical development and that, as age is a major element in ethical maturity, new undergraduate students can realistically be expected to be found hovering between stages 1 and 2 and stages 3 and 4 of Kohlberg's ladder. As a result the dominant emphasis on the pursuit of self-interest within accounting education can be expected to reinforce any tendency to fail to advance through the stages of ethical development. This emphasis is surely self-evident – in agency theory, in positive accounting theory, in the capital asset pricing model (CAPM), in assumptions about investor behaviour in response to financial accounting; and in a predominance of management accounting analysis, self-interest, masquerading as the rational exercise of utility maximization, is an essential assumption. Indeed, viewed in this light, a re-examination of core accounting textbooks is both illuminating and depressing (see also Swanda, 1990).

Even when the self-interest assumption is not so clearly apparent, it is implicitly present within a postulated set of neoclassical economic constructs. More particularly, if, as we have argued, all human action must, by definition, be judged 'good' or 'bad', i.e. ethically, the maximization of shareholder wealth, the assumption of profit maximization, the selection of investment opportunities because of their greater contribution to profit and/or cash flow, the reduction of costs regardless of the social and environmental 'externalities' and so on, are by definition being pronounced 'good'. We are ethically preferring (say) a profit-maximizing investment to other opportunities and encouraging – nay insisting that – our students adopt this view without questioning or analysing it. We are, to follow Loeb (1991) and McCabe *et al.* (1991), indoctrinating our students. What is more, the indoctrination can only claim the ethical high ground to the extent that one believes that self-interest and profit-maximizing behaviour produce the greatest good for the greatest number within a pristine neoclassical framework. That this is not self-evidently desirable and that there is no evidence to suggest that this is what happens in practice removes even this justification (see, for example, Galbraith, 1973, 1991; Hahn, 1984; Williams, 1987; Gray, 1990c, 1992; Jacobson, 1991; Gray and Morrison, 1992).

The essential points here are that we indoctrinate our students, we emphasize and implicitly reinforce self-interest and we implicitly subscribe to a neoclassical paradigm

Kohlberg's levels of ethical development	Modes of ethical reasoning		
	Consequentialism	Motivism	Deontological
Heteronomous morality	The ethical emphasis in accounting and		
Individualism and instrumentalism	finance university teaching		
Interpersonal relationships			
Social system and conscience			
Social contract and individual rights			
Universal ethical principles			

Fig. 1. A matrix of ethical reasoning.

which is both highly contestable and itself founded on self-interest. But there is a further point. Recalling that Table 4 identified three broad ways of assessing 'rightness' and 'wrongness' of action, it will be apparent that accounting education not only emphasizes only one ethical approach – consequentialism – (and thus ignores other approaches) but that it also concentrates on only one small, restricted, subset: self-interested financial utilitarianism. Seen in this way, it should come as no surprise at all that accounting students – and subsequently accounting practitioners and trainees – are unable to demonstrate ethical maturity.

The essence of the ethical focus in accounting education can, we suggest, be usefully illustrated by reference to a matrix of possible ethical positions (see Fig. 1). Figure 1 offers 18 possible approaches to ethical reasoning (of course, many more could be offered by the addition of further ethical schema). While it is probable that university accounting educators vary in their emphasis and that most will use a majority of the options at different stages in their teaching, the evidence we have reviewed suggests, very strongly, that the emphasis in accounting education is on just two of these options: the lower levels of Kohlberg's ladder with an emphasis on consequentialism. This leaves 16 options in Fig. 1 which appear to be treated as marginal at best and irrelevant at worst. This restriction of ethical options must be a serious, if probably unconscious, ethical decision on the part of the accounting educator. It must, we believe, raise substantial questions about the educators' fulfilment of their moral duties *qua* educators (Lehman, 1988, 1992; Hopwood, 1990).

Reviewing these arguments and this evidence, we can see no possible ethical or intellectual justification for much of what currently passes for accounting education – in particular as reflected in the popular textbooks in the mainstream accounting and finance subjects. Without both a major re-examination of core teaching *and* the introduction of more explicit ethical analysis within the core curriculum it seems highly unlikely that accounting education can ever either contribute to ethical development or produce the prior necessity of deep learning.[10] This is not a simple matter to deal with (see, for example, Laughlin et al., 1986). However, we would now like to turn to social and environmental accounting and the ways in which that can be used pedagogically perhaps to mitigate, if not eliminate, these worrying symptoms.

A case for social and environmental accounting teaching?

If the arguments we have summarized above are persuasive, then a wholesale review of both what is taught and how it is taught in accounting degrees will need to be considered most carefully. There would seem to us to be some signs of initial moves in this direction with the emergence of the occasional educational experiment in universities and with the emergence of textbooks which approach core curriculum material from wider and more challenging viewpoints.[11] As these more 'mainstream' areas develop, we believe that there may be much to learn from the area of social and environmental accounting. Such a suggestion goes further than simply reflecting our own interests and experience. Social and environmental accounting teaching has lurked around the fringes of accounting university education for many years and has gained a relevant amount of experience in dealing with the issues we have addressed in this paper.[12]

The developmental possibilities of (and the difficulties arising from) the introduction of courses in social accounting have been discussed in some detail and well documented elsewhere (see, for example, Mathews, 1987; Blundell and Booth, 1988; Lewis et al., 1992). Such courses experience resistance from academic colleagues and students, not least because they are found to be difficult and do not appear to be immediately 'relevant'. Furthermore, a recent study (see, for example, Bebbington et al., 1992) identified an apparent reluctance and inability on the part of accounting practitioners to respond to the emerging environmental accounting agenda – with the potentially devastating effects this might have in the light of, for example, the EC's Fifth Action Plan (see, for example, Bebbington, 1993). In addition, there have been calls in the accounting literature for more study of 'what accounting is not' as means of reflecting upon 'what accounting is' (Choudhury, 1988; Hopwood, 1990; Hines, 1992). Social accounting is largely a study of 'what accounting is not' and 'what accounting can be' (see also Coe and Merino, 1988):

> The use of 'social' in conjunction with 'accounting' does not seem to work as well
> as the addition of 'financial', 'management' or 'tax'. These words add a large

[10] We should emphasize that our concern is more with *how* and *why* material is taught than with *what* is taught. We do not wish to dispute the core accounting knowledge, *per se*, within this paper although, inevitably, some material that has passed into the core of conventional accounting brings with it the 'amoral' baggage to which we refer above.

[11] We believe it would be inappropriate to suggest what we personally see as the manifestations of this change as experience suggests that different faculty will have their different interpretations of what is considered innovative and what is considered to be rubbish.

[12] There may be many reasons for teaching (or not teaching) social and environmental accounting. Moral and intellectual development reasons are only some of those reasons. Furthermore, there are many ways of introducing intellectual and moral development into accounting degrees without teaching social and environmental accounting. In our experience, social and environmental accounting just happens to be the most interesting and productive vehicle for this purpose.

measure of explanation and precision to 'accounting' which 'social' does not. Perhaps one difficulty is the range of total activity included under social accounting. (Mathews, 1987, p. 12)

Social accounting, with its large range of possible activity, its study of what accounting is not and its possible – rather than obvious – 'relevance' has the effect of holding a mirror up to 'conventional accounting'.[13] Social accounting is what we have when the limiting assumptions of conventional accounting (and, in particular, its restriction to particular versions of entity; its emphasis on economic transactions, measured in financial terms for a limited array of users for a limited array of purposes – see, for example, Laughlin and Gray, 1988) are questioned and removed. Put another way, social accounting is the universe of all possible accountings, of which financial accountings are a restricted subset (see, for example, Gray et al., 1987). The pedagogic value of such an examination of accounting, especially in the present context, is that students must make their personal value systems explicit if they are to accept or reject social accounting as a 'good thing'. In doing so, students make explicit the value system implicit in conventional accounting. In other words, if conventional accounting is unproblematic there is no need for social accounting and, conversely, we cannot have social accounting without questioning the values of conventional accounting.

As the study of social accounting develops, a student must, of necessity, come to decisions about the rights of various stakeholders and the 'goodness' or otherwise of both current business structure and the current conventional accounting (see, for example, Puxty, 1986, 1991; Gray et al., 1987; Mathews and Perera, 1990; Tinker et al., 1991). Thus the study of social accounting requires students to expose the ethical values they take for granted and to question – although not necessarily reject – the ethics of their accounting studies. This point can be briefly illustrated by reference to the currently more popular area of social accounting – accounting for the environment.

At a broad and general level, consideration of accounting for the environment requires an examination of whether the accounting profession can and should concern itself with such matters and how it can and should respond (see, for example, Lickiss, 1991). Such an examination inevitably requires an investigation of the role and responsibility of the accountant and the accounting profession (see, for example, Gray et al., 1993). Furthermore, environmental accounting provides a particularly good opportunity to explore the extent of accounting's implication in social issues – in this case environmental degradation (see Gray, 1990b) and the moral imperatives that this implies for accounting's response in terms of pragmatics, ethics, public interest and professionalism (Gray, 1992; Owen, 1992; Gray et al., 1993). This opportunity, in turn, can lead to a recognition of the ultimate limits and responsibilities of anything that we currently recognize as 'accounting' (see, for example, Maunders and Burritt, 1991; Gray, 1992). Such matters challenge student thinking and question the assumptions which they have been taught in other parts of the course. Environmental accounting relates accounting studies to observable events of interest and concern, and consequently captures many of the characteristics that are associated, a priori, with deeper learning and intellectual development.

More particularly, environmental accounting illustrates the major limitations of relying upon consequentialist ethics (and utility maximization/financial utilitarianism in particular) and illuminates both the roles for motivist and deontological reasoning (see, for example,

---

[13] In the sense of permitting 'accounting to reflect upon itself'.

CPPA, 1990) as well as the way progress can be made up Kohlberg's ladder of ethical development. First, consequential reasoning can be shown to be limited in a number of ways. For example, all of the consequences of any action cannot be known – this is especially so in terms of environmental desecration in complex ecologies; *whose* consequences should therefore be considered? To consider only mankind is clearly anthropocentric; and wherein lies the morality of considering, for example, Western well-being when that is gained at the expense of the lesser developed countries? Second, the relative strengths and limitations of motivist and (especially) deontological reasoning will naturally emerge in debate and discussion, and can be well illustrated in the environmental accounting context (see, for example, Gray, 1992). Third, the potential for blending different ethical approaches can be illustrated and the implications this has for policy and for accounting practice can be drawn out (see, for example, Turner and Pearce, 1990). Fourth, consideration of environmental accounting raises the ethical dilemmas of considering whether there is conflict between typical business-centred views and the concerns for the protection of the environment (Schmidheiny, 1992) and how this might be resolved in terms of the resultant conflicts between, for example, shareholders, employees, customers, governments and the planet itself. Indeed such analysis will, almost inevitably, raise the question whether 'business', as currently conceived, can be permitted to continue.[14] Fifth and finally, consideration of environmental accounting is likely to lead to a consideration of sustainability (see, for example, United Nations, 1987) which involves a way of thinking which challenges all current Western 'taken-for-granted' assumptions and demands a much broader conception of the values of man, other species and the planet itself (see, for example, Gray, 1992; Gray *et al.*, 1993). It is a rare student who can remain immune to the conflict in such questions and it is a rare teacher – at least we hope it is – who will be content merely to provide trite repeatable material on these issues for the student to shallow-learn and regurgitate.

These tensions inherent in environmental accounting – and therefore implicitly inherent in conventional accounting – can be reconsidered in relation to Kohlberg's levels of ethical development to enable them to act as a guide to educational and ethical strategy in this area (see Table 7).

Conclusions

The recent growth of research into the ethics of accounting, accounting students and the accounting practitioner and the, currently lesser, but nevertheless parallel, development of research into educational theory and accounting education at a time of increased concern about the parlous state of accounting, accounting education and the activity of accountants have enabled us to look closely at some of the taken-for-granted assumptions in accounting education. The inferences we draw are not flattering. The increased level of concern expressed about the quality of an accounting student's educational experience seems well founded if the research literature and the conclusions we have drawn from it are reliable. Complacency and denial by accounting teachers (in themselves, probably ethically indefensible tactics) can no longer be squared with the evidence as we see it. There is a real need to re-examine honestly what we teach, the educational experience we provide and

---

[14] The political implications of such an outrageous and naive – but potentially crucial question – must also be brought out in any subsequent discussion and analysis.

Table 7. Kohlberg's levels of ethical reasoning and environmental implications

Kohlberg's levels of ethical development	Implications/comments/likely outcomes
1. Heteronomous morality – the avoidance of punishment	This is no way (globally) to avoid 'punishment' for environmentally unsound behaviour. However, if the consequences of environmentally unsound behaviour can be avoided, then an action will be taken. This morality can be successfully applied by a group of people in the short term; however, in the longer term it will lead to environmental collapse
2. Individualism, instrumental purpose and exchange – immediate self-interest	Pursuit of immediate self-interest underlies the current economic framework, and therefore much of accounting theory. Where the environment remains largely unpriced and human existence is not closely tied to it (as it might be in many 'primitive' societies) environmental destruction is inevitable. This is largely reflected in the present state of the biosphere
3. Mutual interpersonal expectations, relationships and interpersonal conformity – conform to what is expected by others, concern for others, desire to be a good person	Environmental actions are dictated by the dominant beliefs of society. In an environmentally considerate society such as Norway, Sweden or Denmark, the environment would be given protection. In a society that does not value the environmental, protection would not be given priority. Accounting, along with much of the developed world, is based on a worldview that until recently excluded the environment. If worldviews change substantially environmentally sensitive behaviour could result
4. Social system and conscience – duty driven, upholding the law and rules becomes very important, cooperation beyond immediate self-interest	At this stage in development the environment is afforded protection that is conferred by law, which in turn is a product of the society's beliefs as identified at the preceding level. Environmental protection is possible but not guaranteed
5. Social contract or utility and individual rights – variety of views held and that values are relative to social groups, recognition of equity and fairness	The concept of sustainability starts to incorporate the idea of equity and fairness so *all* people can satisfy their basic needs. See, for example, Rawl's (1972) conception of justice. This also involved a recognition that a Western world viewpoint as to means and ends is not necessarily valid
6. Universal ethical principles – self-chosen principles on a non-irrational basis derived from general principles	While noting that this level of development is a rare occurrence the 'deep green' or ecocentric approach to the environment is possibly an example of such an approach. It is centred on the independent rightness of care for all life and the planet in particular irrespective of other issues. Although it may also be considered as utilitarian in that such a position may be sufficient to avert an environmental catastrophe

the ethical values we implicitly inculcate through our tendency to concentrate upon the algorithmic, the procedural and the repetitive. If we, as educators, are not excited by our subject, why do we teach it? If we, as educators, are not constantly examining our own ethical position, how can we claim professional status? If we take a large cohort of the (apparently) most intellectually gifted of a nation's youth, how can we justify not passing on that excitement? Not extending that intellect? Not demanding a higher ethical tone? And not turning out potential accountants capable of being 'professional'?

Acknowledgements

We are pleased to acknowledge the especially helpful comments received from John Innes, Alasdair Lonie, other colleagues at the University of Dundee and two anonymous referees on an earlier draft of this paper.

References

Accounting Education Change Commission (1990) *Objectives of Education for Accountants*, Position Statement Number 1, Bainbridge Island, AECC.

Ainsworth, P. and Plumlee, D. (1992) Restructuring the accounting curriculum, *ACCA Education Update*, 22 June, pp. 11–12.

Albrecht, S. (1992) Accounting curriculum changes at Brigham Young University, *ACCA Education Update*, 22 June, pp. 8–10.

Allen, K. (1991) In pursuit of professional dominance: Australian accounting 1953–1985, *Accounting, Auditing and Accountability Journal*, 3 (1), 51–67.

Arlow, Peter (1991) Personal characteristics in college students' evaluations of business ethics and corporate social responsibility, *Journal of Business Ethics*, 10 (1), 63–9.

Armstrong, M. B. (1987) Moral development and accounting education, *Journal of Accounting Education*, 5, 27–43.

Armstrong, M. B. and Vincent, J. I. (1988) Public accounting: a profession at the crossroads, *Accounting Horizons*, March, 94–8.

Baldick, T. L. (1980) Ethical discriminatory ability of intern psychologists: a function of training in ethics, *Professional Psychology*, 11 (2), 276–82.

Bebbington, J. (1993) The European Community Fifth Action Plan: towards sustainability, *Social and Environmental Accounting*, 13 (1), 9–11.

Bebbington, K. J., Gray, R. H., Thomson, I. and Walters, D. (1992) *Accountants and the Environment: Accountants' Attitudes and the Absence of an Environmentally Sensitive Accounting*, Department of Accountancy and Business Finance, University of Dundee, Discussion Paper Series ACC/9211.

Beets, S. D. and Killough, L. N. (1990) The effectiveness of a complaint-based ethics enforcement system: evidence from the accounting profession, *Journal of Business Ethics*, 9 (2), 115–26.

Belkaoui, A. and Chan, J. L. (1988) Professional value system of academic accountants: an empirical inquiry, *Advances in Public Interest Accounting*, 2, 1–28.

Bloom, B. (ed.) (1956) *Taxonomy of Educational Objectives, the Classification of Educational Goals – Handbook 1: Cognitive Domain*, David McKay, New York.

Blundell, L. and Booth, P. (1988) Teaching innovative accounting topics: student reaction to a course in social accounting, *Accounting and Finance*, May, 75–85.

Boyd, C. (1981) The individualistic ethic and the design of organisations, *Journal of Business Ethics*, 6, 145–51.

Brenner, S. N. and Molander, E. A. (1977) Is the ethics of business?, *Harvard Business Review*, **55**, 57–71.

Brokowski, S. C. and Ugras, Y. F. (1992) The ethical attitudes of students as a function of age, sex and experience, *Journal of Business Ethics*, **11** (12), 961–79.

Brooks, L. J. (1989) Ethical codes of conduct: deficient in guidance for the Canadian accountancy profession, *Journal of Business Ethics*, **8** (5), 325–36.

Burton, S., Johnston, M. W. and Wilson, E. J. (1991) An experimental assessment of alternative teaching approaches for introducing business ethics to undergraduate business students, *Journal of Business Ethics*, **10** (7), 507–17.

CPPA (Centre for Philosophy and Public Affairs) (1990) *Studies in Philosophy, Conservation and the Environment*, Vol. 1: *Ethics for Environmentalists*; Vol. 2: *Environmental Philosophy: A Survey*; Vol. 3: *Environmental Philosophy: A Bibliography*; CPPA with the UK Nature Conservancy Council, Edinburgh.

Choudhury, N. (1988) The seeking of accounting where it is not: towards a theory of non-accounting in organizational settings, *Accounting, Organizations and Society*, **13** (6), 549–57.

Chua, F. C., Perera, M. H. B. and Mathews, M. R. (1991) Integration of ethics into tertiary accounting programmes in New Zealand, Paper presented to *Third Asian–Pacific Conference on International Accounting Issues*, Honolulu, October.

Claypool, G. A., Fetyko, D. F. and Pearson, M. A. (1990) Reactions to ethical dilemmas: a study pertaining to certified public accountants, *Journal of Business Ethics*, **9** (9), 699–706.

Coe, T. L. and Merino, B. D. (eds.) (1988) *Future of Accounting Education*, North Texas University, Grant Thornton Conference.

Cohen, J. R. and Pant, L. W. (1991) Beyond bean counting: establishing high ethical standards in the public accounting profession, *Journal of Business Ethics*, **10** (1), 45–56.

Cohen, J. R., Pant, L. W. and Sharp, D. J. (1992) Cultural and socioeconomic constraints on international codes of ethics: lessons from accounting, *Journal of Business Ethics*, **11** (9), 687–700.

Cousins, J. (1991) Accounting for change, Paper given at the *Distinguished Speaker Series*, East London Polytechnic Business School, March.

Curtis, G. (ed.) (1989) *Proceedings of the Computers in Accounting Education Workshop 1988*, CIMA, London.

Davis, R. R. (1984) Ethical behaviour re-examined, *CPA Journal*, **54** (12), 32–6.

Davis, J. R. and Welton, R. E. (1991) Professional ethics: business students' perceptions, *Journal of Business Ethics*, **10** (6), 451–63.

De George, R. and Pilcher, J. (eds.) (1978) *Ethics, Free Enterprise and Public Policy*, Oxford University Press, New York.

Denham, R. A. (ed.) (1991) *Ethical Responsibility in Business and the Accounting Profession: Issues, Opportunities and Education*, University of Alberta.

Donaldson, J. (1988) *Key Issues in Business Ethics*, Academic Press, London.

Elm, D. and Nicolas, M. L. (1990) *Influences on the Moral Reasoning of Managers*, Discussion Paper No. 139, Strategic Management Research Center, University of Minnesota.

Entwistle, N. (1991) Teaching, learning and understanding: implications from recent findings, *ACCA Education Update*, **21**, 10–11.

Entwistle, N., Thompson, S. and Tait, H. (1992) *Guidelines for Promoting Effective Learning in Higher Education*, Centre for Research on Learning and Instruction, Edinburgh.

Ferrell, O. C. and Weaver, K. M. (1978) Ethical beliefs of marketing managers, *Journal of Marketing*, **43**, 69–73.

Flanagan, J. and Juchau, R. (1982) *The Core of the Curriculum for Accounting Undergraduates in Australia*, Flanagan and Juchau, Kingswood, NSW.

French, P. A., Jensen, R. E. and Robertson, K. R. (1992) Undergraduate student research programs: are they as viable for accounting as they are in science and humanities?, *Critical Perspectives on Accounting*, **3** (4), 337–57.

Furman, F. K. (1990) Teaching business ethics: questioning the assumptions, seeking new directions, *Journal of Business Ethics*, **9** (1), 31–8.

Gaa, J. C. (1990) A game-theoretic analysis of professional rights and responsibilities, *Journal of Business Ethics*, **9** (3), 159–69.

Galbraith, J. K. (1991) *The New Industrial State*, Pelican, London.

Gambling, T. (1983) Teaching, learning, examining: time for a fresh approach?, *Accountancy*, February, 109–12.

Gandz, J. and Hayes, N. (1988) Teaching business ethics, *Journal of Business Ethics*, **7**, 661.

Gavin, T. A. and Klinefelter, D. S. (1989) Professional ethics and audit, *Managerial Auditing Journal*, **4** (2), 24–8.

George, R. J. (1987) Teaching business ethics: is there a gap between rhetoric and reality?, *Journal of Business Ethics*, October, 513–18.

George, R. J. (1988) The challenge of preparing ethically responsible managers: closing the rhetoric-reality gap, *Journal of Business Ethics*, **7**, 715–20.

Gerboth, D. L. (1988) Commentary: on the profession, *Accounting Horizons*, **2** (1), 104–8.

Gill, Ravi (1993) Reform needed to build profession's confidence, *Accountancy Age*, 25 February, 10.

Gray, R. H. (1990a) Business ethics and organisational change: building a Trojan horse or rearranging deckchairs on the *Titanic?*, *Managerial Auditing Journal*, **5** (2), 12–21.

Gray, R. H. (1990b) *The Greening of Accountancy: The Profession after Pearce*, ACCA, London.

Gray, R. H. (1990c) Accounting and economics: the psychopathic siblings – a review essay, *British Accounting Review*, **22** (4), 373–88.

Gray, R. H. (1992) Accounting and environmentalism: an exploration of the challenge of gently accounting for accountability, transparency and sustainability, *Accounting Organisations and Society*, **17** (5), 399–425.

Gray, R. H., Bebbington, K. J. and Walters, D. (1993) *Accounting for the Environment: The Greening of Accountancy, Part II*, Paul Chapman, London.

Gray, R. H., Owen, D. L. and Maunders, K. T. (1987) *Corporate Social Reporting: Accounting and Accountability*, Prentice-Hall, Hemel Hempstead.

Greenwood, E. (1957) Attributes of a profession, *Social Work*, July, 44–55.

Gul, F. A., Andrew, B. H., Leong, S. C. and Ismail, Z. (1989) Factors influencing choice of discipline of study: accountancy, engineering, law and medicine, *Accounting and Finance*, **29** (2), 93–102.

Gunz, S. and McCutcheon, J. (1991) Some unresolved ethical issues in auditing, *Journal of Business Ethics*, **10** (10), 777–85.

Gynther, R. S. (1983) The role of tertiary accounting education in today's environment, *Accounting and Finance*, May, 1–19.

Hahn, F. (1984) Reflections on the invisible hand. In *Equilibrium and Macroeconomics* (edited by F. Hahn), Basil Blackwell, Oxford, pp. 109–33.

Harvey, O. J., Reeder, B. L. and Larson, L. M. (1961) *Conceptual Systems and Personality Organisation*, Wiley, New York.

Hauptman, R. and Hill, F. (1991) Deride, abide or dissent: on the ethics of professional conduct, *Journal of Business Ethics*, **10** (1), 37–44.

Hawley, D. D. (1991) Business ethics and social responsibility in finance instruction: an abdication of responsibility, *Journal of Business Ethics*, **10** (9), 711–21.

Hiltebeitel, K. M. and Jones, S. K. (1992) An assessment of ethics instruction in accounting education, *Journal of Business Ethics*, **11** (1), 37–46.

Hines, R. D. (1992) Accounting: filling the negative space, *Accounting, Organisations and Society*, **17** (3), 313–41.

Hopwood, A. G. (1990) Ambiguity, knowledge and territorial claims: some observations on the doctrine of substance over form: a review essay, *British Accounting Review*, **22**(1), 79–88.

Hughson, R. V. and Kohn, P. M. (1980) Ethics, *Chemical Engineering*, **87** (19), 132–47.

Huss, H. F. and Patterson, D. M. (1993) Ethics in accounting: values education without indoctrination, *Journal of Business Ethics*, **12** (3), 235–43.

Institute of Chartered Accountants in England and Wales (1986) *Effective Education and Training for the 21st Century*, ICAEW, London.

Institute of Chartered Accountants in England and Wales (1987) *Training the Business Professional*, ICAEW, London.

Institute of Chartered Accountants in England and Wales (1992) *Business, Accountancy and the Environment: A Policy and Research Agenda* (edited by R. Macve and A. Carey), ICAEW, London.

Jacobson, R. (1991) Economic efficiency and the quality of life, *Journal of Business Ethics*, **10**, 201–9.

Jeffrey, C. (1993) Ethical development of accounting students, non-accounting business students and liberal arts students, *Issues in Accounting Education*, **8** (1), 86–96.

Karnes, A., Sterner, J., Walker, R. and Wu, F. (1989) A bicultural study of independent auditors' perceptions of unethical business practices, *International Journal of Accounting*, **24** (1), 29–41.

Kaye, R. (ed.) (1988) *Proceedings of the Computers in Accounting Education Workshop 1986*, CIMA, London.

Kohlberg, L. (1969) Stages and sequences: the cognitive developmental approach to socialization. In *Handbook of Socialization Theory and Research* (edited by D. Goslin), Rand McNally, Chicago, pp. 347–480.

Kohlberg, L. (1981) *The Meaning and Measurement of Moral Development*, Clark University Press, Worcester, MA.

Kohlberg, L. (1981) *The Philosophy of Moral Development*, Harper and Row, San Francisco.

Kraft, K. L. and Singhapakdi, A. (1991) The role of ethics and social responsibility in achieving organizational effectiveness: students versus managers, *Journal of Business Ethics*, **10** (9), 679–86.

Laughlin, R. C. and Gray, R. H. (1988) *Financial Accounting: Method and Meaning*, Van Nostrand–Reinhold, London.

Laughlin, R. C., Lowe, A. E. and Puxty, A. G. (1986) Designing and operating a course in accounting methodology: philosophy, experience and some preliminary empirical tests, *The British Accounting Review*, **18** (1), 17–42.

Lee, T. A. (1989) Education, practice and research in accounting: gaps, closed loops, bridges and magic accounting, *Accounting and Business Research*, Summer, 237–54.

Lehman, C. (1988) Accounting ethics: surviving survival of the fittest, *Advances in Public Interest Accounting*, **2**, 71–82.

Lehman, C. (1992) *Accounting's Changing Roles in Social Conflict*, Paul Chapman, London.

Lessem, R. (1991) Foreword: greening management. In *Greening Business: Managing for Sustainable Development* (edited by J. Davis), Blackwells, Oxford, pp. 1–16.

Lewis, L., Humphrey, C. and Owen, D. (1992) Accounting and the social: a pedagogic perspective, *British Accounting Review*, **24** (3), 219–33.

Lewis, P. V. (1989) Ethical principles for decision makers: a longitudinal survey, *Journal of Business Ethics*, **8** (4), 271–8.

Lickiss, M. (1991) President's page: measuring up to the environmental challenge, *Accountancy*, January, 6.

Lindblom, C. E. (1984) The accountability of private enterprise: private – no; enterprise – yes. In *Social Accounting for Corporations* (edited by A. M. Tinker), MUP, Manchester.

Loeb, S. E. (1988) Teaching students accounting ethics: some crucial issues, *Issues in Accounting Education*, Fall, 316–29.

Loeb, S. E. (1991), The evaluation of 'outcomes' of accounting ethics education, *Journal of Business Ethics*, **10** (2), 77–84.

Loeb, S. E. and Rockness, J. (1992) Accounting ethics and education: a response, *Journal of Business Ethics*, **11** (7), 485–90.

McCabe, D. L., Dukerich, J. M. and Dutton, J. E. (1991) Context, values and moral dilemmas: comparing the choices of business and law school students, *Journal of Business Ethics*, **10** (12), 951–60.

McDonald, G. M. and Zepp, R. A. (1988) Ethical perceptions of Hong Kong Chinese business managers, *Journal of Business Ethics*, **7**, 835–45.

McKee, A. (1986) The passage from theology to economics, *International Journal of Social Economics*, **13** (3), 5–19.

Mahoney, J. (1990) An international look at business ethics: Britain, *Journal of Business Ethics*, **9** (7), 545–50.

Mahoney, J. (1993) Teaching business ethics, *Professional Manager*, March, 13–15.

Mai-Dalton, R. R. (1987) The experience of one faculty member in a business ethics seminar: what can we take to the classroom?, *Journal of Business Ethics*, **6**, 509–11.

Maklin, R. (1980) Problems in teaching of ethics: pluralism and indoctrination. In *Ethics in Higher Education*, Plenum Press, New York, pp. 61–101.

Martin, T. R. (1981) Do courses in ethics improve the ethical judgement of students?, *Business and Society*, **20** (2), 17–26.

Marton, F. and Saljo, R. (1984) Approaches to learning. In *The Experience of Learning* edited by F. Marton, Hounsell, D. J. and Entwistle, N. J.), Scottish Academic Press, Edinburgh.

Mathews, M. R. (1987) *Social Accounting and the Development of Accounting Education*, Accounting and Finance Discussion Paper No. 68, Massey University.

Mathews, M. R. and Perera, M. H. B. (1990) *Accounting Theory and Development*, Chapman and Hall.

Maunders, K. T. and Burritt, R. (1991) Accounting and ecological crisis, *Accounting, Auditing and Accountability Journal*, **4** (3), 9–26.

Millerson, G. L. (1964) *The Qualifying Association*, Routledge and Kegan Paul, London.

Mintzberg, H. (1983) The case for corporate social responsibility, *The Journal of Business Strategy*, **4** (2), 3–15.

Mischel, W. and Mischel, H. N. (1976) A cognitive social learning approach to morality and self-regulation. In *Moral Development and Behaviour* (edited by T. Lickona), Holt, Reinhart, Winston, New York.

Mitchell, A., Puxty, A., Sikka, P. and Willmott, H. (1991) *Accounting for Change: Proposals for Reform of Audit and Accounting*, Fabian Society, London.

Napier, C. and Power, M. (1992) Professional research, lobbying and intangibles: a review essay, *Accounting and Business Research*, **23** (89), 85–95.

Nelson, D. R. and Obremski, T. E. (1990) Promoting moral growth through intra-group participation, *Journal of Business Ethics*, **9** (9), 731–9.

Owen, D. L. (1992) *Green Reporting: The Challenge of the Nineties*, Chapman and Hall, London.

Paradice, D. B. and Dejoie, R. M. (1991) The ethical decision-making processes of information systems workers, *Journal of Business Ethics*, **10** (1), 1–21.

Patten, R. J. and Williams, D. A. (1990) There's trouble – right here in our accounting programs: the challenge to accounting educators, *Issues in Accounting Education*, **5** (2), 175–9.

Pitt, L. F. and Abratt, R. (1986) Corruption in business: are management attitudes right?, *Journal of Business Ethics*, **5**, 39–44.

Ponemon, L. A. (1990) Ethical judgements in accounting: a cognitive-development perspective, *Critical Perspectives on Accounting*, **1** (2), 191–215.

Ponemon, L. A. (1992) Ethical reasoning and selection-socialization in accounting, *Accounting, Organizations and Society*, **17** (3/4), 239–58.

Ponemon, L. and Glazer, A. (1990) Accounting education and ethical development: the influence of liberal learning on students and alumni in accounting practice, *Issues in Accounting Education*, **5** (2), 193–208.

Power, M. (1991a) Auditing and environmental expertise: between protest and professionalisation, *Accounting, Auditing and Accountability Journal*, **4** (3), 30–42.

Power, M. (1991b) Educating accountants: towards a critical ethnography, *Accounting, Organizations and Society*, **16** (4), 333–53.

Power, M. (1992) After calculation? Reflections on *Critique of Economic Reason* by Andre Gorz, *Accounting, Organizations and Society*, **17** (5), 477–500.

Puxty, A. G. (1986) Social accounting as immanent legitimation: a critique of a technist ideology, *Advances in Public Interest Accounting*, **1**, 95–112.

Puxty, A. G. (1991) Social accountability and universal pragmatics, *Advances in Public Interest Accounting*, **4**, 35–46.

Raines, J. P. and Jung, C. R. (1988) Knight on religion and ethics as agents of social change, *American Journal of Economics and Sociology*, **45** (4), 429–39.

Ramsden, P. (1984) The context of learning. In *The Experience of Learning* (edited by F. Marton, Hounsell, D. J. and Entwistle, N. J.), Scottish Academic Press, Edinburgh.

Reilly, B. J. and Kyj, M. J. (1990) Economics and ethics, *Journal of business ethics*, **9** (9), 691–8.

Rest, J. R. (1974) Judging the important issues in moral dilemmas: an objective measure of development, *Development Psychology*, **10**, 491–501.

Rest, J. R. (1979) *Development in Judging Moral Issues*, University of Minnesota Press, Minneapolis.

Rest, J. R. (1986) *Moral Development: Advances in Research and Theory*, Praeger, New York.

Rest, J. R. (1987) Can ethics be taught to adults?, reprinted in S. M. Mintz (ed.), *Integrating Ethics and Professionalism into the Accounting Curriculum*, California Society of CPAs.

Rohatyn, F. G. (1987) Ethics in American money culture. In *Ethics in American Business: A Special Report*, Touche Ross, New York.

Rosen, B. and Caplan, A. L. (1980) *Ethics in the Undergraduate Curriculum*, The Teaching of Ethics IX, Institute of Society, Ethics and the Life Sciences, New York.

Roslender, R. (1992) *Sociological Perspectives on Modern Accountancy*, Routledge, London.

Ruland, R. G. and Lindblom, C. K. (1992) Ethics and disclosure: an analysis of conflicting duties, *Critical Perspectives on Accounting*, **3** (3), 259–72.

Sangster, A. and Wilson, R. A. (1991) Knowledge-based learning within the accounting curriculum, *British Accounting Review*, **23** (3), 243–61.

Schlachter, P. J. (1990) Organizational influences on individual ethical behaviour in public accounting, *Journal of Business Ethics*, **9** (11), 839–53.

Schmeck, R. R. (1983) Learning style of college students. In *Individual Differences in Cognition*, Vol. 1 (edited by R. F. Dillon and R. R. Schmeck), Academic Press, New York.

Schmidheiny, S. (1992) *Changing Course*, MIT Press, New York.

Schwartz, R. H., Kassem, S. and Ludwig, D. (1991) The role of business schools in managing the incongruence between doing what is right and doing what it takes to get ahead, *Journal of Business Ethics*, **10** (6), 465–9.

Schweikart, J. A. (1992) Cognitive-contingency theory and the study of ethics in accounting, *Journal of Business Ethics*, **11** (5/6), 471–8.

Serwinek, P. J. (1992) Demographic and related differences in ethical views among small businesses, *Journal of Business Ethics*, **11** (7), 555–66.

Shepard, J. M. and Hartenian, L. S. (1991) Egoistic and ethical orientations of university students toward work-related decisions, *Journal of Business Ethics*, **10** (4), 303–10.

Shertzer, B. and Morris, K. (1972) APGA members' ethical discriminatory ability, *Counselor Education and Supervision*, **11** (3), 200–6.

Shute, G. E. (1979) *Accounting Students and Abstract Reasoning: An Exploratory Study*, American Accounting Association, Sarasota, FL.

Sikka, P. (1987) Professional education and auditing books: a review article, *British Accounting Review*, **19** (3), 291–304.

Smith, L. M. (1993) Teaching ethics: an update – part 1, *Management Accounting (US)*, March, 18–19.

Standish, P. E. M. (1983) Accounting education in Australia: 1982–1983, *Accounting and Finance*, November, 1–29.

Stanga, K. G. and Turpen, R. A. (1991) Ethical judgements on selected accounting issues: an empirical study, *Journal of Business Ethics*, **10** (10), 739–47.

Stead, B. A. and Miller, J. J. (1988) Can social awareness be increased through business curricula?, *Journal of Business Ethics*, **7**, 553–60.

Sterling, R. R. (1973) Accounting research, education and practice, *Journal of Accountancy*, September, 44–52.

Stewart, I. C. (1991) The ethics of disclosure in company financial reporting in the United Kingdom 1925–1970, *The Accounting Historians Journal*, **18** (1), 35–54.

Swanda, J. R. (1990) Goodwill, going concern, stocks and flows: a prescription of moral analysis, *Journal of Business Ethics*, **9** (9), 751–9.

Tan, K. and Choo, F. (1990) A note on the academic performance of deep-elaborative versus shallow-reiterative information processing students, *Accounting and Finance*, May, 67–79.

Tinker, A. M. (1984) Theories of the state and the state of accounting: economic reductionism and political voluntarism in accounting regulation theory, *Journal of Accounting and Public Policy*, **3**, 55–74.

Tinker, A. M. (1985) *Paper Prophets: A Social Critique of Accounting*, Holt Saunders, Eastbourne.

Tinker, A. M., Lehman, C. and Neimark, M. (1991) Falling down the hole in the middle of the road: political quietism in corporate social reporting, *Accounting, Auditing and Accountability Journal*, **4**, 28–54.

Trevino, L. K. (1992) Moral reasoning and business ethics: implications for research, education, and management, *Journal of Business Ethics*, **11** (5/6), 445–59.

Turner, Kerry R. and Pearce, David (1990) *The Ethical Foundations of Sustainable Economic Development*, International Institute for Environment and Development/UCL London Environmental Economic Centre.

Tyson, T. (1992) Does believing that everyone else is less ethical have an impact on work behaviour?, *Journal of Business Ethics*, **11** (9), 707–17.

Tyson, Thomas (1990) Believing that everyone else is less ethical: implications for work behaviour and ethics instruction, *Journal of Business Ethics*, **9** (9), 715–21.

United Nations World Commission on Environment and Development (1987) *Our Common Future* (The Brundtland Report), OUP, Oxford.

Waples, E. and Shaub, M. K. (1991) Establishing an ethic of accounting: a reponse to Westra's call for government employment of auditors, *Journal of Business Ethics*, **10** (5), 385–93.

Weber, J. (1990) Measuring the impact of teaching ethics to future managers: a review, assessment, and recommendations, *Journal of Business Ethics*, **9** (3), 183–90.

Weber, J. and Green, S. (1991) Principled moral reasoning: is it a viable approach to promote ethical integrity?, *Journal of Business Ethics*, **10** (5), 325–33.

Williams, B. C. (1991) The impact of IT on basic accounting concepts and accountancy education: an overview. In *IT and Accounting: The Impact of Information Technology* (edited by B. C. Williams and B. Spaul), Chapman and Hall, London.

Willmott, H. (1990) Serving the public interest? A critical analysis of a professional claim. In *Critical Accounts* (edited by D. J. Cooper and T. M. Hopper), Macmillan, Basingstoke, pp. 315–31.

Willis, D. and Clift, J. (1988) Learning for understanding – why is it important?, Paper presented to *NZARE Conference*, Massey University.

Zeff, S. A. (1989) Recent trends in accounting education and research in the USA: some implications for UK academics, *The British Accounting Review*, **21** (2), 159–76.

Zook, D. R. (1982) Learning/instructional theory and accounting instruction: some practical applications, *American Accounting Association News*, 12–17.

Competence is not enough: meta-competence and accounting education

REVA BERMAN BROWN and SEAN McCARTNEY

Abstract

The UK Management Charter Initiative (MCI) movement towards competence-based education is an indication of the growing attention being paid to the notion of the competent professional. There are already developments by the UK accounting bodies to develop detailed programmes to introduce competence-based education to accounting students. Competences have been defined in various ways – a behavioural description of workplace performance; doing rather than knowing; a focus on output (what a person can do) rather than input (what he or she has been taught). The underlying notion is to provide specific skills that are relevant to professional practice. The paper suggests that competences are not enough, and that what is required – meta-competence – can be learned but cannot be taught. Meta-competence is the overarching ability under which competence shelters. It embraces the higher order abilities which have to do with being able to learn, adapt, anticipate and create. Meta-competences are a prerequisite for the development of capacities such as judgement, intuition and acumen upon which competences are based and without which competences cannot flourish. The authors suggest that before syllabuses are created for the teaching of competence-based learning to accounting students, issue should be taken to confront the problematic nature of such teaching, should the existence of meta-competence be ignored.

> The clever men at Oxford
> Know all that there is to be knowed
> But they none of them know one half as much
> As intelligent Mr Toad!
>
> (*The Wind in the Willows*, Kenneth Grahame)

Introduction

The UK Management Charter Initiative (MCI) movement towards competence-based education is an indication of the growing attention being paid to the notion of the competent professional. A number of the UK accounting bodies are in the process of initiating and developing detailed programmes to introduce competence-based education to accounting students. What is intended is to create specifications of skills that are relevant to the usefulness of newly-qualified accountants.

The schemes concerned with the specification of competences being looked at, and worked on, by the Chartered Association of Certified Accountants (ACCA), Chartered Institute of Public Finance and Accountancy (CIPFA), and Chartered Institute of Management Accountants (CIMA) are being designed, developed and carried out largely in conjunction with practitioners, although there is obviously input from university staff. Nevertheless, it would seem that the process of the introduction of competences into accounting education is intended to work outwards from the professional bodies into syllabuses that can be applied by staff at academic institutions.

It is suggested here, however, that before syllabuses are created for the teaching of competence-based learning to accounting students, both those at university and those undertaking professional qualifications, issue should be taken to confront the problematic nature of such teaching. There is still time to question the apparently taken-for-granted assumption that accounting students will benefit from a competence-based approach to their accounting education. It would seem sensible, before boarding the train, to consider whether we wish to arrive at its destination.

The paper takes the following form: first, competences are defined and discussed and their relevance to accounting education is considered. In the second section, the concept of meta-competence is introduced, and its relevance to competence is debated. In the final section, conclusions are drawn about the issues of competence, meta-competence and the accounting student.

Competences

To begin at the beginning, at least in the UK, competence as an educational concept by means of which to accredit ability is linked with the Management Charter Initiative (MCI), a body which emerged in 1988. The MCI wished to address deep-rooted problems in UK management training which, over the years, had been identified in a series of National Economic Development Office (NEDO) and British Institute of Management (BIM) reports, culminating in the Handy Report (1987) and the Constable and McCormack Report (1987).

The MCI competence approach is based on the view that it is possible to define standards which have universal validity and to create tests of those standards. This view is itself based on the assumption that there is a common core of skills and knowledge which all managers or professionals share, which they require in order to perform their roles effectively, and which are capable of fair and impartial assessment.

Frank (1991) suggests that the central principle of assessment is that the onus for providing evidence of competence lies with the candidate, that this will come from more than one source, and that it should adequately reflect his or her unique experience. Competences therefore provide the mechanism to assess whether a particular individual has the ability to fulfil a particular role at work.

An organizational role is a pattern of behaviour by means of which the job is performed. The MCI believes that it is possible to design tests which will allow an individual to demonstrate that he or she is competent – that is, that he or she has sufficient skill and knowledge and is capable (*Concise Oxford Dictionary of Current English*, 1987, pp. 191–192).

Definitions of competence vary – and this itself is part of the problem surrounding the competence movement. Competence appears to be many things, depending on the dictionary or authority being consulted. It can be, *inter alia*:

- a condition of being capable;
- an ability to do;
- a behavioural description of workplace performance;
- doing rather than knowing or being taught.

In embryology, competence is the ability of embryonic tissues to react to external conditions in a way that influences subsequent development. It seems to be this interpretation which guides the ACCA publication *Competences for Registered Auditors* (1990). This document states:

> The elements of competence shown on the following pages define what work a practicing accountant should be able to undertake satisfactorily. They are written in a format consistent with definitions of standards of performance in other professions e.g. engineers, doctors and architects (ACCA, 1990, p. 1).

For ACCA then, 'competence' and 'occupational standard' are synonymous. An occupational standard specifies occupational excellence in a particular employment sector or profession. In the booklet, these standards are expressed at different levels of generalization, moving from the general to the specific. First, a key role is stated, which gives in general terms, the purposes of the whole occupational area. Let us take 'accounting' from the booklet as our example:

Key role

- Prepare and advise on financial information required by a client for management, or external reporting, purposes.

The key roles are then divided into units which describe the major functions associated with the occupation, for example:

Unit

- Develop and monitor accounting systems to produce management information and to meet relevant statutory or other obligations.
- Prepare accounts to meet internal needs and external obligations.

Finally, the units are broken down into elements of competence, which define what an individual should be able to do, for example:

Elements of competence

- Collect and structure the requisite financial data to meet internal needs and external obligations.
- Analyse and appraise financial information and data.
- Produce financial statements and report to client.

The elements of competence are further broken down. For example, in the case of the element 'collect and structure the requisite financial data to meet internal needs and external obligations', the document states:

> this element covers:
> non-incorporated financial agreements
> company non-audit engagements

small company audit and accountancy engagements.
financial data – both internal and external

The element of competence contains the performance criteria which are descriptions of employment expectations and the standards of performance required, for example:

performance criteria – to be met on each occasion:

(a) The client is informed in an appropriate manner of the requisite financial data which must be provided for the compilation of the accounts.
(b) The financial data collected for inclusion in the accounts is as complete as far as it is possible to establish from the available evidence, and a signed certificate to this effect is obtained from the client.
(c) The financial data is [sic] structured in a manner which enables the compilation of financial statements to be carried out efficiently and effectively.

performance criteria – brought into use on every occasion:

(d) Where the practitioner has doubts about the completeness, accuracy or validity of the data which is [sic] presented, a covering letter which identifies the areas of doubt is sent to the client.

It is these performance criteria which allow the individual to deduce whether he or she is competent or not.

The ACCA booklet goes on to explain (1990, p. 1):

> These occupational standards are fully comprehensive and define *all those competences you will need to become a practising accountant* – none is optional. Accordingly, they have to cover more than just routine, task-based work. They also focus on your ability to manage a number of things at once, cope with contingencies, and deal with other aspects of the work environment such as relating to clients and colleagues. *Competence is not restricted to one workplace, but covers other environments and alternative ways of doing things.* It therefore includes the ability to transfer to other situations and changing practice as the need arises (emphasis added).

Where this paper is concerned, the ACCA example is just that – a good example of a well-thought-out competence approach. As the ACCA booklet states, one can find this kind of detailed description of competences and occupational standards wherever the MCI notion of competence has been accepted as a good route to follow for the provision of professional competence. The underlying assumption is that of the MCI – that competences, while work-based, are common to a variety of work situations and work practices. What is eyebrow-raising, however, is that the ACCA booklet asserts with total confidence that it has managed to capture, once and for all, *all* those competences any individual will need to become a practising accountant.

The complex and very detailed scheme developed by ACCA would suggest that the standards being described, and which are to be tested and assessed, are founded upon a solid base of knowledge. There appears to be nothing whatever problematic about what 'an accountant' might be, what 'a professional accountant' might be, or what 'a competent accountant' might be – and whether or not these attributes and abilities can be stripped down to basic skills which can be, and need to be, demonstrated.

The concept of what constitutes accounting knowledge is seemingly more complex than either practising or academic accountants appear to acknowledge. Where accounting's sister-discipline of management is concerned, Hughes (1988) suggests that management knowledge largely consists of an accumulation of empirical evidence and literature from management and related disciplines. This is a partial definition at best, and an indication of the uncertainties surrounding the pinning-down of the elusive concept. This view can be said to apply equally to accounting knowledge.

Another assumption which appears to permeate the competence view is that managers and professionals continuously act in a rational, logical, planning, and goal-seeking manner. The management literature abounds with criticisms and demolitions of this view – for instance, Alvesson (1992), Schön (1987) and Starbuck (1985) – and with researchers putting forward the view that the study of management and its related disciplines is very different from the study of natural sciences – for example, Glaser and Strauss (1967), Mintzberg (1979) and Van Maanen (1979).

The problem where competences are concerned is that, unlike the natural sciences, social science provides evidence and argument, not fact and proof (Lindblom and Cohen, 1979). But competences are being viewed as fact and proof and the ACCA and the other accounting bodies who are about to go down the competence route, seem to consider that its method of assessing the demonstration of 'elements of competence' provides valid, external facts against which accounting competence can be compared.

The limitations of competences have been discussed by a great number of researchers, for example Baker (1991), Brown (1993, 1994), Burgoyne (1989, 1990, 1993), Jacobs (1989) and Thomson (1991). A major criticism is whether the static nature of competences makes them an appropriate measure for professional or managerial ability. The idea that to certificate competence is to certificate ability is problematic. Pressures from the dynamic environment in which the accounting professional or manager operates might require the adjustment of 'elements of competence' or the linkages between certain 'facts and proof' and the creation of others. Does an accountant who has been assessed as competent today stay just as competent over the next five years, increase in competence, or decrease? Is ability, therefore, a static skill which can be assessed once and for all by a static tool?

What this paper suggests is that competences are not necessarily a matter of one level of knowledge and that, in addition, there exist levels which the MCI and the professional accounting bodies appear to disregard – one of which is the level of meta-competence.

Meta-competence

Meta-competence is deeply embedded in learning, in that it is innate and natural to human beings, and can be drawn out of an individual, but cannot, in any traditional sense, be taught. Briefly defined, meta-competences are the higher-order skills and abilities upon which competences are based and which have to do with being able to learn, adapt, anticipate and create, rather than with being able to demonstrate that one has the ability to do. Meta-competences encompass skills such as

> statement, assertion, argument, proof, application and communication (Hills, 1990, p. 19)

and represent the range of perceptions that exist about an individual professional's performance, encompassing also the irrationality and unpredictability of personal feelings. The term 'meta-competences' has been deliberately chosen because the prefix 'meta' means 'above', and meta-competences are those abilities, skills, and capacities which exist above and beyond any competence which an individual may develop, guiding and sustaining them, and from which they originate. *Professional and managerial capacities such as judgement, intuition, and acumen are an essential prerequisite if professionals and managers are to undertake their professional and managerial tasks competently. But such capacities, because they are dynamic and interactive are not competences. If they are anything, they are meta-competences.* In brief, meta-competences are knowledge in all its multi-layered strands and competences are skills, which are knowledge-based.

Bethell-Fox (1992) lists what he calls 'generic competencies', which are what Boyatzis (1982) calls a 'competency' – any personal trait, characteristic or skill which can be shown to be directly linked to effective or outstanding job performance - and what has been defined here as meta-competences. These are illustrated in Table 1.

Kanugo and Misra (1992) in an article considering management skills, suggest that it is possible to distinguish between managerial skills and competences. In terms of this paper's approach, what they define as 'skills' are competences and their definition of 'competences' are meta-competences:

> These attributes include general or specialized knowledge, physical and intellectual abilities, personality traits, motives and self-images (Kanugo and Misra, 1992, p. 1318).

If their explanation of the differences between skills and competences were redefined as the differences between competences and meta-competences, the argument put forward in this

Table 1. Meta-competences (source: Bethell-Fox, 1992)

Cognitive:	*	analytical thinking
	*	pattern recognition (ability to identify patterns and key issues in data or information)
	*	technical expertise
	*	use of concepts (ability to use abstract concepts)
Influencing:	*	interpersonal sensitivity
	*	concern with personal impact
	*	use of influence strategies
	*	relationship building
	*	organizational awareness (understanding the power relationships within organizations)
Managing:	*	group management
	*	directing others (relating to use of unilateral authority)
	*	developing others
	*	concern for order (a concern for minimizing errors and maintaining high quality in one's own or others' work)
Personal:	*	initiative
	*	tenacity
	*	flexibility
	*	self-confidence
	*	self-control
	*	achievement drive

paper is strengthened. Kanugo and Misra provide five areas where distinctions can be made between competences (skills) and meta-competences (knowledge). This is illustrated in Table 2.

The point is that a professional or manager may acquire a number of competences – task-specific skills – all of which can be learned on the job or from participating in professional or management education, but the appropriate or efficient utilization of these competences is dependent on meta-competences, which cannot be so taught.

Competence, meta-competence and the accounting student

The guidelines defining competences put forward by the MCI include the following. Competence is:

1. the ability to perform the activities within an occupational area to the level of performance expected in employment. This embodies the ability to transfer skills and knowledge to new situations, and includes personal effectiveness;
2. an action, behaviour or outcome that can be demonstrated, observed and validly, reliably and objectively assessed, or the demonstrable possession of underpinning knowledge or understanding.

As a result of the above definitions, standards – which form the prime focus of training and the basis of vocational qualifications – are based on:

1. the needs of employment;
2. the concept of competence;
3. the skills, knowledge and levels of performance relevant to the work activity.

Table 2. Comparison of competence and meta-competence (source: Kanugo and Misra, 1992)

Competence	Meta-competence
Ability to engage in an overt behavioural system or sequence	Ability to engage in activities using functional intelligence
Required to handle routine and programmed tasks with established procedures	Ability to engage in non-routine and unprogrammed tasks
Utilized to cope with the demands of the stable aspects of the environment which managers face in their day-to-day organizational life	Necessary to cope with the complex and volatile aspects of of the environment
More specific to particular tasks and situations, e.g. the competence to operate a personal computer	More generalizable or transferable to variety of tasks and situations, e.g. the ability to think analytically or synthetically
Capacities to engage in behaviours that are triggered, elicited, or controlled by the demands of specific tasks and are highly task dependent	Capacities which are non-specific and person dependent

And the factors of point 3 above must be assessable and endorsed by the relevant employment sector or profession.

A point to be considered is that the competence view is concerned to provide accreditation of experience and is not able to evaluate expertise. An effective demonstration of a managerial or professional skill does not simultaneously demonstrate that the manager or practising accountant has the necessary expertise to judge when and if the use of that competence/skill is appropriate in another situation (King, 1992).

In the majority of situations, the complex nature of management and professional knowledge precludes the measuring, in the manner provided by the standards of the MCI, of professional or managerial competence in terms of practical, reliable and objective criteria. Setting aside the extent to which standards focus on the lowest common denominator of a competence, rather than the pursuit of excellence, there tends to be inadequate recognition of the part played by knowledge and understanding. The carrying out of the requirements of the profession of accountancy is a many-layered activity, and while the lower levels may be open to measurement of competences, top management of the profession is more a process of knowledge-realization than the practice of measurable and practical skills. The competent accounting student who qualifies as a practising accountant and aims to become a finance director or a partner will find that competence is not enough.

This becomes clearer if we examine the actual function of qualified accountants. Let us take them in their role as auditors. The key task of the auditor of a UK company is to form an opinion as to whether the financial statements prepared by the directors show 'a true and fair view'. The auditor will plan the audit in the light of prior knowledge of the client, gather evidence, assess the client's system of internal control and so on, in order to arrive at an opinion. Then the opinion is formally communicated in the audit report.

The crucial meta-competences of the competent auditor are those which enable the formation of the opinion. These then inform the other tasks, for example, the nature and quantity of the evidence to be accumulated. Yet a competence-based approach cannot directly capture and assess these meta-competences. For example, in relation to the accumulation of audit evidence, a competence-based approach may specify that 'The auditor must collect relevant and reliable audit evidence, sufficient to enable him or her to form the audit opinion'. This is no doubt true. The competent auditor will not collect insufficient, unreliable or irrelevant evidence. But that is not the essence of the matter. The essence of the matter is the formation of the (subjective by definition) opinion itself.

An example from another discipline may be helpful here. The Cambridge historian, E. H. Carr (1961) rejected the idea that history could be purely factual. Carr suggests that competent historians must do more than get their facts right, because to praise historians for accuracy is like praising architects for using properly mixed concrete in their buildings. It is a necessary condition of their work, but not their essential function.

Similarly, competent professional auditors must 'collect relevant and reliable audit evidence' but that is a 'necessary condition' not an 'essential function'. The problem with the competence-based approach is that, because it cannot capture the 'essential function', it must, of necessity, concentrate on the 'necessary conditions'. A general conclusion from this is that, while competences may be adequate to capture certain functions, they are inadequate for professional and managerial roles. Further, not only are competences 'not enough', a competence-based approach may be positively damaging in that the concentration on what can be defined and explicated ('necessary conditions') under this approach may tend to obscure what cannot. The idea, inherent in the competences movement, that competences are all-encompassing, and contain '... all that there is to be knowed ...' in order for an individual to become a qualified professional, may actually obscure the real problem, rather then making it explicit.

In the professions, the tradition has been to avoid any explication of competence. Rather, those who had qualified were assumed to be competent. While nobody in, for example, the accountancy profession would have argued that passing the professional examinations somehow makes one competent, it was thought that the factual knowledge so demonstrated, together with exposure to good practice during one's training contract, would imbue the aspirant accountant with professional competence, which was then assumed, unless pretty strong evidence to the contrary was forthcoming. Similarly, to take another example which may be more familiar to some readers, teaching has always been a major part of the function of university academics. Yet they were seldom given any training, and never assessed. Their competence was simply assumed. This too has changed, and appraisals and assessments by 'line managers' and 'customers' are all the rage, consuming vast quantities of time, effort and paper, with little observable benefit to anyone. But the object of the exercise is perhaps not to achieve some benefit such as raising the level of professional competence. On the contrary, it would seem that the object of the exercise is achieved by the act of carrying it out, legitimating that action whose legitimacy was once taken for granted. The attempt to reduce professions whose essence is informed judgement to a list of documented competences is out of the same stable and is likely to have as little effect.

The users of competence-based assessment are aware that it provides a partial view of performance. Increasingly, the soft qualities, like sensitivity and creativity, are now seen as critical to an organization's continued survival. The more rigid and inflexible competence-based route cannot provide assistance here (Jacobs, 1989).

A distinction can be drawn between accounting education and accounting training, and competences and meta-competences. Accounting education will incorporate the process of learning the ideas and theories of accounting, and accounting training will provide the knowledge, abilities and skills to perform the various jobs that accountants may be called upon to perform. While it is competences which are being developed during accounting training, meta-competences are not synonymous with accounting education. Instead, they are the higher-order intellectual, cognitive, and emotional capacities without which both accounting education and accounting training are likely to prove ineffectual. Meta-competences exist 'above' both education and training and are called upon during both processes in order for these to contribute to the development of the individual being educated or trained.

It is the meta-competences which come into their own when managers and professionals deal with the complexity of managerial and professional work. Meta-competences represent the range of perceptions that exist about an individual's performance, as well as focusing on the irrationality and unpredictability of personal feelings. Burgoyne (1989, p. 61) points out that the qualitative nature of managerial abilities (meta-competence) requires some other 'certification' which is more effective than

> some spurious claim to the achievement of some absolute and universal standards.

Evaluating and developing the performance of managers and professionals is always going to be a difficult and challenging business (Mangham, 1986). And indeed, management development for managers and professionals in the UK has probably benefited from the introduction of the structure and discipline that competence-based assessment can provide (Jacobs, 1989). Nevertheless, managers and accountants deserve more than the counting and measuring of only those of their abilities that can be narrowly defined into units and elements of competence in order to be demonstrated, observed, and objectively assessed.

When it comes to learning, competences are part of the level where information is received, retained and reproduced as required, and meta-competence is involved in the transformation of information by means of the development of understanding, judgement and creativity.

It is suggested here that the train bearing the competence viewpoint is heading for a destination that is barren and unproductive terrain, and it might benefit the accounting student if the professional bodies left their carriage before the train is travelling too fast for them to jump off and abandon the journey without damage to themselves and their students.

References

Alvesson, M. (1992) Organizations as rhetoric: knowledge-intensive firms and the struggle with ambiguity. Paper presented at the Conference *Knowledge Workers in Contemporary Organizations,* University of Lancaster, September.

Baker, B. R. (1991) MCI management competences and APL: the way forward for management education, training and development? *Journal of European Industrial Training,* **15** (9), 17–26.

Bethell-Fox, C. (1992) *Identifying and Assessing Managerial Competences,* London: Hay Management Consultants Ltd (newly commissioned article for Open University course B884).

Black, H. and Wolf, A. (1990) *Knowledge and Competence: Current Issues in Training and Education,* London: HMSO (Careers and Occupational Information Centre).

Boyatzis, R. E. (1982) *The Competent Manager: A Model for Effective Performance,* New York: John Wiley.

Brown, R. B. (1993) Meta-competence: a recipe for reframing the competence debate? *Personnel Review,* **22** (6), 26–37.

Brown, R. B. (1994) Reframing the competency debate: management knowledge and meta-competence in graduate education. *Management Learning,* **1** (1) forthcoming.

Burgoyne, J. (1989) Creating the managerial portfolio: building on competency approaches to management development. *Management Education and Development,* **20** (1), 56–61.

Burgoyne, J. (1990) Doubts about competency. In *The Photofit Manager: Building a Picture of Management in the 1990s* (edited by H. Devine), London: Hyman.

Burgoyne, J. (1993) The competency movement: issues, stakeholders and prospects. *Personnel Review,* **22** (6), 6–13.

Carr, E. H. (1961) *What is History?* London: Macmillan.

Constable, J. and McCormack, R. (1987) *The Making of British Managers,* London: British Institute of Management.

Frank, E. (1991) The UK's management charter initiative: the first three years. *Journal of European Industrial Training,* **15** (1), 3–12.

Glaser, B. and Strauss, A. (1967) *The Discovery of Grounded Theory,* New York: Aldine.

Handy, C. (1987) *The Making of Managers,* London: National Economic Development Office.

Hills, Sir G. (1990) *The Guardian,* 18 September, p. 19.

Hughes, J. M. (1988) The body of knowledge in management education. *Journal of Management Education and Development,* **19** (4), 301–310.

Jacobs, R. (1989) Getting the measure of management competence. *Personnel Management,* June, pp. 32–37.

Kanugo, R. N. and Misra, S., Managerial resourcefulness: a reconceptualization of management skills. *Human Relations,* **45** (12), 1311–1332.

King, I. (1992) The reality of management knowledge. Paper presented at the conference *Reframing Competences: The Debate In Business and Management Learning,* Bolton Business School, November.

Lindblum, C. E. and Cohen, D. K. (1979) *Usable Knowledge: Social Science and Social Problem Solving,* New Haven: Yale University Press.

Mangham, I. (1986) In search of competence. *Journal of General Management*, **12** (2), 5–12.

Mintzberg, H. (1979) An emerging strategy of 'direct' research. *Administrative Science Quarterly*, **24**, 582–589.

Morgan, G. (1988) *Riding the Waves of Change: Developing Managerial Competences for a Turbulent World*, San Fransisco: Jossey-Bass.

The Chartered Association of Certified Accounting (1990) Competencies for Registered Auditors, London: ACCA

Schön, D. A. (1987) *The Reflective Practitioner: How Professionals Think in Action*, London: Temple Smith.

Starbuck, W. (1985) Acting first, thinking later: theory versus reality in strategic change. In *Organizational Strategy and Change* (edited by J. Pennings) San Francisco: Jossey Bass.

Sykes, J. B. (ed.) (1987) *Concise Oxford Dictionary of Current English*, seventh edition, Oxford: Oxford University Press, pp. 191–192.

Thompson, A. (1991) Ten good things and ten bad things about the MCI. *British Academy of Management Newsletter*, **11**, September.

Van Maanen, J. (1979) The fact of fiction in organizational ethnography. *Administrative Science Quarterly*, **24**, 539–611.

Fostering deep and active learning through assessment

LEN HAND[1], PETER SANDERSON[1] and MIKE O'NEIL[2]

[1]*Nottingham Business School, The Nottingham Trent University*
[2]*Faculty of Education, The Nottingham Trent University*

Abstract

Pressures on the unit of resource within higher education are noted and the possible implications for assessment practice considered. There is a tension between low-cost and high-quality assessments, yet assessment appears to drive the students' agenda and requires careful thought if the programme design is to lead to high-quality learning outcomes. A theoretical framework is presented with the purpose of developing an assessment strategy which will enhance the quality of learning by the student. A case study of an introductory accounting module is described and issues of teaching, learning and assessment are explored. A message of hope is signalled; it may be possible to foster deep learning through assessments which engage the student actively with the subject, despite the apparent constraints acting upon academics.

Introduction

The world of higher education is currently facing a period of immense change. Old styles and methodologies which have served well in the past are having to be re-examined to accommodate a dramatic shift in the framework within which higher education operates. The structure of courses, teaching and learning strategy and the methods of assessment are all open to question in the light of the new demands. It would be easy to be overwhelmed by all the pressures and to adopt a minimalist strategy for survival, to opt for cost-efficient, familiar and safe methods of assessment (for example, end of module examinations). In this paper we wish to posit an alternative strategy of hope with particular reference to the way in which we address the issue of assessment. If tutors wish to maintain quality and ensure that students have an enriching educational experience then new strategies must be developed. We support the contention that one aspect of accommodating the pressures for change is to examine the strategy of assessment (Brown and Knight, 1994). Assessment focuses the attention of both students and staff upon what is important with regard to the content and purpose of an undergraduate's education. For the student the demands of assessment inform and shape the learning strategies she/he will adopt (Biggs, 1989, pp. 21–34), whilst for staff a re-examination of the assessment strategy provides a rationale for determining the style and content of a particular course. If as a starting point the assessment process has a strong theoretical basis then the teaching that follows is more likely to be of a high quality (Brown and Knight, 1994).

Pressures for change

It is universally recognized that the higher education sector has seen a rapid expansion in student numbers during recent years. This has been particularly apparent within departments of accounting which have seen ever rising SSRs to the extent that by subject specialism they represent one of the highest in the sector (see Tables 1 and 2 below). The rise in numbers has been coupled with a decline in the unit of resource. For example, government expenditure plans for 1994–1995 showed a reduction of 45% over 1993–1994 in the class-based student fee income to £750.

As a consequence of the above, student populations within departments have risen and so have class sizes. Methods which would work with small cohorts and small seminar groups do not work as well with very large numbers. Although research shows that the number of 2.1s is

Table 1. Student loads in departments of accounting (within the 'old' universities)

Year	SSR
1984–1985	14.5
1985–1986	15.0
1986–1987	16.1
1987–1988	17.1
1988–1989	17.9
1989–1990	18.6
1990–1991	19.4
1991–1992	20.3
1992–1993	21.4

Source: CVCP and UGC, *University Management Statistics and Performance Indicators in the UK.*

Table 2. Student loads for non-laboratory based subjects (for the 'old' universities)

Cost centre	Subject	SSR	
		1988–1989	1992–1993
28	Planning	9.7	14.4
29	Geography	13.4	18.1
30	Law	18.0	20.9
31	Other social studies	13.5	17.1
32	Business and management	14.2	19.1
33	Accountancy	17.9	21.4
34	Language-based studies	11.4	15.5
35	Humanities	13.4	17.6
36	Creative arts	12.2	16.8
37	Education	11.7	15.7

Source: CVCP and UGC, *University Management Statistics and Performance Indicators in the UK.*

on the increase, it is suggested that this may be more of a reflection of our assessment systems lacking objectivity and reliability, than an increase in the quality of our students (Tarsh, 1990; Knight, 1991). A new way must be found if quality and standards are to be maintained in the face of the above pressures.

We also note the strands of policy being pursued via the 'Enterprise in Higher Education' initiative, the competence movement in general and the GNVQ/NVQ approaches in particular, all of which signal a desire by the government to mould the outcomes of undergraduate education towards a stronger vocational orientation. This is away from the old traditional liberal ethos and towards the needs of employers and the economy. The shift to vocationalism with an emphasis upon 'efficiency' is argued by Preston (1992), who, by drawing on the work of Apple (1985) and Giddens (1985), identified 'instrumental rationality' whereby the concept and criterion of instrumentality is applied to more and more relationships and institutions. In particular it has provoked a crisis for the state so that the scope of politics becomes concerned with 'who can run the economy the best'. Education, as an institution of state, has become enmeshed in this crisis and in this particular way of rationalizing and legitimizing policy. To summarize, Preston (1992) seemed to be saying that politics has become a matter of technical decision making, as opposed to the maximization of social welfare. All of these initiatives represent new forces for change which drive us to assess our students in ways which may be outside our normal methodologies.

Modular courses have been introduced which have provided greater student choice and opportunities for credit accumulation transfer. Whilst recognizing the benefits that modularity can bring it does give rise to concerns that assessment will only be used for summative purposes via the end of module exams. As a result, the range of assessment techniques may be severely restricted and consequently focus only upon particular abilities and thus disadvantage some students. The first criterion for choosing a particular form of assessment may be to achieve an objective yet cost-effective system, rather than one that will be embedded within the design of the curricula. As a result, assessments may all appear towards the end of the semester with the students being generally over-assessed and over-stressed. All of these factors will inevitably erode the quality of the learning experience of undergraduates, whilst at the same time placing greater work-loads upon academic staff.

In conjunction with all of these constraints the HEFCE assessment exercise is designed to ensure that minimum levels of quality are maintained and that 'excellence' in teaching is highlighted. Additionally, ranking exercises will have the effect of stimulating institutional competition. It has been noted by Puxty et al. (1994) that the market language of the 'New Right' with students becoming customers, courses becoming products and the use of mission statements (which sound more like marketing strategies than educational aims), have all contributed to a shift in the way in which academics perceive their individual roles. At the same time their power to contribute and influence has been eroded. The full impact that this has upon the individual lecturer is to change the ethos under which she/he operates. This change has been identified by Puxty et al. (1994) as the 'commodification' of academic labour.

The cumulative effect of all these changes is to place the system under stress. If the participants in higher education are to meet the challenges of the future they will have to develop new and imaginative approaches to meet the demands for higher quality and relevance from undergraduates and employers, yet also achieve the cost savings demanded by the government without compromising the quality of our courses. Assessment is a key feature within this puzzle. On the one hand, assessment is seen as a cost driver; at the same time assessment is a major influence upon the quality of the learning process (Gibbs, 1992).

A suggested framework for development of the teaching and learning paradigm

Within the whole cycle of design and delivery of programmes and assessment there are two learning processes at work. The teaching team are engaged in a continuous refinement process which can be likened to the action enquiry spiral (Elliott, 1991). This refinement leads to a programme design with which the student is invited to engage. The student, in turn, is engaged in his/her own learning process which ultimately leads to learning outcomes. Finally, the cycle begins again as tutors review the visible learning outcomes. Our current view of this cycle is depicted in Figure 1.

General comments on the framework

The model presented above is an attempt to draw upon elements of educational theory and to integrate them into a framework which can form a basis for the development of any educational programme. A number of theorists (including Biggs, Brown and Knight, Carr and Kemmis, Kolb and Marton and Saljo) have shaped the development of the above model and certain of their theories have helped us to define the processes through which both students and staff move in order to improve learning outcomes.

Action inquiry

The starting point for the model offered above (Figure 1) is of the tutors using elements of an action inquiry model. In this tradition a question is posed by the teacher on the lines of 'how can I do this better?'. For example, 'how can my assessment process and content provoke better learning outcomes from students?'. Action research is based on a cycle (or, more accurately, a spiral) which runs along the general lines of – review (of a problem situation) – diagnosis – planning –implementation – reflecting – further review. See, for example Carr and Kemmis (1986), Winter (1989) and Elliott (1991).

Carr and Kemmis (1986) characterized action inquiry as a self-reflective cycle in which the inquirer goes through the process of planning, acting, observing and reflecting. The cycle invokes the sense of continuous improvements to the teaching/learning process rather than of seeking out some ultimate optimal 'solution'. Thus, in the model, the tutor focuses upon the programme design with a view to improving the quality of the learning outcomes. We are not suggesting that tutors engage in a *formal* action inquiry for each of their programmes; rather that considered refinement of the programme requires, at least, a process grounded in the principles of action inquiry.

Programme design

In the design stage, tutors are trying to construct situations that will cause students to adopt particular learning strategies. Piaget (within Flavell, 1963) stated that 'A person is driven to learn when their cognitive structures are unable to handle a particular situation.' The implication is that tutors must create cognitive conflict in order for students to learn. This would mean that a tutor would need to present the student with learning, teaching and

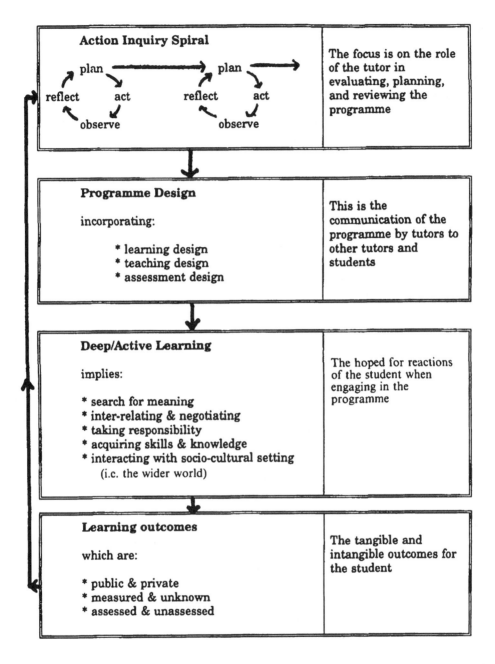

Fig. 1. Framework for development of the teaching and learning paradigm.

assessment situations which cause the student to move outside the normal parameters in which the student knows and views the world. Thus, the students are caused to appraise the new situation and find their preconceptions and previously internalized knowledge challenged. As a result the new learning situation would bring about a change in the students' perceptions and the new learning would become internalized. Piaget's ideas underpin much of our framework, with particular reference to the programme design and the notion of active learning.

As students are undertaking the learning elements of the assessment they bring with them the totality of the experiences which have shaped their cognitive development. Clearly this will be a unique developmental process for each student. Perry (1988) offered insights into how the student develops cognitively; each stage of cognitive development will influence a student's approach to learning and the possible learning outcomes. Perry (1988) observed that students tend to mature and progress through the following main stages.

1. Dualistic – the student sees the world as a place of absolutes with clear rights and wrongs.
2. Multiplistic – the student comes to recognize that there are multiple perspectives to a problem but is unable to evaluate each perspective. A typical response would be 'we are all entitled to our own opinion'.
3. Relativistic – the student sees knowledge as relative to particular frames of reference, shows a capacity for detachment in seeking the overall picture and evaluates his/her own ideas as well as others to seek out alternative perspectives. Under the relativistic view authority (the tutor) is seen as someone who can and should be questioned.

Deep and active learning

The terms surface and deep learning were first identified by Marton and Saljo (1976). They tested the processes and outcomes of learning by asking a group of 40 students to read text and to relate what they had understood and the ways in which they had approached the task. The students (first-year undergraduates) were asked to read three chapters of text. The answers to questions were recorded and categorized into four different levels dependent upon the quality of the response. Level A indicated a deep level of understanding. *All* students were then *given* a level A answer by the researcher. Six weeks later the students were retested and *only those* who had learned in a 'deep sense' appeared to have retained the understanding.

Marton and Saljo (1976) concluded that if there are qualitative differences in terms of the outcome of the learning then this seems likely to be linked into the process by which the students have learned. They identified two types of processes of learning 'which we shall call deep level and surface level approaches' (Marton and Saljo, 1976, p. 7). The surface level approach is a reproductive conception of learning, rote learning of the text, the sign itself. In the case of deep learning the student is directed towards the *intentional* content.

From this early work a body of research has developed. Entwistle and Ramsden (1983), Biggs (1987), Pask (1988) and Entwistle and Tait (1990) all suggested that students who adopt a deep approach to learning (i.e. a meaning orientation) are more likely to achieve successful learning outcomes than those who adopt a surface approach (i.e. a reproducing orientation). Ramsden (1981) introduced a third approach to learning which he labelled 'strategic'. Strategic learning is evidenced by students who are highly motivated and who use both surface and deep strategies dependent upon the learning and/or assessment situation before them.

Presumably tutors will want to design learning programmes that encourage the students to take a holistic and deep approach and to adopt a meaning orientation to study. Assessment procedures which emphasize factual information encourage students to adopt a surface approach (see, for example Thomas, 1986).

Implications of the deep/surface distinction for programme design

The design of the course will signal to the students the type of learning approach which is likely to succeed. Some students on occasions may adopt a strategic surface approach in response to the demands of the course. For example, combinations of, a lack of choice over subjects and methods of study, a heavy work-load with lots of course material, high class contact allied to teacher-centred learning and, finally, an anxiety-provoking assessment (for example, a traditional examination with little or no prior formative feedback) may induce a surface approach and tend to lead to a closed perception of learning (Gibbs, 1992).

In contrast, Biggs (1989), noted four key elements which are conducive to the creation of a deep learning approach. It should be noted that none of these elements are influenced by an individual lecturer's performance. They instead reflect features of the learning environment which in varying degrees are affected by course design and assessment methods.

1. *Motivational context.* This is increased when the students have a need to know; a need to be involved in choosing what they will learn, and how they will learn. They will then take ownership of the learning process. Conservative, teacher-centred approaches to teaching large classes can lead to alienation and low motivation amongst students.

2. *Learner activity.* Deep learning is associated with *doing*, so students need to be active. More connections will be made with past learning and between new concepts if the learner is active together with time for reflection. A 'Kolbian' learning cycle is at

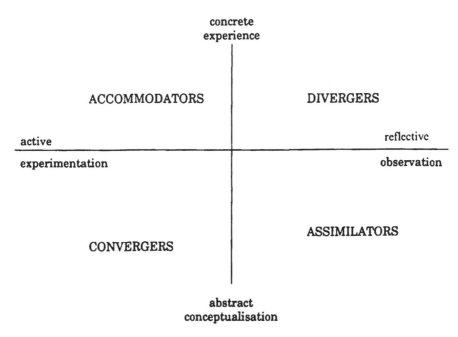

Fig. 2. Kolb's (1974) experiential learning cycle.

work (see later discussion of Kolb's (1974) learning cycle).

3. *Interaction with others.* Students benefit from discussing their ideas with others. This can be done via learning sets, support groups or peer tutoring. In large classes the level of meaningful discussion inevitably falls, yet at the individual level this represents a vital opportunity for personal development.

4. *Well-structured knowledge base.* It is important that the students' current knowledge is used when developing the subject matter. The subject matter needs to be well structured with content taught in integrated wholes. Lecturers are able to signal the structure of the knowledge base but are unable to build upon the personal knowledge and experience that each student brings.

In summary then, deep learning is more likely to emerge when the process is student-centred. Pressure from large student numbers has produced a tendency for courses to become more teacher-centred and for students to see closed perception as good. The students are fearful when faced with the responsibility for taking control of their own learning.

Learning cycles and the work of Kolb

The process of active-deep learning may be facilitated by the reflective activities of 'learning by doing'. This is known as experiential learning within the Kolb framework. It is worth examining the Kolb model in some detail as it helps us to further understand the above framework. It also has a lineage of application to accounting education from which certain principles and conclusions can be drawn.

Kolb's (1974) learning cycle was based upon the work of Jung (1923) who provided the foundation of the learning cycle by examining individual behaviour in terms of the continua of extrovert–introvert and concrete–abstract. The model moves through four stages: concrete experience (CE), reflections and observations (RO), abstract conceptualization (AC) and active experimentation (AE). This process has been referred to as experiential learning or learning by doing. The key feature is that learners interact with their environment and transform it by thinking and doing in a systematic way. Theory and practice are inextricably and creatively linked in the model proposed. The Kolbian model shows how knowledge (knowing how and knowing that) is a function of experience, reflection on this experience by self and others, an active, constructionist search for the meaning of this experience and testing out this new understanding in practice.

The cognitive psychologists Harvey *et al.* (1961) and Flavell (1963) have identified two dimensions for cognitive growth. One dimension is a continuum between concrete experience and abstract conceptualization with active experimentation and reflective observation in the other dimension. Students will develop learning preferences shaped by experience and personality which will reflect a trade-off between CE and AC and between AE and RO. Learners are then categorized by their preferences and have been labelled as accommodators (CE and AE), divergers (CE and RO), convergers (AC and AE) and assimilators (AC and RO). Each of the learning types has certain characteristics. For example, the converger applies deductive reasoning to problem solving and decisions are based upon the practical application of ideas. Hence, they are argued to prefer technical tasks to working with people. The diverger is opposite to the converger and prefers to learn via concrete experience and reflective observation. Consequently, divergers are good at evaluating concrete situations from a variety of perspectives. The assimilators' characteristics are for abstract conceptualization and reflective observation which points towards excellence at inductive reasoning and a preference for sound and logical theories. When practice fails to match theory assimilators are likely to question the facts first. Finally, the accommodator is a person who prefers to learn through concrete experience and active experimentation. Accommodators like to do practical things by experimenting and taking risks and tend to solve problems by trial and error.

Kolb (1976) developed a learning style inventory to measure individual learning styles as proposed by the experiential model and there have been a number of surveys which have sought to discover if students enrolled on particular courses exhibit a dominant learning style. If it could be established that a particular learning style is more in evidence, then curricula may be adapted to accommodate the learning preferences of the students.

Baker *et al.* (1986) surveyed 110 accounting majors in their final year and found a preference (40%) for the converger learning style, with the balance of students evenly split amongst the remaining learning styles. Brown and Burke's (1987) survey of 266 accounting students concluded that there appeared to be an increasing preference for the convergent learning style, as accounting students are exposed over time to a greater concentration of accounting education and related work experience. The same findings were found among accounting practitioners by Collins and Milliron (1987) who, in a sample of 344, found the converger style dominant. These findings were independent of firm type and area of specialization.

Some dissatisfaction has been expressed at the reliability of these original studies. Nunnally (1978) recommended the use of 'α coefficients' to measure the internal consistency of the items comprising the scale within the learning style inventory (LSI). Values of 0.80 and above are recognized as values which would indicate inherent reliability. Stout and Ruble (1991) applied the LSI to a sample of 235 students and 0.56 was the highest value of α coefficient they recorded. A test–retest classification has also been carried out by Sims *et al.* (1986) with only 47% classified in the same learning category after a 5 week period.

Stout and Ruble (1991) concluded with the following recommendations. Firstly, that the early research findings must be treated with a degree of caution. Although the theory of learning styles is helpful we should be wary of the results until psychometric testing is proved to be sufficiently valid and reliable. However, sensitivity to differences in learning styles when designing curricula and teaching within seminar groups is valid as there is no dispute that differing learning styles exist.

To summarize: using Kolb's terminology, a student engaged in an active learning approach will be more likely to use **all** parts of the learning cycle, e.g. following a concrete experience they will reflect upon the outcome and form abstract concepts which will provide the basis for further active experimentation resulting in a new concrete experience. Students who are adopting a surface approach are more likely to use only a small part of the cycle, e.g. concrete experience – reflective observation and back.

Learning outcomes

The final stage in the teaching/learning process is that of learning outcomes – although we recognize that the notion of a 'final stage' is problematic in the context of what is fundamentally a cyclical process. We would support the notion that '... learning should be seen as a qualitative change in a person's way of seeing, experiencing, understanding, conceptualising something in the real world – rather than as a quantitative change in the amount of knowledge someone possesses' (Marton and Ramsden, 1988, pp. 268–86). However, this qualitative emphasis highlights a paradox within the learning outcomes stage: what is public, measured and assessed is recorded and carries weight – yet it is the private, unknown and unassessed outcomes which matter (at least to the student) in the long-term. Any publicly assessed measure can only be a surrogate for the real changes and learning which have occurred.

The case study – assessment of introductory accounting

Having established a framework for analysis, we now move onto a specific case study of accounting assessment. We will use this case study to explore some of the issues which have been discussed in the early part of the paper.

Background to the case
Within the wider higher education context noted earlier, Nottingham Trent University became committed to modularizing and semesterizing first-year undergraduate courses by September 1993. The semestral model adopted by the university had 15 weeks in each semester, though each had a holiday break of several weeks within the semester. The 'introduction to accounting' (ITA) module under review in this paper was one of a batch of six common-core semesterized modules delivered for the first time during semester 1– 1993–1994.

Students and courses
The following numbers show the scale of the ITA module quite graphically.

1. Just under 500 of our own university students, from 12 separate courses took ITA in its first year, along with a further 100 students in franchised colleges.
2. Sixty-seven of our own students were studying by a part-time route and a further 29 were following courses in the design faculty.

Though these numbers are significant, they do not reveal the wide variety of the following.

1. Student academic qualifications: there was a wide range of A level points, BTEC and other non-standard entry qualifications.
2. Prior exposure to business/accounting studies: a minority of students had studied A level accounting, but most knew nothing about the subject.
3. Student comfort with numeric analysis: one course, for example, did not require even GCSE maths as a prerequisite.
4. Student motivation towards the study of finance: accounting undergraduates had chosen the subject as a specialism; while some non-accounting students possibly saw the study of finance as peripheral.
5. Previous business experience: part-time students often had a fair amount of real experience with business accounting statements, while for most 18 year olds the study was far removed from their own experiences.

In summary then, although the module design and the assessment was common for the entire cohort, the students exhibited a wide range of prior experience and learning, basic skills (particularly numeracy) and orientation towards accounting. We should not be surprised then, to use Perry's (1988) terms to discover a wide range in the stages of maturation and cognitive development.

The teaching team

ITA was staffed by a team of 14 seminar tutors taking 35 seminar groups (excluding the five franchised colleges). The team of 14 had the following characteristics: two members were part-time tutors, four tutors were new to first-year UK undergraduate teaching and three of the tutors were involved in writing the set in-house textbook for the module and with delivering the lectures. Tutors in higher education have always been used to the notion of working in teams. However, modular courses such as ITA create larger teams than hitherto and make team working more difficult to manage and to administer. Perhaps a more fundamental problem with large teams of tutors is agreeing and communicating a common approach to the subject.

Approaches to introductory accounting

Previous attempts at establishing a common first-year accounting curriculum were often perceived within the school as either too specialized for the non-accountant (e.g. BABS students) or too general for the specialist (e.g. accounting undergraduates). The redesigned module (ITA) was based on the fundamental notion that all first-year students (whether specialists or not) begin as naive users of accounting information. The accounting-specialist students also took other accounting modules both alongside ITA and following ITA.

Eleven of the 14 tutors had only peripheral input into the in-house textbook and teaching programme and some conflicts arose concerning the content, ordering, assessment and emphasis of the module. Clearly there are tensions here.

1. To invite the involvement of all tutors in the certain knowledge that agreement will be difficult to establish or to use (as with ITA) a small core of designers and run the risk of alienating some team members.
2. Tutors feel the need, naturally, to express their individual preferences in seminar meetings, yet the module should be seen to be offering all students a consistent approach.

Feedback from staff members indicates some fair success in overcoming these tensions through a text written specially for the module, a detailed tutor guide, a common lecture programme, a flexible seminar programme with pre-designed material offering some choice for tutors to match the learning needs of different groups and a common assessment which allowed for student/tutor negotiation on content.

The ITA assessment

Assessment of first-year accounting had previously followed two general patterns: a course-work assignment requiring the student to undertake a 'corporate analysis' (i.e. to analyse the performance of a real company from publicly available information) and a closed book examination. The introduction of a new module within a newly semesterized programme, provided an opportunity for a rethink of the assessment strategy. There had been considerable dissatisfaction with the previous assessment models: staff believed that both had resulted in closed surface-type learning among a large proportion of the students. Closed book exam-inations had led to 'question spotting' and learning about 'how to pass the examination' rather than learning about the subject, while the corporate analysis assignment was typified by mediocre, descriptive, bland and superficial scripts.

The roots of the 'new' assessment model in this case were to be found in an introductory accounting course delivered some years previously to a group of around 30 non-business students at another university. The assessment which had been used on that course took the form of a 'business plan'. The students were asked to imagine setting up a new business of their own choice and to produce financial projections for the first 2 years. The outcomes had been surprisingly positive; students had engaged with the subject, conducted rigorous research and produced relevant and informative information which pulled together various strands of the course. However, that had been for 30 students, with only one tutor who both delivered and assessed all of the students. Could this idea be transferred to a course of some 500 students with a large group of teachers? The tutors most closely involved with the module design, after lengthy consideration of the possible value and risks, decided to adopt the 'business plan' model for assessing the ITA module.

This 'new' assessment approach was, of course, not new at all! We were aware that similar schemes had run on HND courses for several years. However, it was quite novel for most of the staff members on the ITA team and was certainly new for first-year undergraduate courses in this university. Compared with previous assessment patterns, each piece of work would be unique in that students could select different types of businesses (subject to undiscovered plagiarism!) and, hence, the marking scheme would have to address process rather than content and marking time would probably be higher than more conventional work.

We can recognize that the 'new' assessment demonstrated a number of the key features of the framework for analysis offered earlier in the paper (particularly the programme design linked to the work of Gibbs, (1992)). Specifically the 'business plan' assessment was as follows.

1. Required active participation on the part of the student.
2. Allowed for negotiation and student choice regarding the type of business to be studied.
3. Was rooted in the real world of business and required research into, for example, markets, selling prices and costs.
4. Drew together the various threads of material in the ITA module.
5. Required an iterative process to link together in a meaningful way costs, revenues, cvp analysis, accounting statements, ratio analysis, thus seeking to engage the student in the **full** learning cycle as proposed by Kolb (1974).

Students were given the assessment brief early in the semester. Despite advice that the project should be commenced early many students appeared not to take this too seriously. As a result many of the later seminars were taken over by student queries with regard to their assignment. It became clear that the nature of the project provided the students with an alternative agenda, which to a large extent overruled the predetermined seminar programme of the module team and illustrated quite dramatically the notion that assessment drives the students' programme (see, for example Gibbs, 1992).

The marking process followed a fairly traditional pattern with a detailed marking scheme which was refined after sample marking, double marking of random scripts and marginal scripts and detailed feedback to students via a grade plus qualitative comments.

Table 3 summarizes the results for the 482 university students by degree classification and distinguishes results for four broad categories of student: accounting students, following an accounting degree or a foundation course, non-accounting business students, from courses

Table 3. Results summary, 1993–1994

	First	2.1	2.2	Third	Fail	Total
Accounting students	10	32	20	11	7	80
Non-accounting business students	27	72	98	75	34	306
Part-time business students	19	18	11	13	6	67
Non-business students	0	7	9	10	3	29
All students	56	129	138	109	50	482

such as BABS, part-time business students (part-time BABS or HNC) and non-business students, from the design faculty.

Comments on the results

Given the scale of module, the size of the teaching team and the variety of students, the most remarkable aspect of the marks summary appears to be its normality! The grades profile, on the surface, indicates a quite normal spread of marks and suggests that the project discriminated between excellent and weak students.

Though we may have assumed that this particular assignment would play to the strengths of the accounting students, in the event the performance of the part-time students matched the 'specialists' [commitment, maturity and experience possibly making up for lack of special interest? – see again Perry (1988)]. Though there were no firsts from the non-business group, it was pleasing to see that this group did produce solid work and achieved a fair level of understanding. Anecdotally, the design group often exhibited far more flair in their choice of project than their peers in the business school.

Reflections on the case

There are many issues raised by this case study. We have chosen to focus upon the assessment aspects because our experience confirms Brown and Knight's (1994, p. 12) claim that 'Assessment is at the heart of the undergraduate experience. Assessment defines what students regard as important ... (and) ... how they spend their time ... '.

In this final part of the paper we reflect upon the issues which have struck us most forcibly. We were assisted in this reflection by a survey which we undertook with the 14 staff members who delivered the course.

The staff questionnaire

A five-point 'Likert-scale' questionnaire was completed by all staff members relating to their own views and feelings about the ITA module; there were 55 questions in all and we have reported here upon those which relate to the assessment of the module.

The results of this survey (insofar as they relate to assessment) are given in Table 4 below. The alphabetical references a, b, c, etc., are the individual members of staff – thus a vertical scan of the table allows for an overall view of individuals' views. The mean score for each statement provides a simple mean response of the team. A mean of 3 would suggest a response which, overall, was neutral towards the particular statement. The 'ideal' mark is

Table 4. ITA staff opinion survey, Spring 1994

	Staff member														Mean	'Ideal'
	a	b	c	d	e	f	g	h	i	j	k	l	m	n		
A significant number of my students appeared to leave the assessment very late	1	1	1	1	2	2	1	2	1	1	1	3	1	5	1.64	5
Concerns about the assessment detracted from the progress which I could make through the seminar programme	2	4	4	2	2	1	1	1	2	2	1	1	1	2	1.86	5
The assessment was too difficult for the students I taught	2	3	5	5	2	2	3	4	4	2	4	1	4	2	3.07	5
The assessment took too long to mark	1	5	3	5	1	1	2	2	1	1	2	1	4	2	2.21	5
The assessment was a challenging project	2	1	1	1	1	1	2	2	1	1	1	1	1	1	1.21	1
The assessment was very student centred	2	1	3	1	1	1	3	2	1	1	1	4	1	1	1.64	1
My students did a lot better than I would have expected	3	3	3	3	2	2	2	2	2	2	2	2	1	2	2.21	1
Concerns about the assessment took up too much seminar time	3	3	5	4	2	2	1	1	2	2	1	1	1	1	2.07	5
The assessment encouraged students to come to grips with most aspects of the ITA module	4	2	5	1	1	2	2	4	2	2	1	4	1	4	2.50	1
I took an unacceptable amount of 'out-of-class' time in answering student queries about the assessment	2	4	2	4	2	1	1	1	1	2	2	1	2	1	1.86	5
The assessment appeared to discriminate quite well between strong and weak students	2	2	2	1	1	2	2	1	1	2	1	3	1	1	1.57	1
If involved in the review process I would not suggest major changes to the assessment	4	2	4	1	1	5	4	2	3	4	2	5	1	3	2.93	

1, strongly agree; 2, in broad agreement; 3, neither agree nor disagree; 4, broadly disagree; 5, strongly disagree.

more contentious: we have suggested the mean mark which we may have expected to see in a perfect world – a kind of ideal standard! Some statements do not have an ideal as there is some debate about the preferred outcome. Indeed, the reader may question some of our stated ideals! Assuming that the ideal is accepted as a target then the differences between the ideal and the mean and between the ideal and individual scores become important – indicating an experience or expectation gap.

Taking three statements together regarding the students' approach to the project:

> A significant number of my students appeared to leave the assessment very late ... Concerns about the assessment detracted from the progress which I could make through the seminar programme ... Concerns about the assessment took up too much seminar time.

The broad measure of agreement to these statements highlights an apparent contradiction which many tutors will have experienced: students know that the coursework is important, yet often fail to manage their time effectively and frequently leave coursework and revision until (by the tutor's standards) very late. Of course the student may merely be operating to an alternative agenda and may be quite comfortable with a 'last-minute' approach – very few of these students actually missed the final deadline. However, what is raised for us by these statements is the issue of mismatch between, on the one hand, appropriate learning styles for a higher education environment and, on the other, an inexperienced first-year cohort who have not yet had an opportunity to adopt the approaches which will maximize their learning outcomes.

There follows a series of statements which reveal staff views about the general nature and degree of difficulty of the project and about their students' success in tackling it.

> The statements – 'The assessment was a challenging project' ... 'The assessment was very student-centred' ... 'The assessment appeared to discriminate quite well between strong and weak students' ... 'My students did a lot better than I would have expected' – met with widespread agreement.

> The statement – 'The assessment encouraged students to come to grips with most aspects of the ITA module' – met with agreement from most of the team, but five of the tutors disagreed.

> 'The assessment was too difficult for the students I taught' evoked a very patchy response.

We feel that these responses are (generally) encouraging in that students are surprising their tutors with good performance, discrimination is occurring and deeper, student-centred learning is evident. The responses are, of course, merely surrogates for what the students experienced and may tell us more about the variety of staff attitudes and experiences than about the students. Perhaps this batch of questions is opening up the Pandora's box of mixed educational philosophies which will be inevitable within a large teaching team. Our own personal view is that we have a stimulating and powerful assessment vehicle which encourages the student to engage with the subject in an active and responsible manner.

Two final statements are worth considering as they reflect back on one of our initial concerns: the pressures on staff in higher education. The statements 'I took an unacceptable amount of "out-of-class" time in answering student queries about the assessment' and 'The assessment took too long to mark' gained a large measure of agreement. There was certainly a strong feeling amongst some (but by no means all) of the tutors that they were overloaded by the assessment, both in marking time and in responding to student queries and anxieties. It may be that this module (and the unique assessment in particular) was seen as an embodiment of many of the structural and environmental changes which staff were experiencing at the time.

All of our formal and informal feedback tells us that the students found the project a real challenge. They clearly used the project as a valuable learning experience in that it required them to integrate the course material and to relate it to a practical situation. The assessment moved beyond requiring the students to regurgitate material and did encourage them to adopt a deeper active learning style.

Conclusions

Traditional ways of designing and delivering introductory accounting have been built around *inputs*, mainly a syllabus delivered through lectures and seminars. We believe that a more rewarding model can be built around the *learning outcomes* and the *student's learning process*. Although the tightening of resources is inevitably driving academics towards lower contact times, this need not be seen as a threat, but as an opportunity to re-examine our preconceptions about teacher-led programmes. The assessment (form, content and process) is the most powerful signal which we send to students. We agree with Ramsden (1988, p. 21) when he stated that '... perhaps the most significant single influence on students' learning is their perceptions of assessment ... most students try to deliver what they predict their tutors will reward ...'. When tutors design assessments they are explicitly or implicitly sending signals to students which in turn will encourage a particular learning response. If students' responses disappoint us (for example, with mechanistic, instrumental or superficial responses) perhaps we should look again at our assessment design.

References

Apple, M. (1985) *Education and Power*. Boston: Ark Paperbacks.

Baker, R., Simon, J.R. and Bazeli, P. (1986) An assessment of the learning style preferences of accounting majors. *Issues in Accounting Education* **Spring**, 1–12.

Biggs, J.B. (1987) *Student Approaches to Learning and Studying*. Melbourne: Australian Council for Educational Research.

Biggs, J.B. (1989) Does learning about learning help teachers with teaching? Psychology and the tertiary teacher. *University of Hong Kong Supplement to the Gazette*. **36** (1), 21–34.

Brown, H.D. and Burke, R.C. (1987) Accounting education: a learning styles study of professional-technical and future adaptation issues. *Journal of Accounting Education* **Fall**, 207–26.

Brown, S. and Knight, P. (1994) *Assessing Learners in Higher Education*. London: Kogan Page.

Carr, W. and Kemmis, S. (1986) *Becoming Critical: Education, Knowledge, and Action Research*. London: Falmer Press.

CNAA *Improving Student Learning*.

Collins, J.H. and Milliron, V.C. (1987) A measure of professional accountants learning style. *Issues in Accounting Education* **Fall**, 193–206.

Elliott, J. (1991) *Action Research for Educational Change*. Milton Keynes: Open University Press.

Entwistle, N.J. and Ramsden, P. (1983) *Understanding Student Learning*. London: Croom Helm.

Entwistle, N.J. and Tait, H. (1990) Approaches to learning, evaluations of teaching, and preferences for contrasting academic environments. *Higher Education* **19**, 169–94.

Flavell, J. (1963) *The Developmental Psychology of Jean Piaget.* Van Nostrand Reinhold.

Gibbs, G. (1992) *Improving the quality of student learning through course design.* In *Learning to Effect* (edited by R. Barnett), pp. 149–65. Milton Keynes: Open University Press.

Giddens, A. and Habermas, J. (1985) Politics as technology: the return of grand theory V. *Australian Society,* **May,** 17–19.

Harvey, O.J., Hunt, D. and Schroeder, H. (1961) *Conceptual Systems and Personality Organisation.* John Wiley.

Jung, C.G. (1923) *Psychological Types.* London: Pantheon Books.

Knight, P.T. (1991) Value added and history in public sector higher education. *Public Sector History Newsletter* **3** (1), 23–31.

Kolb, D.A. (1974) *On Management and Learning Process Organisational Psychology: A Book of Readings.* Englewood Cliffs, NJ: Prentice Hall.

Kolb, D.A. (1976) *Learning Style Inventory: Technical Manual.* Boston: McBer and Company.

Marton, F. and Ramsden, P. (1988) What does it take to improve learning? In *Improving Learning: New Perspectives* (edited by P. Ramsden), pp. 268–86. London: Kogan Page.

Marton, F.A. and Saljo, R. (1976) On qualitative differences in learning: 1 – outcome and process. *British Journal of Educational Psychology,* **46,** 4–11.

Nunnally, J.C. (1978) *Psychometric Theory.* New York: McGraw-Hill.

Pask, G. (1988) Learning strategies, teaching strategies and conceptual or learning style. In *Learning Styles and Strategies,* pp. 83–100. New York: Plenum Press.

Perry, W.G. (1988) Different worlds in the same classroom. In *Improving Learning: New Perspectives* (edited by P. Ramsden), pp. 145–61. London: Kogan Page.

Preston, N. (1992) Computing and teaching: a socially-critical review. *Journal of Computer Assisted Learning* **8,** 49–56.

Puxty, A.G., Sikka, P. and Willmott, H.C. (1994) Systems of surveillance and the silencing of UK academic accounting labour. *British Accounting Review* **26** (2), 137–71.

Ramsden, P. (1981) A study of the relationships between student learning and its academic context. Unpublished PhD thesis, University of Lancaster.

Ramsden, P. (1988) In *Improving Learning: New Perspectives* (edited by P. Ramsden). London: Kogan Page.

Sims, R.R., Veres, J.G., Watson, P. and Buckner, K.E. (1986) The reliability and classification stability of the learning style inventory. *Educational and Psychological Measurement* **46,** 753–60.

Stout, E. and Ruble, T. (1991) The learning style inventory and accounting education research: a cautionary view and suggestions for future research. *Issues in Accounting Education* **6** (1), 41–52.

Tarsh, J. (1990) Graduate employment and degree class. *Employment Gazette,* **98** (10), 489–500.

Winter, R. (1989) *Learning from Experience: Principles and Practice in Action Research.* London: Falmer Press.

Improving the quality of accounting students' learning through action-oriented learning tasks

RALPH W. ADLER and MARKUS J. MILNE

University of Otago, New Zealand

Abstract

This paper argues that the basis for change in accounting education to more active student involvement is much broader than the need to supply the accounting professions with graduates who possess wider skills and competencies. Active student engagement, in fact, is seen by several educationalists as an essential ingredient to all student learning and the developing of lifelong learning skills. Drawing from our own experiences, the paper illustrates how problem-based and peer-assisted learning tasks can help promote many of the skills and competencies so desired by educationalists, professions, employers and universities alike. The paper also provides student feedback on the effectiveness of these learning tasks in helping to develop those attitudes, skills, and knowledge. Consistent with much of the evidence in the general education literature, and in comparison with more traditional lecture-tutorial based courses, the student feedback overwhelmingly supports the use of action-oriented learning tasks.

Introduction

Within the last decade, accounting education has come under increasing scrutiny and criticism for not providing the type of entrants it is claimed will be needed for the accounting profession of the future. A number of reports from various accounting professions and agencies (e.g. US – Bedford Committee, American Accounting Association (AAA), 1986; 'Big Eight', 1989; Accounting Education change Commission, 1990; Australia – Mathews, 1990; New Zealand – Marrian and Lothian, 1992; International, International Federation of Accountants (IFAC), 1996) have expressed concerns that accounting education has over-emphasized the technical abilities of graduates to the detriment of other competencies. While each report contains its own ideas, two consistent themes are exhibited: (1) the failure of accounting educators to cope with a wider and more general knowledge base, and (2) the failure to promote students' communication, problem solving and interpersonal skills. Some reports admonish accounting educators for their traditional lecture-based approaches and self-contained textbook problems, with the emphasis on conveying specialist content and having memorized facts fed back in examinations. As part of the calls for change in accounting education, prescriptions emerged for educators to move to case-based methods, seminars, role plays, simulations and other techniques for actively involving students in the learning process (AAA, 1986: 178; Big Eight, 1989: 11; AECC, 1990: 309; NZSA, 1995: 6; IFAC, 1996: para 9).

The extent to which this agenda for change will prove successful ultimately depends upon the extent to which accounting educators are persuaded of the nature and need for change. From a survey of US accounting educators, May *et al.* (1995) report a somewhat mixed outlook for those seeking change. While a large majority of respondents (80–90%) agreed that there should be more emphasis on written and oral communication, intellectual, inter-personal, and unstructured problem-solving skills, far fewer (less than 50%) agreed that group and case-based work should be extensively used, and that the textbook-based, rule intensive, lecture/problem solving style should not survive. Whether similar attitudes exist among tertiary accounting educators elsewhere is more difficult to judge. The results from two surveys of New Zealand educators by Adler and Milne (1997a, 1997b), for example, suggest they may be little different there. In over 60% of tertiary accounting courses surveyed, Adler and Milne (1997a) found no educator use of case-based, student group-based, or presentation type activities, for example. Accounting educators, at least in the US and NZ, seem to be widely accepting of the need to expand the competencies of accounting graduates, but far less accepting of the need to change their approaches to educating accounting graduates.

There could be several reasons why accounting educators might be reluctant to switch from the traditional lecture-based to the more action-oriented and student-centred approaches. Such approaches are potentially more time consuming, and may require greater commitment. With reward and incentive structures that emphasize research rather than teaching; a lack of adequate materials, room layouts, and staff training; and a resistance on the part of students to take responsibility for their own learning, such a reluctance may come as no surprise to many. Nonetheless, the point remains that in spite of these difficulties some educators are pursuing action-oriented learning approaches, and the purpose of this paper is to present, from a student learning perspective, good reasons why more educators should seriously consider doing so.[1]

More specifically, by drawing on the student learning and lifelong learning education literature, the paper illustrates that the calls for change in accounting education do, in fact, have a much broader educational basis than simply satisfying the future needs of the profession. Furthermore, by drawing from the education literature, the paper also provides clear links between the learning outcomes that students can achieve (and those desired by others) and the methods that educators use. In this way educators are arguably offered more compelling reasons for why they need to change to case-based, group-based and other active methods of involving students. Following these arguments, the paper then illustrates our own experiences with action-oriented learning methods, and finally reports some student feedback on the effectiveness of these methods.

---

[1]No doubt much work remains to be done on how educators and their institutions can identify and seek to remedy the many individual and structural impediments to more action-oriented learning approaches, but these are issues beyond the scope of this current paper.

An educational basis for higher education change

Accounting education is not alone in questioning whether the right kinds of learning outcomes are being achieved for graduates. Indeed, higher education more generally is being subject to criticism for its failure to adequately provide graduates with the competencies to understand a knowledge base and continue learning long after graduation (see Barnett, 1992; Gibbs, 1992a; Ramsden, 1992; Candy *et al.*, 1994). At fault, according to Candy *et al.*, are the providers of tertiary education for cramming their undergraduate programmes with technical content at the expense of broader and more general aims. Candy *et al.* argue that personal and transferable skills development have been so marginalized in many undergraduate programmes that they are seen by students and staff as incidental to or even interfering with the 'real' purpose of the degree (p. 65). According to Deppe *et al.* (1992), undergraduate accounting programmes are little different:

> the only competency overwhelmingly developed during college experience was "understand[ing] the fundamentals of accounting, auditing, and tax" . . . accounting programmes are heavily oriented toward the development of technical skills to the neglect of broader competencies needed for success in today's practice environment. (Deppe *et al.* 1992: 280–81).

Courses which are typified by a heavy workload, high class contact hours, excessive amounts of course material, no opportunity to pursue subjects in depth, a lack of choice over subjects and methods of study, and threatening and anxiety-provoking assessment systems often lead students to form naive conceptions of learning and teaching (Ramsden, 1987; Crooks, 1988; Biggs, 1989a; Candy *et al.*, 1994: chp 5). Far too many students, these educationalists argue, conceive learning as reproducing (acquiring facts and memorizing) rather than as making sense (understanding relationships). And far too many students believe that teachers are responsible for the learning – they select the content, present it and test whether it has 'stuck', rather than learners being responsible for their own learning (Gibbs, 1992a: 7).

While students with a reproducing conception of learning rarely derive more than a superficial and fragmentary understanding from a learning task (Van Rossum and Schenk, 1984 cited in Gibbs, 1992a: 6), student conceptions of learning and teaching are not fixed. Such conceptions are not individual characteristics of the learner, but appear to be largely developed in response to the teaching context (Ramsden, 1988: 20–21).[2] By experiencing learning tasks and assessment practices in which they take greater responsibility for themselves, students can develop sophisticated conceptions of learning and teaching and go on to derive a deep understanding from the learning tasks (Gibbs *et al.*, 1984).[3] Before examining in more detail why and how educators can modify their teaching contexts to foster different learning outcomes, the next section briefly considers the desirability of promoting skills and attitude development.

Desirable learning outcomes for (accounting) graduates

Candy *et al.* (1994) develop their argument for a broader set of skills and attitude development, in addition to an understanding of applied knowledge, on the basis of a need

---

[2]For recent evidence from the accounting literature on precisely this point, see, for example, Friedlan (1995).

[3]Again, see Friedlan (1995) for recent evidence from accounting education contexts.

to prepare graduates for a lifetime of continuing learning. They argue that, with new occupations and careers, expanding knowledge and technology, dependence on information, and an increasing international focus, graduates need to develop the profile of a lifelong learner illustrated in Appendix A. Their ideal of a lifelong learner with an inquiring mind, helicopter vision, information literacy, a sense of personal agency, and a repertoire of learning skills, together with their emphasis on skills and attitude development, is in fact widely accepted. Frazer (1992b), for example, in attempting to answer the question, 'what is learning in higher education?,' suggests:

> Learning is not just about absorbing (remembering and understanding) knowledge; much more it is about developing positive attitudes and useful skills ... Effective learning induces curiosity, self-confidence and self-awareness with respect to knowledge and how that knowledge is acquired and applied (p. 56).

Similarly, the Council for National Academic Awards (now defunct, but once a major higher education accreditation agency for degrees in the UK), stated the purpose of a higher education as:

> ... the development of students' intellectual and imaginative powers; their understanding and judgement; their problem-solving skills; their ability to communicate; their ability to see relationships within what they have learned and to perceive their field of study in a broader perspective. The programme must aim to stimulate an enquiring, analytical and creative approach, encouraging independent judgement and critical self-awareness (quoted in Gibbs, 1992a: 1).

Many university policies and plans (see, for example, Griffith University, 1993; Victoria University, 1993; University of Otago, 1996), and surveys of employers (see, for example, Smith *et al.*, 1989; NBEET, 1992; Harvey, 1993; Andrews, 1994, 1995) also emphasize that a willingness to learn, teamwork, commitment, oral communication skills, self-motivation, written communication skills, cooperation, self-management, and problem-solving ability are among the most important attributes of graduates. Furthermore, regardless of the graduate's study discipline, employers differ little in their rankings of what is important (Andrews, 1995). Largely consistent with these surveys, Deppe *et al.* (1992) conclude that critical thinking, problem solving, oral and written communication skills, and interpersonal and leadership skills are among the most important competencies for the practice of accountancy.

The call for graduates to possess more than discipline-specific knowledge, and for educators to focus as much (if not more – see Candy *et al.*, 1994: 65) on skills and attitude development is not something peculiar to accounting education. The call applies to all graduates, to all educators in higher education, and is widely echoed by educationalists, professions, employers and universities alike. The question remains, however, how can educators help bring about these desirable learning outcomes?

Learning outcomes related to students' learning approaches and the teaching context

Educators are offered several strategies to help promote skills and attitude development, as well as deeper, more sophisticated conceptions of learning and teaching. A distinguishing feature of many of these strategies is the increased emphasis they place on student learning rather than teaching. Under these strategies, the role of educators becomes radically changed to one of facilitator and coach rather than the one of lawgiver. Ramsden (1988), for example, argues that learning is about changing one's conceptions of the subject matter, and that teaching is (should be) about arranging 'situations where students must confront the discrepancies between their present way of thinking about the subject matter and the new way desired by the teacher' (p. 21).

To enhance their teaching contexts, Biggs (1989a) suggests educators focus on: an appropriate intrinsic motivational context, actively involving the students with the subject matter, promoting co-operation and interaction among the learners, and working from a well structured knowledge base. Similarly, Chickering and Gamson (1987) advocate: encouraging student-teacher contact, encouraging cooperation among students, encouraging active learning, providing prompt feedback, emphasizing time on task, communicating high expectations, and respecting diverse talents and ways of learning. Ramsden (1992), Candy *et al.* (1994), and O'Neil (1995) fully endorse these principles and add to the list: promoting student responsibility for learning, fostering a wide range of approaches to assessment, and learning from one's own students – reflecting on one's teaching practices. There are, of course, a myriad number of ways in which educators may choose to translate these principles into practice including, for example, learning contracts, peer mentoring, role plays, field trips, work experience, problem based-learning, and student-led seminars (Gibbs, 1992b; Candy *et al.*, 1994: Ch. 7). Three such possible approaches that form some basis for our own educational practices are now briefly considered.[4]

Problem-based learning: With problem-based learning students learn by tackling relevant problems. Students who are confronted with a problem experience a need to know something and must learn to develop the means for finding out how to tackle and resolve the problem. Unlike problem-solving, problem-based learning is as much concerned with problem identification or framing the problem, as it is with analysis and solutions. Often, because the problems are assigned as group tasks, much cooperation and interaction occurs: the students share (mis)understandings, divide up the learning, brief each other, and come to learn more about themselves and others. Among the most frequently cited advantages of problem-based learning are 'the ability to access information and apply it to solve problems, as well as experiencing group dynamics through working in a team' (Candy *et al.*, 1994: 145).

Problem-based approaches also have the potential to promote wider multi-disciplinary perspectives by simulating real-world environments and problems. From such approaches students can come to appreciate that problems are messy and uncertain, that outcomes can be many and varied, and that the aim in providing analysis and recommendations is to seek persuasive arguments rather than demonstrate truths. Through problem-based approaches students learn to become self-reliant and develop independent modes of learning. As Ramsden argues:

> Active engagement, imaginative enquiry, and the finding of a suitable level and style [of their own learning] are all much more likely to occur if teaching methods that necessitate student activity, problem solving, and cooperative learning are employed. These kind of methods permit a degree of student control over learning and can thus accommodate individual differences in preferred ways of reaching understanding, as well as having within them the potential to free students from over-dependence on teachers (Ramsden, 1992: 101).

---

[4]As with most strategies discussed in the education literature, they can be implemented to varying degrees by educators. In terms of our own experiences, we would be the first to admit that we have yet to harness these strategies for promoting student autonomy to their full potential.

When combined with presentations, problem-based learning tasks can also help develop students' personal qualities and other skills. For example, such tasks enable students to plan and manage time effectively; to find, assess, and manage information effectively; to develop skills of independent study and autonomy of action; and to build positive self-image and self-confidence (O'Neil, 1995: 118).

Peer-assisted learning: To create a teaching-learning climate that enables individuals to participate responsibly in the learning process, O'Neil (1995) suggests encouraging students to exchange ideas with peers and allowing them to determine what, when, and how they learn in formal as well as informal settings (p. 121). One way to promote such outcomes is through peer-assisted learning. Although it can take various forms (e.g. senior students mentoring juniors, self-help groups, student-led seminars), peer-assisted learning basically involves students teaching other students. From having to teach others, not only do the students gain a deep understanding of the course content, they also gain enormous confidence and acquire valuable organizational, interpersonal and communication skills (Candy *et al.*, 1994: 134).

Group-based peer learning can also potentially boost the exchange of ideas not only within the group doing the instructing or facilitating, but also within the group being facilitated. As Frazer (1992b) points out, students often see their teachers as assessors and so are reluctant to display their ignorance by making mistakes or asking elementary questions. With peer-led groups such inhibitions can be greatly reduced.

Both peer-assisted and problem-based learning approaches, however, require a word of caution. To be effective, teachers need to pursue such approaches with a genuine concern for student learning rather than simply organizing student activity. Doing, Biggs (1989b) argues, is not sufficient for learning. The learning activity must be planned, reflected upon and processed, and related to prior conceptions. In making learning possible teachers face an essential tension between freedom and discipline (Whitehead, 1967). They need to challenge students to do their own learning, but they also need to support students in their endeavours.

Assessment: Whatever strategies educators use to modify their teaching contexts, educators need to be acutely aware that the assessment system has a profound impact on (especially undergraduate) student behaviour (Gibbs, 1992a: 10). Simply assessing an activity or task, however, is not enough. How tasks are assessed, how criteria are used in allocating marks, how these assessment expectations are communicated, and how the students perceive these expectations affect how students approach both assessed assignments and other learning activities (Gibbs, 1992a: 17).

While there are no perfect systems of assessment, a variety of assessment methods will allow students to demonstrate their learning more effectively. To facilitate learning, assessment should be firmly integrated as part of student learning activities, rather than simply tacked on the end. The choice of assessment methods should be based on 'the aims and objectives (including attitudes as well as procedural and conceptual skills) it is supposed to test.' (Ramsden, 1992: 192).

In addition to multiple methods and their integration with course aims, Gibbs (1992a), Ramsden (1992) Candy *et al.* (1994), and others advocate student involvement in the assessment process. Student involvement can take various forms and can offer different advantages. If the student is involved in the design of assessment, the choice of assessment task, and the negotiation of criteria, clear expectations can be communicated and received about what is required. Likewise, allowing student choice in assessment methods can help foster greater responsibility for self-direction in learning. Going further, self- and peer-based assessment can also enable students to be 'weaned away from any tendency towards over reliance on the opinions of others', to come to judge and evaluate their own and others' learning, and so encourage critical self-evaluation so necessary for lifelong learning (Candy *et al.*, 1994, p. 150).

An illustrative example of action-oriented learning in an accounting course

In the remainder of this paper, we discuss the action-oriented learning techniques used in the undergraduate management accounting course we have co-taught over the past six years. In this discussion, we illustrate how specific pedagogical elements of the course are linked with the exemplary teaching practices discussed earlier in this paper's review of the education literature. The paper then proceeds to show how student perceptions of this course, and in particular the learning outcomes the course is intended to engender, compare with student perceptions of a traditional, or lecture taught, course.

The management accounting course (ACCT302) is a required course for our university's bachelor's degree in accounting as well as for entry to the New Zealand Institute of Chartered Accountants. Students take this course along with three other accounting courses, two of which are electives, during their final year of undergraduate studies. The annual enrolment is typically between 180–260 students. Students assign themselves to class sections or streams with class sizes of between 30–36 students. These classes meet during a two-hour period once a week. Student assessment is 75% internal or continuous assessment and 25% final examination. The final examination consists of a case study and essay questions.

Using the teaching context to support intended learning outcomes and approaches

The course has dual objectives: (1) to introduce students to a broad range of management accounting control issues, and (2) to promote lifelong learning. As such, the course is as much concerned about the content it explores as it is with the processes by which students go about building upon their existing knowledge base.

Incoming students are frequently unaccustomed to, and unprepared for, the active role that is expected of them. As a consequence, we spend the initial weeks of the course educating them on the reasons behind the course pedagogy. We point out that the objective of the course is consistent with the accounting profession's expectation that students demonstrate good technical skills and the ability to undertake further independent learning, i.e., learning to learn. We also provide them with an earlier paper of ours (Adler and Milne, 1995) that links together the learning approach adopted by the course and the lifelong learner profile exhibited in Appendix A.

These attempts to educate and reshape students' perceptions of the learning environment commence with a 'preliminary' class that all 200 or so students attend. This meeting is held in a large social function room where light refreshments are served. Also in attendance at this meeting are about 20 recent graduates of the management accounting course. We start the meeting by briefly (in less than 5 minutes) describing the learning outcomes (e.g. skills and attitude, as well as knowledge outcomes) that the course is meant to achieve and the integral role these outcomes play in the workplace. But we quickly say that instead of us *telling* the students that these skills are important, we have invited 20 past graduates,[5] who can be identified by their unique coloured name tags, to mingle with the present cohort of students and talk about their experiences with the accounting course and its relevance to their current work. In other words, we immediately try to signal two important facts: that the course is intended to develop generic learning skills and that our duty as teachers will not consist of *telling* students what is relevant or important but instead will require their active and intimate interaction with the subject matter. This is consistent with both Wight's (1970: 205) belief that the educator should change from being an information or lawgiver to a facilitator or coach of student learning, and Ramsden's (1992) more recent point that teaching is about making learning possible by arranging situations, rather than telling or transmission.

During the week following the preliminary class, students attend their first scheduled class and organize themselves into nine groups composed of 3–4 students. These nine groups coincide with the nine major course topics covered in the course, with each topic being composed of a seminar that is then followed a week later by an illustrative case study. Each group agrees to take responsibility for one of the seminars and one of the cases. When making their seminar and case choices, the students are instructed to select one of the activities from the first half of the course schedule and the other activity from the schedule's second half. We ask this for two reasons. First, we want all students to be actively involved in the course as soon as possible. Second, we have found that as students become more familiar with one another, which primarily results from the intra- and intergroup interactions that the seminars and cases engender, they are better able to undertake the peer-assisted learning element of the course. In particular, the group interactions, and the familiarity this breeds, makes it increasingly possible for students to understand that debate is an essential part of the learning process and should not be viewed as personal attack.

Once the student groups have been formed, and the seminar and case activities assigned, students are further familiarized with our expectations for their performance, the assessment methods to be used, and the encouragement and support mechanisms that are available. Due to the problem-based nature of the course, with its 'messy, unpredictable, and sensitive to context' issues (Ramsden, 1992: 171), and the use of classroom presentations, with the anxious feelings that come from being accountable to one's peers and teacher, it is vital to provide information about expected performance, learning assessment methods, and support mechanisms at the earliest possible opportunity. We have adopted several formal and informal mechanisms for communicating this information, and these are discussed in the following paragraphs.

Using problem-based learning

Problem-based learning is an important feature of the course. Unlike the more typical problem-solving approach that uses learning activities of a discrete, context-free, black and

---

[5]The invited graduates are selected on whether they still reside in the same city as where the university is located and whether they are presently employed. Past graduates who are undertaking further studies as full time students are not seen as appropriate for the purposes of the preliminary class. While no attempt is made to select graduates who favour the learning approach taken in the management accounting course, it is also true that the course generally receives favourable student ratings.

white nature (for example, problems that are normally found at the end of textbook chapters), the course draws upon learning activities that are interdisciplinary, context rich, and are shaded different tints of grey. One way in which the course's problem-based learning approach is promoted is through the liberal use of case studies. Case studies – especially those that simulate real world, messy problems – provide the classic problem-based learning environment. As a teaching method, case studies go well beyond traditional problem solving approaches. Students must first frame the problem, separate the relevant material from the irrelevant, develop alternative courses of action, and then choose one of their identified options for their recommendation.

In addition to the use of case studies, problem-based learning is promoted by the course's seminar experience. The student groups that facilitate the seminars are admonished against lecturing and/or using 'canned' solutions. Instead they are asked to design classroom learning activities that will challenge the class's initial conceptions of the week's topic. In doing this, the facilitating group is encouraged to be controversial, to provide plenty of scope for classroom exploration, and to ground their seminar in theory and practice.

The course, and in particular the seminar readings and case studies used, have been specifically chosen to support a problem-based learning environment and to facilitate student groups' ability to promote an active discussion and involvement of class members. Readings that contain opposing viewpoints are generally favoured. Such readings offer valuable opportunities for students to critically evaluate ideas and develop effective strategies for examining the strengths and weaknesses of given arguments. Although it is true that as course instructors we set the curriculum and choose the main readings, our intent is not to prevent or limit the seminar or case group's creative, critical, or analytical abilities. In fact, we provide very clear messages that a group's efforts should not be limited to the assigned readings or case. Instead they should seek out additional relevant readings and conduct interviews with practising managers. Our expectations about the need for additional readings and interviews are shared with the students during the first formal class meeting and are expressly set out in the instructor-designed grading criteria and feedback sheets used to evaluate seminars and cases. (Refer to Appendix B which contains copies of these grading and feedback sheets.)

Student take-home course assignments are also set in a problem-based framework. Two of the assignments are short (approximately three page) essays, while the third assignment is a case study analysis. Canned solutions or model answers are assiduously avoided. Multiple perspectives are supported in the crafting of the essay questions and case study. As instructors, we welcome and expect the expression of differing views, opinions, and recommendations. Consequently, grades for the assignments are based on the student's ability to mount a forceful, convincing and factual argument.

Using peer assisted learning

The demands of our course, especially its requirement that students facilitate the learning of their peers, is a novel phenomenon for the vast majority of students. While it is true that all of our students have been called upon at some point during their previous years of study to make class presentations, the extent (typically less than 15 minutes) and nature (typically problem solving as opposed to problem-based) of these presentations differ considerably from what they are challenged with in our course. As a result, we use various aids – including practice runs, meetings with the instructor to discuss the student group's activity, and the keeping of a log book that contains instructor and peer feedback on group performances to date – to prepare students for their peer-assisted learning role.

Introductory and course background material are introduced in the first four weeks of classes. During this time, each student group is given the opportunity to experience facilitating a seminar and presenting a case without the pressure of any formal assessment. These practice runs are designed to ease students into the peer-assisted, problem-based learning environment upon which our accounting course is based. Additionally, the practice runs provide feedback that will help the group prepare for their forthcoming formally assessed seminar and case assignments.

The instructors maintain a record, based on what they observed as well as what the class observed, of the strengths and weaknesses of each group's practice performance. These records are referred to when the student groups meet with the instructor to discuss the approach they will take for their coming week's formally-evaluated seminar or case. For example, the instructor may remind the group that during their seminar practice they failed to promote discussion, and instead resorted to lecturing. Or, as another common example, the group's case practice may have included too much regurgitation of case facts and too little analysis, evaluation and recommended courses of action.

Another purpose of the student-instructor meeting is to help equip the group with the teaching skills needed to successfully perform their assigned activity. These skills are especially important for the seminars. Unlike the case presentation, whereby the instructors want the students to formulate a plan of action and persuasively argue it for an uninterrupted length of time (about an hour), the seminars are meant to be highly interactive. Similar to Ramsden's (1992: 171) discussion of the seminar approach in an Italian Art History course, our seminar groups are asked not to lecture on the topic, 'but to explore a range of ideas about a topic, to give necessary information, and to inaugurate questions and discussion related to the key ideas.' In helping students to become more accomplished seminar facilitators, the instructors discuss techniques with the student groups for the active engagement of class members. Some commonly suggested techniques include: highlighting key differences that appear in the companion articles and using these differences to form the basis of a classroom debate, prodding class members to synthesize what appear to be opposing points of view, and conducting role plays that draw upon participation from members of the class at large. In addition to these techniques, a prior year's group framed its entire seminar as a TV 'talkback' show and another group invited local managers to the seminar to help discuss the topic issues and field questions from the class.

A class log book, which consists of the instructor and peer feedback sheets, is on permanent display for class members to inspect at any time. While it is true that the log book contains 'feedback' sheets, it is our hope that the book is used as much for feedforward as it is for feedback purposes. We agree that there are valuable motivational benefits to be gained from providing prompt feedback (Lawler, 1973). Our students are no exception to this rule. They anxiously await the results on their performance because grades for the case and seminar activities form 30% of their overall final course grade.

The benefits from using feedback to modify and improve behaviour should not be underestimated. Student reflection, which can be aided by revisiting past performance, is an important learning tool. As a result of the reflective process, student groups are more likely to correct their past deficiencies and build on their strengths. The student group-instructor meetings that are held prior to the group's second activity always include reference to the peer and instructor feedback that was provided on the group's first activity. Together with the group, the instructor seeks to tease out common feedback themes (for example, a failure to appropriately manage time) and try to facilitate strategies that will improve the group's forthcoming performance.

The log book is also used to promote vicarious learning. While direct learning may be the behaviourists' sole passage to learning (Skinner, 1969), Bandura (1977) clearly shows that this need not be the case. His research reveals that people's learning/reinforcement can occur by virtue of vicariously living or modelling the experience. We feel our students can do the same. By replaying the experiences of other group's performances and comparing this with the feedback they received, another group can learn what they need to do to produce equally effective results or avoid making similar mistakes.

Using assessment to promote lifelong learning

Throughout the six years of teaching the course, we have continued to modify the assessment practices used. As noted by Gibbs (1992a), course assessment practices have a powerful impact on the learning approach students adopt. We have constantly tinkered with the number of assessed activities, the percentage of assessment assigned to each activity and the source of the assessment.

Due care must be exercised when deciding on the number of action-oriented activities to use. There are two considerations we include when deciding on the appropriate number. First, we seek to schedule the activities in such a manner that students are not overly burdened with assignments at any one time. Sufficient spacing between assignments is required to allow students the necessary time to invest in the assignment as well as the ability to reflect on past activities in preparation for their upcoming activity. The need for sufficient time between assignments for students to reflect on prior learning episodes cannot be overstated. Failing to provide these opportunities is likely to condemn the students to repeat their earlier mistakes.

The amount of assessment assigned to a given activity must be sufficiently large to motivate students. We have found that anything less than 10% is often seen by the students as too insignificant to demand their earnest efforts. Obviously, the amount of weight awarded to any one activity must also be based on the pedagogical aims and objectives the activity is supposed to achieve.

The source of assessment is also important for the development of student responsibility in the learning process (Candy *et al.*, 1994). We involve our students in the assessment of the case and seminar activities. Additionally, we allow the students to choose what percentage of the two activities they wish to peer assess. At one extreme the students can choose to assess no portion of the activities, while at the other extreme they can choose to assess the activities entirely themselves. Should they choose the latter option, they would assess 20% of the overall student grade. Our students typically choose to assess 10% of the overall grade, and in the past these student assessments have correlated very highly with our own assessment marks.

Evaluating the effectiveness of the action-oriented approach

There are at least three ways to test how effectively our course contributes to developing students' lifelong learning skills. One way is to measure the students' propensity for lifelong learning at the start of the year, and then to remeasure them at the end of the year. A second way is to wait until after the students have settled into their careers (perhaps five years after graduation) and survey their superiors about our students' (who are now their subordinates) ability to engage in self-directed learning. The self-directed learning scores from the corps of students who studied our course could then be compared against the self-directed learning scores from a similar age and educational background control group. A third way is to survey students about how our course versus another (other) similar level course(s) contribute(s) to developing their lifelong learning skills and attitudes. The first two options suffer from problems of contamination. How, for instance, can we know whether it is our course which contributes to their presumably greater propensities for lifelong learning and higher self-directed learning scores versus some other course that they have studied? Consequently, the present study adopted the third option.

To collect evidence in support of the effectiveness of the course activities in developing students' knowledge, skills and attitudes, a five point scale questionnaire was administered. The questionnaire was not intended to measure the students' appreciation of the course or its particular methods (for these, see Milne and Adler, 1995), but rather to measure the extent to which those attributes considered desirable for competent accounting professionals and lifelong learners were being developed by the course methods.

The instrument was based on one previously used by our own institution and administered on the university's graduates and employers by an external consultant. Likewise, this instrument had been employed at one other university by the same consultant and was largely based on the lifelong-learning work of Candy and Crebert (1991a, 1991b). Using this instrument as a basis, then, permitted the perceptions of our students to be referenced against those of potential employers of our graduates. The original instrument contained 28 items, 18 of which related directly to lifelong-learning attributes and ten of which related to other employment-related attributes. All of these items concerned either skills or personal attitudes and attributes. To the 28 items a further 17 items were added by the authors, and these mostly related to knowledge-based attributes. All 45 items are shown in Table 1 with a key to their origin.

Each student in the course was administered the questionnaire in class by a non-instructing member of staff. Each questionnaire contained three sections with the 45 items repeated in each section.[6] One section asked the students 'To what extent do you believe your involvement in the case study process helped you develop your [the 45 items followed].' The students were asked to rate the items on a five point scale from one (to no extent) to five (to a great extent). Similarly, one section asked the students about the extent to which the seminar facilitation process had helped develop the 45 attributes. And, finally, a third section asked about the extent to which the 45 attributes had been developed by the class activities of one of three other possible courses that the students might have already taken or be taking concurrently with our own. The three 'control' courses were intended for comparative purposes and were deliberately selected because of their use of conventional lecture-tutorial methods. The other courses were also final year courses. To eliminate the possibility of ordering effects, the three sections of the questionnaire were ordered into six possible different formats. The questionnaires were completed voluntarily and anonymously, but, because the sections remained attached, repeated measures analysis

---

[6]Complete copies of the full instrument are available from the authors upon request.

is feasible.[7] The only other information collected from the students were indications of whether, in conjunction with their group members, they had yet facilitated a seminar and had yet presented a case study in class.

From a total course enrolment of 250 students usable responses were obtained from 184 students. Of these 184, 110 students clearly indicated that they had presented a case study, 58 clearly indicated that they had not yet presented a case study, and 16 gave no clear indication either way. In a similar fashion, of the 184 completed questionnaires, 120 students indicated that they had facilitated a seminar, 52 indicated that they had not, and 12 gave no clear indication either way. The section of the questionnaire pertaining to the control section was completed by 136 of the 184 responding students. Finally, of the 136 students who completed the control section of the questionnaire, 43 students had both presented a case study and facilitated a seminar.

Analysis and results

Before proceeding with the main analysis and results, some preparatory analysis was undertaken and is now briefly reported. First, Kolmogorov-Smirnov goodness of fit tests for normality of distributions indicated that the distributions of responses for all of the items for each of the three sections of the questionnaire were not statistically different at the 5% level. Second, to avoid performing several hundred tests, and to make the data more manageable for several control tests, the 45 items were collapsed into 4 scales. The scales were determined on the *a priori* basis of those which fitted the categories of attitudes (12 items), skills (18 items), knowledge (12 items), and course characteristics (3 items). The items that form the basis of each of the scales is indicated in Table 1. Cronbach Alpha scores for the four scales for all three sections of the questionnaire were all above 0.79. Third, to evaluate whether the order in which the three sections were completed affected responses, one-way ANOVA tests were carried out for each of the scales for each of the case, seminar, and other course responses. Of the 12 tests, only one was statistically significant at the 5% level: the skills scale for the other courses.[8] The order in which the sections were completed, then, appears to have had little effect on the mean responses of the scales. Finally, to evaluate if the three other 'control' courses were different from one another, one-way ANOVA tests were performed on each of the four scales. None of the four tests were statistically significant, indicating the responses to these courses are largely similar and can be treated as one.

The mean scores for the 45 skill, attitude, and knowledge items, as reported by the management accounting students, are presented in Table 1. It should be recalled that the mean scores represent students' perceptions of the extent to which the listed skills, attitudes, and knowledge bases have been developed by the case (columns 1–4) and seminar (columns 5–8) activities. Overall student perceptions of the case and seminar activities are presented in columns 1 and 5. The remaining columns of the table show the subgroups of students who have not led the particular activity (see columns 2 and 6), have led the particular activity (see columns 3 and 6), and have led both activities (see columns 4 and 8). The subgroup breakdowns reveal the effect that a student's progression through the course has on his or her skill, attitude, and knowedge development.

---

[7]Under the present circumstances, repeated measures analysis is a preferred, more powerful analytical technique due to its ability to control for the statistical variance attributable to individual students.

[8]The adjusted R^2 value of 5.7% for this ANOVA model, however, is not particularly large.

Table 1. Mean scores for ACCT 302 case and seminar sessions

Skills, attitude and knowledge attributes of students		ACCT 302 case				ACCT 302 seminar			
		All N = 184	Not N = 58	Pres'td N = 110	Both N = 63	All N = 184	Not N = 52	Pres'td N = 120	Both N = 63
Willingness to learn	A*	3.20	3.03	3.26	3.32	3.18	2.87	3.35	3.30
Motivation to work	A⁺	3.13	3.05	3.16	3.22	3.27	2.92	3.47	3.49
Ability to solve problems	S*	3.28	3.14	3.32	3.48	3.17	2.90	3.32	3.30
Oral communication skills	S*	3.31	3.17	3.36	3.43	3.51	3.17	3.65	3.54
Flexibility and adaptability	S*	3.62	3.67	3.60	3.71	3.68	3.38	3.84	3.82
Reliability	A⁺	3.00	2.90	3.06	3.19	3.16	2.81	3.34	3.36
Ability to work as a team member	S*	3.61	3.40	3.72	3.90	3.65	3.11	3.92	3.84
Desire to continue learning in the future	A*	2.96	3.03	2.94	3.14	3.00	2.66	3.18	3.11
Skills to find and assess information	S*	3.32	3.14	3.42	3.52	3.34	2.94	3.55	3.67
Conceptual and analytical skills	S*	3.20	3.28	3.15	3.31	3.18	2.98	3.27	3.25
Written communication skills	S*	2.93	2.78	2.99	3.07	3.04	2.70	3.17	3.06
Ability to interact with others	S⁺	3.37	3.40	3.36	3.52	3.47	3.15	3.66	3.71
Skills to plan your own work	S*	3.28	3.23	3.34	3.52	3.30	3.02	3.49	3.46
Organizational and time management skills	S⁺	3.14	2.88	3.22	3.31	3.16	2.83	3.32	3.41
Computer technology skills	S⁺	2.73	2.58	2.81	3.00	2.78	2.53	2.90	2.94
Ability to make independent judgements	S*	3.35	3.38	3.31	3.45	3.31	3.06	3.44	3.52
Understanding of yourself	A*	2.96	2.71	3.03	3.22	2.98	2.51	3.20	3.24
Ability to be creative	S*	3.22	2.95	3.35	3.49	3.25	2.72	3.53	3.67
Ability to lead others	S⁺	3.05	2.96	3.10	3.44	3.13	2.52	3.45	3.59
Self-confidence	A*	3.26	3.10	3.31	3.49	3.34	2.73	3.59	3.54
Multi-disciplinary perspective	A*	2.92	2.93	2.85	2.98	2.91	2.60	3.08	3.13
Awareness of ethical issues	A*	2.79	2.78	2.76	2.92	2.84	2.53	2.99	3.02
Desire to improve yourself	A⁺	3.32	3.19	3.37	3.53	3.45	3.21	3.57	3.60

Willingness to accept directions from others	A+	3.31	3.34	3.26	3.31	3.38	3.23	3.50	3.54
Skills to implement change	S*	3.10	3.03	3.12	3.36	3.06	2.75	3.23	3.30
Academic rigour	S*	2.78	2.80	2.76	2.83	2.81	2.42	2.96	2.88
Ability to negotiate	S+	3.10	2.91	3.19	3.34	3.24	2.92	3.42	3.49
Assertiveness	A+	3.04	2.91	3.08	3.19	3.23	2.94	3.37	3.36
Ability to judge others	S	3.17	3.22	3.12	3.31	3.24	3.06	3.31	3.38
Confidence to tackle unfamiliar problems	A	3.08	2.98	3.11	3.22	3.19	2.83	3.34	3.31
Understanding of how different firms require different subject outcomes	K	3.55	3.51	3.56	3.74	3.56	3.36	3.67	3.76
Exposed competing points of view	C	3.36	3.19	3.50	3.74	3.35	3.26	3.45	3.46
Understanding of limitations of subject outcomes	K	3.30	3.24	3.32	3.55	3.35	3.06	3.46	3.60
Promoted discussion and exchange of ideas	C	3.44	3.50	3.42	3.56	3.49	3.32	3.62	3.57
Understanding of subject in real organizations	K	3.29	3.30	3.34	3.60	3.24	2.94	3.42	3.48
Knowledge of subject concepts	K	3.23	3.21	3.26	3.38	3.26	2.98	3.40	3.44
Understanding of real organizations	K	3.22	3.26	3.27	3.52	3.12	2.83	3.27	3.25
Ability to critique and improve the design of subject outcomes	K	3.07	2.91	3.19	3.38	3.07	2.70	3.25	3.36
Ability to identify subject problems	K	3.23	3.12	3.27	3.40	3.15	2.86	3.31	3.29
Interest in critiquing and improving subject	K	3.09	3.02	3.16	3.27	3.12	2.85	3.26	3.25
Ability to apply subject concepts to novel situations	K	2.97	2.96	2.97	3.12	2.92	2.66	3.05	3.13
Interest in designing subject outcomes	K	2.85	2.63	2.94	3.09	2.88	2.68	2.98	3.12
Interest in the evolution of subject practices	K	2.95	2.81	3.03	3.08	2.93	2.75	3.02	3.08
Ability to design/prepare subject outcomes	K	2.86	2.77	2.91	3.09	2.82	2.49	2.98	2.95
Injected enthusiasm and excitement into the subject matter	C	2.91	3.02	2.86	2.97	2.97	2.62	3.13	2.96
Mean values for all attributes		3.15	3.07	3.19	3.34	3.19	2.87	3.35	3.37

A: attitude attribute, S: skill attribute, K: knowledge attribute, C: course characteristic.
*indicates original lifelong learning item, +indicates original employment related item.

Table 2. Differences between paired mean scores for ACCT 302 and ACCT 3XX

Skills, attitude and knowledge attributes of students	N = 40 Employers' importance mean	N = 43 ACCT 302 Case and sem mean	N = 43 ACCT3XX mean	Difference between means	Paired-t values
Willingness to learn	4.50	3.45	2.81	0.64	3.11**
Motivation to work	4.45	3.44	2.97	0.47	2.66**
Ability to solve problems	4.10	3.45	2.83	0.62	3.36**
Oral communication skills	3.95	3.57	1.93	1.64	8.23**
Flexibility and adaptability	3.85	3.79	2.45	1.33	6.87**
Reliability	3.85	3.37	2.72	0.65	3.44**
Ability to work as a team member	3.80	4.00	1.77	2.23	12.08**
Desire to continue learning in the future	3.80	3.19	2.90	0.28	1.48
Skills to find and assess information	3.75	3.69	2.81	0.88	5.46**
Conceptual and analytical skills	3.75	3.39	3.11	0.28	1.91
Written communication skills	3.75	3.06	2.19	0.87	4.47**
Ability to interact with others	3.70	3.67	2.35	1.32	6.30**
Skills to plan your own work	3.45	3.57	2.84	0.73	4.25**
Organizational and time management skills	3.45	3.48	2.81	0.67	4.01**
Computer technology skills	3.45	3.01	1.79	1.22	6.03**
Ability to make independent judgements	3.40	3.50	2.71	0.79	4.70**
Understanding of yourself	3.40	3.35	2.70	0.65	3.49**
Ability to be creative	3.30	3.57	2.35	1.22	7.33**
Ability to lead others	3.30	3.57	2.02	1.55	6.66**
Self-confidence	3.30	3.65	2.39	1.26	6.20**
Multi-disciplinary perspective	3.20	3.04	2.50	0.54	2.91**
Awareness of ethical issues	3.20	2.89	2.84	0.05	0.27

Attribute				
Desire to improve yourself	3.15	3.62	3.19	0.43	2.37**
Willingness to accept directions from others	3.15	3.48	2.60	0.88	4.84***
Skills to implement change	3.15	3.30	2.39	0.91	5.94***
Academic rigour	3.15	2.94	2.60	0.34	2.20*
Ability to negotiate	3.05	3.44	2.00	1.44	6.74***
Assertiveness	3.05	3.38	2.39	0.99	5.70***
Ability to judge others	NA	3.30	1.93	1.37	7.90***
Confidence to tackle unfamiliar problems	NA	3.36	3.00	0.36	1.80
Understanding of how different firms require different subject outcomes	NA	3.57	2.65	1.02	4.76***
Exposed competing points of view	NA	3.63	2.20	1.43	6.83***
Understanding of limitations of subject outcomes	NA	3.48	2.67	0.81	3.63***
Promoted discussion and exchange of ideas	NA	3.62	1.91	1.71	8.38***
Understanding of subject in real organizations	NA	3.51	2.39	1.12	4.69***
Knowledge of subject concepts	NA	3.51	2.86	0.65	2.95***
Understanding of real organizations	NA	3.34	2.53	0.81	4.03***
Ability to critique and improve the design of subject outcomes	NA	3.46	2.65	0.81	3.46***
Ability to identify subject problems	NA	3.39	2.83	0.56	2.69***
Interest in critiquing and improving subject	NA	3.23	2.55	0.67	2.67*
Ability to apply subject concepts to novel situations	NA	3.11	2.56	0.56	2.50*
Interest in designing subject outcomes	NA	3.07	2.51	0.56	2.15*
Interest in the evolution of subject practices	NA	3.11	2.55	0.55	2.52*
Ability to design/prepare subject outcomes	NA	3.07	2.51	0.56	2.39*
Injected enthusiasm and excitement into the subject matter	NA	3.01	2.11	0.90	4.08**
Mean values for all attributes	–	3.36	2.45	0.92	–

**Significant at the 1% level, *Significant at the 5% level.
NA: not applicable.

A first conclusion to draw from the table is that the average management accounting student felt that the case and seminar activities developed his or her skills, attitudes, and knowledge bases to 'some extent.' (This interpretation is based on the fact that the scale value of '3' was anchored by the label 'to some extent.') In general, there was very high correspondence between student perceptions of the extent to which specific learning outcomes were developed by the case and seminar activities. The most developed learning outcome for both the case and seminar was flexibility and adaptability, and the least developed learning outcome, again for both the case and seminar, was computer skills.

A closer examination of the table reveals that students who have led a case or seminar perceive themselves as attaining the learning outcomes to a higher degree than those students who have not assumed responsibility for a class activity. For example, the mean score for the entire set of learning outcomes is 3.07 and 2.87 for students who have not led the case or seminar activity, respectively, versus 3.19 and 3.35 for students who have led the case or seminar activity, respectively. This pattern of higher scores for students who have and have not led a given class activity is maintained on the mean scores of the individual items (e.g., the willingness to learn score for students who have presented a case – refer to column 3 – is 3.26, compared with a mean score of 3.03 for students who have not presented a case – refer to column 2). While there are some examples which violate the general pattern for the case activity, it is interesting to note that there is an increase in the development of every learning outcome item associated with the seminar activity. It appears that the seminar facilitation has the greatest influence on the students' learning outcome achievement.

At the time that the course survey was administered, some of the students had both presented a case and facilitated a seminar. In many respects, these students have substantially completed the active-based component of the course. These students are therefore termed quasi-graduates to denote their advanced status. Table 2 reveals that the mean scores on the learning outcomes increase further for these quasi-graduates. The mean score for the entire set of learning outcomes rises to 3.34 for the cases and 3.37 for the seminars. Meanwhile, this general pattern of rising scores repeats itself for the individual case and seminar items (see column 3 versus column 4 and column 7 versus column 8). The increase in individual scores, however, is most pronounced for the cases. This occurrence further supports the contention that the seminars provide the biggest boost to the achievement of students' learning outcomes.

Table 2 compares the quasi-graduates' learning outcome scores on the management accounting course – (ACCT302) with the other third year accounting courses (ACCT3XX) that serve as the control group. The table has been ordered according to the importance that employers have placed on each of the learning outcomes. Based on a five point scale ranging from '1' not important to '5' very important, employers were asked to rate the attributes on the basis of the level of importance they attached to them for successful employment in their organisations.

The table reveals that the management accounting course mean scores are higher on every learning outcome. The total mean value for the management accounting course is 3.36 compared with the control group which is 2.45, a nearly one point scale difference. Furthermore, mean difference tests between the management accounting and control groups shows that all but four of the learning outcomes are significant at the $p < 0.05$ level or better, with the majority being significant at the $p < 0.01$ level.

Table 3. Mean scores for ACCT 302, ACCT 3XX, and paired differences for attitude, skills, and knowledge scales

Skills, attitude and knowledge attributes of students	ACCT 302 case and sem N = 43	ACCT3XX N = 43	Difference means N = 43	Paired-t values N = 43	ACCT 302 case			ACCT 302 sem'r			ACCT 302 case Not pres'td N = 58	ACCT 302 sem Not pres'td N = 52	ACCT 3XX N = 136
					All N = 184	Pres'td N = 110	Both N = 63	All N = 184	Pres'td N = 120	Both N = 63			
Attitude scale (12 items)	3.35	2.75	0.60	4.62**	3.08	3.10	3.23	3.16	3.33	3.33	2.99	2.82	2.77
Skills scale (18 items)	3.46	2.37	1.09	8.88**	3.19	3.24	3.39	3.24	2.41	3.44	3.10	2.90	2.42
Knowledge scale (12 items)	3.33	2.61	0.72	3.90**	3.13	3.18	3.36	3.12	3.26	3.31	3.06	2.85	2.73
Course characteristics scale (3 items)	3.44	2.08	1.36	7?4**	3.24	3.26	3.42	3.27	3.40	3.34	3.23	3.07	2.20
Mean values for all attributes	3.36	2.45	0.92	–	3.15	3.19	3.34	3.19	3.35	3.37	3.07	2.87	2.58

**Significant at the 0.1% level.

Table 3 further examines the students' development of learning outcomes for the management accounting and control group courses, but does so this time by looking at the four scales that comprise the 45 items. Mean scores on all four scales are higher for the management accounting course than the control group, and mean difference tests show that the differences are significant at the $p < 0.001$ level. The table also indicates that there is a steady progression in the students' reported achievements on the four scales as the students undertake case and seminar activities. For example, the mean score on the attitude scale for students that have not presented a case is 2.99. The mean score rises to 3.10 for students who have presented a case, and rises still further to 3.23 for students who have facilitated a case and presented a seminar.

Overall, the results from the students' perceptions of the extent to which their learning outcomes had been achieved demonstrate two things. First, within our own course, at least in the minds of the students, increasing exposure to action-oriented learning tasks does impact on the extent to which lifelong learning attributes are developed. Second, consistent with so much of the education literature that was introduced at the beginning of this paper, in comparison with other more traditionally taught courses, student exposure to action-oriented learning tasks very clearly impacts on their perceptions of the extent to which lifelong learning attributes are developed.

Summary and conclusions

The accounting education literature contains ardent and repeated calls for educators to moderate their emphasis on teaching technical accounting and general business skills and to invest greater attention developing students' organizational, interpersonal, and communication skills. These calls for a changed education go beyond representing the agenda of any particular partisan group (e.g., the accounting profession), and instead appear to be part of the broadly represented educational community's attempt to realign educational values and beliefs with a philosophy of lifelong learning. Sadly, although accounting educators appear to recognize the need to devote more time to developing students' generic learning skills, May et al. (1995) and Adler and Milne (1997a, 1997b) have found that only the smallest minority of educators have embarked on a programme of change.

The failure of accounting educators to change and develop pedagogies that more actively involve their students is unfortunate. There are substantial learning benefits to be gained. Educationalists have written about these gains for a number of years now, and data collected from our course supports the presence of such benefits. As educators we are left with a perplexing situation. On the one hand, the fruits of enhanced learning are clear and abundant. Yet on the other hand, educational regimes appear locked into their old ways and student learning stagnates. An interesting question to research is: What prevents educators from implementing change? Could, for instance, the failure result from institutional influences that recognize and reward research at the expense of teaching? Perhaps the lack of adequate instructional materials, classroom layouts, and staff training might be the cause? Or might the faulure be due to educators' fears that students may rebel against the more empowered role that action-oriented learning demands? Perhaps future research initiatives could shed light on the causes behind the underuse of action-oriented learning and, in the process, provide a useful platform from which educators could begin to work on ways to overcome the current state of educational impoverishment.

Acknowledgements

In preparing this paper, the authors greatly acknowledge the assistance of Garry Heaton, Alan MacGregor and three anonymous referees.

References

Accounting Education Change Commission (AECC) (1990) Objectives of education for accountants: position statement number one, *Issues in Accounting Education*, **5**, 307–12.

Adler, R.W. and Milne, M.J. (1995) Increasing learner control and reflection: towards learning-to-learn in an undergraduate management accounting course, *Accounting Education*, **4**, 105–19.

Adler, R.W. and Milne, M.J. (1997a) Translating ideals into practice: an examination of international accounting bodies' calls for curriculum changes and New Zealand tertiary institutions' assessment methods, *Accounting Education*, **6**, 109–24.

Adler, R.W. and Milne, M.J. (1997b) *Overcoming Obstacles to Improving the Quality of Accounting Students' Learning*. Unpublished report to the Peter Barr Fellowship and Academic Committees of the Institute of Chartered Accountants of New Zealand, Wellington.

American Accounting Association (AAA) (1986) Committee on the future structure, content, and scope of accounting education (The Bedford Committee): future accounting education: preparing for the expanding profession, *Issues in Accounting Education*, **1**, 168–95.

Andrews, R.J. (1994) *Survey of Employer Perceptions of Graduates of Griffith University*, Griffith University, Queensland, Australia.

Andrews, R.J. (1995) *Survey of Employer Perceptions of Graduates of the University of Otago*, University of Otago, Dunedin, New Zealand.

Bandura, A. (1977) *Social Learning Theory*, Englewood Cliffs, NJ: Prentice-Hall.

Barnett, R. (1992) What effects? What outcomes? In *Learning to Effect* (edited by R. Barnett), Bristol: The Society for Research into Higher Education and Open University Press.

Big Eight (1989) *Perspectives on Education: Capabilities for Success in the Accounting Profession*, ('Big Eight' White Paper), New York: Arthur Anderson & Co, Arthur Young, Coopers & Lybrand, Deloitte Haskins & Sells, Ernst & Whinney, Peat Marwick Main & Co, Price Waterhouse, and Touche Ross.

Biggs, J.B. (1989a) Approaches to the enhancement of tertiary teaching, *Higher Education Research and Development*, **8**, 7–25.

Biggs, J.B. (1989b), Does learning about learning help teachers with teaching? Psychology and the tertiary teacher. Supplement to *The Gazette*, **26**(1), University of Hong Kong.

Candy, P.C. and Crebert, G. (1991a) Ivory tower to concrete jungle: the difficult transition from the academy to the workplace as learning environments, *Journal of Higher Education*, **62**, 570–92.

Candy, P.C. and Crebert, G. (1991b) Lifelong learning: an enduring mandate for higher education, *Higher Education Research and Development*, **10**, 3–17.

Candy, P.C., Crebert, G. and O'Leary, J. (1994) *Developing Lifelong Learners through Undergraduate Education*, Canberra: Australian Government Publishing Service.

Chickering, A.W. and Gamson, Z.F. (1987) Seven principles for good practice in undergraduate education, (special insert) *The Wingspread Journal*, **9**.

Crooks, T.J. (1988) The impact of classroom evaluation practices on students, *Review of Educational Research*, **58**, 438–81.

Deppe, L.A., Sonderegger, E.O., Stice, J.D., Clark, D.C. and Streuling, G.F. (1992) Emerging competencies for the practice of accountancy, *Journal of Accounting Education*, **9**, 257–90.

Frazer, M.J. (1992a) *Quality Assurance in Higher Education*, London: Falmer Press.

Frazer, M.J. (1992b) Promoting learning. In *Learning to Effect* (edited by R. Barnett), Bristol: The Society for Research into Higher Education and Open University Press.

Friedlan, J.M. (1995) The effects of different teaching approaches on students' perceptions of the skills needed for success in accounting courses and by practising accountants, *Issues in Accounting Education*, **10**, 47–63.

Gibbs, G. (1992a) *Improving the Quality of Student Learning*, Bristol: Technical and Education Services Ltd.

Gibbs, G. (1992b) Control and independence. In *Teaching Large Classes in Higher Education: How to Maintain Quality with Reduced Resources* (edited by G. Gibbs and A. Jenkins), London: Kogan Page.

Gibbs, G., Morgan, A. and Taylor, E. (1984) The world of the learner. In *The Experience of Learning* (edited by F. Marton, D. Hounsell and N. Entwistle), Edinburgh: Scottish Academic Press.

Griffith University (1993) *Policy on the Structure and Requirements of the Bachelor's Degree*, Griffith University, Queensland, Australia.

Harvey, L. (1993) Employer Views in Higher Education. In *Proceedings of the Second Quality in Higher Education 24-Hour Seminar*, University of Warwick, December.

International Federation of Accountants (IFAC) (1996) Prequalification education, assessment of professional competence and experience requirements of professional accountants, *International Education Guideline* No. 9, Washington: IFAC.

Lawler, E.E. III (1973) *Motivation in Work Organisations*, Brookes/Cole Publishing: Monterey, California.

Knapper, C. and Cropley, A. (1991) *Lifelong Learning and Higher Education*, London: Kogan Page.

Marrian, I.F.Y. and Lothian, N. (1992) *International Review of Admission Policy*. Unpublished report to the Education Committee of the New Zealand Society of Accountants, Wellington.

Mathews, R. (1990) *Accounting in Higher Education: Report of the Review of the Accounting Discipline in Higher Education* (Russel Mathews chair of review panel), Canberra: Australian Government Printing Service.

May, G.S., Windal, F.W. and Sylvestre, J. (1995) The need for change in accounting education: an educator survey, *Journal of Accounting Education*, **13**, 21–43.

Milne, M.J. and Adler, R.W. (1995) Learning to learn in an undergraduate management accounting course: some instructors' experiences, *Accounting and Business Review*, **2**, 125–45.

National Board of Employment, Education and Training (NBEET) (1992) *Skills Sought by Employers of Graduates*, Canberra: Australian Government Printing Service.

New Zealand Society of Accountants (NZSA) (1995) *Admissions Policy: Guidelines for Professional Accounting Schools and Professional Competence Examinations*, New Zealand Society of Accountants Education Committee, Wellington: NZSA.

O'Neil, M. (1995) Towards a model of the learner in higher education: some implications for teachers. In *Research, Teaching and Learning in Higher Education* (edited by B. Smith and S. Brown), London: Kogan Page.

Ramsden, P. (1987) Improving teaching and learning in higher education: the case for a relational perspective, *Studies in Higher Education*, **12**, 275–86.

Ramsden, P. (1988) Studying learning: improving teaching. In *Improving Learning: New Perspectives* (edited by P. Ramsden), London: Kogan Page.

Ramsden, P. (1992) *Learning to Teach in Higher Education*, London: Routledge.

Skinner, B.F. (1969) *Contingencies of Reinforcement: A Theoretical Analysis*, New York: Appleton-Century-Crofts.

Smith, D., Wolstencroft, T. and Southern, J. (1989) Personal transferable skills and the job demands on graduates, *Journal of European Industrial Training*, **13**, 25–31.

University of Otago (1996) *Teaching and Learning Plan*, University of Otago, Dunedin, New Zealand.

Van Rossum, E.J. and Schenk, S.M. (1984) The relationship between learning conception, study strategy and learning outcome, *British Journal of Educational Psychology*, **54**, 73–83.

Victoria University of Wellington (1993) *Draft Strategic Plan Paper: Our Century and Beyond*, Victoria University of Wellington, Wellington, New Zealand.

Whitehead, A.N. (1967) *The Aims of Education and Other Essays*, New York: Free Press. (originally published 1929).

Wight, A.R. (1970) Participative education and the inevitable revolution, *The Journal of Creative Behaviour*, **4**, 234–82.

Appendix A: Profile of a lifelong learner

An inquiring mind
  a love of learning
  a sense of curiosity and question asking
  a critical spirit
  comprehension-monitoring and self-evaluation

Helicopter vision
  a sense of interconnectedness of fields
  an awareness of how knowledge is created in at least one field of study, and an understanding of the methodological and substantive limitations of that field
  breadth of vision.

Information literacy
  Knowledge of major current resources available in at least one field of study
  ability to frame researchable questions in at least one field of study
  ability to locate, evaluate, manage and use information in a range of contexts
  ability to retrieve information using a variety of media
  ability to decode information in a variety of forms: written, statistical, graphs, charts, diagrams and tables
  critical evaluation of information

A sense of personal agency
  a positive concept of oneself as capable and autonomous
  self-organization skills (time management, goal setting etc.)

A repertoire of learning skills
  knowledge of one's own strengths, weaknesses and preferred learning style
  range of strategies for learning in whatever context one finds oneself
  an understanding of the differences between surface and deep level learning
(Candy *et al.*, 1994: 43–44, but also see Knapper and Cropley, 1991; Frazer, 1992a).

Appendix B: Grading sheet for case presentations

Week No. _____   Case _____

Presenters' Names: 1 _____ 2 _____ 3 _____ 4 _____

	Poor	Excellent
Presenters were clear and audible:	⊥_____⊥

Suggestions for
Improvement: _____

_____

	Poor	Excellent
Overhead transparencies were helpful:	⊥_____⊥

	Poor	Excellent
Presentation was well structured:	⊥_____⊥

	Poor	Excellent
Major problems and issues were covered:	⊥_____⊥

	Poor	Excellent
Supporting evidence was provided:	⊥_____⊥

	Poor	Excellent
Feasible alternatives were identified:	⊥_____⊥

	Poor	Excellent
Recommendation was convincing:	⊥_____⊥

	None	Many and relevant
Additional articles were used:	⊥_____⊥

	None	Many and relevant
Interviews with managers done:	⊥_____⊥

What went well in this presentation? _____

_____

_____

What could the group have done to improve its performance? _____

_____

_____

Grading Sheet for Seminars

	D	C− to C+	B− to B+	A− to A+
Demonstrated an embryonic understanding of seminar topic.	■			
Demonstrated a thorough understanding of the seminar topic and did a good job integrating the readings	■	■		
Introduced material from academic and practitioner-based articles in addition to the assigned ACCT 302 readings.	■	■	■	
Provided a practical grounding to the seminar by introducing information supplied from interviews with practising business managers and professionals.	■	■	■	■

Grading Sheet for Case Presentations

	D	C− to C+	B− to B+	A− to A+
Identified the salient case facts and described the case problem.	■			
Offered feasible alternatives and presented a convincing recommendation.	■	■		
Introduced supporting evidence from academic and practitioner-based articles in addition to the assigned ACCT 302 readings.	■	■	■	
Provided a practical grounding to the case study by introducing information supplied from interviews with practising business managers and professionals.	■	■	■	■

Exporting accounting education to East Africa – squaring the circle

PATRICK J. DEVLIN and ALAN D. GODFREY

Glasgow Caledonian University, UK

Abstract

A number of issues associated with exporting accounting education to East Africa are explored. There are four main themes, all of which relate to proper identification of needs. It is argued that the East African context is all-important and that programmes must be designed in the light of that context. However, programmes will be successful only if three other factors are in place. It is essential that those delivering a programme learn from their experiences since the nature of the needs are such that issues will arise which could not have been foreseen. It is necessary – whatever the original intention – for programmes to be more than simply training programmes: there must be a distinct educational dimension to them. It is very important that those delivering a programme avoid imposing values on the participants in circumstances which are very different to those encountered in the 'developed' countries.

Introduction

The World Bank (1989), noting that the inhabitants are almost as poor as they were 30 years ago, describes the situation facing sub-Saharan Africa as one of economic crisis. Whatever the causes of this crisis – and these are strongly disputed – countries in the region have had little alternative but to seek assistance from wherever it might come. Donor assistance takes a variety of forms. This is reflected in the projects which we have undertaken in East Africa. Our involvement mainly has been in the field of education and training but has included: training of public-sector finance staff (from local government in Tanzania, local government and central government in Uganda, and local government, central government and parastatals[1] in Kenya); 'training of trainers' (TOT) programmes (in Tanzania and Uganda); institutional development work (in all three countries). Moreover, in the case of Kenya all the programmes were held in-country whereas in Tanzania and Uganda a combination of in-country and UK training (including placements with local authorities) was used.

These different arrangements reflect the differing needs of the countries concerned. Clearly, 'needs' do not present themselves to you, they must be identified. Great care was taken on all these projects to try to ensure that the needs were correctly identified – lengthy discussions were held with appropriate representatives of the recipient country (for example, government ministers, civil servants, academics) prior to the development of a programme; UK staff involved in these discussions constantly checked to ensure that their 'cultural baggage' did not influence matters; on later projects (some having started as far back as 1982) we became aware of the criticisms levelled at technical assistance – see, for example, Cassen *et al.* (1986), Mosley (1987) and Riddell (1987) – and this served merely to reinforce our concern that we should correctly identify needs. Yet, despite all these efforts, our experience of delivering the early programmes led to significant changes in later programmes. This is not just to say that part of the content of a programme proved to be irrelevant, although both formal and informal techniques were used to identify such errors. It goes deeper than that. We learned over time that technical assistance, which ostensibly should take the form of training, of necessity requires more than training. A whole series of educational issues stemmed from this. In effect, we had to 'square the circle' of education versus training[2] – and had to do so in a very different cultural environment.

Underdeveloped human resources

Human resources in Africa are critically underdeveloped. Two examples should suffice to illustrate the scale of the problem. First, despite considerable progress, particularly in the years immediately following the gaining of independence by many of the countries of the continent, Africa still has the highest illiteracy rate in the world – this varies from 25% in Southern Africa to 63% in West Africa, the average for East Africa (where most of our involvement has been) being 55%[3] (Ghartey, 1993, p. 179). Second, although most of the countries of Africa have higher educational establishments, the proportion of tertiary graduates of age 24 and above is very small – Ghartey (1993, p. 180) cites a World Bank report from 1988 showing that the proportion is 0.4% compared with an average of 6% in other underdeveloped regions.

There is an acute scarcity of trained personnel at many levels in sub-Saharan Africa. This constrains efficiency and the capacity to govern effectively (Tarp, 1993, p. 10). The economic difficulties faced by most countries in sub-Saharan Africa in the 1980s have exacerbated the situation. Inadequate salaries and deteriorating living conditions have led many highly-qualified and trained personnel to take positions in other countries. For the same reasons, professional staff who remain supplement their salary with a second job (irrespective of whether this is authorized), making it impossible to devote their full energies to their duties – we have found this problem to be particularly prevalent in the public sector in East Africa where our experience has been that many accountants, auditors, and accountancy lecturing staff have second jobs (in many instances, the largest

---

[2] In the context of the programmes being discussed, we would define 'training' as surrogate professional accountancy development (i.e. preparation of the participants for employment at their workplaces) and 'education' as the development of the intellectual abilities of the participants. Of course, there is likely to be some degree of overlap between the two. But, as Gray *et al.* (1994) indicate, there is a literature which discusses the potential for conflict – a potential that was realized almost from the outset of our programmes.

[3] Aggregate numbers such as these mask wide variations by country, of course. For example, in 1990 the illiteracy rate in Uganda was 52% while that for Kenya was 31% – no figure is available for Tanzania (Todaro, 1997). Moreover, they take no account of the educational gender gap – for example, while the overall illiteracy rate in Uganda was 52%, the rate for the female population was 65% (Ghartak, 1995).

part of the working day being devoted to the 'second job'). Again for the same reasons, professionally-trained staff in the public sector have sought more lucrative positions in the private sector (see Gujarathi and Dean, 1993, p. 193 for a discussion of salary differentials). This too is a situation we have found to be a regular occurrence – on a number of occasions, institutional development work has been severely set back because staff (lecturers, heads of departments, on one occasion a principal) who have worked closely with us in developing programmes have taken training and other positions in the private sector which significantly increased their salaries. Taken together, these developments have led to lower educational standards, low employee morale, weak loyalty and weakened discipline, and have increased the motivations and temptations for corruption and inadequate accountability (Ghartey, 1993, p. 180). To this, we would add that the development of the institutional capability of training institutions, university departments and governmental departments has been severely thwarted.

In these circumstances, there has been little choice but to rely on advisers who, as Tarp (1993, p. 10) indicates, are willingly supplied through a rapidly-growing international system of technical assistance. Our involvement has been in providing technical assistance primarily in the education and training of accountants in the public sector. The available evidence (see Gujarathi and Dean, 1993) shows that the quantity of governmental accounting personnel is inadequate for underdeveloped countries. Our experience would support this – in Kenya, for example, a consultants' report we prepared for a funding body estimated that 1600 accountants in central government had received no formal training since being employed[4]. Of course, lack of accounting personnel impacts significantly on the quality of work done – there is likely to be inaccurate and delayed record keeping, the breakdown of controls, increased opportunities for financial impropriety, failures in timely reporting for decision-making and a weakening of the system of accountability in general (Gujarathi and Dean, 1993, p. 194). Again, our experience would support this – for example, by the late 1980s/early 1990s in Kenya, Tanzania and Uganda a large number of government ministries and local authorities had not produced accounts for audit since the mid-1970s and problems had been found with many of the accounts which were available for audit.

The acute shortages of qualified and trained accounting personnel and the resultant inefficiencies in financial management (most particularly in the public sector) have led to considerable attention being paid to the issue of training of finance staff. For the same reasons as those discussed above, the quantity and quality of suitably qualified and experienced indigenous trainers is totally inadequate. Hence, there has been reliance on external support.

Background to our involvement

Two notes of caution should be sounded before providing some background information on our involvement in East Africa. First, there is no intention in the paper to suggest that

[4] The best estimate available at the time (1988) showed that there were approximately 1600 staff at Accountant 1, Accountant 2 and Accountant 3 grades within central government. Of these, 200 were at Accountant 1 level. It was estimated that there were approximately a further 180 staff at Accountant 1 level in local government and 200 in the parastatals. Some of our courses in Kenya were designed for staff at Accountant 1/Auditor 1 level i.e 'middle managers'. We were involved also in courses provided for their superiors at 'senior manager' level.

East Africa should be treated as a homogeneous whole. There is no disputing that individual country characteristics exist – but these are not considered critical to a paper which seeks merely to discuss the educational issues faced when exporting accounting education to East Africa. Second, confidentiality prevents us from disclosing some information (such as the names of the donor agencies and the costs of the various projects).

NUMBERS TRAINED

Our first experience of exporting accounting education was in Uganda in 1982. Since then we have been involved in a number of projects in Uganda including: the provision of a series of 12-week courses for staff of the Budget Department of central government held at the Glasgow Caledonian University between 1988 and 1991; the drafting of central government financial regulations; a review of the operation of the Office of the Auditor General in 1986. Our work continues to date – currently, we are helping develop the Institute of Certified Public Accountants and are also providing institutional support to a training institution. The largest project was concerned with the training of local and central government finance staff. Initially designed to last three years, this project ran from 1983 until 1991. A total of 320 staff attended an 11-week course in Uganda and 160 received a further 17 weeks training at the Glasgow Caledonian University (which also included a three-week placement period with a local authority in Scotland).

Between 1988 and 1993 we helped deliver programmes at two government training institutions in Kenya. Finance staff from local government, central government and parastatals attended a four-week course (although this was designed initially as a five-week course – see below). During our involvement, 285 staff were trained (125 from central government, 110 from local government and 50 from parastatals).

Since 1989, we have been involved in a project in Tanzania. During that time, 500 staff from local government (including 100 executive directors) have attended a six-week course in Tanzania, of whom 310 also attended a TOT course of five weeks' duration and 160 received further training at an eight-week course held at the Glasgow Caledonian University (which included a one-week placement period with a local authority in Scotland).

OBJECTIVES

At the start of our involvement, objectives were set by the donor agency – after discussion with appropriate personnel from the recipient country but prior to our becoming involved. We were able to help determine the content of programmes but had no say in determining the overall objectives. That position has changed to some extent – primarily because very good working relationships have been developed – in that we can help shape objectives when a project continues on to a further phase (as has been the case in both Uganda and Tanzania).

Changes have taken place also with respect to the objectives themselves. Initially, broad terms of reference were set. For example, on the Kenyan programme the terms of reference stated that 'the overall objective is to strengthen and expand [the training institution's] contribution to training key personnel in the area of financial management'. The specific objectives were equally broad: '(i) to increase the quality and effectiveness of the short course programmes in financial management; (ii) to develop teaching materials especially case studies; (iii) to provide a wider range of reference books'. Moreover, the terms of reference were set with little regard as to how effectiveness might be measured. Now, the issue of effectiveness is seen as being of critical importance (this is discussed below), reflecting the fact that all concerned have had to learn from experience.

Developing training programmes – context is all

The World Bank (1995, p. 1) argues that education is critical for economic growth and poverty reduction. The contribution that education can make to development is not without controversy, however. For some (Kruger, 1968; Hayami and Ruttan, 1979), education is a central element in political and socio-economic development; others (Morawetz, 1971; Blaug, 1976) are more sceptical about its effectiveness as an instrument for eliminating poverty and underdevelopment. Certainly, any relationship between education and development is bound to be complex and due weight must be given to other factors such as health, nutrition, housing and social welfare. Moreover, given the nature of the problems facing sub-Saharan Africa, there has long been a desire to give priority to primary education – the first United Nations Educational Scientific and Cultural Organisation (UNESCO) conference on policy and cooperation in education in Africa, held in Ethiopia in 1961, identified the development of universal primary education as the first step towards the eradication of illiteracy (Ghartey, 1993, p. 174). (It merits noting that the conference objective of universal primary education by 1980 has not been achieved.)

Given this context, it was important from the outset that we refrained from being over optimistic about the contribution we could make. Even in the best of circumstances, training is only a complement to education. We were very conscious when developing our programmes that the circumstances were far from ideal. For example, the World Bank (1991, p. 11) highlights the decline in sub-Saharan Africa's systems of higher education which has had a particularly severe effect on the region's analytical and management capacity. We therefore recognized that the role which training might play should not be exaggerated.

We were conscious too that, to make even a limited impact, the training of finance staff had to be relevant. Wallace and Briston (1993, p. 216) rightly criticize the exporting to underdeveloped countries of accounting systems which are externally determined and which do not take into consideration the needs of the recipient country. We have always taken great care to avoid this. Of course – as is argued by Parry and Groves (1990), Rivera (1990) and Abayo and Roberts (1991) – the training of more accountants does not necessarily raise the quality of accounting in underdeveloped countries. Nevertheless, it is our contention that bespoke training programmes – as distinct from those which come 'off the shelf' – provide an opportunity for creating more effective financial management.

When developing the first programmes, it was important to ensure that the particular problems imposed by Uganda's recent history were addressed – tyrannical rule in the 1970s had destroyed the functions of accounting and audit throughout the country, partly as a result of the expulsion of the Asian community in 1972 which provided not only most of the commercial enterprise within the economy but also a large proportion of the government's financial skills. At the same time, in developing these programmes we were aware of the potential cultural tension between the recipient and exporter of accounting technology and know-how (later identified by Wallace, 1990) and we tried to adopt what Briston and Wallace (1990, p. 282) subsequently describe as a 'naturalistic' approach –

that is, an approach which seeks to draw upon other countries' systems and experience in a way which meets the recipient country's needs. Our experience shows that, unfortunately, this approach is not adopted by all international consultants and the resulting problem of 'aid distortion' (Godfrey *et al.*, 1996, p. 201)[5] can stifle the impact of multi-aid-funded training programmes by introducing hybrid accounting systems and procedures based on several differing national systems.

Initially, two main elements were deemed important. First, it was accepted that no single curriculum is appropriate for all or most underdeveloped countries (World Bank, 1995, p. 5). Our preparatory discussions indicated that much of the (limited) technical knowledge of public-sector finance staff was almost entirely private-sector oriented, was out-of-date, and was extremely narrowly focused. Accordingly, the curriculum concentrated on agreed areas of importance – financial accounting, auditing and public sector accounting (all adjusted in so far as possible to the realities of the chaotic accounting and auditing systems which had been left).

Second, we identified leading Ugandan academics from Makerere University to join the training team and provide important local knowledge and expertise. In addition, other young academics were encouraged to participate as trainees on the first training programmes and thereafter to join and strengthen the local academic input. It was hoped that these same academics would act as catalysts within their own institutions and introduce curricular changes thereby completing the circle. That is, with the public sector representing the largest employer in the economy, it was considered important that public sector accounting should be included within the curricula of higher education accountancy qualifications – university accountancy education in Uganda at that time concentrated exclusively on commercial accounting.

Learning from experience

The experience of delivering the programmes raised a number of issues which we had not foreseen at the time the programmes were developed.

CURRICULUM

Early attempts to gauge to what extent we had correctly identified 'needs' using formal questionnaires and informal discussions with participants and other interested parties were less effective than was originally anticipated pre-delivery. It would appear that this was due, at least partly, to what we have termed 'aid acquiescence'. This we would define as a reluctance by recipients – especially initially – to question training and associated materials provided by ex-patriate trainers. This acquiescence or reluctance to constructively criticize given situations may also be due to cultural influences which are discussed more fully below. In an attempt to counter this phenomenon, it was decided that the development of skills to encourage group discussion and open-minded questioning of curriculum, materials and other aspects of the courses provided should be integrated into our programmes.

---

[5] It has been our experience that the existence in the field of many international donor agencies, each with its own list of conditions attached to its financial contributions, can result in the implementation of hybrid accounting systems that fail to take sufficient account of local needs and circumstances – a phenomenon we termed aid distortion.

As is indicated above, the curriculum concentrated on what were agreed to be areas of importance based on an assessment of needs. At the same time, in restricting the curriculum to specific public sector accounting and auditing skills (in so far as this is possible) it was hoped that this also would help minimize the labour mobility problems encountered when trained staff are offered a premium to transfer to the private sector. Such leakages from the public to private sector are not unique to Africa but they represent a more damaging resource drain in the short term. (It merits noting that the IMF Structural Adjustment Policy in Uganda has, among other things, improved civil service pay in recent years in an attempt to counter the poor reward and career structure and the corresponding dependence on multi-occupations for economic survival.) In the event, it did not prove possible to restrict the curriculum in this way. Management accounting was introduced into the curriculum (even although its inclusion made the participants more 'marketable') once it became apparent that the future needs of the participants required its inclusion.

Two other examples should suffice to show that needs are not always correctly identified: (i) in Kenya, preparatory discussions indicated that the participants (senior financial managers in local government, central government and parastatals) should be exposed to developments in financial reporting, including those relating to Kenyan Accounting Standards, but delivery of the first course showed that priority should be given more to management- and management accounting-oriented issues; (ii) preparatory discussions at another institution in Kenya failed to indicate that the participants (middle-level financial managers from local and central government) required grounding in book-keeping (most particularly with respect to the closing-off of year-end accounts).

TRAINING OF TRAINER SKILLS

In Uganda, it was hoped, once a reasonable number of staff had been trained, that the informal process of 'learning by sitting next to Waswa' would take place and training would cascade down to junior staff. When assessing the impact of the initial courses, it became evident that informal cascade training to junior finance staff was not taking place to any great extent. A number of factors appeared to contribute to this situation including the lack of both confidence and training skills in the recently trained finance officers. Thus, a series of TOT courses was developed. The intention was that the resulting TOT trained finance officers would provide a part-time team of trainers who would organize a series of formal basic 'cascade' training programmes for junior finance staff, run and financed by the host government. Consequently, the TOT programmes concentrated on developing standard pedagogic skills for use in a classroom situation.

Classroom training of this nature did take place in Uganda. This model subsequently was adopted in Tanzania but internal budgetary constraints made it very difficult for classroom training to take place. It was decided that it would be more effective for finance officers to undertake in-service training of junior staff and the curriculum for the TOT courses was refocused in order to provide the necessary skills to underpin training in the workplace and to concentrate on issues relating to adult learning.

Training for life?

Our experience of delivering the programmes did more than simply raise issues which we had not foreseen. Over time, we found that we were forced into having to reconsider the very nature of what we were doing. According to Wallace and Briston (1993, pp. 206–208), there are three approaches to improving accounting in underdeveloped countries: the Dependency Approach – the main facet of which would appear to be the direct transfer of accounting practices with which the developed country is familiar, regardless of the relevance of the practices to the recipient country; the Self-Reliance (Without Foreign Assistance) Approach – where a country has the ability to conduct its affairs on the basis of three essential requirements (appropriate knowledge, skill and attitude); the Self-Reliance (With Foreign Assistance) Approach – where external assistance (of whatever form) pursues a path between the competing claims of the dependency and absolute self-reliance approaches. We have always adopted the third approach. But, while infinitely preferable to the first approach, this does not of itself guarantee more effective financial management – it is a necessary but not a sufficient condition. During the course of our programmes we have learned that, to be effective, training has to be more than relevant. We have had to face the issue of whether it is possible to train for life.

The purpose of our training has been to enhance the accounting capabilities of finance staff in the public sector. In effect, the training has represented surrogate professional accountancy development. As is indicated above, discussions with the recipient country led to agreement as to the initial orientation of the training. Clearly, what is taught influences how it is taught (Brown and Guilding, 1993, p. 211). Over the years we have used a variety of teaching methods – lectures, seminar/tutorials, group discussions, case studies, role play, workshops. To begin with, the content of a lesson helped determine the most appropriate teaching method(s) – although, as would be expected, an alternative method was introduced if another had been found to be unsuccessful. However, over time our assumptions concerning the nature of the 'training' we should provide began to change – and this had a profound influence on the teaching methods adopted.

Initially, the focus of the training was on accounting practices. This is not to say that the training concentrated only on lower-level cognitive skills. On the contrary, we were able to draw on our experiences of teaching on professional accountancy programmes in the UK to develop challenging teaching materials – for example, case studies were used to help develop analytical and problem-solving skills. But the focus at the beginning was almost entirely on the development of accountancy knowledge and skills in what might be described as a prescribed setting.

It is the notion of a 'prescribed setting' which we began to doubt. Developing analytical and professional judgement skills requires, among other things, enhancing the ability of students to search for the answer (Brown and Guilding, 1993, p. 211). Clearly, this suggests that 'the answer' exists and that a principal aim of training should be problem-solving. Over time, we began to realize that this presupposes that problems present themselves as givens. Thus, although we had developed interesting and challenging case studies – some of which were developed jointly with African counterparts, all of which were suitably 'Africanized' – those case studies made assumptions which were invalid. That is, the world facing the participants on our programmes was more complex, uncertain and dynamic than that represented in our case studies – in which case, as Velaythum and Perera (1993, p. 293) indicate, problems do not present themselves to the professional as givens. On the contrary, as the same authors (p. 293) argue – quoting Schon (1983) – problems must be constructed from situations which are puzzling, troubling and uncertain. While at the time not necessarily articulating our thoughts in the same language, we realized that the training needed to address 'problem setting' (Schon, 1987) in order that problem solving could be properly contextualized.

Differences in the structure of the programmes meant that we had to deal with this in more than one way. In the case of the Ugandan and Tanzanian programmes (both of which included a placement period with a local authority in Scotland during a course delivered at the Glasgow Caledonian University), it was possible for the participants to see for themselves the need to set problems in context – among other things, they attended council meetings, including policy-making meetings. The Kenyan programme did not include such a visit to the UK, placing an even greater onus on the case studies' work done in-country. To ensure that the case studies were suitably contextualized, two members of staff spent two weeks visiting a range of organizations in Kenya (government ministries, local authorities, parastatals) interviewing senior personnel and gathering materials. This information was used subsequently to develop case studies – to help ensure that institutional strengthening took place, the case studies were produced jointly with staff from the two Kenyan training institutions (some of these staff being given time to visit the authors' University for this purpose).

This move towards a focus on problem-setting necessitated a shift in what we were attempting to do. In so far as it is possible to make a clear cut distinction between the two, our programmes initially were designed with training rather than education in mind (see above). We realized almost immediately that there needed to be an educational aspect to our programmes in that the participants needed more exposure to the development of higher-level cognitive skills. With the realization that the participants should be exposed to case studies, etc. which developed problem-setting skills, our programmes became more education-oriented. Thus, although ostensibly training programmes, the programmes aimed at the development of the intellectual abilities of the participants. The primary objective for a programme became the need for learning to learn (Velaythum and Perera, 1993, p. 290). There continued to be techniques acquisition (Gray *et al.*, 1994, p. 5l) since there clearly was a need for it. But the orientation of the programmes moved towards the development of critical thinking skills – that is, towards the development of skills which allowed the participant to address unstructured, ambiguous problems (Kimmel, 1995, p. 299).

It needs noting that the shift just described was not without problems. The participants on the various programmes needed to be persuaded of the efficacy of the approach being adopted. Like students everywhere, they found difficulty in seeing the merit of exploring issues that are uncertain, ambiguous, contested and even subjective. It was only once they were made to realize that their own future needs required such an approach that they were (reluctantly) won over. There was a conflict of interest too with the funding agencies. Each of the programmes had its own specific aims, but common to all was the aim that the participants should receive accountancy training. Again, it was only after the funding agencies were persuaded that the future needs of the participants necessitated more than simply techniques aquisition that this conflict was resolved.

Cultural baggage

In discussing the very many questions posed by numerous theories of development, Leys (1996, p. 107) suggests that these merely testify to the extraordinary degree to which

African reality has been overlaid by theory. He concludes that the motive is good but the pitfalls are many. We would hope that our motive throughout our involvement in East Africa has been good – although we are conscious that there is a 'development community' which arguably constitutes a vested interest. But we would concur that potentially there are many pitfalls. A pitfall we have tried (we hope successfully) to avoid is allowing our 'cultural baggage' to unduly influence matters. We would contend that it is not possible to ditch such baggage. However, it has been an imperative from the outset that we remain conscious at all times of that baggage.

When teaching in East Africa, you become acutely aware of the values and assumptions which you carry. You cannot avoid recognizing that the particular trajectories of histories, politics and nexus of power relations (Puxty et al., 1994, p. 86) have shaped accounting in the countries of the region. Even more so than may have been the case prior to your involvement, you cannot treat accounting as a neutral, technical, value-free activity. Of itself, this cannot guarantee that you do not indoctrinate participants on your programmes and/or emphasize and implicitly reinforce self-interest (Gray et al., 1994, p. 62). But, perhaps more than previously was the case, you are forced to question your own cultural values and assumptions – thereby improving the chances of avoiding the pitfalls identified by Gray et al. (1994). Thus, on all the programmes we have sought both to convey the contested nature of areas of accounting and to refrain from imposing values on the participants.[6]

CONFLICTS OF INTEREST

As has been already indicated, the change in the focus of the programmes led to conflicts of interest both with participants on the courses and with the funding agencies. There also have been such conflicts with staff in the various institutions where the courses have been delivered. These arose, to some extent, as part of the learning experience of working together – common approaches to developing materials and to delivering materials had to be negotiated and developed; the trust of staff in the various institutions had to be gained. Our experience would indicate that a crucial factor in helping resolve such conflicts is that staff need to see the relevance of the programmes being delivered – in some of the institutions, the scepticism of the staff was understandable since they had experienced programmes which were not relevant to the needs of participants; but this scepticism was present even in staff in institutions with no direct experience of donor-funded programmes, illustrating the extent of the repercussions of the Dependency Approach (see above).

It is not being suggested that all conflicts were easily resolved. On the contrary, on some occasions very difficult decisions had to be taken. For example, the attitude of a member

[6] Of course, it might be argued that our very presence in East Africa represents an imposition of values in that not everyone is persuaded of the desirability of exporting education to underdeveloped countries. We would disagree. For us, the (un)desirability of exporting accounting education cannot be determined in advance but instead will depend on the quality of what is delivered. Based on our experiences, we would contend that a crucial factor in determining the quality of the programmes is how well those exporting accounting education refrain from imposing values. This does not mean that educators pretend to be value-free but simply that they desist from suggesting (implicitly or explicitly) that their values are appropriate irrespective of the context. It is extremely difficult to assess how successful one is in refraining from imposing values. We would not claim to have been successful all of the time but we console ourselves with the fact that our continuing presence in East Africa suggests that we have not been totally unsuccessful.

of staff from the authors' University proved to be unacceptable to staff in an institution in Tanzania who insisted that he be removed from the programme; a staff member from an institution in Kenya who had come to the authors' University for a month to help develop case studies proved unwilling to apply himself to the task in hand and had to be removed from the programme once he had returned to his training institution.

CULTURAL DIFFERENCES

Several cultural influences impacted on the effectiveness of the training programmes. Issues such as political and tribal loyalty, the importance of position and seniority, and general misunderstanding of Anglo-Saxon open-management styles can make change difficult to manage. Many people new to Africa tend to underestimate the effects of tribal allegiances. With senior management posts awarded on the basis of political or tribal loyalty, it is often difficult to discipline someone from the same tribe. This feature highlights the danger of trainers carrying their value-laden baggage with them and ignoring the importance of local culture. Many 'mzungos' (strangers) tend to forget that these countries have a relatively short history whereas tribal kingdoms have a history stretching back many hundreds of years. (Sadly, it was the colonial rush to divide the spoils in Africa that split tribes into what for them were unnatural national divisions.)

These cultural problems were not foreseen at the planning stage of the early training programmes. Initially, the mainly young finance officers chosen for training were seen as the main change-agents in updating and modernizing government accounting and auditing systems and skills. In the event, the importance attached to seniority and position made it difficult for these change-agents to introduce new methods and approaches. That is, they were unable to break through the barriers of entrenched ways of operating and, in some cases, the vested interests of higher levels of management. As a response to this problem, on both the Ugandan and Tanzanian programmes, workshops were provided for senior officers and key politicians at both the national and local level to highlight the benefits of improved financial staff and systems.

Another local cultural feature which impacted on the design of the training programmes was the importance to individuals of not losing face. Assessment was an integral part of the Uganda programme from the beginning but it was never the intention to introduce associated qualifications – this would have necessitated the successful completion of all assessments, and the possibility of failing examinations and thereby losing face (as well as promotion prospects) was too strong a disincentive to participants. Instead, documentation was provided which certified completion of a course (as requested by the participants). The programme in Tanzania, on the other hand, operated a similar system to begin with but now includes a more rigorous testing and assessment of competencies to attempt to ensure that proper learning has taken place.

RESOURCE PROBLEMS

Reference has been made already to the dilemma facing governments of underdeveloped economies in terms of education policy. Should scarce resources be concentrated on basic education – primary and lower secondary – or should funding be focused on higher and professional education and training? On the one hand, basic education helps reduce poverty by increasing the productivity of the poor, by reducing fertility and improving

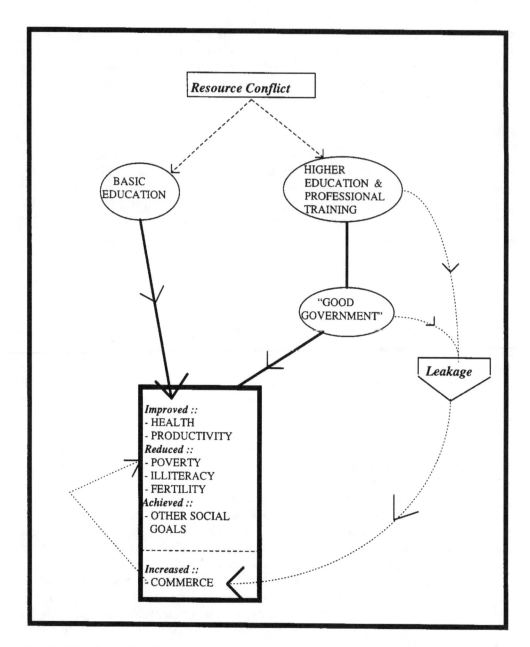

Fig. 1. Education policy dichotomy.

health, and by equipping people with the skills they need to participate fully in the economy and in society. But, at the same time, the acute shortages of qualified and trained personnel require that resources be allocated to higher education. See Figure 1.

Africa provides a good illustration of this dilemma. Spending per student in higher education in Africa generally is about 44 times that per student in primary education; and higher education's share of the total spent on education is now higher than in any other region of the world. Yet one half of Africa's primary school age children are not enrolled in school[7] (World Bank, 1991, p. 3).

Added to this resource dilemma is the problem of leakage of trained government staff into the commercial sector. This potentially reduces the impact of 'good government' (however this may be defined) by lessening effective public accountability and financial controls. At the same time, it could be argued that such leakages benefit society through more efficient commercial activity and associated multiplier effects throughout the economy (see Figure 1). Whatever the relative merits of the arguments, as has been referred to earlier it has been our experience that these leakages have made it very difficult to strengthen and develop training institutions.

Budget problems can also affect the success of aid-funded training programmes where the recipient government is often required to fund the relevant in-country costs. Tight budgetary conditions – particularly if combined with the leakage of trained staff referred to above – may result in training programmes being delayed or cancelled, notwithstanding that such in-country costs normally represent a small proportion of overall costs. Such budget problems can lead to conflicts of interest. In Kenya, courses designed for five weeks had to be reduced to four weeks because the various ministries and local authorities threatened to dock the wages of the participants if they were absent for more than four weeks – a situation which created some tension between the funding agency and the host government. On a number of occasions, problems have occurred because the participants on courses have not received any allowance to pay for accommodation and living expenses – some courses have been delayed, the completion of others has been threatened because the participants threatened to leave part-way through (a situation which created tensions among all concerned – staff, the institution, the employers, the funding body).

In all the circumstances described in this section, we have been extremely careful to refrain from imposing our views of the 'rights' and 'wrongs' of the situation. Of course, we may have held a particular view. But we have long recognized that holding fast to a view in a very different environment benefits no one.

Gauging effectiveness

The assessment of the effectiveness of programmes provides an excellent illustration of how all concerned have had to learn from experience. The objectives for the initial programmes in Uganda (contained in a 'Project Memorandum') were 'input' rather than 'output' focused, little if any reference being made to how the success of a programme might be assessed. This may seem surprising but should not be if the context is taken into consideration – projects of the type being implemented in Uganda were few and far between in 1982; at that time, performance indicators were only beginning to be used to any real extent in some parts of the public sector. It was only later that the issue of effectiveness measurement began to be prioritized.

This is not to suggest that monitoring and evaluation of projects did not take place. On the contrary, projects were assessed – the main project in Uganda, which was designed to

---

[7] Once again, aggregate numbers conceal country variations. In 1986, the primary school enrolment rate in Kenya was 94% while in Uganda it was 58% (Todaro, 1992). Moreover, other critical factors – for example, the average years of schooling, the gender gap, the rural–urban gap – are not reflected in aggregate numbers of this nature.

run from 1983–1986, ran until 1991 because it was considered successful; the project in Tanzania, designed to run from 1989–1992, continues to date for the same reasons; the project in Kenya, on the other hand, was not continued beyond its scheduled end-point of 1993 because, despite the broad nature of its objectives (see above), it was not considered to have been successful. However, while assessment of projects did take place, it was not done in a systematic manner. That is to say, only later was there a framework in place which governed the design, implementation and evaluation of projects.

The first change in gauging effectiveness took place when the reports prepared for the funding bodies were required to include some measure of 'output' (usually the numbers trained on a course). In the first few years of the Ugandan project, there was difficulty in meeting target numbers. It was not unusual for a member of staff from the authors' University to visit ministries and councils some days in advance of a course in order to 'drum up support' for the course. The fact that target numbers were more or less met against a backdrop of continuing civil unrest was a factor in the decision to extend the project beyond its scheduled end-point, as was the fact that classroom training of junior finance staff did take place after finance officers had been TOT trained. At the same time, it merits noting that the Kenyan project was not extended beyond its scheduled end-point despite the fact that target numbers for those attending courses were met. The critical factor so far as the funding body was concerned was the absence of sustainable institutional development. That is to say, the specific objectives of the project had been met – everyone concerned (the funding body, the host government, the host institutions) agreed that the quality of the short course programmes in financial management had improved, that appropriate teaching materials (particularly case studies) had been developed, and that a wider range of reference books had been made available. But salary differentials were such that the indigenous trainers who had helped in various aspects of the project (syllabus development, teaching, case studies' development) left to take up more lucrative positions in the private sector, making it impossible for sustainable institutional strengthening to take place – no doubt, the fact that the funding body had financed post-graduate study in the UK and elsewhere for some of these trainers (thereby making them more marketable) also had a bearing on the decision not to extend the project. (One of the training institutions concerned subsequently has been privatized in order that the problem of salary differentials might be addressed.)

A further refinement in gauging effectiveness took place with the inclusion in the Project Memorandum of a range of targets for programmes ('measurable indicators') – these would include: numbers trained; councils/ministries covered; the proportion of teaching carried out by staff from the indigenous training institution; assessment results. At this time, the progress reports prepared for the funding bodies began to include details of actual achievements against the target outputs. Success in achieving target outputs was a crucial factor in the extension to the Tanzanian project – most of the courses delivered in Tanzania included a substantial input from indigenous trainers; staff from the training institution in Tanzania provided a significant contribution to the writing of a training manual; staff from the same institution helped develop a Financial Memorandum which subsequently was issued by the Prime Minister's Office for use in all local authorities in Tanzania.

A more recent development in gauging effectiveness has been that programmes have begun to focus on 'outcomes'. Projects now include a 'logical framework' which encompasses goals, purposes, outputs and activities. [8] In some ways, this merely represents a refinement in terminology – projects always had objectives (even if these were broad in nature and did not comprise a hierarchy), and always included particular tasks which (on later projects) were intended to produce identifiable outputs. What is new is the emphasis placed on the 'end-of-project impact' – projects now contain reference to the (self-explanatory) terms 'objectively verifiable indicators' and 'means of verification'. Thus, on the present phase of the programme in Tanzania 'tracer studies' are taking place whereby follow-up visits to councils are carried out in order to try to assess the impact of the training courses on a council's financial management systems and procedures and also to assess the extent to which training at the workplace is taking place – it merits noting that staff from the training institution in Tanzania are included in the team conducting the tracer studies. These studies are continuing at the time of writing and it is therefore not possible to provide precise details of the findings. Nonetheless, the studies undertaken to date show that the level of success of the training courses appears to have been variable – that is, some councils have been more successful than others in improving their financial management systems and procedures and in providing workplace training. Once all the local authorities have been visited and a fuller picture has emerged, the next stage of the programme will attempt to determine (i) why there has been this variation; (ii) what needs to be done to overcome this difficulty.

Of course, the answer to the first of these questions may reveal that factors outside our control are responsible for the failure of the project to have the desired impact in certain areas[9]. In such a case, the funding body, the host government and the local authorities will need to determine the answer to the second question. Nonetheless, even if this were so, there can be no doubting that projects are now considered much more systematically than previously was the case. The changes to the design, implementation and evaluation of projects described in this section reflect developments taking place across most of the public sector in recent times. They reflect too the learning experiences of all concerned in the programmes which began in Uganda in 1982. No doubt, that learning will continue so long as the programmes do.

Conclusions

In this paper we have attempted to address a number of educational issues surrounding the exporting of accounting to East Africa. We have, on occasions, described our experiences (which go back to 1982) but this has been done with the intention of illustrating the *educational* difficulties we faced. Based on our experiences, we would make five conclusions. First, given the severe nature of the problems facing Africa, training and education programmes are of paramount importance. (However, those programmes must be relevant – and all the other conclusions relate to this point.) Second, the context of East Africa is a critical factor in determining all aspects of a programme. Provided this is borne in mind, there is a chance that a programme will meet the needs of the recipient country.

---

[8] Goal refers to the 'greater why' (the higher-order objective) of a project; purpose is the 'why' – what does the project hope to achieve? outputs are the 'what' – the specific results produced; activities are the 'how' – the tasks to be undertaken and the resources to be made available to produce the outputs.

[9] Interviews carried out to date have identified the following as reasons for the failure of workplace training to take place in some local authorities – lack of funds; lack of materials; too much work; superiors not cooperative.

Third, those delivering a programme must be prepared to learn from their experiences. No matter how much care is taken, there inevitably will be issues and difficulties which come to the fore which could not have been foreseen when developing a programme. Fourth, there needs to be a very strong educational dimension to a programme, even if initially it was designed more as a training programme. That is, programmes need to attempt to develop the intellectual abilities (in the broadest sense) of the participants, and in particular should aim to develop their problem-setting skills. Fifth, those delivering a programme should beware of their cultural baggage. They should refrain from imposing values on the participants when faced with circumstances very different to their own. We would contend that the possibility exists of exporting something worthwhile if those delivering a programme bear these conclusions in mind.

References

Abayo, A.G. and Roberts, C.B. (1991) Does training more accountants raise the standard of accounting? Further evidence from Tanzania, *Research in Third World Accounting*, **2**, 259–280.

Blaug, M. (1976) Human capital theory: a slightly jaundical survey, *The Journal of Economic Literature*, **14**, 827–856.

Briston, R.J. and Wallace, R.S.O. (1990) Accounting education and corporate disclosure regulation in Tanzania, *Research In Third World Accounting*, **1**, 281–299.

Brown, R.B. and Guilding, C. (1993) A survey of teaching methods employed in university business school accounting courses, *Accounting Education: an International Journal*, **2**(3), 211–218.

Cassen, R.H. (1986) *Does Aid Work?* Oxford: Clarendon Press.

Ghartak, S. (1995) *Introduction to Development Economics*, London: Routledge.

Ghartey, J.B. (1993) Education, accountability and development in the third world, *Research in Third World Accounting*, **2**, 169–186.

Godfrey, A.D., Devlin, P.J. and Merrouche, C. (1996) Governmental accounting in Kenya, Tanzania and Uganda, *Research in Governmental and Non Profit Accounting*, **9**, 193–208.

Gray, R., Bebbington, J. and McPhail, K. (1994) Teaching ethics in accounting and the ethics of accounting teaching: educating for immorality and a possible case for social and environmental accounting education, *Accounting Education: an International Journal*, **3**(1), 51–75.

Gujarathi, M.R. and Dean, P. (1993) Problems of recruiting and retaining qualified government accountants and auditors in developing countries, *Research in Third World Accounting*, **2**, 187–200.

Hayami, Y. and Ruttan, W.M. (1970) Agricultural productivity differences among countries, *American Economic Review*, **60**, 895–911.

Kimmel, P. (1995) A framework for incorporating critical thinking into accounting education, *Journal of Accounting Education*, **13**, 299–318.

Kruger, A.O. (1968) Factor endowments and per capita income, *Economic Journal*, **78**, 641–659.

Leys, C. (1996) *The Rise and Fall of Development Theory*, London: James Currey.

Morawetz, D. (1971) *Twenty-Five Years of Economic Development*, Washington DC: World Bank.

Mosley, P. (1987) *Overseas Aid: Its Defence and Reform*, Brighton: Wheatsheaf.

Parry, M.J. and Groves, R.E. (1990) Does training more accountants raise the standards of accounting in third world countries? A story of Bangladesh, *Research in Third World Accounting*, **1**, 117–140.

Puxty, A., Sikka, P. and Willmott, H. (1994) Reforming the circle: education, ethics and accounting practices, *Accounting Education: an International Journal*, **3**(1), 77–92.

Riddell, R.C. (1987) *Foreign Aid Reconsidered*, Baltimore: The Johns Hopkins Press.

Rivera, J.M. (1990) The accounting profession and accounting education in Panama, in B.E. Needles and V.K. Zimmerman (eds) *Comparative International Accounting Educational Standards* Urbana-Champagne: University of Illinois.

Schon, D.A. (1983) *The Reflective Practitioner: How Professionals Think in Action*, New York: Basic Books.

Schon, D.A. (1987) *Educating the Reflective Practitioner: Toward a Design for Teaching and Learning in the Professions*, San Francisco: Jossey-Bass.

Tarp, F. (1993) *Stabilization and Structural Adjustment: Macroeconomic Frameworks for Analyzing the Crisis in Sub-Saharan Africa*, London: Routledge.

Todaro, M.P. (1992) *Economics for a Developing World*, London: Longman.

Todaro, M.P. (1997) *Economic Development*, London: Longman.

Velayutham, S. and Perera, H. (1993) The reflective accountant: towards a new model for professional development, *Accounting Education: an International Journal*, **2**(4), 287–301.

Wallace, R.S.O. (1990) Accounting in developing countries: a review of the literature, *Research in Third World Accounting*, **1**, 3–54.

Wallace, R.S.O. and Briston, R.J. (1993) Improving the accounting infrastructure in developing countries, *Research in Third World Accounting*, **2**, 201–224.

World Bank (1989) *Sub-Saharan Africa: From Crisis to Sustainable Growth*, Washington DC: World Bank.

World Bank (1991) *The African Capacity Building Initiative*, Washington DC: World Bank.

World Bank (1995) *Priorities and Strategies for Education*, Washington DC: World Bank.

The quality of learning in accounting education: the impact of approaches to learning on academic performance

PETER BOOTH,[1] PETER LUCKETT[2] and ROSINA MLADENOVIC[2]

[1]University of Technology, Sydney, Australia and [2]University of New South Wales, Australia

Abstract

While accounting educators have been increasingly concerned with the quality of accounting education, the accounting education literature has not proposed a coherent framework for addressing this issue. The Approaches to Learning paradigm in the education literature offers such a framework for analysing the ways in which students learn and how the learning context interacts with learning choices. Here we use this paradigm to investigate the learning approaches of accounting students from two Australian universities as compared to previously reported data for Australian arts, education and science students. In addition, we consider the impact of accounting students' approaches to learning on their academic performance. Data about learning approaches, using the Study Process Questionnaire and various attitudinal and performance variables, were collected from accounting students at two Australian universities. The comparison of the learning approach scores of accounting students with previously reported norms for Australian arts, education and science students, indicated that the former had relatively higher surface and lower deep learning approaches. In addition, higher surface approach scores were found to be associated with less successful academic performance, but no association was found for deep approach scores. The implications of these results for accounting educators are discussed and suggestions for future research into students' approaches to learning are considered.

Introduction

The aim of the educational process in accounting, as in all disciplines, is to achieve high quality learning outcomes. Recently, such outcomes have been argued to include not only strong technical competencies, but also a broad understanding of the discipline, the ability to think critically, apply ideas and concepts to problems, and the possession of high communication and other generic skills (Accounting Education Change Commission, 1992; Nelson 1995; Paisey and Paisey, 1996; Beattie et al., 1997). Various critiques of current accounting education, however, have identified deficiencies with respect to such competencies and skills in accounting graduates and have made many recommendations for change (for example, see, Patten and Williams, 1990; Accounting Education Change Commission, 1992; Higher Education Council, 1992; Bauer et al., 1994; Institute of Chartered Accountants in Australia, 1994; National Board of Employment, Education and Training, 1994a, 1994b).

In response to these criticisms, accounting education research has considered a wide range of specific methods that aim to improve students' generic and life-long learning skills. These include the use of case studies (Campbell and Lewis, 1991; Stewart and Dougherty, 1993), group based, intensive and other cooperative learning formats (Cottell and Millis, 1992, 1993; Berry, 1993; Inglis et al., 1993; Peek et al., 1995), and communication and critical thinking techniques (Hirsch and Collins, 1988; Mohrweis, 1991; Gabriel and Hirsch, 1992; Kagan, 1992; Scofield and Combes, 1993). While the aim of these methods is to change how students learn, the studies do not directly address the ways in which accounting students approach their learning tasks and how these impact on the achievement of high quality learning outcomes.

In the education literature, the Approaches to Learning paradigm argues that to improve the quality of learning systematically it is necessary to first understand the process of student learning (Biggs, 1978, 1979, 1987a, 1987b; Entwistle, 1984; Marton and Saljo, 1984; Ramsden, 1992). For example, Biggs (1987a, 1987b) demonstrates that student learning approaches may be crucial in determining the quality of student learning as reflected by factors such as academic performance and satisfaction with the educational experience. But the accounting education literature, with the recent exceptions of two empirical studies (Chan et al., 1989; Gow et al., 1994) and two literature reviews (Lucas, 1996; Beattie et al., 1997), has not explored the implications of this mainstream educational framework for improving the quality of accounting education. These papers call for further consideration of this paradigm in accounting education. For example, Gow et al. (1994, p. 118) argue that an '. . . (e)xamination of the ways students approach their study can provide insights into how students learn and thus provide a guide to the teaching strategies needed to improve their learning'.

In response to these calls, the current study has two aims. First, it provides some evidence relating to claims that accounting students tend to take a superficial approach to learning, characterized by rote memorization, which is not conducive to quality learning outcomes (Bauer et al., 1994; Beattie et al., 1997). Accordingly, the learning approaches of accounting students from two Australian universities are compared to previously reported data for Australian arts, education and science students. Second, the paper considers the impact of accounting students' approaches to learning on their academic performance. The education literature has found that higher academic performance is associated with a deep approach to learning and lower performance with a surface approach (Biggs, 1987a; Trigwell and Prosser, 1991; Eley, 1992). Given that the literature has tended to ignore business education areas such as accounting (Lucas, 1996), we investigate whether similar findings hold in the case of accounting students. Such findings would provide further support for the need for learning environments that encourage deeper learning approaches.

In the next section, the Approaches to Learning paradigm is reviewed. The third section develops the two research propositions. This is followed by a description of the research method. The fifth section presents a discussion of the results. A summary, with implications for teaching practice and future research, forms the final section.

How students learn: the Approaches to Learning paradigm

The current study is informed by the Approaches to Learning literature, which is one of the dominant paradigms in the education literature for examining student learning processes (see Biggs, 1978, 1979, 1987a; Biggs and Rihn, 1984; Entwistle, 1984; Marton and Saljo, 1984; Ramsden, 1988, 1992; Lucas, 1996; Beattie et al., 1997). The main focus is on the influence that the learning environment has on the approach to learning adopted by the student, which, in turn, affects the quality of the learning outcome. The two common learning approaches employed by students are described as deep and surface learning.

A deep approach to learning is characterized by an intention by students to understand and is reflected in a focus on underlying arguments and the identification, organization and classification of new ideas and previous knowledge. In a deep approach the '. . . students are focussing on the content of the task and how it relates to other parts of the course or previous knowledge; they are trying to understand the task and relate its component parts to the whole. The process is internal: the students are concerned with integrating the new material with their personal experiences, knowledge and interests' (Ramsden, 1992, p. 48). Thus, it is argued that a deep approach is more likely to result in quality learning outcomes such as a good understanding of the discipline as well as developing higher order skills such as the ability to think critically and process data at a high level of generality (Biggs, 1987a, pp. 8–13; Trigwell and Prosser, 1991, p. 273; Ramsden, 1992, pp. 38–61; Biggs, 1993, pp. 7–9; Sharma, 1997, p. 143; Sharma, 1998, p. 22).

In contrast, a surface approach is characterized by an intention to complete task requirements. The focus is on the facts rather than arguments, memorization of information and procedures, and an unreflective acceptance of material. In a surface approach to learning '. . . the focus is on reproducing bits and pieces of memorised or textbook knowledge. The process of learning is external to the student: it is one in which alien material is impressed on the memory or manipulated unthinkingly with the intention of satisfying assessment demands' (Ramsden, 1992, p. 46). Consequently, a surface approach usually results in the mere accumulation of unrelated bits of information for reproduction in assessment processes.

In addition, Biggs (1987a) proposed that both the deep and surface approaches to learning interact with the student's orientation to achieving a desired level of performance from learning. An achieving approach is based on competition and ego enhancement where students organize their time and working space in order to obtain the highest grades, whether or not the material is interesting. Biggs suggests that the deep and surface approaches differ from the achieving approach in that the '. . . first two describe ways in which students engage in the context of the task itself, while the achieving strategy describes the ways in which students organise the temporal and spatial contexts surrounding the task' (Biggs, 1987a, p. 12). For example, students can search for meaning in a highly organized way (deep plus achieving approaches) or rote learn in a highly organized way (surface plus achieving approaches). They cannot, however, rote learn and search for meaning simultaneously.

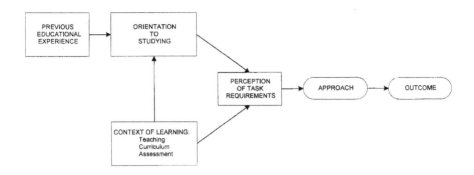

Fig. 1. Student learning in context (source: Ramsden, 1992, p. 83)

The Approaches to Learning literature emphasizes the contextual nature of learning, as illustrated in Figure 1. Learning is not viewed in isolation, but is discussed in relation to a number of factors such as curriculum, assessment, modes of teaching, students' prior experiences and perceptions.[1] The aim is to create an environment that encourages students to employ a deep approach to learning, leading to higher quality learning. A deep approach is to be encouraged, as of the three approaches to learning '. . . only the deep is task-focussed or "natural". Surface and achieving are institutional creations, sanctions and rewards shifting the focus from the task itself to ways of maximising the rewards and minimising the sanctions associated with successful or unsuccessful completion of the task' (Biggs, 1993, p. 7).

Two recent empirical studies in the accounting education literature incorporate the ideas of the Approaches to Learning literature, through the use of the Biggs Study Processes Questionnaire (SPQ), to examine the way in which undergraduate accounting students in Hong Kong approach their study (Chan *et al.*, 1989; Gow *et al.*, 1994). Chan *et al.* (1989) found that '. . . (a)ccountancy students have a tendency to focus on the bare fundamentals and reproduce them through rote learning rather than to organise their time and follow up all suggested readings' (p. 189). Gow *et al.* (1994) reported that the student's enthusiasm and the use of a deep approach to study declined from the first to the second year of the course. They also found that the average scores on the deep approach rose again through the second and third years, but still remained *below* the first year level. These findings provide strong support for the concerns over the quality of accounting education discussed in the introduction to this paper. As potential explanations for their results, Gow *et al.* (1994) identify a number of factors promoting a surface approach such as an '. . . excessive workload, surface assessment demands, lack of intrinsic motivation, a didactic teaching style, high staff / student ratios . . .' (p. 118).

---

[1] Both students' predisposition to learning and the learning environment affect students' perceptions of the task, which affects the learning approach they adopt, and therefore the quality of the learning outcome. However, it is important to point out that while educators cannot do anything about students' predispositions to learning, they do have full control over the learning environment. For this reason, SPQ results can be good indicators of whether the learning environment encourages a deep approach to learning and whether the assessment structure rewards a deep approach.

Table 1. Motive and strategy in approaches to learning and studying

Approach	Motive	Strategy
SA: Surface	Surface Motive (SM) is instrumental: main purpose is to meet requirements minimally: a balance between working too hard and failing.	Surface Strategy (SS) is reproductive: limit target to bare essentials and reproduce through rote learning.
DA: Deep	Deep Motive (DM) is intrinsic: study to actualize interest and competence in particular academic subjects.	Deep Strategy (DS) is meaningful: read widely, inter-relate with previous relevant knowledge.
AA: Achieving	Achieving Motive (AM) is based on competition and ego-enhancement: obtain highest grades, whether or not material is interesting.	Achieving Strategy (AS) is based on organizing one's time and working space: behave as 'model student'.

Source: Biggs, 1987a, p. 11

Research propositions

Following Chan *et al.* (1989) and Gow *et al.* (1994), this paper adopts Biggs' (1987a) model of student learning.[2] As indicated above, Biggs (1987a) describes three approaches to learning; deep, surface and achieving (see also, Entwistle and Brennan, 1971; Entwistle and Wilson, 1977; Entwistle *et al.*, 1979; Hackman and Taber, 1979; Watkins, 1982a; Schmeck, 1993). As shown in Table 1, each approach is defined in terms of the combination of students' *motive* to learn and the *strategy* they use.

The Biggs (1987a) model was developed and tested in a range of Australian tertiary institutions, with norms for approach scores reported for arts, science and education undergraduate university students. This study compares learning approach scores for Australian undergraduate accounting students with these norms to provide some insight into the validity of concerns over the quality of accounting education. In the one prior comparative study of accounting students with those in other disciplines, Eley (1992) found that Australian accounting university students exhibit higher scores for a surface approach and lower scores for a deep approach to learning than biochemistry, chemistry and English literature students. While the Eley (1992) study is based on a small sample (63 accounting students) at only one institution (Monash University), this finding is consistent with the anecdotal evidence from many accounting educators that accounting students seem more interested in surface learning than in understanding the subject. It is also consistent with Beattie *et al.*'s (1997) speculation that accounting attracts a relatively higher proportion of students who adopt a surface approach. Therefore, it is tentatively proposed that accounting students will have higher surface approach scores and lower deep approach scores than the norms reported by Biggs (1987b).

P1   Australian undergraduate accounting students will have relatively higher surface approach scores and lower deep approach scores than Australian Arts, Education and Science undergraduate students

[2] See Beattie *et al.* (1997) for the relationship of the Biggs model to other models in the Approaches to Learning literature.

While P1 proposes that accounting students, in general, have higher scores for the surface approach, this could be an appropriate response to a learning environment that favours such an approach in its design, content and assessment structure. Thus, within the cohort of accounting students, it is important to investigate the impact of different approaches on academic performance.

Biggs (1987a) reported significant negative correlations between a student's self-rating of performance relative to peers and a surface approach, and significant positive correlations with deep, achieving and deep-achieving approaches in all of his three Australian university student samples. In contrast, he reported that student's self-rating of satisfaction with this performance was not as strongly related to the three approach scales. He found significant positive correlations of satisfaction with performance with an achieving approach for all three samples, significant positive correlations with a deep-achieving approach for arts and education students, and a significant positive correlation with a deep approach for arts students.

Watkins and Hattie (1981) examined the relationship between grade point average (GPA) and learning approach scores for arts, science, rural science and economics students in one Australian university. They reported significant negative correlations between a surface approach and GPA for science and rural science students, and a significant positive correlation between a deep approach and GPA for arts students.[3] In commenting on these findings, Biggs (1987a) concluded:

> ... that the science students scored *highest* in Surface Approach yet it is that approach that relates most negatively to performance. In other words, it looks as though the students entering Science are those least likely to do well in that area! (p. 61, emphasis in original).

Finally, and totally consistent with prior findings, Eley (1992) reported that a surface approach to learning was negatively correlated with total percentage marks in a university subject, while both deep and achievement approaches were positively correlated with percentage marks.

This pattern of findings for subjective and objective measures of academic performance, both of which are investigated in this paper, is consistent with a view that higher performance at university level study requires a deep approach to learning, while a surface approach is less successful.[4]

---

[3] Interestingly, for economics students, who could be assumed to be the most similar of Watkins and Hattie's sample to accounting students, there was only one significant correlation, a positive one with deep motive.

[4] It should be noted that a number of studies examining the relationship between students' learning approaches and quantitative measures of learning outcomes at the course, rather than subject, level suggest that the relationship '... is somewhat equivocal, with correlations between approach and outcome being somewhat lower than might be expected. They have tended to confirm the negative association between surface approaches to study and quantitative differences in learning outcomes, but not positive associations between deep approaches and quantitative differences' (Trigwell and Prosser, 1991, p. 265). One explanation for this that research suggests is that measures of quantitative differences do not necessarily relate to measures of qualitative differences. Another is that assessment structures do not sufficiently reward the higher quality of learning arising from a deep approach. Also, quantitative measures of learning only tap one part of learning outcomes and qualitative differences in learning arising from surface and deep approaches may indicate an advantage for a deep approach at the course level.

P2   For Australian undergraduate accounting students, surface approach scores are negatively correlated with academic performance and deep approach scores are positively correlated with academic performance.

Research method

Sample

Data were collected from accounting undergraduates at two major universities in Sydney, Australia – Macquarie University (MU) and the University of New South Wales (UNSW). Two institutions were used to increase confidence that patterns in the learning approaches found from this study were due to disciplinary rather than institutional effects. As the discussion of the 'Approaches to Learning' paradigm in prior sections indicated, the approach to learning adopted by students is affected by many contextual factors. If only one institution is sampled, the pattern of learning approaches found for accounting students may reflect specific aspects of the teaching environment of that institution more than that of the discipline of accounting. Such a chance is significantly reduced by using data from two independent institutions that we believe are generally representative of accounting programmes in Australia.[5] However, following the same line of argument, we acknowledge that our sample may be unrepresentative of accounting approaches to learning in other countries.

The MU students were surveyed during lectures in a second year management accounting subject. As the data for another project was being collected at the same time and there was insufficient time to complete both instruments, the instrument was randomly distributed to half of the 300 students who attended the lecture. The UNSW students were surveyed during tutorials in a third year management accounting subject. Both subjects were compulsory components of the accounting major for both subsamples. Details of the response rates and the gender profile of the final sample are given in Table 2. In both cases the response rate was very high, with the lowest useable response rate being 63.3%. Given such high sampling rates, it is unlikely that any systematic biases from nonresponses have occurred.[6] Our confidence in the sampling process is also increased by the fact that the attendance rates for lectures and tutorials at both institutions were both high (generally greater than 80%) and our sampling time was during a typical lecture and tutorial; that is, not during a prior announced special event where systematic variance in attendance patterns may be found. Importantly, we find no systematic bias in the pattern of cross-institutional results that would suggest that different preferences for lecture versus tutorial attendance imply different learning approaches.[7]

---

[5] The authors' broad knowledge of Australian universities would suggest that there are more similarities than differences between accounting programmes and students across the sector. This increases our personal confidence that our sample is fairly representative of Australian students, in average terms, but we have no systematic evidence to support such a claim.

[6] In any case, it was not possible to test for nonresponse bias as we had insufficient data to profile our samples against the total enrolment profile of the subjects. Also, the early–late split sample comparisons used for such testing in mail surveys could not be used as sampling occurred at one point in time.

[7] We thank one of the referees for pointing out this potential confound in our design.

Table 2. Sample summary statistics

Sample details	MU Sample	UNSW Sample	Total sample
No. surveyed	150	380	530
Instruments returned	104	293	397
	(69.3%)	(77.1%)	(74.9%)
Useable responses*	95	279	374
	(63.3%)	(73.4%)	(70.6%)
No. of males	60	127	187
	(63.2%)	(45.5%)	(50.0%)
No. of females	33	125	158
	(34.7%)	(44.8%)	(42.2%)
No response	2	27	29
	(2.1%)	(9.7%)	(7.8%)

Note: * Respondents answered all the SPQ questions and one or more of the dependent variables.

The survey instrument

A survey instrument composed of two parts – the Study Process Questionnaire (SPQ) as developed by Biggs (1987a) and a post-test questionnaire – was used to collect data on all variables except objective academic performance. The SPQ contains 42 questions, all of which were answered using a fully anchored 5 point scale.[8] The scales of the SPQ instrument have been found to have satisfactory reliability, internal consistency and construct validity (Beattie *et al.*, 1997; see Biggs, 1987b for relevant data and tests). The post-test questionnaire asked for the student's name, gender, plans for further education, ratings of overall performance in accounting subjects and satisfaction with this level of performance (see below).

Measurement of learning approach variables

To determine each student's approaches to learning scores, the 42 SPQ questions were summed in six sets of seven questions. Each set provides either a motive or strategy sub-scale score (theoretical range 7–35) for one of the three main learning approaches (surface, deep or achieving), as described in Table 1. Each matching pair of motive and strategy subscales was then summed into overall surface, deep and achieving approach scales (theoretical range 14–70). These scales represent the relative use of the main three approaches to learning by each student. Within the Biggs (1987a) model, the surface and deep scales can then be independently added to the achieving scale to provide two higher level combined learning approaches labelled surface-achieving and deep-achieving respectively (theoretical range 28–140). Only the first two levels of these scales, the motive/strategy or the three main learning approaches, are analysed in this paper. Both levels are used for considering proposition 1 as the norm data supplied by Biggs (1987b) presents such detail.

[8] The 5 points represented the following: 5 = this item is *always* or *almost always* true of me, 4 = this item is *frequently* true of me, 3 = this item is true of me about *half the time*, 2 = this item is *sometimes* true of me, 1 = this item is *never* or *only rarely* true of me.

For proposition 2 the focus is on the main approach scales only. Descriptive statistics for the motive/strategy and approach scales are given in Table 3, Panels A, B and C, for the MU, UNSW and combined samples respectively.

Subjective measures of performance

Following Biggs (1987a), two subjective measures of academic performance (student's self-ratings of their overall performance relative to that of their peers and their self-ratings of their level of satisfaction with their level of performance) were included.[9] The wording of the two measures was altered to focus upon performance and satisfaction with performance in accounting subjects. The second measure is not a measure of performance *per se*, but an indicator of how students evaluate their level of performance. As university students usually score highly on the achieving approach scale (Biggs, 1987a), their perceptions of their level of performance in a subject and their satisfaction with such a level of performance may not be positively correlated. A consideration of satisfaction with performance may thus add extra insight to any relationships between SPQ scores and perceived academic performance. Descriptive statistics are given in Table 4.

Objective measures of performance (UNSW sample)

In addition, academic performance was measured objectively via subject assessment marks for the UNSW sample. These students were asked to volunteer their names in the post-test questionnaire and, where supplied, their assessment marks were obtained from the third year management accounting subject they were undertaking at the time of the survey.[10] These were available for 128 (46%) of the 279 useable UNSW responses. The final assessment marks were composed of three continuing assessment items, which together represented 35% of the final aggregate mark, and a final examination (30% multiple choice and 70% problem analysis and essay) representing 65% of the final aggregate mark. A breakdown of the mark distribution across the assessment items is shown in Table 5 and descriptive statistics are given in Table 6.

The continuing assessment and final examination components represent the decomposition of the total aggregate mark into different assessment methods that enables a finer discrimination of any relationship between academic performance and surface and deep learning approaches. For example, prior research has indicated that multiple choice questions are likely to encourage surface approaches to learning (Watkins, 1982a, 1982b; Thomas and Bain, 1984; Biggs, 1996). Such a finding, however, would be premised on such assessment items being more likely to reward rote recall than understanding. Thus, the assessment strategy adopted needs to be considered rather than simply the form of assessment used. To provide some indication of the potential linkage between each of the assessment components and a more relevant learning approach, the right-hand column of Table 5 describes the form of assessment and the type of understanding the teaching team

---

[9] Both used fully anchored 5 points scales; the former being 1 = poor, 2 = below average, 3 = average, 4 = above average, 5 = excellent, the latter 1 = very dissatisfied, 2 = dissatisfied, 3 = indifferent, 4 = satisfied, 5 = very satisfied.

[10] Assessment marks were not as easily accessible for the MU students as none of the authors were working at that institution. Also, comparison of the assessment marks across the subsamples would not have been valid due to subject content and assessment structure differences.

Table 3. SPQ summary statistics

Panel A – Macquarie University sample ($n = 95$)

Descriptive statistic	Surface			Deep			Achieving		
	Motive	Strategy	Overall	Motive	Strategy	Overall	Motive	Strategy	Overall
Females ($n = 33$)									
Mean	25.6	24.9	50.6	19.9	19.2	39.1	21.4	19.9	41.3
Std dev	3.4	2.8	4.6	4.6	4.0	8.0	3.9	4.4	7.0
Minimum	20	19	42	12	13	26	13	8	27
Maximum	34	31	59	29	28	57	30	29	56
Males ($n = 60$)									
Mean	26.7	26.8	53.5	22.0	20.3	42.2	24.0	20.1	44.0
Std dev	3.4	3.7	6.4	4.1	3.6	6.1	4.8	4.1	7.3
Minimum	17	14	31	12	13	30	12	12	27
Maximum	35	35	67	34	28	62	32	33	62
Combined									
Mean	26.3	26.1	52.4	21.2	20.0	41.2	23.1	20.1	43.2
Std dev	3.4	3.5	5.9	4.4	3.9	7.0	4.6	4.3	7.4
Minimum	17	14	31	12	13	26	12	8	27
Maximum	35	35	67	34	29	62	32	33	62

Panel B – University of NSW sample ($n = 279$)

Descriptive statistic	Surface			Deep			Achieving		
	Motive	Strategy	Overall	Motive	Strategy	Overall	Motive	Strategy	Overall
Females ($n = 125$)									
Mean	26.3	25.2	51.5	21.9	20.5	42.4	23.4	20.5	43.7
Std dev	4.1	4.1	7.2	4.9	4.7	8.9	5.5	4.9	8.8
Minimum	15	11	32	8	8	23	9	8	26
Maximum	35	35	70	34	33	66	35	32	65
Males ($n = 127$)									
Mean	25.4	25.2	50.6	21.7	21.6	43.3	24.9	19.5	44.4
Std dev	4.5	4.1	7.5	4.5	4.7	8.2	5.5	5.1	8.7
Minimum	9	13	27	11	7	18	10	7	19
Maximum	33	34	65	31	34	64	35	32	63
Combined									
Mean	25.8	25.0	50.8	21.7	20.9	42.6	23.9	19.9	43.7
Std dev	4.3	4.1	7.3	4.8	4.9	8.8	5.6	5.1	8.8
Minimum	9	11	27	8	7	18	7	7	17
Maximum	35	35	70	34	34	66	35	32	63

was trying to reward in its assessment strategy[11] for that item. The possible relation of each item and combinations of items to deep and surface learning approaches is discussed further in the results section.

[11] The general assessment strategy was to try to make it possible to pass the subject with a basic understanding of material, but to require depth of understanding and well-developed analytical abilities to achieve higher

Table 3. Continued

Panel C – Total sample ($n = 374$)

Descriptive statistic	Surface			Deep			Achieving		
	Motive	Strategy	Overall	Motive	Strategy	Overall	Motive	Strategy	Overall
Females ($n = 158$)									
Mean	26.2	25.1	51.3	21.5	20.2	41.7	23.0	20.4	43.2
Std dev	3.7	3.9	6.7	4.9	4.6	8.8	5.2	4.8	8.5
Minimum	15	11	32	8	8	23	9	8	24
Maximum	35	35	70	34	33	66	35	32	65
Males ($n = 187$)									
Mean	25.8	25.7	51.5	21.8	21.2	43.0	24.6	19.7	44.3
Std dev	4.2	4.1	7.3	4.4	4.4	7.6	5.3	4.8	8.3
Minimum	9	13	27	11	7	18	10	7	19
Maximum	35	35	67	34	34	64	35	33	63
Combined									
Mean	25.9	25.3	51.2	21.6	20.6	42.2	23.7	19.9	43.6
Std dev	4.1	4.0	7.0	4.7	4.6	8.4	5.4	4.9	8.5
Minimum	9	11	27	8	7	18	7	7	17
Maximum	35	35	70	34	34	66	35	33	65

Table 4. Subjective student performance summary statistics

Descriptive statistic	Performance relative to peers	Level of satisfaction
MU Sample		
Mean	3.28	3.16
Std dev	0.63	1.12
Range	2–5	1–5
UNSW Sample		
Mean	3.18	2.93
Std dev	0.79	1.12
Range	1–5	1–5
Total Sample		
Mean	3.20	2.99
Std dev	0.75	1.10
Range	1–5	1–5

Manipulation checks

Before exploring the two research propositions, the SPQ scales and dependent variables were examined for any differences between the MU and UNSW samples. There was only one significant difference in the pattern of scores for all SPQ scales and subscales, with

grades. For example, the multiple choice questions used required semicomplex problem solving, not simply the generation of answers from technique application or simple recall of facts. Also, multipart examination questions were designed, where increasing levels of understanding were required to answer later components in the question sequence, and thus achieve higher marks. This strategy was communicated to students and was consistent with the assessment strategy used in a prerequisite management accounting subject.

Table 5. Assessment item structure

Assessment item	Mark out of	Type of assessment
Case study	10 (10% of aggregate mark)	Written analysis of an unstructured case dealing with judgmental application and interpretation of an accounting technique. Requires depth of understanding of material and ability to integrate subject concepts to perform highly on item.
Computing assignment	10 (10% of aggregate mark)	Development of simple spreadsheet model for application of accounting technique. Requires basic understanding of technique and spreadsheet formulae to perform highly.
Class quizzes	15 (15% of aggregate mark)	Multiple choice and short answer questions testing understanding of application of specific subject techniques. Requires reasonable understanding of techniques to perform highly.
Final exam – Part A	30 (19.5% of aggregate mark)	15 multiple choice questions testing understanding of application of specific subject techniques. Requires reasonable understanding of techniques to perform highly.
Final exam – Part B	70 (45.5% of aggregate mark)	Four questions requiring either essay responses or the application of accounting techniques to several semistructured problems and interpretation of student's analysis. Requires depth of understanding of material and ability to integrate subject concepts to perform highly on item.
Aggregate final mark	100	Overall surrogate for subject performance.

Table 6. Assessment item summary statistics

Assessment item	Mean	Std dev	Minimum	Maximum
Case study	6.71	1.10	3.00	10.00
Computing assignment	6.80	1.00	4.00	9.50
Class quizzes	11.87	1.64	6.40	15.00
Total continuing	25.32	2.96	18.00	33.50
Exam – Part A	15.63	5.32	2.00	30.00
Exam – Part B	34.60	8.30	12.00	52.50
Final exam	32.61	7.31	14.30	53.63
Total aggregate mark	57.98	9.36	37.00	87.00

surface approach scores being higher for MU students (52.4 versus 50.8, $t = -2.19$, $p = 0.03$). This difference is minor, but as the surface motive subscale has the lowest reliability rating (Biggs, 1987a, p.31) and a surface orientation bias for accounting students is explored in both propositions, the analysis for both propositions reports results for the individual institution subsamples and for the combined sample. There were no significant differences between the institution sample scores for the students' self-rated performance and level of satisfaction measures.

Finally, for the UNSW sample, the SPQ scores of students for whom objective assessment marks were available were compared to those who did not volunteer their names. No significant differences were found, suggesting that, on average, both groups had similar approaches to learning. To check for construct validity, the total aggregate mark, an indicator of overall academic performance, should be measuring a similar type of performance as the students' self-rating of overall performance. This is supported by a strong, significant positive correlation between the two measures ($r = 0.451$, $p < 0.01$).

Findings and discussion

Accounting students' learning approach profiles

The profile of the accounting students' scores on the SPQ motive and strategy subscales and the three main approach scales are shown in Table 3. These descriptive statistics indicate that the accounting students in this sample have higher surface approach (higher on both motive and strategy) scores than their deep approach or achieving approach scores. In general, this pattern was similar for female and male students, although there were some minor differences.[12] These differences, along with the previously reported surface approach difference between the two institution samples, suggest that the examination of P1 should consider results for both institutional samples and gender differences, as well as the combined sample results.

The pattern of accounting students' SPQ scores in Table 3 can only be interpreted as relative indications of learning approaches. To gain a greater appreciation of any disciplinary/regional/institutional based tendencies towards specific learning approaches they should be compared to norms for other disciplines and other accounting samples. Consistent with this, P1 proposed that Australian accounting students would have relatively higher surface approach scores and relatively lower deep approach scores than Australian arts, education and science students. Biggs (1987b) reports SPQ norms for Australian university students in arts, education and science courses. A limitation of this comparison is the 10 year time difference between the measurement of Biggs' norms and our data. Changes in institutional structures and approaches to education, at least, during this interval may have altered the current SPQ profile in Biggs' disciplines, making our analysis less representative of any discipline differences. Unfortunately, no other norms exist as a basis for comparison and we propose that the analysis provides at least some indication of the relative learning approach profile of accounting students.[13] The means of

[12] The only significant differences were for two sub-scales, deep strategy (male = 21.2, female = 20.2, $t = 2.03$, $p = 0.043$) and achieving motive (male = 24.6, female = 23.0, $t = 2.85$, $p = 0.005$). These differences disappeared for the combined deep approach (male = 43.0, female = 41.7, $t = 1.46$, $p = 0.145$) and achieving approach (male = 44.3, female = 43.2, $t = 1.14$, $p = 0.253$) scales.

[13] While more recent SPQ norms are unavailable for comparative purposes, a more recent study, Eley (1992), found that Australian accounting university students exhibit higher scores for a surface approach and lower scores for a deep approach to learning than biochemistry, chemistry and English literature students. While the Eley study is based on a small sample (63 students) at only one institution (Monash University), this finding is consistent with our findings based on the Biggs' 1987 norms and exhibits the same general pattern. Watkins and Akande (1992) also compare the Biggs norms to SPQ scores for Nigerian university students, but the time difference is about half that of our comparison.

Table 7. Australian SPQ learning approach scores by university course*

Panel A – Macquarie University sample (*n* = 95)

Gender	Surface			Deep			Achieving		
Course	Motive	Strategy	Overall	Motive	Strategy	Overall	Motive	Strategy	Overall
Female									
Acc.	25.6	24.9	50.6	19.9	19.2	39.1	21.4	19.9	41.3
Arts	21.2	19.3	40.5	23.2	22.8	46.1	19.3	21.8	41.2
	[−6.7]	[−9.9]	[−10.7]	[4.0]	[4.8]	[4.8]	[−2.7]	[2.4]	N.S.
Educ.	21.2	19.5	40.7	23.4	23.0	46.6	18.7	21.3	40.0
	[−6.1]	[−8.5]	[−9.4]	[3.9]	[4.6]	[4.8]	[−3.3]	N.S.	N.S.
Sci.	21.8	21.9	43.7	21.7	21.6	43.3	20.2	22.5	42.6
	[−5.2]	[−4.9]	[−6.6]	[2.0]	[3.0]	[2.8]	N.S.	[2.8]	N.S.
Male									
Acc.	26.7	26.8	53.5	22.0	20.3	42.2	24.0	20.1	44.0
Arts	21.4	19.1	40.5	23.8	23.1	46.9	19.9	20.1	40.0
	[−8.3]	[−11.7]	[−11.3]	[3.7]	[4.5]	[4.3]	[−4.9]	N.S.	[−3.3]
Educ.	21.6	19.8	41.4	23.6	22.3	45.9	18.3	18.9	37.2
	[−6.8]	[−9.2]	[−9.1]	[2.1]	[2.9]	[2.9]	[−6.3]	N.S.	[−4.9]
Sci.	21.7	21.9	43.5	21.9	22.1	44.0	20.7	20.4	41.1
	[−8.4]	[−8.0]	[−9.2]	N.S.	[3.1]	[1.7]	[−4.4]	N.S.	[−2.4]

Panel B – University of NSW sample (*n* = 279)

Gender	Surface			Deep			Achieving		
Course	Motive	Strategy	Overall	Motive	Strategy	Overall	Motive	Strategy	Overall
Female									
Acc.	26.3	25.2	51.5	21.9	20.5	42.47	23.4	20.5	43.7
Arts	21.2	19.3	40.5	23.2	22.8	46.1	19.3	21.8	41.2
	[−10.7]	[−12.8]	[−13.5]	[2.5]	[4.8]	[3.9]	[−7.0]	[2.5]	[−2.8]
Educ.	21.2	19.5	40.7	23.4	23.0	46.6	18.7	21.3	40.0
	[−9.1]	[−10.5]	[−11.5]	[2.4]	[4.3]	[3.8]	[−7.3]	N.S.	[−3.5]
Sci.	21.8	21.9	43.7	21.7	21.6	43.3	20.2	22.5	42.6
	[−7.9]	[−6.4]	[−8.5]	N.S.	[2.0]	N.S.	[−4.9]	[3.0]	N.S.
Male									
Acc.	25.4	25.2	50.6	21.7	21.6	43.3	24.9	19.6	44.4
Arts	21.4	19.1	40.5	23.8	23.1	46.9	19.9	20.1	40.0
	[−6.5]	[−10.6]	[−9.7]	[3.6]	[2.5]	[3.4]	[−6.9]	N.S.	[−4.0]
Educ.	21.6	19.8	41.4	23.6	22.3	45.9	18.3	18.9	37.2
	[−5.3]	[−7.8]	[−7.8]	[2.7]	N.S.	[2.1]	[−8.1]	N.S.	[−5.6]
Sci.	21.7	21.9	43.5	21.9	22.1	44.0	20.7	20.4	41.1
	[−6.5]	[−6.3]	[−7.4]	N.S.	N.S.	N.S.	[−6.5]	N.S.	[−3.1]

the scores on the motive, strategy and approach scales of students in arts, education and science courses as compared to our accounting students' scores are shown in Table 7 for the MU, UNSW and combined samples. As Biggs (1987b) reports no combined data

Table 7. Continued

Panel C – Total sample (n = 374)

Gender	Surface			Deep			Achieving		
Course	Motive	Strategy	Overall	Motive	Strategy	Overall	Motive	Strategy	Overall
Female									
Acc.	26.2	25.1	51.3	21.5	20.2	41.7	23.0	20.4	43.2
Arts	21.2	19.3	40.5	23.2	22.8	46.1	19.3	21.8	41.2
	[−11.3]	[−14.1]	[−14.8]	[3.7]	[5.8]	[5.1]	[−7.1]	[3.0]	[−2.5]
Educ.	21.2	19.5	40.7	23.4	23.0	46.6	18.7	21.3	40.0
	[−9.4]	[−11.1]	[−12.3]	[3.3]	[5.0]	[4.7]	[−7.2]	N.S.	[−3.3]
Sci.	21.8	21.9	43.7	21.7	21.6	43.3	20.2	22.5	42.6
	[−8.2]	[−6.9]	[−9.0]	N.S.	[2.7]	[1.7]	[−4.6]	[3.3]	N.S.
Male									
Acc.	25.8	25.7	51.5	21.8	21.2	43.0	24.6	19.7	44.3
Arts	21.4	19.1	40.5	23.8	23.1	46.9	19.9	20.1	40.0
	[−7.9]	[−12.3]	[−11.5]	[3.7]	[3.6]	[4.2]	[−7.1]	N.S.	[−4.3]
Educ.	21.6	19.8	41.4	23.6	22.3	45.9	18.3	18.9	37.2
	[−6.3]	[−9.0]	[−9.1]	[2.7]	[1.8]	[2.6]	[−8.4]	N.S.	[−6.0]
Sci.	21.7	21.9	43.5	21.9	22.1	44.0	20.7	20.4	41.1
	[−8.1]	[−7.9]	[−9.2]	N.S.	[1.9]	N.S.	[−6.8]	N.S.	[−3.3]

Note: * The accounting students' means are compared to each of the other samples using the procedure in Hays (1981, pp. 283–4). The values repored in [] are significant t statistics; critical value at 0.05 level is $z = 1.65$.

for females and males, the analysis reported here does not consider combined female and male data.[14]

Focusing first on the total sample comparison (Panel C in Table 7), the analysis indicates that accounting students were consistently and significantly higher on surface motive, strategy and approach scores than all other students.[15] In contrast, arts, education and science students were significantly higher on deep motive, strategy and approach scores, with the exception of science students (female and male) being similar on deep motive and male science students on deep approach scores.

However, a comparison of the two institution analyses (Panels A and B in Table 7) reveals that some of the Panel C results were due to only one of the institution samples. For the deep strategy scale for males, the lower accounting scores relative to education and science are only significantly lower for the MU sample. Also, the lack of a significant difference between female accounting and science deep motive scores was only present for UNSW students, with MU female accounting students having significantly lower scores than female science students. Similarly, the nonsignificant difference between male accounting and science deep approach scores only held for UNSW students, with MU

[14] Also, Biggs (1987a) reported significant differences in gender on achieving strategy (females had higher scores), on surface approach (males had higher scores) and achieving approach (females had higher scores) for the three disciplinary samples, which reinforces the previous argument for separate analyses of male and female scores in examining P1.

[15] A limitation of this comparison may result from the low reliability of the surface motive subscale. See Biggs (1987b, 1993).

males having significantly lower scores than science males. Further, the significantly lower deep approach score for accounting versus science females was again due to the MU sample, with female UNSW students being similar to female science students. Finally, the significantly higher female accounting student achieving motive scores for all three comparisons and the significantly higher female accounting achieving approach scores compared to arts and education were due only to the UNSW sample. Nevertheless, despite these differences, the overall pattern for males in both institution samples is very similar to the total sample pattern and the only major variations are for various deep scales for MU females. As this is the smallest subsample in the study ($n = 33$), these differences may be due to sample bias.

Overall, the three analyses consistently show higher surface motive, strategy and approach scores for both female and male accounting students. They also indicate a tendency for lower deep motive, deep strategy and deep overall approach scores for male accounting students, but less clearly so for female accounting students. Therefore, there is a reasonable level of support for P1. Nevertheless, the time difference limitation discussed above should be recognized in interpreting this support. Further research comparing current SPQ profiles across disciplines is needed to confirm our findings.

Two other studies of accounting students (Eley, 1992; Gow et al., 1994) report a similar pattern of SPQ scores to those in this study. Eley (1992) reports SPQ approach scales means of Surface = 52.1, Deep = 34.0 and Achieving = 40.1 for accounting students at Monash University. Gow et al. (1994) only graphically reports SPQ means on the three main approach scales for accounting students at Hong Kong Polytechnic.[16] Figure 1 in Gow et al. (1994) indicates the following approximate approach scores: Surface ≅ 43.1, Deep ≅ 44.7 and Achieving ≅ 44.2. Two differences for these two prior studies to the SPQ approach scores reported in Table 7 are relatively lower surface approach scores for the Hong Kong students and relatively lower deep and achieving scores for the Monash students. Consistent with arguments in the Approaches to Learning literature, these differences may be due to different learning environments and cultural backgrounds.

The impact of learning approach on academic performance

P2 proposed that surface approach scores would be negatively correlated and deep approach scores positively correlated with academic performance. This is examined for both subjective and objective measures of academic performance. Data on the subjective measures were available for both the institution samples, but objective measures of academic performance were only available for a subsample of the UNSW respondents.

As P2 is concerned with the surface and deep approaches, and as both are positively correlated with the achieving approach (Biggs, 1987a, p.16), achieving approach scores were controlled for in the analyses. To do so, a series of regressions of surface or deep approach scores on achieving scores for the total sample and appropriate subsamples were run, and the residuals obtained. In all the performance analyses reported in this section, the various academic performance scores were correlated with these residuals.

The first analysis considers the two subjective measures of academic performance; students' self-ratings of their performance relative to peers and their satisfaction with their

---

[16] Only one of the authors could be contacted and he did not have access to any of the original data on which the paper was based. Also note that the Chan et al. (1989) study on Hong Kong accounting students did not report any SPQ means for their sample.

Table 8. Correlations of surface and deep learning approach scores with subjective academic performance measures

Performance variable*	Surface	Deep
Performance relative to peers		
MU sample ($n = 94$)	**−0.237**	−0.119
	$p = 0.021$	$p = 0.252$
UNSW sample ($n = 253$)	**−0.153**	−0.007
	$p = 0.015$	$p = 0.913$
Combined sample ($n = 347$)	**−0.140**	−0.036
	$p = 0.009$	$p = 0.506$
Satisfaction with performance		
MU sample ($n = 94$)	−0.077	−0.143
	$p = 0.460$	$p = 0.170$
UNSW sample ($n = 253$)	−0.085	−0.023
	$p = 0.179$	$p = 0.719$
Combined sample ($n = 347$)	−0.066	−0.075
	$p = 0.222$	$p = 0.162$

Note: * Correlations significant at $p < 0.05$ are shown in bold.

level of performance. Pearson correlation coefficients are reported in Table 8. For reasons discussed previously, the analysis is performed for the MU, UNSW and combined samples.

There is some support for P2 with respect to subjective performance relative to peers. The results for the total sample and the two institutional samples show significant negative correlations with the surface approach scale. This is consistent with the findings for arts, science and education students reported by Biggs (1987a). There was, however, no significant relationship between this measure of performance and the deep approach. Thus, while students who tend to take a surface approach rate their performance below that of their peers, there is no perceived advantage for those who take a deep approach.

In contrast, there were no significant relationships between the learning approach scales and subjective satisfaction with performance. The latter was, however, positively related to performance relative to peers ($r = 0.510$, $p < 0.001$ for the combined sample), suggesting that, as would be expected, students were satisfied when their perceived level of performance relative to peers was average or above, but dissatisfied when it was below average.[17] Taken together, this suggests that satisfaction with performance is only associated with perceptions of relative performance in a subject, and not with the approach to learning adopted.

The second part of the analysis considers the objective measures of academic performance for a subsample of the UNSW accounting students. The correlations of the surface and deep approach scales with the aggregate mark and the various assessment items are reported in Table 9.

The total aggregate mark is the more general measure of academic performance, and the most analogous to the subjective academic performance relative to peers measure discussed above. As for that measure, the significant negative correlation of the total

[17] Note, however, that, on average, students were indifferent about their level of performance (see Table 4).

Table 9. Correlations of surface and deep learning approach scores with objective academic performance measures ($n = 128$)

Performance component*	Surface	Deep
Total aggregate mark	**−0.219**	0.014
	$p = 0.013$	$p = 0.877$
Case study	− 0.009	0.024
	$p = 0.917$	$p = 0.792$
Computing assignment	− 0.137	0.048
	$p = 0.122$	$p = 0.593$
Class quizzes	− 0.090	0.050
	$p = 0.313$	$p = 0.573$
Total continuing assessment	− 0.100	0.053
	$p = 0.262$	$p = 0.555$
Final examination − Part A	**−0.230**	0.095
	$p = 0.009$	$p = 0.288$
Final examination − Part B	**−0.177**	− 0.065
	$p = 0.046$	$p = 0.463$
Total final examination	**−0.240**	− 0.004
	$p = 0.006$	$p = 0.968$

Note: * Correlations significant at $p < 0.05$ are shown in bold.

aggregate mark with a surface approach provides support for P2 and is consistent with those reported by Watkins and Hattie (1981) for the relationship with GPA for science students. The lack of a positive correlation for the deep approach indicates that this part of P2 is not supported. Eley (1992), in contrast, who also used total aggregate subject mark, reported significant correlations consistent with P2 expectations for both the surface and deep approach scales.

The relationships with the total aggregate mark may mask relationships with specific assessment items that favour specific learning approaches. For example, one might argue that the computing assignment, class quizzes and multiple-choice based Part A of the final examination assessment items rely more on recall of concepts and the simple application of techniques and that students should perform highly on them using a surface learning approach. In contrast, the case study and the problem based Part B of the final examination assessment items rely more on depth of understanding and interpretation in applying concepts and techniques, which should require a deep learning approach to perform highly on the items. The correlations of the individual assessment items with the two approach scales allow an exploratory examination of such arguments.[18]

---

[18] It is important to note a caveat on this analysis. When designing the assessment for this subject, the Approaches to Learning literature was not used to explicitly inform the subject or assessment design. However, the teaching team consciously tried to design an assessment structure that would not reward rote learning with high subject performance and would reward depth of understanding of subject. Moreover, the teaching team stressed to students the importance of understanding rather than memorization explicitly during the teaching of the subject. However, the subject assessment was not explicitly informed by the Approaches to Learning literature, and thus does not represent a direct test of the relation between surface and deep learning approaches and academic performance in accounting.

The correlations for the individual assessment items, and their partial aggregation into total continuous assessment and total final examination marks, show a consistent pattern of negative correlations with a surface approach to learning. Three of these are significant, namely both parts of the final exam and, of course, the total final examination mark. The finding for the multiple choice based Part A of the final examination may seem inconsistent with prior findings on such assessment tasks (Watkins, 1982a, 1982b; Thomas and Bain, 1984; Biggs, 1996). This can be attributed to the fact that multiple choice examinations generally test the recall of facts and the application of simple procedures. However, explicit attempts were made to exclude such features from the multiple-choice questions used in this examination (see footnote 10). Our results would suggest some success in this regard, but that this was insufficient to reward greater use of a deep learning approach significantly. In fact, the lack of any significant correlations with the deep approach (especially with respect to the final examination) suggests that the assessment structure did not explicitly reward a deep understanding of the subject.

Overall, the results for the impact of learning approach on the academic performance of accounting students suggest no relationship for a deep approach and a negative relationship for a surface approach.[19] The latter finding, combined with the relative high surface approach scores in our sample, suggests that, consistent with Biggs' (1987a) conclusion for science students, there are some grounds for concern that many students in this study use a learning approach that is least conducive to performing well in the subject.

Concluding comments

This paper has provided some evidence pertinent to the growing concerns about the quality of accounting education, particularly the belief that accounting students focus more on rote learning than on learning to learn (Accounting Education Change Commission, 1990; Bauer et al., 1994). By using the Approaches to Learning framework, it has been possible to gain some insights into the way in which accounting students approach their learning environment and experiences, which in turn can inform educators when designing accounting courses.

Specifically, the paper investigated the learning approach profile of Australian university accounting students. Only three prior studies have reported on learning approach profiles of accounting students. Two of these were for Hong Kong polytechnic students (Chan et al., 1989; Gow et al., 1994) and the other was for a relatively small sample of students from one Australian University (Eley, 1992). This paper also extended this prior work by providing evidence of the relationships of surface and deep learning approaches with a number of measures of academic performance.

In general, it was found that Australian university accounting students had significantly higher surface approach scores and lower deep approach scores than documented norms for Australian arts, education and science university students. Also, while the difference was not quantifiable, they were also more surface learning-oriented than Hong Kong

[19] However, a limitation of our analyses is that they have not controlled for variation in the general intellectual ability of the students. As this has been shown to be related to quantitative academic performance measures (Trigwell and Prosser, 1991), our findings may be confounded by variation in general intellectual ability across our sample. We had no access to measures of general academic ability to control for such effects in this study.

polytechnic students. This finding is of particular relevance to accounting educators as it provides some empirical evidence of widely-expressed concerns that students adopt a predominantly surface learning approach in accounting.

In terms of its potential impact on learning outcomes, higher surface approach scores were found to be associated with less successful academic performance and also with lower self-ratings of performance relative to peers. This finding gives grounds for concern when considered in tandem with the high average scores for this approach amongst accounting students as it suggests that they use a learning approach unsuited to higher performance in the subject. At the same time, a deep approach was not found to be associated with more successful academic performance or higher self-rated performance. The lack of any positive relationships may be due to students' misperceptions of the assessment task or the failure of the assessment structures to sufficiently reward a deep learning approach. These findings reinforce the arguments in the Approaches to Learning paradigm for the need to pay attention to the design of the total learning environment, as indicated in Figure 1. Finally, students' satisfaction with performance was unrelated to their learning approaches.

It is important to recognize the limitations associated with the results reported here. First, as noted above, the validity of the comparison with Biggs' norms is reduced due to the time difference between the two data sets. However, no more recent data was available. Nevertheless, despite the growing concern with improving learning quality in accounting in recent years, the accounting student scores were still significantly higher for surface approach scores that the 'older' norms. Thus, it seems reasonable to conclude that many accounting students tend to adopt a relatively high surface approach, which is supported by the findings of the three other accounting studies referred to above. Second, as the data was obtained from two Sydney universities, the generalizability of the results is limited. However, given that the findings were highly similar for both institutions, there are some grounds for suggesting that accounting students in other Australian universities would display similar profiles. Third, the lack of any observed relationships between the deep approach scores and academic performance measures does not necessarily imply that deep learners did not benefit from a 'higher quality' learning experience. Conventional quantitative measures of learning outcomes based on continuous assessment marks and examination grades are unlikely to capture all dimensions associated with deep learning (Trigwell and Prosser, 1991). Future studies should attempt to develop more complete measures of learning outcomes incorporating aspects such as critical thinking and analytical skills.

The findings have some important implications for educators wishing to improve the quality of learning for accounting students. First, the high surface approach scores found for accounting students highlight the need to make changes in the teaching/learning environment in order to alter students' apparent perceptions that studying accounting is simply a matter of rote learning a set of rules. It is worth noting that the SPQ instrument enables the accounting educator to gain some quantitative information about students' learning approaches, enabling an analysis of the current approaches of students and also providing an *ex post* indicator of the impact of educational interventions aimed at increasing the use of a deep approach.

Second, the mixed findings for impacts of learning approach on academic performance are of concern, particularly the finding that students who rely more on a surface approach tend to have lower levels of academic performance. One implication of these findings is that there is a mismatch between the requirements of assessment tasks and the expectations of students (for example, what students believe is necessary to answer multiple choice questions). It has been shown in prior research that students adapt their learning approach to suit the (perceived) context of a subject area, particularly the assessment structure (Entwistle and Ramsden, 1983; Kember and Gow, 1990). It could be that, despite the intentions by many accounting educators to reward depth of understanding, the nature and form of assessment items and/or students' experience in prior accounting subjects results in a perception that generally a surface approach is appropriate for the study of accounting. Thus, unless assessment items are consistently and explicitly designed to both encourage and reward a deep approach to learning, it is likely that many students will continue to pursue a surface approach to their learning. In addition, a related critical issue for accounting educators is the need to change student perceptions about the study of accounting. A recent study by Mladenovic (1998) argues that the promotion of a deep approach to learning is achieved only through aligning all aspects of the learning environment. When the curriculum and the teaching methods are aligned and assessment is not aligned only limited success is achieved.

Finally, the findings here suggest some further research avenues. First, while we have indicated possible differences in learning approaches between accounting and other disciplines, there is very little comparative research on different disciplinary approaches to learning. Research that considered differences in current learning approach norms, and particularly whether different disciplines attract different mixes of learning approach preferences (as Beattie et al., 1997, speculate is the case for accounting), would increase our understanding of how accounting students approach their learning. Second, while we have provided some evidence of a higher surface learning approach for accounting students, it is not clear why this is the case. In fact, Gow et al.'s (1994) finding that Hong Kong polytechnic accounting students' use of a deep approach suffered an overall decline after completing their first year indicates that the most likely causes are problems with course design, delivery and assessment, and with the teaching approaches used by accounting educators. What factors or combination of factors drives the finding here requires further study. Gow et al. (1994, p. 118) identify a number of factors promoting a surface approach such as an '. . . excessive workload, surface assessment demands, lack of intrinsic motivation, a didactic teaching style, high staff/student ratios . . .'. Finally, studies that consider approaches to learning in their full learning context (see Figure 1) and relate them to broader learning outcomes than merely quantitative subject assessment, as in Trigwell and Prosser (1991), would provide deeper insights into how the quality of accounting education could be improved.

Acknowledgements

We thank Sujatha Perera, Macquarie University, for assistance in the collection of data and John Biggs, Linda English, participants at the 1997 Annual Conference of the Accounting Association of Australia and New Zealand and the two anonymous referees and the Associate Editor for comments on this paper.

References

Accounting Education Change Commission (1992) *The First Course in Accounting*, Position Statement No. Two, Bainbridge, WA: AECC.

Bauer, L., Locke, J. and O'Grady W. (1994) Introducing accounting education change: a case of first-year accounting, *Working Paper*. Department of Accounting, Massey University.

Beattie, V., Collins, B. and McInnes, B. (1997) Deep and surface learning: a simple or simplistic dichotomy? *Accounting Education: an International Journal* **6**(1), 1–12.

Berry, A. (1993) Encouraging group skills in accountancy students: an innovative approach. *Accounting Education: an International Journal* **2**(3), 169–79.

Biggs, J. (1978) Individual and group differences in study processes, *British Journal of Educational Psychology* **48**, 266–79.

Biggs, J. (1979) Individual differences in study processes and the quality of learning outcomes, *Higher Education* **8**, 381–94.

Biggs, J. (1987a) *Student Approaches to Learning and Studying*, Hawthorn, Victoria: Australian Council for Educational Research.

Biggs, J. (1987b) *Study Process Questionnaire Manual*, Hawthorn, Victoria: Australian Council for Educational Research.

Biggs, J. (1993) What do inventories of students' learning process really measure? A theoretical review and clarification, *British Journal of Educational Psychology* **63**, 3–19.

Biggs, J. (1996) Enhancing teaching through constructive alignment, *Higher Education* **32**, 347–64.

Biggs, J. and Rihn, B. (1984) The effects of intervention on deep and surface approaches to learning. In J. Kirby (ed.) *Cognitive Strategies and Educational Performance*, pp. 279–94. New York: Academic Press.

Campbell, J. and Lewis, W. (1991) Using cases in accounting classes, *Issues in Accounting Education* **6**(2), 276–83.

Chan, D., Leung, R., Gow, L. and Hu, S. (1989) Approaches to learning of accountancy students: some additional evidence. In *Proceedings of the ASAIHL Seminar on University Education in the 1990's*, 4–7 December, Kuala Lumpur, pp. 186–93. Bangi, Singapore: Penerbit Universiti Kebangsaan.

Cottell, P. and Millis, B. (1992) Cooperative learning in accounting, *Journal of Accounting Education* **10**(1), 95–112.

Cottell, P. and Millis, B. (1993) Cooperative learning structures in the instruction of accounting, *Issues in Accounting Education* **8**(1), 40–59.

Eley, M. (1992) Differential adoption of study approaches within individual students, *Higher Education* **23**, 231–54.

Entwistle, N. (1984) Contrasting perspectives on learning. In F. Marton, D. Hounsell and N. Entwistle (eds) *The Experience of Learning*, pp. 1–18. Edinburgh: Scottish Academic Press.

Entwistle, N. and Brennan, T. (1971) The academic performance of students. 2 Types of successful students, *British Journal of Educational Psychology*, **41**(3), 268–76.

Entwistle, N. and Wilson, J. (1977) *Degrees of Excellence: The Academic Achievement Game*, London: Hodder and Stoughton.

Entwistle, N. and Ramsden, P. (1983) *Understanding Student Learning*, London: Croom-Helm.

Entwistle, N., Hanley, M. and Hounsel, D. (1979) Identifying distinctive approaches to learning, *Higher Education* **8**, 365–80.

Gabriel, S. and Hirsch, M. Jr. (1992) Critical thinking and communication skills: integration and implementation issues, *Journal of Accounting Education* **10**(2), 243–70.

Gow, L., Kember, D. and Cooper, B. (1994) The teaching context and approaches to study of accountancy students, *Issues in Accounting Education* **9**(1), 118–30.

Hays, W.L. (1981) *Statistics*, 3rd Edition, New York: Holt-Saunders.

Hackman, J. and Taber, T. (1979) Patterns for undergraduate performance related to success in college, *American Educational Research Journal* **16**, 117–38.

Higher Education Council (HEC) (1992) *Higher Education Achieving Quality*, National Board of Employment Education and Training. Canberra: Australian Government Publishing Service.

Hirsch, M. and Collins, J. (1988) An integrated approach to communication skills in an accounting curriculum, *Journal of Accounting Education* **6**(1), 15–32.

Inglis, R., Broadbent, A. and Dall'Alba, G. (1993) Comparitive evaluation of teaching innovation in accounting education: intensive learning in a seminar format, *Accounting Education: an International Journal* **2**(3), 181–99.

Institute of Chartered Accountants in Australia (1994) *Chartered Accountants in the 21st Century: A report of the 21st Century Task Force*, Sydney: ICAA.

Kagan, D. (1992) The social implications of higher level thinking skills, *Journal of Accounting Education* **10**(2), 285–96.

Kember, D. and Gow, L. (1990) A model of student approaches to learning encompassing ways to influence and change approaches, *Instructional Science* **18**, 263–88.

Lucas, U. (1996) Student approaches to learning – a literature guide, *Accounting Education: an International Journal* **5**(1), 87–98.

Marton, F. and Saljo, R. (1984) Approaches to learning. In F. Marton, D. Hounsell and N. Entwistle (eds.) *The Experience of Learning*, pp. 36–55. Edinburgh: Scottish Academic Press.

Mladenovic, R. (1998) An investigation into ways of challenging introductory accounting students' negative perceptions of accounting. Unpublished paper, University of New South Wales, Australia.

Mohrweis, L. (1991) The impact of writing assignments on accounting students' writing skills, *Journal of Accounting Education* **9**(2), 309–26.

National Board of Employment Education and Training (NBEET) (1994a) *Workplace Learning in the Professional Development of Teachers*, Commissioned Report No. 24. Canberra: Australian Government Publishing Service.

National Board of Employment Education and Training (NBEET) (1994b) *Developing Life Long Learners through Undergraduate Education*, Commissioned Report No. 28, Canberra: Australian Government Publishing Service.

Nelson, I. (1995) What's new about accounting education change? A historical perspective on the change movement, *Accounting Horizons* **9**(1), 62–75.

Paisey, C. and Paisey, N. (1996) A wolf in sheep's clothing? Teaching by objectives in accounting in higher education, *Accounting Education: an International Journal* **5**(1), 43–60.

Patten, R. and Williams, D. (1990) Invited editorial: there's trouble – right here in our accounting programs: the challenge to accounting educators, *Issues in Accounting Education* **5**(2), 175–79.

Peek, L., Winking, C. and Peek, G. (1995) Cooperative learning activities: managerial accounting, *Issues in Accounting Education* **10**(1), 111–26.

Ramsden, P. (ed.) (1988) *Improving Learning: New Perspectives*, London: Kogan Page.

Ramsden, P. (1992) *Learning to Teach in Higher Education*, London: Routledge.

Schmeck, R. (ed.) (1993) *Learning Styles and Learning Strategies*, New York: Plenum.

Scofield, B. and Combes, L. (1993) Designing and managing meaningful writing assignments, *Issues in Accounting Education* **8**(1), 71–85.

Sharma, D. (1997) Accounting students' learning conceptions, approaches to learning, and the influence of the learning–teaching context on approaches to learning, *Accounting Education: an International Journal* **6**(2), 125–46.

Sharma, D. (1998) Addressing the student quality problem: some directions for accounting education research, *Asian Review of Accounting* **6** (1), 1–29.

Stewart, J. and Dougherty, T. (1993) Using case studies in teaching accounting: a quasi-experimental study, *Accounting Education: an International Journal* **2**(1), 1–10.

Thomas, P. and Bain, J. (1984) Contextual differences of learning approaches: the effects of assessments, *Human Learning* **3**, 227–40.

Trigwell, K. and Prosser, M. (1991) Relating approaches to study and quality of learning outcomes at the course level, *British Journal of Educational Psychology* **61**, 265–75.

Watkins, D. (1982a) Identifying the study process dimensions of Australian university students, *Australian Journal of Education* **26**, 76–85.

Watkins, D. (1982b) Factors influencing the study methods of Australian tertiary students, *Higher Education* **11**, 369–80.

Watkins, D. and Akande, A. (1992) Assessing the approaches to learning of Nigerian students, *Assessment and Evaluation in Higher Education* **17** (1), 11–20.

Watkins, D. and Hattie, J. (1981) The learning processes of Australian university students: investigations of contextual and personological factors, *British Journal of Educational Psychology* **51**, 384–93.

Identifying and overcoming obstacles to learner-centred approaches in tertiary accounting education: a field study and survey of accounting educators' perceptions

RALPH W. ADLER MARKUS J. MILNE and CAROLYN P. STRINGER

University of Otago, New Zealand

Abstract

Contrary to international accounting bodies' calls for the adoption of learner-centred approaches in accounting education, several recent studies (e.g. May *et al.*, 1995; Adler and Milne, *Accounting Education: an International Journal* **6**(2), 1997) and further survey-based evidence from this paper suggest that learner-centred approaches have not been significantly and seriously adopted by most accounting educators. This paper explores the impediments to adopting learner-centred approaches. The research method began with a series of face-to-face interviews with accounting educators and administrators from four different New Zealand tertiary institutions and progressed to a relatively large-scale mail survey of accounting educators in Australia and New Zealand. The interview and survey data point to three broad groupings of impediments: a lack of student readiness, inadequate educator support mechanisms, and nonreflective teacher practices. The nature and range of these impediments casts doubts on the idea that the lack of learner-centred approaches can be explained in such simple terms as accounting educators not being given sufficient time to translate the professions' calls for change into practice. Instead, positive change is only likely to be realized through the adoption of a more vigorous and proactive approach.

Introduction

To enable accounting students to achieve the skills expected of them, various strategies have been advanced in recent years by, for example, the Bedford Committee Report (AAA, 1986), the 'Big Eight' White Paper (1989), and the Accounting Education Change Commission (AECC, 1990). These were shortly followed up by the Institute of Chartered Accountants of New Zealand's Admissions Policy (ICANZ, 1994), the Australian Society of Certified Practising Accountants, The Institute of Chartered Accountants in Australia, and The International Federation of Accountant's (IFAC) recent Prequalification Requirements (1996).[1] The 1996 IFAC guidelines on prequalification education and experience are quite explicit about actions educators need to undertake to 'provide students with the tools for self-directed learning after qualification.' The guidelines suggest a range of learner-centred teaching methods that include:

- case studies and other means to simulate actual work situations;
- working in groups;
- adapting instructional methods and materials to the ever-changing environment in which the professional accountant works;
- pursuing a curriculum that encourages students to learn on their own;
- using technology creatively;
- encouraging students to be active participants in the learning process;
- using measurement and evaluation methods that reflect the changing knowledge, skills, and values required of professional accountants;
- integration of knowledge and skills across topics and disciplines to address multifaceted and complex situations typical of professional demands; and
- emphasis on problem-solving which encourages identifying relevant information, making logical assessments and communicating clear conclusions.

While examples of accounting educators who have heeded such calls and subsequently redesigned their courses exist (see, for example, Böcker, 1987; Stewart and Dougherty, 1993; Adler and Milne, 1995; Stout, 1996), several surveys of accounting education practice suggest these examples are the exception rather than the norm. For example, May *et al.*'s (1995) survey of over 400 US accounting educators reported that less than half of the respondents believed that group and case-based work should be extensively used. Another finding was that only a minority of educators strongly advocated moving away from the traditional textbook-based, rule intensive, lecture/problem solving approach to teaching.

In New Zealand, the picture appears to be little different. From a survey of 180 tertiary accounting course outlines, Adler and Milne (1997) found that 60% of these courses contained no group, case, oral/presentation, or peer-assessed work. Of the remaining 40% of courses, very few contained all four types of assessed activity, and when courses did include at least one of the assessed activities, it usually accounted for less than 20% of the course grade. Follow-up content analysis and telephone interviews led Adler and Milne to conclude that student learning is 'assessed almost entirely by the instructor's evaluation of the written efforts of individual student's non-case work'[2] (p. 5) and that '... group, peer assessed, and oral presentation work are substantially underused at New Zealand tertiary institutions' (p. 10).

Four years on, little has changed in Australia and New Zealand at least. Evidence from 100 Australian and New Zealand accounting educators surveyed as part of this study

---

[1] The accounting professional bodies in Australia and New Zealand have a strong influence on the content of accounting programmes. In Australia, the accreditation process requires students to have completed a minimum of 25% of their studies in disciplines other than accounting and business. In New Zealand, the ICANZ accreditation process requires four years of study including 35%–40% Accounting Studies, 35%-40% Business-related Studies and 20–30% Liberal Studies (nonaccounting, nonbusiness related studies).

[2] Averaging out the assessment practices across all the course outlines reveals that, on average, accounting students receive less than 10% of their total accounting programme grade from case, group, and presentation work.

suggests that lectures (used in 93% of 153 undergraduate courses) and tutorials (used in 69% of the 153 courses) continue to dominate class room teaching methods. Seminar discussion groups (21% of courses), individual student presentations (13% of courses), student-group presentations (16% of courses), student-facilitated seminars (6% of courses), and unstructured case studies (10% of courses) were used significantly less by these educators.

Why New Zealand and Australian accounting educators have shied away from concerted attention being given to learner-centred education approaches has yet to be comprehensively and directly addressed. Nonetheless, several possibilities have been suggested in the accounting education literature. Stout (1996), for example, highlights the increased time commitment that is involved with the teaching of cases. Meanwhile, May et al. (1995) point to such obstacles as the existing reward structure, which does not reward teaching; the pervasive publish or perish mentality; the failure to view the development of course programmes and materials as important scholarly activity; and the absence of faculty training. Of course, whether these obstacles are the only – or even the main – reasons underlying the reluctance of US accounting educators to adopt case studies and group work is difficult to judge. May et al. (1995) sought educators' perceptions to a *preselected* set of issues that focuses on rewards and training: No opportunity for other possible reasons was provided.

Adler and Milne's (1997) study also provides some further insights into why New Zealand educators might fail to use learner-centred approaches. From semistructured telephone interviews with accounting educators there emerged three main groupings of impediments: resource constraints, incompatible educator attitudes and perceptions, and a lack of student readiness. Adler and Milne's study, however, did not directly or deliberately set out to document those impediments. Rather they emerged as the result of educators who, after describing the teaching approaches they used, proceeded to *voluntarily* disclose the reasons behind their choice of teaching approaches.

There appears to be insufficient evidence of innovative educational approaches to accounting education to believe that the concept of learner-centered learning has been significantly and seriously adopted by accounting educators. This paper focuses on and explores educators' beliefs about the impediments to learner-centered approaches. First, it discusses the method that was used to select the group of interviewed and surveyed tertiary educators and administrators. Next, it presents a detailed discussion of the impediments uncovered. Direct quotations are used to provide the reader with an appreciation for the context and depth of emotion that surrounds these impediments. Integrated into this discussion are the views gained from a larger and broader group of surveyed accounting educators in New Zealand and Australia. The paper concludes with a discussion of how educators, their institutions, and the accounting profession might better strive to achieve a wider adoption of learner-centred approaches in accounting education.

Method

The research method included face-to-face interviews and a large mail-survey. The semistructured interviews[3] were conducted at four New Zealand tertiary institutions. These four institutions represent all the approved (by the Institute of Chartered Accountants of

---

[3] A copy of the interview instrument can be obtained from the authors upon request.

New Zealand) providers of accounting degrees on the South Island of New Zealand. While these organizations were selected on the grounds that they were easily accessible to the researchers, they are not believed to be atypical of the remaining accredited institutions in New Zealand and Australia.

Five individuals were interviewed at each of the four institutions. When selecting the individuals to interview, the following approach was adopted. The business school's senior administrator was always selected. This person's title varied slightly from institution to institution, but in essence this person was the school's 'Dean.' The accountancy department's Head of Department was also always selected. The Deans and Heads of Department were interviewed to gain insights into the institutional context within which the educators operated. The final three individuals were selected using a stratified (albeit nonrandom) sampling technique. In particular, a balanced selection of educators who were using teacher-centred and learner-centred approaches was sought. The teaching approach of the Head of Department was counted, producing an even split of two educators who exhibited each approach. This selection was undertaken as a way of promoting the widest possible range of views.

The identification of teaching approaches was partially guided by the findings from Adler and Milne's (1997) telephone survey of New Zealand tertiary educators' assessment practices. In addition, the 1997 course outlines for all the accounting courses taught at each of the four institutions were closely scrutinized for clues about the teaching approach being used. At every institution it was relatively easy to find (and the subsequent interviews confirmed this ability) two educators who appeared to use a teacher-centred approach and, although slightly more challenging, two educators who appeared to use a learner-centred approach. The courses these educators taught ranged from first year through to final year courses.

Each of the 20 interviews lasted approximately 30–40 minutes and was audio-taped for the purpose of transcribing. The transcriptions remain confidential to the authors and, in the excerpts quoted below, individuals and institutions remain anonymous.

The second stage of the research method included a mail-survey of 400 accounting educators randomly selected from the *Wiley Directory of Accounting* 1999–2000.[4] Stratified random sampling by title of educator was used to select accounting educators involved in course design. The stratification resulted in 50% of the responses from lecturers, 35% from senior lecturers, and 15% from professors and associate professors. The survey was conceived and executed for the purpose of assessing the generalizability of the interview data. Statements made by accounting educators during the face-to-face interviews were selected for the survey instrument. The mail-survey was always meant to play a supporting (either confirming or disconfirming) role to the interview data. The survey instrument was pilot tested by several accounting educators in Australia and New Zealand.

A total of 104 usable responses were received from the mail-survey. This produced a response rate of 28%. Mann–Whitney U and Kruskal–Wallis H nonparametric tests were used to analyse early versus late responses. Results revealed no apparent non-response bias between early versus late survey responses on the 15 items included in Table 1, except for student expectations of student-teacher relationships (*early*, Mean = 2.96; *late*,

[4] The Wiley directory provides details of academic staff in Accounting Departments in Australia and New Zealand.

Mean = 4.1).[5] Similarly, no significant differences were observed for the 15 items on account of educator title (professor, lecturer, etc.); subject area taught (e.g., financial accounting, management accounting, auditing, etc.) and residential base of educator (e.g., New Zealand, Australia). The exceptions were New Zealand and Australian educators (i.e., student numbers, study leave) referred to later in the paper.

Accounting educators in New Zealand and Australia operate in a diverse environment. Typically, accounting educators teach 6–8 contact hours per week. The average teaching load for accounting educators in New Zealand was 173 contact hours per annum compared to the 196 contact hours for Australian educators. In New Zealand, the staff–student ratios range from 1:19 to 1:32. Class sizes may range from 200–1000 students (e.g., first year classes), while third year classes may range from seminar groups of 30–40 students up to larger classes of 200-plus students.

As noted earlier, lectures (93%) and tutorials (69%) are the predominant class room activities in the 153 undergraduate courses reported. Seminar discussion groups, individual student presentations, student-group presentations, student-facilitated seminars and un-structured case studies make up much smaller proportions of course activities. The 153 courses were spread relatively evenly across 100 (20%), 200 (35%) and 300 level (35%) courses, with 10% undisclosed as to level taught. Furthermore, where lectures are used in courses, students seem to receive significantly more contact hours by this method. In New Zealand, for example, average lecture contact time per course per week was 2.6 hours, compared to 1.16 and 1.9 hours for tutorials and seminars respectively. In Australia, average lecture time per course per week was 2 hours, with tutorials and seminars, when used, accounting for 1.4 and 1.7 hours per course.

Possible reasons for the lack of learner-centred approaches in accounting education

The interview and survey data, bar one exception, confirmed the existence of the three general impediments to learner-centred approaches identified in Adler and Milne (1997), i.e., lack of student readiness, incompatible educator attitudes and perceptions, and resource constraints. The one exception pertained to the resource constraints category. The issue of resource constraints appears to be part of a larger and more encompassing category that is labelled educator support mechanisms. This category recognizes the need for adequate resources to support innovative teaching, e.g., classroom layouts, as well as the necessary tertiary educational incentive systems that may encourage such teaching in the first place, e.g., promotion criteria.

Table 1 presents a listing of the reasons or impediments named by interviewed educators and administrators and surveyed educators for the lack of learner-centred approaches. Table 2 shows the percentage of surveyed accounting educators who either 'strongly agreed' or 'agreed' (or 'strongly disagreed' or 'disagreed' for reverse coded statements) with statements made by educators during the face-to-face interviews. It was expected that respondents would differ in the types of impediments experienced depending on the

---

[5] The Type I error was set at 5% for determining statistical significance between early versus late responses. Since 15 tests were conducted, there is a high probability that statistical chance accounts for the one statistically significant result.

Table 1. Percentage of educators and administrators citing a particular impediment to Learner-Centred Approaches in Accounting Education

Impediments	Survey	Field Interviews	
		Educators and Administrators	*Educators only*
Student readiness:			
Student expectations of student-teacher relationships	0.40	0.35	0.44
Cultural/language divides	0.43	0.30	0.38
Student maturity	0.09	0.45	0.56
Educator support mechanisms:			
Room layouts	0.31	0.30	0.38
Staff-student ratios	0.38	0.55	0.75
Australian and New Zealand case studies	0.44	0.20	0.25
Promotion criteria	0.87	0.85	0.81
Teaching prizes	0.44	0.55	0.75
Study leave	0.30	0.55	0.63
University tradition	0.24	0.55	0.56
Nonreflective teaching practices:			
Failing to read	0.29	0.30	0.25
Failing to collect student feedback	0.13	0.45	0.56
Failure to recognise skill and attitude development	0.09	0.30	0.25
Obsession with individual student achievement	0.29	0.30	0.38
Single focus on expanding teaching content	0.21	0.50	0.63

particular context in which they teach. The mean and standard deviations have been provided to indicate the expected diversity in responses.

It is important to note that Tables 1 and 2 are a distillation of educators' perceptions about impediments to learner-centred learning. It is expected that respondents would indicate different impediments to learner-centered learning depending on the particular environment in which they teach. Therefore, these tables should not be interpreted as suggesting that all the respondents implicated all 15 of the impediments. Rather there was a sufficient breadth of responses for any one item to suggest that the item should be included as an impediment. Generally speaking, an item was included as an impediment when approximately one-third or more of the respondents supported the item's inclusion.

STUDENT READINESS

A lack of student readiness can be a substantial barrier to the use of learner-centred approaches. Included in this category are student expectations about 'proper' student-teacher relationships, cultural/language divides, and student maturity.

Students may have a rigid set of expectations regarding the proper role of students and teachers in the learning context. Thirty-five per cent of the interviewed educators and administrators listed this item as an impediment. Meanwhile 40% of the surveyed educators 'agreed' or 'strongly agreed' that student expectations affected their teaching style.

Table 2. Summary of educator survey responses to statements made by interviewees: mean, standard deviation and percentage

	Mean	SD	Impediment Percentage+
Student readiness			
Students like certainty, they like to be told what to do, what's likely to be on the exam. So this is what I give them in my course.	3.09	1.20	40
With more international students now in our courses, the course designs have become more structured, more instructor-led.	2.92	1.04	43
Undergraduates aren't mature enough to take responsibility for running a class discussion or presenting a case solution to their peers.	3.91*	0.86	9*
Educator support mechanisms			
We don't have access to enough rooms for seminar discussions. Time-tabling wouldn't permit seminar-based course designs at this University.	3.29	1.23	31
We have too many undergraduate students to be designing case-based and discussion/seminar style courses.	3.10	1.22	38
There aren't enough relevant Australian and New Zealand case studies to use in my courses.	2.94	1.22	44
The promotions committee/criteria say teaching counts, but we all know publications is what really counts most.	1.77	0.92	87
I try to design my courses to save as much of my time as possible for research activities.	3.77	1.02	15
Teaching prizes don't recognize *good* teachers, they simply recognize popular teachers – you know, good entertainers.	2.91	1.19	44
I wouldn't waste my sabbatical leave trying to improve my teaching.	3.34	1.41	30
The spread of assessment between internal and final exam is standardised in our department.	3.59	1.32	24
Nonreflective teaching practices			
I regularly read the accounting education literature.	2.73*	1.07	29*
I regularly collect and use formal feedback from my students to revamp my courses with new assessment regimes, new materials and new assignments.	2.28*	0.90	13*
Developing technical knowledge is more important than skills like teamwork and communication.	3.87	0.87	9
Case study teaching is a good idea, but it takes up too much time.	3.77	0.10	36
Group work permits weak students to get carried, and that is why I refrain from using group-learning activities.	3.22	1.10	29
It's very hard to apportion marks among group members.	2.44	1.06	65
There is too much emphasis on the profession's body of knowledge in our courses.	3.06*	1.06	41*
I think it is better to include some student-led activities like presentations even if it means leaving out some topics.	2.58*	0.93	21*

Note: +Percentage of respondents who 'agreed' or 'strongly agreed' with the statement. Five-point Likert scale 1 = strongly agree, 2 = agree, 3 = neutral, 4 = disagree, 5 = strongly disagree.
* Denotes reverse coded items where respondents 'disagreed' or 'strongly disagreed' with the statements.

Several of the interviewed educators expressed the view that students do perceive teachers who adopt the role of facilitator as shirking their teaching responsibilities. As one educator stated, students believe their role in class is to be lectured to and not asked questions. Another educator described how student expectations about the 'proper' way, i.e., what students were familiar with, to assess their achievement in the course was the primary reason behind the large number of tests given and the small weighting assigned to each. While noting that the assessment regime was popular with the students, the educator at the same time commented:

> We've got mixed feelings about it at this level because it seems like we're drilling them. [It] seems more a technique for school children.

Breaking students' expectations can be difficult. In fact, most of the interviewed educators relented to these student expectations, feeling that their time was better spent satisfying, versus seeking to change, their students' expectations. The unfortunate result is that educators often end up designing learning activities of a small bite, context free, black and white nature (i.e., using problems straight out of accounting textbooks) versus activities that are interdisciplinary, context rich, and are shaded different tints of grey (e.g., case studies).

The recent expansion of enrolments from full-fee paying overseas students also raises issues for learner-centred approaches, especially those students originating from Asian countries. At some of the visited institutions, the number of overseas accounting students is very high, and it appears that cultural and/or language divides may be having some impact on the approaches that educators are taking. Several educators expressed the opinion that, while the overseas students' technical accounting and general business skills are of a high standard, their English skills fall short. It was also pointed out that many of the overseas students resisted becoming more actively involved in and reflective of their learning. As a result, the educators were loath to use learner-centred approaches that entailed peer-assisted learning, e.g., student-presented cases or student-facilitated seminars. Thirty per cent of the interviewed educators and administrators named this item as an impediment to the greater use of learner-centred approaches. Forty-three per cent of the surveyed educators either 'agreed' or 'strongly agreed' that the growing number of international students had influenced the design of more structured and instructor-led courses.

The resistance to assuming greater learning responsibility was attributed to the students' previous educational experiences and their home culture. For example, one head of department said:

> They [overseas students] are not used to making their own decisions. You really have to force them to make their own comments and give their own views. But that is not the way they are taught [back home]. They believe all they should do is quote what the teacher says because the teacher is the important person. We are trying to change their entire culture. Big thing to do in one year.

The idea that the overseas students saw the teacher's role in terms of what Farnes (1975) has described as a lawgiver is further reinforced by the following educator:

> They [the overseas students] want to get told what they have to do in their exam, and if they do this will we give them the marks to pass? Yes we will. So they want to learn how to do that. To be honest, I don't think it is a very good atmosphere.

> In principle I would like to see myself in a facilitating role. I would like to use case studies and listen to a practical discussion in a tutorial and so on. But that is not what the overseas students want, and they tend to respond rather poorly to that sort of thing. So while I agree in principle that I would like to be seen as a facilitator, at the moment I don't think that is the way we are going, and it is certainly not the way we have gone this year.

A lack of student maturity, especially regarding the need for students to assume greater control for their learning, was a commonly cited impediment. Forty-five per cent of the interviewed educators and administrators pointed to this impediment to learner-centred instruction. Contrary to the interview data, only 9% of the surveyed educators 'agreed' that undergraduates were not mature enough to facilitate class discussion or present case solutions to their peers. Clearly, the 78% of the surveyed educators who 'disagreed' or 'strongly disagreed' with the statement considered undergraduates were mature enough for learner-centered learning. However, the survey indicated that student-facilitated seminars and unstructured case studies were not commonly used in undergraduate courses.

Many of the educators noted (and lamented) the failure of students to commit themselves to the high standards required under learner-centred approaches. Nevertheless, many of these same educators were giving into the students' dislike for the high level of preparation required of them. Rather than trying to reshape the students' attitudes in favour of learner-centred approaches, these educators succumbed to their students' desire for less learning responsibility. As one educator described it:

> Lecturers are giving in and taking the easy way because students resist. [Students] are reluctant to talk even with one another.

It appears that undergraduate students want (and at times actually demanded) learning environments that are teacher-controlled and lecture-driven. The students' dislike for learner-centred approaches was an often cited reason for why educators avoided using cases, role-plays, simulations, and other teaching methods advocated by the AECC and IFAC.

EDUCATOR SUPPORT MECHANISMS

Educator support mechanisms comprise issues that are related to teaching resources and the tertiary institution's structural support and incentive systems. These issues included inadequate room layouts, staff to student ratios, the lack of New Zealand and Australian case studies, promotion criteria, teaching prizes, study leave criteria, and university tradition. It is usually the absence of these mechanisms or the criteria by which they are made available that generally creates problems for educators seeking to implement learner-centred approaches.

Teaching resources

Inadequate room layouts were mentioned as one reason for the under-use of learner-centered approaches. Thirty per cent of the interviewed educators and administrators, and 31% of the surveyed educators pointed to this problem. The interactive learning approach that characterizes learner-centred approaches was seen by many educators as difficult, if not impossible, to achieve in the large-sized, tiered seating lecture theatres that they were usually assigned. Typical comments included about the inadequacies of room layouts were 'rooms . . . are designed for our tutorials, and they are designed to have no more than about

20–25 people. So you couldn't physically get them in', 'That teaching method would be difficult due to [such] simple mechanics like room allocations' or 'It's difficult in terms of venue flexibility' or 'We have a timetable problem here. It is hard enough to get three tutorial rooms that hold 80 people.'

The large number of students in undergraduate courses can also influence the use of learner-centered approaches. Fifty-five per cent of the interviewed educators and administrators, and 75% of the interviewed educators identified this as an impediment. Thirty-eight per cent of the surveyed educators either 'agreed' or 'strongly agreed' that they had too many undergraduate students to be designing case-based and seminar discussion style courses. This problem of large student numbers appears to be more prevalent in Australia than New Zealand (Australia 44.9% and New Zealand 21.9% 'agreed' or 'strongly agreed').

Interviewed educators gave several examples of how large numbers of undergraduate students can be an impediment to learner-centered approaches. Many educators agreed that learning activities should seek to actively involve students, but felt that they were handicapped by a lack of qualified tutors. Typical comments were, 'I would like to assign case studies if I had people who were consistent markers to mark them.' Another educator explained that smaller class sizes required for learner-centered approaches would increase the teaching contact hours for existing staff. The allocation of teaching hours may also provide an incentive towards the large lecture format. Some institutions gave educators more credit for teaching large classes. In one extreme case, an institution's method of teaching allocation was strongly influenced by the inclusion of a rating based on the EFTS [Effective Full Time Students] in particular courses. While the teaching allocation in this institution did take into consideration other factors as preparation time and level of study, it advantaged the larger first-year undergraduate courses.

The lack of relevant New Zealand and Australian-based cases was cited as another reason for educator's unwillingness to use any case studies. Twenty per cent of the interviewed educators and administrators cited this as an impediment. The interviewed educators believed that students would be less able to connect with and appreciate the case study process if the case organisations were foreign-based. Consequently, the educators wanted a sufficiently large and representative repository of home country cases prior to embarking on case study approaches. Forty-four per cent of the surveyed educators either 'agreed' or 'strongly agreed' that there were insufficient Australian and New Zealand cases to use in their courses.

Promotion criteria

The failure of promotion criteria to influence, other than in a negative sense, innovative teaching was referred to time and again. Eighty-five per cent of the interviewed educators and administrators, and 87% of the surveyed educators pointed to this problem. The typical complaint was that only lip service was paid to good teaching. As stated by one educator:

> [The institution] does say it recognizes it [good teaching], but my colleagues interpret it as, 'if you get bad evaluations then you don't get promoted'.

Other educators were more scathing in their remarks about the relationship between teaching and promotion. As one educator said:

> We have very good teachers who can't get over the bar [a promotional step]. I mean they [the good teachers] publish small bits and pieces here and there. But it [the promotion decision] is loaded towards research and how many dollars you can get into the university. If you can manage to attract a lot of research funding you will get promoted.

Another educator stated that teaching not only fails to 'rate very highly in the promotion stakes [but that] teaching activities take away from research which is what promotion is all about.' In a similar vein, a different educator, when asked about the role that good teaching plays in promotion decisions, said:

> It's supposed to be [important], but we all suppose that it's very minute. They [the administrators] say it's a part of promotion and that it's going to be considered equally with research, but really they count up how much research you've done.

This same educator then went on to say, good teaching 'takes too much time. I'm trying to make sure that research takes more time than teaching.' Fifteen per cent of the surveyed educators 'agreed' or 'strongly agreed' that they try to design courses to save time for research activities.

Even the administrators were cynical about the weighting their institutions' promotions committees ascribed to teaching. As one administrator aptly put it, 'Educators are rewarded for their research but paid for their teaching.' This administrator then elaborated by saying:

> There is a strong belief that although teaching counts, it doesn't count very much. Publication in overseas refereed journals is getting even more of a criterion than it was before. I was railing against this the other day when we were making a case for promotion, and we wanted somebody who was a damn good teacher and in fact had been disappointing so far as a researcher. And I would say that there is a form of academic snobbery growing more entrenched as from a fashionable point of view to say that on the whole staff tend to reflect the viewpoint that says that top research and publications is what we're here for. We are here for that but not that alone, and I was having trouble making that point. And I don't think the staffing committee believes it. A good researcher will be aided by being a good teacher. An excellent teacher will not be promoted if not a good researcher.

A similar criticism against the promotion criteria came from a second administrator:

> I can only say that every time I go there they [the promotion committee] look first of all to see what the publication list is. The one thing that is weighted more than anything else would be the publication list.

Other administrators commonly advised their academic staff to trade-off teaching in favour of research. For instance, one administrator was candid enough to describe instances where 'lecturers were too gung-ho with teaching' and were advised 'to back off teaching and pick up the research.'

In sum, promotion criteria appear to be an important influence on educators' adoption, or better yet lack of adoption, of learner-centred approaches. While every educator interviewed, as well as the majority of the administrators, acknowledged that his/her institution had policy documents recognizing teaching, the general feeling was that teaching mattered very little in decisions about promotion, unless the teaching was considered to be very bad. According to one educator, the only way to make good teaching payoff was if you could produce a journal article on the teaching. But even this potential benefit was not unanimously supported. For instance, one administrator said:

> If you've got some rigorous academic research it's easier to get into high power refereed journals. And that's what you get your brownie points for. Whereas if you get in an education journal or something of that nature it may not carry the same weight in terms of the [promotion] committee's findings.

As an aside, an interesting finding of the interviews was that educators who use innovative teaching activities never once mentioned promotion as a reason for their actions. Instead, the motivation invariably stemmed from the educator's pride in being a teacher. For example, when one educator was asked why he had chosen to use learner-centred approaches – even though he admitted to receiving no reward or recognition for their use – replied, 'Because that is why I am here.'

Teaching prizes

Some institutions used teaching prizes to recognize and encourage excellent teaching. While simple intuition would suggest that such prizes would be useful for motivating excellence in teaching, 55% of the interviewed educators and administrators, and 44% of the surveyed educators felt very differently. Interestingly enough, the education research supports these disenchanted educators. Studies by McKeachie (1982) and Miller (1988), for example, found no evidence for a relationship between enhanced quality in US higher education and such rewards as merit pay, teaching prizes, and other awards for teaching effectiveness. In fact, McKeachie found the reverse relationship to hold: teaching awards reduce educator motivation, especially in the long run (cited in Ramsden, 1992, p. 252).

Ramsden (1992), in trying to reconcile why such a negative relationship between teaching rewards and good teaching exists, suggests that 'prizes for teaching are readily interpreted in a cynical light as token and divisive gestures by a fundamentally hostile institutional management (p. 252).' Ramsden's impression accords with the interview data. At one institution, the prize for excellence in teaching was withdrawn. While the stated reason was that no other division [faculty] was offering such a prize, the view held by the teaching staff was that the prize had been the cause of much consternation for senior level management. During the prize's three-year history, no recipient remained at the institution following its award. The award was commonly referred to as 'the kiss of death.' On two of the occasions the winner left to go elsewhere. On one occasion the winner was subsequently denied tenure for his failure to compile a sufficiently strong research record. This latter episode, which was publicized in the media and greeted with much student protest, was a great embarrassment to the institution. As a result the prize was quietly phased out.

At another institution educators referred to the teaching prize as a 'popularity award,' where the members on the award committee did little more than count student votes. As one of the educators said:

> Yes [we have a teaching award] but it is really a popularity award. It's nominated by other lecturers, it is. Students can make nominations as well. But it seems to go to reasonably new people with very large classes, and some of the other teachers

who have had it in the past are unable to get it again. They [the award committee] basically say you've had it before.

Teaching development

Study (sabbatical) leave, which provides an educator with a period of time that is unencumbered by teaching or administrative responsibilities, would appear to be an ideal time for writing a book, performing field research at a distant location, or making improvements to one's teaching and/or courses. According to 55% of the interviewed educators and administrators, their institutions only regard the first two courses of action as proper motivation for study leave. In New Zealand perceptions were less negative about using study leave for teaching innovations (Australia 34.8% and New Zealand 21.2% 'agreed' or 'strongly agreed'). As one administrator put it:

> I have the feeling that the ethos of this university as such is that a request which was wholly phrased in terms of 'I want to develop teaching techniques' would be seen as a novelty and there would be an initial antipathy to the idea. Study leave is for research. Teaching you just do.

The educators seemed well aware of their administrators' views toward study leave. Accordingly, the educators said they would never be so naïve as to request study leave for the purposes of teaching development.

Combining this understanding of the appropriate situations in which study leave can be used with an understanding of how the typical promotion system operates makes it easier to understand – though no less sorrowful – why one educator said, 'I probably would not waste my study leave on something for teaching because you don't get promotion based on it.' Thirty per cent of the surveyed educators either 'agreed' or 'strongly agreed' with this educator.

University tradition

At some institutions there was an expectation, either written or unwritten, about the format of courses taught. Fifty-five per cent of the interviewed educators and administrators raised this issue. Some educators spoke about certain norms that governed the percentage of assessment awarded to internal and final examination components of the course. A typical ratio might be 40% internal and 60% final. Expectations also existed about the type of assignments (e.g., terms test) and the number of assignments (e.g., no greater than three). Some of the educators believed these guidelines were amenable to change at their sole discretion, while other educators said they would need departmental approval before making changes. Similarly, 24% of the surveyed educators either 'strongly agreed' or 'agreed' that assessment practices were standardized in their departments.

NONREFLECTIVE EDUCATOR PRACTICES

Nonreflective educator practices include such impediments as educators' failure to read the education literature, to collect useable feedback on how to improve the classroom learning experience, to break out of the mould of 'teaching as we were taught,' and skill and attitude development to appreciate how lifelong learning skills are developed. Two additional impediments in this category are an obsession with rewarding individual student achievement and a continual compulsion to increase the amount of material covered.

The number of educators pointing to these nonreflective educator practices was generally less than the number of educators who implicated student readiness or educator support impediments. Social desirability bias may be operating here. Thus a lower threshold was accepted for the inclusion of an item under this set of impediments. As expected, not all items are impediments for all accounting educators.

An educator's motivation for not undertaking reflective teaching practices is just as likely to be conscious as it is unconscious. As previously discussed, educators commonly believe that there are few rewards associated with excellence in teaching. As a result, it is not surprising to see that educators might devote little time or attention to such activities as reading the education literature, collecting data on their students' learning experiences, etc. Educators in this instance are taking what is for them a sensible, at least economically so, course of action.

Other educators, however, appear to be less conscious of their teaching shortcomings and omissions. A possible cause for their nonreflective practices may be attributable to the absence of a tertiary educators' teaching profession. Without a sense of belonging to a larger body of teaching professionals, with all the requisite duties and responsibilities that accompany this wider membership, tertiary educators are perhaps disadvantaged in instituting improvements in the learning experiences of their students.

Educator unfamiliarity

The interviews revealed that 30% of the educators and administrators alike were generally nonreaders of the education literature. Similarly, 29% of surveyed educators either 'disagreed' or 'strongly disagreed' with the statement 'I regularly read the accounting education literature'.

Some of the administrators were completely unaware of the accounting profession's calls for changes in curriculum design. For example, one administrator, when asked if he stayed abreast of the New Zealand Institute of Chartered Accountants' or the International Federation of Chartered Accountants' educational guidelines and exposure drafts, said 'Probably not. No.' A second administrator was equally naïve about the New Zealand accounting profession's educational guidelines, and especially their recent pronounce-ments on the need for generic skills development, in spite of the fact the administrator reported that representatives from the Institute had recently visited to outline its new Admissions Policy.

Failure to collect relevant information on how to improve the learning experience of their students was commonplace among the interviewed educators. Forty-five per cent of these educators cited this as an impediment to learner-centered approaches. Among the interviewed educators, there was a fairly common reliance on student evaluation forms that were constructed and sometimes administered by their department or institution. However, the educators recognized that they seldom offered useful insights into ways to successfully redesign learning activities. Most of the interviewed educators did not add questions to the 'standard' student evaluation form, or use separate course evaluations that include questions that probe course redesign issues. However, the surveyed educators did not support this view, as only 13% of the respondents indicated that they failed to collect relevant, course-improving information.

Several educators also suggested that their teaching is largely guided by historical precedence. One educator, for example, most innocently stated, 'that was the way the course was structured before I started here.' For other educators, it appeared that their teaching approach was largely, if not exclusively, a function of what they themselves experienced in the classroom as students. While lectures were used in 93% of the courses, and tutorials in 69% of the courses reported upon by our surveyed educators, they also revealed that lectures (98%) and tutorials (81%) were the methods they were primarily exposed to as undergraduates. Without a tertiary educators' profession and no prerequisite training in higher education teaching and pedagogy, it is perhaps not surprising that so many educators tend to unquestionably teach as they were taught.

Educator misconceptions

When the interviewed educators were asked for their reactions to the New Zealand Institute of Chartered Accountants' and the International Federation of Accountants' calls for the design of courses that foster students' generic learning skills, the educators unanimously supported these objectives. There was, however, a divergence of opinion on how, or more appropriately, who should be developing the skills. Many accounting educators were content to compartmentalize various skill acquisitions. In particular, the accounting educators were content to leave the development of generic learning skills, and the learner-centred approaches that promote their development, to other nonaccounting educators teaching the liberal studies requirements for ICANZ. Accounting educators would then be free to concentrate on the development of technical business skills, typically done through a lecture approach.

Thirty per cent of interviewed educators and administrators cited the failure to recognize the importance of skill and attitude development as another impediment. Contrary to our expectations, only 9% of surveyed educators 'agreed' that developing technical knowledge was more important than skills like teamwork and communication. One reason for this may be that generic skills such as effective communication, analytical and critical thinking and innovative problem solving are required to be incorporated in accounting and business subjects in Australia (Australian Society of Certified Practising Accountants and The Institute of Chartered Accountants in Australia, 1996). While 73% of surveyed educators either 'strongly disagreed' or 'disagreed' that technical knowledge was more important than generic skills, classroom activities such as seminar discussion groups, student presentations, student-facilitated seminars and unstructured case studies remain under-utilized in accounting courses.

Several educators were also loath to adopt group work because of the inability to assess, at least not as accurately as the educator desired, individual student performance. Thirty per cent of the interviewed educators and administrators fell into this category. The difficulty of assigning marks to individual group members and the possibility of a free rider effect were reasons offered for avoiding group work. Similarly, 65% of the surveyed educators agreed that it was hard to apportion marks among group members, and 29% agreed that the possibility of a free rider effect was why they avoided group-learning activities.

The field of accounting is continuing to expand in subject diversity and technical complexity. Many of the educators felt a burning need to cover all the facets of accounting, or certainly the ones that touched on their particular course's subject area. Fifty per cent of the interviewed educators and administrators voiced their need to expand course content. Forty-one per cent of surveyed educators did not consider that there was too much emphasis on the profession's body of knowledge, and 21% did not think it was better to include some student-led activities if it meant leaving out topics. When asked, 'Are there any reasons why the course has been designed this way versus, say, cutting out some content and using some other [teaching] methods?' one educator said:

> The course was designed before I came here. So I was not privy to the original decisions. I suppose I sort of came gradually to taking a bit of control of the content, and we have been reducing the content. But every time I have attempted to say to other people that this course is too full of material – what are we going to cut out – someone will say you can't cut that out.

With so many topics to cover, and no room for any leeway on topics to omit, many of the educators were taken aback with the question of whether they would consider introducing more student-led learning activities. These educators saw student-led activities as time consuming and therefore at odds with obtaining maximum topic coverage. Thirty-six per cent of interviewed educators 'agreed' or 'strongly agreed' that case study teaching was a good idea, but it is time consuming.

There were, however, some educators who showed concern for the obsession with covering an ever-increasing number of topics. For instance, one educator said:

> There is a tension with the [New Zealand Institute of Charted Accountants'] Body of Knowledge, of trying to get through it. I think there is too much emphasis on the Body of Knowledge, just pouring it in.

In general, educators, whether or not they displayed concern with the obsession to include an ever-expanding body of knowledge, were unwilling to trade course content against what they felt were more time-consuming learner-centred approaches. For instance, one educator regretted introducing a student-led activity because it reduced the number of topics that could be covered.

Study limitations and cautionary notes

A few words of caution are required when interpreting the findings of this study. Readers are reminded that the aims of this study were to uncover and shed light on the barriers to learner-centred education. The findings should not be viewed as a condemnation of tertiary accounting education in New Zealand or Australia. Any such interpretation would be a gross misuse of the data. In fact, the visits to the four tertiary New Zealand institutions brought to light many instances of highly innovative and exemplary teaching and learning practices. And these practices were revealed in spite of the intent to look for barriers and not exemplars.

It must be remembered that the impediments catalogued and discussed here may or may not exist at all institutions. This paper also makes no comment or inference about the extent to which these impediments exist at any of the institutions studied. Suffice it to say that while none of the four institutions visited was totally unaffected by the impediments, it was also the case that none of the institutions suffered from all of the impediments. Instead of viewing the data as specific to any one institution, the impediments should be seen as potentially occurring in any given course setting.

Readers should also be careful not to view the impediments as independent of one another. The education literature and the interview data both point to the fact that these impediments are linked together in a web-like manner. Changes in one impediment, either for the better or worse, are likely to impact not only on the type of learning approach chosen (i.e., process versus content driven) but are also likely to have an influence on the nature of one or more of the other impediments. As an example, a greater availability of Australian and New Zealand-based cases is likely to lead educators to use more case studies as part of their teaching pedagogy. Additionally, a greater availability of Australian and New Zealand-based cases is likely to influence, by virtue of the greater perceived relevance of such cases, students' readiness for and acceptance of the more active learning role that cases require.

Finally, readers are warned that the impediments to learner-centred education are best seen as multiplicative in nature versus additive. Even the best attempts to target and alleviate the problems associated with a given impediment will not succeed if certain minimum thresholds are not achieved on the remaining set of impediments. For example, the interviews revealed situations where educators, although attracted by the recognition that their institutions' new promotion criteria gave to teaching, were no closer to promoting learner-centred approaches than they were prior to the newly published promotion criteria. The problem appears to be that these educators have yet to become reflective of their teaching practices. Instead of looking for ways of enabling and empowering students to become more active in their learning, and thereby enhancing the learning experience the students receive, the educators were more interested in enrolling in public speaking courses, such as Toastmaster courses. The obvious and candidly espoused aim was to improve their lecturing styles. Thus, despite tertiary institutions' attempts to align their promotion practices with the goals of lifelong learning, progress toward a wider use of learner-centred approaches will only occur when a certain minimum threshold in educator attitudes and perceptions is also achieved.

Ways forward in overcoming the underuse of learner-centred approaches

There are two strategies for making accounting education more learner-centred. The first strategy involves isolating and overcoming the impediments identified in this paper at their individual level. The second strategy requires rethinking the relationships between accounting educators, the tertiary institutions in which they operate, and the accounting profession they are asked to serve. Without a committed and concerted effort by all three parties to effect change, any improvement in the educational experience is unlikely to occur. Due to the rather obvious and straightforward nature of the first course of action, only the second approach is further enumerated upon.

TERTIARY INSTITUTIONS

Tertiary institutions can begin the process of change by re-examining their promotion criteria. Clearly, one of the more contentious issues to be raised by both the educators and administrators was the failure of promotion systems to promote excellence in teaching. While two of the institutions visited have started down this road, even they have a long way yet to go. The major problem is how to develop educator performance measurements that support the institutions' avowed goals of lifelong learning. If student evaluations are to be used for the purpose of assessing an educator's fostering of lifelong learning, then the evaluations themselves must measure lifelong learning and not educator attributes. The promotion of lifelong, and in particular, learner-centred approaches, is not about lecturing; nor can it ever be. As the old Chinese proverb suggests, 'I hear, I forget; I see, I remember; I do, I understand.' Instead of asking about an educator's ability to transmit information, evaluations must ask about an educator's ability to facilitate student learning. To do otherwise will result in more occurrences of educators being encouraged by their Heads of Department to attend training sessions, such as Toastmaster courses, that help the educator deliver better-packaged and better-rehearsed lectures.

Of course, the development of performance measures that support lifelong learning may prove to be the easy part of the promotion system to fix. The ability to overcome educators' beliefs about the operation of their institutions' promotion system will represent a more difficult task. Over and over again the interviews uncovered an uneasy distrust between what administrators said and what academic staff believed the real intent of their message was. During several of the interviews with the administrators, the reasons behind this distrust became evident. For example, an administrator at one of the institutions said that a weighting of around 40% was formally attributed to teaching, but in reality the true weighting was much lower. It is no wonder, therefore, that academic staff view with suspicion the espoused claims of their institutions' reward systems. As Emerson (1876, p.96) once stated 'What you are stands over you the while, and thunders so that I cannot hear what you say to the contrary'. Consequently, tertiary institutions will need to do more to show that they are sincere in their efforts to bring about greater lifelong learning.

In addition to modifying their promotion systems to give greater recognition to teaching, there is much more that tertiary institutions can do to promote excellence in teaching. Tertiary institutions must not forget that their purpose is both to teach students and to conduct reputable research. While it is true that sufficient funds are needed to properly carry out these activities, and while it is also true that recent years' government funding has made this task increasingly more difficult, it does not follow that opening the floodgates to the 'full fee paying' overseas student is the answer. Overseas students may provide funds to support research; but, as the interviews revealed, this practice may come with deleterious side effects for teaching. Many of the learning approaches that educators say they would like to use, with many of the cited approaches being action-oriented, are not used as a direct consequence of the overseas students' skill level and the attitudes they possess.

Two of the educators interviewed were very blunt in their assessment of the reasons behind their institution's recruitment of overseas students. According to one educator, 'It is bringing them in large dollars. We know that is primarily why.' In a similar vein, a different educator said, 'They [senior management of the tertiary institution] see their mission in terms of satisfying the customers and keeping them pouring in from Malaysia.'

The presence of international students provides an important opportunity for enhancing student learning, but only if academic rigour is maintained. Recruiting practices that are based on the funding they generate versus the enriched learning opportunities they promote should be stopped. Otherwise tertiary institutions are in danger of suffocating the experientially-based learning that is needed in today's accounting programmes, with the likely consequence of jeopardizing their institutions' teaching missions.

Still another step that tertiary institutions can take in their quest to improve their students' learning experiences is to promote an environment that encourages openness, co-operation, and innovation. According to Ramsden (1992), tertiary institutions all too often do quite the opposite and instead create climates that are defensive, competitive, and passive. The new environment that Ramsden talks about will, of course, require much time and effort. According to Ramsden, 'Efforts to innovate in teaching when workloads are heavy are likely to result in superficial outcomes.' If tertiary institutions are really serious about creating beneficial changes in their learning environments, then they must refrain, as one administrator termed it, from seeing 'teaching as something you do.' The time needed to excel in teaching must be put on an equal footing with the time needed to excel in research. As such, study leave that is requested for the purpose of making course innovations should not be seen as an oddity, as it currently is, but as an equally appropriate alternative to study leave that is spent undertaking academic research.

EDUCATORS

Undoubtedly educators have a large role to play in the improvement of tertiary accounting education. Too often educators appear to be conducting their teaching as they were taught versus how it might be taught. Part of the problem stems from their failure to give serious consideration to the act of teaching. Of course, given the operation of their institutions' promotion systems, such behaviour is not surprising. The failings of the promotion system, however, appear to be only part of the problem. It also seems that educators are not sufficiently reflective of their teaching practices. Apart from concerns about content issues, i.e., what topics to include, very little regard appears to be given to improving the process by which students undertake their learning. Educators must move beyond trying to stuff more information into students' heads and begin looking at the processes through which the learning occurs. Continual refinements to these learning processes, versus trying to apply an 'optimal' recipe, represent the task at hand. The search for new ways of enhancing the learning environment will require educators to go outside their individual perceptions of the learning experience. At a minimum, they will to need solicit advice from interested colleagues, survey their students about their reactions to the learning activities, and become more regular readers of the education literature.

The need for educators to reflect on their teaching practices is no different from the need for students to reflect on their learning. This comment is echoed by Ramsden (1992, p. 268), who says, 'Encouraging students to learn and helping lecturers to teach involve identical practices.' Just as students must be encouraged to move away from being passive recipients of a fixed body of knowledge that they will be subsequently called upon to regurgitate, so too must educators become more reflective of their teaching practices.

THE ACCOUNTING PROFESSION

The accounting profession can also play a role in further promoting the lifelong learning approach it appears to so dearly advocate. Greater support, and not just through rhetorical exhortation, is needed. The profession, in New Zealand and Australia, is giving out mixed signals. On the one hand it says it supports learning to learn. On the other hand, the funding it offers is largely, if not exclusively, for the purpose of academic research. For example, the profession commonly offers financial support for students' PhD studies and academics' travel to seminars and conferences. Typically these endeavours are for the purpose of academic research. This is not to say, however, that the profession has a bias toward academic as opposed to educational research. Certainly the profession is supportive of accounting education initiatives. Nevertheless, it is true to say that the profession has yet to develop a strategy for specifically targeting educational research. What educational research does get funded is less a product of forethought and planning and more a product of serendipity.

The profession should be more deliberate in the pursuit of educational developments. One way, for instance, would be to support educators' travel to other institutions for the expressed purpose of promoting the exchange of teaching and learning practices and not the more traditional purpose of presenting academic research. The sponsorship of short-term faculty visits between tertiary institutions could similarly be used to foster the exchange of teaching and learning practices. This latter approach, by virtue of the greater time allotted, offers a fuller and more in-depth collaboration on teaching innovations.

The profession might also wish to rethink its sponsorship of conferences. While it is true that large conferences, such as those of the Accounting Association of Australia and New Zealand, include presentations on topics of accounting education, this is hardly the focus of the conference. Additionally, the sheer size and the consequent impersonal nature of many conferences tends to stifle meaningful exchange. So too do the lecture style formats of the presentations. Instead of providing financial support for large conferences, the profession might find it more beneficial to support smaller, more interactive educational sessions.

Regardless of the role the profession assumes in its support of learning and teaching developments, it must make its stance explicitly known and be willing to financially support projects that are consistent with its intentions. Educators are full of stories about how their institutions have remade students into customers and preached the need to satisfy these customers by offering a high quality of instruction. While plenty of lip service has been paid to improving the students' learning experience, many educators would argue that the remuneration system and, in particular, promotion are still largely based on research output versus teaching quality. The profession needs to be careful that it too is not viewed as paying little more than lip service to the principles of learning to learn. The profession must remember that what it fails to say or financially support can be as important as what it chooses to say and financially support.

Conclusion

This paper attempted to assess directly educators' and administrators' perceptions about the dearth of learner-centred approaches in accounting programmes. In the process, it highlights the tensions that exist between the educators, their institutions and their students and the profession's calls for the adoption of learner-centred approaches.

The interview and survey findings suggest that the perceived impediments to learner-centred approaches can be grouped under three broad headings: lack of student readiness, inadequate educator support mechanisms, and nonreflective education practices. Contained with these groupings are such factors as inadequate resources for teaching, large class sizes, passive and didactic learning preferences of students, and inadequate staff development (e.g., study leave) and incentives (e.g., promotion criteria) in the area of pedagogic innovation.

Today's educators, their institutions, and their profession appear to be at a crossroads. For more than a decade now the accounting education literature has discussed and generally advocated the promotion of learning to learn. Nevertheless, most accounting programmes and educator teaching practices appear to have remained mostly unchanged.

Considering the tensions that exist between the educators, their institutions and their students, and the profession's calls for the adoption of learner-centred approaches it is unlikely that a strategy of simply waiting a bit longer for educators to translate the profession's calls for change into practice will work. Instead, positive change is only likely to be realized through the adoption of a more vigorous and proactive approach. It is probable that this latter approach will require a rethinking of the way accounting educators, their institutions, and the accounting profession operate and co-operate.

Acknowledgements

In providing financial support for this project, the authors wish to gratefully acknowledge the assistance of a Peter Barr Fellowship awarded by the Institute of Chartered Accountants of New Zealand. In addition, the authors are grateful for comments on an earlier draft received from seminar participants at Loughborough University, UK, and the comments from three anonymous reviewers.

References

Accounting Education Change Commission (AECC) (1990) Objectives of education for account-ants: position statement number one. *Issues in Accounting Education* **5**(2), 307–12.

Adler, R.W. and Milne, M.J. (1995) Increasing learner-control and reflection: towards learning-to-learn in an undergraduate management accounting course. *Accounting Education: an International Journal* **4**(2), 105–19.

Adler, R.W. and Milne, M.J. (1997) Translating ideals into practice: an examination of international accounting bodies' calls for curriculum changes and New Zealand tertiary institutions' assessment methods. *Accounting Education: an International Journal* **6**(2), 1–16.

American Accounting Association (AAA) (1986) Committee on the Future Structure, Content, and Scope of Accounting Education (The Bedford Committee), Future accounting education: preparing for the expanding profession. *Issues in Accounting Education* **1**(1), pp. 168–95.

Australian Society of Certified Practising Accountants and The Institute of Chartered Accountants in Australia. (1996). *Guidelines for Joint Administration of Accreditation of Tertiary Courses by the Professional Accounting Bodies*. Melbourne, Australia: Australian Society of Certified Practising Accountants and The Institute of Chartered Accountants.

Big Eight (1989) *Perspectives on Education: Capabilities for Success in the Accounting Profession*, ('Big Eight' White Paper). New York: Arthur Andersen & Co, Arthur Young, Coopers & Lybrand, Deloitte Haskins & Sells, Ernst & Whinney, Peat Marwick Main & Co, Price Waterhouse, and Touche Ross.

Böcker, F. (1987) Is case teaching more effective than lecture teaching in business administration? An exploratory analysis. *Interfaces* **17**(5), 64–71.

Briers, M.L. (1999) *Continuously Improving Management Accounting Education: Change management and Experiential Learning*. International Federation of Accountants Research Monograph.

Emerson, R.W. (1876) *Social Aims*.

Farnes, N. (1975) Student-centred learning. *Teaching at a Distance* **3**, 2–6.

Institute of Chartered Accountants of New Zealand Education Committee (1994) *Admissions Policy*. Wellington: Institute of Chartered Accountants of New Zealand, Wellington.

International Federation of Accountants (IFAC) (1996) Prequalification education, assessment of professional competence and experience requirements of professional accountants. *International Education Guideline* No. 9, Washington, DC: IFAC Education Committee, IFAC.

May, G.S., Windal, F.W. and Sylvestre, J. (1995) The need for change in accounting education: an educator survey. *Journal of Accounting Education* **13**, 21–43.

McKeachie, W.J. (1982) The rewards of teaching. In J. Bess (ed.) *New directions for Teaching and Learning: Motivating Professors to Teach Effectively.* San Francisco: Jossey Bass.

Miller, R.I. (1988) Merit pay in United States postsecondary institutions. *Higher Education* **17**, 219–32.

Ramsden, P. (1992) *Learning to Teach in Higher Education.* London: Routledge.

Stewart, J.P. and Dougherty, T.W. (1993) Using case studies in teaching accounting: a quasi-experimental study. *Accounting Education: an International Journal* **2**, 1–10.

Stout, D. (1996) Experimental evidence and recommendations regarding case-based teaching in undergraduate cost Accounting. *Journal of Accounting Education* **14**(3), 293–317.

A study of students' perceptions of the usefulness of case studies for the development of finance and accounting-related skills and knowledge

SIDNEY WEIL[†], PETER OYELERE[†], JOANNA YEOH[‡] and COLIN FIRER[§]

[†]Lincoln University, New Zealand, [‡]University of Canterbury, New Zealand and [§]University of Cape Town, South Africa

Abstract

Recent accounting and finance education literature indicates a trend towards an increasing use of case studies. The literature in this field is primarily descriptive, with no empirical evidence on the use or effectiveness of the method. This study examines students' perceptions of the use of case studies and the potential influences of gender and prior academic performance on such perceptions. The study focuses, in particular, on students' perceptions about whether case studies develop particular skills suggested in the literature. The questionnaire-based study was conducted in a post-graduate (Honours) class at a South African university. Analyses of the results reveal significant differences in students' perceptions of the benefits of the use of cases. Gender and prior academic performance-based differences in perception were also found. The study is useful for educators who use, or intend to use, case studies, as it highlights issues, such as the learning objectives of the course, which need to be addressed prior to curriculum design.

Introduction

The use of case studies for imparting certain thinking skills and knowledge to students is widespread in education, being employed extensively in medical, legal and business education (Bonk and Smith, 1998). In accounting and finance, case studies are considered to be valuable teaching tools because of the opportunity they present for mimicking real-life practical problems and situations, enabling students to develop and/or improve upon a range of skills required for day-to-day business decisions. Several studies have identified a broad range of skills and abilities that could be imparted, developed or improved through the use of case studies (Campbell and Lewis, 1991; Knechel, 1992; Saudagaran, 1996; Bonner, 1999). Little, however, has been done to investigate and report on the relative usefulness of case studies in meeting course objectives from the point of view of the principal stakeholders – students. This study is aimed at measuring students' perceptions of the relative usefulness of the case method as a tool for developing a set of desirable skills in students.

A questionnaire was employed to collect data on students' perceptions of the usefulness of case studies for developing thinking skills and imparting knowledge. Data were analysed to determine the greatest benefits derived from the use of case studies, as ranked by the students. Nonparametric statistical tests were used to isolate possible differentials in the ranking of the benefits of case studies in developing and imparting individual and subscaled skills and knowledge. Cross-gender and prior performance statistical analyses were also conducted. The results of the analyses show that students perceive the major benefit of the use of case studies to be exposure to real-world complexity, particularly with respect to decision-making. Cross-gender and prior academic performance differences in student perceptions were also found. The findings of the study can assist educators to design more effective teaching approaches.

The rest of the paper is organized as follows. Relevant literature on the subject is reviewed next. This is followed by a presentation of the research design and methodology. The results of the study are then reported and discussed, followed by a summary and conclusions. Suggestions for further research are presented in the final section.

Literature review

This section provides a review of the literature relating to the use of case studies. Case studies have been used in education[1] for many years, their use being particularly wide-spread in management education (Fulmer, 1992; Wines *et al.*, 1994). They are closely associated with the Harvard Business School, which published the first book of written cases in 1921 (Shapiro, 1984). Numerous definitions of case studies are found in the management education literature. Easton (1992) defines a case study as a '[means] to provide practice in problem solving and decision making in a simulated situation . . . The case method is primarily a vehicle for developing skills; skills which are a vital part of a decision maker's armoury . . .' Shapiro (1984) similarly describes the essence of case teaching as the facilitation of student learning, being very useful in the development of skills and a philosophy of real-world management. In an accounting context, Wines *et al.* (1994) describe case studies as typically possessing several features. These are: issues, the consideration of which require the use of judgement and analytical reasoning skills; the inclusion of real or realistic situations, requiring a consideration of the complexity and ambiguity of the business world; and the existence of more than one possible solution to the case problem. Common to all of these definitions are the development of problem-solving skills and the use of either real or realistic contexts.

The use of case studies in accounting education is more recent than in management education. It is, in part, a response to the call by the Accounting Education Change Commission (AECC, 1990) for more innovative teaching of accounting to achieve certain employment-related skills (*Perspectives on Education*, 1989). The AECC (1990) classifies desirable educational outcomes into communication skills, intellectual skills, interpersonal skills, general knowledge, business knowledge, accounting knowledge and attitudes. Intellectual outcomes specified are to locate and organize information, to identify and

---

[1] For examples of case-based learning in the medical field, see Schwartz and Heath (1994) and Johnstone and Biggs (1998). The use of cases is also well established in legal education (Bonk and Smith, 1998).

solve unstructured problems and to exercise judgement. The AECC recommends the use of teaching techniques such as the case method (the use of case studies) to develop such intellectual skills. Despite this pronouncement, only a few studies have examined the usefulness of case studies, with most of the literature being descriptive in nature. Some papers describe the nature of case studies, while others specify how to incorporate the case method into accounting instruction (Libby, 1991; Knechel, 1992; Wines *et al.*, 1994; Bonner, 1999). Another category of studies describes the benefits to be derived by students from the use of case studies (Campbell and Lewis, 1991; Kimmel, 1995).

Case studies take many different forms, varying in length (Campbell and Lewis, 1991), mode (Bonk and Smith, 1998), extent of incorporation of actual business situations (Barkman, 1998), level of detail (Wines *et al.*, 1994) and analytical approach (Knechel, 1992). Irrespective of the types of case studies used, the development of skills is propounded to be their main benefit. The skills most frequently mentioned as being developed by case studies are analytical and judgement skills (Campbell and Lewis, 1991). They argue that the success or failure of the use of cases depends primarily on the specific educational objectives and on practical implementation issues. For example, cases might be appropriate if the course objective is to facilitate the development of analytical and judgement skills, whereas lectures and reading assignments may, but need not exclusively, be more appropriate means of presenting basic accounting techniques. Bonner (1999) presents a comprehensive framework for choosing teaching methods based on specific learning objectives. She specifies the use of cases as being one of a wide variety of teaching methods available to accounting instructors, to be used in conjunction with each other. Hassall *et al.* (1998) specify the aim of using case studies as being 'to develop and apply an integrated approach to problem solving and to provide students with an understanding of the problems inherent in the application of discipline based knowledge to practical situations in a period of change' (p. 326). To achieve this aim, Hassall *et al.* identify several objectives encompassing academic and personal skills, for example, 'students should be able to evaluate, classify and organise information into a suitable format for the application of decision-making techniques' (p. 326).

Bonner (1999) identifies cases as being particularly suitable for the development of complex cognitive skills. Similarly to Hassall *et al.* (1998), Wines *et al.* (1994) identify both cognitive and affective benefits to be derived from the use of case studies. The benefits include organization and comprehension, judgement and analytical reasoning, communication and interpersonal skills, realities of decision-making, student motivation and staff motivation and development. Johnstone and Biggs (1998) identify several ways in which cases can be used in problem-based learning. They view realistic cases as a means of enabling students to practise gathering relevant professional information and integrating that information within the context of the case, as well as being useful for encouraging the development of diagnostic reasoning skills.

Kimmel (1995) regards cases as being very useful for developing critical thinking skills in students. He divides cases into three categories, namely, basic, intermediate and advanced. For each category, he identifies critical thinking elements that can be taught by the use of a case (see Table 1, Panel A).

The critical thinking elements listed in Table 1 increase in cognitive complexity with the level of case used. According to Kimmel (1995), the extent to which an instructor wishes to develop particular skills in students will determine which particular type of case will be used in a given situation. Thus, an instructor wishing to develop students' ability to modify

Table 1. Critical thinking elements and the categorisation of skills, abilities and knowledge into subscales

Panel A: Strategies for developing critical thinking elements (adapted from Kimmel, 1995)

Critical thinking element	Basic case	Intermediate case	Advanced case
Welcoming divergent views	X		
Tolerating ambiguity		X	
Recognizing personal biases		X	
Resisting overgeneralization		X	
Analysing data for value and content			X
Synthesizing			X
Defining problems accurately		X	X
Variety of thinking processes			X
Employing precise terms	X		
Modifying judgments			X
Gathering facts			X
Applying knowledge to new situations		X	X
Distinguishing fact from opinion			X

Panel B: Subscales of skills, abilities and knowledge

Communication skills	Dealing with uncertainty	Active participation	Judgement
Listening skills	Take decisions with incomplete information	Participate actively in the learning process	Improve judgement skills
Written communication skills	Deal with situations involving uncertainty and ambiguity	Ask pertinent questions	Distinguish facts from opinions
Persuasive skills	Awareness of multiple solutions to business problems	Increase motivation to study	Develop problem-solving skills
		Responsibility for own learning	

Consolidation and integration	Data exploration	Problem elaboration	Visualization
Integrate understanding of the different components of the course	Identify the relevant data in a case	Interpret data	Consider different perspectives
Synthesize the essential elements of a problem	Ability to organize data	Think critically	Insight into business decision-making
Consolidate prior knowledge of the discipline	Problem identification skills	Analytical skills	Insight into business operations
Summarize the available information		Think conceptually	Relate theory to real-life practice
Integrate technical knowledge of the discipline		Evaluate ideas	Apply knowledge to new situations

judgments would use an advanced case, whereas an instructor wishing to improve students' ability to use precise terms – a lower-order thinking skill than modifying judgments – might use a basic case. Unlike Kimmel, Bonner (1999) does not classify cases into different levels of complexity.

Empirical research on the use of case studies in accounting education is limited. Saudagaran (1996) uses cases, together with other pedagogically innovative features, to de-emphasize a single solution approach and to stress the need to deal with uncertainty in accounting. Students in his study indicate that they find that the new course improves their perception of accounting. Another perception-based study, Friedlan (1995), examines the effect of teaching approach on students' perceptions of the skills and abilities needed for success in accounting courses and by accounting practitioners. He reports that teaching approach had a significant effect on students' perceptions. In particular, he found that students in a non-traditional course using, *inter alia*, minicases, had perceptions about the skills and abilities required for academic and professional success that were more con-sistent with those identified as necessary by members of the accounting profession than by students in a traditional course. Barkman (1998) reports mixed student reaction on the use of live cases; some students indicate appreciation at being exposed to real businesses, while others find the effort involved in completing the case too demanding. In addition to this evidence, which is anecdotal, questionnaire responses from clients involved in the live cases reflect a high level of satisfaction. Neither Friedlan nor Barkman measured students' perceptions about the proposed benefits of the use of mini- or live cases, respectively.

A study that has measured students' perceptions about the benefits of case studies is that of Hassall *et al.* (1998). Students were requested to indicate the extent to which a module, using only case studies, developed ten specified skills. The five most frequent 'yes' responses, in descending order, were for negotiation skills, ability to work in a group, presentation skills, the ability to apply and integrate subject skills and knowledge and the ability to question assumptions and listen to arguments. The lowest percentage of 'yes' responses was for a question relating to the ability to recognize and accept leadership. When asked about the ability of case studies to develop knowledge, skills and personal qualities, 85% of the students agreed that case studies were the most appropriate teaching tool for developing knowledge; 90% agreed in respect of skills and 62%, personal qualities. No further empirical studies that examine either the use and effectiveness of the case method, or students' perceptions of this teaching method, are available.

The role of gender in accounting and finance education has been examined in numerous studies (see Brazelton, 1998, for a summary). Many of these studies have investigated the relationship of gender to students' performance. Although Brazelton notes that, 'virtually all of these investigations have determined that there are unexplained variables in assessing career success of accounting graduates' (1998, p. 512), it is nevertheless evident that female accounting students frequently outperform male accounting students (Hanks and Shivaswamy, 1985; Mutchler *et al.*, 1987; Tyson 1989; Carpenter *et al.*, 1993).[2]

Brazelton (1998) also investigates gender communication patterns in the accounting classroom. She reports, *inter alia*, that men are involved in more than their share of classroom interactions; that more men are involved more often and that men interrupt more often. As these findings all involve levels of student participation, they may have implications for the use of case studies, which, if used in conjunction with study groups,

---

[2] Some evidence to the contrary, however, also exists in the literature (Doran *et al.*, 1991).

require extensive student participation. Weil *et al.* (1999) found that male students perceive case studies to be more useful than females in developing their knowledge of management accounting. Because of its possible impact on student perceptions about the use of case studies, gender has been incorporated in the current study.

There is little evidence in the literature about the relationship of prior academic performance to student perceptions about the benefits of case studies. Weil *et al.* (1999) report that there are no differences in perception of the use of case studies based on prior academic performance. This potential influence on students' perceptions is included in the study to explore it further, particularly with respect to whether academically strong students perceive the use of case studies differently from academically weak students.

To summarize, this study aims to contribute to the literature by assessing students' perceptions of the benefits of case studies and the association between students' perceptions of the benefits of case studies and certain factors, namely, gender and prior academic performance. The method employed in conducting the research is described next.

Research method

Background to the study

The study was conducted with 72 Honours students, whose course was case study based, at a tertiary institution in South Africa in 1998.[3] The course was an optional unit and students were aware that a case study approach to teaching and learning was to be used. Prior to the course, students had not experienced the case study approach, having been taught primarily through traditional teaching approaches, such as lectures, seminars and tutorials. The decision to offer the course in case study mode was taken to allow students to integrate their prior knowledge and to apply this knowledge in solving real-world problems. Hence, the key learning objectives set for the course were to familiarize students with typical real-world business issues, to encourage students to ask pertinent questions, to develop students' ability to deal with uncertainty and/or ambiguity, and to encourage them to make decisions and recommend courses of action.

The course ran for one semester. There were 12 teaching weeks, with four hours of contact time per week. Students were required to prepare two cases per week. The class was divided into two groups; one group presented cases on Tuesdays and the other on Thursdays. Students within each of the two groups were asked to form their own study groups, of three or four students each. Each study group had to be ready to present the scheduled case on the day for which it was responsible. The groups doing the presentation were randomly selected on the day by being drawn out of a hat. The presentations were used as the introduction to the session and generally lasted a quarter of the class time – approximately half an hour. Thereafter the discussion was open and general. The approaches adopted in the presentation of the cases were interpretational and decision-oriented (Knechel, 1992). The presentations were assessed primarily on a content, rather than a style, basis and contributed 20% towards the final mark for the course.

The case studies were divided into two categories; short (80% of the cases) were between three and five pages long, while the long case studies were between 10 and 15

---

[3] The class, comprising 121 students, was split into two streams – traditional (lectures and tutorial sessions) and case study-based. Students were given the option of choosing between the two streams. Seventy-two students chose the case study-based stream.

pages in length. To avoid the criticism that cases frequently create oversimplified (Bonk and Smith, 1998) or unrealistic contexts (Stoneham, 1995), all of the cases were based on real companies. Specific questions were set for each case study to suggest areas for analysis by students. Approximately 60% of the cases were basic, with the balance being intermediate (as classified by Kimmel, 1995). Most of the cases were issues cases, with a few being appraisals cases (as described by Wines *et al.*, 1994).

As the students had no prior experience of the case study approach to learning, during the first week of the course they were given relevant readings, a sample case together with a suggested solution and a demonstration of the desired analytical approach to case studies, in order to familiarize them with the case method.

Each study group prepared a single written submission, which was marked and contributed 20% of the final mark for the course. The final examination consisted of a four-hour case study. All but one of the students passed the course.

Research aim

The study investigates the usefulness of case studies in teaching as perceived by a group of Honours students. More specifically, the study is designed to observe the perceived relative usefulness of case studies for imparting a set of 31 desirable skills to the students. The study also investigates a possible disparity of opinion among the students across two homogeneously distinct characteristics, namely, gender and prior academic performance.

Instrument design and data collection

A questionnaire was designed for administration to the target population. The questionnaire was based on that used in a previous study (Weil *et al.*, 1999), which examined students' perceptions of the use of case studies and study groups in an Advanced Management Accounting course, using a Malaysian student population. Using this as a pilot study, a more comprehensive questionnaire was constructed. The questionnaire requested demographic information in respect of student name, gender, age, language and prior results in undergraduate courses. The main part of the questionnaire contained questions about the use of case studies in the course.[4] To minimize variations in students' responses due to different interpretations of the term 'case study,' it was defined in the questionnaire as 'an unstructured academic assignment, which requires information to be analysed and organized, in an attempt to determine an answer from available alternatives.'[5]

Thirty-one questions were constructed regarding desirable skills, abilities and knowledge purportedly developed through the use of case studies (see questions 5–35 in Appendix I). The list of questions is not exhaustive, but includes the benefits of case studies most frequently cited in the literature (Campbell and Lewis, 1991; Knechel, 1992; Wines *et al.*, 1994; Kimmel, 1995; Hassall *et al.*, 1998).

The 31 skills, abilities and knowledge can be organized under the following eight headings: *Visualization*, encompassing skills which provide familiarity with the business decision-making environment; *Dealing with uncertainty*, containing questions about situations dealing with incomplete and/or ambiguous information; *Problem elaboration*, including critical thinking elements used when developing an approach to a problem;

---

[4] The questionnaire also contained questions about the use of study groups, which will be reported on separately.
[5] This definition is adapted from those used by Easton (1992) and Wines *et al.* (1994).

Communication skills, listing questions relating to various components of the communication process; *Consolidation and integration*, relating to the skills used to combine different knowledge components of the discipline; *Judgement*, being skills involving assessing and choosing between different alternatives; *Data exploration*, relating to the exploratory phase of problem-solving, and *Active participation*, relating to the student's contribution to the learning process. The classification of the 31 skills, abilities and knowledge into these eight headings is presented in Panel B of Table 1.[6]

The questions do not appear under these headings in the questionnaire, but are randomized. Respondents were asked to indicate the extent to which the use of case studies helped them in realizing or enhancing each of the listed skills, by rating the strength of their preference on a seven-point Likert-like scale ranging from 1 (not at all) through 4 (moderate) to 7 (extensively). In addition to the 31 specific questions, respondents were asked to rank the three most valuable benefits of the case study method from the 31 options. Finally, the respondents were asked to indicate on a scale ranging from 1 (no value) through 4 (some value) to 7 (high value) how valuable overall they found the use of case studies as a learning method in the course.

Data was collected by the administration of the questionnaire to the student population in a classroom setting during the last lecture of the course. Fifty-one respondents, representing 71% of the sample population, completed the questionnaire. Completion of the questionnaire was voluntary.

Data analysis

The mean usefulness of case studies for teaching each skill was computed by adding up the point values assigned by all respondents, and then dividing the total by the number of respondents for the group. The skills were then ranked in descending order of mean importance. Table 3 (Panel A) shows the mean rankings for the five highest and five lowest ranked skills. The table also shows the level of agreement among the students, as measured by the standard deviation of their responses, on each measurement variable. In addition, percentages of all respondents who consider case studies to have been extremely useful (responses 6 and 7 on the Likert-like scale) in developing or improving each skill are presented. Panel B of Table 3 reveals the same information across gender and Panel C for prior performance levels. To aid the analysis, the skills are presented in the order of ranks given by respondents in 'experimental groupings' – female for gender and 'above-average' for performance levels. Based on their performances in the undergraduate Finance paper, respondents were classified into 'above-average' (A) and 'below-average' (B) performers.[7] The ranks given by members of the 'control group' for gender and prior performance are presented, respectively, in Panels B and C of Table 3 for comparative purposes.

Further statistical analysis was carried out to isolate possible gender or performance level differentials in the perceived impact of the case study method on the development or improvement of each type of skill. The *Mann–Whitney U (M–W U)* test of independence was employed to explore possible differences in the effect of the case study method across

---

[6] The subscales are not entirely mutually exclusive, as it is possible to classify some of the skills under more than one subscale. Where this is the case, skills are classified under the 'best-fit' subscale.

[7] Note that this classification is a 'convenience-split' of the respondents into two homogeneous groups for analysis purpose only. Students who qualify for admission into the Honours programme all have records of above-average performance in previous courses. The overall average for this class, on which the split is based, is 60.55%.

gender and performance levels. Summarized (items of significant differences only) results of the tests are presented in Table 4 (Panels A and B).

Factor analysis was used to derive sub-scales for the 31 individual skills. Using both a Varimax and Oblimin rotation, the factor analysis of all 31 questions produced nine factors with eigenvalues of over 1. Four subscales emerged clearly from this initial factor analysis. The remainder of the questions were subjected to a further factor analysis, which yielded five factors. From this analysis, two different subscales were identified clearly. Six of the eight subscales discussed under *Instrument design and data collection*[8] were thus confirmed by the factor analysis. The standardized alpha coefficient for the eight subscales ranged from 0.66 to 0.82, with seven out of eight subscales scoring above 0.70.[9]

The final step in the analysis involved applying appropriate statistical tests to explore the perceived effectiveness of case studies in developing the subscaled skills derived from the factor analysis. Following through from the previous analysis, possible differentials in students' perception of sub-scales were investigated. The *Friedman* test was employed to investigate possible differences in students' overall perceptions, while the *M–W U* test was applied to investigate gender- and performance-based differences. The results of the tests are presented in Table 6.

Results and discussion

The survey and statistical test results are discussed and presented in this section. The preliminary statistics are presented first, followed by substantive statistical tests and discussion. Due to the nature of the data, all tests were nonparametric. The discussion of the results is in the following order: first, preliminary statistics on respondents' demographic details and their ranking (overall, gender- and performance-based) of the 31 individual benefits of case studies are presented; next, the results of substantive non-parametric tests for differences in students' perceptions with respect to individual skills are presented; finally, the results of tests on students' perception of subscaled benefits of case studies are discussed. In all cases, where applicable, overall results are presented first, followed by discussions of differences attributable to gender and prior academic performance.

Preliminary statistics

Some demographic details on the student respondents to this study are presented in Table 2. Of the 51 students, 19 (37.3%) are female, while the remaining 32 are male. The grade obtained in the undergraduate paper completed prior to the Honours programme by the students ranged from 50 to 76%, with a mean of 60.55%.[10] Fifteen (about 31%) of the students fell within the modal performance category of 60–64%. Of these, nine are male, while the rest are female. The next highest cluster of students scored *less than 55%*. Twelve students (about 25 %), one-third of whom are female, fell into this category. Only two students, both male, scored *greater than 74%*. The age of the student respondents ranged between 21 and 25 years. Most of them were either 22 (47%) or 21 (43%) years

---

[8] See Panel B of Table 1.

[9] These scores are considered sufficient and reliable for a study of this nature (Nunnally, 1978).

[10] The degree for which the students were registered, namely a Bachelor of Business Science, is a broadly based one in which they encounter all the functional areas of business, including Accounting and Finance. It was therefore reasoned that students' score in undergraduate Finance would be representative of their abilities.

Table 2. Respondent demographics

| | Gender of respondents | | | | | |
| | Female | | Male | | Total | |
	Count	Per cent*	Count	Per cent	Count	Per cent*
Performance categories						
Less than 55%	4	23.5	8	25.0	12	24.5
55% to 59%	2	11.8	5	15.6	7	14.3
60% to 64%	6	35.3	9	28.1	15	30.6
65% to 70%	1	5.9	5	15.6	6	12.2
71% to 74%	4	23.5	3	9.4	7	14.3
Greater than 74%	–	–	2	6.3	2	5.0
Total	17	100.0	32	100.0	49	100.0
Age of respondents						
21	7	36.8	15	46.9	22	43.1
22	10	52.6	14	43.8	24	47.1
23	2	10.5	2	6.3	4	7.8
25	–	–	1	3.1	1	2.0
Total	19	100.0	32	100.0	51	100.0

* Percentages do not add up to 100 due to rounding errors.

old. One male student was 25 years old. These demographics are typical of the cohort normally registered for a Finance Honours programme.

The results of the analysis of respondents' ranking of the perceived relative usefulness of case studies for the development of the 31 individual skills are summarized in Table 3. The summary highlights the five highest-ranked and five lowest-ranked skills. Panel A of the table presents the results on an overall basis for the 51 students, while Panels B and C are gender- and performance-based segregated rankings respectively.[11]

The results show that, overall, the three highest ranked skills, with means ranging from 6.18 to 5.78, all relate to students being exposed to the reality and complexity of the business world. These skills are developing insight into business decision-making in the real world, envisaging alternative solutions to business problems and applying theory to real-world business situations. Three of the five highest ranked questions are part of the Visualization subscale (except for 'several solutions to business problems' and 'facts versus opinions'). The rating by students of exposure to real-world situations as being of great benefit supports Wines et al.'s (1994) listing of the 'realities of exposure to decision-making' as one of the main benefits to be derived from the use of case studies. This benefit is ranked more highly by students than the development of critical thinking skills, which is listed in much of the literature as being a major benefit of the use of case studies (Kimmel, 1995; Campbell and Lewis, 1991; Wines et al., 1994).

The least perceived benefit of case studies is helping students to improve their written communication skills. This outcome is not unexpected, as students were not required to

[11] For a comprehensive list of respondents' mean rankings (including standard deviations) of skills, see Appendix II. Panel A presents the results on an overall basis for all of the respondents, while B and C report gender- and performance-based rankings respectively.

Table 3. Ranking of skills (summarised) by positive impact of case studies on their development

Panel A: All students ($n = 51$)

Rank	Skills[#]	Mean (S.D.)	Extremely useful[##]
1.	Real-world business decision-making	6.18 (0.62)	88.2
2.	Several solutions to business problems	6.18 (0.99)	46.2
3.	Theory application to real-world	5.78 (0.83)	64.7
4.	Facts versus opinions	5.55 (0.83)	56.9
5.	Application of knowledge	5.51 (1.05)	56.9
27.	Organization of data	4.78 (0.92)	23.5
28.	Listening skills	4.73 (1.20)	27.5
29.	Persuasive skills	4.57 (1.15)	21.6
30.	Motivation	4.49 (1.10)	15.7
31.	Written communication skill	4.16 (1.17)	13.8

Panel B: Gender-based ranking ($n = 51$)

Rank			Female (F)*	Male (M)*
F*	M*	Skills[#]	Mean (S.D.)	Mean (S.D.)
1.	2	Real-world business decision-making	6.26 (0.65)	6.13 (0.61)
2.	1	Several solutions to business problems	6.05 (1.03)	6.25 (0.98)
3.	3	Theory application to real-world	5.89 (0.81)	5.72 (0.85)
4.	6	Facts versus opinions	5.79 (0.79)	5.41 (0.84)
5.	6	Application of knowledge	5.68 (0.89)	5.41 (1.13)
27.	30	Persuasive skills	4.42 (1.39)	4.66 (1.00)
28.	18	Active participation	4.42 (1.50)	5.13 (1.16)
29.	12	Pertinent questions	4.32 (1.42)	5.22 (0.91)
30.	31	Written communication skill	4.26 (1.37)	4.09 (1.06)
31.	29	Motivation	4.16 (1.26)	4.69 (0.97)

Panel C: Prior performance-based ranking ($n = 49$)

Rank			Above (A)**	Below (B)**
A**	B**	Skills[#]	Mean (S.D.)	Mean (S.D.)
1.	2	Real-world business decision-making	6.24 (0.66)	6.12 (0.61)
2.	1	Several solutions to business problems	6.24 (1.09)	6.17 (0.82)
3.	4	Theory application to real-world	6.04 (0.61)	5.46 (0.93)
4.	7	Integration of diverse Finance components	5.76 (0.78)	5.21 (1.44)
5.	5	Application of knowledge	5.68 (1.11)	5.29 (1.00)
27.	28	Listening skills	4.84 (1.31)	4.54 (1.10)
28.	17	Ability to synthesize	4.76 (0.78)	5.00 (1.06)
29.	29	Persuasive skills	4.56 (1.29)	4.50 (1.02)
30.	30	Motivation	4.52 (1.16)	4.38 (1.06)
31.	31	Written communication skill	4.16 (1.11)	4.00 (1.18)

[#] The descriptions of the skills in this table are precis of the questions in the questionnaire. Each question is preceded by the words. 'To what extent did the use of case studies . . .' and is followed by a verb. For example, 'To what extent did the use of case studies encourage you to apply your knowledge to new situations?'
[##] The proportion of respondents indicating that they found case studies extremely useful by ticking either 6 or 7 on the Likert scale.
* n(Female) = 19 and n(Male) = 32.
** n(Above average performers) = 25 and n(Below-average performers) = 24.

present their weekly case study presentations in writing. Although each study group was required to prepare one written submission during the course, the results in Panel A of Table 3 suggest that students perceived little relationship between the regular use of case studies and the improvement of their written communication skills.

With respect to gender-based perceived benefits of case studies for developing the 31 desirable skills (Panel B of Table 3), both male and female students agree on the two major benefits of case studies, although the order is reversed, with females ranking 'several solutions to business problems' higher than 'real-world business decision-making.' The least favourably perceived benefits are also similar. The largest difference in rankings is for the question relating to 'pertinent questions,' which is ranked 29th by females, but 12th by males. This low ranking by female students may suggest that they either did not perceive the case study material as encouraging them to ask questions, or that the group structure for discussing cases inhibited them from doing so. The latter scenario is consistent with Brazelton's (1998) finding that female students communicated less in accounting classes than males, although this occurred in lecture classes, rather than in study groups. This finding needs to be examined further.

The results of the performance-based preliminary analysis (Panel C) are broadly similar to the previous gender-based analysis, with both above- and below-average performers agreeing on the two major benefits of case studies (again in reverse order). Both 'theory application to real world' and 'application of knowledge' also featured prominently in the ranking of both groups of students. Both groups rated 'persuasive skills', 'motivation' and 'written communication skill' as the three skills least developed by their use of case studies.

It is noticeable that every skill in Panel A of Table 3 is rated above the midpoint of the response scale, suggesting that students perceive the case method to be capable of developing every skill included in the study. This outcome is not surprising, however, as these skills, and their development, were identified in the literature as being the primary benefits to be derived from the use of case studies (Campbell and Lewis, 1991; Knechel, 1992; Wines *et al.*, 1994; Kimmel, 1995; Hassall *et al.*, 1998).

Substantive statistics

The summarized *M–W U* test results (Table 4, Panel A) indicate that there are statistically significant differences between male and female students' perceptions for four of the potential case study benefits investigated in this study. At the 5% level, males perceive case studies to facilitate the development of critical thinking ability and pertinent questioning more than do females. The latter result is consistent with the exploratory findings reported in Table 3 previously and the findings of Brazelton (1998). At the 10% level, males perceive case studies to facilitate the development of interpretative skills and dealing with uncertainty and ambiguity more than do females. Interpretative skills and critical thinking ability are part of the *problem elaboration* subscale, while the other two questions belong to other subscales.

The *M–W U* test was also employed to investigate potential prior performance-based differences. The results, as presented in Panel B of Table 4, indicate that there are differences in students' perception of case studies' capacity to facilitate the development of three of the individual skills. At the 5% level, below-average students found case studies more beneficial for 'applying theory to the real-world' than did above-average students. They also found case studies more useful for 'applying knowledge' and for 'developing

Table 4. *Mann-Whitney U* test of differences in students' perception of the positive impact of case studies

Panel A: Gender-based differences

Skills	Mean rank		Corrected for ties	
	Female*	Male*	Z	M–W sig. (p)
Interpretation skills	21.47	28.69	− 1.774	0.076[c]
Critical thinking ability	20.63	29.19	− 2.106	0.035[b]
Pertinent questions	19.61	29.80	− 2.451	0.014[b]
Deal with uncertainty and ambiguity	21.34	28.77	− 1.798	0.072[c]

Panel B: Performance-based differences

Skills	Mean rank		Corrected for ties	
	Above**	Below**	Z	M–W sig. (p)
Theory application to real-world	20.17	29.64	− 2.481	0.013[b]
Application of knowledge	21.92	27.96	− 1.580	0.074[c]
Ability to summarize information	22.15	27.74	− 1.469	0.092[c]

* n(female) = 19 and n(male) = 32.
** n(above-average performers) = 25 and n(below-average performers) = 24.
b and c indicate that differences are significant at the 5% and 10% levels respectively.

the ability to summarize information' at the 10% level. These results are not consistent with Weil *et al.*'s (1999) findings, which found no differences in perception of the use of case studies based on prior academic performance. The results are not necessarily conflicting, however, as the Weil *et al.* (1999) study based its finding on a single question about the overall value, rather than on 31 questions about specific benefits, of case studies.

Students were asked to choose and rank the three most valuable benefits of case studies from the list of 31 possibilities. Their responses were then summarized according to the eight subscales identified previously in the study. The results, as reported in Table 5, are consistent with the mean ratings of each benefit of case studies reported earlier and indicate that students perceive case studies to be most useful in assisting them to visualise real-world business issues. Visualization is followed by help in dealing with uncertainty as the next major benefit of case studies, and then by help in consolidating and integrating students' knowledge of finance. The least frequently ranked benefits of case studies relate to improving students' communication and data exploration skills.

Results of a *Friedman* test (Panel A of Table 6) indicate statistically significant differences in students' perceptions of the efficacy of case studies in developing the eight subscales of skills at the 1% significance level. This is a strong indicator of students' abilities to differentiate between the different types of skills and the degree to which case studies are perceived to be useful for the development of each subscale of skills. In other words, students are perceptively conscious of the level and variety of benefits they obtained from their involvement with this mode of course delivery.

Results of statistical tests to explore the possible influence of gender on students' perceptions of the sub-scaled benefits of case studies are presented in Table 6 (Panel B).

Table 5. Student mean responses and rankings of the three most valuable aspects of case studies according to subscales ($n = 51$)

Subscales	Mean	Most valuable			Second most valuable			Third most valuable		
		Frequency*		Rank	Frequency*		Rank	Frequency		Rank
Visualization (VISUAL)	5.61	24	(49)	1	22	(45)	1	12	(25)	1
Dealing with uncertainty (DEAL_UNC)	5.40	3	(6)	5	6	(12)	2	12	(25)	1
Consolidation/Integration (CONS_INT)	5.26	8	(16)	2	6	(12)	2	7	(15)	3
Problem elaboration (PROB_ELB)	5.10	5	(10)	3	6	(12)	2	5	(10)	5
Data Exploration (DATAEXP)	4.98	1	(2)	8	0	(0)	8	1	(2)	8
Judgement (JUDGEMEN)	4.97	3	(6)	5	2	(4)	7	3	(6)	6
Active participation (ACTPART)	4.84	4	(8)	4	4	(8)	5	6	(13)	4
Communication skills (COM_SKI)	4.48	1	(2)	7	3	(6)	6	2	(4)	7
Total		49	(100)		49	(100)		49	(100)	

* Numbers in brackets indicates percentages. Percentages may not add up to 100 due to rounding errors.

Two significant differences are reported; active participation at the 5% level and problem elaboration at the 10% level. In both cases, namely, facilitating active participation in the learning process and assisting with the development of problem elaboration skills, male students rank the usefulness of case studies higher than females. The finding with respect to active participation confirms the study's findings for female students' low rankings for 'pertinent questions', as reported in Tables 3 (Panel B) and 4 (Panel A), as this skill falls within the 'active participation' subscale.

Although male students (mean = 5.38) perceive the use of case studies as a learning method to be more valuable than females (mean = 5.26), the difference between the genders is not statistically significant. This is not consistent with Weil *et al.* (1999), who found a significant difference between male and female perceptions of the value of case studies as a learning method.

No significant differences were found between students who scored below- and above-average, in their prior undergraduate paper, on any of the eight subscales (see Panel C of Table 6). This is consistent with a Spearman's rank correlation test conducted (not reported here), which found no significant correlation between any of the subscales and prior performance results, as well as with Weil *et al.* (1999). These results suggest that caution needs to be exercised in interpreting the results of the earlier analysis on individual skills reported in Panel B of Table 4. The findings here indicate that prior performance, as proxied in this study, has little or no association with students' perceptions of the development of skills, when these are aggregated into meaningful subscales.

Table 6. Tests of differences in students' mean rating of sub-scaled benefits of case studies

Panel A: *Friedman's* test of overall differences

Subscales	Mean rank	
DATAEXP	3.88	
ACTPART	3.65	
CONS_INT	5.08	
PROB_ELB	4.54	
JUDGEMEN	3.84	
VISUAL	6.68	
DEAL_UNC	5.88	
COM_SKI	2.45	
Test statistics		
Chi-square	111.262 (df = 7)	Significance 0.00[a]

Panel B: *M-W U* test of differences by gender

Subscales	Means		Corrected for ties	
	Female (n = 19)	Male (n = 32)	Z	M–W Sig. (p)
DATAEXP	4.9	5.0	−0.52	0.603
ACTPART	4.4	5.1	−1.97	0.049[b]
CONS_INT	5.3	5.2	−0.01	0.992
PROB_ELB	4.8	5.3	−1.67	0.096[c]
JUDGEMEN	4.9	5.0	−0.27	0.791
VISUAL	5.7	5.6	−0.71	0.484
DEAL_UNC	5.3	5.5	−1.04	0.308
COM_SKI	4.4	4.5	−0.23	0.826
Value of the case study	5.26	5.38	−0.21	0.981

Panel C: *M-W U* test of differences by prior academic performance

Subscales	Means		Corrected for ties	
	Above (n = 24)	Below (n = 25)	Z	M–W Sig. (p)
DATAEXP	4.9	4.7	−1.17	0.24
ACTPART	4.8	4.9	−3.8	0.70
CONS_INT	5.2	5.3	0.00	1.00
PROB_ELB	5.0	5.1	−0.58	0.56
JUDGEMEN	4.9	5.0	0.000	1.00
VISUAL	5.5	5.7	−1.508	0.32
DEAL_UNC	5.4	54	−0.28	0.78
COM_SKI	4.3	4.5	−1.2	0.23
Value of the case study	5.2	5.5	−0.97	0.32

a, *b* and *c* indicate that differences are significant at the 1, 5 and 10% levels respectively.
DATAEXP = Data Exploration; ACTPART = Active participation; CONS_INT = Consolidation/Integration; PROB_ELB = Problem elaboration; JUDGEMEN = Judgement; VISUAL = Visualization; DEAL_UNC = Dealing with uncertainty; COM_SKI = Communication skills.

Summary and conclusion

The results of the study indicate that, according to students' perceptions, the use of case studies enhances student learning by helping to develop certain thinking skills and provide benefits identified in the literature (Campbell and Lewis, 1991; Wines *et al.*, 1994; Kimmel, 1995; Hassall *et al.*, 1998). The major perceived benefit of the use of case studies is in the way in which they expose students to real-world complexity, particularly with respect to decision-making. Three of the five highest perceived benefits fall into the 'visualization' subscale. These benefits all relate to the nexus between theory, practice and the real world. This result validates one of the primary reasons for the course lecturer introducing a case-based stream into the course, namely, to allow students to integrate and to apply their knowledge in solving real-world problems.

The second most highly ranked benefit is in respect of 'several solutions to business problems'. This benefit's high ranking by students is confirmed by the high ranking of the subscale 'dealing with uncertainty', which is ranked second after 'visualization'. The 'dealing with uncertainty' subscale contains questions relating to incomplete information, ambiguity in information and multiple possible solutions.

Although the rankings of the benefits of case studies by gender are similar for males and females, some significant differences are found in the study. For example, at the 5% level, males perceive that case studies facilitate the development of critical thinking ability and pertinent questioning more than do females. The same result applies to the perception of case studies' benefits for the development of 'interpretation skills' and 'dealing with uncertainty and ambiguity', albeit at a weaker (10%) level.

In respect of prior academic performance, three statistically significant differences are found in student perceptions. At the 5% level, below-average students find case studies more beneficial for 'applying theory to the real-world' than do above-average students. At the 10% level, below-average students find case studies more useful for the 'application of knowledge', and for developing the 'ability to summarise information'. While these results suggest that case studies may provide more benefits for below-average students than for above-average students, they should be treated with caution. This is so because, even though the entering grades of students into the Honours programme are spread over a wide range, it would be unusual to classify any of the students entering the programme as being below-average. In addition to this, no significant differences are found on the eight subscales based on students' prior performance.

When the hypothesized benefits of case studies are organized into sub-scales by means of factor analysis, 'visualization' is ranked as the most valuable benefit. This is consistent with the earlier results reported, as specific benefits, such as 'real-world business decision-making' and 'application of knowledge,' which consistently receive high rankings by students, are components of the 'visualization' subscale. This provides strong validation for the aim of Hassall *et al.* (1998) for using case studies, namely, developing and applying an integrated approach to problem solving and providing students with an understanding of the problems inherent in applying discipline-specific knowledge to practical situations.

A significant difference between male and female perceptions is found for the subscales in respect of 'active participation.' This is consistent with females previously ranking 'pertinent questioning' – a component of 'active participation' – much lower than males as a benefit to be derived from the use of case studies. The significant difference for 'active participation' is again reflected by the significant correlation which it has with student perceptions of the overall value of case studies as a learning method.

The results suggest that case studies, as perceived by students, do indeed provide learning benefits. However, on the basis of the findings of the study, accounting educators considering the use of case studies need to reflect carefully on their reasons for using them and the relationship of this educational tool to the course objectives (Bonner, 1999) on the one hand, and the gender and capability profile of the class on the other.

Suggestions for further research

There are possible limitations associated with the current study. Some of these provide scope for further research and extension of the literature in this area. For example, as the study respondents selected themselves, it could be argued that the responses are favourably biased towards case study methods. This need not, however, reduce the validity of the findings, particularly the relative rankings of the perceived benefits of the use of case studies, as some benefits are clearly perceived by students to be more effectively provided by case studies than others. In addition, the statistical differences which emerge in the study provide clear evidence of student preferences across the skills developed by case studies – even if their overall responses are biased favourably towards the use of case studies. Nevertheless, the issue of self-selection in studies of this nature is worthy of further investigation.

At least two findings of the study stand out as deserving consideration for further research. One is the suggestion that below-average students benefit more from the use of case studies than above-average students with respect to three specific skills (namely, applying theory to the real-world, applying knowledge in general and summarizing information). If this is indeed so, then the use of case studies should be encouraged as a tool to assist under-performing students develop these skills. The other finding that can benefit from further study is that females showed less favourable perceptions towards the use of case studies than males. Whether attributable to learning style differences, study group dynamics and/or other factors, further information is needed.

Every skill in Panel A of Table 3 is rated above the midpoint of the response scale, suggesting that the case method is capable of developing every skill included in the study. Although this finding confirms the benefits of case studies propounded in the literature, future researchers may wish to design studies that more clearly distinguish between skills on the high- and low-benefit ends of the scale.

This study has not examined the impact of personality (Hutchinson and Gul, 1997), culture and learning style preferences (Fatt, 1995; Auyeung and Sands, 1996) on students' perceptions about the benefits of case studies. It has also not considered the challenging question of whether the benefits of case study usage are in fact being obtained by students, or are merely perceived by them as being obtained. These are topics for future researchers to explore.

Acknowledgements

The authors wish to thank Associate Professor Trevor Wegner, of the University of Cape Town, for his assistance with the design of the research questionnaire and the data capture.

Thanks are also due to Shireen Zaharudin for her research assistance. We would also like to thank the two anonymous reviewers for their very useful comments and suggestions.

References

Accounting Education Change Commission (AECC) (1990) Objectives of education for accountants: Position Statement No. 1. *Issues in Accounting Education* **5**(2), 307–12.

Auyeung, P. and Sands, J. (1996) A cross cultural study of the learning style of accounting students. *Accounting and Finance* **36**, 261–74.

Barkman, A.I. (1998) Teaching and Educational Note: The use of live cases in the accounting information systems course. *Journal of Accounting Education* **16**(3/4), 517–24.

Bonk, C.J. and Smith, G.S. (1998) Alternative instructional strategies for creative and critical thinking in the accounting curriculum. *Journal of Accounting Education* **16**(2), 261–93.

Bonner, S.E. (1999) Choosing teaching methods based on learning objectives: an integrative framework. *Issues in Accounting Education* **14**(1), 11–39.

Brazelton, J.K. (1998) Implications for women in accounting: some preliminary evidence regarding gender communication. *Issues in Accounting Education* **13**(3), 509–30.

Campbell, J.E. and Lewis, W.F. (1991) Using cases in accounting classes. *Issues in Accounting Education* **6**(2), 276–283.

Carpenter, V., Friar, S. and Lipe, M. (1993) Evidence on the performance of accounting students: race, gender, and expectations. *Issues in Accounting Education* **8**, 1–17.

Doran, B.M., Bouillon, M.L. and Smith, C.G. (1991) Determinants of student performance in Accounting Principles I and II. *Issues in Accounting Education* **6**(1), 74–84.

Easton, G. (1992) *Learning From Case Studies*. Hemel Hempstead: Prentice-Hall.

Fatt, J.P.T. (1995) Learning styles in accounting education. *Asian Review of Accounting* **3**(1), 25–58.

Friedlan, J.M. (1995) The effects of different teaching approaches on students' perceptions of the skills needed for success in accounting courses and by practicing accountants. *Issues in Accounting Education* **10**(1), 47–63.

Fulmer, W.E. (1992) Using cases in management development programmes. *Journal of Management Development* **11**(3), 33–37.

Hanks, G. and Shivaswamy, M. (1985) Academic performance in accounting: is there a gender gap? *Journal of Business Education* (January), 154–56.

Hassall, T., Lewis, S. and Broadbent, M. (1998) Teaching and learning using case studies: a teaching note. *Accounting Education: an international journal* **7**(4), 325–334.

Hutchinson, M. and Gul, F.A. (1997) The interactive effects of extroversion/introversion traits and collectivism/individualism cultural beliefs on student group learning preferences. *Journal of Accounting Education* **15**(1), 95–107.

Johnstone, K.M. and Biggs, S.F. (1998) Problem-based learning: introduction, analysis, and accounting curricula implications. *Journal of Accounting Education* **16**(3/4), 407–27.

Kimmel, P.A. (1995) Framework for incorporating critical thinking into accounting education. *Journal of Accounting Education* **13**(3), 299–318.

Knechel, W.R. (1992) Using the case method in accounting instruction. *Issues in Accounting Education* **7**(2), 205–17.

Libby, P.A. (1991) Barriers to using cases in accounting education. *Issues in Accounting Education* **6**(2), 193–213.

Mutchler, J., Turner, J. and Williams, D. (1987) The performance of female vs. male accounting students. *Issues in Accounting Education* **2**(1), 103–11.

Nunnally, J.C. (1978) *Psychometric Theory*. Second edition, New York: McGraw-Hill Book Company.

Perspectives on Education: Capabilities for Success in the Accounting Profession (The White Paper) (1989) New York: Arthur Andersen & Co., Arthur Young, Coopers & Lybrand, Deloitte Haskins & Sells, Ernst & Whinney, Peat Marwick Main & Co., Price Waterhouse, and Touche Ross.

Saudagaran, S.M. (1996) The first course in accounting: an innovative approach. *Issues in Accounting Education* **11**(1), 83–94.

Schwartz, P.L. and Heath, C.J. (1994) Students' perceptions of course outcomes and learning styles in case-based courses in a traditional medical school. *Academic Medicine: Journal of the Association of American Medical Colleges* **69**(6), 507.

Shapiro, B.P. (1984) *Hints for Case Teaching*. Boston, MA: Harvard Business School Publishing Division.

Stoneham, P. (1995) For and against the case method. *European Management Journal* **13**(2), 230–32.

Tyson, T. (1989) Grade performance in introductory accounting courses: why female students outperform males. *Issues in Accounting Education* **4**, 153–160.

Weil, S., Laswad, F., Frampton, C. and Radford, J. (1999) Cultural and other influences on student perceptions of the use of case studies and study groups in management accounting. Discussion Paper No. 62, Commerce Division, Lincoln University, New Zealand.

Wines, G., Carnegie, G. Boyce, G. and Gibson, R. (1994) *Using Case Studies in the Teaching of Accounting*. Deakin University, Victoria: Australian Society of Certified Practising Accountants.

Appendix I: Extract from survey questionnaire: The usefulness of case studies for learning

We appreciate your help in completing this questionnaire on students' attitudes towards and experiences with case studies.

The data collected in this questionnaire are entirely confidential.

Optional

Name: _____ _____ _

Providing your name is optional. If you do, the research will be able to correlate the survey findings with performance.

The survey findings will NOT identify any student by name.

PART 1: GENERAL BACKGROUND

(Please tick the correct box, or insert the information requested, where appropriate)

1. **Gender:**

☐ Female   ☐ Male

2. **Age** _____ **(in years)**

3. **Language:**

(a) Is English your first language (that is, do you use it at home)?

☐ Yes ☐ No

(b) If English is not your first language, please indicate whether it is your second, third or fourth language _____ _

4. **Results**

Please state your percentage for: Finance I _____

Finance II _____

PART 2: THE USE OF CASE STUDIES IN THE HONOURS PROGRAMME

The following questions relate to your opinions about the use of case studies in the Honours programme only. In answering them, please ignore the impact that the group process (that is, working in study groups) might have had on your perceptions. This part of the questionnaire is concerned only with assessing your opinions about the usefulness of the case study approach as a learning method.

For purposes of the questionnaire, a *case study* is defined as:

an unstructured academic assignment, containing numerous issues, which requires information to be analysed and organised, in an attempt to evaluate and select from alternative courses of action

We would like your opinion on each of the following statements. Please choose a number on the following scale to indicate the *strength of your preference* and enter it in the box next to each question. Please treat the distances between the points on the scale as equal.

1	2	3	4	5	6	7
Not at all		Moderate			Extensively	

To what extent did the use of case studies . . .

5. ☐ improve your *judgement skills* (defined as *identifying and choosing between available alternatives)?*

6. ☐ help you to integrate your understanding of the different components of the course?

7. ☐ help you to develop skills in interpreting (defined as the ability to understand and decipher) data?

8. ☐ help you to develop your ability to think critically about issues?

9. ☐ improve your analytical skills (defined as the ability to think in a logical and enquiring manner)?

10. ☐ develop your ability to synthesize (combine) the essential elements of a given situation?

11. ☐ develop your listening skills?

12. ☐ help you to consolidate your prior knowledge of the discipline?

13. ☐ help you to develop your problem-solving skills?

14. ☐ enable you to take decisions with incomplete information?

15. ☐ develop your skill in evaluating ideas?

16. ☐ increase your motivation to study the course?

17. ☐ develop your skill in asking pertinent questions?

18. ☐ encourage you to be an active participant in the learning process?

19. ☐ encourage you to consider the perspectives of the different parties (for example, managers, shareholders, trade unions) involved in the case?

20. ☐ give you insight into the realities and difficulties of decision-making in business?

21. ☐ develop your written communication skills?

22. ☐ help you relate theory to real-life practice?

23. ☐ encourage you to apply your knowledge to new situations?

24. ☐ give you insight into practical business operations?

25. ☐ develop your ability to identify the relevant data in a case?

26. ☐ develop your ability to organize data?

27. ☐ develop your problem identification skills?

28. ☐ encourage you to think conceptually?

29. ☐ encourage you to distinguish facts from opinions?

30. ☐ develop your persuasive skills?

31. ☐ teach you how to deal with situations involving uncertainty and ambiguity?

32. ☐ develop your ability to summarize the available information?

33. ☐ teach you that there is seldom only one correct solution to business problems?

34. ☐ teach you to integrate your technical knowledge of the discipline?

35. ☐ encourage you to take responsibility for your own learning?

36. From the preceding questions (5 to 35), please select and enter below the three most valuable benefits of the case study method to you. Insert the number of the most

valuable benefit next to number 1, the number of the second most valuable benefit next to number 2 and the number of the third most valuable benefit next to number 3.

1. _____

2. _____

3. _____

Please use the following scale to answer the next question.

1	2	3	4	5	6	7
Not value		Some value			High value	

37. ☐ How valuable did you find the use of case studies as a learning method in the Honours programme?

38. Are there any other learning benefits, not mentioned in the questionnaire, that you gained from the use of case studies in the Honours programme? If so, please specify.

_____

_____

_____

_____

Appendix II: Ranking of skills (all) by positive impact of case studies on their development

Panel A: All students ($n = 51$)

Rank	Skills[#]	Mean (S.D.)	Extremely useful[##]
1.	Real-world business decision-making	6.18 (0.62)	88.2
2.	Several solutions to business problems	6.18 (0.99)	46.2
3.	Theory application to real-world	5.78 (0.83)	64.7
4.	Facts versus opinions	5.55 (0.83)	56.9
5.	Application of knowledge	5.51 (1.05)	56.9
6.	Integration of diverse components of the course	5.50 (1.16)	58.8
7.	Different parties' perspectives	5.35 (1.11)	49.0
8.	Insight into business functioning	5.31 (1.07)	50.9
9.	Critical thinking ability	5.22 (0.94)	37.2
10.	Analytical skills	5.16 (1.01)	43.1
11.	Identify relevant data	5.14 (0.85)	33.3
11.	Decision-making with incomplete information	5.14 (1.10)	35.3
11.	Consolidate prior knowledge	5.14 (1.44)	47.0
14.	Responsibility for own learning	5.12 (1.19)	35.3
15.	Conceptual thinking	5.02 (0.84)	29.5
15.	Skill in evaluating ideas	5.02 (0.95)	29.4
15.	Interpretation skills	5.02 (0.97)	33.4

18.	Problem-solving skills	5.01	(0.88)	27.5
19.	Judgement skills	5.00	(0.77)	27.5
20.	Technical knowledge	4.98	(1.35)	37.2
21.	Problem-identification skill	4.96	(1.15)	33.3
22.	Ability to summarize information	4.92	(1.02)	25.5
22.	Ability to synthesize	4.92	(0.93)	23.5
24.	Deal with uncertainty and ambiguity	4.88	(1.16)	31.4
24.	Pertinent questions	4.88	(1.19)	33.4
26.	Active participation	4.86	(1.33)	33.3
27.	Organization of data	4.78	(0.92)	23.5
28.	Listening skills	4.73	(1.20)	27.5
29.	Persuasive skills	4.57	(1.15)	21.6
30.	Motivation	4.49	(1.10)	15.7
31.	Written communication skill	4.16	(1.17)	13.8

Panel B: Gender-based ranking ($n = 51$)

Rank			Female (F)*	Male (M)*
F*	M*	Skills[#]	Mean (S.D.)	Mean (S.D.)
1.	2.	Real-world business decision-making	6.26 (0.65)	6.13 (0.61)
2.	1.	Several solutions to business problems	6.05 (1.03)	6.25 (0.98)
3.	3.	Theory application to real-world	5.89 (0.81)	5.72 (0.85)
4.	6.	Facts versus opinions	5.79 (0.79)	5.41 (0.84)
5.	6.	Application of knowledge	5.68 (0.89)	5.41 (1.13)
6.	4.	Integration of diverse components of the course	5.53 (1.12)	5.50 (1.19)
7.	9.	Insight into business functioning	5.37 (0.96)	5.28 (1.14)
8.	8.	Different parties' perspectives	5.32 (0.82)	5.37 (1.26)
9.	21.	Decision-making with incomplete information	5.26 (1.05)	5.06 (1.13)
10.	20.	Consolidate prior knowledge	5.21 (1.62)	5.09 (1.35)
11.	26.	Ability to synthesize	5.11 (1.10)	4.81 (0.82)
12.	11.	Analytical skills	5.00 (0.88)	5.25 (1.08)
13.	12.	Identify relevant data	5.00 (0.88)	5.22 (0.83)
14.	24.	Problem-identification skill	5.00 (1.20)	4.94 (1.13)
15.	21.	Problem-solving skills	4.95 (0.97)	5.06 (0.84)
16.	25.	Ability to summarize information	4.95 (0.97)	4.91 (1.06)
17.	10.	Responsibility for own learning	4.89 (1.05)	5.25 (1.27)
18.	5.	Critical thinking ability	4.84 (1.01)	5.44 (0.84)
19.	19.	Judgement skills	4.79 (0.79)	5.12 (0.75)
20.	15.	Skill in evaluating ideas	4.79 (1.03)	5.16 (0.88)
21.	15.	Conceptual thinking	4.79 (0.79)	5.16 (0.85)
22.	12.	Interpretation skills	4.68 (1.06)	5.22 (0.87)
23.	15.	Technical knowledge	4.68 (1.45)	5.16 (1.27)
24.	26.	Organisation of data	4.63 (1.07)	4.88 (0.83)
25.	28.	Listening skills	4.58 (1.02)	4.81 (1.31)
26.	21.	Deal with uncertainty and ambiguity	4.58 (1.12)	5.06 (1.16)
27.	30.	Persuasive skills	4.42 (1.39)	4.66 (1.00)
28.	18.	Active participation	4.42 (1.50)	5.13 (1.16)
29.	12.	Pertinent questions	4.32 (1.42)	5.22 (0.91)
30.	31.	Written communication skill	4.26 (1.37)	4.09 (1.06)
31.	29.	Motivation	4.16 (1.26)	4.69 (0.97)

Panel C: Prior Performance-based ranking ($n = 49$)

Rank			Above (A)**	Below (B)**
A**	B**	Skills#	Mean (S.D.)	Mean (S.D.)
1.	2.	Real-world business decision-making	6.24 (0.66)	6.12 (0.61)
2.	1.	Several solutions to business problems	6.24 (1.09)	6.17 (0.82)
3.	4.	Theory application to real-world	6.04 (0.61)	5.46 (0.93)
4.	7.	Integration of diverse Finance components	5.76 (0.78)	5.21 (1.44)
5.	5.	Application of knowledge	5.68 (1.11)	5.29 (1.00)
6.	3.	Facts versus opinions	5.60 (0.87)	5.50 (0.83)
7.	6.	Different parties' perspectives	5.44 (1.19)	5.25 (1.07)
8.	10.	Insight into business functioning	5.44 (1.04)	5.17 (1.13)
9.	11.	Critical thinking ability	5.24 (0.72)	5.13 (1.15)
10.	16.	Analytical skills	5.20 (0.91)	5.04 (1.12)
11.	13.	Identify relevant data	5.20 (0.91)	5.08 (0.78)
12.	12.	Consolidate prior knowledge	5.16 (1.55)	5.12 (1.42)
13.	24.	Problem-identification skill	5.16 (1.03)	4.71 (1.27)
14.	25.	Ability to summarize information	5.12 (0.88)	4.67 (1.13)
15.	18.	Interpretation skills	5.08 (0.86)	4.96 (1.12)
16.	20.	Problem-solving skills	5.08 (0.76)	4.92 (1.02)
17.	20.	Technical knowledge	5.08 (1.19)	4.92 (1.56)
18.	8.	Decision-making with incomplete information	5.04 (0.89)	5.21 (1.32)
19.	18.	Skill in evaluating ideas	5.04 (0.93)	4.96 (1.00)
20.	9.	Responsibility for own learning	5.04 (1.34)	5.21 (1.10)
21.	25.	Active participation	5.00 (1.26)	4.67 (1.43)
22.	22.	Deal with uncertainty and ambiguity	4.96 (1.06)	4.79 (1.32)
23.	14.	Judgement skills	4.92 (0.81)	5.08 (0.78)
24.	23.	Pertinent questions	4.92 (1.08)	4.75 (1.29)
25.	25.	Organization of data	4.92 (0.91)	4.67 (0.96)
26.	15.	Conceptual thinking	4.92 (0.91)	5.08 (0.78)
27.	28.	Listening skills	4.84 (1.31)	4.54 (1.10)
28.	17.	Ability to synthesize	4.76 (0.78)	5.00 (1.06)
29.	29.	Persuasive skills	4.56 (1.29)	4.50 (1.02)
30.	30.	Motivation	4.52 (1.16)	4.38 (1.06)
31.	31.	Written communication skill	4.16 (1.11)	4.00 (1.18)

The descriptions of the skills in this table are precis of the questions in the questionnaire. Each question is preceded by the words. 'To what extent did the use of case studies . . .' and is followed by a verb. For example, 'To what extent did the use of case studies encourage you to apply your knowledge to new situations?'
The proportion of respondents indicating that they found case studies extremely useful by ticking either 6 or 7 on the Likert scale.
* n(Female) = 19 and n(Male) = 32.
** n(Above average performers) = 25 and n(Below-average performers) = 24.

Accountability of accounting educators and the rhythm of the university: resistance strategies for postmodern blues[1]

RUSSELL CRAIG[1] and JOEL AMERNIC[2]

[1]*Australian National University, Australia and* [2]*University of Toronto, Canada*

Abstract

This paper conducts a wide-ranging and critical interpretative review of the accountability of university accounting educators. The 'idea' of the university is reviewed briefly. Particular attention is given to analysing the implication of accounting and auditing in the ravaging of universities; and to the effect of the *market model* on what we teach, how we teach and how we ought to discharge our accountability, as educators, to society. We explore the implications of regarding 'university accountability' as *ideograph* and *persuasive definition* and draw upon Whitehead (1929/1957) to propose a *re*definition of the descriptive meaning of 'university accountability'. Whereas the principal focus is discipline-specific (accounting education), the central thesis and the themes pursued have strong relevance for university educators in all disciplines. We reflect upon four inter related contemporary issues affecting accounting educators: *globalization, market force hysteria, metaphor and the university as a market-driven business*, and *Internet technology*. We contend that accounting education should focus less on *technical menus* and more on *social critique*; argue that the response of accounting educators to the pedagogical demands of the Internet age has been inadequate; and profess the view that accounting educators might better discharge their accountability by adopting an approach to curriculum development and education which is akin to *critical action learning*.

---

[1] This paper is not fashioned in the usual academic format. It evolved substantively as a series of email interchanges between the two authors (one located in Australia and one in Canada) in the first half of 2001, and represents (according to one of the emails) '... a collaborative journey of mutually challenging self-discovery and articulation. A serendipitously compiled paper: the product of many years of collaboration, of introspection as well as "reaching out." It is "research" in the deep sense of the word, re-searching how we who are members of the accounting professoriate should live our lives. It's about thinking how we can fulfill the role of accounting professors in a more-or-less absurd world.'

> To us, education is a public trust, not a business; knowledge is a gift to give, not a commodity to sell; schools are communities, not corporations; and students are citizens, not consumers.[2]

The complicity of accounting and audit in the ravaging of 'universities'

Here we reflect upon the behaviour of universities and their accounting educators in coping with the demands of a postmodern society. Particular attention is drawn to the need for university teaching to offer 'resistance' to dominant ideologies of 'the market', through the embracing of methods of 'social critique'.

To help understand and assess our arguments, readers should be mindful, at the outset, of the general tenor of the (alleged) effects of postmodernism on society and universities. These effects, and the 'paradox of free will' and the 'cultural prison' that accompany them, have been captured strikingly by Hackney (1999). They deserve immediate scrutiny.

Hackney contends, rightly in our view, that postmodernism:

> . . . has focused our attention on the *paradox of free will*. We are all at the same time products of our culture and also authors of that culture. We are trapped within our particular context of time and place, within the imposed meanings of our race, class, gender and other given traits; yet that *cultural prison* is constantly being renovated, continuously transformed by human thought and action. We are thus simultaneously subjects and objects of culture (1999, p. 978, emphasis added).

Hackney continues by arguing that universities (and we include here university accounting educators) are caught by this same paradox, one that:

> . . . is profoundly conservative in that it is the guardian of the accumulated store of human knowledge; it is profoundly radical because it is the institutionalized instigator of cultural change. The university processes students so as to fit them for service in society as it is, but it also rips those same students out of their comfortable cultural moorings and equips them to choose their own values and their own identities. (1999, p. 978)[3]

Universities, in which we who 'profess' reside, are citizens of perilous times,[4] afflicted by a virulent strain of the 'postmodern blues'. Universities show the symptoms of conflicting values, ideologies, and demands, thereby creating a sort of professorial version of *teenage angst*, along with attendant trauma to body and soul.[5] Ironically, members of the

---

[2] British Columbia Teachers' Federation President David Chudnovsky, protesting outside the 'World Education Market' conference, Vancouver BC, 2000. (Cited by J. Lyon, Conference showcases education in business. *The Australian* 31 May, p. 34.)

[3] Bean (1998, p. 500) views this paradoxical state thus: 'Postmodernism, whatever its benefits in making us more self-critical in our thinking and more aware of hierarchies and power imbalances in the academy, has not made us more secure in our identity as faculty members'.

[4] Most times are 'perilous', at least to a degree, for those who live through them. But it is the sea-change, in our times, arising from the groundswell of moves to confound the very idea of the 'university', that has special discomfort for us.

[5] The phrase 'trauma to body and soul' is not merely a rhetorical flourish. There is now evidence of the impact of our perilous times on stress levels and the general well-being of those who work in universities. Bean (1998, p. 502) writes that in an academia in which '[r]est, reflection, and regeneration are disdained', 'workaholism is a virtue' even though it 'is a pathology'. Barry *et al.* (2001, p. 95) note the growth of 'a "macho" culture of

accounting professoriate seem to bear a rather unique *mea culpa* (at least in a class sense), since the source of many of the significant pernicious features of the ravaging demands of universities on their (accounting and other) professors may be traced to . . . *accounting*! Indeed, mathematician Sir Michael Atiyah, President of the Royal Society of London, complained (justifiably, in our view) that universities have become 'dominated by accountancy procedures and measured by the products they produce' (1992, pp. 157–58). Atiyah cited the President of the British Academy as expressing the view that the 'great divide' in universities was 'not between the arts and sciences but between the scholars and the accountants'; and that 'the great accountancy edifice' was one in which we could have 'little confidence'. As *accounting scholars* it is incumbent upon us not to ignore such views.

In similar vein to Atiyah, anthropologists Shore and Wright (1999) are stingingly critical of the 'audit culture' in (British) higher education.[6] This 'culture' drags with it such jargon as 'quality assurance', 'transparency', 'value for money', 'benchmarks' and 'league tables'. Shore and Wright argue that practices of audit and accountability, now imposed rampantly in higher education, are bizarre perversions with many adverse outcomes: the 'audit culture functions as a political technology', with attendant 'damaging effects on trust', and the meanings of words such as 'quality' and 'performance' are subject to 'radical transformation' (pp. 565–66). The new 'audit culture' accountability replaces a system based on 'autonomy' with one that is argued to be 'coercive', 'disabling', and characterized by 'crude, quantifiable and "inspectable" templates' (Shore and Wright, 1999, p. 557). And, as if referring to some dreaded social virus, Shore and Wright claim that

> The cumulative effect of these audit technologies has been to create a self-referential and self-reinforcing system from which it is very difficult to remain unaffected. As audit spreads to new domains, it acquires momentum for colonizing yet more areas of society. The audit phenomenon thus has a dynamic of its own and, like Frankenstein's monster, once created, is very hard to control. (1999, p. 570)[7]

Shore and Wright suggest the following laudable remit: 'What is needed is a different way of thinking about accountability, one that restores trust and autonomy . . . that uses qualitative, multiple and local measures, and is based on public dialogue' (1999, p. 571).

---

workaholism' amongst academics. Menzies (with Newson, 2001) contends that the global corporate economy and its allied digital lifeworld create an environment in which academics are 'run off their feet' (p. A3). Whilst not denying the privileged position of (many) academics relative to other types of workers, it seems fair to conclude that even academics (especially those under short-term and also pre-tenure contracts) live to at least some degree lives ruled by Bean's 'pathology'.

[6] Such a culture is not the unique preserve of the British: it is characteristic of many national university systems. Australia, for example, has established the 'Australian Universities Quality Agency'. It employs 'academic audit officers' to conduct 'regular audits of Australian universities' and to draft 'fair and rigorous public audit reports' (Advertisement, *The Australian* 18 April 2001, p. 32). For an overview of university 'quality assessment' in 14 countries, see Brennan and Shah (2000), who write that 'the changes taking place as a result [of assessment regimes] are as much to do with power and values as they are to do with quality' (p. 332).

[7] See also Power (1997).

So, as *accounting* members of the university community, we seem to bear a somewhat special duty to pursue Shore and Wright's remit, a task to which we now turn.[8]

The 'idea of a university' and accountability frameworks

Universities are important institutions in society. They have occupied 'a special place in *social imagery* as Ivory Towers inhabited by scholars at liberty to pursue knowledge in a rigorous and critical way, engaging in the independence of means and mind . . . that comes from financial autonomy and intellectual freedom' (Barry *et al.*, 2001, p. 88, emphasis added). They have evolved over time, exist for multiple reasons and fill roles that are conceived in a wide variety of ways.

There is an extensive body of literature, much of it conflicting, about the university, its purpose and its functioning.[9] Indeed, the word 'university' has no standard usage, and is remarkably malleable. Its meanings include: *for-profit corporation training centres* (see Meister, 1994), *on-line niche accredited degree-granting e-schools or virtual universities*,[10] *tertiary institutions with an exclusivist ideology* (for example, Bob Jones University in the USA, brought to prominence in 2001 during President George W. Bush's cabinet selection), *tertiary institutions with strong business ties* (Polster, 1998), *academic production lines on the model of the McUniversity* (Parker and Jary, 1995), and (perhaps yet, at least a bit) *tertiary institutions that still evoke the 'idea of a university'* (with apologies to the memory of Cardinal Newman). This article is concerned principally with this last-mentioned type of university. In order to distinguish it from the others, we will refer to it as the 'University.'

We acknowledge that there are wide and disparate views regarding the roles of the University.[11] But one rough constant in the variety of opinion about Universities (and the accounting educators within them) is that they should operate in some loose (and often

---

[8] Bean (1998, p. 497) makes the perversity of this *accounting language* plain: 'How do we talk about higher education now? This is the language I hear: efficiency, productivity, technology, credit hours generated, grants with overhead received, accountability, assessment, competition, costs, total quality management. This is not the language of education or morality or scholarship or community; it is *the language of counting, accountants, accountability* and, to a greater or lesser extent, it is how we imagine our enterprise.' (emphasis added).

[9] See, for example, Woodhouse (1985, 1999a, 1999b, 2000), Whitehead ([1929]/1957), Newman ([1852–1889]/1996), Polster (1998), Jones (1998a, 1998b), Bean (1998), Hackney (1999), Craig *et al.* (1999), and the *Boyer Commission on Educating Undergraduates in the Research University* (undated), amongst numerous others.

[10] The 'Jones International University', also known as 'The University of the Web', was established in 1998. It is reputedly the first fully accredited, entirely online university in the USA (Confessore, 2001). Pease (2000, p. 627) describes it as '. . . a viable and operational virtual university'. Garnham (2000, p. 139), in contrast, argues that far from serving noble ends driven by the needs of society, 'the current push towards the creation of virtual universities is [driven by] the desire to cut educational labour costs rather than to upgrade the status of so-called knowledge workers'. Maher *et al.* (1999) concern themselves with issues regarding the *design* of a virtual campus.

[11] For example, Jones (1998a, p. 69) argues that '[t]here are both temporal and socio-political dimensions to the idea of the university' . . . [and that] . . . 'the Canadian idea of the university includes the notion of the university as a public, autonomous, secular, degree-granting institution'. He does not 'wish to suggest that these characteristics in themselves define the Canadian university, but rather than (*sic*) they are important components of how Canadians think of this institutional forum and that these facets, combined with the more universal notions of the university as a center for the dissemination and advancement of knowledge, have contributed to the creation of a uniquely Canadian idea of the university' (p. 78). For a criticism, see Kant (1998), and also Jones' response (1998b).

contested) sense so that 'socially useful' outcomes result (see also Polster, 2000). University curricula should be conceived and delivered to produce graduates who will serve a useful purpose in society and thus be better members of the *civitas* than they otherwise would be.[12] University research and scholarly work generally should have a similar end also. In these senses, Universities are *accountable* to society for what they do and (to again invoke ugly metaphor) what they 'produce'. But, in what seems largely a perversion of this sociable, community, sense of 'accountability', throughout the world public institutions of higher education (the Universities) are being coaxed[13] into responding to performance-based state agendas, largely driven by ideology. Their responses, allegedly, are conditioned by national history and 'cultural institutional legacy' (Atkinson-Grosjean and Grosjean, 2000).[14]

With the preceding contexts in mind, this paper explores the broad issue of the *accountability* of modern day University-based accounting educators. In doing so, it includes discussion of fundamental issues of *what* we should teach and *how* we should teach. Evidence from a variety of settings is analysed to tease out policy propositions regarding the nature and delivery of accounting education in coming decades. We explore whether accounting education should continue merely to implement *technical menus* and teach cases (the alleged facilitators of 'judgment') free of social context. Or should accounting education be focused more strongly on *social critique*? Should accounting curricula be untouched by 'the humanities'? Is it possible, within the University, to construct an accounting curriculum that ignores the everyday influence of accounting outputs, processes, language and mindsets, on the people, organizations and societies affected by accounting? This question transcends the recurring accounting pedagogy question of '*should we teach procedures alone, or include cases?*' and renders such a question almost irresponsible. We take our cue from the fundamental question posed by the anthropologists Shore and Wright (1999, p. 571): 'How should anthropologists respond to the 'audit culture' and the neo-liberal norms that are propelling [Universities] ever-onwards?' In doing so, we substitute 'academic accountants' for 'anthropologists'.

The issue of the *accountability* of accounting educators is addressed broadly. In the next section, we engage in an interpretative review of the broad obligations, motivations and mechanisms by which an important part of a community institution, a University, (and a component part, such as a department of accounting) effects *accountability* to society. In the fourth section we analyse the implications arising from regarding the keywords 'university accountability' as *ideograph* (McGee, 1980) and as *persuasive definition* (Walton, 2001). In doing so, we draw upon Alfred North Whitehead ([1929]/1957) and his

[12] Some informed commentators on universities are more specific. For example, Dalton Camp, a respected Canadian journalist has observed: '. . . it would be a tragedy for all society to see our universities give up their most valid role at the hour of society's greatest need. This is the part of education which invites the young to be skeptical of authority and to challenge conformity and convention; it is in the university environment and in the study of humanities that young adults best learn to think for themselves before emerging into a world of relentless propaganda, government and public relations and huckstering' (1997, p. F3).
[13] 'Coaxed' might be too gentle a word – 'coerced' might be more accurate in many instances.
[14] Making universalist comments about universities, such as our phrase '[t]hroughout the world' is fraught with dangers of overstatement and misinterpretation. For example, Quddus and Rashid (2000), in their study of the growth of private universities outside of 'the West', argue that 'for economies in transition and resource-poor nations with underdeveloped political institutions, universities can be important catalysts in building a civil society, a necessity if liberal democracy is to flourish,' (p. 509). The key is, of course, just what is meant by 'liberal democracy'.

interpreters, especially Woodhouse (1999a, 1999b, 2000). Such a perspective on accountability is invoked to critique, and shun, popular notions of accountability that flow from market and quantitative, objectivist rhetoric – notions characterized as 'reductionist and punitive and therefore counterproductive' (Shore and Wright, 1999, p. 571).[15]

In the fifth section we assess the state of University-based accounting education. In particular, our attention is directed to analysing the effects (and responses of accounting educators) to four specific thematic matters: globalization, market force hysteria, metaphor and the 'naturalness' of the university as a market-driven business, and Internet technology. Special attention is given to analysing the pernicious effects of unthinking adoption of the 'market' as the determining overarching metaphor directing university accounting endeavour. We draw upon our assessment and analysis to enter recommendations about the future of accounting education. A general discussion of relevant issues stimulated by the analysis follows in the final section.

Audit culture, disinterested scholarship and discipline-based accountability

The task of a University is agreed widely to be to provide graduates and research of service to society.[16] Universities, especially public universities, are accountable to society for this. But how that accountability ought to be effected is a matter of considerable debate. To what extent should Universities be idiosyncratic, utilitarian, Utopian, diverse or uniform? Should teaching emphasize vocationalism or idealism, or a blend of both? Should research have an 'applied' or a 'pure' focus? Should it give preference to achievement of outcomes that have readily apparent (and immediate) 'commercial' benefit? Should vigorous challenge be given to the colonization of the University by intellectual property regimes[17] (Polster, 2000)? And, furthermore, to whom is accountability owed: to [alleged] 'customers' (who might, in some conceptions, be students), community stakeholders (especially employers), the consciences of educators, or governments, amongst other possibilities?

An Adelaide University law school academic (Gava, 2001, p. 46) paints a depressing picture of the accountability treadmill on which he finds himself; his experience as a 'foot soldier of academe' would be little different to that confronting the preponderance of accounting academics in many countries. Gava argues that opportunities for the disinterested pursuit of scholarship, of reading widely, thinking deeply and discussing ideas with colleagues, are diminishing rapidly as accountability pressures lead many into the 'pointless labour' of 'repeatedly rehash[ing] a topic or writ[ing] articles because they have to, not because they have something to say'. Despite most academics not being entrepreneurs, they are 'pushed away from reading and thinking and towards making money, making links with the community and industry and dreaming up new ideas for new

---

[15] Some commentators go even further in their language; for example, Horn, in the *Canadian Journal of Higher Education*, writes with passion (justifiably, in our view) that '[t]he call for the sort of market-driven universities that neoliberals like has calamitous implications for some of the academy's key functions: the expansion of the realm of knowledge, the quickening of students' minds and sensibilities, and the provision of an informed and disinterested analysis of phenomena and events ...' (2000, p. 174).

[16] But 'service to society' does not mean service to perversions of the moment. For example, although nazified universities and university faculty in the Germany of 1933–1945 served the prevailing perversion, they did not 'serve society' in our sense.

[17] *Intellectual property regimes* are defined by Polster (2000, p. 37) as 'the rules and regulations governing the establishment and protection of intellectual property rights.'

centres and courses to tap into markets for new, preferably fee-paying, students'. He describes this all as 'soul destroying commercialization', undertaken by universities which have not 'maintained their integrity' and which have devalued distinctive academic values. 'Money making' is claimed to 'figure more' in teaching and scholarship as universities jump aboard the entrepreneurial bandwagon.

As depressing as it may seem, Gava's assessment rings true of the university worlds in which most university accounting educators find themselves. Certainly it rings true in our worlds (see also Polster, 2000). It would ring true too in the world of the anonymous, bright, young lecturer in literature, described in the lament by University of Melbourne Professor of English, During (2001):

> . . . he hadn't understood . . . that academe is a business in which each student, each publication, each research grant has a money value . . . [that is] used to manage and assess universities, faculties, departments, individuals.

> But, as he complained, these money values are . . . determined . . . through formulas . . . that clash with academics' real needs and aspirations . . . he wanted to write a book . . . that would allow him to win international recognition . . . [yet he found himself] . . . under pressure to produce quickie, so-called refereed conference papers to help the departmental research quantum.

The pervading paradigm seems to be that a university's accountability and performance should be measured in terms of the extent to which it satisfies some ill-defined 'market' for its services. Such a view is a betrayal of the ideals of a University. We support calls to encourage universities to 'redefine accountability in a way that positions them at the heart of their civic and social responsibilities' (Atkinson-Grosjean and Grosjean, 2000). Clearly, with 'globalization' and the 'cross-border' delivery of education via the Internet, the issue of *to whom accountability should be owed* is a particularly vexing one. The operations of multinational confederations of universities (e.g. *Universitas 21*)[18], major universities

---

[18] The *Universitas21* website (www.universitas.edu.au /introduction.html, visited on 13 April 2001) reveals that '**Universitas 21** is a company incorporated in the United Kingdom with a network of 18 universities in 10 countries. Collectively, it enrolls about 500 000 students each year, employs some 44 000 academics and researchers, and has a combined operating budget of almost US$9 billion.' Member universities are in Canada/USA (McGill, British Columbia, Toronto, Michigan); in Australasia (Melbourne, New South Wales, Queensland, Auckland); in Asia (Singapore, Hong Kong, Peking, Fudan); and in UK/Europe (Birmingham, Edinburgh, Glasgow, Nottingham, Lund, Freiburg). However, on 23April 2001, University of Toronto President Birgeneau announced his university's withdrawal from Universitas 21, clearly concerned by the quality of university education that might emerge: he cited the 'need to protect the value of the University of Toronto degree'. [News release posted to Internet at website: www.utoronto.ca]. Three other universities reported to be on the verge of joining the Universitas 21 network are New York, Virginia and Georgia Institute of Technology (Illing, 2001b, p. 43).

The Universitas21 network is claimed to provide 'a framework for member universities to pursue agendas that would be beyond their individual capabilities, capitalizing on the established reputation and operational reach of each member . . . core business is provision of a pre-eminent brand for educational services supported by a strong quality assurance framework. . . . **Universitas 21** has been established [*inter alia*] for the purposes of:

- Developing international curricula for graduates . . . to operate in a global professional workforce, with credentials that are internationally portable and accredited across a range of professional jurisdictions; [and]
- Providing a quality assurance structure that operates globally to offer *internationally valid processes* for the enrolment, instruction, assessment and certification of students, and an *internationally recognised brand* identifiable with a global network of high quality universities.

offering online courses in other countries (e.g. Duke University),[19] and virtual universities (e.g. Western Governors' University, www.wgu.edu) have created much uncertainty and have muddied the waters. Will national interest be subsumed by cyberage-induced changes in the whole fabric of education? Indeed, just what is 'the national interest', or indeed the 'public interest', in our era of transnational mega-corporations and the attendant emasculation of the nation-state?

Accountability in discipline-based subject areas

Ideally, discipline-based educators, like those in accounting, ought to operate to maximize the 'common weal'.[20] But who is to be the arbiter of the activities that do so? And what value sets should we invoke in effecting accountability in accounting education?

All too often in the professions, as in accounting, a professional body acts as the arbiter, as a proxy for the community, of what is good and bad curriculum design and teaching practice. In many countries, professional accounting bodies have been allowed, by the supine acquiescence of university accounting departments, to dominate debates about *what* accounting educators teach and, to a lesser degree, *how* accounting educators teach. The professional bodies reign supreme, wielding accreditation guidelines, *diktats*, on what is, and what is not, worthy of the imprimatur of accreditation. Those accounting educators who have resolved to chart a more independent path, unfettered by the self-serving pragmatism and expedience of the accounting profession, are put in an invidious situation. Endorsement through accreditation is crucial in a society obsessed with credentialism, as is access to funding in an increasingly underfunded public research environment.

It may seem unwarranted churlishness to cavil at professional bodies being legitimized as surrogate determinators of what variety of curricula and teaching is in society's best interests. But quite often what emerges is that the arbiter, a professional body, is a 'club', an elite 'tribe' with its own language, values and prejudices – sometimes at odds with core values in society. So, a difficulty with notions of such an 'accountability surrogacy' is that professional bodies do not necessarily act in the best interests of the common weal. Strong argument can be entered that professional bodies are poor surrogate arbiters of the common weal: they struggle to see beyond their own self-interested bailiwick (Larson, 1977); they have a penchant for practical rather than conceptual issues; and, in many professions, speak as a dissonant cackle, with many voices competing for primacy. For example, the current interest by four major professional accounting bodies (the American Institute of Certified Public Accountants, the Canadian Institute of Chartered Accountants, the Institute of Chartered Accountants in Australia, and the Institute of Chartered Accountants of New Zealand) in an 'initiative . . . to create a new professional designation, global in scope and focused on knowledge integration that creates economic value' (*The XYZ Concept*, 2000, cover page) seems a far echo from the professional mirage of *public service*.

---

[19] In 2001, Duke's Fuqua School of Business used 'video streaming' technology and the Internet to deliver an MBA unit, 'Global Asset Allocation and Stock Selection', to students on five continents. This application of evolving e-learning technology has been argued to be likely to induce the concept of 'boutique education', where students 'mix and match' courses from a variety of universities into a coherent, customized degree programme. (See *The Star* (Toronto) 27 January 2001).

[20] Checkoway (2001) raises an issue having close connection with the 'common weal': that of commitment to renewing the civic mission of the University.

Furthermore, there needs to be a much better accountability for what we teach in accounting. If Chambers (1999, p. 244) is to be accorded credence [and he should be], accounting pedagogues have 'turned a blind eye' to the 'fallacious arithmetic' which underpins the variety of accounting they teach – an accounting where the symbols do not 'correspond with the observable facts' (p. 242). We have failed, according to Chambers, over many decades, to break free of the insulating 'cocoon' of generally accepted accounting practices (p. 249); 'to defend accounting teaching and practice from the infiltration of vague, vagrant and self-serving ideas' (p. 244). As 'expositors' of a variety of accounting with little regard for discovering the critical 'dated money's worth of property in possession' (p. 245) we are implicated as perpetrators of 'specious arguments' that advance 'fallacious' accounting processes leading to 'error, deviousness and plain deceits' (p. 248). We are, as accounting educators, accused of allowing 'indoctrination' and 'brainwashing' to triumph over 'rigorous enquiry'. We propagate 'illogicalities' and 'inconsistencies', abetted by our 'undisciplined imagination' and failure to focus on the 'observables of real world affairs' (p. 250). We must, according to Chambers, teach an accounting that emphasises 'knowledge of the present money's worth of things in possession' (p. 251). Until we do that we have what is tantamount to an 'educational scandal' (p. 250) in which our 'halls of learning [are] bedeviled by a poverty of accounting discourse' (p. 251).[21]

Accounting educators, notably (dare we allege?) many professors of accounting, seem to have been the profession's lap dogs, their quislings, meekly following the self-interested vocationalism of the accounting profession, and similar pursuits of their host educational institutions.[22] Fewer professors of accounting seem to conceive their role as 'professing the truth without fear or favour', of leading the way, of challenging the status quo, of offering critique, of 'disturbing the peace', of setting the agenda, of being the conscience of the

---

[21] Chambers' admonition that we accounting educators should focus on the 'real world' is prescient and deserves to be taken with the utmost seriousness. Later, we explore some implications of excessive *abstraction* in relation to accountability; here now, we observe that such abstraction – such focusing not on the real world but on abstract, often managerialist, chimera – serves to undercut the worthiness of accounting education. For example, suppose that we are interested in teaching 'transfer pricing' and limited our pedagogy to consideration of economic modelling and teaching cases that ignored activity at the 'coal face' of the organization and its environment. Such an approach would not see, in any serious sense, the implications of transfer pricing on people and nature. A more critical, grounded, approach, perhaps using material such as McAulay *et al.* (2001), seems less fraudulent to us.

[22] We are less-than-delighted to acknowledge our own lap-dog character. But, like many other accounting academics, we are held in thrall by a business school reward system that looks with *dis*favour if lap-dog activities are shunned. Such conflictual dualities seem common in management schools, in which accounting and management educators must confront concerns such as those posed by Walck (1997, p. 474):

> ... Nagging questions nibble at my resolve to deliver management education: Is not management really a euphemism for control and domination? What happens to people who are constructed as resources to be made more productive? ...

Such 'nagging questions' seem grounded in an endorsement of accounting and management teaching in which education is *liberating* rather than *domesticating* (Boyce, 1996, drawing upon Freire, 1972). Boyce writes that 'education liberates when it challenges the dominant ideology, teaches critical literacy, and how to learn' (1996, p. 2). However, she acknowledges that '[m]uch of the work in which faculty in management ... are engaged is domesticating ... we prepare students for the world of work rather than lives of resistance. This is understandable – many of us are in colleges of business [in which] inherent conflicts between our radical convictions, our course content, and our teaching practices are unaddressed.' (p. 2). This, of course, raises issues concerning the 'chilling' (or worse) outcomes arising from accounting academics engaging in criticism of university and business school sponsors. It is even more chilling to acknowledge that this problem is not

profession, and of offering 'resistance' to dominant ideologies.[23] This is not surprising given the 'audit culture' sweeping modern universities (Power, 1997). This 'culture' has helped fragment conceptions of our 'professional self' into the discrete aspects of our work that are being audited: 'research', 'teaching' and 'administration'. We have a crisis of identity, 'caught between two conflicting notions of the professional self: the old idea of the independent scholar and inspiring teacher, and the new model of the auditable, competitive performer' (Shore and Wright, 1999, p. 569).

We contend it is timely to reconsider whether society's interests would be better served by greater 'detachment' and independence between professional bodies that are near the 'coal face' of practice and a disinterested scholarly community that is ensconced in the privileged sanctity of a 'bosky dell'. But we do not subscribe to the 'extraordinary view' (as University of Sydney Vice Chancellor, Brown, might insinuate), of 'any intercourse with industry [and the professions being] corrupting' with accounts of such activity representing a 'roll of shame' (Brown, 2001, p. 33). However, we note Brown's contention that as professions 'have come of age ... [they] have given back to our universities through voluntary tuition and support'. He mentions the professions of medicine, dentistry, veterinary science, computer science, engineering and law. Perhaps, pointedly, there is no mention of the accounting profession in Brown's 'roll of honour', suggesting it is not a profession he regards to have 'come of age'. Whether or not the organized branches of accounting have resulted in a profession that has 'come of age' seems relatively unimportant; accounting itself is both of the ages and of fundamental and enduring social importance, perhaps even more so today than ever.[24] We contend, therefore, that *it is time to engage ideal in the service of practice more deliberately*. This does not imply that accounting academics should retreat into 'ivory towers', cocooned and indifferent to the outside world. It *does imply*, though, that we should teach what we believe to be in the best interests of society, what we value ... and that we should 'profess'.

But what value sets should be engaged to effect accountability as accounting educators? We live in a complex, pluralist society, in which the *market model mentality* is running rampant. We are obsessed by accountability mechanisms that substitute 'targets' and 'appraisal' for trust: such mechanisms invoke quantification and reductionism, rather than qualitative and more humane, social welfare dimensions. We worship financial quantification as the arbiter, the discriminator of what is good and bad financial (and increasingly, higher education) performance. We are locked into a masculine accountability mentality obsessed with symbolic logic, rationality, order, quantification, and 'win at all costs' imperatives. We need to supplement brute financial accountability with dimensions encompassing compassion, multiplicity, social welfare, social responsibility, equity and

---

confined to the business academy: it broaches disciplinary divides. Serious ethical issues arise, for example, in connection with the [corrupting?] relationship between drug companies and their financing of medical research.

[23] Warde (2001, online, emphasis added) roundly condemns a wide swathe of academia for neglect of such issues: 'Academic disciplines that should in theory be concerned about the relations between universities and the marketplace pay scant attention to these issues. Departments of education are busy exploring the latest educational fads. The humanities, obsessed by multiculturalism, have "deconstructed" such concepts as "truth" and forfeited their right to defend disinterested inquiry. The social sciences are mostly preoccupied with quantification and abstraction. *Business schools are cheerleaders for whatever generates profits*'.

[24] As an example of accounting's enduring importance, historian Alfred Crosby has written: 'In the past seven centuries bookkeeping has done more to shape the perceptions of more bright minds than any single innovation in philosophy or science.' (1997, p. 221)

environmental issues. We should be accountable to the public, not to 'markets'. And University knowledge should not be sold off to the highest bidder: it should be kept free for all to savour (Polster, 2000).

Yet we find that the new 'culture of audit' in higher education relishes in assessing the learning experience in terms of a 'paper trail' of things that are measurables and 'inspectables':

> It no longer really matters how well an academic teaches and whether or not he or she sometimes inspires their pupils; it is far more important that they have produced plans for their courses, bibliographies, outlines of this, that or the other, in short all the paraphernalia of futile bureaucratization required for assessors who come from on high like emissaries from Kafka's castle (Johnson, 1994, p. 379).

Such quality assurance mentality, according to Dominelli and Hoogvelt (1996, p. 206) involves much 'unproductive "busywork"'. They cite one estimate that 'six tons of paper per year, £250 000 worth of photocopying and the equivalent of a third of an average sized university in labour hours have been devoted to frantic paper pushing' (p. 206).

From the London School of Economics (LSE), Underwood (2001) reports that there were four visits to academic departments by teams of inspectors from the Quality Assurance Agency (QAA) in a five month period. He cites an unreferenced 'recent national report' that estimated the average cost of each of these visits at 'about £75,000 in direct academic staff time, i.e. not including the cost of support staff or the cost of, for example, photocopying to produce documentation'. The physical documentation demands of the QAA are daunting too. Underwood (2001) claims that the QAA visit to the Department of Politics at the LSE required the assembling of 13 four-drawer filing cabinets of documents.

University accountability as ideograph and persuasive definition

> Nobody argues with the need for accountability ... (Sinclair, 1995, p. 219)

The key word, *accountability*, is close kin to accounting educators and what they 'do'. It deserves closer scrutiny. Insights to the meaning of *accountability* emerge from analysing its use in recent contexts. The examples in Appendix A are two of many thousands of instances of the use of *accountability* in connection with the University. We draw upon these examples to argue the importance of regarding accountability as an *ideograph*.

We do not use the term *ideograph* in the strict sense of its conventional definition as 'a graphic symbol that represents an idea instead of a word, a single morpheme, or a lexical item' (LinguaLinks Library, 1999, emphasis added). That is, we do not use the term in the same sense that would have Chinese characters (*kanji*) defined as *ideographs*. Rather, we draw upon the slightly different interpretation (advanced by McGee, 1980, see below) that an *ideograph* (such as 'university accountability') is an ordinary language term (not a 'graphic symbol') meant to convey an idea. As we argue here, 'university accountability' is an ideograph that conveys a politically and ideologically loaded idea.

The examples in Appendix A, and many others in play, are consistent with the view that the word *accountability*, in general, but most particularly in the context of Universities, has become an *ideograph*. McGee defines an *ideograph* as:

> ... an ordinary-language term found in political discourse. It is a high-order abstraction representing collective commitment to a particular but equivocal and ill-defined normative goal. It warrants the use of power, excuses behavior and belief which might otherwise be perceived as eccentric or antisocial, and guides behavior and belief into channels easily recognized by a community as acceptable and laudable. (1980, p. 15).

Ideographs 'exist in real discourse, functioning clearly and evidently as agents of political consciousness. They are not invented by observers; they come to be a part of the real lives of the people whose motives they articulate' and 'are bound within the culture which they define' (McGee, 1980, pp. 7, 9). The following are claimed also to be examples of ideographs in American culture: 'liberty'; 'equality'; 'impeaching'; 'rule of law'; 'principle of confidentiality'; 'freedom of speech' (McGee, 1980, pp. 9–13).

To show more completely that 'university accountability' is an ideograph, we would have to mirror what Cloud (1998) did in connection with the (related) ideograph, 'family values'; that is, conduct an intensive and extensive text search (using services such as Lexis/Nexis) to document the extent and use of such terms in rhetorical discourse. Although we leave this for possible future research, we wish to explore, tentatively, some aspects of the (alleged) ideograph 'university accountability'.

McGee (1980) contends that ideographs are a link between rhetoric and ideology. This point is elaborated upon by Cloud (1998, p. 389) in her contention that:

> ... ideographic slogans comprise the building blocks of ideology in a system of public commitments; they are persuasive because they are abstract, easily recognized, and evoke near-universal and rapid identification within a culture. Thus, the dimension of social control and coercion in understanding the ideograph is crucial. It is incumbent upon the critic to question the interests motivating ideographic choices, as well as to assess potential consequences of public adherence to a particular vocabulary of motives.

Accountability (and particularly *university accountability*) can (and ought) to be viewed as far from a 'mere' technical accounting term; rather, it should be viewed as a loaded, pliable, rhetoric of ideology. And since '[it] is not remarkable to conceive social control as fundamentally rhetorical' (McGee, 1980, p. 6), such rhetorical ideographic terms evoke both an ideological commitment and a *gestalt* in members of a community (McGee, 1980, p. 7). Thus, ideographic terms such as 'university accountability' can be expected to change over time and to be contestable insofar as their definition is concerned, just as Cloud's example of 'family values' is contestable.[25] For *accountability*, this is no surprise, since '[a]ccountability is subjectively constructed and changes with context' (Sinclair, 1995, p. 219). It is a member of a rhetorical genre known as *persuasive definition* (Stevenson, 1938; Walton, 2001). The importance of this genre derives from the allegation that 'persuasive redefinitions of terms already defined in science, law or everyday usage'

---

[25] Coy and Pratt (1998, p. 541) agree, stating that '... the nature of accountability is mutable and changes over time'. A prominent academic who seemed unmindful of this mutability of meaning of 'university accountability', and suffered the consequences, was the then Chancellor of the University of Sydney, Professor Dame Leonie Kramer. On 6 August, 2001, Kramer was compelled, by a narrow majority of the Senate of the University of Sydney, to resign. Her resignation was attributed, in large part, to her 'ostensibly *outdated view of accountability*' and her 'lack of transparency' (Lawnham, 2001, p. 33, emphasis added). Kramer had not disclosed to the University Senate details of a new remuneration package negotiated with Vice-Chancellor Brown through the Remuneration Sub-Committee.

are very often cleverly and subtly 'deployed to serve the interest of the definer.' (Walton, 2001, p. 117).

Walton (2001) explains that theoretical understanding of the concept of *persuasive definition* in argumentation is based largely upon Stevenson (1938). Such understanding proceeds from the assumption that words used in making argument have two meanings: *emotive* and *descriptive*. *Emotive meaning* 'represents the feelings or attitudes (positive or negative) that the use of the word suggests to respondents', while *descriptive meaning* 'is the core factual or descriptive content' (Walton, 2001, p. 118). Walton goes on to explain that

> How a persuasive definition works, according to Stevenson's theory, is by *redefining the descriptive meaning* of the word, while *covertly retaining its old familiar emotive meaning*. (2001, p. 118, emphasis added)

We contend that the expression 'university accountability' is an ideographic term and a member of the rhetorical genre *persuasive definition*. Thus, 'university accountability' should be regarded as an expression with 'strong emotive connotations' and with a 'somewhat vague and ambiguous' descriptive meaning, capable of semantic manipulation (Aomi, 1985). Where the *descriptive meaning* of 'university accountability' is changed, that change is not noticed easily and the expression's *emotive meaning* is largely retained. Exploration of some possible consequences of our *university-accountability-as-persuasive-definition* contention merit consideration. In particular, what, if anything, are the consequences for University accounting educator accountability? This opens up the possibility of deeper, richer, more persuasive definitions of the ideograph. Such definitions have a stronger link with the *humanness* of the University than the accountability of the 'audit culture' so despised by Shore and Wright (1999) and increasing numbers of others both inside and outside universities.

Whitehead and a definitional frame for 'university accountability'

We begin to construct elements of a definition of 'university accountability' (in connection with accounting educators), based upon some of the ideas of Alfred North Whitehead. We do so because of the appeal of exploring *accountability* from a perch grounded in Woodhouse's (1999b, p. 192) interpretation of Whitehead's theory of the university as 'provid[ing] a cogent account of the rhythm that could restore balance to teaching, learning, and research – a balance that is sadly missing in university education today.'

There is nothing innately extraordinary about Whitehead's commentaries on university education in particular, and education, in general. Nonetheless, what is 'ordinary' to one person might seem 'extraordinary' to another. This is especially likely if that second person is accustomed to operating behind a veil of 'received wisdom and assumptions' or perhaps is shrouded by the inapt requirements of some alleged 'accountability'. We employ Whitehead's ideas as inspiration to construct an *ideograph* of what should constitute *university accounting educator accountability*.[26] Thus, we engage in a persuasive re-definition of the descriptive meaning of 'university accountability'.

---

[26] No claim is entered regarding the comprehensiveness or completeness of our recourse to Whitehead. Indeed, it would be presumptuous to do so. Whitehead has inspired considerable deep reflection about the role of education. See, for example, the special collection in volume 31 (2 and 3) 2000 of the educational journal *Interchange*. We are not specialist Whitehead scholars, but this should not prevent us from making rhetorical use of his ideas in our search for accountability.

The partly-true plaintive admonition of Sinclair (1995, p. 219) 'but how accountability is defined, and seen to be provided, is far from resolved', seems likely to be overtaken by events. The Quality Assurance Agency's requirements in the UK and similar hegemonic 'accountability' impositions elsewhere, render it crucial for accounting academics to become involved centrally in those contests which are (re-)fashioning the *accountability* ideograph's persuasive definition. The process of such ideograph-creation is as important as the 'final' definition itself; indeed, it seems that the ideological pathway travelled is the key, with the frame provided by the 'starting point' especially important.[27] In this sense, *accountability of University accounting educators* is as much a process as it is anything else. It is a process of how we, individually and collectively, live our lives as accounting educators in the University, even (perhaps especially) in a hostile environment. If we frame our process of accountability development using a market metaphor, we arrive at accountability definitions much different than if we chose other alternatives as a frame for our thinking – such as those proffered by Whitehead.

Our reflection on some of Whitehead's ideas, and their appropriation to our (always evolving and unabashedly tentative) definition of the *accountability of University accounting educators*, consists of five imperatives, each with implications for accounting curriculum and allied matters.

(i) REPLACING THE 'FALLACY OF MISPLACED CONCRETENESS'

Whitehead, in *Science and the Modern World* ([1925]/1953), employed the notion of the 'fallacy of misplaced concreteness' (FMC) in his critical analysis of the development of science and the impact of science on society. Thompson (1997, p. 219) describes the FMC 'as a set of variations on the central theme of misplacing concreteness, by mistaking the abstract for the concrete . . . is detrimental both to good science and to good human living'. The FMC is a rich, evocative notion that has several interwoven themes, including '*what lies beyond* inquiry', 'competing *metaphysical* modes of thought that claim to best *support* and guide inquiry', and 'the best general *methodology* for conducting inquiry' (Thompson, 1997, p. 220). Flynn (1997, p. 240), as an example, has shown how the FMC has been manifest, to damaging effect, in the concept of intelligence in psychology:

> Did the abstract conception of human intelligence as a limited number of functional behaviours constitute reality for psychologists working in social eugenics and mental hygienics over the course of the 20th century? Did this

---

[27] Donald Schön's comments on the framing of social issues seem relevant here, since contests over *accountability* are contests about social policy:

> When we become attentive to the framing of social problems, we thereby become aware of conflicting frames. Our debates over social policy turn often not on problems but on dilemmas. The participants in the debate bring different and conflicting frames, generated by different and conflicting metaphors. Such conflicts are often not resolvable by recourse to the facts-by technological fixes, by trade-off analyses, or by reliance on institutionalized forms of social choice. Indeed, these stubborn conflicts of perspective, full of potential for violent contention, have become in their own right issues of public policy. The question then arises as to whether it is possible by *inquiry* to achieve the restructuring, coordination, reconciliation, or integration of conflicting frames for the construction of social problems. If so, what is the nature of this inquiry? ([1979]/1993, p. 139).

While we have no ready answers to Schön's questions, we contend that University accounting educators must construct their own frame(s), vigorously, as part of this overall process. They should not be content with the 'default' frames that are implicit in most accounting teaching materials (especially textbooks), professional pronouncements, and research.

abstraction restrict understanding of the aesthetic experiences fundamental to all intelligence in human beings, understanding that might have emerged from a more open-minded inquiry? The answer on both counts appears to be 'yes'.

Both in accounting education and in accounting research, the FMC seems to run rampant. The degree to which Baudrillarian signs guide, indeed coerce, behaviour in accounting (and thus accounting's influence on people), is enough to make a semiotician's heart soar. In accounting research, metaphor and modelled abstractions obscure accounting's affect on the lives of real, embodied people, other creatures, and nature (Amernic, 1997). In accounting education, students might be tempted to believe that numbers in financial statements preceded by dollar signs ('money of account') are equivalent to 'cold hard cash' ('material money'); a balance sheet *is* a firm; and that net income and costs are somehow *real*, when in fact even a *firm* itself is an abstraction (Guthey, 2001).[28] A balance sheet – even one made robust by following Chambers' various dictums on measurement (1965, 1966, 1972, 1975, 1999) – is certainly *not* a firm.[29] Net income and costs exist *in concreto* only in the imaginings of some economists, with accountants' measures being distinctly 'softer' and more pliable. Interestingly, these abstractions, these accounting numbers, take on a *realness*, a *concreteness* of their own, when they appear in audited financial statements, budgets, or other financial reports. Thus, Whitehead's FMC is especially insidious in accounting and accounting education.[30]

This, then, shows forcefully that accounting educators must consider seriously curriculum strategies that encourage students to regard accounting constructs as *social constructions*, laden with partially hidden ideologies and metaphors. An example of such an accounting curriculum strategy is elaborated by Amernic *et al.* (2000) with respect to Economic Value Added, or EVA®. It is not that we abhor accounting technique. Indeed, such knowledge is important, often crucial, for our students. Rather, what we abhor is the

---

[28] Such abstractions can have all-too-real consequences once they are acted upon (see, for example, Hines, 1988).

[29] And yet many senior managers might think about, and act upon, a sort of balance-sheet mental model of the organization they lead – a cognitive abstraction that has potential for perverse effects. In the accounting education literature, Bailey (1995) has queried whether or not the mental model learned by the 'new generation of accounting professionals . . . may not be either appropriate or in the best long-run interests of the profession or society' (p. 192).

[30] Indeed, the *conceptual frameworks* adopted by many national accounting bodies assume, apparently unintentionally, that an objective 'out there' is waiting to be 'accounted for'. Since these *frameworks* are often included in accounting curricula, unproblematically, Whitehead's FMC is relevant here as well. This insidiousness of the FMC in accounting is even more perverse when we consider the *use* of accounting. Moore's (1994, p. 583, emphasis added) example captures this nicely, if surrealistically:

> . . . In August 1991, I had the dubious honor of being present in a room full of two thousand academic accountants at the Opryland Hotel in Nashville, Tennessee, listening, not to Johnny Cash or Waylon Jennings, but to the distinguished economist Rudiger Dornbusch and his keynote speech to the American Accounting Association on the future of the global economy. Dornbusch . . . felt compelled to address the accounting-economics relationship at the beginning of his talk, and did so by saying, essentially, that the only thing factual that economists talked about was accounting information – everything past that was mere theory.
>
> A ripple of unease with the speaker's ignorance filtered through the large audience as, theoretically aware or not, the assembled accountants noted to themselves how wrong he was, since every accounting number ever produced has been, to say the least, highly contestable. What Dornbusch revealed in his off-the-cuff remark was that *accountants had achieved, at least in the eyes of certain major economists, the ultimate goal of the rhetorician's art: to be perceived as not rhetoric at all.*

absence of scrutiny, by accounting educators, of the ideologies lurking beneath the gloss of accounting abstractions manifest in technique.

(ii) LOOKING BEYOND THE 'LEDGE OF ECONOMICS'

Accounting has been cited as the 'fundamental metaphor of economics' (Klamer and McCloskey, 1991). It is often regarded, educationally, as a practical attempt to make concrete the economic ideal. Whitehead asserts that to understand business (and accounting) we need to look beyond the 'narrow ledge of economics' and take in 'the whole complexity of human motives' (1936, pp. 171–72). Thus, Whitehead alerts us to the desirability of a holistic approach to the content and process of curriculum. Accounting must, therefore, be taught and learned *in situ*, from a variety of perspectives (not just the economic)[31]. It should use a variety of teaching and learning stimuli. This has serious implications not only for traditional, technical approaches to teaching/learning accounting, but also for more *avant garde* approaches. For example, mere use of 'cases' or emphasizing 'judgment' and 'analysis', will not guarantee the adoption of much needed critical perspectives in accounting education.

(iii) SEEING THE WOOD BY MEANS OF THE TREES

Whitehead has argued that 'there is no royal road to learning through an airy path of brilliant generalizations . . . The problem of education is to make the pupil see the wood by means of the trees.' ([1929]/1957, p. 6) For us, in terms of our accountability, this suggests strongly that details matter. Schön's comment: 'But that which seems obvious to the unreflecting mind may upon reflection seem utterly mistaken' ([1979]/1993, p. 148), seems appropriate here. Accounting phenomena, both process and output, do not exist as discrete self-contained objectivities, sanitized from their history and social setting. Most importantly, they do not exist distinct from the people who produced them and who are (directly and indirectly) affected by them. Accountability flows from Whitehead's 'no royal road' assertion to support both the use of history and detailed social setting in accounting education (see, for example, Craig and Greinke, 1994, Amernic and Elitzur, 1992, and Amernic and Craig, 1996).

In accounting education, the current American Accounting Association (AAA) *Quality of Earnings* (QOE) initiative seems to be an illustration of ignoring aspects of both the 'wood' and the 'trees': the AAA QOE website (http://www.aaahq.org/qoe/index.html) ignores both the context and the social construction of QOE. Far from being a mere object of financial reporting (even if subject to qualitative subjective judgments), QOE is a social phenomenon, as much the result of media and other discourse as it is the 'result' of GAAP-based accounting and disclosure. For instance, Nortel Networks[32] is being pummelled by the media for (among other alleged transgressions) poor and misleading accounting choices and less-than-forthright disclosure.[33] Indeed, the editorial artist Theo Moudakis captured the comic irony in Nortel's contemporary social 'earnings' behaviour in a four-panel editorial cartoon in the *The Toronto Star* newspaper (23 April 2001, p. A16) by

---

[31] Of course, there are a variety of economic approaches as well, ranging from Austrian economics to unbridled neo-liberal *cowboy capitalism*.
[32] Nortel was previously the darling of the stock markets and financial analysts. But by August 2001, its shares had collapsed to less than 10% of their July 2000 high on the New York Stock Exchange.
[33] Major accounting issues for Nortel are those of revenue recognition and accounting for in-process R & D arising from acquisitions.

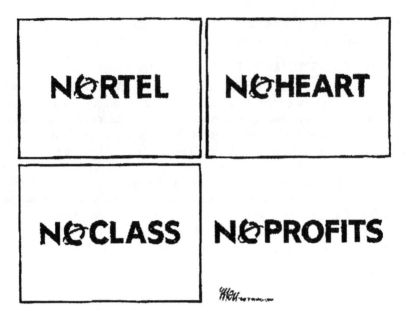

Fig. 1. Nortel corporate logo.

cheeky re-drawings of the Nortel corporate logo (Fig. 1). It is rare for a major, mass circulation, general-audience newspaper to devote an editorial cartoon to criticism of a particular company. Note that the cartoon is anchored (in the unbounded bottom right-quadrant) by visual incorporation of the accounting term '... PROFITS'. Whilst a thorough analysis of this editorial cartoon as visual rhetoric would undoubtedly be valuable, our intent in highlighting it is to proffer it as an unusual and profound piece of evidence of media hostility towards a particular company and its disclosure and accounting.[34]

A plausible reason (a sort of 'proto-hypothesis') for the media to become so hostile towards Nortel and its accounting seems at least partly attributable to a sense of betrayal the media felt in its role as a collaborator in the *social construction* of Nortel's QOE. In 'teaching' about Nortel's QOE, therefore, it seems crucial to investigate the interaction between the company and its leadership on the one hand, and the media on the other. Such investigation might reveal mutually reinforcing ideologies that helped co-construct Nortel's QOE in the first place, well before its shares collapsed.[35] We contend there is merit in contemplating that the 'wood' of QOE is fashioned integrally by the 'trees' of the company and the co-constructing media (the latter perhaps unintentionally). They are both fashioned within the context of overarching ideologies. This suggests that a very complex information and communication process is involved in accounting's QOE. All this has implications for how 'QOE' is 'taught' in accounting. It helps frame our accountability for curriculum choices as accounting educators.

---

[34] An example of an analysis of visual rhetoric in an accounting context is Amernic and Craig (2000a).
[35] Such an approach is akin to 'critical discourse analysis' (van Dijk, 1993).

(iv) BRINGING IMAGINATIVE TEACHERS AND RESEARCHERS INTO INTELLECTUAL SYMPATHY WITH STUDENTS

Whitehead engages in instructive self-interrogation: 'Do you want your teachers to be imaginative? Then encourage them to do research. Do you want your researchers to be imaginative? Then bring them into intellectual sympathy with the young at the most eager, imaginative period of life, when intellects are just entering upon their mature discipline.' (1929/[1957], p. 97)

This quotation raises the hoary old divide in higher education between 'teaching' and 'research'. This divide is artificial and dysfunctional (see, for example, Craig *et al.*, 1999). But aside from platitudes about the 'seamless blend' (Colbeck, 1998) that is *teaching* and *research*, many practical, everyday implications for accounting education and accounting educators' accountability might flow from this quotation. They range from the rich tapestry of creative knowledge that an active researcher brings to teaching (including the sometimes-electric excitement generated when a teacher explains and justifies, with passion, the research for which the teacher *has* passion), to the insight that good research practice has to offer students and educators. As an example of this latter point, accounting and business educators – and indeed educators in most disciplines – might draw from Peshkin (2001). The latter 'develops the idea of consciously using different lenses for the purpose of expanding the perceptual efficacy of the [qualitative] researcher' (p. 238). Peshkin 'offer[s] a sweep of alternative lenses for consideration: patterns, time, emic, positionality, ideology, themes, metaphor, irony, and silence. Each one invites researchers to perceive in a certain way ...' (p. 242).

What is striking about Peshkin's advice for *researchers* is its usefulness for *educators and their students*. We all want our students to 'see' events, issues and business accounting situations from as many 'relevant' perspectives as possible – after all, that is an important part of the essence of cognitive development, maturity and creativity (Amernic and Enns, 1979). It is thus an important frame for our accountability as accounting educators. But what is also striking (although not surprising) is the close resemblance that Peshkin's advice to qualitative researchers has to aspects of Ellen Langer's concept of *mindfulness* (Langer and Moldoveanu (2000). That concept has been shown to have vital implications for education (Ritchhart and Perkins, 2000).

(v) PRESERVING THE CONNECTION BETWEEN KNOWLEDGE AND THE ZEST OF LIFE: UNITING IN IMAGINATIVE CONSIDERATION OF LEARNING

Whitehead (1929/[1957], pp. 92–93) argued that:

> The universities are schools of education, and schools of research. But the primary reason for their existence is not to be found either in the mere knowledge conveyed to the students or in the mere opportunities afforded to the members of the faculty. . . . The justification for a university is that it preserves the connection between knowledge and the zest of life, by uniting the young and the old in the imaginative consideration of learning. The university imparts information, but it imparts it imaginatively. At least, this is the function it should perform for society. A university which fails in this respect has no reason for existence. This atmosphere of excitement, arising from imaginative consideration, transforms knowledge. A fact is no longer a bare fact; it is invested with all its possibilities.

> It is no longer a burden on the memory; it is energizing as the poet of our dreams, and as the architect of our purposes.

These comments of Whitehead help us frame our accountability as University accounting educators in an age characterized by the Internet and allied technology, globalization, and the commodification of knowledge. His assertions, in combination with the general role of Universities in social critique, help us to 'see' how the rhetoric of the University as *edu-mart info-hustler* deserves strident countering at more fundamental levels (see, for example, Clarke *et al.*, 1999). Plainly, the University cannot be either the 'poet of our dreams' or 'the architect of our purposes', especially in this age of specious accountability and intellectual property regimes – unless our dreams are really nightmares and our purposes quite perverse.

As accounting educators in the University, we have a public voice (and ought to exercise it). Coy and Pratt (1998, p. 542) observe that members of the professoriate, presumably including academic accountants, have a special duty in connection with the overall political accountability of the State and other powerful interests. This duty arises since, among other checks on power such as a free press

> ... the existence of academic institutions whose members have the protection of tenure and are expected to act as the critic and conscience of society, are other important ways in which accountability may be demanded of those with delegated responsibility for the control of public assets. ...

Thus, as members of a tenured professoriate, accounting academics have a *public* role to play in overall social and political accountability. That role also has an introspective dimension: regard for the accountability of these self-same accounting academics in the University. This is an integral part of what Harold Innis regarded as 'the social role of intellectuals' (Massolin, 1998, p. 57).[36]

THE UNIVERSITY AS PART OF THE RHYTHM OF LIFE

Whitehead's work is inspiring as we reflect on our own accountability. But we have barely touched the surface: for example, Whitehead ([1929]/1957) contended that University education was the third stage in what he viewed as the *rhythmic cycle of learning*. He commented also on the function of universities to civilize business and on the place of business schools in the University (Whitehead, [1929]/1957; 1936. See also the critical commentaries by Woodhouse, 2000, and Hendley, 2000). Whitehead was also a keen advocate of ideas that the principles of business organizations had no true place in University governance or in the management of Universities. He argued that '... universities cannot be dealt with according to the rules and policies which apply to the familiar business corporations. Business schools are no exception to this law of university life' ([1929]/1957, p. 100). But this view has not prevented the widespread application of

---

[36] Bender (1997, p. 31), writing about the recent history of American universities, offers a somewhat pessimistic view of the current state of this public role:

> The dissolution of the public sphere and the limited role of academic intellect in whatever survives of that sphere is worrisome. A democratic culture and polity invites and needs an open dialogue on all questions pertaining to the human condition. Restoring a place for academic knowledge in the public culture and a role for public discussion in academic culture ought to be a high priority of both academic and public leaders.

the principles of business management to university management, however ill-fitting they may be.[37]

Whitehead's ideas on the 'rhythm of the university', including his ideas on the 'organic' and 'embodied' nature of human understanding, are appealing. They provide a stimulus for curriculum, including both content and process, that resonates well with recent work in cognitive development and metaphor (Lakoff and Johnson, 1980; 1999). Indeed, one of the metaphors associated intimately with Whitehead is 'rhythm'. He applied this to a wide range of phenomena, including education, freedom and discipline (1929/[1957]). Woodhouse (1999a, 1999b) has described and interpreted Whitehead's notion of 'rhythm' in the special context of the university and has asserted that 'Whitehead's theory of the university knits together teaching, learning, administering, and research into a seamless web capable of restoring balance to the postmodern university' (1999b, p. 323). Whilst all these aspects of the university are a seamless, organic whole, Woodhouse illustrates Whitehead's critique by centering on 'research currently conducted at the university', which

> . . . has lost any sense of balance. Its rhythm is one-sided and furthers continuing human domination, rather than appreciation, of nature. *The modern university fails to create knowledge that enhances human beings' relatedness to the universe and to each other.* On the contrary, it generates knowledge that distances them from both. It does so by distinguishing sharply between the subjective and the objective, the inner life of the mind and the outer life of bodily matter. This epistemological dualism creates a rift between mind and matter that cannot be repaired once its assumptions are accepted . . . (Woodhouse, 1999b, pp. 324–25, emphasis added)

This notion of 'rhythm', which courses through Whitehead's analyses[38] is apt, since it evokes such fundamental entailments as 'pulsation', 'life' and 'organic wholeness'. Although we possibly do severe injustice to the beauty and enchantment of Whitehead's 'rhythm', and its resonance with his fallacy of misplaced concreteness (mentioned earlier), the metaphor 'rhythm' impresses upon us, strongly and profoundly, that our accountability as university accounting educators does not exist in a vacuum. 'Accountability', if it can be objectified thus, is not a phenomenon separate from the universe of nature. It is *of* nature, and cannot be otherwise: it must be integrated with, and be responsive to, our embeddedness in the pulsations, the rhythms, of life. Accountability should not, therefore, be manifest by a piecemeal, mechanical and crude set of measures imposed on educators (accountants or otherwise) to satisfy some perverse ideological logic. Yet that is the way accountability is being manifest in contemporary universities. Such imposition has implications, of the most basic kind, for the accountability of our complete university-life. It threatens to fractionate and impair our 'integral whole' as university educators

---

[37] See Dill (1999), on the university as a 'learning organization' in the sense of Garvin (1993). See Birnbaum (2000) on the rise and fall of management fads in the University. And among the 'calamitous implications' that Horn sees in 'market-driven universities' is the 'danger . . . [to] . . . the freedom of professors to determine the content of their courses and the direction of their research . . . [since] . . . [t]hat freedom is an anomaly from a business point of view, in which academics are employees to be managed, and from the neoliberal perspectives, in which they are suppliers of personal services who must seek to "make it" in the market.' (Horn, 2000, p. 174)

[38] Flynn (2000) shows how Whitehead's concept of the rhythm and cycles of mental growth may be good stimulus to self-understanding and practical classroom experience in post-secondary education.

(comprising inextricably-linked aspects of teaching, research, administration and community service) through over-zealous reductionism.

Practical import

What is the *practical* import of such observations regarding our accountability? Perhaps an illustration will suffice: an examination of one recommendation made by Albrecht and Sack in the widely-publicized American Accounting Association monograph *Accounting Education: Charting a Course Through a Perilous Future* (2000):

> **Consider Carefully Your Curriculum and Course Content**
> ... we would encourage you, in your strategic planning, to rigorously challenge curricula and content from your most introductory accounting course to your most advanced course. Focusing on each course, you would ask questions such as:
> 1. Is what we are teaching and the level at which we are covering topics really important in the business world today or has technology, globalization, or increased competition dictated that we make substantive changes to our curriculum?... (p. 63)

Is it even remotely possible to discharge our accountability, in a Whiteheadian sense, if we interrogate curriculum primarily upon 'what is really important in the business world today'? Does the strong implication that we should be passive recipients of curriculum marching orders 'dictated' by 'technology, globalization or increased competition', mesh with our role in facilitating the rhythm of the university? Does the abstract objectification of accounting, underlying the question posed by Albrecht and Sack, seem plausible in an organic world in which accounting, a product of embodied minds, is at the very least an acknowledged social construction (Whitehead, 1929/[1957]; Lakoff and Johnson, 1999)? For us, the answers to these questions are 'No', 'No' and 'No'.

We hold no special brief for the ideas of Alfred North Whitehead other than to show, however tentatively, that the *accountability of accounting educators in the university* is an ideograph of considerable ideological import and complexity. As such it deserves (indeed requires) intensive and broad debate. The simple-minded, inapt, but corrosive accountability measures proffered by a wide range of authoritative agencies, professional bodies and governments worldwide, should be contested vigorously. Whitehead, in a way similar to Cardinal John Henry Newman, stimulates considered thought about 'the very idea of the University'. One doesn't have to accept everything written by a Whitehead or a Cardinal Newman to appreciate the importance of the stimulus they offer. For example, for us, Whitehead stimulates consideration of an important aspect of what we regard as University accounting educator accountability: *corporate critique as an embedded, organic part of accounting curriculum*. This is a matter to which we now turn.

Towards a project of permanent corporate critique

A Whiteheadian interpreter and critic, philosophy professor Howard Woodhouse (1985, 1999a, 1999b, 2000), has been an astute commentator on the University scene for many years. In a recent paper, Woodhouse 'analyzes a debate from 1936 between Alfred North Whitehead and Robert M. Hutchins (then the president of the University of Chicago) over the role of business schools in universities' (2000, p. 135). He then applies his analysis to a recent budget controversy at his own institution (the University of Saskatchewan). He alleges that up to CDN$15 million per year of his university's 1996 base budget was provided as 'an ongoing subsidy to applied research with business ... [thus] reinforc[ing] the university's role as a service agency for the functions of private business, draining money from an already diminished budget ... [and using] ... considerable amounts of public money ... to fund research for private business operations' (pp. 148–49).

We do not know how good an accountant Professor Woodhouse is, so we avoid focusing on the 'reality' of his claim.[39] However, what is disturbing is the seemingly callous disregard the university administration had for the legitimate, collegial enquiries that he and his colleagues raised about this issue. The response, according to Woodhouse, was one of 'deafening silence from the administration' (2000, p. 149). He bemoans '[t]he advent of commercially-driven codes of conduct', rails against the limits this imposes on 'the academic freedom of faculty', and concludes by querying whether Universities are 'seduced':

> ... our dreams and aspirations are shaped by advertising, and our lives molded by banks, business corporations, and governments barely distinguishable from their partners in the private sector. But why universities stay in bed with business corporations whose logic is opposed to theirs, is a continuing source of frustration to me. (2000, p. 152)

Woodhouse's final poignant question: 'But why ...?', is, we contend, perfectly expected from someone dedicated to the University, the *real* University. But why would a University (and its accounting educators) submit to such an *un*University hegemony?

Woodhouse is arguing in support of core, traditional, University values: for the essence of the University.[40] His first hand view from a ringside seat in the humanities is that of a University being perverted into something else – a university consenting to, but powerless in the face of, such a process of perversion.[41] For those of us in the professoriate most closely-allied with the professions and disciplines linked strongly to 'business corporations whose logic is opposed to that of the University' – disciplines such as accounting – it is time to form strong intellectual and practical alliances with colleagues in the humanities and related disciplines, like Professor Woodhouse. We must do so partly by ensuring that accounting curricula do not ignore social context and the philosophy and language within which accounting must necessarily function.[42] In spite of the risks, we must do so partly by committing to a *project of permanent corporate critique*. If we do not, the (true?) University will, most likely, vanish.

Such a project of permanent corporate critique would recognize that all types of corporations (including for-profit, not-for-profit, government, corporate entities, etc.) are

---

[39] We believe Polster (1998) would endorse such a claim. Polster has concluded that academic research in Canadian universities is being subordinated to the needs of industry: that despite the costs of academic research being 'still largely borne by the Canadian public', nonetheless 'the benefits of our universities' research resources are being privatized' (p. 91).

[40] Just what these 'core values' are has sparked intense argument in the humanities and social sciences on a great many issues, including various varieties of *culture wars*.

[41] This within a context in which questions about whether or not the traditional humanities will survive are, chillingly, seen as legitimate. (Tymoczko, 2001). Even more chilling is the inference of a 'friendly critic' of this paper, who draws attention to the likelihood that some would argue 'we are training students to be businesspeople, not ballerinas'; and to their likely conclusion that therefore any thought of 'connection' with the humanities and the ideas of Whitehead, is utterly misplaced. We reject such a view for reasons outlined elsewhere in this paper.

[42] McDonald (2000) argues more generally for a management education reframed within a humanist context.

awash in a language of metaphor and ideology that is inconsistent with community, cooperation, and the *civitas*. It would recognize also that corporations are human social constructions buttressed by law and convention: they are neither by *nature* good nor bad (after all, 'they' have no 'nature'). They require constant monitoring, that is, they require permanent critique. The larger and the more powerful they are, the more remote and abstract they can become (such as new mega cyber corporations like AOLTimeWarner). A project of permanent critique, especially from the perspective of accounting and accounting education, must acknowledge the powerful rhetorical character of the *accountings* of these monitored corporations. Such accountings are usually masked by the twin features of being *technical (and often complex) and seemingly-objective*, and at the same time being *socially sanctioned through GAAP, auditing, and other institutions*. Such a project of permanent corporate critique must ensure the discourse (including the accounting and disclosure) of specific corporations is read and analysed closely. It must also deal with important *contextual* issues such as the four contemporary, inter-related, issues discussed in the next section. Analysis of these issues conditions our pedagogy of permanent corporate critique by ensuring that our students make setting, including ideological mindset, problematic.[43]

Accounting educators and four inter-related contemporary issues

Globalization

> ... globalization ... is changing the nature of the world. (Guillén, 2001, p. 255)

A 'global' (as opposed to an 'international') dimension[44] is an inescapable, omnipresent daily aspect of academic life in the modern university and its accounting departments. Universities, subject to the 'competitive market forces' spawned by globalization (both on site and online), can respond through tapping into the potential for *global convergence* (sameness) or *global divergence* (difference). There is a strong risk that global impacts will force universities to adopt a *convergence* strategy: to achieve international 'benchmark' targets. Universities seem likely to be sucked into a hegemonic vortex, forcing them to adopt 'common patterns of higher education, in which an (idealized) American university model becomes the only possible model' (Marginson, 1999/2000, p. 5). There seems to be strong risk that globalization will promote a 'universalistic' approach to accounting education in which we lose 'locality, contingency and cultural context amid a supposedly transcendent "world culture" subject to continuous reinvention ... [thereby] ... creating a continuous obsolescence and ever-new products and markets, while basic relations of power remain unchanged' (Marginson and Mollis, 1999/2000, p. 56). Indeed, pressures for conformity in accounting are reaching a boiling point. For example, Canadian financial regulators (such as the Ontario Securities Commission) have launched a web-based inquiry into the feasibility of permitting Canadian corporations to use US GAAP standards or

---

[43] We are not merely suggesting that some corporations are 'rogue companies' and therefore deserve 'close reading'. Whilst some companies might be 'rogues', we contend that the very nature of corporatized capitalism as a social and economic phenomenon requires scrutiny because of the power and attendant mindset it bestows on key elites and the behaviours it imposes on many others. Therefore, even 'model citizen' corporations, especially the more powerful ones, require permanent critique, since closer scrutiny may unmask some of the perceptual blinkers by which they were judged to be such 'model citizens.'

[44] Marginson (1999/2000, p. 5) and Pratt and Poole (1999/2000, p. 16.) explain the difference.

International Accounting Standards (IAS), irrespective of the potential superiority of Canadian GAAP in certain areas. (See www.osc.gov.on.ca)

The Canadian experience again raises the question of to whom do accounting educators discharge their accountability? Is it discharged to a body within a nation state? Or is accounting and accounting education regarded as a universal discipline with accountability sloughed off to some supra-national body or the national body of a much more powerful country? If such prospects seem far-fetched, they ought not to be: for these are developments occurring now in the arena of accounting standard setting. The nation-state's responsibility for accounting standards setting is being assumed by the supranational IAS or US GAAP standards. This raises two important questions. Is accounting education something that ought to operate within a global-nation mindset? Or should accounting educators be accountable at local, national levels?

There seems little doubt that globalization is reinforcing the 'market ideology' with which Universities are currently entranced. It is transforming the culture (and the 'mission statements') of universities and their constituent parts, and is fashioning community perceptions of what constitutes a university. As Menzies (with Newson, 2001) observe, it is 'global competitiveness' and a 'specious abstraction', the impact of which on educators is being felt in 'demands for faster turnover, higher productivity, lower costs and 24 hour competitiveness'. The embracing of entrepreneurial endeavour and adoption of the 'business model' of a university is now seemingly mandatory (especially for publicly-funded universities, operating under conditions of extreme financial stringency). This situation is leading increasingly to adoption of the rhetoric of marketing and to endorsement of an *Accounting Degrees 'R' Us* mentality. In such circumstances, 'society' can be forgiven for concluding that the 'university' is just another sort of shopping mall, where a 'product' called 'knowledge', and another called 'a degree' are 'for sale'. Indeed, not only are the 'tangible outputs' of universities for sale – so too are their most important intangible assets … their prestige, reputation and 'masthead badging', their 'brand'! Recently, universities in the global *Universitas 21* consortium (see footnote 18) announced a joint venture with education publisher Thomson Learning in which 'U21 universities provide badging and quality assurance' and 'Thomson develops the course material and is responsible for assessment, student database management and translation' (Illing, 2001a, p. 37).

University educators should be committed to responding appropriately and critically to the subtle and not-so-subtle cajoling and exhortation of senior university administrators. We should give precedence to integrity, ethics and humanitarianism and not be impelled primarily by the tawdry pursuit of money. Yet, increasingly, the latter is what we appear to be doing. We ought to be accountable to society, as accounting educators, for providing critique of aspects of post-industrial global corporate capitalism and postmodern business culture. Yet our capacity to do that is compromised, increasingly, in modern day universities.[45] Boje (2001) notes that as 'linkages' between universities and corporations

---

[45] Few modern day university educators can remove themselves from the commercialization and corporatization of Universities. Recently, the faculty to which the first author belongs has established the new post of 'Business Development Manager'. His university has been troubled by controversy surrounding attempts to commercialize medical research through formation, by the university, of a listed company. Claims (in the listing prospectus) about the health benefits of a new drug have been disputed keenly by a scientist within the university: the debate has raised concerns that the university is so keen to 'cash in', through commercialization of its research, that it has forsaken the scholarly virtues of caution, humility, objectivity and validity. The second author belongs to a

proliferate through sponsored research, endowments and the like, critical analysis of corporations is becoming more difficult – sometimes because of 'corporate intimidation', at other times through more discreet 'muffling' of dissonant voices. In one very notable incident, the Nike Corporation 'canceled a US$40 million dollar donation and lucrative endorsement' to the University of Oregon, University of Michigan and Brown University, because all had been critical of Nike (Boje, 2001). This, of course, presents intriguing possibilities in regard to our urging that a project of permanent corporate critique be an integral aspect of our accountability as accounting educators in the University (see above). Globalized, corporatized capitalism, a fully-emergent and vigorous juggernaut of flexible accumulation (Harvey, 1990), has enormous potential to 'chill' and marginalize serious corporate critique, and thereupon trivialize accounting as little more than an exercise in technological virtuosity. But, even more disturbing, when questions are raised in such a context about whether or not accounting 'belongs' in the university (Zeff, 1989), the sad answer is 'yes', because the university itself will no longer really *be* the University. Indeed, an 'accounting' of the most pernicious sort will have colonized 'the university', and will have remade 'the university' into its own image!

Market Force Hysteria

Contemporary university accounting education is influenced strongly by an almost-unthinking and reverential acceptance of a market-focused philosophy. This organizing philosophy results often in a 'bland, technical' approach to accounting education in the universities, in which educators concentrate on professional pronouncements as *technical menus* to be 'learned' rather than as text for *social critique*. Indeed, we contend that such an approach dominates the content of major scholarly journals in 'accounting education' (for example the American Accounting Association's *Issues in Accounting Education*), and university calendar descriptions of accounting course curriculum.

American Accounting Association (AAA) President, Mary Stone, in the AAA's *Accounting Education News* (Fall 2000), editorialized on the topic: 'What Will We Teach?' Stone's answer reveals herself to be a creature of the MARKET. If 'the market' doesn't want historic-cost based GAAP information, we are entreated to serve society and satisfy the 'market' by teaching something 'the market' does want. (Presumably, according to Stone, this would include such things as a new set of measurement principles encompassing valuation of 'employee and supplier assets, customer assets, intellectual capital, and other intangibles that are the crucial drivers of value in the information economy'). Of course, this presumes that the 'market' is the best indicator of the interests of the society accounting is to serve. Does Stone miss a critical point? Would a better alternative be to reconceptualize accounting in the absence of a (mythical) construct such as the MARKET and see where that takes us? We suspect that Chambers (1999), discussed earlier, would agree strongly with such an approach.

faculty latterly named in honour of a prominent local entrepreneur who has bestowed a monetary endowment on the faculty. His university has recently been subject to accusations that it withdrew a formal written job offer to a world-renowned scientist, Dr. David Healy, because he criticized a drug (Prozac) that is manufactured by the corporate conglomerate, Eli Lilly – an important donor to the university (McIlroy, 2001a). The university has denied it was pressured to take such action by Eli Lilly. Nonetheless, the university is reported to have confirmed that it withdrew the job offer because of a speech Dr. Healy gave that 'was critical of the pharmaceutical industry' and by concerns, *inter alia*, about his 'extremist views' and 'sweeping statements'. (McIlroy, 2001b). The many (so-called) 'extremists' in universities who invoke 'sweeping statements' ought to find little comfort in this.

We must not simply conceive accounting as existing to teach *technical menus* of subject fare that have been identified, captured, and interpreted according to the demands posed by vogue conceptions of capitalism. It is important to encourage *social critique* and 'deviations' from this mainstream. Sadly, the professional pressure on accounting academics to conform to market forces is almost overwhelming. Too few are engaging in social critique. A reading of some of the doctrinaire exhortations to comply with economic market forces that have been made by university Vice-Chancellors and Presidents, helps in appreciating how corrupting and overwhelming such views are and how intimidating they can be for (especially untenured) academic staff.[46]

A chilling example of the enunciation of such market-based imperatives we are being cajoled into accepting is the letter of exhortation to staff of the Australian National University (ANU), written by its (then) Vice-Chancellor Terrell in July 2000 (reproduced in Appendix B). Perhaps we should thank Terrell for being so honest and for using language that reveals his image of the university, however repugnant that image might be. What Terrell provides is a candid announcement of intention that his university should be 'captured' by the market-based interests of its 'prospective clients'; that the university seek to locate itself 'at the centre of a rapidly expanding market place'; and that it should make itself 'attractive to potential investors'. It is a very public declaration of his 'ideology'.[47] Terrell's image is 'totalizing' in one direction only. As Vice-Chancellor, he has the power to see his image (that is, of the ANU firmly in the raging river of the 'market') imposed and to contribute to the construction of a discourse at both the ANU and in Australian higher education generally.

Metaphor and the 'naturalness' of the University as a market-driven business

What seems lacking in the image of the University held by many Vice-Chancellors and Presidents (and business faculty deans) is that members of the University have an obligation to pursue critique of pervasive ideas and ideologies which drive the sundering of social life and the often-passive acceptance of that which is 'natural'. An example, especially pertinent to accounting education, is the nexus of ideas associated with 'rational

---

[46] They can be more than simply 'intimidating' too. Sometimes they possess dire consequences, even for tenured staff. At the University of Wollongong (Australia) in 2001, Associate Professor Steele, a scholar with a strong international reputation for his 'paradigm breaking neo-Lamarckian biological research' (Martin, 2001, p. 35), was summarily dismissed. His dismissal was alleged to be contrary to the terms of an industrial agreement which specified a 'due process' prior to dismissal involving the instituting of 'misconduct' proceedings. Steele 'had been an outspoken critic of the university administration' and, in the Vice-Chancellor's words, was dismissed for 'plac[ing] at serious and imminent risk' the university's reputation over allegations of 'soft marking' for fee paying students. In reviewing Steele's dismissal, Martin (2001, p. 35) observed that it has 'sent a stark warning to others who might want to make public comment "on the issue of commercialization in higher education"'. Tellingly, Martin concludes that 'the sacking of Steele has given the appearance that commercial concerns are more important than free speech and that the University of Wollongong is more a commercial entity that an intellectual community. Ironically, this is precisely the point that Steel was making.' (2001, p. 35). Australia's National Tertiary Education Union (NTEU) has begun a national and international campaign in support of the 'due process' procedures and 'natural justice' denied to Steele. NTEU general secretary, McCulloch (2001, p. 3) has claimed the case is 'yet another example' of a Vice-Chancellor embracing management models more appropriate to the corporate world, thereby undermining 'the universities' roles as sites of independent thinking and freedom of speech'.

[47] That is more than can be said for many other university administrators, who often 'mouthe' the language of the admirable academic but practice (especially during budget dust-ups) the behaviour of the 'money-changer'.

choice' in 'competitive markets'. Lakoff and Johnson (1999, p. 532), in their recent major opus analysing the foundations of Western thought, contest the alleged naturalness of such ideas:

> To bring an area of life into accord with 'rational choice' is to force life into the mould of a specific complex of metaphors – for better or worse, all to often for the worse. An example is *the trend to conceptualize education metaphorically as a business*, or through privatization to make education run by considerations of 'rational choice.' In this metaphor, students are consumers, their education is a product, and teachers are labour resources. Knowledge then becomes a commodity, a thing with market value that can be passed from teacher to student. Test scores measure the quality of the product. Better schools are the ones with higher overall test scores. Productivity is the measure of test scores per dollar spent. Rational-choice theory imposes a cost-benefit analysis in which productivity is to be maximized. Consumers should be getting the 'best education' for their dollar.
>
> This metaphor stresses efficiency and product quality above all else. In doing so, *it hides the reality of education. Education is not a thing; it's an activity.* Knowledge is not literally transmitted from teacher to student, and education is not merely the acquisition of particular bits of knowledge. *Through education, students who work at it become something different. It is what they become that is important. This metaphor ignores the student's role, as well as the role of the student's upbringing and the culture at large. It ignores the nurturing role of educators*, which often can only be very labour-intensive. And it ignores the overall social necessity for an ongoing, maintained class of education professionals who are appropriately reimbursed for the immense amount they contribute to society (emphasis added).

Lakoff and Johnson (1980, 1999) help us to realize that much of what we think, say and do is *metaphorical* and *embodied*; that although much of our thinking may be characterized as 'unconscious conceptual systems' (1999, p. 537), we also have the potential to become more self-aware since '[i]t may be possible to learn to use certain metaphors rather than others and to learn new metaphors' (p. 537). Certainly, *education* – and importantly, accounting education – requires that we strive to help ourselves and our students critically comprehend the metaphors that often-subtly guide our thought, words, and actions. Postman (1996, p. 174) put it bluntly thus: 'Do I exaggerate in saying that a student cannot understand what a subject is without some understanding of the metaphors that are its foundation?' He then fleshes out his thinking about the importance of metaphor in education in the following way:

> A metaphor is not an ornament. It is an organ of perception. Through metaphors, we see the world as one thing or another. Is light a wave or a particle? Are molecules like billiard balls or force fields? Is history unfolding according to some instructions of nature or a divine plan? Are our genes like information codes? Is a literary work like an architect's blueprint or a mystery to be solved? (Postman, 1996, p. 174)

In accounting education, what metaphors underlie (metaphorically) the way accountants think about, and act upon, *assets*, *costs*, and *cash flows* (Walters-York, 1996)? When accountants account for a *corporation*, does the metaphor A CORPORATION IS A PERSON intrude upon the way their accounting is constructed? If the *accounting entity* is the corporation (or, in the case of one corporation controlling other corporations, the corporate group), does the sentient, human *character* of the corporation affect how income is constructed and balance sheets built? Is operating cash flow the *life-blood* of this sentient, *corporeal being*, and, if so, does this cognitive lens affect the way managers and accountants conceive of, and measure, operating cash flow?

We should not be content, as accounting educators, in acquiescing to the (allegedly) 'natural' metaphors of 'rational choice',[48] 'competitive markets', 'the accounting entity', 'economic man' (Shackelford, 1992), and so on, without openly acknowledging the metaphorical nature of such human ideas. Vigorous examination of the implications of such acquiescence for accounting, accountability, accounting education, and our students, seems critical. We need to identify the metaphors that inhabit the conceptual frameworks of financial accounting,[49] and (even more importantly) the various authoritative standards encompassing GAAP, and to be sensitive to the metaphors that slip, perhaps unnoticed, into managers' thinking, talking, and acting about their businesses and its accountings.[50] An appreciation of these metaphors is important for they inevitably influence management's *business* and *accounting* decisions (Lakoff and Johnson, 1999; Amernic and Craig, 2000a, 2000b, 2001; Craig *et al.*, 2001). Accordingly, it seems fundamental and legitimate to examine, in classrooms, the strong ideological footprint that metaphor leaves behind. Far from being just a useful pedagogical device in education, metaphor has foundational implications that we should not ignore.

A CORPORATION IS A PERSON is an example of how a metaphor may become embedded in our culture, including our legal system, and consequently alter profoundly the way we think about, make decisions about, and make policy about, the phenomenon, the *corporation*. A recent editorial from *Multinational Monitor*, reproduced in Appendix C, attempts to explain this metaphor and to argue that it is *metaphor* we are dealing with, and not some feature of *nature*. The editorialists observe that '. . . even more important than the legal protections gained by faux personhood status are the political, social and cultural benefits.' To this we would add that accounting characterizations in turn reinforce and extend such metaphor and its practical, social, and cultural character. For example, a corporation, like a human entrepreneur, is 'a person', has a boundary separating it from the outside world, and thus, is an 'accounting entity'. Such (metaphorical) demarcation results in strong ideological pressure to exclude from the 'entity's' accountings so-called 'externalities'.[51]

---

[48] Indeed, even the 'rational' in 'rational choice' has been contested vigorously. For example, Zafirovski (2000) concludes 'In practical terms, society would likely fall apart' if the rational choice model were 'applied in full' (p. 198).

[49] Of course, the notion of an accounting 'framework' for concepts is, itself, an uncontested metaphor.

[50] For example, recourse to the (misleading) accounting metaphor 'the bottom line' effectively shuts off interchange.

[51] This metaphorical mapping of human characteristics onto the corporation is even more complex and interesting, partly because its significance depends on our view of a 'person'. If we regard a 'person' from a neo-liberal, autonomous, allegedly self-reliant perspective, then the corporation, the metaphorical 'person', might acquire similar features. Further, work in cognitive linguistics suggests that an *accounting* metaphor is basic to (at least Western) thinking (Johnson, 1993), which seems to open additional implications for the A CORPORATION IS A PERSON metaphor. We do not pursue those implications here.

Getting beneath the technical to the ideology of accounting

In curricula, we need to get beneath the technical surface of accounting, and permit our students to 'see' how that which seems purely technical inevitably carries a heavy burden of ideology. An example of an attempt at developing such curricula material could well involve critical assessment of the words used in academic and professional publications. An example follows. It is stimulated by the belief that the juggernaut of corporate business ideology, manifest in accounting and auditing technique, has swaggered across the University landscape and has emerged full-blown in various guises. For instance, Lang (1999) describes 'Responsibility Centre Budgeting' and 'Responsibility Centre Management', as having been 'deployed ... to one degree or another' in numerous universities (p. 81). Here, as an example of possible curriculum material, we analyse some elements of a recent study promoting aspects of this deployment. The publication, prepared by three accounting professors for *The PricewaterhouseCoopers Endowment for The Business of Government*, is:

> Granof, M.H., Platt, D.E. and Vaysman, I. (2000), *Using Activity-Based Costing to Manage More Effectively*, Arlington, Virginia: The PricewaterhouseCoopers Endowment for The Business of Government, 31 pages.

Although not mentioned in the publication's title, the purpose of the study was to 'show how activity-based costing (ABC) can be applied to a single department of a major institution of higher education and thereby provide more management-oriented information than the systems currently employed.' (Granof *et al.*, 2000, p. 6). Specifically, the study focuses on an assessment of the merits of ABC to the authors' (academic) accounting department in their business school. The authors view one of the merits of their study as its rather unique applicability to a university's 'more costly intellectual activities' (p. 6).

Our intent is not to conduct an exhaustive critique of this study. Rather, we draw attention to how such critique might be used in accounting education to raise awareness of the implications of the assumptions and other traces of ideology often obscured within the technical virtuosity of such works. As we examine accounting and allied business management technologies applied in Universities, including within our role as accounting educators, it seems prudent to keep in mind that '[s]elective identification and aggregation of accounting information is a political act.' (Coy and Pratt, 1998, p. 545).

We begin by commenting on the *Foreword* to the study: four paragraphs signed by two partners of PricewaterhouseCoopers who identify themselves as the co-chairs of the *Endowment Advisory Board*. The co-chairs write that 'In this report, Professors Granof, Platt, and Vaysman demonstrate how activity-based costing (ABC) can be used by executives to manage more effectively.' But a close reading of the report shows that all the authors did was to illustrate the mechanics of ABC in the setting of an academic department. Indeed, with all the assumptions and caveats in the report's demonstration, just the opposite conclusion might be more reasonable: that ABC was demonstrated to show how to manage less effectively (see below). Of course, the key words 'executives', 'manage', and 'more effectively' deserve scrutiny, as does the conclusion of the co-chairs about what the study accomplished. For example, who are the 'executives' and the 'non-executives' in an academic department? Isn't governance a shared, collegial responsibility ... or at least should be? Do the 'executives' determine policy as well as execute it? And how is 'more effectively' determined, and what does it mean?

The co-chairs also write that:

> ... This model (i.e., ABC) can clearly be applied to government and nonprofit organizations, as well as universities. Instead of measuring traditional 'inputs' of salary and administrative costs, ABC accounting provides a methodology to measure the costs of 'outputs'. (p. 5)

We confess to holding no particular fondness for extant university accounting, which remains largely fund-based and obscurantist (Amernic, 1985; Coy and Pratt, 1998). Consequently, we suspect it of being a convenient tool for maintaining the *status quo* in extant power structures. But we would argue also it is presumptuous to assert that 'ABC accounting provides a methodology to measure the costs of (university) "outputs".' After all, the concept of *cost* remains one of the most elusive in accounting, economics, political economy and society in general. 'Costs are tricky things', as Chapman and Buckley (1997, p. 229) observe. Thus, to assert blithely that ABC facilitates measuring THE costs reinforces the truth of Coy and Pratt's 'political act' contention quoted above. This seems even more egregious when one considers the positioning of this publication in the firmament of public discourse. This is a short booklet prepared by an organization that identifies itself as an *Endowment*, albeit sponsored by one of the remaining mega-accounting-cum-consultancy firms. It is not a technical study prepared for knowledgeable specialists, rather it seems targeted at university 'managers', and perhaps governing bodies and responsible political and private institutions that fund universities. So, in our view, this *Foreword* is a rhetorical text intended to achieve the goal of branding: of placing the accounting firm's ethos on an emerging area of public practice. But, we move on now, since the point is well made that accounting, and accounting documents published under even ostensibly *public interest* auspices, are dense with ideology, and are perhaps self-serving.

The *Executive Summary* (p. 6) of the report consists of five paragraphs. For brevity, we focus only on the fifth paragraph:

> Although our project was a case study, we believe that we learned several lessons that are applicable not only to universities, but also to other governmental and not-for-profit organizations. These include:
>
> - The primary benefit of ABC may be not that it is an improvement upon an already adequate accounting system, but that it provides the structure for the establishment, for the first time, of a true management-oriented system.
> - To be successful, a system must be flexible. Rigid allocation rules cannot readily be imposed upon organizations, like universities, characterized by decentralized management systems.
> - ABC, by assigning costs to previously-unmeasured factors in decisions and providing a measure of the full cost of programmes and activities, helps identify circumstances in which goals and objectives are out of line with spending decisions.

At least two of the many assertions in this paragraph deserve comment. First, the authors' conclusion that ABC 'provides the structure for the establishment ... of a true management-oriented system' seems refreshing, since it displays openly the ideological underpinnings of all accounting systems, including ABC. Such an assertion places the contentious phrase 'a true management-oriented system' where it should be, at the forefront for close ideological scrutiny, a task not undertaken here. We merely react to the signal from our ideological antennae to argue that the words 'true' and 'management-oriented' need airing out.

The second assertion meriting comment is the entire third bullet point. Notice the rather implicit reasoning chain in this assertion:

> *Decisions* exist → *Factors* in decisions exist, and these *factors* should be taken into account in *decisions* → Some, or perhaps many, of these *factors* had remained unmeasured as to their *cost* → But now, fortunately, *cost* numbers obtained via ABC are available, and they are 'a measure of the full cost of programmes and activities' → And, consequently, having these full costs 'helps identify circumstances in which goals and objectives are out of line with spending decisions.'

Such a reasoning chain presumes that:

- these so-called *factors* and their *full ABC costs* pre-existed before they were named by the ABC technology;
- accounting information is innocent: that is, it is not used as *ex post facto* political justification or to render equivocal situations meaningful according to the hegemony of powerful groups controlling the accounting and other management discourse (Swieringa and Weick, 1987);
- ABC is able, through some technique, to divine (at least satisfactory approximations to) full costs, in spite of the problems of opportunity costs and externalities, and boundary issues (Hines, 1988); and
- *decisions* exist independently of their social/political creation, and await high-quality information so that the optimum choices may be made resolving the decisions (in other words, people and human institutions as we know them do not exist).

We do not intend to belabour critique of this third bullet point. Our thesis is that some considerable antidote to such dressed-up bluster is vital and appropriate to counteract students' fascination with the (at times intricate) mechanics of a rather arbitrary accounting technique such as ABC costing. We must not forget that technologies such as ABC carry with them a persuasive, seductive patina. They are well-lauded in the (mainly professional) accounting and management literature. They are appealing too because they have enduring favourable qualities. They satisfy the attraction in our culture to the quantitative (ABC costing often uses statistical regression, for example) and the market (ABC is alleged to provide better costs than other, older, accounting techniques, so that markets, which depend upon cost data, will function more rationally). Consequently, some perhaps rather blunt counter views seem prudent (Jones and Dugdale (1999) provide a specific example of required counter views regarding ABC).

In our teaching of accounting technologies such as ABC, we should remember vividly Hines' admonition regarding the hidden power of accountants to construct reality (1988, p. 257) in ways similar to how modern finance theory has helped construct what we sometimes believe is the natural world of hyperfinance.[52] We should remember keenly also

---

[52] MacKenzie (2001), a sociologist studying the social implication of option pricing theory, makes the following comment about finance theory that seems every bit as apt for accounting, including ABC: 'That *finance theory makes a world rather than just describes a world* adds a wider significance to its study. It is performative ... but not uniformly and straightforwardly performative.' (p. 138, emphasis added).

that the practising arm of accounting has long been skilled at expanding its web of clientele, just like many other professions. Thus, technical phenomena such as ABC are not *merely* technical in an innocent sense, but serve to assist an expansionist profession in its colonial moves.

Internet technology

There are seemingly impressive growth statistics regarding the embrace of the Internet for delivery of university (including accounting) education.[53] Nonetheless, we contend that accounting educators have responded poorly to the challenges of the Internet Age,[54] and indeed, to the emergence of the so-called 'New Economy'. We sustain this contention by introducing points (i) to (vi) below.

(i) *The need for new ways of thinking about accounting*

Internet corporate financial reporting differs significantly from 'traditional' financial reporting (Amernic, 1998). Yet, as accounting educators, we do not seem to have appreciated this sufficiently or to have responded appropriately. Internet-enabled *virtual* companies imply management control systems and management accounting structures that differ radically from the accountings of *non-virtual* companies. Indeed, the degree to which formerly non-virtual companies are embracing aspects of forms of *e-virtualism* seems an issue of fundamental importance for educators. Such attendant new forms of accounting need public policy attention (e.g. to explore the implications of visual rhetoric and telepresence, among many other phenomena),[55] together with frames of reference that broaden our fascination beyond the mere surface technical virtuosity of *technology*. We need to shift our gaze to stimulate critical reflection on the prime, social, and ideological forces at play – forces that ultimately shape accounting and the impact of accounting.[56]

Indeed, Albrecht and Sack (2000, pp. 56–57) came to a similar (belated?) realization whilst writing *Accounting Education: Charting a Course through a Perilous Future*:

> We understand the need to use technology in our teaching and to expose students to technology. However, do we understand what is meant when we say students need to learn technology? We are not sure we understood when we began this study. Our initial thoughts were that technology meant using various technology tools to solve problems, understanding systems controls and maybe some programming, and understanding technology terminology. While understanding

[53] Bennett (2001, p. 7) reports that 'as of 2000, US (higher education) institutions reportedly offered more than 6000 accredited courses on the Web and, by 2002, over 2 million students will be enrolled'.

[54] Accounting educators are not alone in their need to attend to the implications of the Internet. For example, sociologists DiMaggio *et al.* write (2001, p. 308): 'Many observers allege that the Internet is changing society. Perhaps not surprisingly, given the novelty of the new digital media, there is little agreement about what those changes are.'

[55] A recent article in a hauntingly-titled journal, *Presence*, describes a questionnaire developed to *measure* 'presence' in virtual environments (Witmer and Singer, 1998). Such applications of technical thinking to the emerging 'Internet world' should serve to jolt back to reality those who believe, naively, that the Internet has promise as a 'non-hegemonic, globalized ... coalition' (Hackenberg, 2000, p. 368). Although we 'see' such potential, we 'see' also the fantastic corporate resources being invested in the creation of what AOLTimeWarner calls the 'new world' (AOLTimeWarner website < aoltimewarner.com >, *Internet Public Policy Statement*, visited January 15 2001).

[56] Innis, as well as McLuhan, offer promise for accounting educators in this regard (Amernic and Craig, 1999, 2000a; see also Amernic, 1998).

these aspects of technology are important, *probably even more critical is understanding how technology has reshaped everything we do ... Technology has revolutionized everything, including the way we live and work.* **It should have taught us to completely rethink everything we teach** ... (emphasis added).

We concur, and contend also that a good starting point for accounting educators might be to 're-think' the merits of serving students a diet heavy with conventional accounting technique. Such a diet is lacking in what we would regard as the vital trace elements of critique. If our students are to be nourished intellectually, they ought to be encouraged to critique underlying concepts and the social and ideological forces responsible for fashioning any variety of accounting technique.

Educationally, in the emergent era of 'ubiquitous computing' (Gillette, 2001, p. 42), and its consequent influence on all forms of accounting, teachers would benefit from reconceptualizing their understanding of accounting and reporting. A good starting point might be to consider the advice of Gillette (2001, p. 45) to web designers (on how to respond to an environment of context-sensitive embedded computing devices) as being apt also for accounting educators:

> In reaching beyond standard design theory derived from print, film, and television to incorporate theories from the domains of commercial design, cognitive psychology, and architectural, urban, and landscape design, we need to begin assembling a framework to support a new aspect of online rhetorical analysis. A rhetoric of mobile use would begin with traditional ideas of persuasion, discourse, and structure derived from an examination and development of speech, two-dimensional textual presentation on the printed page, the artist's canvas, and the television and movie screen. But a more expansive, inclusive rhetoric could open its scope of inquiry to include the rhetoric of interaction derived from narrative inter-communication in live theatre, social interaction in architecture and urban design, and usability and human factors study, particularly as applied in the field of commercial design.

In other words, we need new and more-encompassing ways of thinking about accounting and accounting education in an Internet age – one that is replete with new metaphors and new *gestalts*. But all this new thinking should have a critical edge, and the ideologies thereby accepted and rejected should be made explicit, along with the consequences.

(ii) *Deification of the Internet*

Determination of what technology 'should be taught to us' has largely been ignored. Rather than 'rethink what we teach' we have tended to deify the Internet unquestioningly. We have been swept along in a torrent of *technical* issues: rarely have accounting educators subjected Internet technology to critique. Among those wading against the storm surge of popular fascination have been Amernic and Craig (1999): they have raised concerns about students being 'neophytes among metaphors' in the use of the Internet in management education. Many educators have been seduced, all too readily, into deification of the Internet and supplication before the altar of Internet-based distance learning: a setting where classes become 'content', universities become 'providers', professors become 'chief knowledge officers' and universities are possessed with concern for issues of 'branding' and 'badging'. An anonymous Georgetown University professor echoed our concerns in describing many university Internet-based approaches to distance learning as 'a new version of the trade school' (see Confessore, 2001).

For both better and (certainly) worse, 'technology creates new opportunities for the ideological imagination' (Carlisle and Manning, 1999, p. 97). Such imaginings have real impacts on live people, most of whom have had no choice in the matter:

> ... In relation to the ever-decreasing proportion of the world's population able to exercise any ideological preference for this or that technology, the ever-increasing proportion is without its benefit, while still being subject to its unintended consequences. Ideologies ride on the merry-go-round of technological change ... (Carlisle and Manning, 1999, p. 100).

The consequences of Internet technology for accounting educators, and educators generally, are wide-ranging. For managers, students, workers, and indeed everyone, the Internet means the emergence of an 'informationistic worldview ... [that] ... fundamentally alters human experience and the evaluation of, and association with, reality' (De Mul, 1999, p. 69). How can we properly *teach* accounting, management control, and financial reporting, until we comprehend how the context of such accounting has been altered, and in turn how accounting and contexts (re-)constitute each other? The problem seems to be that, whereas the practice of accounting is mutating,[57] accounting education is not responding to the emergent changes in a timely fashion.

(iii) *Concern for humans in* virtual *worlds*

Other consequences involve a wide variety of 'human factors issues', including 'human performance efficiency in virtual worlds'. Human health is an issue of special concern. Stanney *et al.* (1998) express concern about the physical, trauma and psychological 'health and safety issues that may affect users of virtual environments'. This concern transfers easily to Internet use in education in general (Amernic and Craig, 1999).[58] We should be especially concerned as accounting educators about this issue since one of the major objects of our pedagogy (corporate Internet-based financial and business reporting) would necessitate our students sitting, transfixed, in front of computer screens for hours at a time.

As educators we should be concerned too about the effects of the Internet on the quality of our work and of the lifestyles we lead. As the International Labour Organization (ILO) (2001, p. 9) notes, there is potential for the Internet to be liberating by making work 'independent' of location and for it to help us better balance work and family responsibilities. Despite this, the risks and stresses involved are great. We need to cope with the stresses of engaging in a continuous 'learning and re-learning' of computing technology and applications [*WebCT, Blackboard, PowerPoint*] and the increased social isolation accompanying a higher intensity of virtual communications (ILO, 2001, p. 9). Our hours of work and hours of leisure are becoming blurred as we submit to pressures (e.g. those of student e-mails) 'to work everywhere and all of the time' (ILO, 2001, p. 10).

---

[57] Perhaps accounting and accounting education is 'morphing' as much as it is 'mutating'.

[58] The latter argue that 'for many, the reality of using the Internet is of an activity in the reflected glow emanating from a cathode ray tube in a dingy room, in the dead of night. It is an unhealthy, sedentary activity ...' (p. 447).

(iv) Recognizing that the Internet is not universally privileging

How we conceive financial reporting in the Internet age is an important issue too. It is misleading to assume, as we seem prone to do, that all users of web-based financial reporting are equal. We need to acknowledge that the 'digital divide' and levels of Internet connectivity are discriminating. The (so-called) 'information rich', who take advantage of high bandwith technologies and who have access to computing resources, are determined by income, race and geography (Allport, 2001, p. 2. See also DiMaggio, *et al.*, 2001, p. 310. for a summary of recent research on 'the "digital divide" in the United States'). The ILO, in its *World Employment Report* 2001, draws attention to a widening digital divide:

> Use of the Internet . . . is more common among younger people than older people, men than women, the more rather than the less educated, urban rather than rural dwellers, and those with high incomes . . . barely 6% of the world's people have ever logged on to the Internet and 85 to 90% of them are in the industrialized countries (ILO 2001, Overview, p. 3)

Indeed, we will have lapsed into a 'developed world blindness' if we presume, for even a moment, that access to information technology devices is in any way universal. Access to even the basic, taken-for-granted, seemingly ubiquitous telephone is a desperate need in many parts of the world. The World Bank (2001, pp. 239–40), in a comparative study of poverty in 23 countries, has highlighted the plight of people in Jamaica, Kyrgyz Republic, Somaliland and Malawi that arises from their lack of access to a telephone.

Some users are more equal than others, for the Internet is never neutral. Accessors of financial accounting information via the Internet operate under the new false illusion that they are now always watching 'Big Brother'-cum-the-corporation. 'Big Brother' is the new ideology of financial reporting. But 'Big Brother' is always watching 'us', employing among other means tracking technology in which Internet capital has invested heavily. So, contrary to popular perception, the Internet has not given Internet accessors the privileged powers of some corporate viewing Panopticon: such a view, we contend, is a cruel fraud.[59]

(v) Recognizing the rhetoric in web-based accounting

For many decades, accounting has been conceived in terms of 'form' and 'substance', with the latter to take precedence over the former. Indeed, it could be argued that we are witnessing the death of accounting, as we have known it – at least as far as 'form' is concerned. Insofar as the rhetorical (persuasive) role of accounting is concerned (Aho, 1985), that is probably not true. The rhetorical role is perhaps deepened and made more evident by financial accounting's co-optation by Internet technology. But is the Internet and our worship of it reversing this and promoting form over substance? Do we have a visual rhetoric of financial accounting that is likely to prompt the demise of the measurement role of accounting? If so, this is likely to be a semiotician's paradise – the 'sign' demolishing the 'measure'.

Furthermore, we seem uncaring and unresponsive to the impact on accounting and Internet financial reporting of the 'mogulization' of business by the likes of Rupert

---

[59] But see Green (1999, p. 42), who writes 'we can see the Internet as a site of conflict between hegemonic and counter-hegemonic surveillance strategies with radically different agendas and relations to power'. This 'even-handed' approach to Internet analysis seems fanciful to us, given the dramatic power asymmetries involved.

Murdoch, Bill Gates, Larry Ellison, Ted Turner and other moguls who will effectively 'control' the e-world and dictate public policy directions. Their corporate websites (including their accounting and financial reporting pages) are often exercises in metonymy (e.g. BILL GATES IS MICROSOFT? See Craig *et al.*, 2001) and reflect the mogul's personality and ideology.

(vi) *Tailoring accounting education to the acculturation of students*

We should concentrate on critique of contemporary 'corporate culture': to reflect on the issues of what we teach and how we can teach more effectively. Should we be content for our teaching to imply a sort of 'theory of human capital' in which universities have a dominant role in educating, training and supplying factors of production – *human resources*? In this context, the matter of how to best 'equip' students for their role as 'human capital' within an economy has been given renewed impetus by the recent highlighting of the (alleged) paradigmatic shift from the 'old economy' to the (so-called) 'new economy' – the latter allegedly based upon commitment to research and development, technology reliance, computer literacy and being Internet-savvy.

In this context, Owsen (2000) has argued that accounting educators are grossly remiss in persisting with a 'worldview' in which teaching practices are outdated legacies, lacking in 'acculturation'. Persistence with inappropriate clinging to the remnants of an outdated paradigm – the one in which the (so-called) 'Old Economy' operates – was criticized and arguments were entered to the effect that some approaches to teaching (such as creative role play) are more conducive to fostering skills critical in the 'New Economy' ... skills such as 'creativity, group work, public speaking ... [and] socializing by having fun'. Accounting educators should be alert to the need to respond to change (paradigmatic or not); adapt to the acculturation of their students, and recognize the educational benefits of flair, adaptation, creativity, theatre, and regard for emotion in educational settings.

Elements of the contemporary issues discussed above are evident in the reasoning and debate surrounding the Massachusetts Institute of Technology's (MIT) announcement, in April 2001, that it intended to make nearly all of its course materials available free of charge, to all, via the World Wide Web – a decision we, and others,[60] commend. MIT, with rhetorical flourish, alleges it was prompted to do so by 'a deeply ingrained sense of service and mission' and 'incredible idealism'. It draws attention to the 'counter intuitive' nature of its decision in a '*market driven world* ... go[ing] against the grain of current material values [because it] wid[ens] access to information and inspir[es] others to participate' (emphasis added; http://web.mit.edu/ocw/). By utilizing *Internet technology*, MIT claims that it will 'facilitate a new style of national and *global* collaboration in education through the sharing of educational content and the potential of telecommunications for real-time communications' (http://web.mit.edu/ocw/). But perhaps we should not be too sanguine about such seemingly-laudatory endeavours, at least until we analyse, critically, the form and substance of what will be on offer, and the metaphors and ideologies lurking therein.

Perhaps the pace of change has been so rapid that we have lost the capacity (or the resolve?) to adapt curricula and teaching methods appropriately, and in a timely fashion, to the imperatives of the Internet age. The magnitude of information we are confronted

---

[60] Tinker, in a discussion of MIT's decision by subscribers to the Accounting Education using Computers and Multimedia (AECM@LISTSERV.Loyola.edu) mailing list, wrote: 'I would be very pleased to be part of an institution that views open access to education as an urgent social priority' (6 April 2001).

with as educators is burdensome, and the way it is constructed and disseminated are changing so rapidly that it will be difficult for us to ever respond appropriately, especially if our attitudes, mindsets and ideologies are geared to another era.

Discussion: resistance strategies for the postmodern accounting educator's blues

> The idea that we live in a world of people – not a world of machines, systems, or budgets – must not die. The human heart of education must be kept alive no matter how heartless the environment in which we live, learn, and teach. (Smith, 1999, p. 421)

Perhaps, as two scholars who have become desiccated and atrophied by a joint total of six decades of university service, we have 'fallible memory . . . and delude ourselves': perhaps we are guilty of 'looking back wistfully to some golden age – to a world we assume existed once and has now been lost' (Barry et al., 2001, p. 93).[61] Perhaps we are living in the twilight zone of another era. Perhaps we are what Wright (2001, p. 23) describes as 'feudal idyllics' who argue, unreasonably, for the preservation of F2F (an acronym known to the cognoscenti of *webspeak* as *face-to-face*) teaching. If all of that is so, we feel no guilt.

The accountability issues highlighted above should resonate with many university (especially accounting) educators. If they resonate with you, be careful. As an individual, you can make a difference. But, if you contest the new world view of 'university accountability' and challenge its implementation, 'you risk being marginalized or branded a Luddite educator unconcerned with quality, unaware of the economic contingencies, or incapable of reason and commonsense' (Sosteric et al., 1998, p. 12).

Those ailing from postmodern blues who hanker for maintenance of what Mills (1959) has described as a 'scholarly craft-ethic', have an array of 'resistance strategies' available to them (Barry et al., 2001): accommodation, conformity, ignorance, circumvention, renegotiation, mediation, moderation, lip-service and open rejection.[62] We must invoke such strategies to put a halt to 'panoptic controls and one-dimensional educational discourses' (Sosteric, et al., 1998, p. 12). One such strategy might be for accounting educators to draw upon Walton (2001) and Stevenson (1938) to re-define the descriptive meaning of 'university accountability' such that it represents what they regard to be critical. In doing so, we encourage input from the ideas of Whitehead. In particular, to re-define 'university accountability' in such a way that accounting education aspires to Whiteheadian dicta to replace the fallacy of misplaced concreteness; to see the wood by means of the trees; to bring imaginative educators into intellectual contact with students; and to preserve the connection between knowledge and the zest of life.

---

[61] A friendly critic has reminded us, quite rightly, to be alert to the fact that, in the past, some universities were bastions of privilege, sexism and racism.

[62] There is an extensive literature on *resistance* in organizations (Scott, 1990; Gottfried, 1994; Ferguson, 1984; Bell and Forbes, 1994). Much of it focuses on forms of *hidden* resistance (for example, flight attendants flouting company policy when out of the monitoring range of supervisors (Murphy, 1998)); tenured professors seeming to agree with a new managerialist hegemony, but then continuing business as usual (Prichard and Wilmott, 1997). Resistance of university students demonstrating at a conference on *The Corporate University*, in Sydney in February 2001, was expressed per medium of the coarse, inelegant chant: *Bullshit, come off it! Education's not for profit!*

For those who wish to 'resist', to keep 'the human heart of education alive' (Smith, 1999), a path of mediation, moderation, circumvention or rejection, through vigorous social critique[63] appears warranted. We must not resign ourselves to the exclusive inculcation of the current curricula bill of fare dominated by market-driven technical menus. We would fail in our accountability to society, as 'disturbers of the peace', if we responded to the ravaging of higher education through meek, obsequious conformity and complaisance. We would have to be comatose to plead ignorance of the impacts of the Internet, globalization and the market model metaphor on contemporary universities.

But is adoption of mere 'social critique' a sufficient response? Just what might constitute 'real resistance' has been a matter of considerable debate. 'To the critical neo-Marxist, only large-scale changes in material conditions count. Consequently, these critics see what looks like resistance as a psychic coping mechanism which in fact allows individuals to reproduce dominant systems' (Murphy, 1998, pp. 505–6). In this paper, we argue that insofar as accounting academics (or at least the preponderantly non-Marxist, non-anarchist variety) in the University are concerned, such hidden resistance is inconsistent with their role as members of the University. The forms of resistance we have argued for are plain-in-site, ground in the social and humanities bedrock of the university, and are directed more to producing beneficial mutation of the pervading vogue of the newly emerging postmodern university culture and endeavour.

We can resist too by advancing performance indicators that possess 'pedagogical depth', by opposing the view that economic efficiency and accountability are in the best interests of students, and by exposing 'the pedagogical implications of narrow business assumptions and interests' (Sosteric et al., 1998, p. 12). We should seek to stem the culture of 'consumerism' and of 'clientocracy' invading universities; and resist physical, intellectual and spiritual colonization of universities by business interests. We should argue vigorously that rather than express our accountability in terms of 'economic efficiency', it should be related 'to the deeper educational needs of students, to issues of social justice and equity, and to a standard of truth not coupled with hegemonic discourse' (Sosteric et al., 1998, p. 5). We should resist any temptation to expunge offensive, challenging material because it may offend sensibilities. 'Merit, hard work, and actually getting students to learn something' should become more important than simply 'pleasing students' (Sosteric et al., 1998, p. 9).

As accounting educators, we must respond to the pervasive accountability 'audit culture' by exposing 'the deleterious consequences of the current financially-derived model of audit' and the 'assumption that market forces provide the best model of accountability' (Shore and Wright, 1999, p. 571). Salter and Tapper capture the essence of this conflict of accountabilities when writing about the UK's Quality Assurance Agency:

> As part of the continuing power struggle for control over the regulation of high status knowledge, quality assurance combines technical, bureaucratic and value elements in ways which give power to some and remove it from others. (2000, p. 66)

In the vanguard of response, to date, has been the London School of Economics (LSE). Laudably, it has accused the British government's university audit body, the Quality Assurance Agency, 'of infringing academic freedom, imposing its own bureaucratic and

---

[63] Of the type we have illustrated here and elsewhere (e.g., our critique of the concept of 'economic value added' (EVA) in Amernic et al., 2000).

pedagogical agenda, neglecting students' intellectual development, and using incompetent and unprofessional reviewers' (*CAUT Bulletin*, accessible at www.caut.ca/english/bulletin/ 2001–apr/news/london.asp)

Our overriding thesis is that we ought to adopt a human, organic notion of accountability in the university, and encourage an approach to accounting curriculum development and education that is akin to *critical action learning* (Wilmott, 1997). Such an approach is described by Mingers (2000, p. 221) in the following manner:

> ... Action learning moves from the traditional perspective that education is the de-contextualized transmission of abstract and universal knowledge and expertise, to the view that learning should be a process of self-development, in which knowledge is acquired through its relevance to the real-life engagements and struggles of the learner. *Critical* action learning allies to this the recognition that individual experiences and learning always occur within institutional and social contexts, and these both engender and constrain through relations of power and signification.

Mingers (2000, pp. 225–28) then proffers 'four aspects of a critical approach' (which we endorse) as:

(1) Critical thinking – the critique of rhetoric;
(2) Being sceptical of conventional wisdom – the critique of tradition;
(3) Being sceptical of one dominant view – the critique of authority; and
(4) Being sceptical of information and knowledge – the critique of objectivity.

Such stratagems seem quite consistent with Alfred North Whitehead's views, and thus with our tentative attempts to (re-)fashion *accountability of university accounting educators*. This all depends on our acknowledgement that accounting is an important social force, in its many manifestations, and that an educational focus on accounting's ostensible technical character is woefully bankrupt. Balance is needed to help students understand that the budget report they have prepared, the consolidation they have mastered, the ABC calculation they have completed, the profit-centre management control system they have recommended in a case analysis, the accrual accounting system they have recommended for a municipality, are all fine, worthy, but very narrow, accomplishments. Students should also be invited to believe that these 'achievements' mean little beyond some arcane technological virtuosity, unless they are understood and critiqued within a framework that explicitly reveals the ideological assumptions and human consequences within which such *techniques* operate. Recall Moore's conclusion about accounting from footnote 30: that 'accountants had achieved ... the ultimate goal of the rhetorician's art: to be perceived as not rhetoric at all' (1994, p. 583). Moore carefully restricted his comment to 'certain major economists', but he is most likely much too cautious in his claim. It is our obligation as accounting educators to make plain the rhetorical nature of accounting, and to identify the ideology that is served by this rhetoric.

For us, accountability in higher education is no abstraction. It goes beyond even well-intended prescriptions regarding the 'scholarship of teaching' (Boyer, 1990; Kreber and Cranton, 2000), and it involves countervailing resistance to other 'accountabilities' such as that described by Alexander thus:

> ... Once it has been established that the primary purpose of higher education is to serve the economy, then it becomes the responsibility of the state to ensure

that the institution is held accountable in successfully achieving this task. (2000, p. 427)

We encourage accounting educators, very strongly, to employ social critique and to not expunge the prospect that they might become 'counter-hegemonic' or post-modernist intellectuals who see themselves as 'change agents and critical thinkers' working towards a better world' (Dominelli and Hoogvelt, 1996, pp. 208–9). In the end, it seems that *university* accounting educators in a corporatized Internet world must take with profound seriousness the pleas to engage in corporate critique that Boje (2001), amongst others, advocates.[64] Boje 'call[s] for an examination of corporate writing not as a stand-alone text but as part of the web that fabricates management communication, more generally' (p. 507). He argues with passion that '[a]n overlooked author of management communication discourse is the multinational corporation ... whose annual reports, press releases, advertising, sponsored research, and consultant reports become the basis of others' discourses ... [and] ... that corporate writing has been imitated and celebrated by academic writers without much critical reflection regarding the kinds of issues that it raises' (p. 507).[65]

In a world in which even some corporations and their advisors complain loudly about the hegemony of the Internet,[66] accounting education and critique informed by ideological awareness and healthy helpings of scepticism would seem to warrant inclusion in curricula, whether mandated by professional accounting bodies or not. For the rhythm of the (true) University to be restored, there must be a return to a scholarly environment in which freedom to be sceptical and critical of conventional wisdom is not only tolerated, but actively encouraged. We would fail in our accountability to society if we were to become unthinking, uncaring automatons who permit conformism to crowd out critical action. As Bender (1997, p. 31) so nicely puts it:

> The university ought never to be too comfortable in and with society – and vice versa ... There ought to be a degree of friction deriving from the critical spirit that is central to academic intellect.

Acknowledgements

Many people offered constructive comments on earlier drafts of this paper. We would particularly like to thank Frank Clarke, Warwick Funnell, Michael Gaffikin, Mike Gordon, Donna Losell, Neil Marriott, Michael McCrae, Rosa Michaelson, Alan Sangster, Sue Ravenscroft, Wally Smieliauskas and Howard Woodhouse. The usual disclaimer applies.

---

[64] We agree wholeheartedly and have recently subjected the corporate writing in a major press release by a consortium of mega corporations to detailed critical analysis (Amernic and Craig, 2001).

[65] Boje suggests the following reasons for this: 'First, increasing partnerships between corporations and universities – as well as corporate-sponsored writing – fashion a textual web from which academics create their pedagogy. In addition, corporate writing seeps into academic (student, doctoral, and professional) writing, which influences how groups such as unions, the state, women, minorities, and populist movements are characterized' (2001, p. 507).

[66] Business journalist Kathleen Driscoll claims that corporations 'in the Internet Age ... have no control over the flow of information ...' (2000, p. 14) – a claim that studiously ignores corporate wealth and ideology manufacture.

References

Aho, J. (1985) Rhetoric and the invention of double entry bookkeeping. *Rhetorica* **3**(1), 21–43.

Albrecht, W.S. and Sack, R.J. (2000) *Accounting Education: Charting the Course through a Perilous Future*, Accounting Education Series, Volume No. 16. Sarasota, Florida: American Accounting Association.

Alexander, F.K. (2000) The changing face of accountability: monitoring and assessing institutional performance in higher education. *The Journal of Higher Education* **71**(4), 411–31.

Allport, C. (2001) eLearning and our future. *NTEU Advocate* **8**(1), April, p. 2.

Amernic, J.H. (1985) The roles of accounting in collective bargaining. *Accounting, Organizations and Society* **10**(2), 227–53.

Amernic, J.H. (1997) Two readings and an epilogue: a commentary on the voice of seduction. In Mynatt *et al.*, *Critical Perspectives on Accounting* **8**, 693–716.

Amernic, J.H. (1998) 'Close readings' of Internet corporate financial reporting: towards a more critical pedagogy on the information highway. *The Internet and Higher Education* **1**(2), 87–112.

Amernic, J.H. and Craig, R.J. (1996) The sisters, the board and the hospital, *Accounting Education; An International Journal* **5**(4), 321–40.

Amernic, J.H. and Craig, R.J. (1999) The Internet in undergraduate management education: a concern for neophytes among the metaphors. *Prometheus* **17**(4), 437–50.

Amernic, J.H. and Craig, R.J. (2000a) The rhetoric of teaching financial accounting on the corporate web: a critical review of content and metaphor in IBM's Internet webpage *Guide to Understanding Financials*. *Critical Perspectives on Accounting* **11**, 259–87.

Amernic, J.H. and Craig, R.J. (2000b) Accountability and rhetoric during a crisis: an analysis of Walt Disney's 1940 letter to stockholders. *Accounting Historians Journal* **27**(2), 49–86.

Amernic, J.H. and Craig, R.J. (2001) Three tenors in perfect harmony: 'close reading' of the joint letter published by the heads of aluminium giants *Alcan*, *Pechiney*, and *Alusuisse*, announcing their mega-merger plan'. *Critical Perspectives on Accounting*, **12**(6), 763–95.

Amernic, J.H. and Elitzur, R. (1992) Using historical accounting reports in teaching: letting the past benefit the present. *Accounting Historians Journal* **19**(1), 29–50.

Amernic, J.H. and Enns, R. (1979) Levels of cognitive complexity and the design of accounting curriculum. *The Accounting Review* **54**(1), January, 133–46.

Amernic, J.H., Losell, D. and Craig, R.J. (2000) Economic value added as ideology through a critical lens: towards a pedagogy for management fashion? *Accounting Education: An International Journal* **9**(4), 343–67.

Aomi, J. (1985) Persuasive definitions in social sciences and social thought. In E. Bulygin, J.L. Gardies and I. Niiniluoto (eds) *Man, Law and Modern Forms of Life*. pp. 187–190. Dordrecht: Reidel.

Atiyah, M. (1992) Anniversary address of the President. *Notes and Records of the Royal Society of London* **46**(1), 155–69.

Atkinson-Grosjean, J. and Grosjean, G. (2000) The use of performance models in higher education: a comparative international review. *Education Policy Archives* **8**(2), 29.

Bailey, A.D., Jr., (1995) The practicing professional's mental model: are we creating the right mental models for new professionals? *Issues in Accounting Education* **10**(1), 191–95.

Barry, J., Chandler, J. and Clark, H. (2001) Between the ivory tower and the academic assembly line. *Journal of Management Studies* **38**(1), 87–101.

Bean, J.P. (1998) 'Alternative models of professorial roles: new languages to reimagine faculty work. *Journal of Higher Education* **69**(5), 496–512.

Bell, E. and Forbes, L. (1994) Office folklore in the academic paperwork empire: the interstitial space of gendered (con)texts. *Text and Performance Quarterly* **14**, 181–96.

Bender, T. (1997) Politics, intellect, and the American university, 1945–1995. *Daedalus* **126**, 1–38.

Bennett, R.E. (2001) How the internet will help large-scale assessment re-invent itself. *Educational Policy Analysis Archives* **9**(5), February, 14.

Birnbaum, R. (2000) *Management Fads in Higher Education: Where They Come From, What They Do, Why They Fail.* San Francisco: Jossey-Bass.

Boje, D.M. (2001) Corporate writing in the web of postmodern culture and postindustrial capitalism. *Management Communication Quarterly* **14**(3), 507–16.

Boyce, M.E. (1996) Teaching critically as an act of praxis and resistance, *Electronic Journal of Radical Organization Theory* **2**(2). Online at www.mngt.waikato.ac.nz/ejrot.

Boyer, E.L. (1990) *Scholarship Reconsidered: Priorities of the Professoriate*, Princeton, NJ: Carnegie Endowment for the Advancement of Teaching.

Boyer Commission on Educating Undergraduates in the Research University (undated) *Reinventing Undergraduate Education: A Blueprint for America's Research Universities.* http://naples.cc.sunysb.edu/Pres/boyer.nsf

Brennan, J. and Shah, T. (2000) Quality assessment and institutional change: experiences from 14 Countries. *Higher Education* **40**, 331–49.

Brown, G. (2001) 'The rising cost of aiming high. *The Australian* 18 April, 33.

Camp, D. (1997) Universities' job is to challenge cult of marketability. *The Toronto Star* Sunday, 30 November, F3.

Carlisle, Y.M. and Manning, D.J. (1999) 'Ideological Persuasion and Technological Determinism'. *Technology in Society* **21**, 81–102.

Chambers, R.J. (1965) Measurement in accounting. *Journal of Accounting Research* **3**(1), 32–62.

Chambers, R.J. (1966) *Accounting, Evaluation and Economic Behavior.* Houston: Scholars Book Company.

Chambers, R.J. (1972) Measurement in current accounting practices: a critique. *Accounting Review* **47**(3), 488–509.

Chambers, R.J. (1975) Profit measurement, capital maintenance and service potential: a review article. *Abacus* **11**(1), 97–104.

Chambers, R.J. (1999) The poverty of accounting discourse. *Abacus* **35**(3), 241–51.

Chapman, M. and Buckley, P.J. (1997) Markets, transaction costs, economists and social anthropologists. In J.G. Carrier (ed.) *Meanings of the Market: The Free Market in Western Culture*, pp. 225–250. Oxford, UK: Berg.

Checkoway, B. (2001) Renewing the civic mission of the American research university. *The Journal of Higher Education* **72**(2), 125–47.

Clarke, F.L., Craig, R.J. and Amernic, J.H. (1999) Theatre and intolerance in financial accounting research. *Critical Perspectives on Accounting* **10**(1), 65–88.

Cloud, D.L. (1998) The rhetoric of < family values >: scapegoating, utopia, and the privatization of social responsibility. *Western Journal of Communication* **62**(4), 387–419.

Colbeck, C.L. (1998) Merging in a seamless blend: how faculty integrate teaching and research. *The Journal of Higher Education* **69**(6), 647–71.

Confessore, N. (2001) Modem learning. *The Australian* 31 January, 35.

Coy, D. and Pratt, M. (1998) An insight into accountability and politics in universities: a case study. *Accounting, Auditing and Accountability Journal* **11**(5), 540–61.

Coy, D., Fischer, M. and Gordon, T. (2000) Public accountability: a new paradigm for college and university annual reports. *Critical Perspectives on Accounting* **12**(1), 1–31.

Craig, R.J. and Greinke, A.J. (1994) Accounting history and government inquiries: an experiment in adversarial roleplay. *Accounting Historians' Journal* **21**(2), 117–33.

Craig, R.J., Clarke, F.L. and Amernic, J.H. (1999) Scholarship in university business schools: Cardinal Newman, creeping corporatism, and farewell to the 'disturber of the peace? *Accounting, Auditing and Accountability Journal* **12**(5), 510–24.

Craig, R.J., Garrott, L. and Amernic, J.H. (2001) A 'close reading' protocol to identify perception-fashioning rhetoric in website financial reporting: the case of Microsoft. *Accounting and the Public Interest* **1**(1), 1–16.

Crosby, A.W. (1997) *The Measure of Reality: Quantification and Western Society, 1250–1600.* Cambridge, UK: Cambridge University Press.

De Mul, J. (1999) The informatization of the worldview. *Information, Communication and Society* **2**(1), 69–94.

van Dijk, T. (1993) Principles of critical discourse analysis. *Discourse and Society* **4**(2), 249–83.

Dill, D.D. (1999) Academic accountability and the university adaptation: the architecture of an academic learning organization. *Higher Education* **38**, 127–54.

DiMaggio, P., Hargittai, E., Neuman, W.R. and Robinson, J.P. (2001) Social implications of the Internet. *Annual Review of Sociology* **27**, 307–36.

Dominelli, L. and Hoogvelt, A. (1996) Globalisation, the privatisation of welfare, and the changing role of professional academics in Britain. *Critical Perspectives on Accounting* **7**, 191–221.

Driscoll, K. (2000) How do you manage Wall Street's view of your company? *Management Review* **89**(3), March, 14–19.

During, S. (2001) Be still our beating arts. *The Australian* 8 August, 38.

Ferguson, K. (1984) *The Feminist Case Against Bureaucracy.* Philadelphia: Temple University Press.

Flynn, M. (1997) The concept of intelligence in psychology as a fallacy of misplaced concreteness. *Interchange* **28**(2/3), 231–44.

Flynn, M. (2000) Transforming what is there into what is here: the feel of knowledge in a university setting. *Interchange* **31**(2/3), 243–57.

Freire, P. (1972) Education: domestication or liberation? *Prospects* **2**, 173–81.

Garnham, N. (2000) 'Information society' as theory or ideology. *Information, Communication and Society* **3**(2), 139–52.

Garvin, D. (1993) Building a learning organization. *Harvard Business Review* **71**(4), 78–84.

Gava, J. (2001) Too busy writing to think. *The Australian* 28 March, 46.

Gillette, D. (2001) Metaphorical confusion and spatial mapping in an age of ubiquitous computing. *Technical Communication* **48**(1), 42–48.

Gottfried, H. (1994) Learning the Score: the duality of control and everyday resistance in the temporary-help service industry. In J. Jermier, D. Knights and W. Nord (eds) *Resistance and Power in Organizations*, pp. 102–27. London: Routledge.

Granof, M.H., Platt, D.E., Vaysman, I. (2000) *Using Activity-Based Costing to Manage More Effectively.* Arlington, Virginia: The PricewaterhouseCoopers Endowment for The Business of Government.

Green, S. (1999) A plague on the panopticon: surveillance and power in the global information economy. *Information, Communication and Society* **2**(1), 26–44.

Guillén, M.F. (2001) Is globalization civilizing, destructive or feeble? a critique of five key debates in the social science literature. *Annual Review of Sociology* **27**, 235–60.

Guthey, E. (2001) Ted Turner's corporate cross-dressing and the shifting images of American business leadership. *Enterprise & Society* **2**, March, 111–42.

Hackenberg, R.A. (2000) Joe Hill in cyberspace: steps toward creating 'one big union'. *Human Organization* **59**(3), 365–69.

Hackney, S. (1999) Higher education as a medium for culture. *American Behavioral Scientist* **42**(6), March, 987–97.

Harvey, D. (1990) *The Condition of Postmodernity.* Cambridge, MA and Oxford, UK: Blackwell.

Hendley, B. (2000) Whitehead and business education: a second look. *Interchange* **31**(2/3), 179–95.

Hines, R.D. (1988) Financial accounting: in communicating reality, we construct reality. *Accounting Organizations and Society* **13**(3), 251–61.

Horn, M. (2000) 'The wood beyond': reflections on academic freedom, past and present. *The Canadian Journal of Higher Education* **30**(3), 157–78.

Illing, D. (2001a) Online deal will cost unis millions. *The Australian* 21 March, 37.

Illing, D. (2001b) Global e-university gets ready to roll. *The Australian* 23 May, 43.

International Labour Organization (2001) *World Employment Report 2001*. Accessed on 8 August 2001 at http://www.ilo.org/public/english/support/publ/wer/overview.htm

Johnson, M. (1993) *Moral Imagination: Implications of Cognitive Science for Ethics*. Chicago: The University of Chicago Press.

Johnson, N. (1994) Dons in decline. *20th Century British History* **5**, 370–85.

Jones, G.A. (1998a) The idea of a Canadian university. *Interchange* **29**(1), 69–80.

Jones, G.A. (1998b) The idea of a Canadian university: a response to Kant. *Interchange* **29**(2), 225–29.

Jones, T.C. and Dugdale, D. (1999) The ABC bandwagon and the juggernaut of modernity, Accounting Stream, Critical Management Studies Conference, Manchester, UK, 14–16 July.

Kant, I. (1998) Essential presuppositions and the idea of a Canadian university. *Interchange* **29**(1), 81–85.

Klamer, A. and McCloskey, D.M. (1991) Accounting as the master metaphor of economics. *European Accounting Review* **1** (May), 145–60.

Kreber, C. and Cranton, P.A. (2000) Exploring the scholarship of teaching. *The Journal of Higher Education* **71**(4), 476–95.

Lakoff, G. and Johnson, M. (1980) *Metaphors We Live By*. Chicago and London: The University of Chicago Press.

Lakoff, G. and Johnson, M. (1999) *Philosophy in the Flesh: The Embodied Mind and Its Challenge to Western Thought*. New York: Basic Books.

Lang, D.W. (1999) Responsibility centre budgeting and responsibility centre management in theory and practice. *Higher Education Management* **11**(3), 81–111.

Langer, E.J. and Moldoveanu, M. (2000) The construct of mindfulness. *Journal of Social Issues* **56**(1), 1–9.

Larson, M.S. (1977) *The Rise of Professionalism: A Sociological Analysis*. Berkeley, California: University of California Press.

Lawnham, P. (2001) Senate in reform mood as Kramer goes. *The Australian* 8 August, 33.

LinguaLinks, (1999) Library Version 4.0. Accessed on 8 August 2001 at http://www.sil.org/lingualinks/literacy/ReferenceMaterials/GLOSSARYOFLITERACYTERMS/WhatIsAnIdeograph.htm

Lyon, J. (2000) Conference showcases education in business. *The Australian* 31 May, 34.

MacKenzie, D. (2001) Physics and finance: S-terms and modern finance as a topic for science studies. *Science, Technology, and Human Values* **26**(2), 115–44.

Maher, M.L., Skow, B. and Cicognani, A. (1999) Designing the virtual campus. *Design Studies* **20**, 319–42.

Marginson, S. (1999/2000) Living with the other: higher education in the global era. *Australian Universities Review* **42**(2), 5–8; **43**(1), 5–8.

Marginson, S. and Mollis, M. (1999/2000) Comparing national education systems in the global era. *Australian Universities Review* **42**(2), 53–63; **43**(1), 53–63.

Martin, B. (2001) When dollars do all the talking. *The Australian* 18 April, 35.

Massolin, P.A. (1998) Academic modernization and the decline of higher learning: the university question in the later scholarship of Harold Innis. *Canadian Journal of Communication* **23**, 45–64.

McAulay, L., Scrace, A. and Tomkins, C.R. (2001) Transferring priorities: a three-act play on transfer pricing. *Critical Perspectives on Accounting* **12**, 87–113.

McCulloch, G. (2001) Arbitrary dismissal at Wollongong – an issue for all NTEU Members. *NTEU Advocate* **8**(1), April, 3.

McDonald, R.A. (2000) Reframing management education: a humanist context for teaching in business and society. *Interchange* **31**(4), 385–401.

McGee, M.C. (1980) The 'ideograph': a link between rhetoric and ideology. *The Quarterly Journal of Speech* **66**, 1–16.

McIlroy, A. (2001a) Prozac critic sees U of T job revoked. *The Globe and Mail* (Toronto) 15 April. Accessed online at www.theglobeandmail.com

McIlroy, A. (2001b) Hospital confirms MD's views cost him job. *The Globe and Mail* (Toronto), 6 May. Accessed online at www.theglobeandmail.com

Meister, J.C. (1994) *Corporate Quality Universities: Lessons in Building a World-Class Work Force.* Burr Ridge, Illinois and New York, New York: co-publishers, Irwin Professional Publishing and American Society for Training and Development.

Menzies, H. with Newson, J. (2001) The over-extended academic in the global corporate economy, *CAUT (Canadian Association of University Teachers) Bulletin*, January, A3, A6.

Mills, C.W. (1959) *The Sociological Imagination.* Harmondsworth: Penguin.

Mingers, J. (2000) What is it to be critical? teaching a critical approach to management undergraduates. *Management Learning* **31**(2), 219–37.

Moore, D.C. (1994) Feminist accounting theory as a critique of what's 'natural' in economics. In P. Mirowski (ed.) *Natural Images in Economic Thought*, pp. 583–610. Cambridge, UK: Cambridge University Press.

Murphy, A.G. (1998) Hidden transcripts of flight attendant resistance. *Management Communication Quarterly* **11**(4), 499–535.

Newman, J.H. ([1852–1889]/1996) The Idea of a University. In F.M. Turner (ed.) *The Idea of a University, John Henry Newman*, pp. 1–233. New Haven, CT and London: Yale University Press.

Owsen, D. (2000) Commentary on: 'popular television formats, the *Student-as-Consumer* metaphor, acculturation and critical engagement in the teaching of accounting. *Accounting Education: An International Journal* **9**(4), 389–93.

Parker, M. and Jary, D. (1995) The McUniversity: organization, management and academic subjectivity, *Organization* **2**(2), 319–38.

Pease, P.S. (2000) The virtual university: Jones International University™ Ltd. *Information, Communication and Society* **3**(4), 627–28.

Peshkin, A. (2001) Angles of vision: enhancing perception in qualitative research. *Qualitative Inquiry* **79**(2), 238–53.

Polster, C. (1998) From public resource to industry's instrument: reshaping the production of knowledge in Canadian universities. *Canadian Journal of Communication* **23**, 91–106.

Polster, C. (2000) The future of the liberal university in the era of the global knowledge grab. *Higher Education* **39**, 19–41.

Postman, N. (1996) *The End of Education.* New York, Vintage Books.

Power, M. (1997) *The Audit Society.* Oxford: Oxford University Press.

Pratt, G. and Poole, D. (1999/2000) Global corporations 'R' Us'. The impacts of globalisation on Australian universities. *Australian Universities Review* **42**(2), 16–23; **43**(1), 16–23.

Prichard, C. and Wilmott, H. (1997) Just how managed is the McUniversity? *Organization Studies* **18**(2), 287–316.

Quddus, M. and Rashid, S. (2000) The worldwide movement in private universities: revolutionary growth in post-secondary higher education. *American Journal of Economics and Sociology* **59**(3), 487–516.

Ritchhart, R. and Perkins, D.N. (2000) Life in the mindful classroom: nurturing the disposition of mindfulness. *Journal of Social Issues* **56**(1), 27–47.

Salter, B. and Tapper, T. (2000) The politics of governance in higher education: the case of quality assurance. *Political Studies* **48**, 66–87.

Schön, D.A. ([1979]/1993) Generative metaphor: a perspective on problem-setting in social policy. In A. Ortony (ed.) *Metaphor and Thought*, second edn, pp. 137–63. Cambridge, UK: Cambridge University Press.

Scott, J. (1990) *Domination and the Arts of Resistance: Hidden Transcripts.* New Haven, Connecticut: Yale University Press.

Shackelford, J. (1992) Feminist pedagogy: a means for bringing critical thinking and creativity to the economics classroom. *American Economic Association Papers and Proceedings* **82**(2), May, 570–76.

Shore, C. and Wright, S. (1999) Audit culture and anthropology: neo-liberalism in British higher education. *Journal of the Royal Anthropological Institute* (NS) **5**(4), 557–75.

Sinclair, A. (1995) The chameleon of accountability: forms and discourse. *Accounting, Organizations and Society* **20**(2/3), 219–37.

Smith, F. (1999) When irresistible technology meets irreplaceable teachers. *Language Arts* **76**(5), 414–21.

Sosteric, M., Ratkovic, G. and Gismondi, M. (1998) The university, accountability, and market discipline in the late 1990s. *Electronic Journal of Sociology* **3**(3). Accessible at www.sociology. org/Vol003.003/sosteric.article.1998.html

Stanney, K.M., Mourant, R.R. and Kennedy, R.S. (1998) Human factors issues in virtual environments: a review of the literature. *Presence* **7**(4), 327–51.

Stevenson, C.L. (1938) Persuasive definitions. *Mind* (New Series) **47**(187), 331–50.

Swieringa, R.J. and Weick, K.E. (1987) Management accounting and action. *Accounting Organizations and Society* **12**(3), 293–308.

The XYZ Concept: Turning Knowledge into Value (2000) 16 November.

Thompson, H.E. III (1997) The fallacy of misplaced concreteness: its importance for critical and creative inquiry. *Interchange* **28**(2/3), 219–30.

Tymoczko, M. (2001) Will the traditional humanities survive in the 21st century? *Organization* **8**(2), 285–97.

Underwood, S. (2001) QAA – the latest round, *News and Views* (LSE newsletter). Accessible at www.lse.ac.uk/Press/newsandviews/12–03–2001.htm

Walck, C.L. (1997) A teaching life. *Journal of Management Education* **21**(4), 473–82.

Walters-York, L.M. (1996) Metaphor in accounting discourse. *Accounting, Auditing and Accountability Journal* **9**(5), 45–70.

Walton, D. (2001) Persuasive definitions and public policy arguments. *Argumentation and Advocacy* **37**, Winter, 117–32.

Warde, I. (2001) For sale: US academic integrity. *Le Monde Diplomatique* March. [online at www.monde-diplomatique.fr.en].

Whitehead, A.N. ([1925]/1953) *Science and the Modern World.* New York: The Free Press.

Whitehead, A.N. ([1929]/1957) *The Aims of Education and Other Essays.* New York: The Free Press.

Whitehead, A.N. (1936) Harvard: the future. *Atlantic Monthly* **158**(3), 260–70.

Wilmott, H. (1997) Critical management learning. In J. Burgoyne and M. Reynolds (eds) *Management Learning: Integrating Perspectives in Theory and Practice*, pp. 161–176. London: Sage Publications.

Witmer, B.G. and Singer, M.J. (1998) Measuring presence in virtual environments: a presence questionnaire. *Presence* **7**(3), 225–40.

Woodhouse, H. (1985) Time to draw the line: universities must do more than feed the economy. *The Globe and Mail* Toronto, 13 May.

Woodhouse, H. (1999a) The rhythm of the university: part one – teaching, learning, and administering in the Whiteheadian vein. *Interchange* **30**(2), 191–211.

Woodhouse, H. (1999b) The rhythm of the university: part two – Whitehead's break with the mechanistic materialism of 17th century science. *Interchange* **30**(3), 323–46.

Woodhouse, H. (2000) The seduction of the market: Whitehead, Hutchins, and the Harvard Business School. *Interchange* **31**(2, 3), 135–57.

World Bank (2001) *Voices of the Poor: Crying Out for Change.* Accessed on 10 August, 2001 at www.worldbank.org/poverty/voices/reports/crying/cry.pdf

Wright, P. (2001) eLearning emerges. *NTEU Advocate* **8**(1), April, 23–24.

Zafirovski, M. (2000) Extending the rational choice model from the economy to society. *Economy and Society* **29**(2), 181–206.

Zeff, S.A. (1989) Does accounting belong in the university curriculum? *Issues in Accounting Education* **4**(1), 203–10.

Appendix A

Example (a)

On 20 March 2001, the provincial government of Ontario released the report of the *Investing in Students Task Force*, titled *Portals and Pathways: A Review of Postsecondary Education in Ontario*. A government news release stated that the report:

> ... could help Ontario's postsecondary education system ... increase *accountability* to taxpayers ... The Task Force ... recommended that colleges and universities promote open and transparent public *accountability* by publishing an annual report containing information about their mission, key strategies and accomplishments, audited financial statements, and outcomes on performance indicators. (emphasis added)

The cover of the report contained a prominent graphic in which the word 'ACCOUNTABILITY' was one point on an ellipse (near the bottom, an anchor-point). The ellipse also contained the words 'STUDENTS', 'ACCESSIBILITY', 'AFFORDABILITY' and 'COLLABORATION'. In the Executive Summary, the following heading appeared:

'ACCOUNTABILITY AND REPORTING
... Cutting Through the Clutter'

The second paragraph under this heading stated:

> It is important that publicly funded institutions have a clear *accountability* framework within which to operate. All elements of the framework need to be linked from the publicly stated goals and objectives, to the institutional mission, to the requirements for an annual public report, to relevant and comparable performance measures, and to the application of best practices using benchmark information. Whatever performance measures, indicators or benchmarks are developed for Ontario, they must enable international comparisons with the best institutions in the world (p. vii, emphasis added).

Example (b)

Coy, Fischer and Gordon (2001, p. 1) have argued that a 'stewardship' orientation rather than a 'decision-usefulness' orientation, 'would move college and university external reporting decision usefulness towards true public accountability.'

Appendix B

VC'S VIEW

(From *The ANU* [*Australian National University*] *Reporter* 21 July 2000).

Understanding our markets and developing carefully targeted strategies are central planks in equipping the University for growth.

Our core activities are research and teaching and we must have a clear idea of what our prospective clients want in both activities. We have to know not only why the clients who chose us did so, but also why the ones who did not turned away.

As a university, we have a lot to offer our clients. But we have to make our merits known and have them appreciated.

The first and foremost question in an ANU marketing drive for the future, alarmingly simple though it may be, is 'Why ANU?' A response of 'Because it's your best local university' will be found to be speaking to a shrinking pool of listeners. The local student market is not a growing one. Year twelve enrolments in New South Wales, Victoria and Queensland have seen gradual increases from 1996 to 2000 and are projected to remain basically stable until 2005. However, in the ACT, while year twelve enrolments have taken a sharp rise from just below 4300 in 1996 to about 4450 in 2000 they are then projected to decline over the next five years to 4000 in 2005. This means that the growth market for recruitment is outside our region. For that market we must define what ANU offers as an institution that others do not – and what would justify the seemingly greater expense, for many, of coming to ANU. We must also pay serious attention to what students want from their university experience.

If we expect that the interest of people will flow to us if we simply tell them that we are a great university and explain what we do and how good we are at it, we are bound for disappointment. We must form our assumptions by looking through the eyes of prospective students, their parents, and the prospective employers to whom our students look for their future.

Our commitment to basic research is one of our most distinctive qualities. This commitment makes us attractive to potential investors because we are at the forefront of discovery.

In marketing the University's intellectual property and in commercializing the outcomes of our excellent basic research activity, it is equally important that the University understand the market for that intellectual property. We must understand how the commercial world operates and what the expectations of investors are.

Of course, the fact that we are now rated by *AsiaWeek* as the top Australian university and as the eighth among 77 universities in the whole Asian region should be highlighted at every opportunity. So should our inclusion by the *London Times Higher Education Supplement* in a global elite of seven along with such institutions as Oxford and Cambridge in the UK and Harvard and Stanford in the US.

Individual elements in the AsiaWeek ratings, such as our top performance in citations, give us the opportunity to target differentiated markets with evaluative data.

How we present ourselves in market places will in many cases be determined by differences in the expectations and requirements of our clients. Different markets may require different approaches.

The University Council has now adopted my recommendation that a Working Party be established to prepare a detailed project brief for a study of our market for students, consulting and commercially contracted research. This is to enable us to correctly position ourselves in our market places to reap growth. That brief will be returned in August and a tender will be let for a study, which will in turn be the basis of a marketing strategy for the University. The Working Party will bring together the Director of Public Affairs Division, as Chair, the Directors of Student Recruitment and International Education and Student Administration and Support Services, the Business Development Office, the Endowment Office, the Research Services Office, the University's commercial arm Anutech and The Faculties.

ANU is poised in front of a new window of opportunity. The ACTEW initiative TransACT, through which residential properties in the ACT are being connected to broadband capacity, is the first of its kind in Australia and at the leading edge internationally. As the ACTEW TransACT initiative matures, it will connect with developing national infrastructure which will, in turn, interface with global networks. This puts the University at the centre of a rapidly expanding market place. It will be essential that we are ready and that we understand it. The Working Party project will be a significant step in ensuring that we do.
Deane Terrell

Appendix C

EDITORIAL from *MULTINATIONAL MONITOR* – VOLUME 21, NUMBER 12, DECEMBER 2000

EDITORIAL

Natural vs Artificial 'Persons'

Corporations are fundamentally different than you and me.

That's a simple truth that Big Business leaders desperately hope the public will not perceive.

It helps companies immeasurably that the law in the United States and in many other countries confers upon them the same rights as human beings.

In the United States, this personhood treatment, established most importantly in a throwaway line in an 1886 Supreme Court decision, protects the corporate right to advertise (including the tobacco companies' right to market their deadly wares), corporations' ability to contribute monetarily to political campaigns, and interferes with regulators' facility inspection rights (via corporate rights against unreasonable search and seizure).

But even more important than the legal protections gained by faux personhood status are the political, social and cultural benefits.

Companies aggressively portray themselves as part of the community (every community), a friendly neighbor. If they succeed in that effort at self-characterization, they know what follows: a dramatically diminished likelihood of external constraints on their operations. If a corporation is part of the community, then it is entitled to the same freedoms available to others, and the same presumption of non-interference that society appropriately affords real people.

Especially because corporations work so aggressively and intentionally to obscure the point, it is crucial to draw attention to the corporation as an institution with unique powers, motivations and attributes, and to point to the basic differences between human beings and the socially constituted and authorized institutions called corporations.

For example:

- Corporations have perpetual life.
- Corporations can be in two or more places at the same time.
- Corporations cannot be jailed.
- Corporations have no conscience or sense of shame.
- Corporations pursue a single-minded goal, profit, and are typically legally prohibited from seeking other ends.
- There are no limits, natural or otherwise, to corporations' potential size.
- Because of their political power, they are able to define or at very least substantially affect, the civil and criminal regulations that define the boundaries of permissible behavior. Virtually no individual criminal has such abilities.
- Corporations can combine with each other, into bigger and more powerful entities.

These unique attributes give corporations extraordinary power, and makes the challenge of checking their power all the more difficult. The institutions are much more powerful than individuals, which makes all the more frightening their single-minded profit-maximizing efforts.

Corporations have no conscience, or has been famously said, no soul. As a result, they exercise little self-restraint. Exacerbating the problem, because they have no conscience, many of the sanctions we impose on individuals – not just imprisonment, but the more important social norms of shame and community disapproval – have limited relevance to or impact on corporations.

In our annual Ten Worst Corporations of the Year feature, we try to highlight in stark terms the consequences of unrestrained corporations: despoilment of the natural environment, infliction of preventable disease on people, smashing of workers' democratically controlled unions, retaliation against the whistleblowers who seek to call attention to egregious corporate abuses, invasions of privacy, denial of care to the sick, needless endangering of consumers, and more.

The fact that corporations are not like us, their very unique characteristics, makes crucially important the development of an array of controls on corporations. These include: precise limits on corporate behaviors (actively enforced environmental, consumer, worker safety regulations, etc.); limits on corporate size and power (through vigorous antitrust and pro-competition policy, including limits on the scope of intellectual property protections); restrictions and prohibitions on corporate political activity (including through comprehensive campaign finance reform); carefully tailored civil and criminal sanctions responsive to the particular traits of corporations including denying wrongdoing companies the ability to bid for government contracts; equity fines – fines paid in stock, not dollars; creative probation, with a court-appointed ombudsman given authority to order specific changes in corporate activities; and restrictions on corporations' ability to close or move facilities.

There is also the permanent challenge of building countervailing centers of people power to balance concentrated corporate power: unions above all, plus consumer, environmental, indigenous rights and other civic groups, organized in conventional and novel formations.

And there is the imperative of directly confronting the corporate claim to personhood and community neighbor status – both in the law and in the broader culture.

This is the beginning of a sketch of an ambitious agenda, but there is no alternative, if democracy is to be rescued from the corporate hijackers who masquerade as everyday citizens.

A comparison of the dominant meta programme patterns in accounting undergraduate students and accounting lecturers at a UK business school

NIGEL BROWN

University of Glamorgan, Glamorgan, UK

Abstract

Meta programmes are a means of describing the behavioural traits that a person exhibits when interacting with other people. An understanding of meta programmes can improve communication between individuals and this may have implications for teaching. The purposes of this study are first to identify the dominant meta programme patterns of first year accounting undergraduates at a UK business school. An earlier pilot study validated use of the Motivation Profile Questionnaire (MPQ) to elicit the dominant meta programmes of accounting lecturers at the same Business School (Brown, 2002). Secondly, the students' meta programmes are compared with those of their accounting teachers to identify whether there are any differences or similarities between the two groups. The matching of the meta programmes of the teachers and students would enhance communication whilst major differences in meta programmes would make communication more difficult. A sample of 62 first year accounting undergraduates and 20 accountancy teachers completed the MPQ. The results indicate that, on average, the accounting students have similar dominant meta programme patterns to their accounting teachers. The implications of the findings for improving communication and therefore teaching are discussed, along with the scope for further research.

Introduction

The use of meta programmes represents a new area of investigation based on recognizing individual differences in personality which are reflected in the ways in which individuals behave and select language for communication. The model on which it is based is Neuro Linguistic Programming (NLP), which originates from cognitive psychology and linguistics. Meta programmes are a model for describing personality or behavioural preferences that a person exhibits when interacting with other people. This study explores how an understanding of meta programmes can improve communication and is therefore placed within the theoretical framework of communication theory.

The purposes of this study are initially to identify the meta programmes of first year accounting undergraduates using a questionnaire-based measuring tool, the Motivation Profile Questionnaire (MPQ). The results of the MPQ are then used to identify whether the accounting undergraduates exhibit any dominant meta programmes and to compare these results with the meta programmes of the accounting teachers. A knowledge of students' dominant meta programmes makes it possible to improve communication on the part of teachers by reflecting those dominant meta programmes in the language used when conveying information to those students. Implications of any similarities and differences for improving the teaching/ learning experience of the students are then discussed.

Literature review

Meta programmes represent a new approach to describing personality preferences. Meta programmes lie within the field of Neuro Linguistic Programming (NLP), which is a model developed from cognitive psychology and linguistics (James and Woodsmall, 1988). NLP is relevant to improving an understanding of communication and how it may be enhanced through study of thinking patterns, language and behaviour. NLP was developed in the early 1970s by Richard Bandler, a computer scientist, and John Grinder, a linguist, and may be defined as: 'The study of what works in thinking, language and behaviour' (Knight, 1995, p.1).

An individual's meta programme preferences influence the language patterns and behavioural preferences chosen when communicating with and relating to others. Charvet (1997, p.11) defines meta programmes as:

> specific filters we use to interact with the world. They edit and shape what we allow to come in from the outside world. They also mould what comes from inside ourselves as we communicate and behave in the world.

Meta programmes operate at an unconscious level, at a level 'meta' to or above the content of the individual's conscious thoughts, and are powerful determinants of personality. This study explores the relevance of meta programmes to communication within the theoretical framework of communication theory, a theory which has roots as diverse as literature, mathematics, engineering, sociology and psychology (Craig, 1999). Communication theory models what happens when two or more people interact.

Communication may be described as 'the process of human beings responding to the symbolic behavior of other persons' (Adler and Rodman, 2000, p.2) where the symbols can be the letters used to construct the language we use (Griffin, 2000). The nature of the response of one person to another person's behaviour will be determined by his/her individual cognitive style where cognitive style is the distinctive way in which the individual acquires, stores, retrieves and transforms information when communicating with others. Meta programmes determine an individual's cognitive style.

The earliest articulation of a communication model was a linear model (Shannon and Weaver, 1949), a one way approach to communication, involving a sender in some way encoding a message which is sent via a communication channel to a receiver who decodes the message. The sender of a message has to encode the message, he/she has to convert the information he/she wants to communicate to the other person or people into a form that can be externally expressed through, for example, speech. The receiver of a message carries out the process of decoding the message by physically accepting the external signals and constructing meaning from those signals, or not (Burton and Dimbleby, 1988).

A refinement to this linear model is a transactional model, which is a more realistic representation of human communication based on the concept that 'communication involves a mutual exchange of information or influence based on negotiation and reciprocity' (O'Sullivan *et al.*, 1994, p. 318). A transactional model acknowledges that most personal communication involves two way exchanges: messages are sent and received simultaneously. The sender of the communication is simultaneously receiving messages from the receiver and may be influenced by the receiver's response. See Figure 1 (also Figure 1.2 Adler and Rodman, 2000, p. 12).

The ability to communicate with people is a crucial part of an accountant's role (Bhamornsiri and Guinn, 1991; Maupin and May, 1993), and oral and written communication skills are the most important skills to be developed within higher education (Deppe *et al.*, 1991). Earlier accounting education research has identified the importance, for accountants, of improving interpersonal skills (for example Peek *et al.*, 1995; Doost, 1999). It is possible to improve communication skills by understanding an individual's personality traits. Meta programmes, which are a way of describing character traits, have a fundamental influence on the way people communicate with each other by determining, at an unconscious level, the language used in that communication.

To date, some educational research in accounting has recognized differences in individual students by focusing on and measuring characteristics those students exhibit such as learning styles (for example: Wilson and Hill, 1994; Apostolou *et al.*, 2001) and approaches to learning, (for example: Gow and Kember, 1994; Kember and Sivan, 1995; Lucas, 1996; Duff, 1997, 1999; Lucas, 2001; and Mladenovic, 2002). Such methods of identifying characteristics of students can have problems and lack sophistication (Duff, 1997; Mladenovic, 2002).

Other research in the accounting education context has attempted to identify the elements that make up a person's personality including Jung's Psychological Types (1999) and the Myers–Briggs Type Indicator (MBTI). Studies that have utilized the MBTI include Hutchinson and Gul, 1997; Wolk and Nikolai, 1997; and Ramsay *et al.*, 2000). Another approach, the Sixteen Personality Factor Questionnaire (SPFQ), (Cattell *et al.*, 1970) measures personality traits and has been used for examining the relationship between personality and approaches to learning (Duff *et al.*, 2002). Hutchinson and Gul, (1997) examined the relationship between cognitive style, as measured by the MBTI, and cultural beliefs on students' group learning preferences. Wolk and Nikolai, (1997) used the MBTI to examine differences in personality preferences of undergraduate and graduate accounting students as

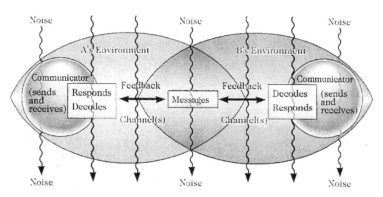

Fig. 1. Transactional communication model

well as faculty members; their aim related to the type of students attracted to accounting programmes. Further research has examined the relationship between cognitive style, as measured by the MBTI, and teaching methods in accounting education (Ramsay *et al.*, 2000). They focused on whether an individual's cognitive style impacts upon his/her preference for co-operative learning techniques. Other research examines the significance of personality to learning, using a five factor model for describing personality (Duff *et al.*, 2002). This study identifies personality traits, as measured by meta programmes, in order to explore communication between teachers and students.

Satisfying communication arises in part as a result of a match in communication style (Adler and Rodman, 2000) and, therefore, a match between the meta programme preferences of the teacher and the meta programme preferences of the student would be a sound basis for good communication. In communication theory, 'noise' refers to any forces that interfere with effective communication. Psychological 'noise' is attributable to forces within an individual that impair his/her ability to express or understand a message accurately. A mismatch of meta programmes may increase the psychological noise that occurs when a teacher is attempting to communicate to a student or group of students.

Identification of student meta programmes and matching of those meta programmes by the teacher would improve what can be done in the classroom, with the objectives of enabling the teacher to be more versatile (Street, 1998; Doost, 1999), enhancing communication and encouraging students to learn. Matching of meta programmes could also enhance the ability of the teacher to empathize with the student. Empathy is viewed as an important requirement of a teacher (Lucas, 2000), where empathy is 'the ability to understand each student's reactions from the inside' (Rogers, 1980)

A teacher's natural tendency is to explain things to others in ways that correspond with his/her own perceptions of how best to understand. This understanding will have been developed/sorted through the teacher's own individual meta programmes which may not coincide with the meta programmes of the students. This may lead to difficulties for students whose way of thinking is different from that of the teacher. This could be improved by using language that matches the meta programme preferences of those students (Lawley, 1997). To achieve this improvement requires meta cognition on the part of the teacher, an ability to be conscious of her/his own thinking styles and language patterns (Eraut, 1993) as a first step to developing the versatility to change language patterns to suit the students' needs.

In communication, appropriate use of language to match a person's meta programmes can enhance communication with that individual and increase his/her intrinsic motivation. In a recent study of the meta programmes of baseball players Miller and Deere (2000, p. 70) found that:

> Coaches could learn from this instrument (MPQ) to help 'impossible' players by communicating with them in appropriate language at the right time.

'Appropriate language' refers to the idea of matching the language used in communicating with someone to the meta programme patterns of the person to enhance the quality of the communication at an unconscious level.

Once a person's meta programmes have been identified, communication with that person can be improved by using language that reflects the person's meta programme preferences. In the teaching context, enhanced communication between the teacher and students has the potential to improve teaching and to increase students' intrinsic motivation to learn; intrinsic motivation is related to a deep approach to learning which is to be encouraged (Gow and Kember, 1994).

Meta programmes

Meta programmes may be classified into two categories as 'simple meta programmes', which are the four 'basic meta programmes', and the 'complex meta programmes'. The complex meta programmes were originally developed by Richard Bandler and later expanded by Rodger Bailey (James and Woodsmall, 1988).

The first three 'simple meta programmes' correspond directly with the distinctions regarding personality in Jung's work: Introvert/Extrovert, Sensor/Intuitor, Thinker/Feeler. The fourth element is implied by Jung's work and appears in Myers–Briggs' work as the Judger/Perceiver preference. The complex meta programmes are the foundation for this research. Meta programmes differ from Myers-Briggs' profiles in that 'meta programmes are not personality types, they are ways of processing or sorting information and communicating in the moment' (Lawley 1997, p.2).

Meta programmes or sorting principles have a direct impact on the content of the messages sent when individuals communicate with each other as they influence the language chosen by the sender and the way the message is interpreted or sorted by the receiver. The sender of a message will sort the information available to them to construct the message using language that reflects their meta programme preferences.

Meta programmes can be identified in the language people use and the behaviours they display. When two people are communicating, if their meta programmes, and therefore their language patterns, are not aligned then they will find it difficult to understand each other (Lawley, 1997).

The meta programmes exhibited may be affected by our state and can be changed. Some meta programmes, referred to as 'driver' meta programmes, can have a significant or dominant effect on an individual's behaviour in all contexts, whilst other meta programmes may vary from one context to another (for example, behaviour patterns of students while with friends at college may or may not differ from their behaviours displayed while at home with their families). The dominant meta programmes may help or hinder individuals in achieving their outcomes (Hall and Belnap, 1999).

Method

Elicitation of meta programmes, which involves study of an individual's language and behaviour patterns, is a complex process. A highly-trained individual can identify meta programmes when in conversation with another individual whilst it is also possible to use the Language and Behaviour (LAB) Profile, which is a semistructured interview technique (Charvet, 1997). Both of these methods involve significant training and expertise, and are very time-consuming. A more practical method that may be applied economically in the context of education is the MPQ.

The MPQ, which is a self-inventory questionnaire developed by Arthur and Engel, (2000) and validated in an earlier pilot study (Brown, 2002), identifies meta programmes from behaviour patterns. The MPQ elicits nine of the total of 51 meta programme patterns that have been identified (Bodenhamer and Hall, 1997). However, some potentially important meta programmes cannot be measured using the MPQ. For example, with the meta programme 'match'/'mismatch', someone who has a preference for 'mismatch' will, when told something by someone, have a tendency to disagree and think of the opposite to what has been said. This process of disagreement is necessary for the person with that preference to make sense of what they are hearing. Teachers may perceive students with that preference as awkward or argumentative because of their tendency to disagree. Someone with the 'match' preference will naturally tend to match the new information to what they already know and then see where it does not match, a potentially easier way to learn.

The MPQ lists examples of behaviour patterns which the subjects identify as being applicable to themselves or not. The MPQ was selected as it is a method which, unlike the Language and Behaviour (LAB) Profile used in the pilot study, can easily be used for larger numbers of students. The MPQ is economically viable to purchase compared with alternatives such as the 'Thinking Styles Questionnaire' (Beddoes-Jones, 1999). However, a questionnaire-based instrument that will identify all 51 meta programmes is not available at the present time.

Sixty-two first year accounting students (total 67) and 20 accounting teachers (total 22) completed the MPQ. As this is the first work on meta programmes in accounting, the initial samples are taken from one university. The MPQ comprises sets of questions on nine meta programmes and the student/teacher reads a series of statements, each of which describes a behaviour, and chooses those statements, if any, that apply to him or her. These behaviours are typical of each of the particular meta programme patterns. The results derived from the questionnaire are therefore dependent on the individual's perception of the applicability of the listed behaviours to himself/herself. The meta programmes that can be identified by the MPQ are shown in Table 1. Each of the first five meta programme patterns in Table 1 can be conceptualized as a continuum stretching between the two extremes. Each individual is likely to exhibit different types of behaviour along that continuum. The sixth pattern 'sameness'/'difference' is also a continuum, with the central part of the pattern described as 'progress'. Patterns seven and eight refer to what is paid attention to whilst pattern nine – 'seeing'/'hearing'/'sensing' – refers to sensory system preferences.

The MPQ is divided into sections, one for each meta programme pattern, each containing nine questions. Each question has alternative answers. The person completing the MPQ chooses as many of the alternative answers that apply to him/her, so a person can select some, all or none of the alternative answers to each question.

The study attempts to identify dominant meta programmes. Dominance was identified in two ways: first the mean scores for each meta programme were identified for each group and

Table 1. Summary of meta programmes

Summary of the meta programmes identified using the MPQ

1. Towards		Away from
2. Internal		External
3. Options		Procedures
4. Proactive		Reactive
5. Detail		General
6. Sameness	Progress	Difference
7. Past/Present/Future		
8. People/Places/Activities/Knowledge/Things		
9. Seeing/hearing/sensing		

ranked (Table 2). Mean scores enabled statistical comparison of those means to assess whether there were any significant differences.

One concern with solely using mean scores is that, with meta programmes, each individual is likely to run 'driver' meta programmes and these, as far as they are identified with the MPQ, would be revealed by high scores for one end of a meta programme relative to the score for the opposite end of that meta programme. Hence the second method of identifying dominance, the difference between the scores for the two extremes of each meta programme, was calculated so as to best identify which four meta programme patterns were dominant for each individual.

A high score, with a maximum of nine for each meta programme pattern, could occur in one of two ways:

1. Subject A scores 9 'towards' and 7 'away from'.
2. Subject B scores 7 'towards' and 2 'away from'.

Both of these scores indicate a preference for 'towards' relative to 'away from'. The second score indicates a stronger preference for 'towards' and may be one of the more dominant meta programmes for that person. Hence the differences between the scores for a pattern (in the example above, the differences are 2 for subject A and 5 for subject B) may provide a better indication of the dominant meta programmes of each individual than the mean values which suggest which meta programmes are dominant for the group as a whole.

Results

The meta programme patterns are ranked in order of popularity based on the mean score for (Table 2) each meta programme pattern. These rankings are compared using Spearman's rank correlation coefficient. Spearman's rank can be used to test the strength of correlation between the two rankings since each group has answered the same set of meta programme questions.[1]

'Proactive', 'people', 'internal' and 'detail' appear in the first six for students and teachers whilst 'away from', 'sensing', 'sameness', 'difference' and 'things' appear in the lowest six for both students and teachers. This suggests a high degree of similarity between the two groups. The high ranking meta programmes with high mean scores are likely to be the preferred or driver meta programmes of the two groups and it is significant that there is such a strong similarity between the two groups. Both groups have a strong preference for several of the same meta programmes and a weak preference for many of the same meta programmes. Spearman's rank correlation coefficient is 0.827 indicating a high degree of correlation between the rankings of the meta programme preferences of the two groups. This suggests there is a good match between the meta programmes of the two groups as a whole, leading to good communication between the teachers and the students whose meta programmes are similar to the group mean.

---

[1] The mean scores of the respective groups of students and teachers were compared using ANOVA to identify if there was a significant difference between the two mean scores. With the exception of 'proactive' (p value: 0.018), which is ranked highest by both groups, there are no significant differences between the scores of the two groups for the top ten ranked patterns.

Table 2. Comparison of rankings based on mean scores

Teachers		Students	
1. Proactive	7.7	1. Proactive	6.5
2. People	6.2	2. People	6.4
3. Internal	6.1	3. Towards	6.2
4. Detail	6.0	4. Internal	6.2
5. Seeing	5.8	5. Options	5.9
6. Places	5.6	6. Detail	5.5
7. Towards	5.6	7. Hearing	5.0
8. Options	5.5	8. Seeing	5.0
9. Progress	5.3	9. Past	4.9
10. Past	4.8	10. Places	4.7
11. Procedures	4.7	11. Progress	4.7
12. Activities	4.5	12. General	4.7
13. Hearing	4.4	13. External	4.5
14. General	4.4	14. Procedures	4.3
15. Future	4.4	15. Present	4.3
16. External	4.3	16. Reactive	3.9
17. Present	4.3	17. Future	3.9
18. Knowledge	4.2	18. Activities	3.4
19. Sensing	3.9	19. Away from	3.3
20. Away from	3.5	20. Sensing	3.2
21. Difference	3.5	21. Difference	3.0
22. Reactive	2.1	22. Sameness	2.8
23. Things	2.0	23. Knowledge	2.6
24. Sameness	1.8	24. Things	2.5
Spearman's rank correlation coefficient: 0.827			

Discussion

The consequences of these results for teaching are discussed in detail, starting with the most dominant meta programmes.

Proactive (or active)/ reactive (or passive)

The teachers' highest score is for 'proactive' (7.7), which is an extremely high average given that the maximum score is 9. Similarly for students, 6.5 is very high and is also their highest score. In the pilot study the score for 'proactive' was identified as unusually high when using the questionnaire, compared with an interview-based method of assessment, possibly indicating an element of questionnaire bias (Brown, 2002). Whilst this casts doubt over the reliability of the absolute reading for 'proactive' (and consequently on the reading for 'reactive'), this bias is likely to affect the results for staff and students uniformly. As a potential for bias has been identified for this measure, it may not be possible to conclude that 'proactive' is the strongest meta programme preference. However, it can be asserted that the staff are more 'proactive' than the students.

A high 'proactive' score suggests that both groups prefer to take action rather than reflect on things. The students may learn best by doing rather than listening to others and reflecting on their opinions. This preference could, if it is a consistent preference, explain the liking students on the accounting degree programme have for learning in smaller group workshops/tutorials which involve students undertaking activities rather than in larger group lectures where the students' role is more static and reflective. This raises the issue of what students actually 'do' or can be required to 'do' in lectures.

The higher student score for 'reactive' and lower student score for 'proactive' compared to that of the teachers may indicate a more passive culture among students. It may be linked to the fact that students have, in the main, just passed through the school system in which they are perhaps encouraged to be more 'reactive'. A 'reactive' approach is necessary as part of the process of synthesizing information and making informed decisions.

People/places/activities/knowledge/things

'People' is the second highest score for teachers (6.2) and students (6.4). This score indicates a strong preference for 'people' over 'places' (teachers 5.6 and students 4.7), 'activities' (teachers 4.5 and students 3.4), 'knowledge' (teachers 4.2 and students 2.6) and 'things' (teachers 2.0 and students 2.5). A crucial aspect of the teachers' role is the communication of knowledge to others, which involves establishing effective working relationships with students and fellow staff so a preference for 'people' is desirable. The strong 'people' preference amongst students suggests that they may enjoy class contact, prefer working in groups and other team-building activities and may be motivated by opportunities to enhance their communication skills. This preference suggests, unsurprisingly, that the students' motivation for attending university may be strongly related to contact with people and further developing their relationships with others.

Teachers' 6th highest preference is for 'places' (5.6), suggesting a concern for where they live and/or work with a strong sense of connection with their locality. The mean score the students exhibited for 'knowledge' (2.6) is significantly below the mean score for teachers of 4.2, with both scores indicating a low preference for 'knowledge' being 18th for teachers and 23rd for students. The low score for 'knowledge' is of great importance in the context of higher education where pursuit of 'knowledge' should be a core aim. A key part of the teachers' role is to seek new knowledge and assimilate that knowledge for onward communication to students and to pursue research objectives. A high preference for 'knowledge' would therefore be desirable. The score for teachers, though higher than the students' score, is low considering the maximum possible is 9. It would be interesting to compare this result with the score for teachers in a more research-based university. The preference for 'knowledge' may be partly a function of the subject. Accounting, with the majority of the staff having a professional qualification, may be less academically-grounded than other subject areas.

The low student score for 'knowledge' is of concern. It indicates that the students as a whole do not have a high motivation to gain more knowledge and may not have a natural interest in researching for information. The low 'knowledge' score could indicate that student-centred learning may be difficult to adopt and that time may be needed in tutorials/workshops for students to read articles and case studies. Again, it would be extremely interesting to compare this result with students in more research-led universities.

Both students and staff showed a low preference for 'things' which is consistent with the high preference for 'people'. A preference for 'things' would indicate an interest in having possessions such as cars, clothes, and collections.

Internal/external

The third highest preference for staff (6.1) is 'internal' and this is the fourth highest preference for the students (6.2). It could be posited that staff, being professionally-qualified accountants, would tend to be highly 'internal' as they are relied upon to establish expert opinions on topics and to communicate their opinions to others. They need to have the confidence to know what information is needed in order to prepare lecture notes and course materials for students' use.

The high 'internal' preference amongst students suggests that they place a strong reliance on their own judgement. They have a preference for collecting the information they think they need. In lectures and tutorials they may be more likely to sit and listen and not say much unless they hear something they do not understand. This may be frustrating for teachers, particularly those with an 'external' preference, who need external feedback to convince them they are doing a good job. Students with an 'internal' preference may take instructions from the teacher as information, which they themselves will decide whether to follow. They may read other opinions and listen to the teacher's opinion before making up their own minds. If highly 'internal', the students may pay insufficient attention to the opinions of the teachers or the other experts in the fields of academic work they are studying. A high 'internal' preference (an extreme example being Margaret Thatcher who knew she was right!) may limit the ability to take on new learning. Students with a high 'external' preference could also be interpreted as exhibiting 'communication reluctance' since it could lead to a reluctance to participate in group discussions if they are very unsure of their own opinions (Hassall *et al.*, 2002).

The teacher's score for 'external' (4.3) was lower than the score for students (4.5). This score, especially when compared with the score for 'internal', would suggest that staff are less likely to seek the opinion of others or to seek external feedback on whether they are right. They are more likely to rely on their own judgement as to whether they are right and whether they are doing a good job. Against this, it could be preferable that some notice should be taken of feedback from students, peers and superiors so that ongoing improvements can be made to the teaching experience. The score of 4.5 for students suggests that, although the score for 'external' is lower than 'internal', there is a higher degree of 'external' referencing present among the students than amongst the staff.

General (or big picture)/detail (or specific)

The 'detail' score for staff (6.0) is their fourth highest preference and for students (5.5) is their sixth highest. The 'general'/'detail' meta programme may influence a student's approach to learning. A strong preference for 'detail' indicates a preference for starting with the details and working inductively up to the general overview or to broad concepts and a preference for detailed information. The teachers' score for 'detail' (6.0) is higher than their score for 'general' (4.4), which is ranked 14th and therefore a relatively low preference, though the difference is only 1.6, indicating a fairly balanced score. For students the difference is only 0.8 with 'detail' (5.5) and 'general' (4.7), which is a more balanced score. A reasonably even score would be desirable as there are situations where an ability to see the big picture is beneficial in, for example, essay planning and subjects such as strategy or information systems. An ability to focus on detail is necessary when involved in the more technical aspects of accounting. Also, if the teacher's 'detail' preference matches that of the students, this could contribute to good communication in the teaching context.

There could be a link between the 'detail'/'general' meta programme and the functioning of the two hemispheres of the brain. The left hemisphere is used to process 'logic, sequence, computation, categorization and verbal skills and starts with the pieces first' whereas the right hemisphere is used to process 'intuition, emotion, vision, humour, rhythmic movement, image formation and other gestalt brain capacities and sees the whole picture first' (Hannaford, 1995 pp. 79, 178). Exercises, such as those suggested by Dennison and Dennison (1994), can be used to increase the neural connections between the two hemispheres of the brain which may impact on this meta programme pattern.

Seeing (or visual)/hearing (or auditory) /sensing (or feelings or kinaesthetic)

'Seeing' (5.8) is the teachers' fifth strongest preference. This suggests a liking for visual information, for example in the form of diagrams or mind maps. People with a preference for 'seeing' may prefer visual internal processing which involves use of pictures inside the head for learning and recalling information, and use of more visual language. Visual processing is fast processing and can result in fast speech and a relatively detached unemotional approach. The students' 'seeing' score (5.0) was ranked eighth which, whilst below the score for staff, is not significantly different. This suggests a general level of compatibility between the staff and the students with respect to 'seeing'. The teachers' score for 'hearing' (4.4) is 13th and a relatively low preference whilst the students' score (5.0) is similar and ranked seventh, which is just above their score for 'seeing'. The students' preference suggests they may prefer to receive information by listening to it. From a teaching viewpoint this implies they may favour hearing staff explain topics to them and like to learn from videos or audiotapes rather than via reading.

The scores for 'sensing' are both very low with staff averaging 3.9, ranked 19th, and students averaging 3.2, ranked 20th. This suggests a high degree of compatibility with a low preference for kinaesthetic processing. Kinaesthetic processing would result in a preference for taking notes and incorporating movement into the learning process. A low kinaesthetic preference suggests that students may like attending lectures and tutorials but prefer to be given copies of handouts and slides rather than taking notes.

There is a tendency to teach reflecting one's own preferences for 'seeing'/'hearing'/'sensing' and therefore the degree of similarity between the scores of the two groups could be beneficial for communication between the teachers and the students.

Towards/away from

'Towards' is ranked seventh for staff (5.6) and third for students (6.2). These high scores suggest a preference for setting goals and working towards achieving outcomes. Students are therefore more likely to be motivated by having targets to work towards with incentives such as prizes having a positive motivational effect. The students' score for 'towards' is higher, though not significantly higher. The opposite preference to 'towards' is 'away from' in which the staff scored an average of 3.5, ranked 20th and the students scored 3.3 which was ranked 19th so again the scores are similar indicating a high degree of compatibility between the two groups. A low preference for 'away from' may result in a lack of awareness of problems or things that could go wrong and a low motivation to meet deadlines. This may explain why some students fail to hand in work on time or fail to schedule their studies, particularly if they also have a 'reactive' preference.

Options/procedures

The teachers' score for 'options' (5.5), ranked eighth, is similar to that for students (5.9), ranked fifth. These are relatively high scores compared with the score for 'procedures' in which the teachers' mean was 4.7, and ranked 11th, and the students' mean was 4.3, ranked 14th. Though the options scores are higher, these scores are relatively balanced. An 'options' style of thinking is useful when dealing with such issues as systems design or solving unstructured problems whereas a 'procedures' approach is more appropriate if dealing with technical areas such as preparation of tax returns, using accounts preparation packages or solving structured problems. Students with an 'options' preference are likely to prefer case studies and open-ended questions; those students with a 'procedures' preference are likely to struggle in that context.

Sameness/progress/difference

The teachers' score for 'progress' of 5.3, ranked ninth compared with a student score of 4.7, ranked 11th. The teachers and students show a preference for progress over 'sameness' and 'difference'. This suggests a preference for making gradual changes, an evolutionary approach rather than revolutionary. This is appropriate in the context of a degree course where it is desirable for staff continually to improve on their teaching and the students should aim for ongoing improvements in their performance. The teachers' score for difference of 3.5 is ranked 21st which compares with 3.0 for the students which is ranked 21st, indicating a low preference and a good match between the two groups. The teachers' score for 'sameness' is 1.8, which is their lowest score. The students' score is similarly low (2.8) and ranked 22nd. People with a 'sameness' preference want the world to stay the same and, when learning, will attempt to find consistencies between new information and what they already know. This is a good result since it is preferable that the staff and students have a low preference for 'sameness' as the accounting environment is one of constant change.

Past/present/future

The teachers' score for 'past' is 4.8, ranked tenth whereas the students' mean score was 4.9 and ranked ninth, so very similar scores for the two groups. This suggests a tendency to be focused on events that have taken place in the past, a preference for reminiscing and perhaps to be dissociated from the present. The teachers' score for 'future' is slightly lower at 4.4, ranked 15th which is similar to their 'present' score of 4.3, ranked 17th. The students' 'future' score is 3.9, ranked 17th and is lower than their 'present' score of 4.3 which is ranked 15th. There may be a lack of attention on the future, though the scores for the three patterns are similar within each group and between the two groups.

Further analysis

As this research focuses on nine meta programmes, exploratory factor analysis was used to gauge whether certain of the meta programmes appear to be correlated and therefore may be measuring the same underlying dimension or factor. In this context, if a particular combination of meta programmes is correlated and identified as one factor this could indicate the existence of particular personality types common to a number of students (Field, 2000). Alternatively, this could indicate that certain combinations of meta programmes tend to go together.

The factor analysis results in Table 3 reveal that, for this group of students, the first factor explains approximately 20% of the variation in meta programme patterns and is mainly a function of the meta programmes: 'people', 'towards', 'options' and 'proactive'. These four meta programme patterns are correlated and may therefore be describing different aspects of students with common personality traits. These meta programmes are, not surprisingly, ranked highly (1st, 2nd, 3rd and 7th) suggesting this factor relates to the

Table 3. Rotated component matrix year 1 accounting undergraduates

	Component			
	1	*2*	*3*	*4*
Seeing	–	0.667	–	–
Hearing	–	–	–	–
Sensing	–	–	–	–
People	0.655	–	–	–
Places	–	0.664	–	–
Activities	–	–	–	–
Knowledge	–	0.835	–	–
Things	–	–	–	–
Away from	–	–	–	–
Towards	0.808	–	–	–
Internal	–	–	–	–
External	–	–	–	–
Options	0.662	–	–	–
Procedures	–	–	–	–
Proactive	0.635	–	–	–
Reactive	–	–	–	–
Sameness	–	–	0.847	–
Progress	–	–	–	–
Difference	–	–	–	–
General	–	–	–	–0.751
Detail	–	–	–	0.887
Past	–	–	0.682	–
Present	–	–	–	–
Future	–	0.671	–	–
Eigen value	4.894	4.144	2.278	1.755
% of variance	20.39	17.267	9.494	7.311

For ease of presentation only values 0.6 or above or –0.6 or below have been reported.

dominant meta programmes of the group. The second factor, which explains 17% of the variation, predominantly comprises of 'seeing', 'places', 'knowledge' and 'future' all of which appear 14th or lower in the rankings, based on the four highest scores for each student. These are all different meta programme patterns to the components in the first factor. This second factor, which is uncorrelated with factor 1, may indicate that there is a separate subgroup of students who have a different set of personality traits. Factor 3 is mainly a function of 'sameness' and 'past'. Within factors 1 to 3, there are only two meta programme patterns that are common to the same meta programme: 'future' and 'past'. Factor 4 is a function of the 'detail'/'general' meta programme. Overall, it appears, unsurprisingly, that the students are not one homogeneous group and that different subgroups of students within the group may exhibit different combinations of dominant meta programmes. If the staff are one homogeneous group, which is extremely unlikely, at least some of the students may experience difficulties with understanding their teacher as a result of having different meta programme preferences.

Table 4. Comparison of rankings based on four most popular meta programmes, using differences

Teachers			Students		
1. Proactive	22%	18	1. Towards	14%	35
2. Detail	12%	10	2. Proactive	12%	30
3. Towards	11%	9	3. Options	10%	25
4. People	10%	8	4. Internal	9%	23
5. Options	9%	7	5. Detail	9%	22
5. Internal	9%	7	6. Progress	7%	18
7. Progress	7%	6	7. Past	6%	16
8. General	6%	5	7. People	6%	16
9. Procedures	4%	3	9. General	4%	11
10. External	2%	2	9. Procedures	4%	11
11. Seeing	1%	1	11. External	3%	8
11. Past	1%	1	11. Reactive	3%	8
11. Away from	1%	1	13. Present	2%	5
11. Difference	1%	1	14. Hearing	2%	4
11. Reactive	1%	1	14. Seeing	2%	4
16. Places	0	0	14. Difference	2%	4
16. Present	0	0	17. Away from	1%	3
16. Knowledge	0	0	18. Places	0.4%	1
16. Sensing	0	0	18. Future	0.4%	1
16. Activities	0	0	18. Activities	0.4%	1
16. Future	0	0	18. Sensing	0.4%	1
16. Hearing	0	0	18. Sameness	0.4%	1
16. Things	0	0	23. Knowledge	0	0
16. Sameness	0	0	23. Things	0	0
Total		80			248

Spearman's Rank Correlation Coefficient: 0.899

In the initial analysis, shown in Table 2, the meta programme scores are compared based on mean scores. Table 4 shows the results of comparing the teachers and students by taking the difference between the scores for the two extremes of each meta programme to best identify the dominant or 'driver' meta programmes. Table 4 reveals a different ranking to Table 2, with a higher rank correlation and more common patterns in the top six (five rather than four), and therefore indicates a stronger similarity between the teachers' and students' dominant meta programmes.

Conclusions

When considering the meta programmes that are measurable by the MPQ, there is some matching of meta programme preferences between the accounting undergraduates and the accounting teachers. For teaching and learning, this demonstrates a certain level of compatibility on some meta programmes. This matching of meta programmes could contribute to good communication between the teachers and the students, and enhanced motivation.

With regard to the accounting undergraduates, the results, as would be expected, show that they are not a homogenous group. This suggests that, for teaching, there is a need for flexibility of approaches to accommodate the different preferences. For high quality class teaching, teaching approaches could be extended to accommodate different meta programme preferences, to match those preferences by using language that matches the different meta programme patterns within the student group, and therefore communicate more effectively.

This could be achieved by first raising awareness amongst the staff of their own meta programme preferences and increasing the flexibility of the teaching approach by including alternative language patterns in lectures and handouts to match various student preferences. It would be interesting to assess whether, from a student's perspective, having similar dominant meta programmes to the teacher has any beneficial effects on the learning experience or on their perception of the learning experience. This could be carried out by interviewing students individually or in small groups. It would also be useful to assess whether raising awareness of meta programme preferences contributes to the ability of the students to reflect on their own thinking processes (meta cognition) with a resultant improvement in their learning experience.

Further work could identify meta programme patterns of students at other universities and address whether there are any differences between meta programmes in, on the one hand, teaching-led and, on the other hand, research-led universities. Another interesting issue is whether there are differences between cultures in which the issue of language is relevant, particularly where students who are being taught have English as their second language.

Finally, the meta programmes people run also apply to how individuals learn (Lawley, 1997) so there is potential for examining meta programmes in the context of students' approaches to learning and to assess the relationship between meta programme preferences and learning styles.

References

Adler, R.B. and Rodman, G. (2000) *Understanding Human Communication,* 7th Edn., London: Harcourt College Publishers.

Apostolou, B., Watson, S.F., Hassell, J.M. and Webber, S.A. (2001) Accounting education literature review (1997–1999), *Journal of Accounting Education* **19** (1), 1–61.

Arthur, J. and Engel, G. (2000) *The Motivation Profile Questionnaire*, Denver, CO: Lifestar.

Beddoes-Jones, F. (1999) *Thinking Styles, Relationship Strategies That Work!* Stainby, Lincolnshire: BJA Associates Ltd.

Bhamornsiri, D. and Guinn, R.E. (1991) The road to partnership in the 'Big Six' firms: implications for accounting education, *Issues in Accounting Education* **6** (1), 9–24.

Bodenhamer, B.G. and Hall, L.M. (1997) *Figuring Out People. Design Engineering With Meta-Programs,* Camarthen: Anglo American Book Company.

Brown, N. (2002) Meta programme patterns in accounting educators at a UK Business School, *Accounting Education: an international journal* **11** (1), 1–13.

Burton, G. and Dimbleby, R. (1988) *Between Ourselves. An Introduction to Interpersonal Communication,* London: Edward Arnold.

Cattell, R.B., Eber, H.W. and Tatsuoka, M.M. (1970) *Handbook for the Sixteen Personality Factor Questionnaire*, Champaign, Illinois: Institute for Personality and Ability Testing.

Charvet, S.R. (1997) *Words That Change Minds, Mastering the Language of Influence,* 2nd Edn., Dubuque, Iowa: Kendall/Hunt.

Craig, R.T. (1999) Communication theory as a field, *Communication Theory* **9** (2) May, 119–61.

Dennison, P.E. and Dennison, G.E. (1994) *Brain Gym: Teacher's Edition Revised*, Edn-Kinesthetics, Ventura, CA, USA.

Deppe, L.A., Sonderegger, E.O., Stice, J.D., Clark, D.C. and Streuling, G.F. (1991), Emerging competencies for the practice of accountancy, *Journal of Accounting Education* **9** (2), 257–90.

Doost, R.K. (1999) The missing links in accounting education, *Managerial Auditing Journal* **14** (3), 93–114.

Duff, A. (1997) Validating the learning styles questionnaire and inventory of learning processes in accounting: a research note, *Accounting Education: an international journal* **6** (3), 263–72.

Duff, A. (1999) Access policy and approaches to learning, *Accounting Education: an international journal* **8** (2), 99–110.

Duff, A., Boyle, E. and Dunleavy, K. (2002) The relationship between personality, approach to learning, emotional intelligence, work attitude and academic performance. Paper presented at British Accounting Association Special Interest Group on Accounting Education Annual Conference, Glasgow, May.

Eraut, M. (1993) The characterisation and development of professional expertise in school management and in teaching, *Educational Management and Administration* **21** (4), 223–32.

Field, A. (2000) *Discovering Statistics Using SPSS for Windows,* London: Sage Publications.

Gow, L. and Kember, D. (1994) The teaching context and approaches to study of accountancy students, *Issues in Accounting Education* **9** (1), 118–30.

Griffin, E.M. (2000) *A First Look at Communication Theory,* Fourth Ed, London: McGraw-Hill.

Hall, L.M. and Belnap, B. (1999) *The Sourcebook of Magic: A Comprehensive Guide to the Technology of NLP*, Camarthen: Crown House Publishing Ltd.

Hannaford, C. (1995) *Smart Moves: Why Learning is not all in the Head*, Camarthen: Great Ocean Publishers, Anglo American.

Hassall, T., Joyce, J. and Ottewill, R. (2002) Similar problem: different solutions? A comparative study of communication apprehension in English and Spanish business and accounting students. Paper Presented at Accounting and Finance Research Unit, Open University, Milton Keynes March.

Hutchinson, M. and Gul, F.A. (1997) The interactive effects of extroversion/introversion traits and collectivism/individualism cultural beliefs on student group learning preferences, *Journal of Accounting Education* **15** (1), 95–107.

James, T. and Woodsmall W. (1988) *Time Line Therapy and The Basis of Personality*, Capitola, California: Meta Publications.

Jung, C.G. (1999) *Psychological Types. A Revision by R.F.C. Hull of the Translation by H.G. Baynes*, London: Routledge.

Kember, D. and Sivan, A. (1995) An analysis of the learning process of business students at Hong Kong Polytechnic, *Journal of Education for Business* **70** (3), 172–84.

Knight, S. (1995) *NLP at Work: The Difference that Makes the Difference in Business,* London: Nicholas Brealey Publishing Ltd.

Lawley, J. (1997) The application of meta programmes in the classroom, *Rapport* **37**, Autumn, 7–11.

Lucas, U. (1996) Student approaches to learning – a literature guide, *Accounting Education: an international journal* **5** (1), 87–98.

Lucas, U. (2000) Worlds apart: students' experiences of learning introductory accounting, *Critical Perspectives on Accounting* **11**, 479–504.

Lucas, U. (2001) Deep and surface approaches to learning within introductory accounting: a phenomenographic study, *Accounting Education: an international journal* **10** (2), 161–84.

Maupin, R.J. and May, C.A. (1993) Communication for accounting students, *International Journal of Educational Management* **7** (3), 30–38.

Miller, F.C. and Deere, R. (2000) Meta-programs in sports: the profiles of two college baseball teams, *NLP World* **6** (4), 65–71.

Mladenovic, R. (2002) The approaches to learning paradigm: theoretical and empirical issues for accounting education research. Paper Presented at British Accounting Association Special Interest Group in Accounting Education Annual Conference, Glasgow, May.

O'Sullivan, T., Hartley, J., Saunders, D., Montgomery, M. and Fiske, J. (1994) *Key Concepts in Communication and Cultural Studies,* 2nd Edn, London: Routledge.

Peek, L.E., Winking, C. and Peek, G.S. (1995) Cooperative learning activities: managerial accounting, *Issues in Accounting Education* **10** (1), 111–25.

Ramsay, A., Hanlon, D. and Smith, D. (2000) The association between cognitive style and accounting students' preference for cooperative learning: an empirical investigation, *Journal of Accounting Education* **18** (3), 215–28.

Rogers, C.R. (1980) A *Way of Being*, Houghton Mifflin: Boston.

Shannon, C. and Weaver, W. (1949) *The Mathematical Theory of Communication*, Champaign, IL: University of Illinois Press.

Street, D.L. (1998) A framework for the development of accounting education research revisited, *Accounting Education: an international Journal* **7** (Supplement Issue), S135–52.

Wilson, R.M.S. and Hill, A.P. (1994) Learning styles – a literature guide, *Accounting Education: an international journal* **3** (4), 349–58.

Wolk, C. and Nikolai, L.A. (1997) Personality types of accounting students and faculty: comparisons and implications, *Journal of Accounting Education* **15** (1), 1–17.

Encouraging a deep approach to learning through curriculum design

LINDA ENGLISH[1], PETER LUCKETT[2] and ROSINA MLADENOVIC[1,*]

[1]The University of Sydney and [2]University of New South Wales, Australia

Abstract

Accounting educators are concerned by research suggesting that accounting students frequently adopt a surface approach to learning given that this approach has been shown to result in undesirable learning outcomes (Eley, 1992; Booth *et al.*, 1999). Despite mixed empirical evidence, the possibility of encouraging students to adopt a deep approach to learning through interventions in the learning context is suggested by the approaches to learning and metacognition literatures. Functional Linguistics (Halliday, 1985) provides principles upon which such interventions might be based. This paper, first, provides a rich description of an intervention in an introductory accounting course to encourage a deep approach to learning by improving students' written communication skills. Second, the effectiveness of the intervention is examined by comparing students' approaches to learning, using Biggs' (1987a) Study Process Questionnaire, with those at another leading Australian university offering a more 'traditional' course. The findings broadly confirm the effectiveness of the intervention, both in encouraging a deep approach, and in improving overall course results.

Introduction

This paper describes and analyses the effectiveness of an intervention in an introductory accounting course aimed at encouraging students to adopt a deep approach to learning. The intervention is based on Functional Linguistics (FL) and the literatures on metacognition and approaches to learning. This research makes two contributions to the extant literature. First, it provides a rich description of the intervention, which involved developing introductory accounting students' writing skills. To our knowledge, prior studies have not assessed the effectiveness of developing writing skills in changing students' learning approaches. Second, in order to analyse the effectiveness of the intervention, Biggs' (1987a) Study Process Questionnaire (SPQ) was used, by comparing SPQ scores of the students who studied the course to those of similar students at another university who undertook a more traditional introductory accounting course.

This paper draws on previous empirical studies that have used Biggs' (1987a) SPQ to examine the ways in which undergraduate accounting students approach their learning. There have been two major strands of inquiry in these studies. The first strand seeks to document the learning approaches of accounting students, both in comparison with students' approaches in other disciplines (Eley, 1992; Booth *et al.*, 1999), and by comparing the approaches of 'local' students with those of international students from Asia (Chan *et al.*, 1989; Biggs, 1990; Kember and Gow, 1991; Gow *et al.*, 1994; Ramburuth, 2001). Research using the SPQ suggests that accounting students demonstrate relatively lower deep approach scores and relatively higher surface approach scores than students in other disciplines (Eley, 1992; Booth *et al.*, 1999), and score relatively higher on the surface approach measure compared with their scores on the deep approach measure (Chan *et al.*, 1989; Gow *et al.*, 1994; and Booth *et al.*, 1999). These findings are consistent with the argument by Beattie *et al.* (1997) that accounting attracts students who tend predominantly to adopt a surface approach to learning. However, as prior research shows that a surface approach to learning is more likely to result in unsatisfactory learning outcomes in a university environment, this finding is of concern to accounting educators and has motivated research into how to mitigate the problem.

The second strand of SPQ-based research examines whether it is possible to encourage students to adopt a deep approach to learning through interventions in the learning context (Biggs and Rihn, 1984; Marton and Saljo, 1984; Ramsden *et al.*, 1986; Kember and Gow, 1989; Gordon and Debus, 2002; Hall *et al.*, this issue; Cope and Staehr, forthcoming 2005). This paper forms part of this second strand. Research into attempts to encourage students to adopt a deep approach to learning suggests that this presents educators with serious challenges. Nevertheless, a number of interventions into the learning context have been identified that may support this goal (Gordon and Debus, 2002; Hall *et al.*, this issue; Cope and Staehr, forthcoming 2005).

In the next section of this paper the theoretical perspectives and empirical evidence underpinning this study are described. A discussion of the interventions introduced at the University of Sydney (USYD) follow. Subsequently, the research questions, research design and results are reported and the limitations, conclusions and suggestions for future research are presented in the final section.

Theoretical perspectives and empirical evidence underlying the intervention

This section first outlines how the approaches to learning and metacognition literatures provide the theoretical grounds for the proposition that students can be encouraged to adopt a deep approach to learning through interventions in the learning context. Second, empirical studies of the effectiveness of such attempts are reviewed. And third, a rationale is provided for the intervention which was introduced to engage students in reflection-based writing tasks that demanded more complex levels of analysis over time. The interventions were based on the Functional Linguistics and the metacognition literatures.

Encouraging a deep approach to learning – theoretical grounding

The approaches to learning literature indicate that learning is a function of both student and context (Trigwell and Prosser, 1991; Gow *et al.*, 1994). According to Ramsden's (1992) Model, located at the centre of Fig. 1, the *approach to learning* adopted by individual students

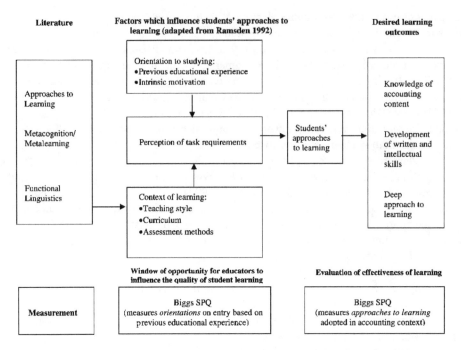

Fig. 1. Theoretical Rationale for Curriculum Redesign and its Evaluation. (Augmented and adapted from Ramsden's Model of Student Learning in Context (1992, p. 83)).

is primarily affected by their perception of the *task requirements*, which is itself influenced by two main factors—students' *orientation to studying* and the *context of learning* within individual courses. Biggs (2001) defines students' orientations as preferences or predispositions to use a particular approach. Ramsden (1992, p. 51) states that '(a)lthough it is abundantly clear that the same student uses different approaches on different occasions it is also true that general tendencies to adopt particular approaches, related to . . . previous educational experiences, do exist. Variability in approaches thus coexists with consistency'. While educators cannot influence the orientations to learning that students' *bring* to their studies, they are able to manipulate the learning *context*, providing a *window of opportunity* to influence the approach students adopt, and therefore the quality of student learning.

The *learning context* includes both the *nature of the course* and the *teaching within the course*. Early research identified a number of contextual factors that influence the learning approach adopted by students, including: the nature of curriculum and assessment (Entwistle and Ramsden, 1983; Thomas and Bain, 1984; Gow *et al.*, 1994) student-centred teaching style (Ramsden and Entwistle, 1981; Entwistle and Ramsden, 1983); and workload levels (Ramsden and Entwistle, 1981; Gow *et al.*, 1994).

Interventions to improve student learning have also been informed by the literature on metacognition or metalearning, that is the learner's *awareness of his/her learning processes* and *control of those processes*. It suggests that even relatively young students can perceive the motive and strategy options associated with the three approaches to learning (deep, surface, and achieving) (Biggs, 1987a), indicating a level of control and self-awareness sufficient to enable students to change their approach to learning in response to modifications of the external environment.

According to Biggs (1987a), an individual's control of his/her learning processes is related to maturity and experience and is not necessarily uniform, but is positively associated with high quality learning. Such high quality learning is fostered by a pedagogy that regards students as active, reflective and central participants in the learning process (Ramsden, 1998; Trigwell *et al.*, 1998). Without the ability to reflect on one's own learning and to transfer skills to novel tasks, it is unlikely that the learner will develop skills for intentional learning (Francis *et al.*, 1995; English and Ihnatko, 1998).

Together, these two research strands suggest that it may be possible to influence some students' approaches to learning in a particular course by designing teaching materials, assignments and assessment tasks that promote quality learning, that is learning which involves students in a conscious and reflective search for personal understanding. However, as students' approaches to learning are also influenced by their orientation to studying, which is related in turn to their previous educational experiences (Ramsden, 1992), the redesign of curricula and teaching materials will not be universally effective. For students with a predisposition to adopt a surface approach to learning, even the most supportive learning contexts will not necessarily be sufficient to encourage them to adopt a deep approach (Biggs and Rihn, 1984; Marton and Saljo, 1984; Ramsden *et al.*, 1986, Ramsden, 1988; 1992; Kember and Gow, 1989). It is possible to discourage a predisposition to rote learning by ensuring that learning activities and assessments require the demonstration of understanding, analysis and critical evaluation (Laurillard, 1984; Biggs, 1985; Ramsden, 1992).

Encouraging a deep approach to learning – prior research

Drawing on many case studies, Kember and Gow (1989) conclude that it is possible to influence students' approaches to learning, but that opinion is divided over how this is achieved. They identify three possible methods for reorienting students with surface predispositions to deep predispositions, one of which – consistently presenting students with deep level study tasks– formed the basis for the intervention at the University of Sydney (Kember and Gow, 1989). Whilst there has been much discussion about the need for changes in the learning context to promote a deep approach to learning, there are few recently published empirical studies of this issue. Those few have reported some success. For example, Gordon and Debus (2002) explored the impact of a series of interventions in all subjects throughout a three-year teacher-training course, which included using more learner-centred strategies, altering task requirements and assessment methods to reduce the emphasis on examinations, and setting more reflection-based assignments. They reported significant shifts to a deep approach to learning in the third year of study. Cope and Staehr (forthcoming 2005) introduced, over a five-year period, small scale interventions into the learning context of a first year information sciences subject, reducing student workload and concentrating on 'educationally critical' areas within the curriculum. In the fifth year, the researchers found a statistically significant increase in the proportion of students adopting a deep approach.

Hall *et al.* (this issue) report on the outcomes of an intervention in the learning context that required accounting students to work on three group activities, each of which was designed to promote the adoption of a deep approach to learning. Using the Biggs (1987a) SPQ to measure approaches to learning at the beginning and end of a one-semester course, their analysis of 159 usable responses (a 37% response rate) found that students significantly increased their use of deep strategies but did not significantly reduce their use of surface strategies. These results, while not as expected (i.e. students' use of the surface strategies did not decrease), appear to be consistent with the arguments of Birkett and Mladenovic (2002), and with other accounting education research including English *et al.* (1999), Jackling (1999) and Lucas (2002). The overall conclusion of these papers is that encouraging the adoption of a deep approach to learning *is* possible but that, in accounting, as in many other disciplines, lower level strategies (such as rote learning, paraphrasing and describing) are required to underpin progression to higher levels of understanding. As Hall *et al.* state '(i)n accounting, students first must learn terminology, basic concepts and procedures before being able to apply knowledge to novel problems and reflect/evaluate on the appropriateness of various treatments and methods' (this issue, p. 502). These two insights – evidence that a deep approach to learning can be encouraged through modifications to the learning context, and that lower level strategies form prerequisites for higher level ones, suggesting the need for a staged progression of learning activities – informed the USYD intervention.

Functional Linguistics – the role of language and writing

A third strand of educational research influencing the design and development of the USYD intervention was Functional Linguistics (FL), which is concerned with the *role of language* in representing a discipline (Halliday, 1985). The learner accesses subject matter through language, and becomes familiar with a subject by mastering the language of the discipline. In using language to know, understand and in turn explain a subject, the learner develops the skills of consciously reflecting on learning that subject. Using language to know and understand a subject is usually a product of the private domain of learning, and includes iterative processes of reading, summarising, drafting, and self-testing. When a student explains a subject to others, orally or in writing, his/her level of understanding is demonstrated.

The linguistic framework also explains how the socio-cultural purpose of a piece of writing is embodied in its language and structure (Street, 1984; Halliday, 1985). Clanchy and Ballard (1988) note that becoming literate involves becoming acculturated through learning to read and write within a given culture. Each discipline, each subject, and each academic has specific ways of ordering and presenting written knowledge (Lea and Street, 1998). Lea (1994) suggests that academic staff can help students to develop critical language awareness of their own practices as writers in higher education by explicitly identifying how knowledge should be ordered and processed in written form within their own subject areas. The significance of writing as a means of engaging with, and understanding content, was reported by researchers at Harvard University (Light, 1991). They found that the more writing students were required to do in their undergraduate courses, the better they learned, and the more they reported being intellectually challenged. All these studies suggest that setting writing tasks that require reflection and independent engagement should be a central tool of interventions to encourage students to adopt a deep approach to learning. Such a finding is supported by the metacognition literature, which emphasises the centrality of self-conscious reflection to the learning process.

At university, however, complex writing tasks are not just a *means of encouraging* a deep approach to learning, but also the prime *measure* of students' adoption of such an approach (seen in the centrality of writing both as a determinant of progression and as a measure of students' critical thinking abilities). Yet the quality of a written piece of work is the result of not only the writer's approach to the task, but also the nature of the task itself, as well as the writer's perception of the standard expected. For example Biggs and Telfer (1987), show that students who perceive an essay as an ordered arrangement of facts and ideas adopted a surface approach to writing and produce a fragmented, unrelated and regurgitated piece of writing. By contrast, students who perceive writing as a deep search for meaning tend to produce essays that are well argued and supported by evidence. As Bereiter and Scardamalia (1987) note, students must progress from surface understanding ('knowledge telling') to a deep understanding that reflects critical engagement with the subject matter ('knowledge transforming') if they are to progress successfully at university.

This overview has highlighted how the approaches to learning and metacognition literatures provided a conceptual framework for the USYD intervention, by suggesting the plausibility of supporting a deep approach to learning through interventions in the learning context. The importance of language and writing to learning processes highlighted by FL, combined with the emphasis on conscious reflection as a learning tool in the metacognition literature, provided a rationale for setting reflection-based writing tasks as the basis of our intervention. A number of principles arise from these literatures including: the staged progression of learning activities and tasks from lower order cognitive processes such as memory and recall to higher cognitive processes such as analysis and evaluation (Bloom, 1956); attempts to lead the learner towards a deep approach to learning through the design of appropriate learning activities and assessment tasks (Ramsden, 1992); the elaboration of metacognitive learning strategies through modelling of thinking and writing processes (Collins and Gentner, 1980); and the use of individual and peer review to foster individual reflection on the quality of learning as displayed in written work.

The most appropriate strategy for teaching language and writing skills is within the regular subject curriculum (rather than by running a specialised course) and flows logically from the FL literature's emphasis that the development of language and writing skills are intimately tied to knowledge formation within a discipline (Lea and Street, 1998; English *et al.*, 1997). This integration is supported by the focus on modifications to the learning context as a means of encouraging the adoption of a deep approach to learning in both the accounting literature (Gabriel and Hirsch, 1992; Hall *et al.*, this issue), as well as in the higher educational literature (Ramsden *et al.*, 1986; Ramsden, 1992; Prosser and Webb, 1994; Cope and Staehr, forthcoming 2005).

The interventions in the first-year course at The University of Sydney[1]

The theoretical perspectives outlined in the previous section informed attempts to structure experiences within USYD's two-semester first-year accounting course to facilitate the development of critical thinking and writing skills, whilst simultaneously helping students to learn the subject matter. Over 700 students were enrolled in the first year accounting course. Of these over 40% came from non-English speaking backgrounds, some as full fee-paying foreign students, but most, reflecting Australia's multicultural policies, as local students whose first language at home was not English. For students enrolled in a commerce degree, first year accounting is compulsory. Slightly less than half of those enrolled in first year were expected to proceed to major in accounting. Few, if any, had previously studied accounting.

The interventions were not solely motivated by perceived weaknesses in the writing of students from non-English speaking backgrounds, as it was acknowledged that, although writing

---

[1]The material in this section of the paper relies heavily on English *et al.* (1999, pp. 230–239). The interventions to improve students' writing were supported by intervention to facilitate the development of oral presentation skills (Jones *et al.*, 1995) and team skills (Bonanno *et al.*, 1998).

can be culturally determined (Kaplan, 1966; Clanchy and Ballard, 1981; Becher, 1994), within Australian education itself there are cultural differences between school and university regarding expectations about writing (Webb *et al.*, 1995; English and Ihnatko, 1998). Many criticisms of student writing by academics, such as a tendency to conceive of an essay as a list of what they know about the topic, are directed as much at Anglo-Australian students making the transition from school to university, as at students from non-English speaking backgrounds. Jackson (1991) explains that one of the underlying causes of this inadequacy is the respect with which school students treat knowledge, such that presentation of an array of content knowledge about the topic becomes the goal, rather than the start of a piece of written work.

Despite a growing emphasis in the first-year accounting course on written work (reflected in the growing number of marks devoted to it in tutorials and assignments), the outcome in terms of students' development of writing skills had been disappointing. As a result the course co-ordinator sought help from the University's Learning Centre.[2] Through analysis of student writing and discussion between the Learning Centre and accounting staff, it was determined that the identified problems – lack of wide and critical reading, of clear focus and comprehensive treatment of subject matter, and of reasoned argument (three areas identified by Clanchy and Ballard (1981) and by FL (Halliday, 1985)) – should be addressed by redesigning the tutorial programme to ensure that task requirements were made explicit, and that the development of content knowledge and critical thinking as demonstrated in student writing was supported and rewarded. The remainder of this section explains how these decisions were translated into the development of the teaching and learning context.

The conceptual approach was based on a number of principles that were then put into practice. As the language of the discipline is complex, dense and can seem formidable for the novice reader, the interdisciplinary team decided to prepare interactive reading guides. Unlike the typical end-of-chapter summaries, the guides were essentially visual summaries of readings, and required students to fill in key words and phrases. The ultimate purpose of the guides was threefold: first: to help students comprehend subject matter; second: to introduce them to a particular type of discipline-based writing; and third: to provide an exemplar of how they could approach a new reading and make sense of it for themselves. A second aspect of heightening students' awareness of 'acceptable' writing at university level was a strategy to explicitly reveal 'appropriate' and 'inappropriate' answers so that students were in the position to more fully comprehend why one answer is 'better' than another. These aides were introduced in the first four tutorials. Two of the first tutorials focused on how to answer a 'discuss' question, one genre with which students seem to have great difficulty; the third tutorial involved writing a business letter, and the fourth a report interpreting financial statements of two business opportunities, neither of which obviously represented the optimal investment choice. Further detail of the development of writing skills within the course is provided in English *et al.* (1999).

The interdisciplinary team then turned its attention to considering *how* this material should be taught. Typically, discipline-based teachers concentrate on teaching content; they are less aware of the need to teach the process of writing, often because they have little difficulty

---

[2]The mission of the Learning Centre is to improve the quality of students' learning. The primary role of the centre in pursuing this objective is to develop in students those skills necessary for the acquisition and communication of knowledge and ideas in a university setting. The dual concerns of the centre are to equip individual students with skills and attributes that will enable them to learn and communicate effectively at university and beyond; and to facilitate improvements in learning environments within which these enabling skills and attributes can be fostered.

with writing, or have forgotten how learned an activity it is. Accordingly, there was a need to help tutors to facilitate the learning of both content and process. Tutors were requested to cover the content aspect first. The teaching plan developed for tutorials suggested that the first activity should concentrate on 'answering the question' – that is on the content. As the content was not straightforward, tutors were requested to allow the students to brainstorm and to write their ideas on the board as they called them out; a process intended to highlight that different responses are both valid and acceptable, to encourage questions and clarification, and to help break the ice in this early stage of students' university experiences. Essentially we also wanted to indicate very early in their experiences that accounting, although numbers-based, does not always result in one undisputedly 'right' answer.

Content covered, tutors were then directed to focus attention on the *process* of writing an appropriate response. Again the brainstorming technique was adopted to stimulate students to think what answering the question actually required. Should terms be defined? If so, which terms and how to define them? Do discuss questions require a particular type of response? If so, what features should that response contain? Finally, did they agree, disagree, or partly agree with the statement to be discussed? How would their understandings shape their answer? After students had been given the opportunity to consider these matters as a group (with no 'solution' given at this stage by tutors), they were presented with four possible answers to the question and asked to consider which they thought represented the most appropriate response, and why. In each of the first four tutorials students were prompted in this way to consider the need for definitions, tone, structure and genre (in this context, genre means different types of written responses, for instance, business letters, discuss questions and reports feature different types of writing irrespective of subject matter).

In the case of both discussion questions, four model answers were introduced (see Appendix A). Care was taken to ensure that two of the 'more appropriate' models in each case presented a case for or against the proposition in the question. The purpose of the model answers was not to provide the definitive answer, but to capture the type of answers students may write themselves, or could aspire to write in this early stage of their academic careers. Students were then asked to distinguish between the models. After prompting they could see that the subject matter in each answer was essentially the same. What distinguished them was *how* they were written; how the writer had controlled understanding of subject matter to answer the question in the most effective manner, including how in text referencing should be handled. To support these understandings, students were finally shown the structures of the model answers (Appendix A). The purpose of revealing the structure of the answers was to show students that the appropriate answers were more complex in structure, as reflected in the greater sophistication of their argument and analysis. These answers, together with their structures, also revealed to students the difference between 'knowledge telling' and 'knowledge transforming' (Bereiter and Scardamalia, 1987) and gave them something tangible to aspire towards.

For many students, uncertainty regarding the 'correct' answer to a tutorial question is unnerving, particularly in a class setting. They prefer to 'please' tutors by giving the correct answer, and they like to leave the room with *the* right answer. As one of the objectives of the interventions was to foster confident independent thinkers who are able to argue a position coherently and to understand that their comprehension of subject matter and the quality of their argument are the most important factors, these strategies were designed to help students understand that being right or wrong in their overall conclusion is relatively immaterial.

The learning activities described above were designed to support the development of skills in information acquisition, organisation and basic analyses of discipline-based knowledge.

Tutorial question: 'If resources were not scarce, there would be no need for accounting information'. Discuss. (Martin, 1994, p. 14)

Skills Objectives	Learning Activities	Prompts To Support Learning
1. *Accessing and processing of information: ensuring that students understand content*	a. Pre-tutorial preparation: students read relevant text, complete reading guide and draft a response to the question b. Students' collective understandings of content revealed to the whole tutorial group	a. Reading guide requiring completion by students to aid understanding of content and to introduce students to the language of the discipline b. Content covered through students responding to carefully staged questions in a brainstorming session in the tutorial
2. *Focusing on the writing process: determining the requirements of the task*	Students explore the demands of the task in the tutorial, what do they think actually answering the question requires in terms of both content and genre?	Further brainstorming and task analysis check list
3. *Critical analysis and synthesis of ideas: making it all come together in a written response*	a. Students evaluate and analyse model answers in groups using an evaluation check list b. Students analyse structure of model answers prior to being given a structure hand out	a. Model answers evaluation check list b. Structure of model answers c. Class discussion of answers and structures allows students to understand why two of the answers are more appropriate, and to comprehend that it is possible to provide exemplary answers arguing both for and against the proposition
4. *Self evaluation and reflection: an opportunity to improve writing prior to summative assessment*	Students individually evaluate their own draft answer which is to be redrafted in final form in their own time after the tutorial	Feedback from and tutorial activities reinforces individual reflection on learning activities and tasks and how to use them to improve student's writing

Fig. 2. Relationship between sequence of learning activities and skills objectives for one writing task (Adapted from English *et al.* (1999).)

Subsequently, more sophisticated problem-solving activities in the form of case studies were introduced to develop higher cognitive skills and associated writing skills. The case studies supported the use of a deep approach to learning; were ambiguous, unstructured and unfocused to heighten awareness of the roles of uncertainty (Mayer-Somer, 1990) and professional judgement in unfamiliar settings (Subotnik, 1987). They were written in less academic English to imbue a more informal style, and presented facts in random order to mirror the vagaries of life. Where possible, the cases were framed so as not to present one obvious 'right' answer, in terms of analysis and conclusions, including failure to provide a definitive 'correct' numerical answer.

In line with the overall teaching philosophy of supporting understandings of both content and how to write about content, and to draw attention to expectations, case study analysis and presentation was supported in various ways, including the provision of analysis grids to model an approach to thinking and organisation, and notes on how to write a report. In addition, students were guided by criteria-based grading sheets which focused on their understanding of content in the context of task requirements – that is, on their ability to write about content in terms of four broad linguistic categories relating to the original analysis of weaknesses in student writing discussed above (Clanchy and Ballard, 1981; Halliday, 1985). The four categories were: (1) retrieval and processing of information; (2) organisation of a written text; (3) control of academic style of writing; and (4) communicating without grammatical interference (Webb *et al.*, 1995).

Examinations also reinforced the emphasis on writing in the course. For instance, about 50 percent of total marks in the final examination were assigned to questions that required written responses demonstrating critical thinking and analysis. The emphasis on written answers requiring the demonstration of understanding and analysis in examinations reflects the view that assessment is an aid to learning; a means to engender interest, commitment, and intellectual challenge; and capable of influencing students' approach to learning. As Ramsden (1992) notes, assessment plays a critical role in defining the way students see a course and the quality of learning it demands.

Finally, the curriculum redesign included the preparation of a detailed manual for tutors to ensure a uniform approach to teaching to support both teaching and student learning by avoiding the problem of students facing differing interpretations of what constitutes 'appropriate' writing. Lea and Street's (1998) project highlighted the difficulties encountered by students where expectations about appropriate writing remain unarticulated, and in which feedback is incomprehensible. The detail contained in the criteria-based grading sheets went some way to alleviate the latter problem because expectations were explicit and reinforced messages about writing that the students had received consistently in tutorials.

Testing the effectiveness of the intervention

Research propositions

In order to provide some evidence on the effectiveness of the initiatives introduced at USYD, Biggs (1987a) SPQ data was collected and analysed. Ramsden's Model (adapted Fig. 1) suggests that the approach to learning adopted is related to students' perceptions of the task requirements and these are influenced by a student's *orientation to studying* (related to previous educational experiences) and the *context of learning* which includes teaching processes, curriculum and assessment. It was necessary to control for such factors by comparing USYD students with another similar cohort of students, who were studying first-year accounting in a similar course, but using a more traditional teaching approach. To achieve this control the accounting course at the University of New South Wales (UNSW), a university also in the Sydney metropolitan area with similar admission requirements, subject matter and delivery mechanisms was selected. At UNSW, however, there was no specific attempt to foster a deep approach to learning of the subject matter through writing as documented in the previous section. A detailed comparison of the USYD and UNSW learning contexts is provided in Appendix B.

The comparison reveals that, for the purposes of examining the effectiveness of the intervention at USYD over the period of a year, UNSW students can be considered to be a control group in terms of the context of learning. Thus, given the similarities between the two student cohorts, apart from the writing intervention at USYD, it is proposed that:

> P1   Compared to students in a traditional learning context, those subjected to interventions in a learning context designed to encourage the adoption of a deep approach to learning will have lower surface approach scores and higher deep approach scores at the end of year.

While demonstrating the effectiveness of the intervention in terms of its impact on the adoption of a deep approach to learning, it is also of interest to investigate the extent to which students at USYD benefited from these experiences. Previous studies have reported that students adopting a deep approach to learning also achieve more successful learning outcomes, such as examination grades and results. For example, Watkins and Hattie (1981) examined the relationship between grade point average (GPA) and learning approach scores for arts, science, rural science and economics students in an Australian university. They found significant negative correlations between a surface approach and GPA for science and rural science students, and a significant positive correlation between a deep approach and GPA for arts students. In commenting on these findings, Biggs (1987a) concluded:

> ...that the science students scored *highest* in Surface Approach yet it is that approach that relates most negatively to performance. In other words, it looks as though the students entering Science are those least likely to do well in that area! (p. 61, emphasis in original).

Eley (1992) reports that tendencies to display surface approaches to learning correlated with lower marks and tendencies to display either deep or achieving approaches both correlated with higher marks, suggesting this is a straight forward affirmation of previous research findings. Similar findings were reported by Booth *et al.* (1999), who also found a significant negative correlation between the final aggregate grade and a surface approach to learning. In a recent study, Davidson (2002) examined the relationship between approach to learning (measured using the SPQ) and examination performance. Findings revealed a significant positive relationship between the use of a deep approach to learning and complex examination questions, but no relationship between a deep approach and less complex examination questions. For a surface approach to learning, no significant relationships were reported.

Based on these research findings it is expected that:

> P2   For the students at USYD, surface approach scores will be negatively correlated with academic performance and deep approach scores will be positively correlated with academic performance.

Research sample

SPQ data was collected from undergraduate students enrolled in Economics and Commerce degrees at USYD and UNSW. Students at both universities complete a number of core introductory courses in Accounting, Business Statistics, Economics and Commercial Law. These core courses ensure that students have the essential foundations for their studies in their respective business majors. Students at both institutions were surveyed during lectures both at the beginning of their introductory accounting course (week 1) and at the end of their first year of accounting studies. In total, for USYD (UNSW) there were, for the initial survey, 718 (1004) responses and, at the end of the year, 430 (765) responses.

Table 1. Details of survey sample

Sample details	USYD sample	UNSW sample	Total sample
Males	176	314	490
Females	177	390	567
Missing	1	2	3
Total	354	706	1060

Students were asked to record their student identity number for both surveys. With the student identity number, it was possible to match student responses for subsequent analysis, but as the disclosure was voluntary, not all student responses could be utilised. As a result of the matching process, the final useable sample was 354 cases for USYD (49% of the beginning responses and 82% of the end responses) and 706 for UNSW (70% of beginning responses and 92% of the end responses). Details of the sample and the male/female profile of the final sample are given in Table 1. Proportions of males and females were similar at both universities (Pearson Chi-square = 2.612, not significant).

Variable measurement and descriptive statistics

The importance of measuring students' approaches to learning derived from the SPQ is that they can serve as indicators in a number of research contexts. First, the SPQ can measure students' *orientations* to learning (that is, their predispositions to adopt particular approaches). Second, SPQ scores can be used descriptively to indicate the *approach to learning* students employ in various educational settings or tasks. Third, measures of students' approaches to learning, when used in comparative studies, can indicate the *effect of the learning context* on students' learning processes (that is, the effects of curriculum, teaching methods and assessments on the approaches to learning adopted by students). As stated by Ramsden (1992, p. 53):

> (q)uestionnaires of this type can be used as a form of course evaluation, because they provide direct information about students' responses to particular curricular and the way they are taught and assessed.

In this study, the SPQ was employed to explore both students' *general orientations* to learning at the commencement of their accounting studies at university, and to assess the effects of an intervention introduced in the learning context to encourage a deep approach to learning on students' *approaches to learning*. A survey instrument composed of two parts–the Study Process Questionnaire (SPQ) as developed by Biggs (1987a) and a post-test questionnaire–was used to collect data for the variables used in the following analysis. The SPQ contains 42 questions, all of which are answered using a fully anchored 5-point scale.[3] The post-test questionnaire asked for demographic information including the student's name and gender as well as perceptions of workload and academic success. To determine students' orientations to learning and their approaches to learning in accounting contexts, the 42 SPQ questions were summed for each student in sets of seven questions to derive scores (range 7–35) on three motive and three strategy sub-scales (surface, deep and achieving in each case). Each pair of motive and strategy

---

[3]The 5 points represented the following: 5 = this item is *always* or *almost always* true of me, 4 = this item is *frequently* true of me, 3 = this item is true of me about *half the time*, 2 = this item is *sometimes* true of me, 1 = this item is *never* or *only rarely* true of me.

Table 2. SPQ summary statistics

	Mean (SD)	
	USYD	UNSW
PANEL A – 'pretest' scores		
Surface Motive	25.70 (3.81)	25.95 (3.90)
Surface Strategy	23.17 (3.61)	23.32 (3.66)
Deep Motive	22.22 (4.74)	22.49 (4.48)
Deep Strategy	22.51 (4.22)	22.26 (4.30)
Achieving Motive	25.73 (4.23)	25.75 (4.27)
Achieving Strategy	23.66 (5.52)	23.35 (5.10)
Surface Approach	48.87 (6.30)	49.27 (6.44)
Deep Approach	44.73 (8.01)	44.76 (7.90)
Achieving Approach	49.38 (8.15)	49.10 (7.66)
PANEL B – end of first year studies scores		
Surface Motive	25.81 (4.09)	26.29 (3.92)
Surface Strategy	23.17 (3.80)	24.08 (3.74)
Deep Motive	21.74 (4.60)	21.03 (4.46)
Deep Strategy	21.77 (4.19)	20.84 (4.40)
Achieving Motive	24.81 (4.32)	24.31 (4.60)
Achieving Strategy	20.89 (5.42)	20.12 (5.11)
Surface Approach	48.97 (7.00)	50.38 (6.60)
Deep Approach	43.51 (7.86)	41.87 (8.01)
Achieving Approach	45.70 (8.28)	44.44 (8.00)

sub-scales then were summed into surface, deep and achieving approach scales (range 14–70). Descriptive statistics for the two levels of SPQ scores were collected from each institution at two points in time. The first data set was collected at the commencement of studies and reflects the orientation to studying as influenced by previous educational experiences and thus constitutes "pretest" scores (see Table 2, Panel A). The second set of data was collected at the end of Session 2 when students had completed a year (two semesters) of accounting studies (see Table 2, Panel B).[4]

---

[4]A comparison of USYD pre-test and post-test scores is somewhat problematic given the pre-test scores represent students' general orientations to learning and the post-test scores represent students' learning in an accounting context. However, there are a number of possible explanations for why students' scores on the deep approach scale are lower at the end of the year than at the beginning of the year. First, longitudinal studies of students SPQ scores show '...an increasing disposition for a surface approach (Biggs, 1987a; Gow and Kember, 1990; Stokes Balla and Stafford 1989; Watkins and Hattie 1985)' (Biggs 1993, p. 10). In accounting, Gow et al. (1994) reported that students' enthusiasm for a deep approach to study declined from the first year to the second year of the course. Given this trend, the USYD intervention appears to have mitigated the downward trend to some extent when one compares the change in USYD (44.73 to 43.51) and UNSW scores (44.76 to 41.87). Second, Meyer and Eley (1999 p. 198) argue: '...that individual students might well adopt differentiated patterns of learning behaviours that are attributable to the learning contexts shaped by different subjects. That is, perceptions and experiences of learning contexts might be shaped also by the epistemology of a discipline and they might therefore vary considerably from one discipline to another.' Thus, students might adopt quite different approaches in their accounting course when compared with subjects such as biology, art mathematics, English, history etc. studied at secondary level.

Table 3. Independent samples t-tests for equality of means for – 'pretest' SPQ scores between the two universities

	t	Sig. (2-tailed)*	Mean difference	Std. error difference	95% Confidence interval	
					Lower	Upper
Surface Motive	0.985	**0.325**	0.25	0.252	−0.246	0.743
Surface Strategy	0.665	**0.506**	0.15	0.235	−0.308	0.623
Deep Motive	0.928	**0.354**	0.27	0.298	−0.308	0.860
Deep Strategy	−0.881	**0.379**	−0.25	0.278	−0.791	0.301
Surface Approach	0.976	**0.330**	0.40	0.416	−0.411	1.223
Deep Approach	0.052	**0.959**	0.03	0.517	−0.988	1.042

*df $= 1058$ for all t-tests with significant $p < 0.05$, 2-tailed shown in bold type.
Note: Levene's tests for homogeneity indicated no significant difference between the two samples.

In addition, for USYD students, objective measures of academic performance were collected in order to test Proposition 2. Students were asked to volunteer their student identification number in the post-test questionnaire and, where supplied, their assessment marks were obtained for the accounting course they were undertaking at the time of the survey. Marks were obtained for 316 students (89% of the merged sample), with the mean grade being 61.22% (standard deviation, 11.77, minimum 20 and maximum 86).

Findings and discussion

As approaches to learning are related to student's orientations to learning and the learning context, to ensure the validity of the comparison between the end-of-year scores, the orientations to learning for the students from the two universities were compared prior to the intervention (that is, in terms of the 'pretest' SPQ scores). For the purposes of the pretest, students were asked to respond to the SPQ questions as follows: 'We would like you to relate your responses to the subjects you have most recently studied'.[5]

A comparison of the means of the pretest SPQ scores for the two universities indicated no significant differences in students' learning orientations (see Table 3). Students were also asked to rate their overall academic performance relative to peers on a scale of 1 (poor) to 5 (excellent). A t-test indicated no difference between the two groups (means: UNSW 3.65, USYD 3.58, $t = 1.38$, $p = 0.168$). Thus, these findings, in combination with the similarities between the degree programmes, course content (see Appendix B), admission criteria and gender profile, as discussed at the beginning of this section, provide a defensible basis for considering the UNSW group

[5]For the majority of students their most recent studies would include the subjects studied at secondary school which could include any combination of the following areas: mathematics, English, history, economics, geography, art, biology, chemistry, media studies, drama, etc. Some students complete an introductory business studies subject at secondary school which would provide them with some experience of an accounting learning context. However, most of the subjects completed at secondary school are not similar/related to the accounting context of learning which students experience at university.

Table 4. Independent samples *t*-tests for equality of means for end of first year studies SPQ scores between the two universities

	t	*Sig. (1-tailed)**	*Mean difference*	*Std. error difference*	*95% Confidence interval*	
					Lower	*Upper*
Surface Motive	1.890	**0.030**	0.48	0.259	−0.019	0.998
Surface Strategy	3.741	**0.000**	0.91	0.245	0.436	1.398
Deep Motive	−2.424	**0.008**	−0.71	0.294	−1.288	−0.135
Deep Strategy	−3.294	**0.000**	−0.93	0.282	−1.481	−0.375
Surface Approach	3.208	**0.000**	1.41	0.438	0.546	2.267
Deep Approach	−3.163	**0.001**	−1.64	0.519	−2.658	−0.623

*df = 1058 for all *t*-tests with significant p < 0.05, 1-tailed shown in bold type. (Note, that as Proposition 1 is directional, 1-tailed *t*-test results are appropriate).
Note: Levene's tests for homogeneity indicated no significant difference between the two university samples.

to be the baseline group with respect to examining the impact of the learning interventions at the USYD.

Proposition 1 is concerned with examining the extent to which the learning initiatives at the University of Sydney, as described in detail in section 3, were effective in encouraging students to adopt a deep approach to learning and, as a corollary, reducing the tendency of students to employ a surface approach. Table 4 indicates that there were significant differences between the mean scores for the cohorts from the two universities, and the differences are in the directions predicted in Proposition 1. With respect to the individual surface approach to learning scores (motivation and strategy), those for USYD were lower relative to the control group at the end of the year, indicating that there was a significantly lower tendency to adopt this approach, given the intervention. In contrast, the deep approach to learning scores (motivation and strategy) were significantly higher for the USYD students by the end of the year, which is also consistent with Proposition 1. Similar results hold for the combined, learning approach scores. Thus, the results support a conclusion that interventions, such as the writing initiatives undertaken at USYD that are carefully designed to encourage students to take a more critical and reflective appreciation of the subject matter, can result in students adopting a deep approach to learning as well as reduce the tendency to employ a surface approach[6].

Proposition 2 is concerned with performance results. USYD surface and deep approach scores were correlated with students' final grades at the end of their first year of introductory accounting. A summary of these correlations is presented in Table 5.

---

[6]The results may have been mitigated by the high workload of the intervention. Feedback mechanisms at USYD, indicated that the workload was perceived by students as being very high (English *et al.*, 1998). Further, in the questionnaire, students were asked to rate the workload in their accounting course relative to other subjects. A significant difference was found between the institutions (means: USYD = 3.81, UNSW = 3.64, $t = 3.161$, $p = 0.002$). Thus the perceptions of workload were higher with USYD students. High workload is a factor recognised as contributing to a surface approach to learning in the literature (Ramsden and Entwistle, 1981; Gow *et al.*, 1994).

Table 5. Correlation coefficients of SPQ approach scores with final grade

	Final grade
Surface Approach	$r = -0.096$ (**p = 0.045**)*
Deep Approach	$r = 0.078$ (p = 0.082)

Note: *1-tailed significance.

The results indicate some tentative support for Proposition 2. In the case of the surface approach, there was a negative correlation with performance scores, although the correlation coefficient is very small, suggesting that the impact on grades is minimal. A marginally significant positive correlation (p = 0.082) was found for the deep approach, and again the correlation coefficient was small. Taken together, while the findings are consistent with previous research (Watkins and Hattie, 1981; Eley, 1992; Booth *et al.*, 1999; and Davidson, 2002) and indicate that there are benefits to students where they are encouraged to take a deep approach to learning and are successful in doing so, aggregate assessment grades were not very sensitive to the level of deep and surface approach scores. As recommended by Davidson (2002), analysis using disaggregated data for individual assessment tasks may have revealed clearer results; however, only aggregate assessment data was available. Disaggregated data would have enabled a closer examination of the *nature* of each of the assessment tasks in terms of eliciting a deep or a surface learning outcome.

Summary, conclusions and future research

This study aimed to describe and explore the effects of an intervention in the learning context designed to encourage students to adopt a deep approach to learning in introductory accounting. This is an important area of research as prior studies using Biggs (1987a) Study Process Questionnaire (SPQ) have reported that accounting students tend to display relatively higher surface approach scores and relatively lower deep approach scores.

This paper makes two contributions to the literature. First, based on recommendations and findings derived from research in the approaches to learning, metacognition and Functional Linguistics literatures, a rich description of the interventions introduced in the learning context aimed at developing introductory accounting students' writing skills was provided. Second, using Biggs (1987a) SPQ, evidence of the effectiveness of the interventions is reported.

The approaches to learning literature suggests, at the macro level, that teachers may be able to manipulate students' approaches to learning through the learning context, particularly through assessment, which, in turn influences students' perceptions of task requirements and hence their approach to learning. The FL literature influenced how the interventions to improve students' writing at the micro level were formulated and developed. The interventions introduced in the context of learning centred on a guided and staged development of students' writing skills.

In order to provide some evidence on the effectiveness of the intervention, introductory accounting students at two leading Australian universities were surveyed using the SPQ at the beginning and end of their first year of accounting studies. At the University of Sydney, students were introduced to a learning context designed to encourage a deep approach, while the other university offered a more 'traditional' course. A comparison of SPQ scores at the commencement of the first year of accounting for students at the two universities indicated that they had very similar orientations to learning. By the end of their first year, however, the students in the learning context aimed at encouraging a deep approach to learning scored significantly higher on the SPQ deep approach to learning scale and significantly lower on the surface approach scale than did students attending the more traditional course. Further, for the USYD students, there was some evidence of a significant negative correlation between students' use of a surface approach and their performance, as measured by their final examination grades. The suggestion that students with lower surface approach scores may experience a positive impact on grades (as well as the marginal finding here that higher deep approach scores have a similar effect) supports the calls of those advocating learning interventions to encourage a deep approach to learning.

While it is important to provide empirical evidence about the effectiveness of various learning interventions designed to encourage accounting students to adopt a deeper approach to their learning, the nature of these 'educational experiments' poses some problems to researchers. Accordingly, the findings reported here are subject to some limitations. Firstly, in order to judge the impact of the learning intervention, a comparison against a benchmark was necessary. One possibility was to compare the USYD students' SPQ scores at the beginning and end of the period. Such a comparison, however, is problematic as the initial scores were collected prior to any experience with accounting studies and therefore reflect a general orientation to learning. For this reason, a comparison with a similar group of students from another university was chosen. While care was taken to ensure similarity between the two groups, it is possible that other variables may account for the observed differences in SPQ scores. Nevertheless, steps were taken to minimise the threat. As documented, the two groups faced a very similar course were subjected to the similar admission requirements, and, importantly, were shown to have the same initial orientations to learning. The major difference is the learning intervention for USYD students, and, in the absence of other obvious differences, it thus seems reasonable to infer that the intervention had the predicted effect.

Secondly, while the course content and textbook was virtually the same for both universities, the assessment regime was wider at USYD (see Appendix B). This reflected the wider set of assessment tasks that students undertook as a result of the learning intervention. Thus, the assessment tasks were an integral part of the intervention package and the results of Proposition 1 reflect the impact of this package. It was not possible to separate the independent effect of the assessment process with the data available, but an important research opportunity exists in attempting to assess the influence of assessment procedures to the overall success of a learning innovation. Further, the demands of the assessment tasks on the overall student workload should be examined as previous research shows that a high workload encourages a surface approach (Ramsden and Entwistle, 1981; Gow et al., 1994) which may mitigate the effects of supportive learning interventions.

Thirdly, the impact of learning approaches on performance in terms of final aggregate grades is, at best, marginal. This raises a question about the appropriateness of using such grades as a measure of the effectiveness of an intervention designed to encourage a deep approach to learning. Overall grades reflect the aggregation of performance on a variety of tasks, which is likely to mask the impact of engaging in a deep approach to learning. Future research investigating the effectiveness of learning interventions using more focused performance measures (e.g. disaggregated assessment grades or learning outcomes measured using Biggs and Collis (1982) SOLO taxonomy) offers the potential to demonstrate more forcefully the benefits to be gained when students adopt a deep approach. Further, assessment tasks could be also evaluated using the Biggs and Collis (1982) SOLO taxonomy to determine the level of cognitive processing required to complete each task.

Finally, the results of this study should not be automatically generalised to other possible learning interventions. Further research exploring the effectiveness of alternative interventions across diverse learning contexts would be useful given the success of the intervention explored in this paper and given that in the absence of positive interventions students show an '...increasing predisposition for a surface approach (Biggs 1987a; Gow and Kember, 1990; Stokes *et al.*, 1989; Watkins and Hattie, 1985)' (Biggs, 1993, p. 10). In particular, qualitative and quantitative comparative research of alternative interventions (outlined in the literature review), aimed at supporting students in adopting deep approaches to learning, is needed in order to assess the relative merits of the alternatives that are currently being discussed in the literature.

Acknowledgments

The authors would like to thank Ursula Lucas and two anonymous reviewers for their very helpful comments on earlier drafts of the paper.

References

Beattie, V., Collins, B. and McInnes, B. (1997) Deep and surface learning: a simple or simplistic dichotomy?, *Accounting Education: an international journal* **6** (1), 1–12.

Becher, T. (1994) The apprenticeship approach to advanced academic literacy: graduate students and their mentors, *English for Specific Purposes* **13** (1), 23–24.

Bereiter, C. and Scardamalia, M. (1987) *The Psychology of Written Composition*. Hillsdale, NJ: Lawrence Erlbaum Associates.

Biggs, J. (1985) The role of metalearning in study processes, *British Journal of Educational Psychology* **12** (1), 73–85.

Biggs, J. (1987a) *Student Approaches to Learning and Studying*. Hawthorn, VIC: Australian Council for Educational Research.

Biggs, J. (1987b) *Study Process Questionnaire Manual*. Hawthorn, VIC: Australian Council for Educational Research.

Biggs, J. (1990) Asian students' approaches to learning: implications for teaching and learning. Keynote Discussion Paper, 8th Australasian Tertiary Learning Skills and Language Conference, 11–13 July, Queensland University of Technology.

Biggs, J. (1993) What do inventories of students' learning process really measure? A theoretical review and clarification, *British Journal of Educational Psychology* **63** (1), 3–19.

Biggs, J. (2001) Enhancing learning: a matter of style or approach? In R. Sternberg and L. Zhang (eds) *Perspectives on Thinking, Learning and Cognitive Styles*, pp. 73–102. Mahwah, NJ: Lawrence Erlbaum.

Biggs, J. and Collis, K. (1982) *Evaluating the Quality of Learning: The SOLO Taxonomy (Structure of the Observed Learning Outcome)*. New York: Academic Press.

Biggs, J. and Rihn, B. (1984) The effects of intervention on deep and surface approaches to learning. In J. Kirby (ed.) *Cognitive Strategies and Educational Performance*, pp. 279–93. New York: Academic Press.

Biggs, J.B. and Telfer, R. (1987) *The Process of Learning*. Sydney: Prentice Hall.

Birkett, W. and Mladenovic, R. (2002) The approaches to learning paradigm: theoretical and empirical issues for accounting education research. Paper presented at the AAANZ Conference, Perth, Australia, 7–9 July.

Bloom, B. (ed.) (1956) *Taxonomy of Educational Objectives, the Classification of Educational Goals–Handbook 1: Cognitive Domain*. David McKay: New York.

Bonanno, H., Jones, J. and English, L. (1998) Improving group satisfaction: making groups work in a first year undergraduate accounting course, *Teaching in Higher Education* **3** (3), 365–82.

Booth P., Luckett P. and Mladenovic, R. (1999) The quality of learning in accounting education: the impact of approaches to learning on academic performance, *Accounting Education: an international journal* **8** (4), 277–300.

Chan, D., Leung, R., Gow, L. and Hu, S. (1989) Approaches to learning of accountancy students: some additional evidence. Proceedings of the ASAIHL Seminar on University Education in the 1990's, Kuala Lumpur.

Clanchy, J. and Ballard B. (1981) *Essay Writing for Students*. Melbourne: Longman Cheshire. (international edition: *How to Write Essays* [1993]).

Clanchy, J. and Ballard, B. (1988) Literacy in the university: an anthropological approach. In R. Gordon *et al.* (eds) *Literacy by Degrees*, pp. 7–23. Milton Keynes: Open University Press.

Collins, A. and Gentner, D. (1980) A framework for a cognitive theory of writing. In L.W. Greg and E.R. Steinberg (eds) *Cognitive Processes in Writing*. Hillsdale, NJ: Lawrence Erlbaum Associates.

Cope, C. and Staehr, L. (forthcoming 2005) Improving students' learning approaches through intervention in an information systems learning environment, *Studies in Higher Education* **30** (1).

Davidson, R. A. (2002) Relationship of study approach and exam performance, *Journal of Accounting Education* **20** (1), 29–44.

Eley, M. (1992) Differential adoption of study approaches within individual students, *Higher Education* **23** (3), 231–54.

English, L. and Ihnatko, T. (1998) Curriculum innovation: assessing the effectiveness of the explicit teaching of communication skills in a large first-year accounting course. In C. Rust (ed.) *Improving Students as Learners*. Oxford: Oxford Centre for Staff and Learning Development, Oxford Brookes University.

English, L., Bonanno, H., Ihnatko, T. and Webb, C. (1999) Learning through writing in a first-year accounting course, *Journal of Accounting Education* **17** (2/3), 221–54.

English, L., Bonanno, H., Jones, J. and Webb, C. (1997) Curriculum innovation: teaching communication, intellectual and interpersonal skills in a large first-year accounting course. In C. Rust and G. Gibbs (eds) *Improving Student Learning Through Course Design*, pp. 120–43. Oxford: Oxford Centre for Staff and Learning Development, Oxford Brookes University.

Entwistle, N. and Ramsden, P. (1983) *Understanding Student Learning*. London: Croom Helm.

Francis, M.C., Mulder, T.C., and Stark, J.S. (1995) Intentional learning: a process for learning to learn in the accounting curriculum. Accounting Education Change Commission and American Accounting Association, Education Series, No. 12.

Gabriel, S. and Hirsch Jr, M. (1992) Critical thinking and communication skills: integration and implementation issues, *Journal of Accounting Education* **10** (2), 243–70.

Gordon, C. and Debus, R. (2002) Developing deep learning approaches and personal teaching efficacy within a preservice teacher education context, *British Journal of Educational Psychology* **72** (4), 483–512.

Gow, L. and Kember D. (1990) Does higher education promote independent learning?, *Higher Education* **19** (3), 307–322.

Gow, L., Kember, D. and Cooper, B. (1994) The teaching context and approaches to study of accountancy students, *Issues in Accounting Education* **9**, 118–30.

Hall, M., Ramsay, A. and Raven, J. (this issue) Changing the learning environment to promote deep learning approaches in first year accounting students, *Accounting Education: an international journal* **13** (4), pp. 487–505.

Halliday, M.A.K. (1978) *Language as Social Semiotic: The Social Interpretation of Language and Meaning*. Baltimore, MD: University Park Press.

Hoggett, J. and Edwards, L. (1996) *Accounting in Australia*, 3rd edn. Brisbane: John Wiley.

Jackling, B. (1999) Students' motives, strategies and perceptions in studying financial accounting: implications for quality learning outcomes. Paper presented at AAANZ Conference, Cairns, Australia, 4–7 July.

Jackson, M. (1991) Writing as learning: reflections on developing students' writing strategies, *Higher Education Research and Development* **10** (1), 41–52.

Jones, J., Bonanno, H., Webb, C. and English, L. (1995) Development of oral communication skills in first-year–a collaborative project, *Research and Development in Higher Education*, HERDSA **18**, 422–27.

Kaplan, R. (1966) Cultural thought patterns in intercultural education, *Language Learning* **16** (1), 66–77.

Kember, D. and Gow, L. (1989) A model of student approaches to learning encompassing ways to influence and change approaches, *Instructional Science* **18** (4), 263–288.

Kember, D. and Gow, L. (1991) A challenge to the anecdotal stereotype of the Asian student, *Studies in Higher Education* **16** (2), 117–28.

Laurillard, D.M. (1984) Learning from problem solving. In F. Marton *et al. The Experience of Learning*, pp. 124–43. Edinburgh: Scottish Academic Press.

Lea, M. (1994) 'I thought I could write until I came here': student writing in higher education. In G. Gibbs (ed.) *Improving Student Learning: Theory and Practice*, pp. 216–28. Oxford: The Oxford Centre for Staff Development.

Lea, M. and Street, B. (1998) Student writing in higher education: an academic literacies approach, *Studies in Higher Education* **23** (2), 157–72.

Light, R.J. (1991) Harvard assessment seminars: excerpts from the second report. A supplement to *Harvard University Gazette*, 8 November.

Lucas, U. (2002) Rote learning in accounting? De-bunking a myth. Paper presented at British Accounting Association Accounting Education Special Interest Group Annual Conference, Glasgow Caledonian University, 29–31 May.

Martin, C. (1994) *An Introduction to Accounting*, 4th edn. Sydney: McGraw Hill.

Marton, F. and Saljo, R. (1984) Approaches to learning. In F. Marton *et al.* (eds) *The Experience of Learning*, pp. 36–55. Edinburgh: Scottish Academic Press.

Mayer-Somer, A. P. (1990) Substance and strategy in the Accounting curriculum, *Issues in Accounting Education* **5** (1), 127–142.

Meyer and Eley (1999) The development of affective subscales to reflect variation in students' experiences of studying mathematics in higher education, *Higher Education* **37** (2), 197–216.

Prosser, M. and Webb, C. (1994) Relating the process of undergraduate essay writing to the finished product, *Studies in Higher Education* **19** (2), 125–38.

Ramburuth, P. (2001) Cross cultural learning behaviour in higher education: perceptions versus practice. *ultiBASE Publication*. Melbourne: RMIT.

Ramsden, P. (ed.) (1988) *Improving Learning: New Perspectives*. London: Kogan Page.

Ramsden, P. (1992) *Learning to Teach in Higher Education*. London: Routledge.

Ramsden, P. (1998) *Learning to Lead in Higher Education*. London: Routledge.

Ramsden, P. and Entwistle, N. (1981) Effects of academic departments on students' approaches to studying, *British Journal of Educational Psychology* **51**, 368–83.

Ramsden, P., Beswick, D. and Bowden, J. (1986) *An Investigation of First Year Assessment*. Report on Research Promotion Grant 1987: University of Melbourne.

Stokes M., Balla J. and Stafford K. (1989) How students in selected degree programmes at CPHK characterise their approaches to study, *Educational Research Journal* **4** (1), 85–91.

Street, B.V. (1984) *Literacy in Theory and Practice*. Cambridge: Cambridge University Press.

Subotnik, D. (1987) What accounting can learn from legal education, *Issues in Accounting Education* **2** (2), 313–24.

Thomas, P. and Bain, J. (1984) Contextual differences of learning approaches: the effects of assessments, *Human Learning* **3**, 227–40.

Trigwell, K. and Prosser, M. (1991) Improving the quality of student learning: the influence of learning context and student approaches to learning on learning outcomes, *Higher Education* **22**(3), 251–266.

Trigwell, K., Prosser, M., Ramsden, P. and Martin, E. (1998) Improving student learning through a focus on the teaching context. In C. Rust (ed.) *Improving Students as Learners*. Oxford: Oxford Centre for Staff and Learning Development, Oxford Brookes University.

Watkins, D. and Hattie, J. (1981) The learning processes of Australian university students: investigations of contextual and personological factors, *British Journal of Educational Psychology* **51** (3), 384–93.

Watkins, D. and Hattie, J. A longitudinal study of the approach to learning of Australian tertiary students, *Human Learning* **4** (2), 127–42.

Webb, C., English, L. and Bonanno, H. (1995) Collaboration in subject design: integration of the teaching and assessment of literacy skills into a first-year accounting course, *Accounting Education: an international journal* **4** (4), 335–50.

Appendix A (Adapted from English *et al.*, 1999)

Model Answers and Structures for the Following Discuss Question:

'If resources were not scarce, there would be no need for accounting information.' Discuss (Martin, 1994, p. 14)

Model answer (i)

Accounting is the process of identifying, measuring and communicating economic information to permit informed judgements and decisions by users of the information.

If resources were not scarce, there would be no need for accounting. Scarce means 'insufficient to meet the demand' and resources refers to any source of economic wealth such as mineral resources and labour. These resources are scarce and so we need accounting. Accountants help to make decisions about how to use scarce resources, like also about whether to expand the business, sell out or cease operations. Thus, accounting is necessary because decisions have to be made about how to use scarce resources.

Model answer (ii)

The definition of accounting which has won widespread acceptance is 'the process of identifying, measuring and communicating economic information to permit informed judgements and decisions by users of the information' (Martin 1994, p. 4). Accounting is needed because resources are scarce. If resources such as minerals and labour were not scarce there would be no need to make choices and therefore no need for accounting information. The choices that need to be made are between two or more alternatives to ensure the best outcome. In making decisions, the first step is to decide what objective is to be achieved. Then the alternative actions are evaluated and a decision is made. Accounting provides us with the information we need to evaluate the alternative actions. Some examples of types of decisions users of financial reports will make are:

1. whether to invest more capital or withdraw capital from the business;
2. how much profit to withdraw;
3. whether to expand the business, sell out or cease operations;
4. whether the business is financially stable;
5. should the directors be reappointed;
6. what cash will be available if the managers decide to liquidate the company.

Model answer (iii)

Of the many definitions of accounting, the one most accepted in the accounting field (Martin 1994, p. 4) is the definition of the American Accounting Association as:

'the process of identifying, measuring and communicating economic information to permit informed judgements and decisions by users of the information'.

This definition highlights the fact that the essential purpose of accounting is to provide information so that choices can be made. There is nothing in the definition to imply that the reason that choices need to be made is because resources are finite.

Even in a scenario of abundant resources, information about those resources will be needed to enable rational decisions to be made about their disposition. For instance, information will be required about what resources are actually controlled and their location. This could involve the preparation of an inventory, continuously updated to reflect resource acquisition and use so that decision makers are able to plan for efficient resource use. In such a world it would be more efficient to send raw materials from the nearest geographical location to a factory when they were needed. To make such a decision, information is required about the raw materials used in a particular production process at a particular factory, the timing of their use and the most convenient location from which they could be obtained. Other possible uses of accounting information in a world of abundant resources would be to enable the evaluation of performance and efficiency of a particular manufacturing process; to convert data into meaningful information so that it can be interpreted and compared and to ensure that information is accessible within a convenient time-frame.

Thus, even in the case in which resources are not scarce, decisions need to be made about resource use to enable rational planning and those decisions are based, in part, on accounting information.

Model answer (iv)

Of the many definitions of accounting, the one most accepted in the accounting field (Martin 1991, p. 3) is the definition of the American Accounting Association as:

> 'the process of identifying, measuring and communicating economic information to permit informed judgements and decisions by users of the information'.

This definition highlights the fact that the essential purpose of accounting is to provide information so that choices can be made. The reason why choices must be made is that resources are finite.

The scarcity of resources such as minerals and labour means that choices must be made between two or more alternatives to ensure the best outcome. In making decisions, the first step is to decide what objective is to be achieved. Then the alternative actions are evaluated and a decision is made. Accounting provides us with the information we need to evaluate alternative actions. Some examples of types of decisions users of financial reports make include investment decisions such as whether to invest in a particular project, either by taking over an existing project or starting a new project from scratch. Information is also needed in order to make financing decisions, such as how to finance new projects through borrowing, or through increasing shareholders' contributions. Finally, management decisions must be made, for example, about how to cost the project, about whether there is enough cash to support the day to day operations of the project, and about what sort of information should be given to shareholders.

If resources were not scarce, these choices would not be necessary, and so there would be no need for accounting information.

Model Answers: Structures

The structure of **model answer (i)** can be described as follows:

Overall structure	Function of each stage	Stages of the answer
INTRODUCTION	ACCOUNTING DEFINITION	Accounting is the process of...
	POSITION STATEMENT	If resources were not...
BODY	DEFINITION OF TERMS	Scarce means...
	RESTATEMENT OF POSITION	These resources are scare and so...
	EXPLAIN ACCOUNTING FUNCTION	Accountants help to make decisions...
CONCLUSION	SUMMARY AND CONCLUSION	Thus, accounting is necessary because...

The structure of **model answer (ii)** can be described as follows:

Overall structure	Function of each stage	Stages of the answer
INTRODUCTION	ACCOUNTING DEFINITION	The definition of accounting which...
	POSITION STATEMENT	Accounting is needed because...
BODY	REASON 1	If resources such as mineral and...
	DESCRIPTION OF PROCESS	In making decisions, the first step...
	EXAMPLES	Some examples of types of decisions...

The structure of **model answer (iii)** can be described as follows:

Overall structure	Function of each stage	Stages of the answer
INTRODUCTION	ACCOUNTING DEFINITION	Of the many definitions of accounting, the one most accepted...
	EVIDENCE FOR POSITION STATEMENT (THESIS STATEMENT)	This definition highlights the fact that the essential purpose of...
	POSITION STATEMENT	There is nothing in the definition to imply...
BODY	REASON 1	Even in a scenario of abundant...
	EXAMPLES	For instance, information will be required about
	REASON 2 AND EXAMPLES	Other possible uses of accounting information...
CONCLUSION	PROVING OF STATEMENT	Thus, even in the case in which...

The structure of **model answer (iv)** can be described as follows:

Overall structure	Function of each stage	Stages of the answer
INTRODUCTION	ACCOUNTING DEFINITION	Of the many definitions of accounting, the one most accepted...
	EVIDENCE FOR POSITION STATEMENT (THESIS STATEMENT)	This definition highlights the fact that the essential purpose of...
	POSITION STATEMENT	The scarcity of resources such as minerals and labour means...
	LINK BETWEEN DEFINITION AND THESIS STATEMENT	In making decisions...
BODY	REASON 1	Accounting provides us with...
	EXAMPLES	Some examples of the types of...
	REASON 2	Information is also needed in order to...
	REASON 3 AND EXAMPLES	Finally, management decisions must be made, for example...
CONCLUSION	PROVING OF STATEMENT	If resources were not scarce, these choices would not be necessary...

Appendix B

Comparison of the Teaching/Learning Contexts at the University of Sydney (USYD) and the University of New South Wales (UNSW)

	USYD	UNSW
Economics/Commerce Degree Programmes		
Admission Requirements*		
English	Yes	Yes
2 unit Mathematics	Yes	Yes
Compulsory First Year Courses		
Accounting 1A and 1B	Yes	Yes
Business Statistics 1A and 1B	Yes	Yes
Commercial Law	Yes	Yes
Economics 1A and 1B	Yes	Yes
Computer Information Systems	No	Yes
Elective unit – student's choice	Yes	No
Core Accounting Course		
Text Book		
Hoggett, John and Edwards, Lew *Accounting in Australia*, 3rd Edition, John Wiley and Sons	Yes	Yes
Topics Covered		
First semester		
The accounting equation and debits and credits	Yes	Yes
The accounting cycle	Yes	Yes
Internal control and cash	Yes	Yes
Receivables and bad and doubtful debts	Yes	Yes
Payables and Equity	Yes	Yes
Non-current assets (cost, depreciation, disposal)	Yes	Yes
The social sphere and the competing interests of stakeholders	Yes	Yes
Second semester		
External reporting and regulation	Yes	Yes
Assets, including intangibles	Yes	Yes
Liabilities, including off-balance sheet financing	Yes	Yes
Revenue, expenses and the profit and loss statement	Yes	Yes
Partnerships and companies	Yes	Yes
Statement of cash flows	Yes	Yes
Financial statement analysis	Yes	Yes
Securities and financing decisions	Yes	Yes
Cost-volume profit analysis		Yes
Budgeting		Yes

(continued)

	USYD	UNSW
Teaching/Face to Face Class Time (first & second semesters)		
Lectures	2 hours	2 hours
Small group tutorial	1 hour	2 hours
Large group workshop	1 hour	
Total	**4 hours**	**4 hours**
Assessment Regime		
First semester		
Mid-semester examination	8%	30%
Final examination	50%	60%
Practice set		10%
Case Study	12%	
Tutorial assessment	20%	
Computer assignments	10%	
Total	**100%**	**100%**
Second semester		
Mid-semester examination	10%	20%
Final examination	50%	60%
Tutorial assessment	4%	10%
Essay		10%
Group case study	6%	
Individual case study	8%	
Major group assignment	10%	
Computer assignments and tests	12%	
Total	**100%**	**100%**

*All students are required to study English at secondary level. UNSW required a minimum HSC mark 2 unit General/Contemporary English (60/100), 2 unit English (53/100), 2 unit Mathematics (60/100)

It can be seen from the information in Appendix B above that the degree programmes and core accounting courses at USYD and UNSW were similar in many ways.

The majority of students in this study are first year undergraduate students enrolled in Economics and Commerce degrees at USYD and UNSW (only a small proportion of students complete the introductory accounting units explored in this study when they are enrolled in degrees in other faculties, such as the Faculty of Science). Economics and Commerce students at both universities must complete a number of core introductory courses in Accounting, Business Statistics, Economics and Commercial Law. These core courses ensure that students have the essential foundations for their studies in their respective business majors.

It is also evident that the two-semester introductory accounting courses at USYD and UNSW were similar in many ways. They used the same text book, covered most of the same topics (except for 2 management accounting topics at UNSW in the second semester) and had similar contact hours. At USYD technical material was covered in large weekly workshops, each of about 70 students. The interventions took place in the weekly tutorial, which contained

20 or fewer students and focused exclusively on fostering a deep approach to learning through improving students' written literacy skills. At UNSW the weekly two-hour tutorial contained about 30 students and covered all aspects of the content.

The assessment regimes reflect the differences in approaches to teaching. At UNSW in the first semester the multiple choice mid-semester examination was worth 30 marks, and the major assignment was a practice set, suggesting that the focus of the course was the grasp of technical material. At UNSW in the second semester the multiple choice mid-semester examination was worth 20%, the tutorial participation was worth 10% and there was an essay worth 10%. In contrast, at USYD in both semesters there was considerably less emphasis on the multiple choice mid-semester examination, and considerably more emphasis on assessing various writing tasks. In first semester there was an individual case study report and tutorial assessment that included group-based oral presentations of case study solutions. The computer assignments in both semesters tested technical competence. In the second semester at USYD 18 tutorial marks were devoted to activities and tasks that tested written literacy skills development.

Perceptions of the Learning Context and Learning Approaches: Implications for Quality Learning Outcomes in Accounting

BEVERLEY JACKLING

Deakin University, Australia

ABSTRACT   *This study analyses learning approaches, course perceptions and learning outcomes of a group of second year accounting students at an Australian university using qualitative data analysis techniques. The research method involves the development of a series of matrices linking types of motives and strategies used by students in their study, together with their perceptions of the learning context associated with learning outcomes. The study focuses on assessing the links between learning approaches and a qualitative assessment of students' conceptual understanding of aspects of financial accounting studied at the undergraduate level. The results confirm how individual differences in the perceptions of the learning context relate to study motives and strategies. The findings show how different forms of memorisation relate to study strategies and how the completion of accounting tasks link to students' perceptions of course requirements. There was also some evidence that, in terms of learning outcomes, students with sophisticated levels of understanding of concepts, tended to have consistent deep and achieving approaches to learning. This result was compared with students' academic performance as a measure of learning outcome. Discrepancies between these two measures of learning outcome are highlighted in the conclusions. The findings strengthen the case for further investigation of the use of measures other than academic performance in examining relationships between learning approaches and learning outcomes.*

Introduction

The higher education literature recognizes that, in order to improve the quality of student learning, there is a need to develop a better understanding of student learning approaches. In particular, there is a well-established body of educational research, which supports the contention that students' approaches to learning are related to their perceptions of the learning environment and that the approaches adopted are linked to the quality of the learning outcomes (Ramsden, 1992, 2003; Marton and Booth, 1997; Prosser and Trigwell, 1999).

In studies across various discipline areas, deep learning approaches have been associated with positive perceptions of the learning environment (Ramsden, 1992, 2003). Surface learning approaches have been associated with perceptions of high workload requirements and the perception that assessment tasks require rote learning of factual material (Entwistle and Ramsden, 1983; Ramsden, 1991; Trigwell and Prosser, 1991a; Prosser and Trigwell, 1999; Lizzio et al., 2002). Aspects of the learning environment, including good teaching, clear goals, appropriate workload, appropriate assessment and emphasis on independence in learning, have been linked with the quality of learning approaches and learning outcomes achieved by students (Ramsden, 1992, 2003). These findings, in the main, have been derived from models of learning and associated inventories. For example, Study Process Questionnaire, (Biggs, 1987a), Approaches to Study Inventory developed by Entwistle and Ramsden, (1983). Much of the educational research has had a general focus. Specific discipline studies, however, enable an examination of possible variations from the general models of learning and have the potential to provide more practical applications for educators in that discipline (Eley and Meyer, 2004).

Some studies have suggested that, given the nature of the tasks in accounting that build on prior knowledge and the recording of transactions following particular algorithms, a surface approach to learning may be more predominant among accounting students (Beattie et al., 1997). More recently, research has suggested that the use of surface approaches, particularly linked with memorisation and rote learning, are over-simplifications of the learning approaches adopted by accounting students (Lucas and Meyer, 2003a). The work of Meyer (2000a) identified contrasting deep and surface forms of memorising that may assist in explaining further refinements to models of student learning, particularly as it relates to the accounting discipline.

Differing approaches have been used to test the relationship between students' approaches to learning in accounting and measures of the quality of learning outcomes, including the use of examination performance as a measure of learning outcomes (for example, Duff, 1996; Booth et al., 1999; Byrne et al., 2002; English et al., 2003) and qualitative data analysis related to perceptions of accounting (Gow et al., 1994; Sharma, 1997; Lucas, 2001; Lucas and Meyer, 2003b). Although assessing student learning outcomes is described by Lucas and Meyer (2003a) as 'more an art than a science' (p. 6) as the influences that lead to a particular learning outcome are not directly observable, it is generally agreed that qualitative measures of learning outcome are better indicators of student learning than quantitative measures such as examination performance (Trigwell and Prosser 1991a; Ramsden, 1992, 2003).

This study adds to the body of accounting education literature on learning approaches by exploring qualitatively the relationships between the contexts of learning and learning approaches with particular reference to the role of memorisation in studying accounting. Additionally, the study examines the relationships between learning approaches and learning outcomes as measured by the understanding of concepts taught in accounting. The study uses interviews with twelve second-year undergraduate accounting students to examine these relationships.

The remainder of this study is organized as follows. First, Biggs 3P learning model which is used as the basis for this research is outlined, as well as prior research on learning approaches, the context of learning and learning outcomes is explored; second a description of the research method employed is provided. Third, the findings are presented and discussed and the study concludes with a consideration of the implications of the findings for accounting educators.

Learning Model Approach

There has been a substantial body of research developed around relations between students' perceptions of learning, their perceptions of the learning environment, their approaches to learning and learning outcomes in higher education (Marton *et al.*, 1984; Trigwell and Prosser, 1991b; Ramsden, 1992, 2003). In this study, a relational approach is used to incorporate the ideas of educational researchers in the area, particularly Biggs (1993, 1999) and Prosser and Trigwell (1997, 1999). The Biggs 3P model of learning is a view of learning and teaching that emphasises the interrelationships and interactions between presage, process and product factors in learning. The study process consisting of motives and strategies in learning that mediate between presage factors which exist before the student enters the learning situation (e.g. personal characteristics) and institutional characteristics (e.g. teaching method, assessment and course structure) and the product factors, identified as learning outcomes. As such, the Biggs 3P model of learning is seen as a means of understanding individual variations in the learning experience.

The relational learning research approach adopted in this study is illustrated in Figure 1. It proposes that the elements of the model are simultaneously present in students' awareness as they contemplate the learning tasks presented in an undergraduate accounting unit of study.

Approaches to Learning

Research on student learning has shown how the context of learning (broadly defined to include teaching, assessment, learning materials, and discipline areas) influences student-learning outcomes (Entwistle and Smith, 2002). The findings originate from the early research by Marton and his colleagues in Gothenburg (Marton *et al.*, 1984). These researchers identified qualitative differences in the way in which students went about their learning tasks. The main distinction was between deep and surface approaches to learning. The

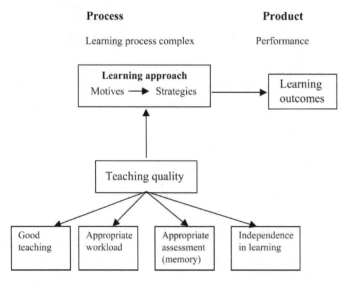

Figure 1. Relationships between perceptions of teaching, learning approach and learning outcome

learning approach adopted by a student depends upon his/her intentions and motives and on his/her perceptions of the task demands. The intention to seek meaning (deep approach) or to reproduce the information (surface approach) is seen as a consequence of how students interpreted the context of learning. Traditionally the surface approach has been described as involving the use of rote memorisation, while the deep approach has drawn on making connections with previous knowledge and involving logical reasoning. The link between memorisation and the surface approach has, however, proved an oversimplification as research by Kember (1996), and Watkins and Biggs (1996) on Chinese student learning has demonstrated. Additionally, work by Meyer (2000a, 2000b), Lucas (2002) and Lucas and Meyer (2003a) has provided support to the view that memorizing may be used as a first step towards developing understanding.

In Figure 1 a motive-strategy combination defines a distinct approach to learning, although students may use a mix of strategies depending on their perceptions of the context of learning and their motives in study. Based on previous research findings three strategies, Deep, Surface and Achieving will be related to the quality of learning outcomes. The *Surface strategy* is likely to be identified with accurate but disjointed recall of detail; the *Deep strategy* to structural complexity of the subject; and the *Achieving strategy* is likely to be associated with whatever goals the student sees as most pertinent to high grades in the unit (Biggs, 1987b).

Figure 1 shows that learning motives and strategies are hypothesised as being linked with learning outcomes. The assessment of the quality of learning outcomes will be determined from students' descriptions of their conceptual understanding of a series of second year financial accounting tasks.

The Learning Context and Approaches to Learning

The research on learning approaches has indicated that the learning context impacts on learning approach. Ramsden (1991) in the development of the Course Experience Questionnaire (CEQ) initially derived five scales measuring students' perceptions of teaching quality that can be identified more broadly with the context of learning. These scales included perceptions of good teaching, clear goals, workload, assessment and independence. Each of the scales sought to identify aspects of students' perceptions of the teaching/ learning environment that led to a deep approach to learning. Prior studies suggest that the most consistent finding is that perceptions of heavy workloads are associated with a surface or reproducing approach to learning (Entwistle and Tait, 1990; Trigwell and Prosser 1991a,b; Eley, 1992). Lizzio *et al.* (2002) found that perceptions of heavy workload were associated with surface approaches to learning, but there was no such relationship between the perceptions of the appropriateness of workload and a deep approach to study. However, their findings indicate that perceptions of quality teaching and appropriate assessment were strongly related to a deep approach to learning.

Recent studies have reported experimentation in changing aspects of the learning environment to promote a deep approach to learning. Various studies (for example, Gordon and Debus, 2002; Hall *et al.*, 2003; English *et al.*, 2003; Cope and Staehr, 2005) have demonstrated that changes in the learning environment impact on the learning approaches of students. Other studies have demonstrated that students studying the same course may perceive it in radically different ways (for example, Prosser and Trigwell, 1997; Lucas, 2001). Further work by Mladenovic (2000) explored ways of facilitating change in the negative preconceptions held by introductory accounting students. Studies of this type serve to demonstrate that students' perceptions of the context of learning potentially have an important role in influencing learning approach.

Approaches to Learning and Learning Outcomes

Numerous studies have shown that the outcomes of learning are associated with the approaches students adopt in their study (Dahlgren, 1984: Van Rossum and Schenk, 1984; Marton and Säljö, 1997). Ramsden (1992, 2003) indicates that various studies of the quality of students' understanding in academic disciplines shows that many students achieve low level content-related outcomes, linked with retention of vast quantities of information that are soon forgotten. This type of learning outcome has been aligned with surface approaches to learning. Deep approaches to learning have been more closely associated with relational or extended abstract learning outcomes defined in terms of grades or in terms of qualitative measures of learning (Van Rossum and Schenk, 1984).[1] Trigwell and Prosser (1991a) however, have drawn an important distinction between the types of learning outcomes that students derive from a course. They found that a deep approach to learning was more strongly related to qualitative learning outcomes (measured by the complexity of students' understanding of the aims of a course of study) than to quantitative outcomes (academic grades). Studies that have used examination results as a measure of learning outcome when investigating the link between learning approach and learning outcome have produced mixed results (Watkins and Hattie, 1981; Entwistle and Ramsden, 1983; Ramsden et al., 1986; Newble et al., 1988; Trigwell and Prosser, 1991a,b). Ramsden (1992) suggests these variations in results may be explained by the potential inappropriateness of examination marks as a means of measuring differences in the quality of learning outcomes.

Similarly in accounting, recent studies have produced mixed results in terms of the relationship of study approach and student performance in accounting. Booth et al. (1999) found that higher surface approach scores on Biggs SPQ were associated with less successful academic performance while there appeared to be no association between performance and deep approach scores. In contrast, Davidson (2002) found a significant positive relationship between performance on complex examination questions and the use of a deep learning approach. Other studies using assessment of learning outcomes via examination performance also provide mixed results, for example Byrne et al. (2002) and English et al. (2003). This study examines the relationship between learning approach and learning outcome where the learning outcome is measured by the level of understanding of the concepts taught in the unit of study, rather than using performance on formal assessment tasks.

Method

Subjects

Interviewees were selected from students studying the second year of a three-year Bachelor of Commerce degree at a university in Australia. Second-year students were chosen for this study because at this stage in their studies, in most instances they have chosen accounting as part of a major study towards meeting recognition requirements of professional accounting bodies such as the Institute of Chartered Accountants in Australia and CPA Australia. It was therefore anticipated that students would be motivated in their studies of accounting, having selected accounting as a major field of study.

The qualitative data were acquired from a pool of 121 second-year students who completed the Study Process Questionnaire (SPQ) as part of a larger study of second year students (Jackling, 2001). Twelve of these 121 students were invited to be interviewed about their experiences and understanding of concepts in learning financial accounting. Interviews of approximately 45 minutes' duration with twelve students provided sufficient coverage of a range of issues related to learning in accounting for the researcher to be satisfied that there had been adequate re-occurrence of themes and perceptions (Guba and Lincoln, 1994; Lucas, 2001).

Gender Issues

Prior studies have produced varying results for tests of gender differences in approaches to learning. For example, in terms of learning approaches, Hassall and Joyce (1997) and Byrne *et al.* (2002) found a significantly higher score for surface learning for female students compared to male students, while Booth *et al.* (1999) and Byrne *et al.* (1999) found no significant differences in approaches to learning of male and female students in first year accounting courses.

Similarly, gender differences have been reported in the academic performance of accounting students. Early studies (Mutchler *et al.*, 1987; Tyson, 1989) found that female accounting students outperformed male students. In contrast, more recently Buckless *et al.* (1991), Gist *et al.* (1996), and Jackling and Anderson (1998) found that gender had no impact on performance.

In examining gender issues and the relationship between learning approaches and learning outcomes, Byrne *et al.* (2002) found that a significant relationship existed for female students in terms of deep and achieving (strategic) approaches to learning and high academic performance. Additionally, there was a relationship between surface (instrumental) learning and poor performance for females. However, there was little evidence of a relationship between performance and learning approaches for male students.

Prior research on gender issues related to learning approaches and performance warranted consideration of the possible differences in males and females in the interviews conducted in this study. Consequently, an equal number of males and females were included in the study.

Administration of the Interviews

The qualitative data were collected following the completion of the semester's study of financial accounting. There were two reasons for this approach. First, student interviews of approximately 45 minutes duration were considered less taxing on students' time following the timetabled examination period rather than in the weeks prior to examinations. Second, this approach meant that the content-specific questions related to financial accounting tested longer-term levels of understanding.

There were non-evaluative responses from the interviewer to the answers given by students throughout the interview. All interviews were taped and transcribed verbatim.

Data Analysis Strategies

The analysis of data follows a framework of identification of distinctive aspects of learning experienced by the learner. This approach followed the model presented by Prosser and Millar (1989) where learning was seen as a two-pronged approach. The 'how' of learning being related to the learning approach (deep or surface) and the 'what' of learning related to the concepts held of subject content in the learning task (explanation of concepts). The interview questions were designed to identify, firstly, 'how' students went about their learning to establish whether Deep, Surface or Achieving motives and strategies were used.[2] For example, students were asked the following question 'Thinking about the way you studied financial accounting in Semester 1 this year, tell me about your approach to lectures'. This section of the interview dealing with learning approaches specifically sought to gain an understanding of the way in which students approached their learning of tasks.

The second part of the interview examined 'what' students had learned, that is, the outcome of learning. This involved students providing descriptions of their understanding of some of the concepts covered in the unit of study. These descriptions were used to identify qualitatively different perceptions of understanding of particular aspects of the course content and constituted a measure of the extensiveness of the learning outcomes achieved by each student.[3]

A pilot study was undertaken to test for the suitability and structure of the questions together with testing the appropriateness of the level of difficulty of the content-specific questions. In the final version of the interview protocol, each part of the interview contained a series of general questions and potential probes to explore themes more fully. (See Appendix 1)

Preliminary Data Analysis

In conducting the analysis of interview data, the credibility of the work relies on attention to rigorous, complete, and impartial analysis of the interview transcripts (Miles and Huberman, 1994, p. 10). This section of the study outlines the protocol used for the development of the variables from the interview transcripts that form the basis of the data analysis.

Data Reduction

In this study interview transcripts were coded by associating the sentences with one or more of the process and product components formulated in the model of learning (see Figure 1). This resulted initially in the development of three broad categories: student motives in learning, student strategies used in learning, and perceptions of teaching. Subsequently, interview extracts were examined for recurring themes, for example, recurring motives and strategies in earning and grouping of common perceptions of teaching (Abbott, 1992; Ragin, 1987). The data were then classified into categories of learning motives and strategies, as well as perceptions of the quality of the teaching.

Analysis of Motives and Strategies

The classification of students' motives in learning was developed with reference to the literature, describing surface, deep and achieving motives. Re-reading of all interview transcripts revealed that there were four main recurring *motives* utilized by students when learning, which were: obtaining high grades; just doing enough work to pass; completing the course with minimum effort; and seeking depth of understanding.

The motive 'high grades' was clearly identifiable as an Achieving motive, described by Biggs (1987a) as an intention to obtain high marks and as an intention to excel regardless of interest in the course (Evans *et al.*, 2003). The categories 'completion of course' and 'pass the unit' were labelled as Surface motives. These categories were created from comments such as 'I am concerned about just getting enough marks to pass this subject'. Typically, a surface motive is characterized by a balance between failing and not working more than necessary, being an aspect of extrinsic motivation in study. According to Biggs (1993), students having a surface motive have a desire to obtain a qualification and a fear of failure. The category 'depth of understanding' was labelled as a Deep motive as the learner's aim is to extract maximum meaning from completing a task (Biggs, 1987b). This variable was identified with the intention to understand underlying concepts and the aim of maximising understanding by focusing on meaning (Evans *et al.*, 2003).

Similarly, learning **strategies** used in preparing for examinations were displayed for all interviews as a basis for further classification.[4] The interview extracts revealed a number of common strategies such as reading notes, completing past examination questions, re-doing tutorial exercises, completing computer assisted learning tasks and re-writing notes.

Classification into Surface, Deep and Achieving strategies in examination preparation were made with reference to Biggs' (1987a) classifications. A strategy is a tactic for handling a procedure; therefore, a surface tactic is limited to bare essentials and reproduction of these essentials via rote learning. As such, re–writing notes and memorising tactics were categorised as Surface strategies. The Achieving strategy classification relates to student involvement with time management, completing all set tasks including completion of suggested reading, seeking cues from instructors, planning ahead and prioritising (Biggs, 1993). Completion of examination solutions and re-doing tutorial exercises were labelled as Achieving strategies as interview data analysis demonstrated that these activities were linked to the motive of maximising success, based on the ego-enhancement that results from high grades (Biggs, 1993).

Reading and making notes were categorised as Deep strategies, where the intention was to engage in activities that enhance depth of understanding, e.g. by reading and/or inter-relating topic knowledge by making notes. It is reasonable also to consider making notes as an Achieving strategy as this may be a way of organising work. Clearly identifiable distinctions between Deep/Achieving strategies were not always attempted as this combination of motive and strategy is considered reasonable, particularly in students undertaking tertiary studies (Biggs, 1989). Consequently, an additional category 'Deep/Achieving' strategy was created.

Analysis of Perceptions of Teaching Quality

Perceptions of Teaching Quality revealed in the data display, related to four of the five scales in the Course Experience Questionnaire inventory (Ramsden, 1991). These variables were perceptions of the Workload, perceptions of Good Teaching, appropriateness of Assessment (sub-scale item in the CEQ related to memorising) and Independence in learning.

Analysis of Learning Outcomes

Students were asked a number of questions specific to the course content, hereafter called 'content-specific questions' (see Appendix 1). Responses were initially coded according to the order of the question, e.g. Question 1 being the first content-specific question. Further examination resulted in classifying the response as adequate or inadequate for each question as a form of first-order data analysis.[5,6]

The preliminary data analysis and classification outlined above was checked using data analysis sheets described by Miles and Huberman (1994) as a means of minimising the impact of interviewer bias in the analysis of transcripts. The data analysis sheets provided an overall check on the coding of text, as well as a summary that incorporated quotations of significant points in the areas of investigation. Inconsistencies between data analysis sheets for each interviewee and coded data were corrected prior to data analysis by re-reading interview scripts and recoding according to the guidelines established by the literature supporting the classification codes.

Data Analysis and Results

Data analysis involved the formation of matrices to show the cell location of each student's response to variables in the model of learning shown in Figure 1. The tabular format provides a form of data reduction to aid the interpretation of trends and clusters in the analysis of the data. A number allocated at the time of interview identified each student in the summary tables. From the summary tables, extracts from the extended text were used to illustrate the responses within cells of the relevant matrix. The following parts of this section provide the analysis of the matrices together with a selection of quotations from students to illustrate the descriptive content in some of the cells in the matrix.

First, the matrices were used to test the relationships between perceptions of the Teaching Quality and Motives and Strategies in learning. The second part of the analysis examines the relationships between Motives/Strategies in learning and the quality of learning outcomes. Table 1 provides a brief summary of some of the background features of the interviewees, including details of study mode (part-time or full-time) and the responses to the content specific questions asked in interviews.

The Learning Context and Approaches to Learning

Learning Context and Motives in Study

Table 2 shows the combination of Deep, Achieving and Surface motives which students used in their learning of financial accounting, together with their perceptions of the learning context, in terms of perceptions of various aspects of Teaching Quality. The results show that students who perceived Teaching Quality less favourably tended to have Surface motives in learning. For example, there was some evidence that students who

Table 1. Summary of background characteristics and learning outcomes

Student	Sex	Mode of study	Biggs' learning approach classification[a]	Q.1	Q.2	Q.3	Q.4
1	F	P/T	Surface predominant/exclusive	✓[b]	✓	✓	✗
2	M	F/T	Surface predominant/exclusive	✓	✓	✓	✓
3	F	F/T	Surface-achieving	✓	✓	✓	✓
4	M	F/T	Surface-achieving	✓	✓	✗[c]	n/a[d]
5	F	P/T	Deep-achieving	✓	✗	✗	n/a
6	M	F/T	Deep-achieving	✓	✓	✓	✗
7	M	F/T	Low achieving	✓	✗	n/a	n/a
8	F	F/T	Low achieving	✓	✗	✗	n/a
9	F	F/T	Achieving predominant/exclusive	✓	✓	✓	✗
10	M	P/T	Achieving predominant/exclusive	✓	✓	✓	✗
11	F	F/T	Deep predominant/exclusive	✓	✓	✓	✓
12	M	F/T	Deep predominant/exclusive	✓	✓	✓	✓

Note:
[a] The categories of learning profiles (Biggs 1987a) determined from scores on SPQ inventory completed by interviewees.
[b] ✓ = adequate response.
[c] ✗ = inadequate response.
[d] n/a = question not attempted.

Table 2. Perceptions of learning context and motives and strategies

		Measures of learning context							
		Teaching		Workload		Memory		Independence	
	Student No.	Satisfactory	Unsatisfactory	Approp.	Not aprop.	Import.	Not import.	Import.	Not import.
MOTIVES									
Deep – Depth of understanding	6	✓		✓				✓	
	8	✓		✓				✓	
	10	✓		✓		✓		✓	✓
	11	✓		✓			✓	✓	
	12	✓		✓			✓	✓	✓
Achieving – High grades	8	✓		✓		✓		✓	
	9		✓[a]	✓			✓	✓	✓
	10	✓						✓	
Surface – Complete course	1	✓		✓		✓			
	2	✓			✓	✓	✓[b]		
	3	✓	✓[a]		✓	✓			✓
	4	✓			✓	✓	✓[b]		
	5	✓			✓	✓	✓	✓	
	7				✓			✓	
STRATEGIES									
Deep – Read	2	✓[a]				✓[b]		✓	
	3	✓			✓	✓		✓	
	5		✓			✓		✓	✓
	6					✓		✓	✓
	7				✓		✓	✓	
	8				✓		✓	✓	
	12				✓		✓	✓	

Achieving –
Complete exercise 1 2 5 8 9 10 11 12

Achieving –Exam.
solutions 2 4 5 6 8 12

Deep/achieving –
Make notes 5 11

Surface – Memorize 2 3 4 5 9

Surface – Read 1 9

Surface – CAP 1 2 8

Surface – Rewrite notes 3

---

[a] As there was more than one lecturer in the unit, some students (e.g. Students 3 and 9) perceived the teaching both satisfactory/unsatisfactory owing to their differences in perceptions of the quality of teaching by different lecturers.

[b] Students 2 and 4 perceived that memory was important in the learning context in certain situations, while in other situations they perceived that memory was not important.

perceived that the assessment tasks in the unit merely required a good memory tended to be motivated simply to pass the unit (a Surface motive). Importantly, students who perceived the Workload was inappropriate (too heavy) tended to have Surface motives in learning, for example, Students, 3, 4, 5 and 7. Table 2 matrix cell surface motive (Complete course)/Perception of course – (Workload not appropriate).

Students who viewed aspects of Teaching Quality more favourably tended to have Deep motives in learning accounting. For example, Students 10, 11 and 12 generally had favourable perceptions of the learning context together with Deep motives in learning. See Table 2 Matrix cells motive deep (depth of understanding)/perception (teaching satisfactory); motive deep (depth of understanding)/perception (memory not important). Students who were motivated to seek depth of understanding (a deep motive) in their studies, perceived that the course required more than just knowledge of facts for examinations. As an example of the association between deep motive and perception that the course required more than memorising of material, Student 11, stated:

Student 11 (quotation taken from Table 2 matrix cell motive deep/perception –memory)

> It's better if you learn about a subject instead of just cramming for the exam, because then when you get to your next subject, sometimes there's something that you've learnt already. If you spend time on doing it properly, you sort of benefit from it.... Rather than just pass and get a good grade, it is better to have learnt something from the unit.

There was also a relationship between perceptions of independence in learning and deep/achieving motives in learning. For example, Table 2 shows that Students 6, 8, 10 and 12 believed that they had a degree of independence in their learning and they used deep/achieving motives in learning.

Learning Context and Study Strategies

The analysis shows that students with favourable perceptions of the Teaching Quality tended to utilize deep and achieving strategies in preparing for assessment tasks. However, a display of the node in NUD*IST[7] relating to reading as a learning strategy revealed that this variable needed further refinement in coding. The interviews transcripts showed that, for some students, 'reading' was a preliminary step to memorising, while others read to gain understanding. The transcripts showed that Students 1 and 9 read for memorising purposes. For example:

Student 9 (extract taken from Table 2 matrix cell: surface strategy (read)/perception (memory important)

> A few days before the exam I read through the book once again, and when I prepare my work, I highlight some of the points, I read those points again, and see what points I should memorise and then prepare another shorter one (summary) memorise those ... I need to refresh my memory for all the calculation and all the theories. When I am in the exam I couldn't open a book to look what items they are, I have to memorise which area they belong to.

In contrast, Student 2 read for understanding, as he perceived that the assessment tasks required more than memorisation of procedures. As such, 'reading' as a strategy was further classified into two components: reading for understanding, a deep strategy, and reading with the aim of memorizing, a surface strategy. This classification is consistent with the recent work of Meyer (2000a) and Lucas and Meyer (2003a) that examines various levels of memorisation in student learning.

The pattern of associations between perceptions of Teaching Quality and strategies in learning was repeated in relation to perceptions of workload requirements. For example, Student 12, with favourable perceptions of aspects of Teaching Quality, in terms of good teaching and appropriateness of the workload, utilized achieving-type strategies, such as completing tutorial exercises and past examination studies. In contrast, Student 3, who had a fairly consistent pattern of unfavourable perceptions of Teaching Quality (workload heavy, memory important and independence in learning not important), used more surface-type strategies in learning, such as re-writing notes and memorizing. This pattern of relationships between deep and achieving strategies and perceptions of the learning context was also demonstrated in terms of perceptions of good teaching and independence in learning. For example, Students 8, 10, 11 and 12 tended to have favourable perceptions of overall Teaching Quality in terms of good teaching and independence in learning. These students utilised achieving and deep strategies in their studies.

The matrix analysis for learning strategies also showed that a number of students perceived that memory was an important strategy in learning financial accounting. The importance of memorising as a strategy may be partly attributable to the nature of the course content, given that the course of study was perceived by students to have a procedural orientation, together with a sequential processing of data. These characteristics were similar to an algorithm-based approach to course content in accounting described by Umapathy (1984 p. 142) and Birkett and Mladenovic, (2002).

A more detailed investigation of the results revealed that the perception of the importance of memory often related to the type of learning task that the student was referencing. For example, Student 2 used memorising as a strategy to learn definitions, while Student 4 used memorising when he believed that it helped in preparing for procedural-type questions in the examination. These students both indicated that the use of memory as a strategy was influenced by the learning context and they acknowledge that memorizing was not always appropriate in their learning. For example, Student 2 stated:

> Just trying to remember as much as you can is one way of going in this subject. It's probably not the right way to go about it – you should be trying to understand it.

While Student 4 stated:

> I found in this subject compared to other subjects, you have to understand what is going on, because to memorise is not enough.

The findings relating to the use of memory in terms of perceptions of course requirements and learning strategies were consistent with previous research that shows that the context of learning influences the adoption of learning strategies (Ramsden, 1984; Meyer *et al.*, 1990; Eley, 1992; Lucas and Meyer, 2003b).

Approaches to Learning and Learning Outcomes

The aim in this matrix analysis was to examine the interaction between learning approaches and the ability to verbalise conceptual knowledge acquired in the study of financial accounting. A summary of students' responses to the four content specific questions was given in Table 1. Of interest is that only three students (Students 2, 11 and 12) were able to provide adequate explanations for Question 4. This question was considered to require a more detailed conceptual knowledge of the topic than the earlier questions.[8]

The first part of Table 3 shows the relationship between motives in learning and learning outcomes. It demonstrates that, if students had surface motives (pass the unit or complete the course) then, generally, they were unable to answer the more conceptual type questions, such as Question 4. Although very few students were able to give a satisfactory

Table 3. Learning motives, strategies and learning outcomes

	Student No.	Q.1	Q.2	Q.3	Q.4
MOTIVES					
Deep – Depth of understanding	6	✓	✓	✓	
	8	✓			
	10	✓	✓	✓	
	11	✓	✓	✓	✓
	12	✓	✓	✓	✓
Achieving – High grades	8	✓			
	9	✓	✓	✓	
	10	✓	✓	✓	
Surface – Complete course	1	✓	✓	✓	
	2	✓	✓	✓	✓
	3	✓			
	4	✓			
	5	✓			
	7	✓			
STRATEGIES					
Deep – Read	2	✓	✓	✓	✓
	3		✓		
	5	✓			
	6	✓	✓	✓	
	7	✓			
	8	✓			
	12	✓	✓	✓	✓
Achieving – Complete exercises	1	✓	✓	✓	
	2	✓	✓	✓	✓
	5	✓			
	8	✓			
	9	✓	✓	✓	
	10	✓	✓	✓	
	11	✓	✓	✓	✓
	12	✓	✓	✓	✓
Achieving – Examination solutions	2	✓	✓	✓	✓
	4	✓	✓		
	5	✓			
	6	✓	✓	✓	
	8	✓			
	12	✓	✓	✓	✓
Deep/achieving – Make notes	5	✓			
	11	✓	✓	✓	✓
Surface – Rewrite notes	3		✓		
Surface – CAP	1	✓	✓	✓	
	2	✓	✓	✓	✓
	8	✓			
Surface – Memorize	2	✓	✓	✓	
	3	✓			
	4	✓	✓		
	5	✓			
	9	✓	✓	✓	
Surface – Read	1	✓	✓	✓	
	9	✓	✓	✓	

✓ = adequate response.

response to Question 4, those best able to answer this question had Deep/Achieving motives in their learning (for example, Students 11 and 12). However, Student 2, identified with predominantly surface motives and strategies in learning, was also able to demonstrate considerable conceptual knowledge, providing satisfactory responses to all four questions. A mitigating factor in this result may have been due to Student 2 being a mature-age student returning to full-time study. Biggs' (1987b) early work shows that deep and achieving approaches to learning increase with age. Although using predominantly surface approaches to learning, it would appear that Student 2 used surface and deep strategies when required (Kember, 1996).

Students with few satisfactory responses to the content specific questions used a number of surface strategies in learning. For example, Student 3 was only able to provide one satisfactory response. In answering questions, the student tried to rely on memory. For example:

Student 3: (extract from Table 3 matrix cell: surface motive/question 3)

Now, I'm looking back and I can't remember how to do it... but I remember doing certain techniques ... I'm thinking back to the computer programme now, I'm trying to think why. I will probably stumble.

Similarly, Student 4 with surface motives (pass the unit) and surface strategies demonstrated a reliance on memory in answering the content specific questions. In response to Question 3, the elimination of inter-company transactions in company consolidations, the student stated:

Student 4: (extract from matrix cell Table 3 surface strategy/question 3)

I'm just trying to think now.. ... Stuff like you've got to add on or take a few things like stuff like say that inter-company transactions and stuff like that ... say that subsidiary bought from the actual company, the parent company, or bought things off the other company sort of thing, and there's a few things you gotta [sic] use though. The inter-company transactions and a lot of other things that went on between the company or like you don't want to double count things, stuff like that, you know its just not as simple as adding and subtracting, I'm trying to think of a good example.. ...

These quotations show that students with Surface strategies, had difficulty verbalising some of the concepts covered in this unit of learning. Students 1, 3, 4 and 7, who had predominantly Surface motives in their learning, were not able to answer the more complex questions. The results shown in Table 3 suggest that surface **motives** did not lead to appropriate strategies or enable satisfactory responses to a number of questions testing conceptual knowledge.

The findings also show that achieving/deep **strategies** in learning were associated with answering the more sophisticated questions in the interview (for example, Students, 10, 11, and 12). Table 3 shows that Students 10, 11 and 12 used a combination of deep strategies (deep read, making notes) and achieving strategies (complete exercises; prepare examination solutions).

The results also lend some support to the findings reported by Trigwell and Prosser (1993). They argued that deep approaches to learning were more closely related to *quality* learning outcomes rather than the *quantity* of learning outcomes, represented by grade-level performance. In this study, the quality learning outcomes, as measured by ability to answer conceptual questions, were not necessarily replicated in performance on formal assessment tasks. Only three students gave adequate responses to the question considered to test the most complex concepts. One of these students (Student 12) with a predominantly deep approach to learning failed the unit, yet provided an adequate explanation for Question 4. Student 12 had a high level of interest in content of the course, was motivated to achieve high grades, but attributed his academic failure to a lack of time management and concentration on the finer details required in answering some examination questions. In contrast, some students with typically surface approaches to their learning had been successful academically, but were not able to answer the more sophisticated questions put to them in interview (e.g. Students 1 and 9). The results suggest that, in this instance, the examination was less likely to test depth of conceptual understanding. This suggests that deep approaches to learning may be more strongly identified with qualitative measures of learning outcomes rather than quantitative measures of learning outcomes. Given the mixed results in this study using both quantitative and qualitative measures of learning outcome, and prior studies using academic performance as a measure of learning outcome (Booth *et al.*, 1999; Byrne *et al.*, 2002; English *et al.*, 2003), the case is strengthened for further investigation of the measures of the relationship between learning approaches and learning outcomes.

This study incorporated an equal number of males and females to examine possible gender differences in learning approaches and learning outcomes previously identified in some of the literature. The results were inconclusive in terms of both learning approach and learning outcomes as there were both males and females with various motives and strategies in learning. Additionally, no consistent pattern was identifiable in terms of superiority of either males or females in levels of understanding of concepts.

Conclusions

This study examined the relationships between context of learning and learning approaches using qualitative data analysis techniques. The analysis demonstrated that favourable perceptions of the learning context, tended to be associated with deep and/ or achieving approaches to learning. There was also evidence that students perceived memory as being important in the context of learning accounting in financial accounting. A number of students perceived that the assessment tasks required memorisation techniques hence they used surface strategies. This finding demonstrated how a surface approach to learning in accounting might be a response to the student's perception of the learning tasks in the unit of study rather than a characteristic of the learner.

The use of surface strategies, in particular memorisation, is consistent with the view expressed by Birkett and Mladenovic (2002). They proposed that it is possible, in the accounting discipline, lower level strategies, such as rote learning, paraphrasing and describing aligned with a surface approach to learning, may well underpin the progression to higher levels of understanding, associated with a deep approach to learning. Additionally, students in adapting their learning approach to the context of the learning environment may maintain relatively high levels of a surface approach to learning as part of the process of meeting procedural task demands often required in their accounting studies.

The results also revealed that memorisation was important for students in different ways. Some students relied on memory exclusively, utilizing what Meyer (2000a) refers to as 'memorising for rehearsal'. This approach is consistent with the surface learning strategy identified in responses from some students in this study, where they indicated that they had to read material over and over in order to 'rehearse' for assessment tasks (for example, Student 3 surface strategy – read). The findings also showed that some students used memorizing as a preliminary step to understanding (for example Student 2 used memory for learning definitions), while it was evident that others exercised the use of memory when they perceived that the assessment tasks required this approach. The results provided further evidence of the need for 'finer grained individual difference models of student learning especially in proposing additional sources of variation in terms of "memorisation" that can directly influence learning outcomes' (Meyer 2000b, p. 174), particularly as applied to the accounting discipline.

Furthermore, this study examined the relationships between learning approach and the quality of learning outcomes, as tested by content specific questions designed to examine the level of conceptual understanding. The results showed that deep/achieving motives and strategies were generally associated with more appropriate responses to questions related to course content. In contrast, students with surface motives using surface strategies showed a distinct lack of knowledge of concepts that had been taught. These results lend support to findings from previous studies that have used qualitative measures of learning outcome, other than examination performance (Dahlgren, 1984; Van Rossum and Schenk, 1984; Marton and Säljö, 1997). In particular, the results provide evidence that, in the discipline of accounting, there is an association between deep motives and strategies and the quality of learning outcomes. The findings also provide further impetus for the development of experimental studies to investigate the ways of increasing deep approaches to learning, building on the recent work in this area (Gordon and Debus, 2002; Hall et al., 2003; English et al., 2003; Cope and Staehr, 2005).

Methodological Limitations

Although providing a rich source of interpretation about students' ways of learning, the qualitative data analysis had some limitations. For instance, the interviews conducted with students were subject to content analyses focused on data reduction, display and interpretation of substantial bodies of unedited text. There are limitations about the way in which rich data can be condensed into variables reflected in a model of student learning. Säljö (1997) claims that coded and classified statements may have little or no meaning in isolation from the associated conversational discourse of an interview. Although some of the qualitative data that related to the most critical propositions were quoted more fully within this study, a great deal of data remains 'hidden' within the classification and coding system.

Checks were made on data coding and classification using an independently maintained data sheet for each interview, but there were also potential problems with the nature of data collection and coding. For instance, the potential for interview bias attributable to the 'teacher/pupil' environment was unable to be completed removed in this study. The interviewer, although not the instructor for the interviewees, was known to students as a member of the academic staff. This limitation in data collection was largely unavoidable given the technical nature of some aspects of the interviews and the need for the interviewer to have familiarity with the concepts being tested in the interview setting. Additionally, the researcher was also the sole coder of interview data, which produces a further potential bias. Although multiple independent coders potentially contribute significantly to the reliability and validity of the coding process, there are cost/benefit trade-offs in their use that need to be determined in the context of the study (Lillis, 1999). As this was an exploratory study, designed to inform future research, the limited use of validation processes need to be viewed in this context.

Implications for Accounting Educators

The results of this study suggest that elements of the learning environment, which are under the control of the academic teacher, have the potential to influence positively both the way in which students approach their learning of accounting and the learning outcomes they achieve. There is a need to extend recent research on teaching interventions that have been undertaken to increase the use of deep approaches to learning as a means of increasing the quality of teaching and learning of accounting students (English *et al.*, 2003; Hall *et al.*, 2003).

The present study strengthens the case for using measures, other than academic performance in accounting, to examine relationships between deep learning and the quality of learning outcomes. As outlined previously, studies using examination results as a measure of learning outcome have produced mixed results when investigating the link between learning approach and learning outcome. Further studies investigating the complexity of students' understanding of the concepts taught in accounting courses, would provide a firmer basis for the structuring of teaching that encourages conceptual learning.

Notes

[1] Van Rossum and Schenk (1984) analysed the quality of student learning responses from reading text using a taxonomy developed by Biggs and Collis (1982). The Structure of Observed learning Outcome (SOLO) taxonomy contains five levels of outcome which are used to classify the structural complexity of students' responses. At levels 4 (Relational) and 5 (Extended Abstract) responses involve evidence of understanding in the sense of integrating and structuring parts of the material learned which are readily identifiable with deep approaches to learning.

[2] The specific variables identified in this study are referred to throughout this study using capitalised names e.g. Surface motive, Surface strategy, to distinguish the variables from general reference to e.g. surface motives and strategies in learning.

[3] The content specific questions related to financial accounting were compiled in consultation with the Lecturer in Charge of the unit.

[4] The data related to studying for examinations provided the richest descriptions of students' strategies. Consequently these were used in the analysis of study strategies.

[5] The Lecturer in Charge of the unit, who was not associated with this study, rated the specific content questions in terms of difficulty.

[6] It is acknowledged that a more detailed analysis of responses to the specific content questions would be achieved by sorting the data into sub-groups and grading the quality of the responses in each cell of the matrix.

[7] Qualitative data analysis package known as NUD*IST which is an acronym for Non-numerical Unstructured Data-Indexing, Searching and Theorizing.

[8] The Lecturer in Charge of the unit provided an assessment of interview response to the specific content questions.

References

Abbott, A. (1992) What do cases do? Some notes on activity in sociological analysis, in: C. Ragin and H. Becker (Eds) *What is a Case? Exploring the Foundations of Social Inquiry*, pp. 53–82 (New York: Cambridge University Press).

Beattie, V. *et al.* (1997) Deep and surface learning: a simple or simplistic dichotomy?, *Accounting Education: an international journal*, 6(1), pp. 1–12.

Biggs, J. B. (1987a) *Study Process Questionnaire: Manual* (Melbourne: Australian Council for Educational Research).

Biggs, J. B. (1987b) *Student Approaches to Learning and Studying* (Australian Council for Educational Research, Hawthorn, Victoria).

Biggs, J. B. (1989) Approaches to the Enhancement of Tertiary Teaching, *Higher Education Research and Development*, 8(1), pp. 7–25.

Biggs, J. B. (1993) What do inventories of students' learning process really measure? A theoretical review and clarification, *British Journal of Educational Psychology*, 63(1), pp. 3–19.

Biggs, J. B. (1999) *Teaching for Quality Learning* (Buckingham: Society for Research into Higher Education & Open University Press).

Briggs and Collis (1982) *Evaluating the Quality of Learning: The SOLO Taxonomy (Structure of the Observed Learning Outcome)* (New York: Academic Press).

Birkett, B. and Mladenovic, R. (2002) The approaches to learning paradigm: theoretical and empirical issues for accounting education research, Study presented at the *International Association for Accounting Education and Research 9th World Congress of Accounting Educators* (Hong Kong, November).

Booth, P. *et al.* (1999) The quality of learning in accounting education: the impact of approaches to learning on academic performance, Accounting *Education: an international journal*, 8(4), pp. 277–300.

Buckless, F. *et al.* (1991) Do gender effects on accounting course performance persist after controlling for general academic aptitude?, *Issues in Accounting Education*, 6(2), pp. 248–261.

Byrne, M. *et al.* (1999) Approaches to learning: Irish students of accounting, *Irish Accounting Review*, 6(2), pp. 1–29.

Byrne, M. *et al.* (2002) The relationship between learning approaches and learning outcomes: a study of Irish accounting students, *Accounting Education: an international journal*, 11(1), pp. 27–42.

Cope, C. and Staehr. L. (2005) Improving students' learning approaches through intervention in an information systems learning environment, *Studies in Higher Education*, 30(2), pp. 181–197.

Dahlgren, L. O. (1984) Outcomes of learning, in: F. Marton *et al.* (Eds) *The Experience of Learning*, pp. 19–35 (Edinburgh: Scottish Academic Press).

Davidson, R. A. (2002) Relationship of study approach and exam performance, *Journal of Accounting Education*, 20(1), pp. 29–44.

Duff, A. (1996) The impact of learning strategies on academic performance in an accounting undergraduate course, in: G. Gibbs (Ed.) *Improving Student Learning: Using Research to Improve Student Learning*, pp. 50–62 (Oxford: Oxford Centre for Staff Development).

Eley, M. G. (1992) Differential adoption of study approaches within individual students, *Higher Education*, 23(3), pp. 231–254.

Eley, M. G. and Meyer, J. H. F. (2004) Modelling the influences on learning outcomes of study processes in university mathematics, *Higher Education*, 47(4), pp. 437–454.

English, L. *et al.* (2003) Encouraging a deep approach to learning through curriculum design. Study presented at Accounting Educators Forum, (Sydney, November).

Entwistle, N. and Ramsden, P. (1983) *Understanding Student Learning* (London: Croom Helm).

Entwistle, N. and Smith, C. (2002) Personal understanding and target understanding: Mapping influences on the outcomes of learning, *British Journal of Educational Psychology*, 72(3), pp. 321–342.

Entwistle, N. and Tait, H. (1990) Approaches to learning, evaluations of teaching, and preferences for contrasting academic environments, *Higher Education*, 19(2), pp. 169–194.

Evans, C. J. *et al.* (2003) Approaches to learning, need for cognition, and strategic flexibility among university students, *British Journal of Educational Psychology*, 73(4), pp. 507–528.

Gist, W. *et al.* (1996) The influence of mathematical skills and other factors on minority student performance in principles of accounting, *Issues in Accounting Education*, 11(1), pp. 49–60.

Gordon, C. and Debus, R. (2002) Developing deep learning approaches and personal teaching efficacy within a preservice teaching education context, *British Journal of Educational Psychology*, 72(4), pp. 483–512.

Gow, L. *et al.* (1994) The teaching context and approaches to study of accountancy students, *Issues in Accounting Education*, 9(1), pp. 118–130.

Guba, E. G. and Lincoln, Y. S. (1994) Competing paradigms in qualitative research, in: N. K. Denzin and Y. S. Lincoln (Eds) *Handbook of Qualitative Research*, pp. 105–117 (Thousand Oaks, CA: Sage).

Hall, M. *et al.* (2003) Changing the learning environment to promote deep learning approaches in first year accounting students, study presented at the *Discipline of Accounting and Business Law Seminar Series*, (The University of Sydney).

Hassell, T. and Joyce, J. (1997) What do the examinations of professional bodies reward? Some preliminary evidence, in: G. Gibbs and C. Rust (Eds) *Improving Student Learning through Course Design*, pp. 529–538 (Oxford: The Oxford Centre for Staff and learning Development).

Jackling, B. (2001) Learning Approaches of Tertiary Accounting Students. Unpublished doctoral dissertation (University of Melbourne).

Jackling, B. and Anderson, A. (1998) Study mode, general ability and performance in accounting, *Accounting Education: an international journal*, 7(1), pp. 65–73.

Kember, D. (1996) The intention to both memorise and understand: another approach to learning?, *Higher Education*, 31(3), pp. 341–354.

Kember, D. (2000) Misconceptions about the learning approaches, motivation and study practices of Asian students, *Higher Education*, 40(1), pp. 99–121.

Lillis, A. (1999) A framework for the analysis of interview data from multiple field research sites, *Accounting & Finance*, 39(1), pp. 79–105.

Lizzio, A. *et al.* (2002) University students' perceptions of the learning environment and academic outcomes: implications for theory and practice, *Studies in Higher Education*, 27(1), pp. 27–52.

Lucas, U. (2001) Deep and surface approaches to learning within introductory accounting: a phenomenographic study, *Accounting Education: an international journal*, 10(2), pp. 161–184.

Lucas, U. (2002) *Rote Learning in Accounting? De-bunking a Myth* (Glasgow: British Accounting Association, Accounting Education Special Interest Group Annual Conference).

Lucas, U. and Meyer, J. H. F. (2003a) Understanding students' conceptions of learning and subject in 'introductory' courses: the case of introductory accounting. Study presented at the Symposium *Meta learning in higher education: taking account of the student perspective* (Padova, August: European Association for Research on Learning and instruction, 10th Biennial Conference).

Lucas, U. and Meyer, J. H. F. (2003b) *Towards Disciplinary Models of Learning. Improving Student Learning: Theory and Practice 10 Years on* (Oxford: OCSLD).

Marton, F. and Booth, S. (1997) *Learning and Awareness* (Mahwah, NJ: Lawrence Erlbaum Associates).

Marton, F. *et al.* (Eds) (1984) *The Experience of Learning* (Edinburgh: Scottish Academic Press).

Marton, F. and Säljö, R. (1976) On qualitative differences in learning. I. Outcome and process, *British Journal of Educational Psychology*, 46(1), pp. 4–11.

Marton, F. and Säljö, R. (1997) Approaches to learning, in: F. Marton *et al.* (Eds) *The Experience of Learning*, 2nd edn. (Edinburgh: Scottish Academic Press).

Meyer, J. H. F. (2000a) Variation in contrasting forms of "memorising" and associated variables, *British Journal of Educational Psychology*, 70(2), pp. 163–176.

Meyer, J. H. F. (2000b) The modeling of 'dissonant' study orchestration in higher education, *European Journal of Psychology of Education*, 15(1), pp. 5–18.

Meyer, J. H. F. *et al.* (1990) Individual study orchestrations and their association with learning outcome, *Higher Education*, 20(2), pp. 67–89.

Miles, M. B. and Huberman, A. M. (1994) *Qualitative Data Analysis: An Expanded Sourcebook* (Thousand Oaks, CA: Sage Publications).

Mladenovic, R. (2000) An investigation into ways of challenging introductory accounting students' negative perceptions of accounting, *Accounting Education: an international journal*, 9(2), pp. 135–155.

Mutchler, J. *et al.* (1987) The performance of female versus male accounting students, *Issues in Accounting Education*, 2(1), pp. 103–111.

Newble, D. I. *et al.* (1988) Towards the identification of student learning problems: the development of a diagnostic inventory, *Medical Education*, 22(6), pp. 518–526.

Prosser, M. T. and Millar, R. (1989) The "how" and "what" of learning physics: a phenomenographic study, *European Journal of Psychology of Education*, 4(4), pp. 513–528.

Prosser, M. T. and Trigwell, K. (1997) Using phenomenography in the design of programs for teachers in higher education, *Higher Education Research & Development*, 16(1), pp. 41–54.

Prosser, M. T. and Trigwell, K. (1999) *Understanding Learning and Teaching* (Buckingham: Society for Research into Higher Education & Open University Press).

Ragin, C. C. (1987) *The Comparative Method: Moving Beyond Qualitative and Quantitative Strategies* (Berkeley, CA: University of California Press).

Ramsden, P. (1984) The context of learning, in: F. Marton *et al.* (Eds) *The Experience of Learning*, pp. 144–164 (Edinburgh: Scottish Academic Press).

Ramsden, P. (1991) A performance indicator of teaching quality in higher education: the Course Experience Questionnaire, *Studies in Higher Education*, 16(2), pp. 129–150.

Ramsden, P. (1992) *Learning to teach in higher education* (London: Kogan Page).

Ramsden, P. (2003) *Learning to teach in higher education* (2nd edn) (London, New York: Routledge Falmer).

Ramsden, P., Beswick, D. and Bowden, J. (1986) Effects of learning skills interventions on first year university students' learning, *Human Learning*, 5(3), pp. 151–164.

Säljö, R. (1997) Talk as data and practice – a critical look at phenomenographic inquiry and the appeal to experience, *Higher Education Research & Development*, 16(2), pp. 173–190.

Sharma, D. S. (1997) Accounting students' learning conceptions, approaches to learning and the influence of the learning-teaching context on approaches to learning, *Accounting Education: an international journal*, 6(2), pp. 125–146.

Trigwell, K. and Prosser, M. (1991a) Improving the quality of student learning: the influence of learning context and student approaches to learning on learning outcomes, *Higher Education*, 22(3), pp. 251–266.

Trigwell, K. and Prosser, M. (1991b) Relating approaches to study and quality of learning outcomes at the course level, *British Journal of Educational Psychology*, 61(3), pp. 265–275.

Trigwell, K. and Prosser, M. (1993) Relating approaches to study and quality of learning outcomes at the course level, *British Journal of Educational Psychology*, 61(3), pp. 265–275.

Tyson, T. (1989) Grade performance in introductory accounting courses: why female students outperform males, *Issues in Accounting Education*, 4(1), pp. 153–160.

Umapathy, S. (1984) Algorithm-based accounting education: opportunities and risks, *Issues in Accounting Education*, pp. 136–143.

Van Rossum, E. J. and Schenk, S. M. (1984) The relationship between learning conception, study strategy and learning outcome, *British Journal of Educational Psychology*, 54(1), pp. 73–83.

Watkins, D. and Biggs, J. B. (1996) *The Chinese Learner: Cultural, Psychological and Contextual Influences* (Hong Kong and Melbourne: CERC and ACER).

Watkins, D. and Hattie, J. (1981) The learning processes of Australian university students: investigations of contextual and personalogical factors, *British Journal of Educational Psychology*, 51(3), pp. 384–393.

Appendix 1

Part B of Interview – Specific Content Questions

Assume a person with a small shareholding in a large public company approaches you for an explanation about the annual reports of the firm.

Question 1

They first ask you 'What is meant by the term consolidated reports?' How would you respond to this question?

(The response to the question should demonstrate the student's basic understanding of the concept of consolidations: i.e. consolidated reports enable a combined account of the progress of the group of companies linked by share ownership. Reference to a group entity with a parent company having control over the operations of one or more subsidiary entities.)

Question 2

If the shareholder then says that he believes the preparation of consolidated financial reports is simply a matter of adding together the financial reports of the individual companies that make up the group entity, how would you respond?

(The objective is for students to be able to demonstrate a slightly more sophisticated level of understanding than for Question 1. The response given should demonstrate that adding together the information from each subsidiary will not take care of the distorting effects of inter-entity transactions, nor does it take into account relevant items that exist only at a group entity level.)

Question 3

Why are inter entity dealings or transactions eliminated when preparing consolidated financial reports?

(The answer should demonstrate the concept of the consolidated entity operating as a group. A single group entity cannot deal or transact with itself. Thus, inter-entity transactions are eliminated in order to prepare accurate consolidated financial reports.)

Question 4

Would you explain to the shareholder what portion, if any, of the shareholders' equity of a subsidiary company appears directly on a group balance sheet?

(This question is considered to require greater depth of understanding and in some instances may not be asked if the student appears to have struggled with the prior questions.)

Note: The specific content questions were designed to get students to explain in their own words the meaning of some of the concepts taught in the topic of company consolidations. The questions were designed to encourage students to provide a response to a person without technical knowledge of consolidated reports (in this instance a shareholder).

Using Dimensions of Moral Intensity to Predict Ethical Decision-making in Accounting

DEBORAH L. LEITSCH

Goldey-Beacom College, USA

ABSTRACT   *Many ethical decisions are based on the intensity of the moral conflict. Embezzling large sums of money is seen as more unethical, by most people, than stealing a pen or a piece of paper from one's workplace. This study examines the importance of the underlying characteristics of moral issues and how they directly affect accounting students' ethical decision-making process (moral sensitivity, moral judgment and moral intentions). A four stage model presented by Rest (1986) and expanded by Jones' (1991) was used to measure the moral decision-making process. The study highlights the results of a sample of 110 accounting majors in a small business college in the USA. The research suggests that moral intensity appeared to have two dimensions: "perceived corporate concern" and "perceived involvement effect". These dimensions did not significantly predict moral sensitivity. However, when they were combined with moral sensitivity they did significantly predict the students' moral judgment. Likewise, moral judgment and the dimensions of moral intensity significantly predicted accounting students' moral intentions. The findings presented here extend current understanding of the influence of the moral intensity components on the moral decision-making process. The results can also be used to enhance ethics coursework and training programs in educational and industrial settings.*

Introduction

For centuries, the accounting profession has had a significant impact on the business environment. As key providers of financial information, the profession has held an important role. Historically, most have agreed that accountants were individuals who practiced honest principles and performed an efficient and valuable service for their clients, contemporaries and the public. However, such recent accounting scandals as those surrounding Enron, WorldCom, and GlobalCrossing have undermined the public's confidence in the accounting profession. In fact, some question whether accountants practice without regard to the profession or society that they supposedly serve.

Recent events have stimulated public and professional concern to restore integrity to the bottom line (net income) and investor confidence in the accounting profession. In the light of the problems and concerns that have generated interest in business ethics and the accounting profession, an increased stream of academic research has emerged.

Previous studies have addressed the ethical decision-making process of accountants faced with moral conflicts (Shaub, 1994; Armstrong, 1987; Jeffery, 1993). These studies have examined various individual, situational, and organizational factors that can influence the moral decision-making process. An important aspect that has received less attention in accounting studies involves the assessment of the moral issue itself and its influence on the moral decision-making process. The moral intensity of the issue, as defined by Jones (1991), captures the heightened feelings and emotions of a particular ethical conflict. Jones (1991) believed that moral intensity is an important concept and significantly influences all aspects of an individual's decision-making process. Weber (1996) noted, 'Conclusions and implications presented in prior research which ignores the moral issue when assessing decision-making may be limited or misdirected' (p. 3). Therefore, extending the issue-contingent model to the moral decision process in the field of accounting represents an important area for future research.

Research focusing on the moral intensity of a particular issue, within the field of accounting, will provide a better understanding of which constructs are most important in the moral decision-making process. It is thought that the more that is understood about the factors influencing these decisions, the better business educators will be able to develop ethical training programs to improve moral awareness in the accounting profession.

Background of the Study

Jones (1991) significantly contributed to the literature by noting that the ethical decision-making process, within an organization, was dependent upon many organizational factors as well as the issue itself. He suggested that moral issues could vary from situation to situation in terms of intensity. Issues of high intensity capture the individual's attention more often than issues of low intensity. Alternatively, issues of low intensity may not be viewed as unethical by the decision-maker.

Jones (1991, p. 373) extended Rest's (1986) four stage model by identifying specific issue-related components that are also important in moral decision-making. This model is presented in a logical sequence of steps and it represents a framework for considering what must happen in order for moral behavior to occur. These four stages were moral sensitivity, moral judgment, moral intentions, and moral behavior. Rest (1986) noted that his model's four stages have distinct functions, which interact with each other.

According to Jones (1991, p. 374) moral intensity can be defined as consisting of six components. *Magnitude of consequences* is the sum of the harms (benefits) felt by victims arising from a moral act. *Social consensus* refers to the level of social agreement of the proposed act as being either ethical or unethical. *Probability of effect* is the likelihood that the act will in fact take place and cause harm (benefit). *Temporal immediacy* is defined as the perceived length of time between the act and its consequences. *Concentration of effect* relates to the inverse function of the number of people affected by an act. *Proximity* refers to how close (socially, culturally, physically) the victim is to the decision-maker. Jones (1991) believed that these moral intensity components interacted with each other to signal a situation as being more as opposed to less 'morally intense' (see Figure 1).

Jones (1991) stated that the level of moral intensity in a specific situation is described by the combined effects of moral intensity components. Empirical research has confirmed

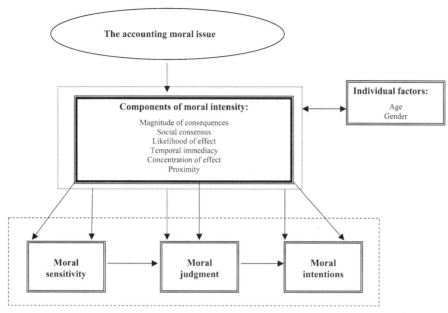

Adapted from Jones (1991) and Frey (2000a).

Figure 1. A model of the accounting students' moral decision-making process in accounting scenarios

that a relationship seems to exist between the six components of moral intensity. However, there exists some controversy over whether the components are one-dimensional or multi-dimensional as Jones (1991) asserts. Valentine and Silver (2001) and Frey (2000a,b) suggested that the components of moral intensity were one-dimensional rather than multi-dimensional. They believed that this result emerged because of the inter-relationships among the components. However, other studies have supported Jones' (1991) contention that the components of moral intensity are multi-dimensional. For example, two dimension solutions were found by Dukerich *et al.* (1993), and Singhapkdi *et al.* (1996).

According to Jones (1991), the moral intensity of the issue significantly influences each stage of the moral decision-making process. Previous research has examined the influence of the dimensions of moral intensity on moral sensitivity, moral judgment, and moral intentions (Singhapakdi *et al.*, 1996, 1999; Frey, 2000a,b; May and Pauli, 2000). In these studies, the dimension(s) of moral intensity were found to significantly influence the moral decision-making process of various respondents. However, limited research has examined the importance of these dimensions and how they affect the specific steps of the moral decision-making process of accounting students.

The present study will examine first the dimensionality of the moral intensity construct in different ethical scenarios. Second, it will examine if a particular dimension(s) of moral intensity is a better predictor of the accounting students' moral decision-making process.

Research Question Development

Jones (1991) stated that moral intensity is a multi-dimensional construct that is defined through six components. He proposed that if the moral intensity of a situation were strong in terms of the sum of these components, it would be recognized as an ethical issue. Several studies have examined the dimensionality of the moral intensity components. Dukerich *et al.* (1993) examined the components of moral intensity on moral sensitivity to determine whether they represented a single one-dimensional construct as suggested by Jones (1991). The results of a factor analysis, using business managers, suggested a two-factor dimension. The first dimension consisted of magnitude of consequences, social consensus, proximity, and concentration of effect, while the second dimension consisted of temporal immediacy. These researchers labeled the first factor organizational moral intensity (OMI) since each component was organizational or interpersonal in nature. They treated the second dimension as a separate factor for analysis.

Similarly, Singhapakdi *et al.* (1996) found that moral intensity also had two dimensions in their study using a slightly different population of marketing professionals. The first dimension was composed of magnitude of consequences, probability of effect, temporal immediacy, and concentration of effect. These authors labeled this dimension as the 'perceived potential harm/no harm' dimension. The second-dimension consisted of social consensus and proximity and it was labeled as the 'perceived social pressure' dimension.

In a later study, Valentine and Silver (2001) assessed the dimensionality of the moral intensity scale developed by Singhapakdi *et al.* (1996). These authors noted that the one-factor solution might be emerging because of several reasons. First, the presence of one component of moral intensity may stimulate thinking about the other components. Second, and a related point, the components of moral intensity may be closely associated to each other (Valentine and Silver, 2001). For example, an individual might sense an increase in social consensus that may also trigger thinking about the magnitude of consequences and the likelihood of effect or proximity in a particular situation. In this sense, several associated components may be successively stimulated because of a single issue.

Empirical research has confirmed that a relationship seems to exist between the six components of moral intensity. However, there exists some controversy over whether the components are one-dimensional or multi-dimensional as Jones (1991) asserts. In addition, limited efforts have examined whether these dimensions are situation specific. Given the limited evidence suggested by past research, the following research question is presented:

Research Question 1: Will a single dimension of moral intensity emerge that is situation specific, or is moral intensity multi-dimensional?

Jones (1991) proposed that the dimensions of moral intensity would directly affect each of the stages of the moral decision-making process. Empirical evidence has offered supporting evidence that a relationship may exist between a dimension(s) of moral intensity and an individual's moral decision-making process. Using four marketing scenarios, Singhapakdi *et al.* (1996) suggested the two dimensions of moral intensity (perceived potential harm (no harm) and perceived social pressure) were significant determinants of moral sensitivity and moral intentions of marketing managers. These authors noted that the marketer's decision-making process appeared to be influenced by situation-specific issues.

In a later study, May and Pauli (2000) examined the influence of moral intensity on three stages of the moral decision-making process: moral sensitivity, moral evaluation/ judgment and moral intentions as defined by Rest (1986). These authors suggested that a moral intensity dimension, composed of probable magnitude of harms, social consensus, and concentration of effect, was significantly related to the moral decision-making process. This is consistent with the findings of the Singhapakdi *et al.* (1996) study.

Likewise, Frey (2000a) also conducted a factor analysis of the six components of moral intensity but found different results than Dukerich *et al.* (2000) and Singhapakdi *et al.*'s

(1996) two-factor solution. He indicated that magnitude of consequences, social consensus, likelihood of effect, proximity, and temporal immediacy loaded on the first factor while concentration of effect loaded on the second factor. Since three components (magnitude of consequences, social consensus, and likelihood of effect) yielded the highest factor scores in his study, Frey concluded that they played a more important role in influencing the moral decision-making process.

These studies confirm Jones' (1991) assertion that the dimension(s) of moral intensity would directly affect each of the stages of the moral decision-making process. Therefore, it seems reasonable to anticipate that the dimension(s) of moral intensity may also influence the accounting students' moral decision-making process. Therefore, the following research question will be investigated:

> **Research Question 2**: A dimension(s) of moral intensity will be predictive of the accounting students' moral decision-making process.

Methodology

The survey was distributed to students in accounting classes at one college in the Northeast of the USA. Participation in this study was voluntary and students were assured that all results would be kept confidential. The surveys were distributed in class and students were instructed to complete and return them to the instructor at the end of the class meeting. One hundred and twenty-four students were eligible to participate (accounting majors). Of these, 110 students completed the survey instead of an alternative assignment for a response rate of 89%. The demographic characteristics of the sample are presented in Table 1.

Survey and Questionnaire

The survey used in this study consisted of four scenarios and the related questions. Each scenario, adapted from the Flory *et al.* (1992) study, depicted a different ethical accounting issue found in the workplace. The accounting issues included approving a questionable expense report (Scenario 1), manipulating company books (Scenario 2), by-passing company policy (Scenario 3), and extending questionable credit (Scenario 4). Flory *et al.* (1992) noted that Scenarios 1 and 4 represents issues (approving a questionable expense report and extending questionable credit) that most accountants may not perceive as being ethical or unethical. Therefore, the respondents in this study may not perceive these scenarios as involving an ethical or unethical action, which is what is called for in these scenarios.

A questionnaire was used to assess the dependent variables (stages of moral decision-making process: moral sensitivity, moral judgment, and moral intensity) and the independent variables (dimension(s) of moral intensity) for each scenario. For the questions, respondents indicated their agreement on a 7-point Likert-type scale to the action statement. The questions contained statements from previous researchers (see below) regarding the respondents' moral sensitivity, moral judgment, moral intention, and the moral intensity of the dilemma. Information was also captured on the demographic variables of age and gender.

Moral sensitivity.   The accounting student's moral sensitivity was measured directly by asking them to respond to whether the situation in each scenario involves an ethical problem. Students were asked to indicate their degree of agreement or disagreement regarding the statement, 'The situation above involves an ethical problem' (Singhapakdi *et al.*, 1996).

ACCOUNTING EDUCATION RESEARCH

Table 1. Selected demographic characteristics of the sample

Characteristics	Number	Percentages
Gender		
Male	32	30
Female	78	70
Age		
Under 21	37	33.9
21–30	53	47.7
31–40	16	14.7
41–50	3	2.8
51–59	1	0.9
Academic year		
Freshman	3	2.8
Sophomore	30	27.5
Junior	40	35.8
Senior	35	33.9
Ethnicity		
African–American	15	13.8
Caucasian	59	54.1
Hispanic	7	6.4
Asian	18	16.5
Other	11	9.2
US citizen		
Yes	90	82.6
No	20	17.4
Employed		
Full-time	38	34.9
Part-time	49	45.0
Do not work	23	20.2
Type of company		
Retail	19	17.4
Wholesale	3	2.8
Manufacturer	8	7.3
Financial institution (bank)	28	25.7
Educational institution	6	5.5
Other	24	22.0

Moral judgment. The accounting students' moral judgment was measured directly by asking them to respond to their level of agreement with the action statement in each scenario. Students were asked to indicate their degree of agreement or disagreement regarding the statement, '(The decision-maker) should (not) do the proposed action' (reverse-coded) (May and Pauli, 2000).

Moral intentions. Moral intention was measured by asking accounting students to indicate their degree of agreement or disagreement regarding the statement, i.e. 'If I were the (decision-maker), I would make the same decision' (reverse-coded)

(Singhapakdi *et al.*, 1996). An agreement with the action taken in the scenario will indicate less ethical intentions.

The components of moral intensity. The dimensions of moral intensity were measured using items based on Jones' (1991) work and adapted from previous research (Singhapakdi *et al.*, 1996; May and Pauli, 2000). *Magnitude of Consequences* was measured by 'The overall harm (if any) done as a result of the (decision-maker's) decision will be small' (reversed-coded). *Social Consensus* was measured by '"Most people would agree that (the decision-maker's decision) is wrong.' *Probability of effect* was measured by 'There is a very small likelihood that (the decision-maker's) decision will actually cause any harm' (reverse-coded). *Temporal immediacy* was measured by '(The decision-maker's) decision will cause harm in the immediate future' (reversed-coded). *Concentration of effect* was measured by '(The decision-maker's) decision will harm a few people (if any)' (reverse-coded). *Proximity* was measured by '(The decision-maker's) decision will affect his/her co-workers'.

The responses to each question were averaged to yield a total score for that component of moral intensity. They were later combined into dimension(s) through factor analysis for further analysis.

Results

Table 2 presents the means and correlation coefficients for the scenarios studied. The accounting students' perceived Scenario 1 (approving questionable expense report) to be the most unethical action (m = 5.79), they also recognized the ethical nature in the other scenarios. The descriptive statistics suggest a moderate perceived moral intensity (averaging the means over all moral intensity components) ranging from 4.06 to 5.05 where neutral ratings = 4 (see Table 2). Overall, the perceived moral intensity seemed to vary depending on the nature of the situation within the scenario. This supports Jones (1991) theory that individuals tend to perceive some situations as being more 'morally intense' than others.

Correlation coefficients, presented in Table 2, were computed for moral sensitivity, moral judgment, and moral intensity components for each scenario. As expected, there was a significant degree of intercorrelation between each step of the moral decision-making process (moral sensitivity, moral judgment, and moral intentions). Likewise, the components of moral intensity (magnitude of consequences, social consensus, probability of effect, and temporal immediacy) were positively associated with most of the other moral intensity components in each of the other scenarios.

These results were consistent with Singhapakdi *et al.* (1996) and Barnett's (2001) results, where the components of moral intensity, for the most part, were highly correlated. Likewise, significant correlations between the components of moral intensity and the moral decision-making process were suggested by May and Pauli (2001) and this was confirmed here (see Table 2). They also support Jones' (1991) contention that moral intensity components are expected to have interacting effects.

The moral intensity scale reliability was assessed using Cronbach's coefficient alpha, a common measure used to test the consistency among scales. Hair *et al.* (1998) suggest that a reliability of 0.70 or higher is acceptable for group research. In this study, the reliability analysis yielded acceptable individual alpha coefficients for each scenario. They were, Scenario 1 $\acute{a} = 0.7649$, Scenario 2 $\acute{a} = 0.8818$, Scenario 3 $\acute{a} = 0.8596$, Scenario 4 $\acute{a} = 0.8639$. Similarly, the moral intensity components were summed to yield a global alpha score of moral intensity ($\acute{a} = 0.9204$).

Table 2. Means and correlation matrix by scenario

Components of moral intensity	Means	MC	SC	PE	TI	CE	PR
Scenario 1: Approving a questionable expense report							
MC Magnitude of consequences	4.78	–					
SC Social consensus	4.53	0.272**	–				
PE Probability of effect	4.60	0.446*	0.141	–			
TI Temporal immediacy	4.40	0.352*	0.191*	0.347**	–		
CE Concentration of effect	3.94	0.164	0.077	0.231*	0.062	–	
PR Proximity	4.67	0.221*	0.218*	0.324**	0.201*	0.050	–
Scenario 2: Manipulating company books							
MC Magnitude of consequences	4.69	–					
SC Social consensus	4.73	0.435**	–				
PE Probability of effect	4.62	0.592**	0.458**	–			
TI Temporal immediacy	4.49	0.252**	0.167	0.409**	–		
CE Concentration of effect	4.18	0.412**	0.173	0.234*	0.132	–	
PR Proximity	4.84	0.173	0.218*	0.320*	0.318**	0.132	–
Scenario 3: Violating company policy							
MC Magnitude of consequences	5.06	–					
SC Social consensus	4.73	0.302**	–				
PE Probability of effect	4.93	0.564**	0.244*	–			
TI Temporal immediacy	4.95	0.415**	0.375**	0.573**	–		
CE Concentration of effect	4.52	0.241*	0.283**	0.326**	0.253**	–	
PR Proximity	4.99	0.165	-0.066	0.261**	0.221*	0.056	–
Scenario 4: Extending questionable credit							
MC Magnitude of consequences	4.59	–					
SC Social consensus	4.06	0.496**	–				
PE Probability of effect	4.40	0.671**	0.609**	–			
TI Temporal immediacy	4.19	0.527**	0.440**	0.562**	–		
CE Concentration of effect	4.36	0.247*	0.159	0.320*	0.231*	–	
PR Proximity	4.86	0.177	0.204*	0.286	0.236	0.194*	–

*Correlation is significant at the 0.05 level (two-tailed).
**Correlation is significant at the 0.01 level (two-tailed).

Research Question 1 addressed the relationship between the components of moral intensity for accounting issues. In order to address this, the dimensionality of the components of moral intensity was analyzed using principal component analysis, which was rotated using the Varimax rotation procedure. The Kaiser–Meyer–Olkin (KMO) measure of sampling adequacy was 0.764, which falls within the acceptable range (Hair *et al.*, 1998).

Table 3 presents the results of factor analysis on all scenarios separately and combined. Factor analysis resulted in a two-factor solution which explained 62.86% of the variance. Factor one loaded on magnitude of consequences, social consensus, probability of effect, temporal immediacy, and proximity, and explained 40.84% of the item variance. This factor could be labeled 'perceived corporate concern' as each of the components, in some way, relates to the effect of the unethical issue on the corporation itself. Concentration of effect loaded on factor two and accounted for 22.02% of the item variance. This factor could be labeled 'perceived involvement effect,' since this component focuses on the number of stakeholders affected by the unethical action. The answer to

Table 3. Factor analysis by scenario and combined scenarios rotated factor matrix

	Scenario 1 components	Scenario 2 components	Scenario 3 components	Scenario 4 components	Combined scenarios components
First dimension (perceived corporate concern)					
MC Magnitude of consequences	**0.647**	**0.843**	**0.701**	**0.827**	**0.707**
SC Social consensus	**0.597**	**0.619**	0.277	**0.789**	**0.592**
PE Probability of effect	**0.582**	**0.633**	**0.821**	**0.841**	**0.771**
TI Temporal immediacy	**0.643**	0.131	**0.783**	**0.735**	**0.760**
CE Concentration of effect	−0.072	**0.698**	0.250	0.159	0.041
PR Proximity	**0.639**	0.058	**0.628**	0.120	**0.654**
Second dimension (perceived involvement effect)					
MC Magnitude of consequences	0.360	0.178	0.267	0.119	0.455
SC Social consensus	−0.099	0.264	**0.691**	**0.053**	0.247
PE Probability of effect	0.508	0.529	0.204	0.268	0.454
TI Temporal immediacy	0.133	**0.768**	0.275	0.204	0.049
CE Concentration of effect	**0.903**	−0.101	**0.657**	**0.742**	**0.899**
PR Proximity	−0.029	**0.772**	−0.591	**0.772**	−0.193

Note: Factor loadings of 0.50 and greater are in bold.

the Research Question 1 is that, in this study, moral intensity appears to have two-dimensions that are situation specific.

In order to test Research Question 2 a multiple regression analysis was conducted to evaluate the predictive power of the dimensions of moral intensity on the accounting students' moral sensitivity. The results of this analysis suggested that the dimensions of moral intensity were not significantly related to moral sensitivity in any of the scenarios, separately or combined.

Then, a multiple regression analysis was conducted to evaluate the predictive power of moral sensitivity and the dimensions of moral intensity on the accounting students' moral judgment (Table 4). The results suggest that the dimensions of moral intensity were significant predictors of moral judgment in all of the scenarios, separately and combined.

For the scenarios combined, 35.8% of the variance in moral judgment could be explained by moral sensitivity and the dimensions of moral intensity. An examination of the standardized beta coefficient, ranging from 0.285 to 0.481, suggests that the first dimension (perceived financial harm) had a somewhat significant influence on moral judgment depending upon the issue. Likewise, the second dimension of moral intensity was statistically significant in Scenarios 3 and 4, and the combined scenarios (Table 4). Moral sensitivity was statistically significant for all scenarios separately and combined except for Scenario 3. An examination of the standardized beta coefficients, ranging from 0.123 to 0.455, suggests that moral sensitivity did influence moral judgments as much as the first dimension. From this analysis, the first dimension along with moral sensitivity appears to offer most of the predictive power for the accounting students' moral judgment (Table 4).

Next, multiple regression was conducted to evaluate how well the dimensions of moral intensity and moral judgment could predict the moral intentions of accounting students

Table 4. Multiple regression: moral sensitivity, moral intensity dimensions and moral judgment

Variables	β	R^2	ΔR^2	F
Scenario 1: Approving questionable expense report				
Perceived corporate concern	0.285*			
Perceived involvement effect	0.039			
Moral Sensitivity	0.209*	0.84	0.110	
F (2.107)				4.308*
Scenario 2: Falsifying external financial statements				
Perceived corporate concern	0.287*			
Perceived involvement effect	0.108			
Moral sensitivity	0.455*	0.283	0.303	
F (2.107)				15.238*
Scenario 3: Violating company policy				
Perceived corporate concern	0.318*			
Perceived involvement effect	0.223*			
Moral sensitivity	0.123	0.143	0.167	
F (2.107)				6.993*
Scenario 4: Extending questionable credit				
Perceived corporate concern	0.407*			
Perceived involvement effect	0.295*			
Moral sensitivity	0.225*	0.303	0.322	
F (2.107)				16.658*
Scenarios combined				
Perceived corporate concern	0.481*			
Perceived involvement effect	0.249*			
Moral sensitivity	0.290*	0.358	0.376	
F (2.107)				21.094*

Perceived corporate concern = magnitude of consequences, social consensus, probability of effect, temporal immediacy, proximity. Perceived involvement effect = concentration of effect. β = standardized beta coefficients; R^2 = total variance explained; ΔR^2 = change in R-squared; * = $P < 0.05$.

(Table 5). The results suggest that the factors of moral intensity were significant predictors of accounting students' moral intentions in all of the scenarios, separately and combined.

In the combined scenarios, 59.7% of the variance in moral intentions could be explained by moral judgment and the dimensions of moral intensity. In an analysis of the scenarios separately, only the first dimension was statistically significant for Scenarios 1 and 3. However, moral judgment was statistically significant in all scenarios separately and combined. From this analysis, the accounting students' moral judgment appears to offer most of the predictive power for the accounting students' moral intentions (Table 5). Based on these findings, Research Question 2 is supported for Scenarios 1 and 3.

Discussion

The purpose of this study was to gain a better understanding of the impact of moral issues on the moral decision-making process within the field of accounting. The present study examined the importance of the underlying characteristics of issues and how they directly

Table 5. Multiple regression: moral judgment, moral intensity dimensions and moral intentions

Variable	β	R^2	ΔR^2	F
Scenario 1: Approving questionable expense report				
Perceived corporate concern	0.234*			
Perceived involvement effect	0.057			
Moral judgment	0.369*	0.219	0.241	
F (2.107)				11.086*
Scenario 2: Falsifying external financial statements				
Perceived corporate concern	−0.018			
Perceived involvement effect	0.090			
Moral judgment	0.609*	0.375	0.393	
F (2.107)				22.628*
Scenario 3: Violating company policy				
Perceived corporate concern	0.146*			
Perceived involvement effect	0.123			
Moral judgment	0.636*	0.522	0.536	
F (2.107)				40.384*
Scenario 4: Extending questionable credit				
Perceived corporate concern	−0.076			
Perceived involvement effect	0.052			
Moral judgment	0.797*	0.612	0.623	
F (2.107)				57.818
Scenarios combined				
Perceived corporate concern	0.087			
Perceived involvement effect	0.115			
Moral judgment	0.697*	0.597	0.609	
F (2.107)				54.427*

Perceived corporate concern = magnitude of consequences, social consensus, probability of effect, temporal immediacy, proximity. Perceived involvement effect = concentration of effect. β = standardized beta coefficients; R2 = total variance explained; ΔR2 = change in R-squared; * = $P < 0.05$.

affect the perceptions of moral sensitivity, moral judgment, and moral intentions of accounting students at a small business college in the USA.

In the current study all issues represented unethical actions, of varying degrees, which could be commonly found in the work settings of those engaged in the accounting profession. The results of the factor analysis of the scenarios combined suggested that moral intensity appeared to have two dimensions. The first dimension, 'perceived corporate concern,' was composed of magnitude of consequences, social consensus, probability of effect, temporal immediacy, and proximity. The second dimension, 'perceived involvement effect,' was composed of concentration of effect. A similar two-factor solution was suggested in previous studies. Dukerich *et al.* (2000) examined business managers and the first dimension was composed of magnitude of consequences, social consensus, concentration of effect, and proximity. Temporal immediacy formed its own dimension. Similarly, Singhapakdi *et al.* (1996) studied marketing professionals and suggested a two-dimension solution. The first dimension included magnitude of consequences, concentration of effect, probability of effect and temporal immediacy while social consensus and proximity formed the second dimension. These differences in composition of moral intensity dimensions may be due to the different types of samples and scenarios used in each of these studies. In general, these findings support Jones (1991) contention that moral intensity is a multi-dimensional construct. In fact, the six moral intensity components can be synthesized into two dimensions when examining particular accounting situations.

In analyzing accounting issues, however, accountants must consider the magnitude of the financial consequences, referred to as materiality, within a given act. They also must consider the degree of social agreement in terms of other co-workers. The accounting profession is seen as an authoritative institution that guides and expects moral behavior among its members. For example, Lampe and Finn (1992) used the Defining Issues Test (DIT) to analyze accounting students and certified public accountants (CPAs). They suggest that the highest percentage of scores tended to fall in Rests' (1986) Stage 4. Accountants in this stage are cognizant of the feeling and agreement of others (Rest and Narvaez, 1994). Likewise, they must also take into consideration the probability that a financial situation will in fact happen in the immediate or distant future (probability of effect). Finally, accountants must consider the effects of the financial consequences on all stakeholders involved whether they include co-workers, investors, or the community. Since many accounting issues have a significant affect on individuals beyond those close to the situation, concentration of effect is an important component and must be included in this model as was done in the present study. Jones (1991) included concentration of effect in his moral intensity construct for the sake of completeness. In fact, it can easily form its own factor in describing the importance of the dimensions of moral intensity.

Two dimensions of moral intensity, 'perceived corporate concern' and 'perceived involvement effect,' were evaluated to determine if they would be better predictors of accounting students' moral sensitivity, moral judgments and moral intentions. In the present study, these moral intensity dimensions did not significantly predict the ability of the accounting students to recognize a moral conflict. It is possible that, for the accounting issues used here, the students did not have to take into account the components of moral intensity in deciding the ethical nature of the conflict because they were a little more obvious.

In testing this hypothesis, however, when moral sensitivity was combined with the dimensions of moral intensity, it was a significant predictor of moral judgment. Barnett (2001) and May and Pauli (2001) also suggested similar results with regard to the dimensions of moral intensity relating to moral judgment. Consistent with Jones' (1991) theory, the ability to recognize that an issue represents a moral conflict, along with the perceived moral component dimensions, influences moral judgment in individuals. The first dimension, here 'perceived corporate concern,' along with moral sensitivity, significantly predicted moral judgments in all scenarios, except for violating company policy (Scenario 3). With this issue, students seemed to recognize the ethical content of the issue. However, it did not significantly predict moral judgment as the two dimensions did together. Since this issue was also considered more intense, it is possible that students recognized the issue immediately without taking into account any moral intensity dimensions.

The second dimension (perceived involvement effect) significantly predicted moral judgment in issues involving violating company policy (Scenario 3) and extending questionable credit (Scenario 4). Since this dimension was composed of concentration of effect, it is likely that students did not perceive this dimension as being important in approving a questionable expense report or violating company policy. It is possible that, because of the limited work experience, which students possess, they may not consider the number of people that would be affected by their actions in these unethical scenarios.

The dimensions of moral intensity and moral judgment were also significant predictors of moral intentions. Similar results were suggested by Barnett (2001). While moral judgment significantly predicted moral intentions in all scenarios, the first dimension (perceived corporate concern) significantly predicted moral intentions in issues involving approving a questionable expense report (Scenario 1) and violating company policy (Scenario 3). In these issues, students may have perceived the potential financial harm to be greater than in the other issues involving falsifying financial statements and extending questionable credit. Again, the limited work experience that students possess, may have been a factor in their moral decision-making process. Apparently, the components in the first dimension (perceived corporate concern) helped students decide how they would act in a similar situation. These findings were similar to Barnett (2001) who suggested one dimension consisting of magnitude of consequences, social consensus, and proximity along with moral judgment significantly predicted moral intentions. Likewise, the results do support the findings in the May and Pauli (2001), Harrington (1997), and Singhapakdi *et al.* (1996) studies and seemed to support the notion that the moral intensity construct can be synthesized into two dimensions that do, in fact, influence and predict moral intentions in different business contexts, at least in marketing and accounting!

Limitations

Several limitations should also be noted. First, a small sample of students was drawn from only one college in the northeastern part of the USA. Therefore, any generalizations to the entire accounting student population must be made with caution.

A second limitation is that four hypothetical scenarios were used in this study, rather than actual moral situations. However, the use of hypothetical scenarios is common in business ethics research, but the findings may have been different if actual moral situations had been used.

A third limitation is that moral intensity was narrowly defined within the context of each scenario. These components may have been more or less intense depending upon the issue without the researcher detecting these differences.

A fourth limitation is that students' perceptions of the issues presented in this study may have been influenced by the recent publicized events of Enron and WorldCom. As a result, students may have been more likely to report higher ethical sensitivity, judgments, intentions, and perceptions of the components of moral intensity than under other circumstances.

A fifth limitation is the potential for gender effects. Previous research has examined the effects of gender on moral decision-making. Their findings suggest that females appear to score higher on moral sensitivity and judgment than males (Shaub, 1989). Future research should attempt to replicate these findings in other samples of students to ensure their generalizability.

Implications

This study contributes to the literature in two primary ways. It addresses whether a dimensionality of moral intensity components, in fact, exists which are situation-specific. Second, it examined whether particular dimension(s) of moral intensity were better predictors of accounting students' moral decision-making processes.

The accounting profession in the USA has recently taken the initiative to examine skills (competencies and values) that it believes accountants need to meet the demands of the future. In 2000, the American Institute of Certified Public Accountants (AICPA) published

The CPA Vision Project (the Vision) that identified integrity as a core value that CPAs must possess in order to meet the challenges of the future (AICPA, 2000a). In order to achieve the skills identified in the Vision, the AICPA developed *The AICPA Core Competency Framework for Entry into the Accounting Profession*. An important area in this framework, addressed in the area of personal competencies, is the ability of accounting professionals to demonstrate commitment towards integrity and ethical behavior (AICPA, 2000b).

It is hoped the results of this study will help educators who are integrating ethical instructional components into their curriculum to satisfy professional initiatives. Educators could design ethical components within their accounting courses that could introduce students to different types of unethical issues and help them to identify the components of moral intensity in each situation. Role-playing, essay responses, and open discussions may be excellent vehicles within which to examine various moral issues in accounting. For example, in an accounting information systems course, students may study ethical issues relating to computer and network practices while emphasizing the ethical intensity issues and how they may affect the decision-making process. The consequences of unethical behavior could be examined in the light of the intensity elements (especially the magnitude of the consequences, the social consensus and the concentration of effects).

The results of this study could also contribute to business organizations and professional associations that are developing training programs, policies and procedures, and educational programs geared towards accountants. In response to the Sarbones-Oxley Act of 2002, some companies are considering on-going training programs (Myers, 2003). For example, in ethical awareness seminars and workshops, specific case studies could be developed to focus on different types of unethical behavior, the intensity of different elements of a problem, and the decision-making processes that may occur in the practice of accounting within business settings. Concentration on these elements may highlight different moral intensity issues and stress the various parts of the decision-making process.

Directions for Future Research

Many opportunities for future research are suggested in this study. Future research may also find it fruitful to examine other potential covariates of moral intensity and decision-making such as the threat of sanctions, organizational culture, norms, codes of conduct, legislation, and type of industry, etc. There exists limited research concerning the contribution these variables may have on moral decision-making.

Similarly, in light of the current media attention given to the accounting scandals of Enron and WorldCom, an experimental post-test design may provide additional insight into the interaction effects of the accountant's moral decision-making process and moral intensity issues. Students could be exposed to several of these scenarios and then a discussion of the ethical implications of moral behavior could occur. This could bring into the classroom the current events surrounding the recent accounting scandals, and it is hoped, influence ethical decision-making.

The study could be conducted using real life ethics' issues developed into cases. This would give students the opportunity to discuss moral intensity components and identify how they influence the situation. Studying different samples of undergraduates and graduate students would also provide additional interesting feedback into the moral decision-making process.

Conclusion

The findings presented above add to the existing business ethics literature. In addition, they extend the existing understanding of the influence of the components of moral intensity on the ethical decision-making process for accounting profession also. These findings can be used to enhance ethics coursework and training programs in educational settings and industry. As was mentioned above, Merritt (2002) notes what is needed, is a return to the fundamental basics to restore confidence in Corporate America. A renewed emphasis must be placed on ethics in accounting in order for the public's confidence in the integrity of their financial information to be restored. The present study may help steer us in the right direction.

References

American Institute of Certified Public Accountants (AICPA) (2000a) *CPA Vision Project*. Available at http://www.cpavision.org/vision.htm (accessed 1 March 2004).

American Institute of Certified Public Accountants (AICPA) (2000b) *Core competencies framework*. Available at http://www.aicpa.org/edu/corecomp.htm (accessed 18 March 2004).

Armstrong, M. B. (1987) Moral development and accounting education, *Journal of Accounting Education*, 5(1), pp. 27–43.

Barnett, T. (2001) Dimensions of moral intensity and ethical decision making: an empirical study, *Journal of Applied Social Psychology*, 31(5), pp. 1038–1057.

Dukerich, J. M. *et al.* (2000) Moral intensity and managerial problem solving, *Journal of Business Ethics*, 24(1), pp. 29–38.

Flory, S. M. *et al.* (1992) A multidimensional analysis of selected ethical issues in accounting, *The Accounting Review*, 67(2), pp. 284–302.

Frey, B. F. (2000a) The impact of moral intensity on decision making in a business context, *Journal of Business Ethics*, 26(2), pp. 181–195.

Frey, B. (2000b) Investigating moral intensity with the world-wide web: a look at participant reactions and a comparison of methods, *Behavior Research Methods, Instruments & Computers*, 32(3), pp. 423–431.

Harrington, S. J. (1997) A test of a person-issue contingent model of ethical decision-making in organizations, *Journal of Business Ethics*, 16(4), pp. 363–375.

Hair, J. *et al.* (1998) *Multivariate Data Analysis* (Englewood Cliffs, NJ: Prentice Hall).

Sarbones-Oxley Act (2002) Available at http://frwebgate.access.gpo.gov/cgibin/getdoc.cgi?dbname=107_-cong_bills&docid=f:h3763enr.txt.pdf (accessed 4 February 2003).

Jeffery, C. (1993) Ethical development of accounting students, non-accounting business students, and liberal arts students, *Issues in Accounting Education*, 8(1), pp. 86–97.

Jones, T. M. (1991) Ethical decision making by individuals in organizations: an issue-contingent model, *Academy of Management Review*, 16(2), pp. 366–395.

Lampe, J. and Finn, D. (1992) A model of auditors' ethical decision process, *Auditing: A Journal of Practice and Theory*.

May, D. R. and Pauli, K. P. (2000) The role of moral intensity in ethical decision making: A review and investigation of moral recognition, evaluation, and intention. *Academy of Management Meeting* in Toronto, CA.

Merritt, J. (2002) For MBAs, Soul-searching 101, *Business Week*, 3799, pp. 64–65.

Myers, R. (2003) Ensuring ethical effectiveness, *Journal of Accountancy*, 195(2), available at www.aicpa.org/pubs/jofa/feb2003/index.htm (accessed 5 February 2003).

Rest, J. R. (1986) *Moral development: advances in research & theory* (New York: Praeger).

Rest, J. R. and Narvaez, D. (1994) *Moral Development in the Profession* (Englewood Cliffs, NJ: Lawrence Erlbaum Associates).

Shaub, M. K. (1989) An empirical examination of the determinants of auditors' ethical sensitivity. Unpublished doctoral dissertation. Texas Technological University, Lubbock.

Shaub, M. K. (1994) An analysis of the association of traditional demographic variables with the moral reasoning of auditing students and auditors, *Journal of Accounting Education*, 12(1), pp. 1–26.

Singhapakdi, A. *et al.* (1996) Moral intensity and ethical decision-making of marketing professionals, *Journal of Business Research*, 36(3), pp. 245–255.

Singhapakdi, A. *et al.* (1999) Antecedents, consequences, and mediating effects of perceived moral intensity and personal moral philosophies, *Journal of the Academy of Marketing Science*, 27(1), pp. 19–36.

Valentine, S. L. and Silver, L. (2001) Assessing the dimensionality of the Singhapakdi, Vitell, and Kraft measure of moral intensity, *Psychological Reports*, 88(1), pp. 291–294.

Weber, J. (1996) Influences upon managerial moral decision-making: nature of the harm and magnitude of consequences, *Human Relations*, 49(1), pp. 1–22.

Accounting Textbooks: Exploring the Production of a Cultural and Political Artifact

JOHN FERGUSON, DAVID COLLISON, DAVID POWER
& LORNA STEVENSON

University of Dundee, UK

ABSTRACT   *This paper explores the production of introductory financial accounting textbooks in the UK. Despite being a pervasive pedagogical device (see Brown and Guilding, 1993, Accounting Education: an international journal, 4(2) pp. 211–218), there has been little research carried out which examines the role or contents of textbooks in accounting education. This is a surprising gap in the literature when one considers the numerous concerns that have been expressed regarding the content of accounting education, the values which it projects and the type of student which it produces. Drawing on contemporary research into textbooks, this paper considers accounting textbooks to be 'cultural artifacts' which may reflect the cultural, ideological, and political interests of particular groups in society. In this regard, introductory financial textbooks have the potential to reinforce cultural homogeneity through the advancement of shared attitudes. This study is based upon 12 semi-structured interviews with both textbook authors and commissioning editors. Results indicate that the contents of textbooks are the product of complex social and cultural relations. Whilst conflicts and negotiations may characterize the production process, the knowledge that is considered most 'legitimate' tends to be mandated, either directly or indirectly, by professional accounting bodies through course accreditation requirements. Furthermore, this knowledge reflects wider cultural issues and assumptions regarding the structure of society and of how it should be organized.*

1. Introduction

Crawford (2003, p. 5) argues that 'the symbolism of the textbook is well established in the English Language', with metaphors such as 'it was a textbook operation,' 'it was a textbook takeoff' and 'it was all done by the textbook' reinforcing the notion that the textbook reflects or depicts an idea of convention and procedure. However, as Apple and Christian-Smith (1991, p. 1) note, textbooks are not merely a 'delivery system of facts' but are 'the result of political, economic, and cultural activities, battles and compromises' (Apple and Christian-Smith, 1991, p. 1). Whilst progress has been made in terms of understanding the relationship between school knowledge and wider society, 'little attention has actually been paid to that one artifact [sic] that plays a major role in defining whose culture is taught—the textbook' (Apple and Christian-Smith, 1991, p. 1). Although textbook research has been fairly well established throughout Europe since the beginning of the 20th century, studies that consider the political and cultural role of textbooks are generally restricted to school history textbooks.

The aim of the present study is to explore how the contents of introductory financial accounting textbooks are decided upon and what influences this text production process. Concerns have been raised in earlier literature regarding the content of accounting education, in particular, the values that it projects and the type of student that it produces (AAA, 1986; Loeb, 1988; AECC, 1990a,b; Power, 1991; Lewis et al., 1992; Gray et al., 1994; Puxty et al., 1994; McPhail and Gray, 1996; Kelly et al., 1999; McPhail, 1999; Albrecht and Sack, 2000; McPhail, 2001). These criticisms have been extended to include the textbooks used in accounting degree curricula, where the dominance of a neo-classical economics worldview that emphasizes the interests of shareholders has been noted (Kelly and Pratt, 1994; Ferguson et al., 2005). These studies suggest that, in order to help develop the critical faculties of students, they should be made aware of the contested nature of this perspective and introduced to other possible ways in which society can be, and is, organized (see, Doyle, 1994; Hutton, 1996; 2002; Collison, 2003, for an overview of alternative perspectives). By exploring the production of accounting textbooks, this study considers the factors that influence the contents of accounting texts and, in particular, the selective decisions that determine which knowledge is deemed appropriate/inappropriate for inclusion. A further aspect of this research, drawing on the extant literature in the area, considers whether textbook authors and publishers perceive accounting textbooks to be ideological, reflecting the interests of particular (powerful) social groups. In this sense, the present study starts with the assumption that financial accounting textbooks are a cultural and political artifact the contents of which are shaped by the struggles and compromises which characterize the 'social relations of production' (Apple, 1986, p. 83).

Semi-structured interviews with authors and commissioning editors were conducted to identify the processes, sites of conflict and compromises that influence the contents of introductory financial accounting textbooks, hence the cultural, political, and economic relations, which texts reflect, are considered. The paper is structured as follows: section 2 reviews the extant literature in the area, beginning with a description of how textbook research emerged through the work of supra-national bodies such as the United Nations, before turning to more recent studies, which examine the ideological role of textbooks in education. The remainder of this section reviews the relatively scarce literature addressing the role of accounting, business, and management textbooks and it is followed by a consideration of the theoretical literature on ideology. Section 3 describes the research method employed, whilst a discussion of the research findings is outlined in section 4, and section 5 concludes.

2.   Literature Review

Explicit recognition of the political role of textbooks can be traced at least as far back as the 1920s when the League of Nations highlighted the need for comparative studies of textbooks (Pingel, 1999; Nicholls, 2003). Following World War II, such projects were overseen by the United Nations Educational, Scientific, and Cultural Organization (UNESCO). The principal aim of these projects was to highlight how nations (often former enemies) represented themselves and 'the other' in educational (mainly history) textbooks in order to 'combat mutual xenophobia and to help in avoiding stereotypes' (Pingel, 1999, p. 6). UNESCO's commitment to textbook research was further developed through its partnership with the Georg Eckert Institute (for International Textbook Research) in 1974 (Pingel, 1999; Nicholls, 2003).

In addition to the Georg Ekert Institute, Johnsen (1993, p. 73) acknowledges the importance of the work of Horst Schallenberger and Gerd Stein, from the University of Duisburg whose 'systematic investigation of textbooks as political media' generated considerable interest in textbook research and led to the development of the Institut Für Schulbuchforchung in Duisburg. The assumptions that guide much of the work undertaken by the Duisberg School were developed by Franz Poggeler (1985) who maintained that political influence in textbooks is not limited to social science and may occur in subjects thought to be apolitical: he argued that both textbook authors and educators were insufficiently aware of this influence.

Textbooks and Ideology

According to Crawford (2003, p. 5), textbooks are crucial in the process of 'constructing legitimated ideologies and beliefs and are a reflection of the history, knowledge and values considered important by powerful groups in society'. In this respect, textbooks epitomize what Raymond Williams (1989, p. 58) refers to as the 'selective tradition':

> From a whole possible area of past and present, in a particular culture, certain meanings and practices are selected for emphasis and certain other meanings and practices are neglected or excluded. Yet within a particular hegemony, and as one of its decisive processes, this selection is presented and usually successfully passed off as "the tradition", "the significant past." What has then to be said about any tradition is that it is in this sense an aspect of contemporary social and cultural organization, in the interest of the dominance of a specific class.

Whilst it is important to realize that the selection of knowledge is never a neutral activity, it is neither, nor need it be, a *complete* 'mirror reflection of ruling class ideas' (Apple, 1991, p. 10). In order to maintain its own legitimacy, the ruling power must integrate many interests, 'even opposing groups under its banner' (Apple, 1995, p. 27). In describing how powerful groups may set about incorporating the views of oppositional cultures, Apple and Christian-Smith (1991) argue that one trend in textbook production is apparent; very little ever is dropped from textbooks. In this sense, 'progressive *items* are perhaps mentioned... but not developed in depth' (Apple and Christian-Smith, 1991, p. 11, emphasis in original). Therefore, by simply *mentioning* alternative perspectives, dominant cultures can maintain hegemonic discourse (Apple and Christian-Smith, 1991; MacIntosh, 2002).

The Production of Textbooks

In order to understand both the role and content of textbooks it is necessary to consider the perspectives of those involved in the production process, in particular both authors and editors/publishers (Apple, 1991; Crawford, 2001, 2003). One increasing feature of textbook publishing is that publishers often create their own books, through extensive market research. In essence, the contents of a textbook may be decided almost before an author puts pen to paper. However, Apple (1991, p. 31) cautions that 'it is not ideological

uniformity or some political agenda which accounts for many of the ideas that are ultimately made or not made available to the general public. Rather, it is the 'bottom line'
that counts'.

When studying a cultural artifact, such as a textbook, one must also consider the social
and economic relations within the publishing industry and how this affects 'the politics of
knowledge distribution' (Apple, 1991, p. 24). For example, as Apple and Christian-Smith
(1991, p. 5) point out, textbooks are:

> Not only cultural artifacts [sic], they are economic commodities as well. Even though texts
> may be vehicles of ideas, they still have to be "peddled on the market" ... decisions about
> the "bottom-line" determine what books are published and for how long.

Moreover, there will be structured differences between different types of publisher: for
example, whether the firm is a trade publisher, text publisher or university press will often
determine the technology employed, the bureaucratic and organizational structures
adopted and attitudes to risk (Apple, 1991; Thompson, 2005).

In his detailed study of the book publishing industry in the UK and USA, Thompson
(2005) distinguishes between academic publishing and higher education publishing.[1]
Drawing on the concept of field from French sociologist Pierre Bourdieu, Thompson
(2005, p. 31) explains that both these fields are distinct, with their own 'structured
space of social positions' and their own 'logic.' The field of academic publishing is
'bound up with the world of scholarly and scientific research' and publishes books and
monographs primarily for scholars and researchers (Thompson, 2005). Speaking at a
recent conference on book publishing, Secretary to the Delegates and Chief Executive
of Oxford University Press, Henry Reece, described the principal role of academic publishing as knowledge advancement. Quoting Cathy Davidson (2003, p. 4), Reece (2005)
argued that 'Scholarly publishing isn't financially feasible as a business model—never
was, never was intended to be, and should *not* be.' By contrast, the field of higher education publishing is characterized by large media conglomerates with strong financial/
profit motives. Publishing in this field is concerned primarily with the development of textbooks to be used in higher education. Competition in this field is intense and tends to be
concentrated at the lower levels of the curriculum where there are greater student numbers;
therefore, publishers can generate a large profit by securing adoptions at this level
(Thompson, 2005). Hence, whilst 'academic' authors have greater freedom to develop
the contents of their manuscripts, this is much more limited for 'textbook' authors, who
are constrained by market pressures and their publisher's desire to secure as many adoptions as possible.

Accounting, Business and Management Textbooks

Only a handful of studies within the accounting, business and management literature have
given any explicit consideration to the textbook or its role in the education process
(Scapens *et al.*, 1984; Kelly and Pratt, 1994; Cuganesan *et al.*, 1997; Feige, 1997;
Laidler and Pallet, 1998; Cameron *et al.*, 2003; Mir, 2003; Ferguson *et al.*, 2004;
Aisbitt, 2005; Davidson, 2005; Ferguson *et al.*, 2005). In the accounting literature, such
studies concentrate predominantly on the contents of management accounting textbooks,
often questioning the relevance of the material which they contain (Scapens *et al.*, 1984;
Kelly and Pratt, 1988, 1992, 1994; Cuganesan *et al.*, 1997). One common feature of all
these studies is that they identify the prevalence of a neo-classical economic framework,
which informs the decision-making models covered by the textbooks examined. For
example, as Scapens *et al.* (1984, p. 34) point out, the underlying assumptions of these

models imply 'that the decision maker is either the owner or shares the owner's goals' and is a profit maximiser. However, as Kelly and Pratt (1994) note, there is a general absence within management accounting textbooks of any explicit discussion of the (neo-classical) framework or paradigm that informs the text: this is taken as given.

Expanding upon prior investigations into management accounting textbooks, Ferguson *et al.* (2004, 2005) considered the selection and contents of introductory conventional accounting textbooks, including financial accounting, management accounting, and financial management texts. Findings from these exploratory studies indicated that accounting educators believed that primacy was accorded to shareholders and managers within accounting textbooks and, accordingly, supplemented their recommended textbooks with additional material (Ferguson *et al.*, 2004). The analysis of recommended textbooks supported this belief, indicating that the interests of shareholders were predominant within financial accounting and financial management textbooks, while management accounting texts had a more pronounced managerial orientation. In this respect, Ferguson *et al.* (2004, 2005) provided further support to claims made in prior studies that the primary ethical perspective conveyed to accounting students is that of financial utilitarianism[2] (see Gray *et al.*, 1994).

In a special edition of the *Journal of Management Education*, four prominent textbook authors were asked to consider whether their textbooks were 'propaganda' or reflected a particular 'ideology' (Cameron *et al.*, 2003). The study concluded that 'authors espouse mostly conservative ideologies' which was 'not surprising given the level of success of the group and their rational self interest in maintaining the status-quo' (Cameron *et al.*, 2003, p. 728). In his commentary on this paper, Mir (2003, p. 736) argues that a significant amount of management is about controlling employees and is 'imbued with power' whilst being located in a definite hierarchy. However, this is seldom ever questioned in management textbooks and is made to appear natural (Mir, 2003). For example, 'when management texts talk about 'effective management practice', they seldom (if ever) point out that this effectiveness is judged from the point of view of a limited set of stakeholders—most often the owners, shareholders and (top) managers' (Mir, 2003, p. 737). Finally, Mir (2003, p. 737) claims that textbooks engender hegemony, stating that 'textbooks and other such artifacts [sic] attempt to shape our cognitive and affective interpretations of the world through their ideological apparatus'.

The Concept of Ideology—Some Theoretical Considerations

The concepts of 'ideology' and 'hegemony' are central to the majority of studies outlined in the preceding review of the extant literature on textbooks. In particular, these studies highlight a number of salient themes concerning unequal relations of power and the production/ reproduction of meaning in the service of power, which form the basis of analysis in the present study. More specifically, three main issues emerge from this prior literature: first, that textbooks often reflect the interests of particular social groups, and authors (as well as publishers) are, arguably, insufficiently aware of this limitation. Second, textbooks have the potential to render alternative discourses ineffectual through 'mentioning' them without sufficient discussion. Third, in terms of accounting, business, and management textbooks, the dominant discourse tends to be managerialist and reflects the interests of a limited set of stakeholders (i.e. shareholders and managers). This perspective appears to be natural in accounting, business, and management textbooks, partially because of insufficient discussion of alternative viewpoints (Kelly and Pratt, 1994; Ferguson *et al.*, 2005).

In keeping with the earlier literature in this area, the concept of ideology will play an important role in our analysis of the production of accounting textbooks. However, when using contested terms such as ideology, care must be taken to specify the way in which these terms are being employed, since, as Eagleton (1991, p. 1) points out, ideology 'has a world of useful meanings, not all of which are compatible with each other'. For example, ideology has been variously used to refer to specific kinds of beliefs, such as fascism, communism, or nationalism (Eagleton, 1991; Thompson, 1990); beliefs which are in some way false or which legitimate (political) power (Eagleton, 1991; Thompson, 1990); and discourse which constrains what is said or thought (Bourdieu, 1991; Fairclough, 2003; Van Dijk, 1998; Wodak and Meyer, 2001).

Drawing on Thompson (1990, p. 7) the term ideology is used in this study in a critical or pejorative sense to refer to 'meaning in the service of power'. However, whilst this use of the term retains the 'criterion of negativity' inherent in a number of contemporary Marxist approaches to ideology, Thompson's (1990, p. 56) account differs in that it does not imply that ideology need be 'erroneous or illusory'. Whilst acknowledging that ideology '*may* operate by concealing or masking social relations,' Thompson (1990, pp. 56–57) notes that these are only 'contingent possibilities,' adding:

> What we are interested in here is not primarily and not initially the truth or falsity of symbolic forms, but rather the ways in which these forms serve, in particular circumstances, to establish and sustain relations of domination.

Furthermore, Thompson (1990, p. 91) takes care to distance himself from some popular approaches to ideology, which view ideology as a kind of 'social cement . . . binding individuals to a social order which oppresses them.' One problem with this 'dominant ideology' conception is that it downplays the 'prevalence and significance of dissensus and disagreement, of skepticism and cynicism, of contestation and conflict' (Thompson, 1990, p. 90). Therefore, the reproduction of unequal power relations does not necessarily require an underlying consensus of values and beliefs: as Thompson (1990) points out, skepticism and rejection of ideas is often 'interfused' with traditional values. Similarly, in his neo-Gramscian analysis of the reproduction of dominant values in schools, Apple (1995) acknowledges the role of conflict and contestation, arguing that, in order to maintain their own legitimacy, dominant interests will often incorporate oppositional cultures in order to maintain ideological hegemony.

Key to Thompson's (1990, p. 8) reformulation of the concept of ideology is his contention that cultural artifacts (or 'symbolic forms')[3] are not ideological in themselves. Whether they are ideological or not, or the extent to which they are 'depend[s] on the ways in which they are used and understood in specific social contexts' (Thompson, 1990). In particular, Thompson (1990, p. 8), outlines a 'depth hermeneutics' methodological framework, which highlights the necessity for researchers interested in studying the ideological characteristics of symbolic forms (such as accounting textbooks) to consider whether they 'serve to establish and sustain relations of domination in the social contexts within which they are *produced, transmitted and received*' (*emphasis added*). More specifically, Thompson (1990, p. 306) stresses that researchers should pay attention to the ways in which individuals involved in the production and reception of symbolic forms understand what they are doing, how they make sense of symbolic forms and 'incorporate them into their lives'.

Whilst Thompson's (1990) framework emphasizes both the production and reception of symbolic forms, the analysis in the current study will concern itself primarily with the everyday understanding of individuals involved in the production and transmission of accounting textbooks. This is for two reasons. First, whilst there is a paucity of research that considers accounting textbooks in the literature, the studies that do exist tend to focus on either the contents (Scapens *et al.*, 1984; Kelly and Pratt, 1994; Cuganesan *et al.*, 1997; Ferguson *et al.*, 2005) or the use (Kelly and Pratt, 1994; Ferguson *et al.*, 2004) of accounting texts. Therefore, by focusing on the production of texts, this study addresses a gap in the accounting literature. Second, since earlier studies into accounting textbooks have highlighted problems with content (Scapens *et al.*, 1984; Kelly and Pratt, 1994; Cuganesan *et al.*, 1997; Ferguson *et al.*, 2005) and noted that users of texts employ supplementary material in order to overcome these perceived deficiencies (Ferguson *et al.*, 2004), this study addresses the issue of why the contents of texts are as they are—i.e. who decides upon the contents and what influences this process.

Developing the insights provided by the preceding review of the literature, the present study has two main research questions.[4]

1. How are the contents of accounting textbooks decided upon and what influences this process?
2. Do authors and publishers perceive accounting textbooks to be ideological?

The following section delineates the research method employed in the study to address these research questions, and is followed by a discussion of the main research findings.

3. Research Method

Drawing on the prior research outlined in Section 2, this study aims to explore how the contents of textbooks are decided upon and what influences the process. The views of authors and publishers were sought for two reasons. First, as discussed in Section 3, when exploring the ideological character of 'symbolic forms' (such as accounting textbooks) it is important to consider their production and diffusion by exploring the everyday understanding of individuals involved in the process (Thompson, 1990). Second, authors and commissioning editors were deemed the key actors in terms of decisions regarding the contents of textbooks. Whilst other individuals play an important part in the process of production and diffusion of accounting textbooks, such as printers, sales representatives, wholesalers and retailers, it was felt that these roles were less focused on content development. It was decided to undertake an exploratory study for this research because of the relative paucity of empirical evidence concerning the content development and production of textbooks in accounting education. As discussed in the literature review, whilst there are a few studies that consider the contents and use of accounting textbooks, the authors are not aware of any studies that focus on the production of accounting texts. Semi-structured interviews were chosen as the principal method of data collection. Such an approach was deemed appropriate given the exploratory nature of the investigation being undertaken (Parker *et al.*, 1998). In this study, therefore, 'the intention then is not to generate empirically generalisable statistical outcomes, but rather to generate the beginnings of holistic understandings of the area under investigation' (Parker *et al.*, 1998, p. 375).

Twelve semi-structured interviews with introductory financial accounting textbook authors and commissioning editors were conducted between June 2004 and August 2005. Authors and publishers were contacted directly; interviewees were selected based on access and by virtue of having authored or commissioned an introductory financial accounting textbook in the UK.[5] Each interview lasted between 45 min and 1 h. A summary of interviewees' details is provided in Table 1. Before the start of each interview a statement of the objectives of the project and a list of possible discussion points and questions were given to the interviewee. The interviewees were not restricted to these topics but instead were encouraged to expand on other issues that they felt were important.

Table 1. Interviewee background[a]

Author	Gender	Professional accounting qualification	In print
(a) Authors			
A	M	Yes	No
B	F	Yes	Yes
C	M	Yes	Yes
D	M	Yes	Yes
E	M	Yes	Yes
F	F	Yes	Yes
G	F	Yes	Yes
H	M	Yes	Yes
Publisher	Gender	Subject area	Type of publisher
(b) Commissioning editors			
A	M	Marketing and Accounting	Higher Education
B	M	General Accounting	Higher Education
C	F	General Accounting	Higher Education
D	F	Business, Management and Accounting	Higher Education and Academic

[a]Whilst it would be useful to provide further background details on the authors and publishers interviewed for this study, it was felt that in order to preserve interviewees' anonymity, further information should not be disclosed.

All interviews, except for two, were tape-recorded, with two of the interviewers usually present. Interviews were conducted on a strictly non-attributable basis.

4. Findings

The views of the authors and publishers that emerged from the interviews can be summarized into separate areas and will be discussed under the following headings: the contents of financial accounting textbooks; homogeneity in financial accounting textbooks; ideology and accounting textbooks.

The Contents of Financial Accounting Textbooks

Authors and commissioning editors were asked a number of questions regarding the decisions surrounding content and the publishing process in general. A number of issues emerged from this aspect of the discussion: namely, that the contents of textbooks, to an extent, were 'planned' by publishers, and that, whilst the market was defined in terms of what was taught on undergraduate accounting education courses,[6] there was an indirect influence on textbook content by professional accounting bodies.

All of the commissioning editors noted that the contents of introductory financial textbooks were driven predominantly by perceived market demand. When asked to comment on whether textbooks were written to cover both professional *and* higher education markets, respondents suggested that it would be commercial suicide to try to cover two markets at once. However, Publisher A noted:

> I personally wouldn't go and look at professional courses. I would rely much more on the modules that are taught in higher education. If *they* are influenced by professional [syllabi], then I guess, indirectly I would be as well.

Therefore, the publishers defined their markets almost entirely by reference to university accounting curricula: textbook content was principally derived from what was taught on university degree courses. Whilst publishers acknowledged that they paid little attention to the professional market or professional accounting syllabi, all of the commissioning editors interviewed acknowledged that it was likely that professional accreditation[7] influenced the content of what was taught at university and what would, therefore, affect decisions regarding textbook content. This issue will be explored further in the following section ('Homogeneity in Financial Accounting Textbooks').

Both authors and publishers were asked to consider how much each had influenced the content of the textbook. Publisher C explained:

> It's a mixture of both really. We do get people approaching us, usually with an idea rather than actually having written a manuscript . . . it's a mixture of that and us thinking "well, where is the gap, what do we need, what's happening in the market, what kind of book are people asking for?" and then going out and finding an author to write it for us.

Publisher A noted that it was more common for the contents of textbooks to be planned by the publisher for introductory level courses, whilst authors were more likely to submit scripts for textbooks at more advanced levels, such as accounting theory. He stated:

> We will know what we want to do, it's just a question of finding [an author], and really, you pick those up as you go along. If somebody has got [an idea] in that area, that's when you will sit down . . . and start shaping the contents to what you want—which is really driven by the market.

Some of the authors agreed with this sentiment. For example, Author F explained that textbooks were written for the market and they very rarely reflected the author's own ideas of the subject. Both Authors B and G were not involved in the initial editions of their textbooks and therefore explained that they were not privy to any negotiations that may have taken place between the original authors and publishers regarding the contents of their textbooks. However, both of these authors noted that their respective publishers had never suggested that they include or remove any material on the editions on which they have worked.

Three of the authors interviewed indicated that decisions regarding content were entirely up to them, subject to a few minor changes, which resulted from the review process. Author C explained:

> I was quite clear on what the book I wanted to write was, and they basically went along with it. Basically, they have a review process . . . and the reviewers had some comments, and where possible, I incorporated them into my book. Ninety percent of the content of the textbook was decided by me.

The review process was quite rigorous for introductory financial accounting textbooks because the market is much larger at this level. Typically, there would be around ten reviewers for an accounting textbook at an introductory level, whilst there would probably only be about three for a more specialized, higher level textbook. The process was detailed by Publisher A as follows:

> The author will get to see the reviews. They will be anonymised. We will sit down and say, three reviewers have picked up on this, and then basically it is give and take. The only thing that drives our need for an extra chapter or not is whether we think we will hit a slightly bigger market by having it. Whereas, I think authors feel sometimes a bit more personally that that is how the subject should be taught. I'm not saying that that is right or wrong; I mean I don't have a formal accountancy qualification. My knowledge of accounting is all about what is

taught and how it is taught. ... I don't necessarily know what it is, if I did then I would be writing the books. So it needs to go to an academic [for review] ... Everything is a compromise. I mean, we are in publishing to make money. It is as simple as that. We are not here to disseminate information or whatever, this is just how we choose to make money. If we thought that adding another 30 pages, which means adding 30 pages worth of paper to every unit we produce ... will bring a greater return, then we will do it.

This quotation highlights the negotiations that take place regarding decisions about content, and how these processes are affected by the social and economic relations within the publishing industry (Apple, 1991). It seemed clear from the comments made by three of the commissioning editors interviewed that financial capital (as opposed to symbolic capital)[8] dominated editorial decisions. Only one of the commissioning editors interviewed perceived his publishing firm as something other than a profit-motivated business: Publisher D viewed her firm's activity as contributing to knowledge in the subject areas in which they operated, although acknowledging that profit was important in terms of survival. Again, it would appear that publishing organizations do not have a particular political agenda that shapes the contents of their textbooks Apple (1991). Instead, existing market structure and the 'bottom line' are influential in this regard. From the publisher's perspective, the knowledge that is deemed important is the knowledge that sells.

With an increasing focus on the bottom line, the marketing of textbooks was viewed by Publishers B and C as being as important as content development. For example, Publisher B explained, 'to be honest, it's less to do with the content of the book, although it has to be right or thereabouts. ... It is more dependent on your commercial power in the market, how many representatives you have, how good they are at getting round and seeing lecturers and getting them to accept books.' The prominent role of marketing within higher education publishing is the consequence of an 'institutionalized' aspect of the field: namely, the adoption system (Thompson, 2005). In this sense, sales of textbooks depend not on the purchasing decisions of students, but on whether the text is recommended for a course by the lecturer. Therefore, lecturers act as 'gatekeepers,' giving a textbook a form of 'authorization' by adopting it as the core course text and ultimately influencing students' decisions to purchase. Marketing activity in this field tends to be directed primarily at course lecturers (see Smith and DeRidder (1997) for a discussion of the marketing of accounting textbooks in the USA).

Homogeneity in Financial Accounting Textbooks

Pointing to a lengthy shelf filled with introductory financial accounting textbooks, Author A exclaimed rather exasperatedly that, 'they are all the bloody same!' However, in spite of being the most vehement, he was not alone in making this observation. Authors A, B, C, D and E acknowledged that most of the financial accounting textbooks tended to cover the same material, even though there appeared to be a wider choice of financial accounting textbooks on the market in comparison to other accounting subject areas (see Ferguson *et al.*, 2004). Although sometimes keen to distance themselves from any influence exerted by professional accounting bodies, it would appear that accreditation requirements, whether directly or indirectly, impacted upon the contents of financial accounting textbooks (see also, Green and Everett, 2003; Ferguson *et al.*, 2004, 2005).

A number of the authors consciously consulted professional accreditation requirements in order to make sure that 'everything was covered.' For example, Author D stated: 'We literally took the syllabuses of the major professional bodies and went through the introductory syllabuses and ticked off what we thought should be in it, and made sure we covered everything' (see Table 2).

However, in most cases the role of the profession was viewed as having little influence on the contents of introductory textbooks—although an 'indirect' relationship was acknowledged by nearly all of the authors interviewed. In this sense, authors tended to view the act of writing an introductory textbook as an 'autonomous' rather than a 'heteronomous' activity (see Green and Everett, 2003). Green and Everett (2003) use a 'sociology of education perspective' based on the work of Bourdieu to explain the relationship between the accounting profession and accounting education in Canada. Their paper suggests that autonomy in accounting education is undermined by the profession and has implications for the 'effective and equitable' education of accounting students. They state that the 'university is an important site for the reproduction of the accounting profession' and stress that, given the importance of universities in this production function, criticisms of accounting education 'are regularly levied in the direction of this institution' (Green and Everett, 2003, p. 1). However, as Green and Everett (2003, p. 2) point out: 'few [accounting academicians] view the profession as interrelated.' In this respect, accounting education is viewed as 'autonomous' rather than a 'heteronomous' field, which, according to Green and Everett (2003, p. 2), is

Table 2. Textbook features

Interviewee	Professional syllabus/ accreditation consulted?	Intended audience	How is active independent learning achieved?
A	Yes	Level 1, UK accounting undergraduate	Learning objectives and outcomes, questions/ self-test
B	Yes	Level 1, UK accounting undergraduate	Questions/self-test
C	Yes	Level 1, UK accounting undergraduate	Questions/self-test, web-based questions
D	Yes	Level 1, UK accounting undergraduate[b]	Questions/self-test
E	[a]	Secondary school accounting students	NA
F	No	Level 1, UK business undergraduate	Questions/self-test
G	No	Level 1, UK accounting undergraduate	Learning contract, reflection of learning experience, questions/ self-test
H	No	Level 1 UK business undergraduate	Learning objectives and outcomes, questions/ self-test

[a]Secondary school standardized test curriculum consulted. Whilst author E's textbook was aimed at secondary schools, it is, none the less, the most widely adopted textbook on accounting degree programs in the UK. For this reason, it was felt that the views of this author were of importance to the paper.
[b]First edition of textbook intended for professional students.
NA, not answered.

misleading because the accounting profession places considerable pressure on accounting departments.

Consistent with Green and Everett's (2003) insights, Author C viewed the authorship of his text as autonomous. He stated:

> I have been influenced very little by professional bodies. Only indirectly in the sense that I might want to be in the market to reach first year accounting students, whose syllabus in turn might be dictated by the fact that the accreditation bodies might want them to cover partnerships

Similarly, Author B explained that you do not write a textbook to specifically get exemptions but you 'hope to [meet] exemption requirements' in the process. She felt that most authors would try to meet accreditation requirements because:

> You can't market your book properly if you can't meet the exemption requirements. They are a sub-conscious influence if you know what I mean. For example, I didn't go back to fundamentals of accounting for Association of Chartered Certified Accountants (ACCA) [to check] what was in the syllabus [and whether] I was covering every single thing. . . . But, being a qualified accountant and being aware of accreditation requirements, then that is always in the back of your mind.

Two of the authors interviewed indicated that another reason for the homogeneity in financial accounting textbooks was the reticence of lecturers to engage with alternative approaches. In describing the reception of his 'alternative approach' to the financial accounting textbook, Author A stated:

> One of the things that I realized, much to my horror, was that accountants, and accounting lecturers in particular, are far more conservative than other academics. In other [disciplines], if someone takes a more radical approach to teaching and they find that it is effective, they may think "oh, this is great" and it would be more quickly adopted. . . . But accountants— no. [The financial accounting textbook market is] by and large, saturated with the same sort of stuff. Nobody takes a radical approach. Some take minor, minor differences, with "unique selling features." But essentially, it's the same material you get no matter what.

Author G suggested that such reticence, in some cases, is down to people 'looking for an easy life' and not wanting to do anything that is different. Talking specifically about her own textbook (which also takes a more alternative approach), author G suspected that some of the negative reactions to her textbook arose because 'it just offends sensibilities, in that it is chatty . . . and quirky and some people find that very threatening.'

The homogeneity in financial accounting textbooks was noted by the majority of interviewees and was attributed, in part, to professional accreditation requirements. Whilst professional accounting bodies do not directly determine the contents of financial accounting textbooks, their 'symbolic capital' is enough to ensure that courses adhere to accreditation requirements (Green and Everett, 2003). As mentioned in the previous section, if textbooks are designed to match course content, and course content is designed to cover professional accreditation requirements, then it is likely that textbooks will match closely the content and knowledge that professional accounting bodies deem to be relevant.

Ideology and Accounting Textbooks

Drawing on Cameron *et al.* (2003), authors were asked whether they viewed their textbook as reflecting a particular ideology. Responses indicated that most authors felt that, due to the nature of the subject, financial accounting textbooks reflected a capitalistic view of the world: therefore, maximization of shareholder wealth assumptions were implicit throughout. For example, author F explained that students are taught capital market accounting at university whether they like it or not. This view was expressed succinctly by author E, who stated:

> This book is purely and simply based on the philosophy that people studying accounting should learn how to do it. Because accounting traditionally is profit and loss and balance sheet, produced for the shareholders and the owners; that is the focus of the book.

Authors who adopted this particular view of the world in their text were asked whether they felt that such an approach was desirable. Author H explained that you could not get away from the fact that accounting 'is the handmaiden of capitalism' although students are insufficiently aware of this relationship. The majority of responses suggested that introductory level accounting was not the place to introduce wider contextual issues (such as the relationship between accounting and the economic structure of a society).

For example, author D stated 'I think if you are learning accounting it is better to learn accounting first and then you [can] develop your own critical faculties, which is broader than just the accounting question'. Author B supported this comment, stating that students at an introductory level 'find it difficult just to understand the basic fundamental principles. For some of them that's hard enough.' However, authors differed in their views on how much later these wider issues should be taught. For most, final year courses on corporate governance or social and environmental accounting were the appropriate places to cover this material on an accounting degree. Author A disagreed, stating:

> I am not saying leave it until the third year. That's what most of the accountancy degrees do. That's the influence of the profession. You learn all the techniques in the first two years, then in the third year we will tell you what it [really] is.

However, three of the authors made an explicit attempt to explain the context of financial accounting and to introduce alternative perspectives in their textbooks. For example, author F explained that stakeholder perspectives were 'killed off' by UK Prime Minister, Margaret Thatcher, who scrapped a green paper, drafted under the previous Labour government, which considered corporate reporting for wider stakeholders.[9] Whilst the rights of shareholders have explicit primacy in UK company law, author F attempted to introduce the perspectives of other stakeholders by including a conversation between different constituencies right through the text, so that their perspectives were considered throughout.

Similarly, author G attempted to make students aware of relationships between stakeholders, other than simply financial relationships. She explained that, in her textbook, she:

> [Tried] to get students to understand that financial information flows always follow physical moves, or exchanges. So the systems perspective on teaching book-keeping, means that we start off with the physical [flows]. So that kind of flow is the first thing. And after, we say, are we going to capture this physical flow in a financial way and can we measure it, in which case we are actually doing something in the accounts. It does of course mean that we immediately say, oh there is pollution—but actually, we don't measure that, because even though it physically happens, there are no financial flows as a result of it [because] it is not part of our accounting system. So right from the very outset we say, there are all of these flows, and we are going to catch a subset of them. In that respect, those relationships become explicit right up front.

In this respect, students became aware not only of the relationships that exist between stakeholders but also of the limitations of accounting information. However, it seemed authors were limited in terms of the extent they could introduce contextual issues into their textbooks. One of the most common reasons cited was that there was no market for such issues and, in particular, reviewers were not asking for such things to be included.

Interestingly, some authors explained that the worldview presented in their textbook was different to their own. For example, author A stated:

> I think both [the other author] and I would be regarded as more left wing in our thinking. I think a lot of academics are. But the book isn't. I think the book is aimed at more traditionalist business models. It is essentially capitalist with the odd dot of red, where we could get it in.

One other limitation, frequently cited by interviewees, was the length of the textbook. In terms of minimizing production costs, both authors and publishers were aware that if something additional were to be added, then something would usually have to be removed. If that something happened to be included for accreditation purposes, then there was an inherent danger that sales would be adversely affected.

5.   Conclusions

This paper considers the societal significance of texts and explores the factors that influence the contents of, in particular, introductory financial accounting textbooks. Textbooks are commonly viewed as vehicles which disseminate legitimate knowledge: however, interviewees' responses indicated that the contents of introductory financial accounting textbooks, and how this content is decided upon, was the result of a complex set of social and cultural relations. Many constituents in the production of introductory financial accounting textbooks were identified by the interviewees, including authors, publishers, universities, accounting professional bodies, lecturers, and students. In addition, more abstract cultural factors were identified in the textbook production process—in particular, 'the market' and an Anglo-Saxon model of capitalism. The textbook and its contents emerge through a series of complex interactions and struggles involving cultural factors and these constituents.

These findings shed some light upon a number of important issues regarding the production of accounting textbooks and the knowledge (and interests) which they reflect, issues that have much broader implications for accounting education in general. Prior studies have expressed concern over the ethical and moral development and the lack of critical awareness of accounting students (Gray *et al.*, 1994; Puxty *et al.*, 1994; McPhail and Gray, 1996; McPhail, 1999; Collison and Frankfurter, 2000). In particular, these studies claim that the theoretical underpinnings of accounting education are restricted to only one subset of ethical reasoning: financial utilitarianism (Gray *et al.*, 1994). Restricting learning in this way, without offering an alternative perspective from which students can exercise their own reasoning and judgment, can be viewed as indoctrination (Loeb, 1999), a means of advancing hegemonic discourse (Van Dijk, 1998) or propaganda (Mir, 2003).

Given the rhetoric of professional accounting bodies that repeatedly call for graduates with critical thinking skills (Albrecht and Sack, 2000), or students who are 'active, independent learners and problem solvers rather than passive recipients of information' (AAA, 1986), it seems reasonable to suggest that a good start to engendering such qualities would be to introduce students to the broader context of the subject which they are studying at an early stage. Some of the authors interviewed in the current research argued that an introductory level should not be the place for such a discussion, although others felt that this should not be left until the final year of the students' studies. In respect of the latter view, the influence of the accreditation requirements of the professional accounting bodies was noted as an obstacle to introducing wider issues at an earlier stage of a degree and in introductory textbooks.

This is not to suggest that students should learn nothing but broader contextual issues at the beginning of their studies. However, if students are made aware that what they are learning reflects a particular view of the world (the Anglo-Saxon model of capitalism) and that there are other possible ways in which capitalist society can be, and is, organized (Doyle, 1994; Hutton, 1996, 2002; Collison, 2003) then it may improve the likelihood of the profession getting the type of student they (claim to) want. That these very fundamental and basic issues are not made explicit to students at the beginning of their studies suggests that accounting educators and the accounting profession are contributing to the maintenance of the ideological *status quo*, and act as a bulwark of a discourse which maintains acquiescence in a deeply contestable privileging of certain interests within society.

This study represents an initial step in furthering our understanding of a pervasive instructional device used in accounting education—the textbook. Whilst this study addresses some cultural and political factors, which affect the production of introductory financial accounting textbooks (and, therefore, what many perceive as legitimate accounting knowledge), much more work is required in the area in order to facilitate a more comprehensive understanding. In particular, more work needs to be carried out on the use of textbooks from the perspectives of both lecturers and students. As Apple and Christian-Smith (1991, p. 14) point out, one 'cannot assume that what is "in" the text is actually taught . . . nor can we assume that what is taught is actually learned.' Whilst there is a great need to understand about 'whose' knowledge gets taught, the influence of textbooks cannot be fully understood until an attempt is made to understand how they are used and how students actually interact with them (Apple and Christian-Smith, 1991; Manninen, 1997). Finally, the present study has limited its focus to a particular subject area. Further research could consider other accounting subject areas as well as other learning resources such as lecturers' notes and the internet (Johnsen, 1993) as well as the business media.

Acknowledgements

The authors gratefully acknowledge the financial support from the Institute of Chartered Accountants of Scotland. The authors also wish to thank Michael Fraser, Prem Sikka, Crawford Spence and the four anonymous reviewers for their insightful comments. This paper has also benefited from the comments provided by participants at the Critical Perspectives on Accounting Conference, New York, April 2005; the British Accounting Association Accounting Education Special Interest Group Annual Conference, Aberdeen, May 2005; and the British Accounting Association Scottish Regional Group Conference, August 2005.

Notes

[1]Thompson (2005) notes that there is considerable overlap between higher education publishing in the UK and the USA given that the same publishers are predominant in both countries. However, he outlines a number of key differences, which include the size of the market and the pedagogical culture in each country. Thompson (2005) emphasizes that the most significance difference is the size of the market-given that in 2002, the total number of students in higher education in the UK was around 14% of the US total. One consequence of this difference is that in the UK "the stakes are much lower, and the struggle for adoptions has not been waged as intensively" (Thompson, 2005, p. 268). In addition to market size, Thompson (2005) also comments upon differences in pedagogical cultures. More specifically, the culture in the USA is to structure a course round a textbook and effectively 'teach the book', whereas, in the UK, there is a tendency to structure courses in ways that are interesting, 'rather than follow the structure

that is laid down by a particular textbook' (Thompson, 2005, pp. 263–264). In this respect, there tends to be a greater match between course content and textbook content in the USA, and students are more strongly encouraged to buy a particular text. By contrast, in the UK, students are 'more commonly given a reading list in which several books may be recommended' (Thompson, 2005, p. 264).

[2]Gray *et al.* (1994) assess three modes of ethical reasoning: consequentialism (of which financial utilitarianism is a subset), motivism, and deontology. They argue that no particular mode is inherently superior to any other, and that it is quite often the case that individuals could apply all three. However, by emphasizing one particular mode, accounting education may restrict the development of ethical reasoning.

[3]Thompson (1990, p. 59) uses the term 'symbolic forms' to refer to a 'broad range of actions and utterances, images and texts, which are produced by subjects and recognized by them and others as meaningful constructs'. These may include linguistic utterances, both spoken and inscribed, as well as visual images: hence, accounting textbooks are a symbolic form.

[4]It was felt that the authors' and publishers' perceptions of the production process and their views on whether accounting texts were ideological should be considered separately—as they reflect two distinct, or analytically separable dimensions to the study. Whilst the former considers reflections upon a *process*, the latter is concerned with perceptions regarding the *values*, or worldview, which the texts embody.

[5]Whilst the study focuses on the publication of accounting textbooks in the UK, the issues that are addressed in the paper are of relevance to a wider, non-UK audience. (For example, see Zeff, 1988; Herring, 2003).

[6]In the UK, textbooks are typically used by undergraduate students, whilst students studying for professional examinations will normally use 'manuals,' which are targeted at specific professional bodies' accounting syllabi.

[7]In the UK, university accounting degrees may be 'accredited' by professional accounting bodies such as the Association of Chartered Certified Accountants (ACCA), the Chartered Institute of Management Accountants (CIMA), the Institute of Chartered Accountants in England and Wales (ICAEW) or the Institute of Chartered Accountants of Scotland (ICAS). By completing an accredited degree, students may obtain exemptions from sitting certain stages of their professional accounting examinations.

[8]Drawing on the work of French sociologist Pierre Bourdieu, Apple (1991) distinguishes between symbolic and financial capital. Apple (1991) claims that the type of capital a publisher pursues will depend on the objectives of the firm. For example, firms that are primarily concerned with short-term objectives are likely to pursue a strategy more congruent with the accumulation of financial capital. In contrast, some publishing firms pursue longer-term objectives and attempt to nurture symbolic capital (although such firms may not be uninterested in the 'logic of profitabilities') (Apple, 1991).

[9]The Green Paper was entitled 'The Future of Company Reports' published in July 1977 (HMSO, 1977). Amongst other things, the Green Paper outlined the requirement to report to a wider group of stakeholders such as employees, customers, the public, etc. as well as making it a requirement to include value added statements in company accounts.

References

AECC (Accounting Education Change Commission) (1990a) Objectives of education for accountants: position statement number one, *Issues in Accounting Education*, 5(2), pp. 307–312.

AECC (Accounting Education Change Commission) (1990b) AECC urges priority for teaching in higher education, *Issues in Accounting Education*, 5(2), pp. 330–331.

Aisbitt, S. (2005) International accounting books: publishers' dream, authors' nightmare and educators' reality, *Accounting Education: an international journal*, 14(3), pp. 349–360.

Albrecht, W. S. and Sack, R. J. (2000) *Accounting Education: Charting the Course through a Perilous Future* (Sarasota, FL: American Accounting Association).

AAA (American Accounting Association) (1986) Future accounting education: preparing for the expanding profession, *Issues in Accounting Education*, 1(1), pp. 168–195.

Apple, M. (1986) *Teachers and Texts: A Political Economy of Class and Gender Relations in Education* (London: Routledge).

Apple, M. (1991) The culture and commerce of the textbook, in: M. Apple and L. Christian-Smith (Eds) *The Politics of the Textbook*, pp. 22–41 (London: Routledge).

Apple, M. (1995) *Education and Power* (London: Routledge).

Apple, M. and Christian-Smith, L. (1991) The politics of the textbook, in: M. Apple and L. Christian-Smith (Eds) *The Politics of the Textbook*, pp. 1–22 (London: Routledge).

Bourdieu, P. (1991) *Language and Symbolic Power* (Cambridge: Polity Press).

Brown, R. B. and Guilding C. (1993) A survey of teaching methods employed in university business school accounting courses, *Accounting Education: an international journal*, 4(2), pp. 211–218.

Cameron, K. *et al.* (2003) Management textbooks as propaganda, *Journal of Management Education*, 27(6), pp. 711–729.

Collison, D. J. (2003) Corporate propaganda: its implications for accounting and accountability, *Accounting, Auditing and Accountability Journal*, 16(5), pp. 853–886.

Collison, D. J. and Frankfurter, G. M. (2000) Are we really maximizing shareholders wealth? Or: what investors must know when we do, *The Journal of Investing*, 9(3), pp. 55–63.

Crawford, K. (2003) The role and purpose of textbooks, *International Journal of Historical Learning, Teaching and Research*, 3(2), pp. 5–11.

Crawford, K. (2001) Researching the ideological and political role of the history textbook—issues and methods, *International Journal of Historical Learning, Teaching and Research*, 1(1), available at: www.centres.ex.ac.uk/historyresource/journal1/journalstart.htm

Cuganesan, S. *et al.* (1997) Exploring accounting education's enabling possibilities: an analysis of a management accounting text, *Accounting, Auditing and Accountability Journal*, 10(3), pp. 432–453.

Davidson, C. N. (2003) *American council of learned societies' annual meeting*, available at: www.acls.org/03am/davidson.pdf.

Davidson, R. A. (2005) Analysis of the complexity of writing used in accounting textbooks over the past 100 years, *Accounting Education: an international journal*, 14(1), pp. 53–74.

Doyle, P. (1994) Setting business objectives and measuring performance, *European Management Journal*, 12(2), pp.123–132.

Eagleton, T. (1991) *Ideology: An Introduction* (London: Verso).

Fairclough, N. (2003) *Analysing Discourse: Textual Analysis for Social Research* (London: Routledge).

Feige P. (1997) How 'uniform' is financial reporting in Germany?—The example of foreign currency translation, *European Accounting Review*, 6(1), pp. 109–122.

Ferguson, J. *et al.* (2004) Values implicit in accounting education: an investigation into the role of the textbook in introductory accounting, Dundee University Discussion Paper (ACC/0301).

Ferguson, J. *et al.* (2005) What are recommended textbooks teaching students about corporate stakeholders, *British Accounting Review*, 38(1), pp. 23–46.

Gray, R. H. *et al.* (1994) Teaching ethics and the ethics of teaching: educating for immorality and a possible case for social and environmental accounting, *Accounting Education: an international journal*, 3(1), pp. 51–75.

Green, D. L. and Everett, J. (2003) Accounting education and the reproduction of the accounting profession, Haskayne School of Business working paper, available at: wwwdocs.fce.unsw.edu.au/accounting/news/seminars2003_s1/paper4.pdf

Herring III, H. (2003) Conference address: the accounting education change movement in the United States, *Accounting Education: an international journal*, 12(2), pp. 87–95.

Her Majesty's Stationery Office (1977) *The Future of Company Reports: A Consultative Document* (London: HMSO).

Hutton, W. (1996) *The State We're In* (London: Vintage).

Hutton, W. (2002) *The World We're In* (London: Vintage).

Johnsen, E.B. (1993) *Textbooks in the Kaleidoscope: A Critical Survey of Literature and Research on Educational Texts* (Oslo: Scandinavian University Press).

Kelly, M. *et al.* (1999) Contemporary accounting education and society, *Accounting Education: an international journal*, 8(4), pp. 321–340.

Kelly, M. and Pratt, M. (1988) *The Gaps Between Theory, Current Practice and Best Practice in Management Accounting* (Canberra: The Accounting Association of Australia and New Zealand).

Kelly, M. and Pratt, M. (1992) Purposes and paradigms of management accounting: beyond economic reductionism, *Accounting Education: an international journal*, 1(3), pp. 225–246.

Kelly, M. and Pratt, M. (1994) Management accounting texts in New Zealand: the need for a paradigm shift, *Accounting Education: an international journal*, 3(4), pp. 313–329.

Laidler, J. and Pallett, S. (1998) International accounting; a review of books available to support UK courses: a teaching note, *Accounting Education: an international journal*, 7(1), pp. 75–86.

Lewis, L. *et al.* (1992) Accounting and the social: a pedagogic perspective, *British Accounting Review*, 24(3), pp. 219–233.

Loeb, S. E. (1988) Teaching students accounting ethics: some crucial issues, *Issues in Accounting Education*, 3(2), pp. 316–329.

McPhail, K. J. (1999) The threat of ethical accountants: an approach of Foucault's concept of ethics to accounting education and some thoughts of ethically educating for the other, *Critical Perspectives On Accounting*, 10(6), pp. 833–866.

McPhail, K. J. (2001) The dialectic of accounting education: from role identity to ego identity, *Critical Perspectives On Accounting*, 12(4), pp. 471–499.

McPhail, K. J. and Gray, R. H. (1996) Not developing ethical maturity in accounting education: hegemony, dissonance and homogeneity in accounting students' world views, Dundee University Discussion Paper (ACC/9605).

MacIntosh, N. B. (2002) *Accounting, Accountants and Accountability: Poststructuralist Positions* (London: Routledge).

Manninen, A. (1997) Critical reading in accounting, *Accounting Education: an international journal*, 6(4), pp. 281–294.

Mir, A. (2003) The hegemonic discourse of management texts, *Journal of Management Education*, 27(6), pp. 734–738.

Nicholls, J. (2003) Methods in school textbook research, *International Journal of Historical Learning, Teaching and Research*, 3(2), pp. 11–27.

Parker, L. *et al.* (1998) Accounting and management research: passwords from the gatekeepers, *Accounting, Auditing and Accountability Journal*, 11(4), pp. 371–406.

Pingel, F. (1999) *UNESCO Guidebook on Textbook Research and Textbook Revision* (Hannover: Verlag Hahnsche Buchhandlung).

Pöggeler, Franz. (1985) *Politik im Schulbuch* (Bonn: Bundeszentrale für Politische Bildung).

Power, M. (1991) Educating accountants: towards a critical ethnography, *Accounting, Organizations and Society*, 16(4), pp. 333–53.

Puxty, A. G. *et al.* (1994) (Re)forming the circle: education ethics and accountancy practices, *Accounting Education: an international journal*, 3(1), pp. 77–92.

Reece, H. (2005) *The Future of University Presses*, Paper presented at The Third International Conference on the Book, Oxford, September.

Scapens R. W. *et al.* (1984) *Management Accounting, Organisational Theory and Capital Budgeting* (Macmillan Press: London).

Smith, K. J. and DeRidder J. J. (1997) The selection process for accounting textbooks: general criteria and publisher incentives, *Issues in Accounting Education*, 12(2), pp. 367–384.

Thompson, J. B. (1990) *Ideology and Modern Culture* (Cambridge: Polity).

Thompson, J. B. (2005) *Books in the Digital Age* (Cambridge: Polity).

Van Dijk, T. (1998) Critical discourse analysis, in: D. Tannen *et al.* (Eds) *Handbook of Discourse Analysis*, pp. 352–372 (London: Blackwell).

Williams, R. (1989) Hegemony and the selective tradition, in: S. DeCastell *et al.* (Eds) *Language, Authority and Criticism: Readings on the School Textbook*, pp. 56–61 (London: The Falmer Press).

Wodak, R. and Meyer, M. (2001) *Methods of Critical Discourse Analysis* (London: Sage).

Zeff, S. A. (1988) Economic consequences in intermediate textbooks: A review after eight years, *Issues in Accounting Education*, 3(2), pp. 433–445.

Concept Mapping in a Financial Accounting Theory Course

JON SIMON

University of Hull, UK

ABSTRACT *This paper assesses the usefulness of concept mapping (an educational learning, assessment, and curriculum development technique developed by Novak, widely used in the natural sciences) within an accounting education context. It shows how an accounting-based concept map can be constructed by students and educators to provide a visual, conceptually transparent graphical representation of an individual's understanding of a particular knowledge domain. The method is firmly routed in Ausubel's theory of meaningful learning and its emphasis upon the hierarchical structure of concepts is particularly relevant to accounting. While concept mapping has been used extensively in many (particularly science) disciplines, it has received relatively little attention within accounting education. The paper's contribution is to extend its application within an accounting education context by focusing upon how concept mapping can enhance students' learning by evaluating student-prepared concept maps, showing how concept mapping can be used at different levels within a course (i.e. curriculum, topic and activity) and reporting feedback of its use with two cohorts of students, within a financial accounting theory component. The use of educator-prepared concept maps, with concepts omitted, proved popular as tutorial quiz exercises and increased the quantity and quality of participation. However, students were less willing to construct their own concept maps and engage in meaningful learning. While most students were able to build upon aspects of their prior knowledge, stronger students used a greater range of concepts, a richer set of linkages and more examples than weaker students did. Concept maps were useful in diagnosing students' and instructors' misconceptions. Many students found concept mapping relatively easy to use, provided a better understanding of complex issues, liked the visual representation and holistic view, and so supported their learning. However, educators need to become proficient in constructing maps and using appropriate software, not make the maps too complex, provide students with some initial training in the technique and consider the fit between using the techniques as a learning tool and as an assessment tool. While no significant differences were found in the usefulness of the method for students of different ages and gender, Asian students generally found the method to be more useful than did UK students.*

Introduction

Novak (1993) first used concept mapping to understand schoolchildren's knowledge of science. Since then concept maps have been used extensively to assist students' to learn meaningfully in many disciplines (Novak and Gowin, 1984). They have also been used in organising, planning and displaying information, such as a lecture, a topic, a course and an entire curriculum, so providing an overview of a domain of knowledge (Canas, 2003; Plotnick, 2001).

A concept map provides a visual, conceptually transparent graphical representation of a person's understanding of the whole or a part of a knowledge domain at a particular period in time (Novak and Gowin, 1984). Ovals are used to represent concepts and labelled lines are used to represent the relationship between concepts (Plotnick, 2001; Novak and Gowin, 1984). A central concept provides the context for a map and examples are used to help clarify the meaning of concepts (Canas, 2003; Novak and Gowin, 1984).

Concept maps provide a framework (or scaffolding) for the learner and educator to mentally interact with the subject matter (Canas, 2003, p. 9), to structure the subject matter (Jonassen and Grabowski, 1993) and make knowledge explicit (Novak and Gowin, 1984). Schau and Mattern (1997) use the term 'connected understanding' citing the cognitive education literature (e.g. Ausubel, 1963; Farnham-Diggory, 1992 and Anderson, 1995) which lead us to believe that knowledge must be organised if it is to be learned successfully and accessible from long-term memory (Pendley *et al.*, 1994, p. 1). Concept mapping provides such a method to organize knowledge.

Despite the widespread use of concept mapping within natural science education, it is not widely known in the accounting area and its use within accounting education is limited. There have been relatively few reported uses of concept mapping in accounting education (Hackner and Tschudi, 1994; Leauby and Brazina, 1998; Chen and Ching, 2003; Maas and Leauby, 2005). This paper's contribution is to extend its application within an accounting education context by focusing upon how concept maps can be used to enhance students' learning by evaluating student-prepared concept maps and reporting feedback of its use with two large groups of students. Other papers have focused on how concept mapping might be introduced in accounting education and/or applied with a small student group. This paper also shows how concept mapping can be used at different levels (i.e. curriculum, topic and activity) within a final year financial accounting theory course as compared with Maas and Leauby (2005) who used it within an introductory accounting course.

This paper is divided into a number of sections. The first section shows how an accounting-based concept map might be constructed. The second section shows how this construction process is firmly rooted in Ausubel's theory of meaningful learning. The third section consists of a literature review, which focuses upon the use of concept mapping in educational contexts and supports a constructivist epistemology. The fourth section describes the context of this study, a final year undergraduate financial accounting theory course component. The fifth section reviews examples of student-prepared concept maps according to the criteria discussed in the previous sections. The sixth section reports students' assessment of the usefulness of concept mapping in enhancing their learning, from both quantitative and qualitative perspectives. Finally, conclusions are outlined, together with limitations of the study and areas for future research are identified.

How to Construct a Concept Map

The process of constructing concept maps can be conceptualised as a series of interconnected stages. To illustrate the construction process we will consider the initial map used with my final year accounting undergraduate degree students at the University of Hull as shown in Figure 1.

First, a central concept or theme is identified, such as 'financial accounting theories' and placed near the top of the page. A concept is defined as *regularities in real world objects and events* (Novak and Gowin, 1984, p. 4). Novak and Gowin (1984, p. 24) contend the notion of a concept 'is a simple but profound idea' which students need to understand; everything 'they hear, see, touch, or smell [and taste] is in part dependent upon the concepts they have in their minds'. Concepts are seen as building blocks, which allow knowledge to be constructed.

Second, important concepts related to the central concept are identified. For example, positive, normative and critical financial accounting theories, as well as the financial reporting world representing users of financial reports and regulators amongst others, and value judgments, are seen as important concepts related to 'financial accounting theories'. A careful study of the relevant literature should reveal the key concepts related to a particular knowledge domain. This choice of concepts will inevitably be a personal one as we all perceive specific knowledge domains as being composed of different concepts, which can change as our understanding develops. Disagreement concerning the choice of which concepts to include might occur with 'others' claiming some important concepts are missing while 'trivial' concepts have been included. The beauty of concept mapping is that the creator(s) are forced to be explicit about which concepts (and linkages between concepts) they view as important and are therefore accountable for the way they perceive the specific knowledge domain. The concept map shown in

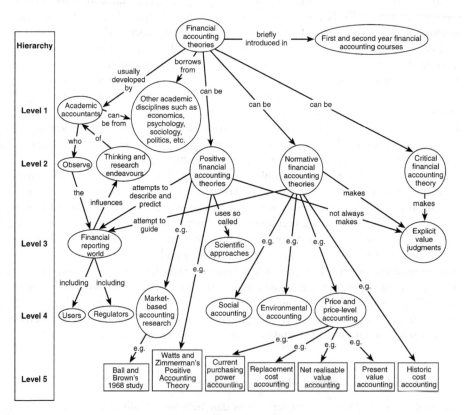

Figure 1. Instructor-prepared concept map of a four-week financial accounting theories component

Figure 1 is used as a *road map* for a four-week financial accounting theory component, so no attempt is made at a comprehensive coverage of the knowledge domain, even though concept mapping could be used for this objective.

Third, illustrative examples of concepts are identified. For example, current purchasing power accounting, replacement cost accounting, net realisable value accounting and present value accounting are all examples of price and price-level accounting. These examples are put in square boxes so they can be differentiated from concepts. Just what is classified as a concept or an example is a function of the knowledge domain focused upon.

Fourth, concepts (and examples) are arranged into a hierarchy with more-inclusive concepts placed towards the top of the map and less-inclusive concepts lower down (Novak and Gowin, 1984, p. 16). In addition, related concepts should be positioned close together. For example, the normative financial accounting theories concept is seen as including social, environmental and price and price-level accounting. We will have more to say about these hierarchical relationships in the next section of the paper, when we consider the learning theory underlying concept mapping.

Fifth, related concepts and examples are connected with lines, using a few words to specify the nature of the relationship. In this way, linking phrases and concepts conveys meaningful constructs or propositions, which are seen as basic units of knowledge (Novak and Gowin, 1984, p. 17). For example, positive accounting theories attempt to describe and predict the financial reporting world. This proposition is made up of the two concepts 'positive accounting theories' and 'financial reporting world' and the linking words 'attempts to describe and predict'. So propositions as shown in concept maps allow meaning to be shared among academic staff (e.g. in curriculum development), between academic staff and students, and among students to enhance learning and improve teaching effectiveness. Such visualized representations can facilitate learning, as humans are highly-skilled at identifying and using patterns (Novak and Gowin, 1984, p. 28). Arrows are used to indicate the direction of the relationships and, as we will see when reviewing student-prepared concept maps, such relationships between concepts might be valid or invalid.

Sixth, 'cross-links' are used, to link different sections of the map (Novak and Gowin, 1984, p. 37). For example, critical and normative accounting theories make underlying value judgments explicit while this is not always the case with positive accounting theories. Cross-links are highly valued as they are seen as evidence of creative thinking and learners should be praised for making such connections (Novak and Gowin, 1984). Finally, the map is reviewed for completeness and accuracy.

The construction process is greatly facilitated by the use of concept mapping computer packages such as *Inspiration* (www.inspiration.com/uk) used to prepare the concept maps shown in this paper or *Cmap* (www.cmap.ihmc.us). Such packages facilitate efficient map construction and revision. It is unlikely that a first attempt at preparing a concept map will be the final product, as numerous revisions are usually needed. To ensure concepts (and examples) are arranged in an appropriate hierarchy, related concepts are positioned close together, appropriate linkages are made with a minimum of overlapping linkages, correct spelling, and so on (Novak and Gowin, 1984, p. 35). Such software allows concepts to be moved around the map with established linkages (i.e. the constructors' thought processes) maintained. New concepts and examples can be added and the map reconstructed to ensure an appropriate fit.

Students (and faculty) are likely to require training in the construction of concept maps and access to appropriate software. Such training might be included in an initial study skills module and staff training provision. Maas and Leauby (2005) suggest a step-by-step process to introduce concept mapping to accounting students. The software is not difficult to master and reasonable proficiency can be attained within a few hours. *Cmap* is free software while *Inspiration* software is available on 30-day free trial and then costs £69 for a single licence. Some universities make concept mapping software available as part of their learning support.

Concept maps share similarities with other forms of visual representation, such as:

- Flow-charts, used widely in accounting and auditing contexts as time- efficient methods of showing how to apply standards and procedures, presenting a comprehensive structure of alternative actions or considerations, and as an aid to decision-making (Buckner *et al.*, 1978; Porter *et al.*, 2003). They differ from concept maps, as their aim is to present the sequence in which tasks need to be performed, rather than a conceptual hierarchy (Novak and Gowin, 1984, p. 37).
- Organization charts that show how administrative units are linked within an organizational hierarchy. While a hierarchical structure is used, no attempt is made to represent concepts and linkages are rarely labelled (Novak and Gowin, 1984, p. 37).
- Decision trees, which show options within a decision-making process (Novak and Gowin, 1984, p. 37). Decision trees are widely used in a financial management and management accounting context, so hierarchical features are present, but only as they relate to the focused decision. While concept maps can be used to assist in decision-making, particularly when used in curriculum design, this paper is primarily concerned with their use in a learning context.
- Cycles, which show how ideas or procedures are related in a circular manner, such as a working capital cycle. Concept maps are used occasionally to show feedback loops. For example, in Figure 1 'academic accountants' are seen as 'observing' the 'financial reporting world' which influences their 'thinking and research endeavours'.

Perhaps, the closest and most widely known visual representations akin to concept maps are Buzan's *mind maps* (Buzan, 2002). Concept maps differ from mind maps in that the former are explicitly based upon Ausubel's theory of meaningful learning, which stresses a hierarchical relationship among concepts. Mind maps, like concept maps, have numerous linkages from individual ideas or concepts but emphasise a radiant rather than hierarchical structure.

Ausubel's Theory of Meaningful Learning

Concept mapping is based upon David Ausubel's theory of meaningful learning proposed in 1963 and further developed in 1968 and 1978. Ausubel contends that we think in terms of concepts in contrast to behavioural approaches, which attempt to explain learning in terms of laws that focus upon functional relationships between environmental stimuli and behavioural responses (McShane, 1991, p. 3). Such behavioural approaches emphasised experimental and quantitative approaches to the study of learning (Khan, 1993, p. 47). Ausubel's theory, as interpreted by Novak (1998), emphasised the need to study learning in its natural, classroom environment using qualitative research methods (Khan, 1993, p. 51).

Ausubel stresses the importance of meaningful learning as opposed to rote learning (Novak and Gowin, 1984). Meaningful learning is non-arbitrary, non-verbatim and involves the substantive incorporation of new knowledge into an individual's cognitive structures (Novak, 1998). Students must make a conscious or active effort to build upon what they already know (i.e. their existing knowledge). That is, they must develop a cognitive disposition to construct linkages between new and existing concepts to anchor the new knowledge with existing knowledge. The material must be in itself inherently meaningful and presented in clear language (Novak and Gowin, 1984). Concept maps provide evidence of meaningful learning having taken place, as the students are required to describe explicitly what they have learnt and how it relates to what they already known (Khan, 1993, p. 48).

The alternative to meaningful learning is rote learning, the memorisation of fragmentary facts. As no significant connection with existing knowledge is made, such learning is unsatisfactory and does not stay with us for extended periods. Novak and Gowin (1984, p. 8) contends that, in most instances, rote learning can only be recalled over an 8-week period and within that period the ability to recall diminishes.

Ausubel *et al.* (1978) argue that much school learning is of the rote kind, with the memorisation of teacher-presented or textbook facts and definitions without any serious consideration of their meaning. In addition, verbatim repetition is often required for assessment. A learner can easily come to believe that such rote learning is the accepted method of learning and so inhibit meaningful learning taking place.

Novak (1998) considers rote and meaningful learning as two ends of a learning continuum, with individual learning and teaching methods falling along the continuum. He also contends that the rote—meaningful learning continuum is different from, but associated with, reception and discovery learning. Reception and discovery learning are seen as strategies that can be used to encourage students to learn. The former involves 'information being provided directly to the learner' while discovery learning in its pure form involves the learner identifying and selecting which information is to be learnt (Novak and Gowin, 1984, p. 7). This reception-discovery choice of learning strategy also forms a continuum, where the instructor exercises increasingly less influence and the learner greater influence over what is learnt as we move from reception to discovery learning. Discovery learning, by allowing students to select the information they choose to learn, can increase their motivation to learn meaningfully. However, it is generally accepted that, while students should have some say in what they learn, they do not have the knowledge to specify an entire curriculum and, as learning can be idiosyncratic, discovery learning can be extremely time-consuming. Also, in accounting (and in many other) educational contexts, considerable information is specified in syllabuses of professional accountancy bodies and, in the UK, in the Quality Assurance Agency for Higher Education (2000).

Novak and Gowin (1984, p. 8) show the rote-meaningful and reception and discovery learning continuums in graphical form. Figure 2 adapts their presentation to an accounting (and business) education context.

Certain aspects of accounting can lead to rote learning (including the memorization of which accounts to debit and credit for common transactions, such as sales and purchases). While a certain amount of rote learning is useful, such as the recall of multiplication tables, learning should be mainly meaningful (Novak and Gowin, 1984). Concept maps facilitate meaningful learning as learners are required to be explicit about and required to justify relationships between concepts (Novak and Gowin, 1984).

The main principle of Ausubel's learning theory will be illustrated using the concept map show in Figure 1.

Ausubel (1968, p. vi) considers the 'most important single factor influencing learning is what the learner already knows'. The instructor should 'ascertain this and teach him [sic] accordingly'. Ausubel uses the term 'subsumption' to describe the process of relating less inclusive concepts to more inclusive concepts. Therefore, subsumption is used to create a 'hierarchical structure' of concepts, starting with the most general or inclusive, through the less inclusive to the least inclusive and most specific (Novak and Gowin, 1984).

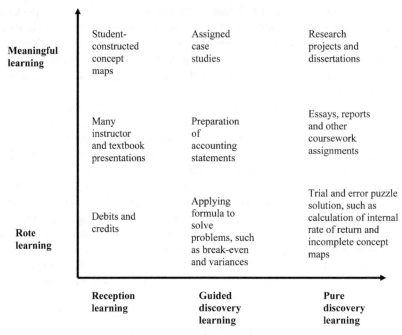

Figure 2. Novak and Gowin's (1984, p. 8) rote-meaningful and reception-discovery learning continuums, adapted to an accounting (and business) education context. *Source:* Adapted from Novak and Gowin's (1984, p. 8).

For example, financial accounting theories represent a knowledge framework, and so are the most general or inclusive concept (i.e. hierarchy 1) in Figure 1. Positive, normative and critical financial accounting theories are less inclusive concepts (i.e. hierarchy 2). Price and price-level accounting theories being examples of normative accounting theories are less inclusive, so they are positioned at a lower level.

The process of adding new concepts (to the map) and the resultant changes to the meaning of existing concepts (i.e. those already included in the map) is called 'progressive differentiation' and shows how knowledge deepens (Novak and Gowin, 1984). Progressive differentiation is a dynamic process, which we are constantly undertaking in all aspects of our lives (Khan, 1993, p. 76). For example, the addition of social and environmental accounting (as examples of other normative financial accounting theories) changes the meaning of what we understand by normative financial accounting theories. This process of progressive differentiation reveals which are the key concepts within any knowledge structure.

The process of adding a new concept to a person's existing cognitive structure is not simply the addition of a new piece of knowledge. Its addition requires the learner to consider new (and sometimes novel) linkages with existing concepts, which modify not only the meaning of the new concept and those it is linked to, but also the meaning of other concepts within the knowledge structure (Novak and Gowin, 1984). Ausubel calls this process 'integrative reconciliation'. Integrative reconciliation leads to all concepts within the framework taking on (marginally or significantly) new meanings. Khan (1993, p. 77) argues that the addition of a new relationship can 'enable the learner to see everything in a new light'. For example, the learner might consider the nature of 'value judgments' made by proponents of different financial accounting theories and see that, while normative and critical financial accounting theories usually make their underlying value judgments explicit, this is rarely so with positive financial accounting theories. This is particularly so when linkages are made between two previously unconnected sections of the knowledge structure. Such linkages on concept maps are called cross-links. Novak and Gowin (1984) attach great importance to such cross-links as they represent important evidence of integrative reconciliation. Students should be encouraged to search for significant cross-links between sections of their concept maps and to label these cross-linkages appropriately. They can represent significant similarities or differences between previously unreconciled or distinct bodies of knowledge (Khan, 1993, p. 78).

Concept maps are never complete as learning about any knowledge structure is an ongoing process. Researchers and learners can discover new concepts, linkages between concepts and illuminating real world examples. Khan (1993, p. 77) draws the corollary between life-long learning and meaningful learning. He describes meaningful learning as an evolutionary process of defining and redefining concept meaning and sometimes the complete overthrow of an accepted knowledge structure, when a new concept significantly changes the meaning of established concepts. The ideas of Thomas Kuhn's (1962) periods of 'normal science' and 'paradigm shifts' are clearly embedded within Ausubel's theory of meaningful learning and Novak's concept mapping process.

We have seen how Novak's concept mapping approach can be used as a practical, graphical application of Ausubel's theory of meaningful learning. Concept mapping attempts to mirror how people naturally learn and can be used as a proxy to represent what the learner knows (Khan, 1993, p. 56). Of course, it is not possible to know exactly what the learner knows as this knowledge is (currently) invisible, living inside the brain.

The quantity and quality of relevant concepts, linkages and examples are seen as the extent to which learning has occurred (Khan, 1993, p. 53). Novak and Gowin (1984) operationalize (or measure) such learning by adopting the following scoring conventions when assessing concept maps:

- Valid relationships between concept = 1 point each.
- Valid hierarchy = 5 points each.
- Valid cross-link = 10 points each.
- Examples = 1 point each.

Novak and Gowin (1984) place considerable weight upon the learner developing valid cross-links and, to a lesser extent, on determining a valid hierarchy as evidence of meaningful learning. Khan (1993, p. 74) contrasts this emphasis with that of a more behaviourally oriented hierarchical model, such as Bloom's (1956) *taxonomy*, which implies that learners need to progress from lower to higher order levels. Novak and Gowin (1984) consider students capable of performing at all learning levels within the same learning task, such as the construction of a concept map.

A further method of assessing students' concept maps is to compare their maps against one constructed by a subject expert (e.g. the instructor). A score can be derived by dividing the student's map score by the instructor's map score and multiplying by 100% (Novak and Gowin, 1984). This opens up the possibility of students scoring in excess of 100%.

Literature Review

Novak and Gowin (1984) contend that concept mapping addresses four objectives (or commonplaces) of education (Schwab, 1973). These objectives address issues relating to enabling learners to learn, enabling teachers to teach, developing effective curricula, and ensuring educational governance. We will use these four commonplaces as a structure to consider the uses of concept mapping and related research within accounting and other educational contexts. However, as the focus of this paper is the use of concepts maps to enhance learning, this commonplace will be considered in considerably more detail than the other three

Enabling Teachers to Teach

Novak and Gowin (1984) first used concept maps constructed by the teacher from student interviews to assess students' learning, pre- and post-instruction. They were in effect using the technique as a qualitative research tool. Rowell (1978) also used the technique to assist in the planning, undertaking and analysis of interviews as well as to plan his lectures. Moreover, the technique has considerable potential as an aid to theory construction (Novak and Gowin, 1984) and research project management (Canas, 2003, p. 19). A number of studies have also utilised concept mapping within the context of teacher training and development (Bolte, 1999; Butler, 2001; Beyerbach and Smith, 1990; Ferry et al., 1998; Jones et al., 1999: Lang and Olson, 2000; Winitzky and Kauchak, 1995; Morine-Dershimer, 1993).

Enabling Learners to Learn

After focusing upon instructor-prepared concept maps, Novak and Gowin (1984) then required their students to construct their own concept maps. This involved some training in how to construct concept maps but it was considered essential to support a constructivist or active approach to learning, allowing students to engage actively with the material. Learning was not considered a 'spectator sport' as students were required to construct knowledge. This involved them in the translation of a lecture or text material, often presented in a linear structure, into a hierarchical structure and thinking of new relevant concepts, and linking words to represent new relationships (Khan, 1993, p. 75). Such a process, embedded in a constructivist epistemology, was considered essential for meaningful learning to occur. Students when preparing concept maps, need to understand that they have to make choices regarding which concepts to include, their hierarchical positioning, which concepts to link together to form constructs, which linking words to use, the direction of the relationship and which examples to include. Different choices will lead to different nuances of meaning. As Novak and Gowin (1984, p. 35) state:

> Concept maps are ... powerful tools for observing the nuances of meaning a student holds for the concepts embedded in his or her map.

Positivist epistemologies might lead students to believe that there are single correct choices for all these decisions. Therefore, constructivist epistemology embraces multiple perspectives reflecting the constructor's world-views.

Novak and Gowin (1984) argue that the process of constructing concept maps is more important than the produced map, as it is within the constructing process that learning takes place. The resulting map should be seen as nothing more than how one person understands a particular conceptual framework at one period. The teacher's role is seen as the manager of an educational environment in which meaningfully learning can take place. In fact, Khan (1993, p. 65) argues that concept maps can be used to move students from rote to meaningful learning strategies. Leauby and Brazina (1998) support this view.

There is a considerable amount of evidence that concept mapping, when used appropriately, enhances learning (Horton *et al.*, 1993; Esiobu and Soyibo, 1995; Schmid and Telaro, 1990; Bascones and Novak, 1985; Pankratius, 1990; Czerniak and Haney, 1998; Jegede *et al.*, 1990; Nicoll *et al.*, 2001; Chang *et al.*, 2001). Many of these studies use the scoring system developed by Novak and Gowin (1984) which is described above.

Students have been required to construct concept maps in a number of educational contexts:

- To assess the quantity and quality of learning, students have been required to construct their own maps at the end of a unit of learning. Chen and Ching (2003) found concept mapping to be a useful method to improve the learning and problem solving skills of 50 Taiwanese university freshmen after five weeks of accounting learning.
- Concept maps are also useful as a reflective or feedback tool after students experience an educational event such as a lecture, tutorial or reading an article, to help students monitor their learning (Canas, 2003, p. 8). The process of constructing a concept map forces students to reflect upon their learning, so consolidating the educational experience. For example, Canas (2003, p. 22) suggests using concept mapping to structure notes and Gurley (1982) has used concept maps as tutorial and homework assignments to summarise book chapters. Such exercises occasionally revealed inadequacies in lectures and texts.
- Other studies have required students to construct maps before and after instruction. Pre-maps are used to represent initial knowledge structures and post-maps to represent new learning. Pre-maps are particularly important within Ausubel's learning theory, as learners arrive at a learning experience (e.g. lecture, tutorial, reading a text) with a massive body of knowledge, which needs to be built upon if meaningful learning is to occur (Novak and Gowin, 1984, p. 22). Concept maps provide an educational device for externalising this cognitive position (Novak and Gowin, 1984, p. 40). Novak and Gowin (1984, p. 34) do not claim any student-prepared concept map is an exact representation of their cognitive position, but do claim that it can be a useful approximation.
Hackner and Tschudi (1994) required students in an MBA accounting module to produce such maps, one at the start and one at the end of the module. Of the five students who participated in the research, three produced final maps. While Hackner and Tschudi (1994) report significant changes in students' understanding of accounting, the limited sample size limits the usefulness of their results. A number of other studies outside an accounting context have used this approach (Songer and Mintzes, 1994; Adamczyk and Wilson, 1996; Pearsall *et al.*, 1997; Hoz *et al.*, 2001).
- Student-produced concept maps have been used to diagnose learner mis-understandings (Edwards and Fraser, 1983; Gonzalez, 1997; Regis and Albertazzi, 1996; Trowbridge and Wandersee, 1994; Kinchin et al., 2000). Concept maps are explicit pictures of concepts and constructs held; hence, they allow a dialogue between learners and educators concerning the validity of identified linkages and the absence of possible linkages. Such a dialogue can reveal misunderstandings and so lead to new learning (Novak and Gowin, 1984, p. 19). Novak and Gowin (1984, p. 20) define misunderstanding as linkages between two concepts that are generally 'unaccepted (but not necessarily wrong) interpretation' or ones that miss the key notion of how the two concepts are related. Unlike most other learning methods, concept maps allow such misconceptions to be exposed. Such misconceptions are particularly damaging if they occur at or near the beginning of a unit of study since they can form part of the foundations upon which future learning is constructed.

- Concept maps can be used to negotiate meaning through effective communication between learners (Novak and Gowin, 1984, p. 20). Learners can construct maps individually and then compare maps discussing key differences. Alternatively, a group of learners can construct a map together, jointly deciding which concepts to use, where in the hierarchy they are to be placed, and how they are to be connected. Learners must be committed to the process of collaboration if meaning is to effectively negotiated (Van Neste-Kenny *et al.*, 1998, p. 23). Novak and Gowin (1984, p. 20) are clear that negotiating meaning is a different but related activity to 'learning' since learning is an individual activity for which only the individual is responsible. The old adage of leading a horse to water but only the horse can decide drink is an important principle, which both learner and educator need to understand, and which strikes at the heart of the student-educator relationship.
- The process of constructing a concept map can help clarify the role and responsibilities of the student and educator in any educational environment (Novak and Gowin, 1984, p. 23). The learner actively seeks to understand shared meaning, while the educator seeks to share their meaning of some knowledge domain. As we are all learners, this interaction can also lead educators themselves to adapt their meaning of a knowledge domain. Therefore, all student-educator interaction should occur in an environment of mutual respect and cooperation (Novak and Gowin, 1984, p. 23).
- Novak and Gowin (1984, p. 23) claim that the construction of concept maps requires learners to function at all six levels of Bloom's learning objective hierarchy and a particularly useful device to encourage students to perform at the three highest levels (of analysis, synthesis and evaluation).
- Concept maps can be used to assist students in extracting meaning from texts (Novak and Gowin, 1984, p. 43). Accounting students frequently complain that financial accounting theory texts and articles can be difficult to read and understand. The problem can be traced to the author(s)' making implicit assumptions that are not held by the learner (Novak and Gowin, 1984, p. 44). They are assuming that the reader understands certain key concepts that they consider, often implicitly, to be well understood within a specific research community. As learners are often not (or new) members of such research communities, meaningful learning is halted. Novak and Gowin (1984, p. 43) call this the 'meaning impasse' cycle (i.e. something is difficult to understand so it is hard to read, and as it is hard to read it is difficult to understand). This 'impasse' will continue until some intervention occurs to break the cycle. The process of constructing a concept map can identify where such impasses might lie and where the need for intervention highlighted.
- Concept maps can be used prior to undertaking practical exercises to ensure that students understand what they are supposed to do. Much of accounting education involves students engaging in numerical procedures such as recording transaction, preparing of single company and group financial statements and budgets, investment appraisal, and so on. Students can find themselves undertaking such work without a clear understanding of what they are supposed to do or what the end product means. Students might be successful in following a series of procedures (e.g. entering transactions) with little understanding of what they are doing. This is similar to how Novak perceived many natural science students undertook experiments (Novak and Gowin, 1984, p. 47). Using concepts maps to understand the major concepts and relationships prior to undertaking such practical exercises can make such procedures meaningful (Novak and Gowin, 1984, p. 48).
- Concept maps can be used to identify the main ideas, and how these ideas are interrelated, when planning a piece of independent work, such as an assignment, essay,

report, project, dissertation or research paper. While writing is necessarily a linear activity involving the sequencing of concepts, constructs and examples, starting with a hierarchical structuring can be useful (Novak and Gowin, 1984, p. 53). Some concept mapping software, such as *Inspiration*, allows the text within a concept map to be converted into a Word text file, using the logic of the constructed map to structure the text. This paper was constructed using this method. This facility addresses the frequently encountered student question: where do I start?

- Canas (2003, p. 7) has suggested using concept maps as alternatives to traditional writing assignments. As concept maps require students to use less text than traditional written assignments (such as essays or reports), issues of plagiarism might be less frequently encountered. The process might also be less discriminatory towards students originating from countries and educational environments where English is not the first language.

- Canas (2003, p. 9) has suggested that concept mapping might be particularly useful to lower-ability learners who have difficulty in structuring knowledge. As the process of constructing a concept map forces students to consider explicitly the structure of a knowledge domain, it might be useful to learners who originate from educational environments where knowledge structure has not been emphasized.

- Other learning-based uses for concept mapping include brainstorming and other knowledge elicitation and exploration exercises (Plotnick, 2001), structuring and solving problems, assisting critical thinking, and as a revision aid (Canas, 2003).

Concept mapping is not without its problems. We have already noted the time needed to train students in the use of concept maps and the difficulties of constructing such maps without appropriate computer software. Pattern *et al.* (1986) contend there are many different types of relationships between concepts (e.g. conceptual, prepositional, procedural, cause-effect, etc.) which students might have difficulty in identifying and so inhibit their ability to construct effective concept maps. Stewart *et al.* (1979, p. 174) doubt students' ability to identify more subtle linkages. Horton *et al.* (1993), when reviewing several concept mapping research studies, report that the benefits can diminish when they are used in conjunction with other learning approaches.

Effective Organization of the Curriculum

Concept maps have been used in curriculum development in a number of academic disciplines: quantitative methods in business (Canas and Arguea reported in Canas, 2003, pp. 30–31); applied statistics (Schau and Mattern, 1997); nursing (Daley, 1996 and All, 1997); medicine (Edmondson, 1994; 1995); teacher training (Martin, 1994); structural geology (Clark and James, 2004); health education (Wooley, 1995). Figure 1 is an example within an accounting curriculum context. Curricula concept maps can be used to create a sense of coherence and conceptual integration across the curriculum, which allows students to focus upon key themes (Edmondson, 1995, p. 785). They can assist students in avoiding getting lost in a morass of facts and ideas and enable concepts to be prioritised in some order of importance. Textbooks naturally present material from the perspective taken by their authors and may not provide such a 'connected understanding' (Schau and Mattern, 1997, p.171). This is particularly relevant to a UK-based financial accounting theory component, where many of the texts and readings are authored and oriented in a US context. The onus is placed on the educator to provide such topic coherence, which concept mapping can be used to facilitate.

Effective Educational Governance

The context in which learning and teaching take place can be referred to as 'milieu' (Schwab, 1973) or [educational] 'governance' (Gowin, 1981) and covers such aspects as the hard and soft resources which provide the context of any educational environment. Computer and library facilities, web sites, and other administrative support facilities are important examples. We have already outlined the importance of suitable software to support the construction of concept maps. Another potentially important use of concept maps is to facilitate web site design for educational institutions, faculties, departments, programmes, modules and module components (Conklin, 1987).

Using Concept Maps to Learn Financial Accounting Theory

This paper describes and assesses a specific application of concept mapping in a financial-accounting theory component lasting four weeks within a final year financial accounting module. This contributes towards the core of an undergraduate accounting degree at a UK university. The financial accounting theory component represents 40% of a 20-credit one-semester module. This section describes how concept mapping was integrated into this component, the next section illustrates this application by examining three student-constructed maps, and the final section contains students' assessment of the usefulness of concepts maps in enhancing their learning experience.

While the application was focused upon financial accounting at the undergraduate level, concept mapping could be applied to any accounting and business-related knowledge domain at any level. Many of the lessons learnt from the particular application described in this paper might relate to such other potential applications.

Novak and Gowin (1984, pp. 25–34) suggest many different ways of introducing concept maps to students. The two student cohorts that participated in this application had slightly different introductions. The 2004–05 student cohort was introduced to the method in the opening financial accounting theory lecture and tutorial using a similar concept map to that shown as Figure 1. The 2005–06 student cohort was introduced to the method within a second year research methods module designed to support independent study and, particularly, a final year project, and then reintroduced in the final year in a similar way to the previous year's cohort.

The financial accounting component was chosen as an appropriate knowledge domain to apply concept mapping for a number of reasons:

- Experience has shown that students initially find financial accounting theory to be difficult and challenging since their previous financial accounting studies have focused mainly upon record-keeping, financial statement construction and the regulation of financial reporting. A different mind-set is required in thinking about and assessing theoretical constructs to that involved in numerically based topics. Concept mapping was selected as previous research had identified its usefulness in supporting learners to think in conceptual and theoretical terms (Novak and Gowin, 1984).
- For the 2005–06 student cohort it was possible to build upon students' previous use and experiences of concept mapping in a previous year's research methods module. Time was spent in one lecture and two tutorials in preparing/discussing concept maps.
- The author was involved in teaching the final year financial accounting theory component and the second year research methods module, thereby facilitating access to appropriate student groups. Gummerson (2000) considers access to appropriate

participants to be a significant research issue and it should not be underestimated in any empirically based research study.

- The process of conceptually mapping a subject such as financial reporting is useful in assisting students to understand its cumulative nature. Certain, often sizable, units of learning need to be learnt before other units. For example, basic double entry bookkeeping and financial statement construction need to be understood before proceeding to study group accounting. Also, financial reporting, like other accounting (e.g. management accounting) and non-accounting subjects (e.g. research methods), has a significant dualist nature. Students are asked to master mechanical procedures (e.g. double entry bookkeeping) while also understanding philosophical issues (e.g. the nature of what is and is not an asset, liability, etc.). There is a considerable danger that students may internalise the mechanical aspect of the subject and fail to appreciate the need for some philosophical underpinning. Concept mapping can assist students in incorporating the latter into their financial reporting 'world view' (Gowin, 1981).

Table 1 outlines the structure of the financial accounting theory component as presented to students, with the integration of concept mapping shown in italics. No attempt was made to cover all aspects of the financial accounting theory knowledge domain in the revised module, which was first implemented in 2003. Topics were chosen as important examples, which sample the domain. Concept mapping was used in the following points in the components:

- In the initial lecture, students were provided with an instructor-prepared concept map, which summarized some of the major ideas of the component and was similar to the one shown as Figure 1. The map was used in the lecture to provide an outline of the component and to (re)introduce students to the nature of concept maps. It was then used in supporting tutorials to discuss the major concepts embedded in the component. Novak and Gowin (1984, p. 42) draw the analogy between a curriculum and driving a motor car from one end of the country to the other. First, you need a country map to identify major roads; then you need more detailed maps of counties and cities at which you plan to stop along the way. This is supported by Ausubel's idea of using 'advanced organizers' to enhance meaningful learning; that is providing an overview of the material to be learnt (Canas, 2003, p. 29). More specific topic-based maps were used later in the component.
- The second half of the initial lecture also covered Watts and Zimmerman's *Positive Accounting Theory* (1986) as a specific example of a positive accounting theory. At the end of the lecture, students were presented with a instructor-prepared incomplete concept map of the theory as shown in Figure 3. Students were required to match the concept labels listed at the foot of the page with those omitted from the map (Canas 2003, p. 9). The map was constructed as described in the previous section and then selected concept labels were extracted from their appropriate map location and listed at the foot of the page before being given to students. Students were tasked with undertaking prescribed reading on positive accounting theory, identifying the appropriate concepts from the listing for each of the thirteen missing concepts (labelled A to M) and encouraged to add their own concepts to the map based upon their own perceptions and reading.

About 75% of students attempted to complete the map before attending the tutorial. However, very few added their own concepts. In the following tutorial students first participated in a quiz to identify the missing concepts. The quiz approach proved to be a less threatening environment than the one in which students were immediately required

Table 1. Four-week financial accounting theory component

Week	1	2	3	4
2-hour lecture	Introduction to financial accounting theory using *a concept map similar to Figure 1 as a handout.* Watts and Zimmerman's positive accounting theory	Market-based accounting research.	Price and price-level accounting.	Environmental and social accounting. Critical accounting.
Pre-tutorial work	Read Chapter 7 in Deegan and Unerman (2006) *and complete an incomplete concept map of Watts and Zimmerman's positive accounting theory*	Read Chapter 10 in Deegan and Unerman (2006) *and construct a concept map of market-based accounting research.*	Read Chapter 5 in Deegan and Unerman (2006) and complete a numerical Question on replacement cost and current purchasing power accounting.	Read Chapters 9 and 12 in Deegan and Unerman (2006).
Tutorial work (note: tutorials took place in the week following the lecture)	*Discussion of the nature of financial accounting theories and Watts and Zimmerman's positive accounting theory, using concept maps.*	*Discussion of student-constructed concept maps of market-based accounting research.* *These student-constructed concept maps were taken in by the lecturer and formative feedback provided in following week's tutorial.*	Discussion of numerical question on replacement cost and current purchasing power accounting, with particular focus on the underlying assumptions used in determining asset valuation, profit and capital maintenance.	Discussion of specific examples of environmental and social accounting from the above reading. Discussion of students' thinking and feelings towards critical accounting.

Note: The earlier edition of the Deegan and Unerman (2000) text was used with the student cohorts in this study.

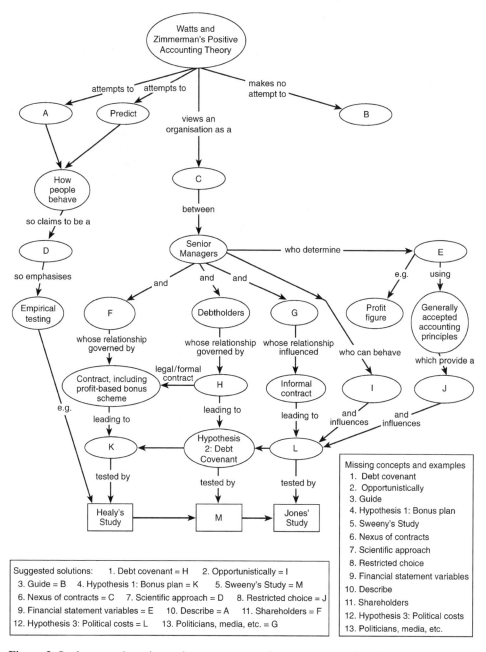

Figure 3. Student exercise using an instructor-prepared concept map at the activity level of Watts and Zimmermsan's positive accounting theory

to discuss elements of the theory and most students took part. Students were asked to justify their decision and, in some cases, where there was disagreement an argument resulted. After participating in the quiz students seemed more willing to volunteer their thoughts and engage in discussion regarding the nature of Watts and Zimmerman's *Positive Accounting Theory*. This was the case for many students who generally were unwilling to answer such discursive questions and appeared to spring from the positive feedback and confidence they received from identifying an appropriate concept label. The quality of discussion within the tutorial was thus enhanced. The exercise also enabled issues involved in the process of constructing concept maps to be addressed.

- The second week's lecture covered market-based accounting research. Students were then required to read relevant sections of the component text and prepare their own concept map of this knowledge domain. These concept maps were collected by the instructor and formative feedback provided in the following week's tutorial. As the map did not form part of the students' formal assessment, only about one third of the students chose to prepare concept maps and only one student used concept mapping software to construct his map. This poor participation rate was similar to that experienced on other modules when asking busy students to undertake work outside of class, which is not formally assessed. Three of these student prepared concept maps are shown as Figures 4, 5 and 6 and discussed in the next section of this paper. Market-based accounting research was selected as this topic is generally considered difficult and it was hoped that the process of constructing concept maps would lead to better understanding.

  The transition from asking students to consider an instructor-prepared concept map, with or without concept labels omitted, to asking them to prepare their own maps should not be underestimated. The former can be seen either as a passive activity or as a quiz exercise and is supportive of rote learning, as shown in Figure 2. Asking students to construct their own concept map from a lecture, with or without providing them with a concept listing, requires them to engage in meaningful learning, also shown in Figure 2. If students are not used to engaging in meaningful learning this type of activity can be a daunting experience. Therefore, it is not surprising that so few students took up the challenge.
- The 2005-6 examination contained the following question:

Critically analyses and assess the knowledge structure of either Watt's and Zimmerman's *Positive Accounting Theory* or market-based accounting research.

This represented one of three financial accounting theory questions from which students had to answer one. The question was worded in such a way that student could answer it with or without providing a concept map. Of the 38% of students who answered this particular question, only 11% chose to provide a concept map. This lack of willingness to provide a concept map might be considered disappointing, but can be explained by the relatively limited exposure to concept mapping and the limited time available in the examination (only 40 minutes were available to answer this question). A significant danger in requiring students to prepare a concept map in an examination is the encouragement to learn an instructor-prepared concept map by rote, which defeats the constructivist learning objects of the approach. The time involved in constructing a concept map should not be underestimated and its use for assessment purposes should perhaps be restricted to assignments.

Assessment of Student Prepared Concept Maps

This section will review three student-prepared concept maps shown as Figures 4, 5 and 6, prepared by students from the 2005–06 cohort, according to the criteria discussed in the concept mapping literature relating to enabling learners to learn. All three maps were prepared during the week following a lecture on market-based accounting research and they may have been influenced by reading the appropriate chapter in the core text. Students were provided with a list of concepts relating to the lecture topic to encourage them to prepare their own concept map, but told that they were free to add any other concepts

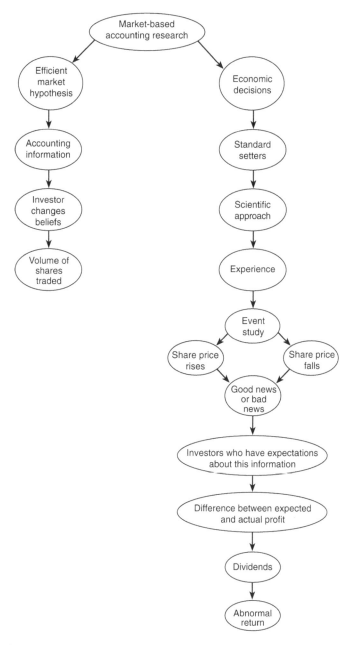

Figure 4. Student W's concept map of market-based accounting research

they considered relevant. The student-constructed maps were collected in by the instructor prior to an instructor-prepared map of the knowledge domain being distributed. The instructor-prepared map is shown as Figure 7. See Maas and Leauby (2005) for illustrations of more instructor-prepared concept maps.

The concept maps shown in Figures 4 and 5 were produced by individual students, and were selected as examples of poorly- and well-constructed concept maps. Two students

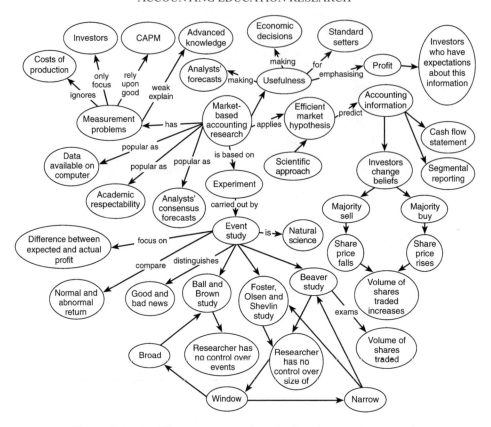

Figure 5. Student X's concept map of market-based accounting research

working together produced the concept map shown in Figure 6, even though such group work was not explicitly requested. The two students said that they negotiated the meaning of concepts by firstly writing the concepts on separate small oval-shaped pieces of paper, then jointly arranging them on a blank sheet of paper before gluing them down and inscribing the linkages.

These student maps were hand drawn and transcribed into electronic form by the author for presentation in this paper. Students were informed that I was assessing the use of concept mapping in their module and permission was obtained to use these maps in this paper. In order to protect the students' identities we will refer to the student who constructed the concept map shown in Figure 4 as Student W, the student who constructed the concept map shown in Figure 5 as Student X, and the students who constructed the concept map shown in Figure 6 as Students Y and Z. The comments below relate in the main to the three maps exhibited.

The hierarchical positioning of concepts seems to be a difficult idea for many students to operationalize. Student W produced a largely linear map with little attempt at showing hierarchical relationships and linkages between some closely-related concepts, such as volume of shares traded and share prices rising or falling. The map constructed by Student X, while not positioning the central concept, market-based accounting research at the top of the page, has some hierarchy features. The map produced in collaboration between Students Y and Z positions the central component in the middle of the page in Mind Map style.

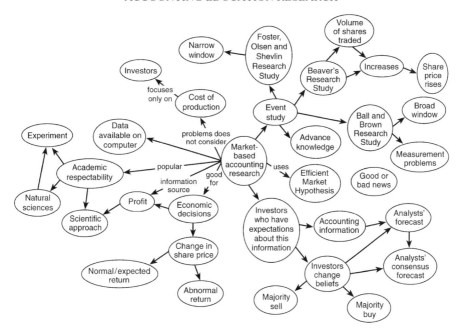

Figure 6. Student's Y and Z concept map of market-based accounting research

Weaker students tended to use a limited number of concepts and linkages, often with no attempt at labelling links between concepts. For example, Student W has used 17 concepts and 17 links with no attempt to label the linkages. Stronger students tended to use a greater range of concepts and linkages, showing greater progressive differentiation, but still omitted to label all relationships. For example, Student X has used 41 concepts and 43 linkages labelling 21 linkages, and Students Y and Z have used 33 concepts and 37 linkages labelling only six linkages.

While most students identified some important constructs, such as the link between market-based accounting research and the efficient market hypothesis, stronger students produced a richer set of constructs. For example, Student X and Students Y and Z both included weaknesses of market-based studies, such as ignoring costs of producing accounting information and only focusing upon investors. Student X's critique was more extensive including identifying measurement problems in using the Capital Asset Pricing type models (to measure companies' expected returns).

However, even the better students' concept maps did show some misconceptions, which were addressed in the following tutorial. For example, Student X considered market-based accounting research to be based upon experiments carried out by event studies. While event studies do have some similarities to experiments, the researcher is unable to exert the same control over the treatment variable (i.e. the announcement of profit/earnings) in the same way that a natural scientist can exercise control in a laboratory experiment. Such examples not only revealed students' misconceptions but also inadequacies in the supporting lecture and/or text(s). In this case, the instructor drew an analogy between events studies and experiments, but failed to emphasize clearly the key differences. Student-constructed maps enabled such misconceptions to be identified (and addressed) which would otherwise be difficult to diagnose.

Weaker students tended to omit examples of concepts, while stronger students included them. For example, Student W did not include any examples, while both Student X and

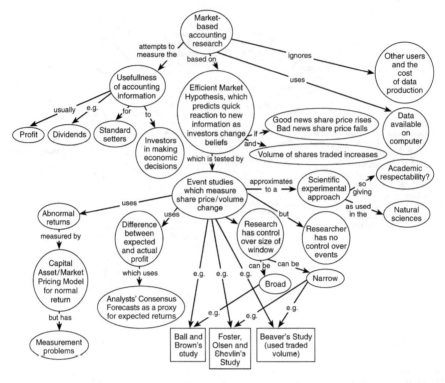

Figure 7. Instructor-prepared concept map at the topic level of market-based accounting research

Students Y and Z identified a number of empirical research studies (e.g. the Ball and Brown 1968 study) as examples of the concept, event studies, thus showing a better understanding of the concept.

While students were not requested to construct pre-maps to identify their level of understanding prior to instruction in the new knowledge domain, the efficient market hypothesis was revised early in the market-based accounting research lecture. The concept of efficient markets had been included in a second year financial management module and now students were being asked to see the concept had important implications in a financial reporting context. Building upon prior knowledge is a key feature of Ausubel's *Theory of Meaningful Learning* and Novak's concept mapping application of that theory.

The concept map constructed by Student X shows (s)he is operating at all six levels of Bloom's learning hierarchy and particularly at the three highest levels of analysis, synthesis and evaluation. The elements or concepts of the knowledge domain have clearly been examined in detail, combined together to form a coherent whole, and the latter's usefulness addressed.

The instructor-prepared concept map of the market-based accounting research knowledge domain is shown as Figure 7.

Students' Evaluations of Concept Mapping

Students were asked to evaluate the usefulness of concept mapping as a method of assisting their learning. All students attended one lecture, which illustrated the use of concept mapping, and two tutorials where they were required to use concept maps. This was considered sufficient exposure for them to make informed judgments regarding its usefulness. Students were then required to complete a one-side A4 questionnaire in the final tutorial. For the 2004–05 cohort 77 students attended and completed the questionnaire (69% of those registered for the module), while for the 2005–06 cohort 92 students attended and completed the questionnaire (63% of those registered for the module). Therefore, all students who attended completed the survey with a few students omitting to answer some of the discursive questions as expected (Saunders *et al.*, 2000). The short questionnaire was handed out, completed and returned at the end of a teaching session; students did not go away and complete the questionnaire. The completed questionnaires were collected in by the students' representatives to preserve anonymity and given to the researcher.

The questionnaire consisted of both qualitative and quantitative question sections and took about five minutes to complete.

Qualitative Analysis

The qualitative section (Section A on the questionnaire) simply asked students to note down the two things they liked best, and the two things they liked least, about concept mapping. Some of the students' responses are recorded below after being grouped around key issues.

Many students (2004–05: 27%, and 2005–06: 26%) found the method relatively ease to use and enabled them to better understand complex issues. The ability to summarise the main ideas of a topic in a single side of A4 paper was consider particularly important by some students. Examples of students' responses were:

> Easy to follow rather than pages and pages of lecture notes.
> Easy to understand the relationship between different concepts.

A considerable number of students (2004–05: 24%, and 2005–06: 26%) viewed the technique as a support for learning, which was consistent with prior research in other subject areas. Examples of students' responses were:

> Allows me to reflect on things learnt and gives a clear understanding of the topic
> Makes us use our brain in the tutorial.
> Made me think and made me link one thing with another, visually.
> Makes you think about the reading you have done and highlights the key points.
> It gave a short and discrete answer—which you can build on later.

Some students (2004–05 16%, and 2005–06: 12%) liked the visual representation of the topic. Examples of students' responses were:

> Eye catching.
> It will help you look at things in a bigger picture.

Some students (2004–05: 11%, and 2005–06: 2%) also appreciated the holistic view of the topic. Examples of students' responses were:

> Provides a whole picture of the topic taught.
> Showed a good overview of whole topic to help understanding.

Some students (2004–05: 10%, and 2005–06: 3%) focused upon the assistance concept mapping might provide with memorising and revising topics for the examination. Examples of students' responses were:

> It's the same method I use for revising
> Maps are useful to have as a revision tool before the exam.

Students were then asked to note the two things they liked least about concept mapping. The key issues were as follows.

In 2004–05, the focus was more on interpreting instructor-prepared concept maps than preparing their own maps. Therefore, more attention was paid to the way some of the concept maps were presented, and 19% of students made such comments, which included:

> Font type too small.
> Background on some maps can be hard to read.

These issues were largely resolved in the maps used with the 2005–06 cohort as no significant adverse comments were received. However, the 2004–05 responses show that educators need to spend some time becoming proficient in preparing concept maps and using concept-mapping software, prior to using it in their teaching.

A number of students (2004–05: 21%, and 2005–06: 28%) found some of the maps to be too complex, containing too many concepts and so difficult to understand. The brevity of the words used (seen as an advantage by some students) compounded the problem. Examples of students' responses were:

> Can be difficult to follow with lines going everywhere.
> Sometimes confusing to follow if the map is too large.
> A bit busy and hard to digest sometimes.
> Not enough detailed information/explanation.
> Hard to understand without explanation.
> Difficult to go back and remember what was talked about—should have made more notes.

Future research might consider the balance between concepts maps containing too many and too few concepts and what is considered a suitable amount of explanation.

Some students (2004–05: 6%, and 2005–06: 10%) commented that initial training in concept mapping would have been useful. Examples of students' responses were:

> It took time to get used to.
> Initially confusing—but OK after discussion.

This problem can be addressed by providing short concept mapping learning units (possibly within a study skills module) located early on in a degree programme.

A final criticism (2004–05: 5%, and 2005–06: 8%) focused upon the fit between concept mapping and the module's assessment criteria. Examples of students' responses were:

> I don't think it is very useful for our exams.
> Too time-consuming, particularly in an exam situation.

While the assessment for this module did not explicitly require students to construct concept maps, it did not explicitly exclude them. A few students did provide concept maps in their assessments and they were given credit for doing so. A future development might require the preparation of concept maps as part of the module assignment rather than in an examination.

Quantitative Analysis

The quantitative section (Section B of the questionnaire) asked students to respond to three questions. The questionnaire given to 2004–05 students requested responses on a three-point scale ('very useful', 'quite useful' and 'of no use'), while the questionnaire given to 2005–06 students requested responses on a five-point scale ('strongly agree', 'agree', 'uncertain', 'disagree' and 'strongly disagree'). The statistical analysis is presented in Tables 2 to 5.

Table 2 reports the results of students' responses to three quantitative questions on the usefulness of concept mapping. The vast majority of 2004–05 students (96%) found concept mapping to be at least 'quite useful' as a visual representation for their learning. The results for the 2005–06 cohort were similar in that 83% of students agreed or strongly agreed with the statement that concept mapping was a 'useful' visual representation for learning in a particular knowledge domain. Similarly, the vast majority of 2004–05 students (92%) found concept mapping to be at least 'quite useful' in helping them identify any misunderstandings they might have had from the lectures. The results for the 2005–06 cohort were similar in that 63% of students agreed or strongly agreed with the statement that concept mapping was 'helpful' in identifying any misunderstandings they might have had from the lectures. In addition, the vast majority of 2004–05 students (99%) found concept mapping to be at least 'quite useful' in enabling them to better understand the structure of a topic. The results for the 2005–06 cohort were similar in that 84% of students at agreed or strongly agreed with the statement that concept mapping was 'useful' in enabling them to understand the structure of a topic. Responses to all three questions/statements were statistically significant at the 0.1% level, when tested using Chi-squared statistics.

Table 3 reports the results of students' responses to the three quantitative questions on the usefulness of concept mapping by gender. The 2004–05 data was analysed using Mann-Whitney tests as there were only three categories while the 2005–06 data was analysed using t-tests as there were five categories (Black, 1999). None of the statistical tests proved significant, so it is concluded that gender is not a significant discriminating factor in assessing the usefulness of concept mapping.

Table 4 reports the results of students' responses to the three quantitative questions on the usefulness of concept mapping by age. Again, the 2004–05 data was analysed using Mann–Whitney tests as there were only three categories while the 2005–06 data was analysed using t-tests as there were five categories (Black, 1999). As only one of the six statistical tests proved significant at the 5% level, and this was only just significant, it is concluded that age as defined in this study (i.e. students aged 21 and under compared with students aged 22 and over) is not a significant discriminating factor in assessing the usefulness of concept mapping.

Table 5 reports the results of students' responses to the three quantitative questions on the usefulness of concept mapping analysed between UK and Asian students. Students from other countries were involved in the study but their numbers were too small to be analysed statistically. Again, the 2004–05 data was analysed using Mann-Whitney tests, as there were only three categories while the 2005–06 data was analysed using t-tests as there were five categories (Black, 1999). While the vast majority of both 2004–05 UK and Asian students found concept maps to be at least 'quite useful' as a visual representation to support their learning, significantly more UK students (at the 5% level) found it to be 'very useful' as a visual representation useful for their learning. However, no significant difference was found when this question was asked of students from the 2005–06 cohort. It should be remembered that the 2004–05 students did not

Table 2. Results of students' responses to quantitative questions on the usefulness of concept mapping for both 2004–05 and 2005–06 cohorts

	Student cohort 2004–05 Relative frequency (n = 77)				Student cohort 2005–06 Relative frequency (n = 92)					
	Very useful	Quite useful	Of no use	Chi-sq. statistic	Strongly agree (= 5)	Agree (= 4)	Uncertain (= 3)	Disagree (= 2)	Strongly disagree (= 1)	Mean and Chi-sq. statistic
Usefulness of concept mapping as a visual representation for your learning	47	49	4	31.089[a]	13	70	9	6	2	3.85 144.087[a]
Usefulness of concept mapping in helping you identify any misunderstandings you might have had from the lectures	30	62	8	35.418[a]	8	55	27	7	3	3.57 85.868[a]
Usefulness of concept mapping in enabling you to understand better the structure of the topic	61	38	1	42.709[a]	28	56	9	4	3	4.01 90.935[a]

[a]Statistically significant at the 0.001 level.

Table 3a. Results of students' responses to quantitative questions on the usefulness of concept mapping by gender for the 2004–05 cohort

Quantitative questions	Female students: relative frequency (n = 43)			Male students: relative frequency (n = 34)			Mann–Whitney statistic
	Very useful	Quite useful	Of no use	Very useful	Quite useful	Of no use	
How useful was concept mapping as a visual representation for your learning?	45	50	5	47	50	3	733.500
How useful was concept mapping in helping you identify any misunderstandings you might have had from the lectures?	29	64	7	33	59	8	729.000
How useful was concept mapping in enabling you to better understand the structure of the topic?	69	31	0	50	47	3	605.500

Table 3b. Results of students' responses to quantitative questions on the usefulness of concept mapping by gender for the 2005–06 cohort

	Female students: relative frequency (n = 57)						Male students: relative frequency (n = 35)						
	Strongly agree (= 5)	Agree (= 4)	Uncertain (= 3)	Disagree (= 2)	Strongly disagree (= 1)	Mean	Strongly agree (= 5)	Agree (= 4)	Uncertain (= 3)	Disagree (= 2)	Strongly disagree (= 1)	Mean	t-test
Concept mapping provided a useful visual representation for my learning	14	67	10	9	0	3.86	11	74	6	3	6	3.83	0.171
Concept mapping was useful in helping me identify misunderstandings I might have had from the lectures	4	61	26	9	0	3.60	15	44	29	3	9	3.53	0.324
Concept mapping was useful in enabling me to understand better the structure of a topic	32	51	10	5	2	4.05	23	63	6	3	5	3.94	0.543

Table 4a. Results of students' responses to quantitative questions on the usefulness of concept mapping by age for the 2004–05 cohort

Quantitative questions	Students aged 18–21: relative frequency (n = 42)			Students aged 22 and over: relative frequency (n = 35)			Mann–Whitney statistic
	Very useful	Quite useful	Of no use	Very useful	Quite useful	Of no use	
How useful was concept mapping as a visual representation for your learning?	53	45	2	37	57	6	530.500
How useful was concept mapping in helping you identify any misunderstandings you might have had from the lectures?	26	67	7	34	57	9	551.000
How useful was concept mapping in enabling you to better understand the structure of the topic?	74	24	2	43	57	0	467.000[a]

[a]Significant at the 0.05 level.

Table 4b. Results of students' responses to quantitative questions on the usefulness of concept mapping by age for the 2005–06 cohort

	Students aged 18–21: relative frequency ($n = 38$)						Students aged 22 and over: relative frequency ($n = 54$)						
	Strongly agree ($= 5$)	Agree ($= 4$)	Uncertain ($= 3$)	Disagree ($= 2$)	Strongly disagree ($= 1$)	Mean	Strongly agree ($= 5$)	Agree ($= 4$)	Uncertain ($= 3$)	Disagree ($= 2$)	Strongly disagree ($= 1$)	Mean	t- test
Concept mapping provided a useful visual representation for my learning	16	71	5	8	0	3.78	11	68	11	6	4	3.95	−1.015
Concept mapping was useful in helping me identify misunderstandings I might have had from the lectures	11	58	18	10	3	3.53	5	53	34	4	4	3.63	−0.554
Concept mapping was useful in enabling me to understand better the structure of a topic	29	50	10	8	3	4.06	28	59	7	2	4	3.95	0.542

Table 5a. Results of students' responses to quantitative questions on the usefulness of concept mapping for UK and Asian 2004–05 cohort

Quantitative based questions	UK students: relative frequency ($n = 35$)			Asian students: relative frequency ($n = 30$)			Mann–Whitney statistic
	Very useful	Quite useful	Of no use	Very useful	Quite useful	Of no use	
How useful was concept mapping as a visual representation for your learning?	62	38	0	34	59	7	412.000[a]
How useful was concept mapping in helping you identify any misunderstandings you might have had from the lectures?	35	55	10	22	71	7	539.500
How useful was concept mapping in enabling you to better understand the structure of the topic?	69	28	4	56	44	0	527.000

[a]Significant at the 0.05 level.

Table 5b. Results of students' responses to quantitative questions on the usefulness of concept mapping for UK and Asian 2005–06 cohort

	UK students: relative frequency (n = 34)						Asian students: relative frequency (n = 46)						
	Strongly agree (= 5)	Agree (= 4)	Uncertain (= 3)	Disagree (= 2)	Strongly disagree (= 1)	Mean	Strongly agree (= 5)	Agree (= 4)	Uncertain (= 3)	Disagree (= 2)	Strongly disagree (= 1)	Mean	t-test.
Concept mapping provided a useful visual representation for my learning	12	70	6	9	3	3.79	15	70	11	4	0	3.96	−0.902
Concept mapping was useful in helping me identify misunderstandings I might have had from the lectures	3	55	24	12	6	3.36	11	61	26	2	0	3.80	−2.280[a]
Concept mapping was useful in enabling me to understand better the structure of a topic	20	53	12	9	6	3.74	37	59	2	2	0	4.30	−2.745[b]

[a]Statistically significant at the 0.05 level.
[b]Statistically significant at the 0.01 level.

have as much encouragement to prepare their own concept maps as did students in the 2005–06 cohort, so this significant result should be treated with caution.

The most interesting differences between UK and Asian students are to be found in the other questions asked of the 2005–06 student cohort. Significantly more Asian than UK students considered concept mapping to be 'useful' in identifying misunderstandings derived from instructors (at the 5% level) and in enabling a better understanding of the structure of a topic (at the 1% level). Maybe this is due to the restricted use of words in concept maps compared with other learning sources such as lectures and texts. As Asian students are less likely to be familiar with the subtle use of English language, particularly when describing theoretical constructs, the brevity of word use in concept maps may be of significant assistance. However, as Asian students tend to be more respectful towards their elders (and teachers), and to be more inclined not to offend by saying they liked the technique; these results could be culturally related. In addition, as these results are based upon a relatively small number of students studying at one university and no such significant results were found with the previous year's cohort of students, they should be read with caution.

Conclusions, Limitations and Areas for Future Research

This paper was divided into a number of sections. After a brief introduction, the first section showed how an accounting-based concept map might be constructed by students and educators to provide a visual, conceptually transparent graphical representation of an individual's understanding of a particular knowledge domain (Novak and Gowin, 1984).

The second section showed how this construction process was firmly rooted in Ausubel's theory of meaningful learning. This theory places great emphasis upon the hierarchical structure of concepts, which is particularly relevant to many areas of accounting where students need to understand certain concepts and topics before progressing to more advanced concepts and topics.

The third section consisted of a literature review of the use of concept mapping in accounting and in other educational contexts. While concept mapping has been used extensively in many disciplines, it has received little attention within accounting education.

The fourth section described the context of this study, which consisted of two cohorts of final year undergraduate students studying financial accounting theory. Both student- and instructor-constructed concept maps were used in the study. The use of instructor-prepared concept maps, with concepts omitted, proved popular tutorial quiz exercises and increased the quantity and quality of participation. However, students were less willing to construct their own concept maps and engage in meaningful learning.

The fifth section assessed student-prepared concept maps according to the criteria discussed in the previous sections. Most students were able to build upon aspects of their prior knowledge. However, stronger students used a greater range of concepts, a richer set of linkages and more examples than weaker students, showing greater progressive differentiation and an ability to operate at all six of Bloom's learning levels when preparing concept maps. Nevertheless, even the stronger students omitted to label all linkages and all students found the notion of the hierarchical positioning of concepts to be a difficult idea to operationalize. Concept maps were useful in diagnosing students' misconceptions for all students, which could then be addressed in tutorials. Even the stronger students' concept maps revealed some misconceptions, some of which could be traced to inadequacies in lectures.

The sixth section reported students' assessments of the usefulness of concept mapping in enhancing their learning, from both quantitative and qualitative perspectives. Answers to qualitative questions indicated that many students found concept mapping relatively easy to use, enabled them to gain a better understanding of complex issues, liked the visual representation and holistic view and so supported their learning. However, educators need to become proficient in constructing maps and using appropriate software, not making the maps too complex, providing students with some initial training in the technique (maybe in a study skills module) and considering the fit between using the techniques as a learning and assessment tool. The effect of these quality criteria in the production of concept maps could be examined in further research studies.

Answers to the quantitative questions showed the vast majority of students agreed that concept mapping was useful in providing a visual representation to enhance their learning; useful in helping them identify misunderstandings; and in understanding the structure of a topic area. While no significant differences were found in the usefulness of the method for students of different ages and gender, Asian students appeared to find the method to be more useful than UK students did in identifying misunderstandings derived from the lectures and in enabling them to understand the structure of a topic better. This might be due to the brevity of words used in concept maps and may be linked to their limited proficiency in the English, (which is likely to be their second language). However, due to potential confounding cultural factors and the limited number of students in this study, this result should be treated with caution.

While all students had considerable exposure to, and opportunities to use, concept mapping there was no requirement for it to be used in their formal assessment, which can be considered a limitation of the study. Another limitation was the inability to compare students' responses to performance criteria such as ability since it was decided to make student feedback anonymous to encourage participation. Requiring students to prepare concept maps using appropriate computer software would also assist the construction and assessment process. Another limitation is that the paper does not address the key question of whether concept mapping helps students to learn better. Future research studies might assess the usefulness of concept mapping in enhancing learning when all students are required to answer questions based upon 'incomplete' concept maps (see Figure 3) or prepare their own concept maps as part of their formal assessment.

Other areas for future research are as follows. Researchers might also like to investigate the use of concept mapping with different types of student (such as students from different cultures and educational backgrounds, with different learning styles, those who prefer using visual techniques, and with students of different levels of ability). In addition, researchers might like to consider how to encourage students to structure concepts into appropriate hierarchical levels. Concept maps could alternatively be used to show how standard accounting texts structure specific accounting topics to assess the quality and possible inadequacies of explanation. Another potentially interesting line of inquiry would be to consider the maximum number of concepts that students can adequately consider on single maps, and what constitutes adequate levels of explanation. In addition, educators are encouraged to experiment using concept maps in combination with other learning and teaching methods or prior to undertaking practical/quantitative accounting exercises to see if their use can make such procedures more meaningful. The need to maximise the time available for students to become familiar with using concept mapping might be addressed by introducing the technique in a first year study skills module.

This paper has shown how concept mapping, a method widely known in science education but not widely known in accounting education, can be used to encourage students to learn meaningfully. The paper's contribution is to extend its application within an accounting education context by having focused upon how concept mapping can enhance students' learning as evidenced by the evaluation of student-prepared concept maps, by showing how concept maps have been used at different levels within a course (i.e. curriculum, topic and activity) and reporting feedback of its use with two groups of students. While a financial accounting theory component was used as illustration, the method is as applicable and offers considerable potential to enhance other areas of accounting education. While the majority of students in this study liked the approach, there have not been enough studies in the accounting education domain to be confident that it really does lead to improvements in learning. Therefore, accounting educators are encouraged to experiment with concept mapping within their teaching, assessment and curriculum development practices and assess how it might encourage their students to learn meaningfully.

References

Adamczyk, P. and Wilson, M. (1996) Using concept maps with trainee physics teachers, *Physics Education*, 31(6), pp. 374–381.

All, A. C. (1997) Cognitive/concept mapping: a teaching strategy for nursing, *Journal of Advanced Nursing*, 25(6), pp. 1210–1219.

Anderson, J. R. (1995) *Learning and Memory: An Integrated Approach* (New York: John Wiley).

Ausubel, D. P. (1963) *The Psychology of Meaningful Verbal Learning* (New York: Grune and Stratton).

Ausubel, D. (1968) *Educational Psychology: A Cognitive View* (New York: Holt, Rinehart and Winston).

Ausubel, D. P., Novak, J. D. and Hanesian, H. (1978) *Educational Psychology: A Cognitive View*, 2nd edn (New York: Holt, Rinehart and Winston).

Ball, R. and Brown, P. (1968) An empirical evaluation of accounting income numbers, *Journal of Accounting Research*, 6(2), pp. 159–178.

Bascones, J. and Novak, J. D. (1985) Alternative instructional systems and the development of problem solving skills in physics, *European Journal of Science Education*, 7(3), pp. 253–261.

Beaver, W. (1968) The information content of annual earnings announcements, *Journal of Accounting Research*, 6(Supplement), pp. 67–92.

Beyerbach, B. and Smith, J. (1990) Using a computerized concept mapping program to assess pre-service teachers' thinking about effective teaching, *Journal of Research in Science Teaching*, 27(10), pp. 961–971.

Black, T. R. (1999) *Doing Quantitative Research in the Social Sciences* (London: Sage).

Bloom, B. S. (Ed.) (1956) *Taxonomy of Educational Objectives: The Classification of Educational Goals, Handbook 1: Cognitive Domain* (New York: McKay).

Bolte, L. A. (1999) Using concept maps and interpretive essays for assessment in mathematics, *School Science and Mathematics*, 99(1), pp. 19–30.

Buckner, K. C., Dillon, R. D. and Hermanson, R. H. (1978) Mapping the method: FASB No. 13, accounting for leases. *The Woman CPA*, 40(3), pp. 8–11.

Butler, A. (2001) Pre-service music teachers' conceptions of teaching effectiveness, microteaching experiences, and teaching performance, *Journal of Research in Music Education*, 49(3), pp. 258–272.

Buzan, T. (2002) *How to Mind Map* (London: Harper Collins).

Canas, A. J. (2003) *A Summary of Literature Pertaining to the use of Concept Mapping Techniques and Technologies for Education and Performance Support* (Florida: The Institute for Human and Machine Cognition).

Chang, K. E., Sung, Y. T. and Chen, S. F. (2001) Learning through computer-based concept mapping with scaffolding aid, *Journal of Computer Assisted Learning*, 17(1), pp. 21–33.

Chen, M. and Ching. S. (2003) Using concept mapping in accounting learning, *Delta Pi Epsilon Journal*, 45(2), pp. 133–145.

Clark, I. F. and James, P. R. (2004) Using concept maps to plan an introductory structural geology course, *Journal of Geoscience Education*, 52(3), pp. 224–230.

Conklin, E. J. (1987) Hypertext: an introduction and survey, *Computer*, 20(9), pp. 17–41.

Czerniak, C. M. and Haney, J. J. (1998) The effect of collaborative concept mapping on elementary preservice teachers' anxiety, efficacy, and achievement in physical sciences, *Journal of Science Teacher Education*, 9(4), pp. 303–320.

Daley, B. J. (1996) Concept maps: linking nursing theory to clinical nursing practice, *The Journal of Continuing Education in Nursing*, 27(1), pp. 17–27.

Deegan, C. (2000) *Financial Accounting Theory* (Sydney: McGraw-Hill).

Deegan, C. and Unerman, J. (2006) *Financial Accounting Theory: European Edition* (Maidenhead: McGraw-Hill).

Edmondson, K. M. (1994) Concept maps and the development of cases for problem-based learning, *Academic Medicine*, 69(2), pp. 108–110.

Edmondson, K. M. (1995) Concept mapping for the development of medical curricula, *Journal of Research in Science Teaching*, 32(7), pp. 777–793.

Edwards, J. and Fraser, K. (1983) Concept maps as reflectors of conceptual understanding, *Research in Science Education*, 13(1), pp. 19–26.

Esiobu, G. and Soyibo, K. (1995) Effects of concept and Vee mapping under three learning modes on students' cognitive achievement in ecology and genetics, *Journal of Research in Science Teaching*, 32(9), pp. 971–995.

Farnham-Diggory, S. (1992) *Cognitive Processes in Education*, 2nd edn (New York: Harper Collins).

Ferry, B., Hedberg, J. and Harper, B. (1998) How do pre-service teachers use concept maps to organise their curriculum content knowledge?, *Journal of Interactive Learning Research*, 9(1), pp. 83–104.

Foster, G., Olsen, C. and Shevlin, T. (1984) Earnings releases, anomalies, and the behavior of security returns, *The Accounting Review*, 59(4), pp. 574–603.

Gonzalez, F. M. (1997) Evidence of rote learning of science by Spanish university students. *School Science and Mathematics*, 97(8), pp. 419–428.

Gowin, D. B. (1981) *Educating* (Ithaca, NY: Cornell University Press).

Gummerson, E. (2000) *Qualitative Methods in Management Research* (London: Sage).

Gurley, L. I. (1982) *Use of Gowin's Vee and Concept Mapping Strategies to Teach Responsibility for Learning in High School Biological Sciences* (Unpublished PhD thesis, Cornell University).

Hackner, E. and Tschudi, F. (1994) Note on cognitive mapping in the teaching of management, *Scandinavian Journal of Management*, 10(3), pp. 281–289.

Horton, P.B., McConney, A.A., Woods, A.L., Senn, G.L. and Hamelin, D. (1993) An investigation of the effectiveness of concept mapping as an instructional tool, *Science Education*, 77(1), pp. 95–111.

Hoz, R., Bowman, D, and Kozminsky, E. (2001) The differential effects of prior knowledge on learning: a study of two consecutive courses in earth sciences, *Instructional Science*, 29(3), pp. 187–211.

Jegede, O. J., Alaiyemola, F. and Okebukola, P. A. (1990) The effect of concept mapping on students' anxiety and achievement in biology, *Journal of Research in Science Teaching*, 27(10), pp. 951–960.

Jonassen, D. H. and Grabowski, B. L. (1993) *Handbook of Individual Differences: Learning and Instruction* (Hillsdale, NJ: Lawrence Erlbaum Associates).

Jones, M. G., Carter, G. and Rua, M. (1999) Children's concepts: tools for transforming science teachers' knowledge, *Science Education*, 83(5), pp. 545–557.

Khan, K. M. (1993) *Concept Mapping as a Strategy for Teaching and Developing the Caribbean Examinations Council (CXC) Mathematics Curriculum in a Secondary School* (Unpublished PhD Thesis, The University of the West Indies).

Kuhn, T. (1962) *The Structure of Scientific Revolutions* (Chicago, IL: University of Chicago Press).

Kinchin, I., Hay, D. and Adams, A. (2000) How a qualitative approach to concept map analysis can be used to aid learning by illustrating patterns of conceptual development, *Educational Research*, 42(1), pp. 43–57.

Lang, M. and Olson, J. (2000) Integrated science teaching as a challenge for teachers to develop new conceptual structures, *Research in Science Education*, 30(2), pp. 213–224.

Leauby, B. A. and Brazina, P. (1998) Concept mapping: potential uses in accounting education, *Journal of Accounting Education*, 16(1), pp. 123–138.

Martin, D. J. (1994) Concept mapping as an aid to lesson planning: a longitudinal study, *Journal of Elementary Science Education*, 6(2), pp. 11–30.

Maas, J. D. and Leauby, B. A. (2005) Concept mapping—exploring its value as a meaningful learning tool in accounting education, *Global Perspectives in Accounting Education*, 2, pp. 75–98.

McShane, J. (1991) *Cognitive Development: An Information Processing Approach* (Oxford: Basil Blackwell).

Morine-Dershimer, G. (1993) Tracing conceptual change in preservice teachers, *Teaching and Teacher Education*, 9(1), pp. 15–26.

Nicoll, G., Francisco, J. and Nakhleh, M. B. (2001) An investigation of the value of using concept maps in general chemistry, *Journal of Chemical Education*, 78(8), pp. 1111–1117.

Novak, J. D. (1993) How do we learn our lesson? Taking students through the process, *Science Teacher*, 60(3), pp. 50–55.

Novak, J. D. (1998) *Learning, Creating, and Using Knowledge: Concept Maps® as Facilitation Tools in Schools and Corporations* (Mahwah, NJ: Lawrence Erlbaum Associates).

Novak, J. D. and Gowin, D. B. (1984) *Learning How to Learn* (New York: Cambridge University Press).

Pankratius, W. J. (1990) Building an organized knowledge base: concept mapping and achievement in secondary school physics, *Journal of Research in Science Teaching*, 27(4), pp. 315–333.

Pattern, J. V., Chao, C. I. and Reigeluth, C. M. (1986) A review for sequencing and synthesising instruction, *Review of Educational Research*, 56(4), pp. 437–471.

Pearsall, N. R., Skipper, J. and Mintzes, J. (1997) Knowledge restructuring in the life sciences: a longitudinal study of conceptual change in biology, *Science Education*, 81(2), pp. 193–215.

Pendley, B. D., Bretz, R. L. and Novak, J. D. (1994) Concept maps as a tool to assess learning in chemistry, *Science Education*, 71(1), pp. 9–15.

Plotnick, E. (2001) A graphical system for understanding the relationship between concepts, *Teacher Librarian*, 28(4), pp. 42–45.

Porter, B., Simon, J. and Hatherley, D. (2003) *The Principles of External Auditing*, 2nd edn (Chichester: John Wiley).

Quality Assurance Agency for Higher Education. (2000) *Accounting Benchmarking Statement* (Gloucester: QAA).

Regis, A. and Albertazzi, P. G. (1996) Concept maps in chemistry education, *Journal of Chemical Education*, 73(11), pp. 1084–1088.

Rowell, R. M. (1978) *Concept mapping: evaluation of children's science concepts following audio-tutorial instruction* (Unpublished doctoral dissertation, Cornell University: New York).

Saunders, M., Lewis, P. and Thornhill, A. (2000) *Research Methods for Business Students* (London: Financial Times Prentice Hall).

Schau, C. and Mattern, N. (1997) Use of map techniques in teaching applied statistics courses, *The American Statistician*, 51(2), pp. 171–175.

Schmid, R. F. and Telaro, G. (1990) Concept mapping as an instructional strategy for high school biology, *Journal of Educational Research*, 84(2), pp. 78–85.

Schwab, J. J. (1973) The practical 3: transformation into curriculum, *School Review*, 81(August), pp. 501–522.

Songer, C. and Mintzes, J. (1994) Understanding cellular respiration: an analysis of conceptual change in college biology, *Journal of Research in Science Teaching*, 31(6), pp. 621–637.

Stewart, J., Van Kirk, J., and Rowell, R. (1979) Concept maps: a tool for use in biology teaching, *American Biology Teacher*, 41(3), pp. 171–175.

Trowbridge, J. E. and Wandersee, J. (1994) Identifying critical junctures in learning in a college course on evolution, *Journal of Research in Science Teaching*, 31(5), pp. 459–473.

Van Neste-Kenny, J., Cragg, C. E. and Foulds, B. (1998) Using concept maps and visual representations for collaborative curriculum development, *Nurse Educator*, 23(6), pp. 21–25.

Watts, R. L. and Zimmerman, J. L. (1986) *Positive Accounting Theory* (Englewood Cliffs, NJ: Prentice-Hall Inc).

Winitzky, N. and Kauchak, D. (1995) Learning to teach: knowledge development in classroom management, *Teaching and Teacher Education*, 11(3), pp. 215–227.

Wooley, S. F. (1995) Behavior mapping: a tool for identifying priorities for health education curricula and instruction, *Journal of Health Education*, 26(4), pp. 200–206.

Introducing a Learning Portfolio in an Undergraduate Financial Accounting Course

GRANT SAMKIN and GRAHAM FRANCIS

University of Waikato, New Zealand

ABSTRACT *This paper evaluates changes made to the internal assessment component of a third year financial accounting course at a university in New Zealand. A learning portfolio was designed to supplement existing coursework. The aim was to engender in students a deep rather than a surface approach to learning. As a record of the students' learning, the learning portfolio was an attempt to produce an innovative development in the assessment of what was a traditionally taught financial accounting course. Within their learning portfolios, students were required to complete a number of tasks, each aimed at improving critical thinking skills and creativity. Students were also required to maintain a personal or reflective section aimed at personalising and deepening the quality of their learning.*

1 Introduction

The increasing complexity of the environment in which accountants operate has meant that, in recent years, the accounting profession has undergone significant and rapid change. Pressures facing the modern accounting professional include globalization, rapid changes in information and communication technologies, as well as the expansion of stakeholder groups, including regulators and oversight boards (IFAC, 2003, para. 17). Professional accountants are no longer solely responsible for the information needs of investors and creditors, but are seen as having a responsibility to the wider community. Coupled with this change, the growth in size and complexity of corporations has led to a proliferation of accounting standards issued by both local and international accounting standard-setting bodies.

As with other countries, New Zealand has not been immune from these changes. Of particular significance from a New Zealand perspective was a 2003 decision by the

Accounting Standards Review Board to adopt International Financial Reporting Standards (IFRS). IFRS are to be adopted by 2007, although entities were permitted to implement them from 2005 onwards. From an accounting education perspective, and the perspective of teaching financial accounting in particular, the number and complexity of financial reporting standards means that it is impractical for all of them to be covered in detail over a three or four year semesterized programme. As a result, the technical and procedural details of individual standards taught during this transition period may not necessarily be applicable in the workplace.

This situation presents a challenge to accounting educators. Consequently, a change in teaching emphasis is required to ensure that prospective accountants are equipped with the necessary skills to function effectively in this environment. Although the teaching of traditional technical accounting remains important, and its position in syllabi is emphasized by organizations such as the International Federation of Accountants (IFAC), this required shift in teaching emphasis has been recognized. Harwood (1999, p. 52) sees that there needs to be a change in focus from what teachers teach, to what students learn. The aim should be to engender life-long learning skills in students (that is, teaching students to learn how to learn). This change in emphasis is consistent with Haigh's (2001, p. 170) belief that a university education is more than mere discipline-specific training. Rather it is an encounter with new ideas and new ways of thinking and the critical assessment of these.

While the responsibility for the change in emphasis rests primarily with teachers, students must also embrace the change for it to be successful. Beattie *et al.* (1997) suggest such a change can be achieved by ensuring students take an active rather than passive role in their education. Course content and methods of instruction should be critically evaluated by teachers. At a minimum, an accounting course should be predicated on the following assumption: namely that, students are responsible for their own learning and that they should actively participate in this process.

The aim of this paper is to describe the implementation and experience of using a learning portfolio and to evaluate its impact in an undergraduate financial accounting course. In particular, the paper describes the simultaneous use of multiple strategies aimed at encouraging a deep approach to learning through the development of critical and creative thought in undergraduate financial accounting students.

Although the use of a learning journal exercise in an accounting theory course has been described by Day *et al.* (2003), and Howieson (2004) describes the implementation and use of a self-reflective learning journal in a postgraduate accounting theory course, little, if any, research on the use of learning journals in technical accounting courses has been reported. This paper attempts to establish whether the introduction of the learning portfolio into a third year undergraduate financial accounting course was successful in encouraging a deep approach to learning. It draws on extracts taken from individual portfolios maintained by students, responses to an anonymous online-administered questionnaire, and interviews with students and tutors.

This paper is structured as follows. In the next section, the background to the course is provided. Thereafter, the relationships between learning, critical and creative thinking, reflection and meta-cognition are considered. The learning portfolio and its various components are then described. Finally, the support provided to students, the assessment and the evaluation of the learning portfolio are then considered.

2   Course Background

Financial Accounting is a 200 hour, third year financial accounting course delivered at a New Zealand university. The course is primarily technical in nature and complements a

Table 1. Learning outcomes

By the end of the semester, it is expected that students will be able to:

---

1. Prepare financial reports for limited liability companies in accordance with generally accepted accounting practice and which comply with the financial reporting standards detailed in the topic list below.
2. Understand the fundamental accounting principles and practices in accounting for business combinations.
3. Prepare consolidated financial statements in accordance with generally accepted accounting practice.

---

third year accounting theory course. Its successful completion is a prerequisite for those students wishing to fulfil the New Zealand Institute of Chartered Accountants' (NZICA) educational requirements. The course objectives described in the outline are:

> ... to foster critical and independent thinking, [and to] enhance analytical ability, creativity and initiative in students. In highlighting policy issues involved in the choice of accounting methods, the [course] attempts to take students beyond a mere mastery of technical skills. Although the development of technical skills is important, students are encouraged to develop intellectual ability so as to be in a position to reflect upon current accounting practice in a critical manner.

While the objectives of the course include the fostering of critical and independent thinking, enhancing analytical ability, creativity and initiative, as a financial accounting course, the mastery of technical skills is also important. As such, the learning objectives were structured to describe the knowledge, skills, or attitudes students should possess by the end of the semester. The aim of the learning outcomes was to direct students towards what it was they should be able to accomplish by the end of the semester. The course's learning outcomes, which are in line with the NZICA's educational requirements, are detailed in Table 1.

The course is divided into 12 modules each of which is a separate topic. The topics covered in this course are detailed in Table 2. These are consistent with those covered

Table 2. Financial accounting syllabus outline

- Financial statement disclosure and events after balance sheet date
- Statement of financial performance and statement of movements in equity
- Revenue recognition including construction contracts
- Accounting for heritage assets
- Accounting for taxation
- Earnings per share
- Accounting for liabilities
- Accounting for leases
- Financial instruments
- Foreign currency transactions
- Accounting for groups
- Translating financial statements of foreign operations

---

in most New Zealand universities at either the second or third year level and represent a progression of topics covered in the first and second financial accounting courses.

Prior to making the changes to the internal assessments described in this paper, the internal assessments comprised two tests held during the fourth and tenth teaching weeks of the semester. The first test usually accounted for 40% of the internal assessment, while the second test made up the balance. These assessment items were largely summative and predominately quantitative in nature, which meant that students who found quantitative work difficult often struggled to perform in the assessments.

One factor behind the decision to introduce the learning portfolio was motivated by the experience associated with the amount of time students spent on the course. Over previous presentations of this course, it had become apparent that a large number of students failed to spend the required 200 hours on the course. Informal discussions with different students together with feedback from tutors suggested that, on average, students spent around 120 hours per semester on the course. Students often failed to complete appropriate readings prior to lectures and did not adequately complete or attempt tutorial work. Teaching staff and, in particular, those who conducted the weekly tutorials, had become disillusioned, as their role had developed into one of merely providing solutions rather than facilitating discussions or debates. Tutorial classes had become forums for 'copying down' solutions and answering the inevitable question: 'How do you get that figure?' The impression obtained from students was that lectures and lecture overheads had become substitutes for their own reading of the prescribed textbook. A recent study by Hall *et al.* (2004, p. 493) identifies a similar lack of engagement on the part of students. They suggest that this lack of engagement contributes to 'a mechanical and superficial (surface learning) approach' to studying accounting being adopted by students (see also Booth *et al.*, 1999).

Before changes were made to the course, a number of discussions were held between the course controller and a senior staff member of the Teaching Learning and Development Unit (TLDU) at the university in an attempt to develop strategies aimed at encouraging students' participation in the course. Following these discussions, it was decided that any strategies adopted or changes made to the course should not only re-energize the teaching and assessment associated with the course, but also aim to engender lifelong learning skills in students and to take responsibility for learning away from the course controller and associated support staff and to place it in the hands of the students. Any changes made to the course, therefore, would need to be consistent with the course objectives and, at the same time, be beneficial to both students and staff.

3 Approaches to Learning, Critical and Creative Thinking, Reflection and Meta-cognition

Effective learning should be an active and dynamic process. Students need to be proactive and engage personally with the subject by taking responsibility for the development of their own study habits and learning. The approaches students take to learning were initially identified in the pioneering work of Marton and Säljö (1976), and considered further by Ramsden (2003); Biggs (1987; 1989; 1993); Entwistle (1981); Beattie *et al.* (1997); and Warburton (2003). These approaches have generally been described as a deep approach to learning and a surface approach to learning. These two approaches to learning produce different qualities of learning outcome. When engaged in a deep approach to learning, a student focuses on the underlying meaning of the material studied, resulting in learning with understanding.

Table 3. Deep and surface approaches to learning distinguished

Deep approach	Surface approach
Intention to understand material for oneself through wide reading	Intention simply to reproduce parts of the content through rote learning.
Vigorous and critical interaction with content	Acceptance of ideas and information passively
Relation of ideas to previous knowledge and experience	Concentration on assessment requirements only
Use of organizing principles to integrate ideas	Lack of reflection on purpose or strategies in learning
Relation of evidence to conclusions	Routine memorization of facts and procedures
Examination of the logic of the argument	Failure to recognize guiding principles or patterns
Likely outcomes: Deep approach	Likely outcomes: Surface approach
Better retention and transfer of knowledge	Lack of engagement with the subject
Quality outcomes including sound understanding of the discipline and critical thinking skills	Reduced ability to experience high-quality learning outcomes or develop appropriate skills and competencies

A review of the literature (see, for example, Biggs, 1987 and 1989; Beattie et al., 1997; Booth et al., 1999; Ramsden, 2003; Warburton, 2003; de Lange and Mavondo, 2004; Hall et al., 2004; Elias, 2005) details the differences between a deep approach and a surface approach to learning. These differences are summarized in Table 3.

A surface approach to learning is not flexible and does not empower the student to develop a capacity to work effectively with knowledge. As the aim of this approach to learning focuses on the memorisation and reproduction of material (Sharma, 1997), students adopting a surface approach are unlikely to experience satisfactory learning outcomes, or to develop appropriate skills or competencies (Biggs, 1987, 1989; Ramsden, 2003; Sharma, 1997; Booth et al., 1999; Hall et al., 2004).

In contrast, a deep approach to learning is characterised by personal commitment to learning and an interest in the subject on the part of the student (Hall et al., 2004). Students adopting this approach to learning make use of previous knowledge and experiences to develop a framework to understand how the different parts of the discipline fit together (see Sharma, 1997; Hall et al., 2004). To be successful, a deep approach to learning should be flexible (Ramsden, 2003; Trigwell et al., 1999) and make use of a wide variety of teaching techniques. These include the development of analytical skills, cross-referencing, imaginative reconstruction and independent or reflective thinking. The development of these skills is necessary to solve practical problems and promote professional growth and, as Sharma (1997) suggests, they are competencies necessary to become a professional accountant. Ramsden (2003) argues that a deep approach to learning leads to quality learning outcomes. These include a sound understanding of the discipline, the development of higher order skills such as critical thinking (Booth et al., 1999; Hall et al., 2004), better developed conceptions of reality (Sharma, 1997) and the processing of data at a high level of generality (Biggs, 1987, 1989; Ramsden, 2003; Sharma, 1997). In the context of a deep approach to learning, Plack and Greenberg (2005, p. 1546) explain that reflection 'gives meaning to experience and promotes a deep approach to learning'. Reflection then assists students to develop a questioning attitude as well as the ability to update their knowledge and skills continually.

Biggs (1987; 1989) identified a third approach to learning—an achieving approach. This approach has also been called a strategic approach to learning. Warburton (2003, p. 46) explains the strategic approach as being characterised by competitiveness. Under this approach students make use of various techniques which emphasize mark maximisation in an attempt to maximise academic achievement with minimum effort (Moon, 1999).

Some authors (Hogan, 1995; Cunningham, 1996) have emphasised the importance to education of creative and critical thinking. The ways in which reflection impacts on the learning process has been considered by Kalliath and Coghlan (2001), MacFarlane (2001), Kalliath (2002) and Plack and Greenberg (2005), while meta-cognition has been considered by Baird (1991) and Dart et al. (1998). Baird (1991) also emphasized the relationship between reflection and meta-cognition. This relationship is illustrated through the interaction of processes (reflection and action) and outcomes (levels of meta-cognitive knowledge, awareness and control). That is, meta-cognition is an outcome of reflection (Dart et al., 1998; Kalliath, 2002). Meta-cognition can be described as the understanding and knowledge students have of how they think and learn. Dart et al. (1998, p. 295) describe meta-cognitive knowledge as incorporating:

> a person's knowledge of learning; recognition of strengths and weaknesses, assets and liabilities in learning; understanding of task characteristics which influence approaches to learning; and information about effective learning strategies [that is, knowing what they are (declarative knowledge), how to use them (procedural knowledge), and when, where, and why to use them (conditional knowledge)].

This relationship suggests that learning follows a continuum. The approach to learning that a student takes dictates the point on the continuum at which learning ends. Figure 1 illustrates the idea that a deep approach to learning is a prerequisite for creative and critical thinking, which in turn, is a prerequisite for meta-cognition. However, a deep approach to learning on the part of the student does not necessarily result in creativity or critical thinking and the existence of these does not necessarily result in meta-cognition. In the case of a deep approach to learning, learning may end before creative or critical thinking occurs, or it may end before meta-cognition occurs.

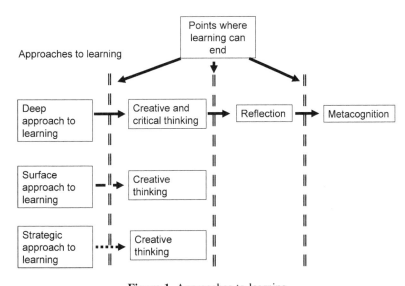

Figure 1. Approaches to learning

Each of the deep, surface and strategic approaches to learning depicted in Figure 1 requires different cognitive approaches, as represented by the different arrows. Students adopting a deep approach to learning must actively engage with the subject material. While a deep approach to learning is necessary to develop creative and critical thinking skills, it does not necessarily follow that reflection and meta-cognition take place, meaning that learning can end at any point. Creative and critical thinking are skills that require development in order for a deep approach to learning to take place. Although a deep approach to learning can be seen as the most desired approach to learning, there may be situations where it is appropriate for students to adopt a surface or strategic approach to learning. However, it is unlikely that critical thinking, reflection or meta-cognition takes place when a surface or strategic approach to learning is used.

Techniques for developing critical thinking skills in accounting students have previously been considered by Bonk and Smith (1998), Cunningham (1996) and Kimmel (1995). Abdolmohammadi and McQuade (2002, p. 181) describe critical thinking as an 'active, purposeful and organised process of thinking about one's own thinking'. Critical thinking requires students to evaluate the logic and validity of information, develop evidence to support or refute a point of view, analyse situations and discuss subjects in an organised way (Cunningham, 1996; Abdolmohammadi and McQuade, 2002; Kimmel, 1995; Bonk and Smith, 1998). In an educational context, critical thinking requires students to examine their ideas against predetermined criteria to determine whether they will work, to establish what problems are associated with them, and to determine whether they can be improved and to decide which ideas are better than others are (Cunningham, 1996). From a slightly different perspective, Abdolmohammadi and McQuade (2002, p. 182) explain that 'critical thinkers do not only seek evidence to support their own views, but also other alternative perspectives'. Creative thinking entails original or imaginative thinking capable of producing innovative solutions to alternative courses of action, which prove useful for problem solving and decision-making (Abdolmohammadi and McQuade, 2002; Cunningham, 1996; Bonk and Smith, 1998).

Accepting then that a deep approach to learning ideally requires the development of critical and creative thinking skills, and that these are a prerequisite for reflection, it was thought necessary to develop a strategy to incorporate techniques that develop these skills into the *Financial Accounting* syllabus. In addition, it was thought that any developments should require students to engage actively with the course.

The importance of fostering creative and critical thinking into the accounting syllabus has been reviewed by Kimmel (1995) and Bonk and Smith (1998). Hence, it was decided that the development of a learning portfolio would be an appropriate pedagogical technique through which critical and creative thinking could be developed. Various instructional strategies used successfully to develop creative and critical thought and described by Bonk and Smith (1998) are shown in Table 4.

While it was impractical to include all of the techniques shown in Table 4 in the learning portfolio, it was decided that a number of the strategies could successfully be incorporated. Techniques for developing critical thinking that could usefully be included in the learning portfolio were know-what-learn, summing up (module summaries), critiques (in the form of mini-cases) and minute papers, while creative thinking could be encouraged through free writing. Incorporating a personal journal that required an element of reflection into the learning portfolio was seen as contributing to the development of critical and creative thinking. The ways in which the individual components of the learning portfolio were used to develop those skills are summarised in Table 5.

The next section considers in more depth the design of the learning portfolio and its implementation into the course.

Table 4. Strategies for developing critical and creative thinking. *Source:* Bonk and Smith (1998)

Developing critical thinking	Developing creative thinking
Nominal group process	Brainstorming
Plus-minus-interesting and considering all factors	Reverse brainstorming
Know-what-learn	Alternatives-possibilities-choices
Summing up	Free writing (or wet-inking)
Minute papers	Simulations and role-plays
Reflective logs	Assigning thinking roles and six hats
Critiques and rebuttals	Semantic webbing and linking of ideas
Case-based reasoning and problem-based learning	Idea spurring questions and checklists
Pruning the tree, 20 questions, and working backwards	Synectics, analogies, metaphor and forced associations
Mock trials and debates	Checker boarding and morphological synthesis
Graphic organizers	Personal journal logs
Socratic questioning	

Table 5. Range of skills learning portfolio was designed to develop

Component of learning portfolio	Skills attempting to develop
Personal journal	Reflection and meta-cognition: Evidence of personal journals being used in other disciplines to develop critical and creative thinking skills. Students are able to record and track their development over a course that encourages reflection.
Classroom assessment techniques	
Background knowledge probe	Reflection: Enables students to complete feedback loop by reflecting on how knowledge has increased over the semester.
Feedback form	Critical and creative thinking: Reflection through the provision of feedback. Requires the use of knowledge obtained during lectures and in previous courses to develop a practical illustration of a key point.
One minute paper	Critical thinking: Requires students to reflect on and elaborate on information and relate it to prior knowledge.
Module summary	Critical thinking: Requires students to develop the ability to search, evaluate, record, summarize and communicate key information.
Know-what-learn	Critical thinking: Requires students to evaluate their initial knowledge deficits, strengths and primary concerns.
Free writing	Creative thought: Requires students to consistently evaluate solutions to a problem.
Mini cases	Critical and creative thought: Requires students to evaluate the thinking of others and recognise that alternative points of view and ambiguities exist in accounting.
Summary and reflection	Reflection: Provides a reflective account of the student's experience over the semester.

4 The Learning Portfolio

Before describing the implementation of the learning portfolios, it is instructive to distinguish between learning journals, learning logs and reflective diaries, and the learning portfolio considered in this paper. Moon (1999) explains that, while the terms learning journals, learning logs and reflective diaries are terms often used interchangeably, their purposes differ. Learning journals are used to record the learning that occurs, while reflective diaries require students to reflect on an experience. Learning logs provide a record of events that occurred. Moon (1999), however, suggests that all these items require an element of reflection.

The advantages of students using personal journals have been widely reported in the literature (see, for example, McCrindle and Christensen, 1995; Barclay, 1996; November, 1996; Moon, 1999; Haigh, 2001; MacFarlane, 2001; Langer, 2002; Loo and Thorpe, 2002; Howieson, 2004; Plack and Greenberg, 2005). Moon (1999, p. 40–45) details these advantages as including: recording course experience; facilitating learning from experience; supporting understanding and the representation of understanding; developing critical thinking; encouraging meta-cognition; increasing active involvement and ownership of learning; and increasing reflective thinking ability. Furthermore, as a means of assessment, personal journals enhance reflective practice for personal development and self-improvement, enhance creativity, improve writing, and support communication.

One immediate difficulty was deciding what to call this item of assessment. The terms 'diary' and 'log' were considered inappropriate as they could perhaps be viewed by some students as having negative connotations. The number of different tasks required by this item of assessment suggested that the term 'learning portfolio' would perhaps most accurately describe the assessment. Another major factor when deciding to introduce the learning portfolio was the need to ensure that individual assessment components could clearly be tied to the course objectives, namely that they would 'foster critical and independent thinking and enhance analytical ability, creativity and initiative'. The learning portfolio described here is more than a learning journal, learning log or reflective diary. The learning portfolio was to be viewed as a personalized collection of work that included a personal journal along with classroom assessment techniques, mini-cases, and it was to conclude with a summary and reflective essay. Each of these components is considered further in the sections that follow.

The learning portfolio, as an item of assessment reported in this paper, was used twice. It was first used in a 14-week (12-week teaching and two-week mid-term break) long course delivered in our B semester, and it was used for the second time in a six-week long summer school semester. One hundred and nine students completed the semester B course while 62 completed the Summer School semester course.

The learning portfolio assignment requirement was detailed in the course outline as follows: 'For the duration of this [course] you will be required to create and maintain a learning portfolio of your work'. In the course's first class, students were advised that the portfolio had to be more than a descriptive journal. It was not to be a collection of items thrown together with little or no thought; rather the aim was for students to put together a collection of work designed to reflect their efforts, progress and achievements. This expectation was detailed in the course outline as follows: 'This learning portfolio will be a record of your personal learning journey as you progress through [this course]'. The learning portfolio serves a number of purposes: (1) it helps synthesize learning over the duration of the course; (2) it documents the depth and breadth of personal growth; (3) it confirms the practical applications of what students have learned; and (4) it forms a component of the course-work for the course.

Table 6. Weighting of portfolio components
for assessment purposes

	%
Personal journal	30
Classroom assessment techniques	20
Summary and reflection	40
Creativity	10
	100

For assessment purposes, the individual components of the learning portfolio were weighted as follows (Table 6):

To increase the emphasis on the classroom assessment techniques and to encourage students to engage seriously, the weighting of the marks attributable to these items was changed. During the Summer School semester, the marks attributed to the classroom assessment techniques were increased to 30%, with the marks for the summary and reflection being decreased to 30%. Beyond the individual components and recommendation that students maintain five sections in their learning portfolios, guidance on what additional items individual students might include was deliberately limited. The intention was to ensure that students did not merely produce an item of work in a format they thought was required. As an unstructured item of assessment, it was hoped that in developing their critical and creative thinking and enhancing their reflective skills, students would take some intellectual risks, and be adventurous and curious.

Design and Implementation

The learning portfolio was to be a record of students' learning over the semester. Within their portfolios, students were required to complete a number of tasks, one of which was the maintenance of a personal journal. At the outset, two decisions had to be made:

- What guidance should be provided; and
- Whether this assignment would be assessed.

Guidance was obtained from Brookfield (1995, p. 97) who states:

> If students are to take journal writing seriously, three conditions must be met: (1) they must be given some specific guidelines on what a learning journal should look like, (2) they must be convinced that it is in their best interests to keep a journal, and (3) their effort must in some way be publicly acknowledged and rewarded.

Following Brookfield's (1995) advice, the instructions to students were specific while at the same time permitting individual choice. In the B semester, each student was to acquire a hard cover lecture book in which to maintain his/her learning portfolio. In the Summer School semester, students were required to maintain the personal journal component of the learning portfolio online through the 'electronic diary' function of the university's MyWeb™ facility. This mechanism was to ensure that, throughout the semester, students made regular entries in the personal journal component of their learning portfolio rather than completing it at a single sitting.

November (1996) details the attributes that good learning portfolios should possess. These are width, depth, and distance. Width, explains November (1996, p. 119), refers to the breadth of topics covered by a student in his or her journal. This breadth should consider items other than interpersonal factors. Depth is analogous to a deep rather than surface approach to learning. A student who shows depth in his or her journal will examine issues more thoroughly and comprehensively than students who take a surface approach to learning. November (1996, p. 119) describes distance as the length of a student's journey with a topic. Distance is evidenced when a student returns to a particular topic, notes changes in his or her understanding, and is able to describe the interrelationship of the topic with other topics.

The course outline also suggested that students maintain five sections in the learning portfolio as follows: (1) personal journal; (2) module summaries; (3) classroom assessment techniques; (4) mini-cases; and (5) summary and reflection. However, the course outline did reiterate that students could maintain their portfolios in a format that best suited them. By providing this option, it was hoped that if they could be personalized, students would view their portfolios as being relevant and useful. This instruction was not included in the Summer School semester course outline. Students taking this course, however, did request detailed guidance, which was provided. Almost all the students in both semesters maintained their portfolios as suggested. For students who took the course during the shorter Summer School semester, one classroom assessment technique—the self-monitoring log—was discarded. This decision was taken after informal discussions with a cross-section of B semester students who felt that this particular classroom assessment technique provided no benefit and was an excessive administrative burden.

Figure 2 shows the relationships between the various components of the learning portfolio. For the purposes of this course, module summaries were considered a classroom assessment technique. Figure 2 also details how the summary and critical reflection which students were to prepare at the end of the course were drawn from the other components of the learning portfolio and how the attributes of width, depth and distance apply to the learning portfolio as a whole. Students were encouraged to use their imagination to personalize their learning portfolios. This personalization could take any form and include

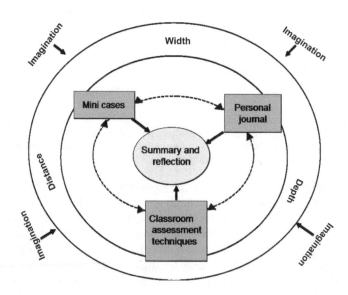

Figure 2. Structure of learning portfolio, detailing interrelationship between main components

the use of colour, pictures, mind-maps, media item cuttings, quotations, and even poems. The only limitation was the individual student's imagination.

The Personal Journal

As detailed in Table 7, the use of personal journal writing has been widely used as a form of assessment in a number of academic disciplines. These studies were explored for insights into how they may be used in an accounting context.

The essence of a personal journal has been captured by Hogan (1995, p. 6) who describes it as follows:

> The aim is to enable students to monitor their learning goals, processes and progress; interrelate ideas; develop understanding of themselves at work; describe learning plateaux and blocks and how they overcome these and free up the writing process so that it can become a source of freedom, relaxation and fun. The journal can include phrases, passages, words, quotes, sketches, scribbles, cartoons, collage, mind maps, mandalas, prose and poetry, graphs and charts, colours, images and symbols.

While the above quotation illustrates how personal journals can be used in an academic environment to develop creativity, personal journals have also been used to assist students develop reflective skills (Barclay, 1996; MacFarlane, 2001; Langer, 2002; Loo and Thorpe, 2002). Extending the principle of a personal journal, McCrindle and Christensen (1995, p. 172) suggest that journals 'provide a mechanism to increase metacognition through both students' awareness of their cognitive processes as well as their management of these processes'.

The literature on the use of personal journals in Accounting is limited. Their use to develop the writing skills of accountants have been described by Wygal and Stout (1989) and Hoff and Stout (1989). There is limited evidence, however, of their use to develop creative and critical thinking skills in students, or for self-reflection. A possible reason is that accounting may be seen as a technical discipline that does not lend itself to critical and reflective thinking. This view, however, is not shared by some authors including Cunningham (1996) and Bonk and Smith (1998). Cunningham (1996) and Bonk and Smith (1998) suggest that journal writing by accounting students can foster and enhance creative and critical thinking. Day *et al.* (2003) use a five-act play to describe

Table 7. Research where the use of journal writing is detailed

Discipline	Author
Biology	McCrindle and Christensen (1995)
Business ethics	MacFarlane (2001)
Business management	Barclay (1996); Rosier (2002)
Computer technology	Langer (2002)
Education	Morrison (1996); Dart *et al.* (1998)
Geography	Haigh (2001)
Human resource management	Hogan (1995)
Marketing	November (1996)
Nursing science	Hahnemann (1986)
Occupational therapy	Routledge *et al.* (1997)
Organizational development	Kalliath and Coghlan (2001)
Team performance	Loo and Thorpe (2002)

their own reflection on what an accounting theory student's personal journal exercise revealed to them about their attempts to employ critical accounting perspectives in their teaching and research activities. Day *et al.* (2003), Cunningham (1996) and Bonk and Smith (1998) do not describe the details and techniques they used to conduct their personal journal exercises but, more recently, Howieson (2004) has described the implementation and use of a self-reflective personal journal in a postgraduate accounting theory course.

It was hoped that the introduction of the personal journal component of the learning portfolio would benefit both students and teaching staff. From the students' perspective, it was hoped it would contribute to the development of their creative and critical thinking, and assist them in developing reflective thinking skills. From the lecturers' perspective, it was hoped that it would develop students who think more deeply about financial accounting issues. If this could be achieved, the personal journal would be a useful pedagogical technique that could help students to become more reflective and to participate actively in their own learning.

Classroom Assessment Techniques

Assessment can be broadly classified into two types: programme level (Gainen and Locatelli, 1995) or outcomes assessment (Herring and Izard, 1992), and classroom assessment (Harwood, 1989; Harwood and Cohan, 1999). Programme level or outcome assessment refers to large-scale efforts that assess students periodically at key points in a course. Harwood (1999, p. 52) explains that the focus of these assessments is to identify changes that will improve the learning of future students. This form of assessment can be contrasted with classroom assessment, which typically comprises continuous small-scale efforts initiated and controlled by the lecturer and designed to improve the learning of students currently enrolled in the course. Cottell and Harwood (1998, p. 552) consider that this continuous assessment supplements the traditional evaluative techniques of formal examinations and written assignments. The main advantage of this type of technique is that it can provide regular and timely feedback on how the class is progressing and provide a more comprehensive view of the level and dispersion of the group's learning at a particular point in time (Cottell and Harwood, 1998; Harwood, 1999). Furthermore, providing feedback and direction to students encourages a deep approach to learning (Sharma, 1997).

Classroom assessment techniques (CATs) have become a well-established and accepted method of continuous assessment (Angelo and Cross, 1993; Beard, 1993; Almer *et al.*, 1998; Cottell and Harwood, 1998; Harwood, 1999). To ensure that regular feedback was obtained and to encourage active participation, it was decided to incorporate into the course a range of different CATs described by the literature. To ensure that students took the CATs seriously, they had to be included in their learning portfolios. The following classroom assessment techniques were used at various times during the course.

A self-monitoring log. A self-monitoring log was developed and provided to students online. This self-monitoring log was designed to provide students with a structured approach to working through course material from reading chapters prior to class, to the completion of the tutorial work. As indicated previously, this particular CAT was discarded after the B semester.

Background knowledge probe. The use of a background knowledge probe (BKP) has been described by Cottell and Harwood (1996, 1998). BKPs are designed to establish what knowledge a student brings to class. Cottell and Harwood (1998, p. 556) explain the importance of a BKP as follows:

> Knowing what students know before we start teaching can increase teaching efficiency and effectiveness. Teaching efficiency increases when we discover that students know something we thought they didn't and we now have time to cover other material. Teaching effectiveness increases when we target the learning needs, both in terms of coverage and level, of each class.

The BKP was designed so that it covered the whole *Financial Accounting* syllabus. Twelve short-answer-type questions were developed and distributed at the first lecture. Students were given 15 min of class time to answer the questions. The aim here was not to obtain immediate feedback but rather to make students aware of the extent of the syllabus and required knowledge. Students were asked to paste this BKP in the front of their learning portfolio so that at the end of the semester they could go back and reflect on the progress they had made during the course. Students going back and reflecting on their initial knowledge is important and useful in closing what Cottell and Harwood (1998, p. 563) describe as the 'feedback loop'. The BKP was seen as a particularly useful CAT—especially when students came to completing the summary and reflection component of the learning portfolio.

Feedback form. Cottell and Harwood (1998) and Harwood (1999) considered the benefit of feedback forms as a CAT in an Accounting course. For this course a feedback form for each module was developed, based on the examples provided in Cottell and Harwood (1998) and Harwood (1999). These feedback forms were made available to students online. The feedback forms contained a question that required students to use knowledge obtained during lectures and in previous courses to develop a practical illustration of a key point. Examples of the questions students were required to answer include: 'Explain to the managing director what information should be disclosed when a statement of financial performance is prepared for external reporting purposes' and 'Explain to a fellow student in the fine arts department at the University why a company would wish to make use of an interest rate swap. Use an example in your explanation'.

By relating prior knowledge to the practical application of a key point, students were given the opportunity to reflect on the module to establish whether they understood it. This use of the feedback form was a deliberate attempt to stimulate a deep approach to learning. Making use of previous knowledge and experiences to develop a framework to understand how the different parts of the accounting discipline fit together (see Sharma, 1997 and Hall *et al.*, 2004), students completed the feedback forms at the end of each module and forwarded them to their tutors. The feedback forms were reviewed by tutors on a weekly basis to identify underlying problems, answer queries (administrative and course-related) in a personal manner, and review and provide direction to student attempts to the set problems. Any problems identified were raised by the tutors with the lecturing staff at the weekly tutors' meeting, thus enabling tutorials and workshops to focus on questions that addressed student-identified problems. An example of a completed feedback form reproduced without correction is provided in Appendix 1.

One minute paper. The use of one minute papers as a CAT has been described by Almer *et al.* (1998), Cottell and Harwood (1998) and by Bonk and Smith (1998) as a technique that can assist in the development of critical thinking skills. Where the one-minute paper is used to develop critical thinking skills, students are required to write a brief one-minute reflection concerning the day's lecture or presentation. Using the one-minute paper in this manner enables students to identify what was unclear or crucial in the lecture (the 'muddiest' or most important point) or provide an example they have developed that illustrates the key lecture points (Bonk and Smith, 1998, p. 278). Where a one-minute paper is used in this manner, Bonk and Smith (1998, p. 278) explain that the reflections should be seen as simple tools to elaborate on information and relate it to students' prior knowledge.

Based on Almer et al.'s (1998) suggestions the one-minute paper was used to ask students to respond to the following two questions:

- What was the main point you learned in class today?
- What is the main unanswered question you leave the class with today?

While the above questions can also be used by students to elaborate on information and relate it to prior knowledge, the intention here was that where students had unanswered questions they would take the responsibility for having them answered by approaching either the tutors or the lecturer.

Topic summary. Building on the research of Hidi and Anderson (1986) and Winograd (1984), Bonk and Smith (1998) explain that one useful strategy for developing critical thought is the principle of summing up. Bonk and Smith (1998, pp. 277–278) argue that a student's ability to search, record, summarise and communicate information is critical for success both at university (possibly not to a great extent in this course) and in the work environment. Activities including the creation of review notes, abstracts, outlines or module summaries assist students in their ability to prioritise information or grasp key lecture points (Bonk and Smith, 1998, pp. 277–278).

At the end of each topic, (see Table 2 for a listing of topic) students were required to prepare a summary of the topic in which they identified in their own words the key points covered. This summary could include a review of a theoretical issue or the format could be used to deal with a particular technical issue. While the literature suggests that students share these summaries with their peers, in this case this option was considered impractical. As a significant number of students already prepared topic summaries for their own use, requiring students to maintain them in their learning portfolio merely formalised an arrangement already frequently in place.

Know-what-learn (K-W-L). K-W-Ls were described by Bonk and Smith (1998) as a technique useful for developing critical thought. At the beginning of a lecture, students may be asked to record the answers to the following three questions: What do you know? What do you want to know? What did you learn? Bonk and Smith (1998, p. 277) explain that the answers to a K-W-L completed at the beginning of the lecture provide a record of the student's initial knowledge deficits, strengths and primary concerns.

In order for critical thinking to be able to occur, students need to be able to identify problem areas and recognise when additional information is needed to solve the problem. For example, the aim of asking the question, 'What do you know about finance leases?' at the beginning of a lecture was to identify whether students knew what a finance lease was, identify whether they able to differentiate between a finance lease and operating lease, or were able to calculate the amount at which a finance lease should be capitalized in financial statements. By asking the question, 'What do you want to know about finance leases?' encourages students to identify deficiencies in their knowledge. Responses to this question could include 'When should a lease be capitalised and at what amount?' When asked the question, 'What did you learn about finance leases?' at the end of the lecture, students should be able to review and analyse a particular scenario to establish whether a lease dealt with in the problem is a finance lease and correctly calculate the amount that should be capitalized.

Free-writing. During free writing exercises students are asked to write all they know about a topic, or answer a question, for a period not exceeding five minutes. The aim of this creative thinking exercise is to evaluate possible solutions to a problem (Bonk and Smith, 1998, p. 271). Examples of free-writing exercises include, 'How should a heritage asset, (that is an asset a community intends preserving because of its unique historical, cultural or environmental attributes), be treated for accounting purposes?' and 'If an active market does not exist for heritage assets, what approaches could be used to value them?'

During this five-minute period, students are not to lift their pen from the paper, or pause or reflect. As a result, the writing is unlikely to be polished. The idea is to write down the first ideas that come into your mind. In the first example students could consider alternative methods of recording heritage assets, either capitalising them in the financial statements or providing a supporting narrative description. Ideally, a conceptual framework would be drawn on to justify their position. In the second example, students could identify alternative approaches to valuing heritage assets. Following the free writing a class debriefing and discussion took place on the characteristics of heritage assets and the various approaches that could be used to value them.

Even though the techniques identified by Bonk and Smith (1998) and described above were aimed at developing critical and creative thinking for the purposes of this course, they were described as CATS.

Mini Cases

One strategy described by Cunningham (1996) to develop creative and critical thinking skills in students is that of analysing media-related items. During the B semester, students were asked to analyse a single article, which was provided by the lecturer, on accounting for heritage assets. Students were not to write more than 300 words. During the Summer School semester, students were required to analyse three articles, one of which was an exhibit taken from the prescribed text. Some guidance in the

Table 8. Questions that may assist preparation of the mini case. *Source:* Cunningham 1996, p. 58–59

---

1. What is the main point, problem, or issue addressed by the article?
2. What evidence does the article offer that supports the main point or shows that there is an issue or problem?
3. Is the evidence credible? Why or why not?
4. What would make the evidence stronger?
5. What additional evidence could help support the main point or show that there is an issue or problem?
6. Does the article address more than one point of view?
7. Does the article support opposing arguments or points of view with evidence?
8. If there is an issue or problem, what solutions does the article offer?
9. Are the solutions feasible?
10. Would the solutions resolve the issue or solve the problem?
11. Would other issues or problems be created by the solutions?

---

form of questions students could use was provided in the course outline. These questions are detailed in Table 8.

The rationale for including a mini case requirement in the learning portfolio was for students to appreciate that not all accounting issues were 'cut and dried' and to recognise that alternative points of view and ambiguous issues do exist.

Summary and Reflection

The use of reflective reports has been described by Routledge *et al.* (1997) and Rosier (2002). Rosier (2002) describes the use of written reflective reports submitted after a postgraduate management course class discussion. Rosier (2002) explains that a written report requires more than careful listening and learning from class discussion. Rather, the aim is to encourage students to report on what they might have done differently if they had been provided with a second opportunity to analyse the case and explore other lessons learnt from the case study process. Routledge *et al.* (1997) describes this process as the 'distillation of the whole assignment'.

In the course, the aim of the summary and reflection (maximum of 1000 words) was for students to provide a summary of and reflection on their experiences in the course to be submitted two days after the final examination. The course outline provided the following motivation for the summary and reflection as follows:

> In this reflection you should indicate what aspects of the course you found useful or unhelpful for your own needs. Self-reflection is a useful method of consolidating any learning that has occurred through this course.

The questions detailed in Table 9 were included in the course outline to provide students with a starting point for their summary and reflection. It was emphasized that students were not limited to these questions but were free to develop their summary and reflection in any manner they chose.

A carefully designed learning portfolio that is sincerely engaged with can assist students to develop a range of skills. These include reflection, self-assessment, awareness of learning patterns (metacognition), self-awareness about knowledge, as well as the development of critical and creative thinking skills.

Support Provided to Students

When significant changes are made to assessment, especially where those changes include items not traditionally associated with an Accounting course, it is essential that

Table 9. Questions useful for reflections

---

1. What was my best work?
2. How did I go about accomplishing the task?
3. If I had to do this paper again, what would I do differently?
4. Where do I go from here?
5. What do I feel proudest about regarding my learning activities over the duration of this course?
6. What do I feel most dissatisfied about with regard to my learning activities over the duration of this course?
7. What classroom assessment techniques did I find most useful and why?

---

appropriate and adequate support structures be put in place to assist students. New items of assessment also engender uncertainty and anxiety—especially if the activity is a solitary and personal one. In recognizing this fact, Barclay (1996) stressed the importance of specific guidelines being provided at the outset of the course. In addition, the importance of support in the form of discussions with the lecturer/tutors and fellow students was emphasized.

A senior staff member of the Teaching Learning and Development Unit (TLDU) at the university provided a number of training sessions to both the lecturer and tutors. This individual was available at all times to provide guidance to the academic and support staff. This same TLDU staff member talked to both the B semester and Summer School semester classes and provided them with guidance on what was expected. A series of PowerPoint™ slides was also made available to students online. The TLDU also set aside time for students to drop in to obtain guidance; individual students could make appointments with the staff member who had spoken to the class for one-on-one guidance and assistance.

In addition to the above support, during B semester, the lecturer conducted four separate workshops on reflective thinking, and during the last lecture of the semester included a session for students on how to complete their summary and reflection. In addition, a set of notes detailing how learning portfolios should be maintained and how reflection takes place was made available to all students. Finally, continuous guidance in the form of regular e-mails from the lecturer was provided to the class. Although no formal sessions on critical thinking were provided to students, the concept was discussed regularly in class during the semester.

Despite this support, it would be fair to say that a significant number of students did not take the opportunity to avail themselves of this support. In both the B semester and the Summer School semester attendance at the drop-in and individual one-on-one guidance sessions was disappointing. A breakdown of the number of sessions attended by students is detailed in Table 10 as follows.

Table 10 shows that 3.7% students attended at least three sessions, 17.5% of students attended at least two sessions, while 38 or 47.5% of students attended at least one session. The data provided in Table 10 can be broken down further. Of those B semester students who completed the questionnaire, only 27 out of 54 students attended a session, while only 11 out of 26 Summer School semester students attended a session. This lack of interest in the support provided to students may suggest that, even in a third year course, students may not be prepared to take responsibility for their own learning. However, there may be a number of other reasons why students did not attend these sessions. Possible reasons include the relatively small weighting attributed to the learning portfolio as a whole, meaning students focus their attention on those items of assessment with the greatest weighting; students not being convinced of the benefits of maintaining a learning

Table 10. Use made by students of help sessions

Number of sessions attended	Frequency	Per cent	Cumulative per cent
Four or more	1	1.2	1.2
Three	2	2.5	3.7
Two	11	13.8	17.5
One	24	30.0	47.5
Zero	42	52.5	100.0
	80	100.0	

portfolio in a discipline like Accounting; or that students obtained support from peers who did attend one or more sessions.

Assessment of Portfolio

A question faced by those who require students to maintain learning portfolios is whether these items should be assessed. Moon (1999, p. 91) considers that journal assessment can be either formative or summative. Formative assessment provides students with feedback on their work while summative assessment occurs at the end of the semester and results in an overall mark.

In her work on learning journals, Moon (1999) identifies a number of sources, which argue that personal journals should not be assessed. Supporters of this position question whether personal reflections or individual development can be appropriately assessed, and suggest that to do so is intrusive. While these may be valid concerns, it was always the intention to assess the learning portfolio. The reasons for this decision were two-fold. First, the rise in the number of strategic students (Moon, 1999; Warburton, 2003) meant that, if it was not assessed, students would not complete the assignment. Hogan (1995, p.14) and Howieson (2004) provide evidence that where maintaining a personal journal was voluntary and no marks were allocated, students failed to complete the assignment as there was no incentive for them to do so. Second, where lecturing staff do not evaluate students' attempts, then there may be a perception that their efforts are not being taken seriously.

As the learning portfolio was a new item of assessment, and taking into account the difficulties associated with reflective work, only a small proportion of the overall assessment mark was allocated to this assignment. The aim of this assessment was not to provide a mechanism for scoring significant numbers of marks for mere compliance, but rather to provide an item of assessment that was both formative and summative and, if taken seriously, one that would benefit overall performance. The assessment instrument developed from guidelines provided in Klenowski (2002, p. 94) and November (1996) is detailed in Appendix 2.

Evaluating the Learning Portfolio

Having developed the learning portfolio, we considered it appropriate to carry out an evaluation of its introduction (Hounsell, 2003). In this section, we examine students' responses taken from a variety of sources (including an online questionnaire, interviews and the portfolios themselves) in an attempt to establish whether the learning portfolio contributed to the development of critical and creative thinking skills, as well as to understand students' perceptions of this item of assessment.

It should be noted at this stage that the nature of the ethical approval granted by the Ethics Committee of the university limited the opportunities for evaluating the success of implementing the learning portfolio as an item of assessment. To ensure the confidentiality of students' responses, the online questionnaire was constructed in such a way that made it impossible to identify individual respondents and so the relationship between individual responses and the respondent's result in the course could not be determined.

Demographics and non-response bias. In total 80 students (49.1% of the cohort) completed the online questionnaire. The average age of the respondents was 24.8 years. Four per cent of students were under 20 years; 70% were between 20 and 24 years; 9% were between 25 and 30 years, while 17% were over 30. The respondents were evenly

Table 11. First language profile of the respondents and the sample

First language	Percentage of students taking course $(n = 163)$	Percentage of respondents $(n = 80)$
English	77% $(n = 126)$	70% $(n = 56)$
Non-English	23% $(n = 37)$	30% $(n = 24)$

split in terms of gender, with 39 male and 41 female students responding. Of the 80 respondents, 24 did not have English as their first language.

It was possible to test for non-response problems with reference to known population characteristics (Viswesvaran *et al.*, 1993). In this case, the data available permitted tests based on gender and first language. In order to test for the representativeness of the respondents to the overall cohort, the profile of the respondents was compared to the profile of the overall sample in terms of the students' first language and gender. Overall the Chi-square test showed that the profiles of students' first languages (see Table 11) were not significantly different to the profile of the samples at the 5% level ($\chi^2 = 2.43$, not significant), although there appears to be a slight tendency for international students to be more likely to respond.

The representativeness of the respondents was also checked by comparing the gender split of respondents to that of the students taking the course (see Table 12). Again the Chi-square test showed that the respondents' profile was not significantly different from the profile of the sample at the 5% level ($\chi^2 = 0.073$, not significant). The distribution in terms of gender was a very good match between the respondents and the sample.

Students' Perceptions of the Learning Portfolio

In addition to collecting background data such as gender and first language (used above), the online questionnaire collected data on the students' perceptions of the learning portfolio. A five-point Likert scale was considered the most appropriate method (Robson, 2002; Oppenheim, 1992) to collect this data. The mean and standard deviations of the responses are shown in Table 13 (with the raw data shown in Appendix 3). In addition to the Likert scales questions, the online questionnaire gave the students the opportunity to make open-ended comments.

The questionnaire responses provided an interesting insight into different students' perceptions of the learning portfolios. Overall, international students tended to give higher rankings to them than did home students (see Appendix 4). Additionally, there was a degree of correlation between responses and age with older students tending to give slightly more favourable responses to the learning portfolio (Appendix 5). There were some differences in the mean responses between the use of the learning portfolio in the main B semester and the shorter Summer School semester (see Appendix 6). It might

Table 12. Gender of the respondents and the sample

Gender	Percentage of students taking course ($n = 163$)	Percentage of respondents ($n = 80$)
Male	47% $(n = 77)$	49% $(n = 39)$
Female	53% $(n = 86)$	51% $(n = 41)$

Table 13. Responses to online administered questionnaire. Overall mean and standard deviations of the combined B semester and Summer School Semester

	Overall mean response	SD	n
Maintaining my learning portfolio assisted me in the development of my written communication skills.	2.9	1.1	79
Maintaining my learning portfolio assisted me to develop critical thinking skills.	3.1	1.2	79
The tutors answered the questions that I raised on my feedback form to my satisfaction.	3.8	0.9	79
The learning portfolio encouraged a deeper, more personal engagement with the course learning.	3.3	1.3	79
Completing the learning portfolio encouraged regular, active participation in learning in this course.	3.4	1.3	78
Regular entries in the learning portfolio enabled me to evaluate consistently the progress of my learning.	3.3	1.2	78
The questions contained on the feedback forms were useful for revision purposes.	3.7	0.8	78
The feedback forms enabled me to identify areas in which I was weak and needed to focus on.	3.6	0.9	78
By completing the feedback forms and making entries in my learning portfolio, I was able to engage in an ongoing dialogue with the lecturer and tutors.	3.2	0.9	78
The learning portfolio mark-plan provided me with an adequate indication of how the individual components of my portfolio would be assessed.	3.5	0.9	78

Mean and standard deviations (SD) are from a 5-point Likert scale where 5 = strongly agree; 4 = agree; 3 = neutral; 2 = disagree; 1 = strongly disagree. n = number of responses to each individual question, in this case the combined B semester and Summer School Semester.

be expected that the shorter presentation would be less suitable for students to develop the learning portfolios; however, the difference between the means tended to be small. This result indicated that the use of learning portfolios over the shorter delivery period of the six-week Summer School semester was not particularly problematic.

Table 13 shows the overall mean and standard deviation for questions for the combined B semester and Summer School semester students. The split between the two semesters is detailed in Appendix 6.

In response to the question: *Maintaining my learning portfolio assisted me in the development of my written communication skills*, 38% of students either strongly agreed or agreed with this statement. Female and international students had a higher tendency to agree to this statement (see Appendices 4 and 7). There was a degree of correlation between responses and age with older students being more likely to agree.

In response to the question: *Maintaining my learning portfolio assisted me to develop critical thinking skills*, of those who responded, 48% either agreed or strongly agreed (see Table 13 and Appendix 3) that the learning portfolio contributed to their critical thinking skills. However, of concern were the 20% of respondents who provided a neutral response to this question. Again, female, international and older students had a higher tendency to agree with this statement.

In response to the question, 'The tutors answered the questions that I raised on my feedback form to my satisfaction', 67% of students either strongly agreed or agreed with this statement. When examining the Summer School semester results, this percentage increased to 76%. Although the reasons for this difference are uncertain, there are a number of possible explanations. The Summer School semester was the second time the learning portfolio was used; as such, both the tutors and teaching staff had become more familiar with its implementation. In addition, tutors only taught a maximum of one course over the Summer School semester and were themselves in a better position to provide fuller explanations and more timely feedback to students.

In response to the question, 'The learning portfolio encouraged a deeper, more personal engagement with the course learning', 54% of respondents either strongly agreed or agreed with this statement. However, when examining the Summer School semester responses on their own, 72% of respondents concurred with the statement. The difference between the two results can perhaps be put down to the fact that students usually complete only one course over the six-week Summer School semester period and are, therefore, more likely to have a deeper engagement with the course than when completing three or four courses in a semester. It is possible that the busier students are the less likely it is they will fully engage with the learning portfolio. When looking at responses cross tabulated to students' demographics, a similar pattern of female, international and older students being more likely to agree with this statement emerged.

In response to the question, 'Completing the learning portfolio encouraged regular, active participation in learning in this course', 53% of B semester students and 72% of Summer School semester students either strongly agreed to agreed with this statement. Thirty-two per cent of B semester students disagreed or strongly disagreed with this statement, while only 8% of Summer Students strongly disagreed with it. Again, possible explanations for the differences in responses between the B semester and the Summer School semester students include the number of courses taken. Summer School semester students take only one course and, therefore, are in a better position to participate actively in the learning in the course. In addition, it is possible that Summer School semester students are more enthusiastic participants as they have sacrificed their summer holidays to take the course. Finally, as the Summer School semester was the second time the learning portfolio was used as an item of assessment, teaching staff and tutors were more familiar with its implementation. When responses were related to students' characteristics, there was little difference between international and home students, but marked differences between genders, with female students having a higher mean response. The mean response of female students was 3.8 compared to the mean response of 3.0 for male students. There was an overall mean response of 3.4 (see Appendix 7).

In response to the question, 'Regular entries in the learning portfolio enabled me to consistently evaluate the progress of my learning', 53% of B semester and 48% of Summer School semester students strongly agreed or agreed with this statement. Thirty per cent of B semester and 12% of Summer School semester students strongly disagreed or disagreed with this statement. Whilst many students strongly agreed or agreed with the statements relating to how beneficial the students found the feedback forms (see Table 13), not all the respondents agreed. There were only limited differences between home and international students (see Appendix 4). There was a tendency for female students to give more favourable responses (see Appendix 7).

In response to the question, 'The questions contained on the feedback forms were useful for revision purposes', 64% of respondents either strongly agreed or agreed with this statement. There was no difference in the responses between B semester and Summer School semester students.

In response to the question, 'The feedback forms enabled me to identify areas in which I was weak and needed to focus on', 62% of respondents either strongly agreed or agreed with this statement. There was no great difference in the responses provided by B Semester and the Summer School semester students.

In response to the question, 'By completing the feedback forms and making entries in my learning portfolio, I was able to engage in an ongoing dialogue with the lecturer and tutors', 45% of B semester and 32% of Summer School semester students either strongly agreed or agreed with this statement. The other difference was in the neutral responses. Those students enrolled in the Summer School semester were generally more likely to provide a neutral response to this question than students enrolled in the B semester programme were. The shorter duration of the Summer School semester programme combined with the smaller class size may have contributed to the differences in responses.

In response to the question, 'The learning portfolio mark-plan provided me with an adequate indication of how the individual components of my portfolio would be assessed', 58% of B semester respondents either strongly agreed or agreed with this statement. This compared to only 28% of Summer School semester respondents. The other significant difference came from those respondents who provided a neutral response to this question. Of those who responded 60% of Summer School respondents provides a neutral response to this question while only 30% of B semester students provided a neutral response to this question. While the reasons for the differences in responses are uncertain, perhaps the Summer School semester students thought the mark plan could have been clearer.

The students were also asked about the amount of time spent each week on their learning portfolios. The modal response was between one and one-and-a-half hours per week, with international and female students on average (mean) spending longer on their portfolios. There was a positive correlation (correlation coefficient = 0.41) between age and time spent on their portfolios. The mean response to the question, 'Maintaining my learning portfolio assisted me to develop critical thinking skills', cross-tabulated against the time spent on the learning portfolio is detailed in Table 14.

The cross-tabulation in Table 14 suggests that respondents who spent more time on their learning portfolios rated its impact on critical thinking skills progressively more highly. The responses to four further questions also suggest that those students who spent longer on their learning portfolio appreciated its benefits more highly.

In response to the question, 'Maintaining my learning portfolio assisted me in the development of my written communication skills', respondents who spent more than 120 min per week gave a mean response of 4.0 to the question compared to a mean response of 2.2 for those who spent less than 30 min per week on their learning portfolio believed.

In response to the question, 'Maintaining my learning portfolio assisted me to develop critical thinking skills', respondents who spent more than 120 min per week provided a

Table 14. Mean responses to the question: Maintaining my learning portfolio assisted me to develop critical thinking skills, cross-tabulated against time spent on learning portfolio

Time spent on portfolio	Mean response
Less than 30 min	2.3
More than 30 min but less than 60 min	2.8
More than 60 min but less than 90 min	3.5
More than 90 min but less than 120 min	3.6
More than 120 min	4.1

mean response 4.1 to the question compared to a mean response of 2.3 for those who spent less than 30 min per week on their learning portfolio.

In response to the question; 'The learning portfolio encouraged a deeper, more personal engagement with the course learning', respondents who spent more than 120 min per week provided a mean response of 4.1 compared to a mean response of 2.3 for those spending less than 30 min per week on their learning portfolio.

In response to the question, 'Completing the learning portfolio encouraged regular, active participation in learning in this course', respondents who spent more than 120 min per week answered with a mean rating of 4.3 to the question compared to a mean response of 2.6 for those who spent less than 30 min per week on their learning portfolio.

In response to the question, 'Regular entries in the learning portfolio enabled me to consistently evaluate the progress of my learning', students who reported spending more than 120 min per week had a mean response of 3.9 to the question compared to a mean response of 2.6 for those who spent less than 30 min per week on their learning portfolio.

From the above analysis, the responses to the Likert scale part of the questionnaire can be viewed as partially supporting the view that the learning portfolio contributed to the development of some students' critical thinking skills. However, a possible limitation of the study is that no quantitative measure of increase in critical and creative thinking skills was undertaken. The written responses of students extracted from their learning portfolios, reflective essays and open-ended questions to the on-line administered questionnaire perhaps provide most insight into the feelings of some students.

A number of students were unhappy with this new form of assessment. The reaction of the student body to the learning portfolio item of assessment was mixed, with some students openly hostile to the assignment. The most scathing criticism came from a more mature student who commented:

> This is the most stupid thing I have ever had to do. I am over 30 and treated like a 14 year old. 3rd and 4th year students should not have to have their hand held, they should already know how to learn and if they don't then they shouldn't be studying.

Other students did not find this item of assessment to be of any benefit to them. These comments reflect their perceptions:

> I thought that the journal was a waste of time given the fact that I work and study full time. I found it a bit irrelevant.

> This was a serious waste of time for me, it was more like an admin. burden on my other work, it was a case of filling it out to get marks. Seriously I got nothing out of this piece of assessment, apart from some marks.

The attitude of those who considered the item of assessment to be a waste of time is perhaps consistent with the findings of Booth *et al.* (1999) and Hall *et al.* (2004) who found evidence that certain students did not wish to engage with the subject and adopted a surface approach to the study of Accounting. These views are also consistent with the findings of Biggs (1999, p. 35) who argues that 'although students have excellent ideas about what understanding means in real life, in practice understanding becomes whatever they see will meet assessment requirements'. In other words, from a student's perspective doing well on an item of assessment means regurgitating or retelling the material provided by the lecturers.

This position must, however, be tempered with the positive views expressed by other students. In the following quotations, students articulate the view that the learning portfolio permitted them to take ownership or control of their learning and create something unique to them:

> I feel that my best work and the most useful tool in this [course] was the learning portfolio. I decided early on that I would devote several hours per week to keeping this as up-to-date and as relevant as possible to the course. I used the personal journal as a way of tracking my progress and as a schedule of what needed to be done before the next lecture (readings, tutorial work, mini-cases, CATS, etc.). It kept me focused on what I needed to do in the immediate future rather than looking too far down the track as this often led to feelings of panic. I also enjoyed the opportunity to create something unique for my own use and to be able to personalize it with quotes, cartoons and articles which were relevant to me. (Summer School semester student.)

> The learning portfolio has been an excellent experience for me as this is the first time I feel I have really followed and been in control of my own learning. (B semester student.)

From these comments, it appears that certain students engaged with the learning portfolio as an item of assessment. For these students being in control of their own learning was important, a view supported by Biggs (1999).

The personal journal component of the learning portfolio assisted students to identify behaviour patterns as evidenced in the following comment by a student:

> For the learning portfolio I found that it was no use at all and was just a hassle to do every few days. I didn't use it at all for revision and never went back and read it again during the semester as I didn't feel what was in it was relevant . . . . Looking back at my learning journal I see that there's a theme of not turning up to lectures and not doing any preparation for tutorial and workshops and also there's a lot of comments about not doing any of the readings. (B semester student.)

There were students who found maintaining their learning portfolios difficult. A number of students who completed the questionnaire specifically referred to difficulties keeping up, with the following comment received by a B semester student being typical, 'the continuous nature of the learning portfolio, hardest part was keeping up'.

Additionally a number of students found the concept of reflection difficult and, as shown in the following quotation, felt that more regular, formal feedback could have been useful:

> I found it challenging to truly reflect, rather than approaching the journal as a descriptive piece of work. This is fundamentally different to previous learning approaches in other courses. Although we had a workshop and a number of resources, it would have been useful to have two hand-in's before the final due date as it would have been good to have a progress comment so that we could evaluate it better, especially as this assessment is so much different to other [courses].

Other students came to appreciate the concept of reflection. The following comment illustrates how a student found the reflective process useful, if not the vehicle through which the reflection took place:

> Perhaps more than any other course, [this course] has linked things together. During the semester I have often remembered past [courses], such as auditing, accounting theory and others. To be honest, I am not totally convinced this is the fault of [this course], or of being third year, where things *should* start falling into place. I think Grant has attempted to link things together, so perhaps it is a combination.
> In examining the impact of this 'learning experience' on my performance, I am afraid that it has been minimal. However, while I may not have felt that the actual writing of the journal was useful, the fact that I was thinking about it was. Like good art, it is not the representation, but the idea behind it that is important.
> Following on the above, I do not feel that the actual journal has aided my understanding of

course content, but the thought processes behind it has. In some ways, this exercise has had a much wider benefit than can be expressed in a journal or summary, it helped me understand the *why* as opposed to simply *how*. The value of that is immeasurable [emphasis in original] (B semester student).

The personal journal section of the learning portfolio was used by a number of students to express their frustration with their own learning, and with the course, as well as expressing dissatisfaction with teaching staff. It also provides a form of course evaluation that is perhaps more timely and ultimately more honest and perhaps more beneficial than the traditional evaluation completed at the end of the course.

It was envisaged that the development and implementation of the learning portfolio would provide students with a set of skills that they could use in later life. Indeed, some students even commented that they would continue to use the learning portfolio concept in other courses.

Assessing Levels of Reflective Thinking

In order to assess the level of reflection undertaken by students, an attempt was made to evaluate the level of reflective thinking contained in students' learning portfolios. While there is extensive literature dealing with the concept of reflection (see, for example, Baird, 1991; Kalliath and Coghlan, 2001; MacFarlane 2001; Kalliath, 2002; Plack and Greenberg, 2005), concern has been expressed by both Wong *et al.* (1995) and Kember *et al.* (1999) on the lack of published studies dealing with methods of reliably assessing reflection. Any course that contains a reflective component, according to Kember *et al.* (1999), should contain a valid and reliable procedure to assess this reflection. This assessment should include a process to establish whether students do in fact reflect upon their practice as well as the depth of that reflective thinking.

Before the level of reflective thinking can be assessed, it is necessary to identify the various levels of reflective thinking against which assessment will take place. This must include the ability to distinguish reflective thinking and writing from that which is non-reflective. To achieve this, Kember *et al.* (1999) developed a coding framework for assessing level of reflective thinking based on the work by Mezirow (1977; 1985; 1991; 1992).

Non-reflective action. Mezirow (1991) identifies three types of non-reflective action namely, habitual action, thoughtful action and introspection. Habitual action is that which is learnt before and, as it is performed automatically or with little conscious thought, it requires no thinking about the action while performing it. Examples of this include riding a bicycle or driving a car and as such they should not be recorded in a journal. As a cognitive process, according to Kember *et al.* (1999, p. 21), thoughtful action makes use of existing knowledge, without attempting to appraise that knowledge, so learning remains within pre-existing meaning schemes and perspectives. Mezirow (1991, p. 107) more fully describes thoughtful action as requiring a 'selective review of prior learning rather than a deliberate appraisal or reappraisal of it'. Kember *et al.* (1999, p. 21) suggest that much of the 'book learning' which takes place at universities is best classified as thoughtful action.

Introspection, according to Kember *et al.* (1999, p. 21), lies in the affective domain.

It refers to feelings or thoughts about ourselves. The feelings can be personal, such as recognizing that we feel happy, upset or bored with something. It can involve the recognition that we have feelings towards others such as liking or disliking them. It does not, however, encompass us deciding how or why these feelings developed as that becomes reflective think-ing. Introspection remains at the level of recognition or awareness of these feelings.

Introspection is not reflective, as it does not attempt to re-examine or test the validity of prior knowledge (Mezirow, 1991).

Reflective action.   Reflective action, as explained by Mezirow (1991, p. 108), is 'making decisions or taking other action predicated upon the insights resulting from reflection'. Reflective action starts with the posing of a problem and concludes with the taking of action.

Mezirow (1991) divides reflective thinking into three categories, namely content: reflec-tion, process reflection, and premise reflection. Kember *et al.* (1999, p. 23) consider content reflection and process reflection to be equivalent in level. They differ in the subject matter of the reflection. Mezirow (1991, p. 107) considers content reflection as reflection on 'what we perceive, feel or act upon'. It is concerned with *what*. Process reflection according to Kember *et al.* (1999, p. 23) 'is concerned more with our method or manner in which we think'. Mezirow (1991, p. 108) defines process reflection as being an 'examination of how one perform the functions of perceiving, thinking, feeling, or acting and an assessment of efficacy in performing them'.

Premise reflection is a higher level of reflective thinking. It is through premise reflection that an individual's meaning framework can be transformed as the possibility or perspec-tive transformation is opened. Mezirow (1991, p. 108) views premise reflection as invol-ving 'us becoming aware of why we perceive, think, feel or act as we do'. Kember *et al.* (1999, p. 24) suggest that it is unlikely that premise reflection would be observed within students' journals as this would require evidence of a significant change of perspective.

The categories described above translate into the coding framework developed by Kember *et al.* (1999) for assessing levels of reflective thinking. This is detailed in Figure 3 below. Distinguishing reflective action from non-reflective action is necessary to assess the content of reflective writing accurately.

Kember *et al.* (1999, p. 24) also provide the following additional description of the coding scheme:

> Categories shown on the same horizontal level are regarded as being equivalent in the level of reflective thinking. The shaded lower levels indicate non-reflective action while the upper unshaded ones are reflective.

Implementing the assessment framework.   Rather than attempting to code the whole learning portfolio, only the summary and reflection component of the learning portfolio was coded. This is consistent with the method reported by Kember *et al.* (1999). The

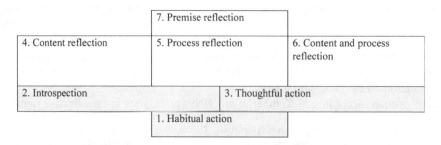

Figure 3. Coding categories for reflective action. *Source:* Kember *et al.* (1999, p. 25)

summary and reflection was for students to provide a summary of and reflection on their experiences in the course. This self-reflection was seen as being a useful method of consolidating any learning that occurred through the course.

Consistent with the approach used by Kember *et al.* (1999), a sample of 20 individual summaries and reflections were obtained and were coded by the course controller using the coding scheme described above. Each summary and reflection was assessed as a whole and categorized according to the highest level of reflective shown. It was found to be beneficial to code the summaries and reflections twice. Of the sample assessed, nine of the summaries and reflections were rated as introspection. In these summaries and reflections, students provided emotional responses rather than providing evidence of reflective writing. Three of the samples were graded as providing evidence of thoughtful action. Although these summaries and reflections provide evidence of students drawing on prior knowledge to make generalizations, judgements and evaluations, as with those graded as introspection there was no evidence of reflective writing.

The remaining eight of the sample showed some evidence of either content reflection or process reflection or both content and process reflection. One of the summaries and reflections graded provided evidence of content reflection in how the student thought, felt and acted upon his/her feelings. Three of the sample provided evidence of process reflection. Evidence of how students identified shortcomings in their knowledge and how they acted to overcome these deficiencies was provided in their summaries and reflections. Four of the students provided evidence of both content and process reflection. As suggested by Mezirow (1991), no evidence of premise reflection was identified in any of the summaries and reflections.

This test provided a convenient mechanism through which the extent and depth of written students' reflections can be evaluated. However, a limitation of this approach is that written reflections may only partially represent the students' thought processes.

Teaching Staff Reflections

From the perspective of the course convenor and the sole lecturer and tutors in this course, perhaps the single biggest consideration in introducing the learning portfolio was the demand it made on staff time. If regular feedback is to be provided, teaching staff must appreciate the time it takes to review all personal journal entries, CATS, feedback forms, module summaries and make meaningful comments on them. This additional workload requires careful time management—particularly with large classes. A further demand on time was the support and on-going assistance a number of students required in learning how to reflect. In the B semester, this need for assistance necessitated special workshop sessions as well as the majority of one lecture period being dedicated to reflection.

In spite of the demand on staff time, the introduction of the learning portfolio re-energised the teaching in the course. It was also enlightening. The personal journal component of the learning portfolio provided an intimate insight into the lives of individual students, into how they learn and into the individual circumstances that may impact negatively on their learning. The personal journal component of the learning portfolio enabled teaching staff to get to know individual students and to understand how they felt about the course and individual staff members. It is important, however, that staff members learn not to take things said by individual students in their learning portfolio personally.

The development of the additional questions for inclusion in the feedback forms required the course controller to reassess what was expected from students. The completed feedback forms provided teaching staff with insight into students' understanding that perhaps would not normally have been apparent until after summative assessment had taken place at the end of the semester. It was also rewarding to note the development in each individual student's reflective skills over the course. The entries in their personal journals went from the reporting of events and the content of lectures to showing signs of reflecting on particular issues. For this reason, the personal journal components of the learning portfolio would be used again.

Introducing a learning portfolio in a technical financial accounting course was considered an assessment risk. This risk was, however, unfounded and the item of assessment will be repeated in the future. Modifications will include a reduction in the overall number of CATs that will be used.

Including the learning portfolio as an item of assessment in a six-week Summer School semester programme will not be repeated. The time constraints associated with a Summer School semester course meant that teaching staff were unable to provide the same level of resources to these students as they did in the B semester. The authors do not believe a six-week period is sufficient time for students to develop fully the skills necessary for them to use a personal journal for reflective thinking.

Senior students who had successfully completed the course in previous semesters acted as tutors. Tutors found the review of the questions included in the feedback forms and the module summaries useful to establish whether students understood a particular concept. This information was then used to identify particular tutorial questions that became the focus of the weekly tutorial. For this reason, these particular CATs will continue to be used in future courses. When reflecting on the usefulness of the concept of the learning portfolio one tutor specifically commented on the qualitative aspect of the assessment. This tutor felt that an item of assessment that was completed over a semester benefited a number of students who perhaps had weaker quantitative skills. While tutors supported the concept of the learning portfolio, the additional workload associated with reviewing and commenting on students' CATs caused one tutor some concern.

5   Concluding Remarks

The paper has described the implementation and experience of introducing a learning portfolio in an undergraduate financial accounting course. It demonstrates how multiple strategies can simultaneously be used to encourage a deep approach to learning through the development of critical and creative thought.

A number of students found this item of assessment beneficial. This point of view is perhaps best expressed by the following comments:

> This learning portfolio is a learning tool, which will help students better understand, learn and reflect on issues covered in class and in other relevant areas. This portfolio brings together the essence of the course and provides students with a place of revision, and communication. A learning portfolio takes adjustment in mind, time, and discipline as it needs to be kept up-to-date and re-read to be able to reflect on earlier entries. (B semester student.)

For those students who did engage with this item of assessment, learning portfolios did seem to offer pedagogical benefits compared to benefits from more traditional forms of assessment used in the course. As such, the authors suggest that, for those students who engage with them, learning portfolios can contribute by facilitating a deep approach to learning.

The results of the questionnaire and entries in students' personal journals suggested that the new form of assessment requiring students to reassess their learning was not universally popular. In particular, the concept of reflection caused students difficulty. Some students found maintaining their learning portfolios to be tedious and not worth the marks allocated to it. The learning benefits of this item of assessment were not fully understood or appreciated by all students. The fact that a number of students did not attend the workshop or any of the drop-in support sessions may have contributed to this situation.

From a faculty perspective, the introduction of a learning portfolio sought to assist students in the development of their critical and creative thinking and to foster a deep approach to learning. Particularly useful for teaching purposes were the feedback form and the module summaries as they could be used to identify shortcomings in students' knowledge, allowing tutorials to be tailored accordingly. The Kember *et al.* (1999) coding framework was used to test of the extent and depth of a sample of students' reflections contained in their summary and reflection essays. This framework proved useful in that it provided confirmation of reflective thought by some students as well as a being a measure of the depth of reflective thinking. Taken as a whole, from the entries in their personal journals and summary and reflection essays, it appeared that some students did indeed start to develop a deep approach to learning. However, methods capable of identifying reflective thought and measuring the depth of reflective thinking by individual students remains worthy of further research.

The authors encourage others to consider the use of this form of assessment to develop a deep approach to learning on the part of accounting students, particularly in situations where they enjoy the luxury of small class sizes.

Acknowledgements

Dorothy Spiller of the Teaching Learning and Development Unit at the University of Waikato, and Dr Jackie Fry of the Open University Business School, UK, are thanked for their assistance. The three anonymous referees are also thanked for their very constructive comments.

References

Abdolmohammadi, M. and McQuade, R. J. (2002) *Applied Research in Financial Reporting* (New York: McGraw-Hill).

Almer, E. D., Jones, K. and Moeckel, C. L. (1998) The impact of one-minute papers on learning in an introductory accounting course, *Issues in Accounting Education*, 13(3), pp. 485–497.

Angelo, T. A. and Cross, K. P. (1991) *Classroom Assessment Techniques: A Handbook for College Teachers* (San Francisco, CA: Jossey-Bass).

Baird, J. (1991) Individual and group reflection as a basis for teacher development, in, P. Hughes (Ed.) *Professional Development*, pp. 95–111 (Hawthorne, Victoria: ACER)

Barclay, J. (1996) Learning from experience with learning logs, *Journal of Management Development*, 15(6), pp. 28–43.

Beard, V. (1993) Classroom Assessment Techniques (CATs): tools for improving accounting education, *Journal of Accounting Education*, 11(2), pp. 293–300.

Beattie, V., Collins, B. and McInnes, B. (1997) Deep and surface learning: a simple or simplistic dichotomy?, *Accounting Education: an international journal*, 6(1), pp. 1–12.

Biggs, J. (1987) *Student Approaches to Learning and Studying* (Hawthorn: Australian Council for Educational Research).

Biggs, J. (1989) Approaches to the enhancement of tertiary teaching, *Higher Education Research and Development*, 8(1), pp. 7–25.

Biggs, J. (1993) What do inventories of students' learning process really measure? A theoretical review and clarification, *British Journal of Educational Psychology*, 63(1), pp. 3–19.

Biggs, J. (1999) *Teaching for Quality Learning at University* (Philadelphia: Society for Research into Higher Education and Open University Press).

Bonk, C. J. and Smith, G. S. (1998) Alternative instructional strategies for creative and critical thinking in the accounting curriculum, *Journal of Accounting Education*, 16(2), pp. 261–293.

Booth, P., Luckett, P. and Mladenovic, R. (1999) The quality of learning in accounting: the impact of approaches to learning on academic performance, *Accounting Education: an international journal*, 8(4), pp. 277–300.

Brookfield, S. D. (1995) *Becoming a Critically Reflective Teacher* (San Francisco, CA: Jossey-Bass).

Cottell, P. G. and Harwood, E. M. (1996) Background Knowledge Probes: An example of the synergy between co-operative learning and classroom assessment techniques, *Co-operative Learning and College Teaching*, 1(7), pp. 6–8.

Cottell, P. G. and Harwood, E. M. (1998) Using Classroom Assessment Techniques to improve student learning in accounting classes, *Issues in Accounting Education*, 13(3), pp. 551–564.

Cunningham, B. M. (1996) How to restructure an accounting course of enhance creative and critical thinking, *Accounting Education: A Journal of Theory, Practice and Research*, 1(1), pp. 49–66.

Cunningham, B. M. (1999) Energising your teaching: a view from deep in the trenches, *Issues in Accounting Education*, 14(2), pp. 307–321.

Dart, B. C., Boulton-Lewis, G. M., Brownlee, J. M. and McCrindle, A. R. (1998) Change in knowledge of learning and teaching through journal writing, *Research Papers in Education*, 13(3), pp. 291–319.

Day, M. M., Kaidonis, M. A. and Perrin, R. W. (2003) Reflexivity in learning critical accounting. Implications for teaching and its research nexus, *Critical Perspectives on Accounting*, 14(5), pp. 597–614.

De Lange, P. and Mavondo, F. (2004) Gender and motivational differences in approaches to learning by a cohort of open learning students, *Accounting Education: an international journal*, 13(4), pp. 431–448.

Elias, R. Z. (2005) Students' approaches to study in introductory accounting courses, *Journal for Education for Business*, 80(4), pp. 194–199.

Entwistle, N. (1981) *Styles of Learning and Teaching: An Integrated Outline of Educational Psychology for Students, Teachers and Lecturers* (Chichester: John Wiley).

Gainen, J. and Locatelli, P. (1995) *Assessment for the New Curriculum: A Guide for Professional Accounting Programs* (Florida: American Accounting Association).

Hahnemann, B. K. (1986) Journal writing: A key of promoting critical thinking in nursing students, *Journal of Nursing Education*, 25(5), pp. 213–215.

Haigh, M. J. (2001) Constructing Gaia: using Journals to foster reflective learning, *Journal of Geography in Higher Education*, 25(2), pp. 167–189.

Hall, M., Ramsay, A. and Raven, J. (2004) Changing the learning environment to promote deep learning approached in first-year accounting students, *Accounting Education: an international journal*, 13(4), pp. 489–505.

Harwood., E. (1999) Student perceptions of the effects of classroom assessment techniques (CATs), *Journal of Accounting Education*, 17(1), pp. 51–70.

Harwood, E. M. and Cohen, J. R. (1999) Classroom Assessment: Educational and research opportunities, *Issues in Accounting Education*, 14(4), pp. 691–724.

Herring, H. C., and Izard, C. D. (1992) Outcomes assessment of accounting majors, *Issues in Accounting Education*, 7(1), pp. 1–17.

Hidi, S. and Anderson, V. (1986) Producing written summaries: task demands, cognitive operations, and implications for instruction, *Review of Educational Research*, 56(4), pp. 473–493.

Hoff, K. T. and Stout, D. E. (1989) Practical accounting/English collaboration to improve student writing skills. The use of informal journals and the diagnostic reading technique, *The Accounting Educators' Journal*, 2(2), pp. 83–96.

Hogan, C. (1995) Creative and reflective journal processes, *The Learning Organization: An International Journal*, 2(2), pp. 4–17.

Hounsell, D. (2003) The evaluation of teaching, in H. Fry, S. Ketteridge and S. Marshall (Eds) *A Handbook for Teaching and Learning in Higher Education*, pp. 200–211 (London: Kogan Page).

Howieson, B. (2004) *The Use of Self-reflective Study Journals in a Postgraduate Accounting Theory Course: A Case Study*. Paper presented to the 2004 IAAER/Southern African Accounting Association Conference, Durban 30 June–2 July.

International Federation of Accountants (IFAC) (2003) *Introduction to International Education Standards* (New York: IFAC).

Kalliath, T. and Coglan, D. (2001) Developing reflective skills through journal writing in an OD course, *Organization Development Journal*, 19(4), pp. 61–70.

Kalliath, T. (2002) Implementing action learning in an OD classroom, *Organization Development Journal*, 20(3), pp. 62–73.

Kember, D., Jones, A., Loke, A., McKay, J. Sinclair, K., Tse, H., Webb, C. Wong, F., Wong, M. and Yeung, E. (1999) Determining the level of reflective thinking from students' written journals using a coding scheme based on the work of Mezirow, *International Journal of Lifelong Education*, 18(1), pp. 18–30.

Kimmel, P. (1995) A framework for incorporating critical thinking into accounting education, *Journal of Accounting Education*, 13(3), pp. 299–318.

Klenowski, V. (2002) *Developing Portfolios for Learning and Assessment* (London: Routledge Falmer).

Langer, A. M. (2002) Reflecting on practice: using learning journals in higher and continuing education, *Teaching in Higher Education*, 7(3), pp. 337–413.

Loo, R. and Thorpe, K. (2002) Using reflective learning journals to improve individual and team performance, *Team Performance Management: An International Journal*, 8(5–6), pp. 134–139.

MacFarlane, B. (2001) Developing reflective students: evaluating the benefits of learning logs within a business ethics programme, *Teaching Business Ethics*, 5(4), pp. 375–387.

McCrindle, A. R. and Christensen, C. A. (1995) The impact of learning journals on metacognitive and cognitive processes and learning performance, *Learning and Instruction*, 5(2), pp. 167–185.

Marton, F. and Säljö, R. (1976) On qualitative differences in learning—1: outcome and process, *British Journal of Educational Psychology*, 46(1), pp. 4–11.

Mezirow, J. (1977) Perspective transformation, *Studies in Adult Education*, 9(2), pp. 153–164.

Mezirow, J. (1985) A critical theory of self-directed learning, in S. Brookfield (Ed.) *Self-directed Learning: From Theory to Practice*, pp. 17–30 (San Francisco, CA: Jossey-Bass).

Mezirow, J. (1991) *Transformative Dimensions of Adult Learning* (San Francisco, CA: Jossey-Bass).

Mezirow, J. (1992) Transformation theory: critique and confusion, *Adult Education Quarterly*, 42(4), pp. 250–252.

Moon, J. A. (1999) *Learning Journals: A Handbook for Academics, Students and Professional Development* (London: Kogan Page).

Morrison, K. (1996) Developing reflective practice in higher degree students through a learning journal, *Studies in Higher Education*, 21(3), pp. 317–332.

November, P. (1996) Journals for the journey into deep learning: a framework, *Higher Education Research and Development*, 15(1), pp. 115–127.

Oppenheim, A. (1992) *Questionnaire Design, Interviewing and Attitude Measurement* (London: Cassell).

Plack, M. M. and Greenberg, L. (2005) The reflective practitioner: reaching for excellence in practice, *Paediatrics*, 116(6), pp. 1546–1552.

Ramsden, P. (2003) *Learning to Teach in Higher Education* (London: Routledge Falmer).

Robson, C. (2002) *Real World Research* (Oxford: Blackwell Publishing).

Rosier, G. (2002) Using reflective reports to improve the case method, *The Journal of Management Development*, 8, pp. 589–597.

Routledge, J., Willson, M., McArthur, M., Richardson, B. and Stephenson, R. (1997) Reflection on the development of a reflective assessment, *Medical Teacher*, 19(2), pp. 122–128.

Sharma, D. S. (1997) Accounting students' learning conceptions, approaches to learning, and the influence of the learning-teaching context on approaches to learning, *Accounting Education: an international journal*, 6(2), pp. 125–146.

Trigwell, K., Prosser, M. and F. Waterhouse. (1999) Relations between teachers' approaches to teaching and students' approaches to learning, *Higher Education*, 37(1), pp. 57–70.

Viswesvaran, C., Barick, M. R. and Ones, D. S. (1993) How definitive are conclusions based on survey data: estimating robustness to non-response, *Personnel Psychology*, 46(3), pp. 551–567.

Warburton, K. (2003) Deep learning and education for sustainability, *International Journal of Sustainability in Higher Education*, 4(1), pp. 44–56.

Winograd, P. (1984) Strategic difficulties in summarising texts, *Reading Research Quarterly*, 19(4), pp. 404–425.

Wolcott, S. K. and Lynch, C. L. (1997) Critical thinking in the accounting classroom: a reflective judgment development process perspective, *Accounting Education: A Journal of Theory, Practice and Research*, 2(1), pp. 59–78.

Wong, F. Y. K., Kember, D., Chung, L. Y. F. and Yan, L. (1995). Assessing the level of student reflection from reflective journals, *Journal of Advanced Nursing*, 22(1), pp. 48–57.

Wygal, D. E. and Stout, D. E. (1989) Incorporating writing techniques in the accounting classroom: experiences in financial, managerial and cost courses, *Journal of Accounting Education*, 7(2), pp. 245–252.

Appendix 1

Feedback form
Financial Accounting
Module: Accounting for groups

Name and ID number: Date:
Tutorial group (include tutors name):

1. **I have the following questions relating to:**

Text material (Page/section)	
Lecture material	
Tutorial	
Workshop	

My question is

✓ ..... I Don't have a question for today – I'm all set.

2. What does minority interest represent and how should it be disclosed in the financial statements?

The other parties that have an investment Intrest in a company (equity) within your control It should be disclosed as a liability in your accounts as that would be the parties entitlement If the Company was liquidated

Forgot to change the text book so Learn't wrong thing made notes and corrected Book.

3. Explain using an example, how the downstream inter-entity sale of a fixed asset should be accounted for in the economic entity's financial statements year after the initial sale. You may find it useful to develop a short problem and use journal entries to assist in your explanation.

(A) Parent
↓ downstream
(B) Sub

Company A fully owns Company B On July 94 B buys a plant from Company A for $340,000. This had originally cost Company A 500,000 & was depreciated over 10yrs Accumulated depreciation was 200,000 at time of Sale. Account for the Sale asset In the accounts for the July 96 assume tax rate 30%

DR Plant   500,000
DR Retained Earn 40,000
* CR Acc depreciation 200,000*
* CR Plant   340,000*
° reverse Sale.

DR Tax Deferred - FTB 12,000
* CR Tax expense Retained E 12,000*
° record tax effect Sale reversal

DR Depreciation   16,000
DR RIE - beg   16,000
* CR Accumulated Depreciation 32,000*
To account for depreciation in the two yrs:
DR Deferred tax   4800
DR Retained Earn - beg 4800
* CR Tax expense   9600   To record tax effect of dep*

Figure A1. Exemplar of feedback form

Appendix 2

Table A1. Learning portfolio assessment instrument

Name: . . . .   Mark
ID Number: . . . .   awarded

Personal day to day journal

0–6   No entries made in journal.

7–12   Evidence of sporadic entries made in journal. No evidence of self-evaluation or use of classroom assessment techniques to provide evidence of learning development. Journal provides no evidence of width, depth or distance.

13–18   Some entries made in the journal. Some evidence of self-evaluation and classroom assessment techniques used to provide evidence of learning development. Journal provides some evidence of width, depth or distance.

19–24   Entries made in the journal on a regular basis. Self-evaluation and classroom assessment techniques provide evidence of learning development. Journal shows substantial evidence of width, depth and distance.

25–30   Journal kept up to date through consistent entries. Self-evaluation and classroom assessment techniques provide comprehensive evidence of learning development. Journal contains compelling evidence of width, depth and distance.

Classroom assessment techniques

0–4   Classroom assessment techniques not completed or seldom completed and with no care.

5–8   Classroom assessment techniques completed sporadically and with little care.

9–12   Classroom assessment techniques generally completed. Evidence of some care in their completion provided.

13–16   Evidence provided of most of the classroom assessment techniques being completed in a satisfactory manner.

17–20   Completion of all classroom assessment techniques in a consistently excellent manner.

Summary and reflection

0–8   The summary and reflection make assertions without supportive evidence and arguments.

9–16   The summary and reflection is simply a recall of facts with little or no supporting evidence provided. Where evidence is provided, there is no effort to supplement evidence with own critical reflections.

17–24   There is little evidence of independent reflection in the summary and reflection and research is superficial with a minimum attempt at analysis and or synthesis.

25–32   Arguments are used in the summary and reflection to support the student's point of view and references are used appropriately.

33–40   The summary and reflection demonstrates deep and original thinking, interpretation, critical thinking and synthesis. Cogent arguments are used and supported by well-selected references.

Creativity

0–2   No evidence of creativity provided in the development of the learning portfolio.

3–4   Minimal evidence of creativity used in the development of the learning portfolio.

5–6   Student has used creativity in the development of learning portfolio.

7–8   Student has been highly creative in the development of the learning portfolio.

9–10   Outstanding creativity used in the overall development of learning portfolio.

                                                                        Total marks

---

Appendix 3

Table A2. Responses to evaluation questionnaire. Raw data

		Strongly agree	Agree	Neutral	Disagree	Strongly disagree	n
Maintaining my learning portfolio assisted me in the	B	0	20	14	12	8	54
development of my written communication skills.	S	1	9	9	3	3	25
Maintaining my learning portfolio assisted me to develop	B	3	22	9	11	9	54
critical thinking skills.	S	4	9	7	4	1	25
The tutors answered the questions that I raised on my feedback	B	8	26	17	3	0	54
form to my satisfaction.	S	6	13	2	3	1	25
The learning portfolio encouraged a deeper, more personal	B	7	21	6	12	8	54
engagement with the course learning.	S	6	8	6	3	2	25
Completing the learning portfolio encouraged regular, active	B	10	18	8	10	7	53
participation in learning in this course.	S	4	14	5	0	2	25
Regular entries in the learning portfolio enabled me to evaluate	B	7	21	9	9	7	53
consistently the progress of my learning.	S	3	9	10	1	2	25
The questions contained on the feedback forms were useful	B	6	28	16	2	1	53
for revision purposes.	S	4	12	7	2	0	25
The feedback forms enabled me to identify areas in which I	B	7	27	15	3	1	53
was weak and needed to focus on.	S	3	11	4	7	0	25
By completing the feedback forms and making entries in my	B	2	22	15	13	1	53
learning portfolio, I was able to engage in an ongoing dialogue with the lecturer and tutors.	S	2	6	11	5	1	25
The learning portfolio mark plan supplied provided me with an	B	7	24	16	6	0	53
adequate indication of how the individual components of my portfolio would be assessed.	S	1	6	15	1	2	25

From a 5-point Likert scale where 5 = strongly agree; 4 = agree; 3 = neutral; 2 = disagree; 1 = strongly disagree. B = Second Semester, S = Summer School, n = number of responses to each question.

Appendix 4

Table A3. Responses to evaluation questionnaire. Responses split between home and international students

	Origin	Mean response	*n*
Maintaining my learning portfolio assisted me in the development of my written communication skills.	H	2.8	56
	I	3.4	24
Maintaining my learning portfolio assisted me to develop critical thinking skills.	H	2.9	56
	I	3.7	24
The tutors answered the questions that I raised on my feedback form to my satisfaction.	H	3.7	56
	I	3.8	24
The learning portfolio encouraged a deeper, more personal engagement with the course learning.	H	3.0	56
	I	3.7	24
Completing the learning portfolio encouraged regular, active participation in learning in this course.	H	3.4	56
	I	3.5	24
Regular entries in the learning portfolio enabled me to evaluate consistently the progress of my learning.	H	3.2	56
	I	3.4	24
The questions contained on the feedback forms were useful for revision purposes.	H	3.7	56
	I	3.7	24
The feedback forms enabled me to identify areas in which I was weak and needed to focus on.	H	3.6	56
	I	3.6	24
By completing the feedback forms and making entries in my learning portfolio, I was able to engage in an	H	3.1	56
ongoing dialogue with the lecturer and tutors.	I	3.4	24
The learning portfolio mark plan supplied provided me with an adequate indication of how the individual	H	3.4	56
components of my portfolio would be assessed.	I	3.7	24

Mean and standard deviations are from a 5-point Likert scale where 5 = strongly agree; 4 = agree; 3 = neutral; 2 = disagree; 1 = strongly disagree. H = home students, I = international students, *n* = number of responses to each question.

Appendix 5

Table A4. Responses to evaluation questionnaire. Responses split between those under 24 and those 25 years and over

	Age	Mean response	n
Maintaining my learning portfolio assisted me in the development of my written communication skills.	24 years and younger	2.6	58
	25 and over	3.6	22
Maintaining my learning portfolio assisted me to develop critical thinking skills.	24 years and younger	2.9	58
	25 and over	3.7	22
The tutors answered the questions that I raised on my feedback form to my satisfaction.	24 years and younger	3.7	58
	25 and over	4.0	22
The learning portfolio encouraged a deeper, more personal engagement with the course learning.	24 years and younger	3.0	58
	25 and over	3.0	22
Completing the learning portfolio encouraged regular, active participation in learning in this course.	24 years and younger	3.2	58
	25 and over	4.0	22
Regular entries in the learning portfolio enabled me to consistently evaluate the progress of my learning.	24 years and younger	3.1	58
	25 and over	3.8	22
The questions contained on the feedback forms were useful for revision purposes.	24 years and younger	3.6	58
	25 and over	3.9	22
The feedback forms enabled me to identify areas in which I was weak and needed to focus on.	24 years and younger	3.6	58
	25 and over	3.7	22
By completing the feedback forms and making entries in my learning portfolio, I was able to engage in an ongoing dialogue with the lecturer and tutors	24 years and younger	3.1	58
	25 and over	3.5	22
The learning portfolio mark-plan provided me with an adequate indication of how the individual components of my portfolio would be assessed	24 years and younger	3.4	58
	25 and over	3.6	22

Mean and standard deviations are from a 5-point Likert scale where 5 = strongly agree; 4 = agree; 3 = neutral; 2 = disagree; 1 = strongly disagree. n = number of responses to each individual question.

Appendix 6

Table A5. Responses to evaluation questionnaire. Responses split between B semester and shorter Summer School semester

	Semester response	Mean	SD	n
Maintaining my learning portfolio assisted me in the development of my written communication skills.	B	2.9	1.1	54
	S	3.1	1.1	25
Maintaining my learning portfolio assisted me to develop critical thinking skills.	B	3.0	1.2	54
	S	3.4	1.1	25
The tutors answered the questions that I raised on my feedback form to my satisfaction.	B	3.7	0.8	54
	S	3.8	1.1	25
The learning portfolio encouraged a deeper, more personal engagement with the course learning.	B	3.1	1.3	54
	S	3.5	1.2	25
Completing the learning portfolio encouraged regular, active participation in learning in this course.	B	3.3	1.3	53
	S	3.7	1.0	25
Regular entries in the learning portfolio enabled me to consistently evaluate the progress of my learning.	B	3.2	1.3	53
	S	3.4	1.0	25
The questions contained on the feedback forms were useful for revision purposes.	B	3.7	0.8	53
	S	3.7	0.8	25
The feedback forms enabled me to identify areas in which I was weak and needed to focus on.	B	3.7	0.9	53
	S	3.4	1.0	25
By completing the feedback forms and making entries in my learning portfolio, I was able to engage in	B	3.2	0.9	53
an ongoing dialogue with the lecturer and tutors.	S	3.1	1.0	25
The learning portfolio mark plan supplied provided me with an adequate indication of how the	B	3.6	0.9	53
individual components of my portfolio would be assessed.	S	3.1	0.9	25

Mean and standard deviations are from a 5-point Likert scale where 5 = strongly agree; 4 = agree; 3 = neutral; 2 = disagree; 1 = strongly disagree. n = number of responses to each question.

Appendix 7

Table A6. Responses to evaluation questionnaire. Responses split between male and female students

	Gender	Mean response	n
Maintaining my learning portfolio assisted me in the development of my written communication skills.	M	2.6	39
	F	3.3	41
Maintaining my learning portfolio assisted me to develop critical thinking skills.	M	2.8	39
	F	3.3	41
The tutors answered the questions that I raised on my feedback form to my satisfaction.	M	3.8	39
	F	3.7	41
The learning portfolio encouraged a deeper, more personal engagement with the course learning.	M	3.0	39
	F	3.5	41
Completing the learning portfolio encouraged regular, active participation in learning in this course.	M	3.0	39
	F	3.8	41
Regular entries in the learning portfolio enabled me to consistently evaluate the progress of my learning.	M	2.9	39
	F	3.6	41
The questions contained on the feedback forms were useful for revision purposes.	M	3.6	39
	F	3.8	41
The feedback forms enabled me to identify areas in which I was weak and needed to focus on.	M	3.4	39
	F	3.8	41
By completing the feedback forms and making entries in my learning portfolio, I was able to engage in an	M	2.8	39
ongoing dialogue with the lecturer and tutors.	F	3.5	41
The learning portfolio mark plan supplied provided me with an adequate indication of how the individual	M	3.3	39
components of my portfolio would be assessed.	F	3.6	41

Mean and standard deviations are from a 5-point Likert scale where 5 = strongly agree; 4 = agree; 3 = neutral; 2 = disagree; 1 = strongly disagree. M = male students, F = female students, n = number of responses to each question.

Moral Intensity and Ethical Decision-making: An Empirical Examination of Undergraduate Accounting and Business Students

BREDA SWEENEY* and FIONA COSTELLO**

*NUI Galway, Ireland, **KPMG

ABSTRACT   *Ethical decision-making is theorised to consist of four stages: identification of an ethical dilemma, ethical judgement, ethical intentions and ethical actions. The moral intensity of the situation has been found to influence the ethical decision-making process. Using a survey consisting of four scenarios, this study examined the relationship between perceived moral intensity and the first three stages of the ethical decision-making process for undergraduate accounting and other business students. Findings showed that the nature of the ethical dilemma in the scenarios impacted on perceived moral intensity and the ethical decision-making process. Moral intensity was found to be multi-dimensional in the study and the social consensus component of moral intensity demonstrated the strongest relationship with the ethical decision-making process. Differences were found between accounting and non-accounting students, though gender was not found to be significant. Implications of the findings and areas for future research are discussed in the paper.*

Introduction

In response to accounting scandals that have rocked the accounting profession worldwide, the area of ethics has attracted increased attention and has led many to question the ethical reasoning of accountants. Much of the research in the area has focused on developing numerous models to better understand individuals' ethical decision-making process as 'understanding why and how individuals and groups make ethical decisions in a business context should improve the ethical decisions made in the organizational context' (Loe *et al.*, 2000, p. 200). The benefits of improved ethical decision-making are wide-ranging and, for example, better ethical decision-making processes may have resulted in a different audit opinion on Enron (Jones *et al.*, 2003). Overall, if ethical behaviour in business is to be improved, it is essential that the factors affecting ethical decision-making are understood (Barnett and Valentine, 2004) and are incorporated into the moral education of accountants.

Rest (1986) developed a model of ethical action consisting of four sequential steps that must occur if moral behaviour is to be observed (identification of an ethical dilemma, ethical judgement, intention to act ethically and ethical action/behaviour). Previous research has examined the impact of individual, situational and organizational factors on this ethical decision-making model (Wright *et al.*, 1997; Douglas *et al.*, 2001). Many ethical decision-making models assume the same decision process regardless of the type of ethical dilemma facing an individual (Jones, 1991). An assessment of the ethical dilemma itself and its influence on the ethical decision process is an important topic that has received little attention to date (Leitsch, 2004). Jones (1991) theorised that the characteristics of an ethical dilemma (moral intensity) significantly impact on all stages of the ethical decision-making process. For example, as Leitsch (2006) pointed out, stealing a pen or a piece of paper from one's workplace would be regarded by most people as less unethical than embezzlement of large sums of money. Knowledge of, and empirical support for, Jones's (1991) model will help increase our understanding of the ethical decision-making process and will have important implications for educators and employers. Both education and training programmes can be designed around the components of moral intensity to benefit individuals and, in the context of accountancy, restore the image of the profession. Empirical research on Jones's (1991) model in the field of accounting represents an important avenue for future research (Leitsch, 2006).

The purpose of this study is to extend Jones's (1991) theoretical model to the ethical decision-making process of accounting and other business students using business scenarios. Insights into the ethical decision-making process of business and accounting students is expected to have implications for third level educators and employers such as accounting firms which recruit directly from college. Specifically, the study will explore the relationship between the perceived moral intensity and the ethical decision-making process of accounting and business students. The study will also examine differences in perceived moral intensity and the ethical decision-making process between different types of business scenarios. Finally, the study will examine the effect of both gender and academic major on perceived moral intensity and the decision-making process.

Background Literature

Ethical Decision-making

Research in accounting ethics has been significantly influenced by the work of Rest (1979; 1986). Rest (1986) maintained that, in order to incorporate an ethical dimension into a decision, an individual must proceed through four sequential steps as shown in Figure 1.

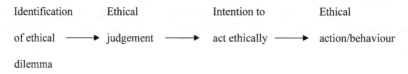

Figure 1. Rest's (1986) model of ethical action

The first stage, identification of an ethical dilemma, involves an awareness that a dilemma may affect the welfare of others. An individual must first identify an ethical dilemma before he/she can behave morally. Chia and Mee (2000, p. 255) explain that 'when individuals recognize the moral dimension of an issue, this recognition has the potential to influence their judgements, intentions and decisions'.

Once a dilemma is identified, an individual comes to an ethical judgement (second stage) based on evaluating the outcomes that ought to occur in a given situation. Ethical judgement is determined in part by an individual's moral development, which is often described using Kohlberg's (1969) six-stage model. Much criticism exists of Kohlberg's theory and these criticisms (summarized by White, 1999) have focused on the number of stages in the model (Gibbs, 1979; Habermas, 1979); the existence of a western cultural bias in the model (Sullivan, 1977; Snell, 1996); the excessive focus on cognitive aspects of moral reasoning and lack of focus on emotional and affective aspects (Guertin, 1986); and the existence of a gender bias in the model towards the male perspective (Gilligan, 1982). Despite these criticisms, however, Kohlberg's work remains perhaps one of the most distinguished theories of moral development.

Once an ethical judgement is made, the individual formulates an intention to act ethically (third stage) based on an assessment of the 'right' choice versus other alternatives. The establishment of ethical intentions is critical to Rest's (1986) model as previous research by Fishbein and Ajzen (1975) has concluded that intentions are important determinants of behaviour. The final stage is the actual carrying out of the ethical action and little research has been carried out on this stage due to difficulties in measuring and observing behaviour (Jones *et al.*, 2003). Rest (1986) outlined that success in one stage does not imply success in any other stage, as each stage in the process is conceptually distinct. The simplistic links between judgement and action presented in Rest's model have been questioned. Brown and Hernstein (1975) suggested that moral action develops independently of moral judgement and White (1999) referred to a number of studies, which suggest that individuals under pressure may act immorally despite capacity for at least conventional moral reasoning.

Questions over the links between the steps in Rest's model led many researchers to suggest variables that they believe impact on Rest's (1986) model (Cohen *et al.*, 1996; Trevino, 1986). Jones (1991) theorised a six dimensional construct, moral intensity, which he believed impacted on the decision-making process. This construct of moral intensity characterises the ethical dilemma itself and is theorised by Jones (1991) to be an independent variable affecting all four stages of Rest's (1986) model of ethical action.

Moral Intensity

Jones (1991, p. 372) defined moral intensity as 'a construct that captures the extent of issue-related moral imperative in a situation'. Moral intensity is composed of six components (magnitude of consequences, social consensus, temporal immediacy, probability of effect, proximity and concentration of effect) that help to describe the characteristics of a moral issue. According to Jones (1991, p. 373), 'moral intensity is likely to vary substantially from issue to issue, with a few issues achieving high levels and many issues achieving low levels'. A situation will not be viewed by a decision-maker as having an ethical element if the moral intensity of that situation is viewed as weak in terms of the components of moral intensity (Singhapakdi *et al.*, 1996).

Jones (1991, p. 374) defined magnitude of consequences as 'the sum of the harms (or benefits) done to the victims (or beneficiaries) of the moral act in question'. The more serious the consequence, the more likely a person is to become morally outraged.

Social consensus is defined by Jones (1991, p. 375) as 'the degree of social agreement that a proposed act is evil (or good)'. If a person does not know what constitutes good ethics in a given situation, then it is difficult for them to act ethically (Jones, 1991). When individuals are unsure what constitutes good ethics they turn to others for guidance on the degree of social acceptability of the action. As a result, Jones believed that any ambiguity that may exist over the ethically correct course of action is reduced when a high degree of social consensus exists. Empirical studies have found the greatest support for the impact of these two dimensions on the ethical decision-making process (Carlson *et al.*, 2002; Barnett and Valentine, 2004). Findings, however, have been inconclusive on the relative importance of these dimensions and Barnett and Valentine (2004) suggested that one of the reasons for this may be differences in the moral development of the samples used. Many of the studies showing perceived social consensus as the key dimension use student samples, whereas studies finding perceived magnitude of consequences as the more significant dimension have sampled practicing managers or professionals (Barnett and Valentine, 2004).

Probability of effect is a 'joint function of the probability that the act in question will actually take place and the act in question will actually cause the harm (benefit) predicted' (Jones, 1991, p. 375) with lower probability implying lower moral intensity. Jones (1991, p. 376) defined temporal immediacy as 'the length of time between the present and onset of consequences of the moral act' and the shorter the length of time, the greater the moral intensity. According to Jones (1991, p. 377), concentration of effect is an 'inverse function of the number of people affected by an act of given magnitude'. People are more concerned about acts that cause greater harm and have a more concentrated effect than those which do not. Proximity is defined by Jones (1991, p. 376) as 'the feeling of nearness (social, cultural, psychological or physical) that the moral agent has for victims (beneficiaries) of the evil (beneficial) act in question' with greater proximity implying greater moral intensity. Mixed empirical evidence has been found on the significance of these components in the ethical decision making process.

Jones (1991) maintained that the six components all represent characteristics of the moral issue itself and are all expected to have interactive effects. He theorized that if any component increases, it is generally expected that the overall level of moral intensity will also increase, and vice versa, assuming all remaining components are constant. However, for moral intensity to vary significantly threshold levels of all components would need to be reached and measurement is probably possible only in terms of large distinctions (Jones, 1991).

Hypotheses Development and Research Method

Ethical Decision-making Process

Ethical reasoning is theorised to consist of four stages in Rest's (1986) Model of Ethical Action and, in order to incorporate an ethical dimension into a decision, an individual must proceed through the four sequential steps. This paper will examine the link between the first three stages of the model. The last stage has been excluded due to difficulties in measuring actual behaviour. Barnett and Valentine (2004) found that recognition of an ethical issue was significantly related to ethical judgement and both variables were significantly related to behavioural intentions. Accordingly, it is hypothesized that:

H1(a)   Identification of an ethical dilemma will be positively correlated with ethical judgement;

H1(b)   Identification of an ethical dilemma will be positively correlated with ethical intentions;

H1(c)   Ethical judgement will be positively correlated with ethical intentions.

Identification of an Ethical Dilemma

Jones (1991, p. 383) theorized that 'issues of high moral intensity will be recognized as moral issues more frequently than will issues of low moral intensity'. He maintained that the identification of ethical dilemmas is due to their salience and vividness and items are salient to the extent that they stand out from their backgrounds. Ethical dilemmas with these traits tend to elicit more information from our memories and capture our emotional interest, dominating our attention and thus making the recognition of ethical dilemmas more probable (Nisbett and Ross, 1980). Findings on the relationship between moral intensity and identification of an ethical dilemma have been mixed. Singhapakdi et al. (1996) found that a two factor solution (and each of the individual components) of moral intensity was significantly related to moral identification in all four scenarios examined. Marshall and Dewe (1997), however, found only social consensus and magnitude of consequences to be positively related to identification. May and Pauli (2002) found that moral intensity was significantly related to identification in only one of their two scenarios and the social consensus component was not significant in either scenario. Given these mixed findings, further testing is necessary and the following relationship is hypothesized:

H2(a)   Perceived moral intensity will be positively related to identification of an ethical dilemma.

Ethical Judgement

Jones (1991) suggested that moral agents would economize on efforts devoted to ethical judgement where less ethical issues are concerned because ethical judgement takes time and energy. He theorized that 'issues of high moral intensity will elicit more sophisticated moral reasoning (higher levels of cognitive moral development) than will issues of low moral intensity' (p. 385). The relationship between this stage of the ethical decision process and moral intensity has received the greatest attention empirically with social consensus and magnitude of consequences emerging as the most significant components of moral intensity (Jones and Huber, 1992; Singer and Singer, 1997; Morris and McDonald, 1995). Singhapakdi et al. (1996) found magnitude of consequences, social consensus, temporal immediacy and probability of harm to be significantly related to ethical judgement. Barnett and Valentine (2004) found magnitude of consequences and social consensus to be significantly related to ethical judgement but not proximity of harm or temporal immediacy. The following relationship is hypothesized:

H2(b)   Perceived moral intensity will be positively related to ethical judgement.

Ethical Intentions

Jones (1991) noted that moral intensity also plays a role in establishing ethical intentions through proximity, a desire to avoid aversive consequences where social consensus is high and also the influence on affect (emotions, feelings and mood). This led Jones (1991, p. 387) to postulate 'that moral intent will be established more frequently where issues of high moral intensity are involved than where issues of low moral intensity are involved'. A number of studies found a significant relationship between ethical intentions and social consensus (Jones and Huber, 1992; Harrington, 1997) and between ethical intentions and magnitude of consequences (Cohen et al., 2001; Chia and Mee, 2000; Flannery and May, 2000). Cohen et al. (2001) also found that both proximity and concentration of effect impacted on intentions though proximity was not found to be significant by Singhapakdi et al. (1996). The following relationship is hypothesized:

H2(c)   Perceived moral intensity will be positively related to ethical intentions.

Moral Intensity of the Issue

Previous research has suggested that the perceived importance of the moral intensity components along with their effect on the ethical decision-making process was influenced by the type of situation and was likely to vary between less unethical and more unethical issues (Leitsch, 2004). Leitsch (2004) found that the sensitivity towards the ethical nature of the issue, ethical judgement, ethical intentions and the perceptions of moral intensity, varied between less unethical and more unethical issues. Other researchers have identified differences in ethical judgements depending on the nature of the situation facing individuals with differences being observed between less unethical and more unethical issues (Weber, 1990; Barnett and Brown, 1994). Studies by both Robin et al. (1996) and Shafer et al. (2001) concluded that the importance of ethical issues influenced behavioural intentions. As a result it is hypothesized that:

H3   The type of situation will influence the perceived importance of the moral
            intensity components and the ethical decision-making process.

Demographic Variables

The impact of gender on the ethical decision-making process is a widely researched variable in ethics literature with the majority of studies either revealing no significant differences between males and females (Hegarty and Sims, 1978; Dubinsky and Levy, 1985; Browning and Zabriskie, 1983; Singhapakdi and Vitell, 1990; Sikula and Costa, 1994; Serwinek, 1992) or finding males to be less ethically sensitive compared to females (Clarke et al., 1996; Etherington and Schulting, 1995; Shaub, 1994; Cohen et al., 1998; Thorne, 1999). Silver and Valentine (2001) concluded that, overall, women tended to be more ethically oriented than men and found gender differences to be evident across all components of moral intensity. Cohen et al.'s (1998) study also identified gender differences with results revealing that women viewed dilemmas as less ethical than men, and results also indicated that women had a lower intention of performing the actions compared to their male counterparts. The impact of gender on moral intensity and the ethical decision-making process will be examined in this study.

Mixed evidence exists in accounting ethics literature dealing with the impact of a student's major on the ethical decision-making process (Cohen et al., 1998) and Borkowski and Ugras (1998, p. 15) concluded 'no relationship between major and ethics can be discerned given the research to date'. Barnett and Brown (1994) found that academic major did not significantly explain differences in the ethical judgements of the students while Silver and Valentine (2000) found that only the social consensus component of moral intensity was significantly different between business and non-business majors with business majors reporting greater social consensus on the unacceptability of the action. Results of Cohen et al.'s (1998) study indicated that accounting students believed the actions to be less ethical when compared to their business and liberal arts counterparts, contradicting findings by Ponemon and Gabhart (1993). Cohen *et al.* (1998) suggested that their result could be attributed to a particularly strong emphasis on ethics in the accounting curriculum in the particular university. The impact of academic major on moral intensity and the ethical decision-making process will be examined in this study.

Research Method

Quantitative analysis was considered most appropriate to address the hypotheses formulated in the study. Questionnaires 'are a convenient way of obtaining views of large numbers of individuals quickly and economically' (Brennan, 1998, p. 39) prior to quantitative analysis and were used in this study. The sample consisted of all students enrolled in the financial accounting class, the marketing class and the management of human resources class in third year commerce at the National University of Ireland, Galway. Prior to its administration, the questionnaire was pilot-tested using 10 students from the above classes. Based on the pilot-test results, some minor changes were made to the wording of two scenarios.

The questionnaires were self-administered to the students during three formal lecture periods by the second author in March 2005. Participation in the study was voluntary and students were assured that all results would remain confidential, and that there were no right or wrong answers. These details were included in the written instructions on the cover page to the questionnaire and were repeated verbally when the questionnaire was distributed. The rationale for these instructions was to attenuate the social desirability response bias that occurs in behavioural ethics research (Randall and Fernandes, 1991). The questionnaire took approximately 10–15 min to complete.

Research Instrument

Four scenarios were used in this study, which were adopted from Flory and Phillips (1992) and previously used by Leitsch (2004; 2006) to examine the ethical decision-making of accounting students. Each scenario, averaging 200 words, detailed a business dilemma (approving questionable expense report, manipulating company books, bypassing capital expenditure policy, and extending questionable credit) judged to be representative of issues found in the workplace. While students are inexperienced in the workplace and would not have exposure to the types of pressures, which individuals face when making these decisions, it would be expected that their educational experience should prepare them for likely workplace dilemmas. Each scenario ended with an action taken in response to the dilemma to ensure all respondents were reacting to the same stimulus (Flory and Phillips, 1992). Nine statements followed each scenario, and for each of the nine, the respondents indicated their agreement/disagreement on a seven-point Likert-type scale in each scenario (see Appendix). Statement 1 based on Singhapakdi *et al.* (1996) measured identification of an ethical dilemma. Statement 2 based on May and Pauli (2002) measured ethical judgement. Statement 3 based on Singhapakdi *et al.* (1996) measured ethical intentions. Statements 4–9, measuring each of the components of moral intensity (magnitude of consequences, social consensus, and probability of effect, temporal immediacy, proximity and concentration of effect) were based on Singhapakdi *et al.* (1996).

Data Analysis

Once all data was collected, it was reviewed and prepared for inputting into SPSS. Responses to all statements were coded 1–7 with responses to statements 3, 4, 6, 7 and 9 reverse-coded.

Any missing data in questionnaires was left blank when inputted into SPSS. Once inputted, the data was checked for errors by both crosschecking from questionnaires to computer file and computer file back to questionnaires at random. Consistent with many of the previous studies on moral intensity, parametric tests were used to analyse the findings.

The only multiple item measure in the study was moral intensity and Cronbach's coefficient alpha (Cronbach, 1951) was calculated to determine the moral intensity scale reliability for each of the four scenarios. For the moral intensity scale to be classified as reliable, it is generally recommended that a Cronbach coefficient alpha of 0.7 or greater should be observed (Pallant, 2001). However, Nunnally (1967) argued that for measures in the preliminary stages of development, a coefficient alpha of between 0.5 and 0.6 is an acceptable level of reliability. Further to this, Van de Ven and Ferry (1980) suggested that alpha values of between 0.35 and 0.55 are acceptable for broad constructs. This study yielded acceptable individual alpha coefficients for two of the four scenarios in this study. Scenarios 3 and 4 had coefficient alphas of 0.724 and 0.728 respectively. However, the coefficient alphas for scenarios 1 and 2 were 0.467 and 0.551 respectively. The moral intensity components for all scenarios were summed to yield a global alpha score of moral intensity of 0.762.

Findings

Demographics

One hundred and ninety-one questionnaires were returned representing all students who attended lectures and comprising 104 accounting students and 87 non-accounting students (human resources and marketing). Total numbers enrolled in these streams were 186 and 181 thereby yielding response rates of 56% and 48% respectively. Males comprised 37% and females comprised 63% of the sample (of the population males comprised 39% and females 61%). The demographic profile of respondents is presented in Table 1.

Moral Intensity

Moral intensity was comprised of six components and correlation analysis of these moral intensity components was carried out for all four scenarios. Proximity was not significantly correlated with all other components in the four scenarios and social consensus was not significantly correlated with all components in scenarios 1 (questionable expense report) and 2 (manipulating company books). Otherwise, results revealed that the components of moral intensity were highly correlated.

Contradictory findings exist on whether moral intensity is uni-dimensional (Valentine and Silver, 2001) or multi-dimensional (Singhapakdi et al., 1996) and therefore an exploratory factor analysis, using varimax rotations, was performed on the six individual components of moral intensity for each of the four scenarios. The results identified two factors for moral intensity with an eigenvalue greater than 1. The components of moral

Table 1. Demographic profile of sample

	Total	Male	Female
Accounting	104	42	62
Non-accounting	87	29	58
Total	191	71	120

Table 2. Principal components analysis of moral intensity items

	Scenario 1		Scenario 2		Scenario 3		Scenario 4	
	Approving questionable expense report		Manipulating company books		Bypassing expenditure capital Policy		Extending questionable expenditure credit	
	Factor 1	Factor 2	Factor 1	Factor 2	Factor 1	Factor 2	Factor 1	Factor 2
Magnitude of consequences	**0.783**	.090	**0.772**	0.128	**0.841**	0.042	**0.820**	−.075
Social consensus	0.003	**0.775**	0.371	**0.699**	0.470	**0.516**	**0.607**	0.330
Probability of effect	**0.687**	0	**0.743**	−0.140	**0.766**	−0.196	**0.813**	−0.155
Temporal immediacy	**0.665**	−0.229	**0.601**	−0.319	**0.777**	−0.206	**0.690**	−0.018
Proximity	−0.206	**0.700**	−0.184	**0.714**	0.107	**0.838**	0.038	0.956
Concentration of effect	**0.696**	0.322	**0.757**	0.092	**0.849**	−0.067	**0.829**	−0.045
Eigenvalue	2.053	1.254	2.254	1.145	2.852	1.057	2.865	1.055
% of variance explained	34.2%	20.9%	37.5%	19.1%	47.5%	17.6%	47.8%	17.6%

intensity included as part of each factor were those loading at 0.50 or greater and are highlighted in Table 2. One factor was composed of magnitude of consequences, probability of effect, temporal immediacy and concentration of effect. Based on the empirical work of Singhapakdi *et al.* (1996), this factor was labelled the 'perceived potential harm' factor. It explained between 34% and 47% of the variance depending on the nature of the specific scenario in this study. The second factor was composed of both the social consensus and proximity components of moral intensity. This was labelled 'perceived social pressure', again adopted from the work of Singhapakdi *et al.* (1996). Depending upon the specific scenario, this factor explained between 17% and 20% of the variance.

The same two-factorial outcome was observed in three of the four scenarios. Only scenario 4 (extending questionable credit) resulted in a difference with the second factor consisting only of proximity. The other five components of moral intensity loaded on the first factor. To be consistent with the other three scenarios, however, it was decided that the same division of the moral intensity scale would be used for scenario 4 as for the other scenarios. The two factors (perceived potential harm and perceived social pressure) are used for subsequent testing of moral intensity.

Correlation Analysis

Relationships between the three stages of ethical decision-making and between moral intensity (using two factors) and each of the stages were examined using correlation analysis. The results of these investigations are shown in Table 3.

No significant correlations were identified between the three stages of ethical decision-making in scenario 1. A significant correlation was found to exist between judgement and intentions in scenario 2 and the relationship between identification and judgement was marginally insignificant in scenario 2. The three variables were significantly correlated with each other in both scenarios 3 and 4. These results provide support for H1(c) in scenarios 2, 3 and 4 and support H1 (a) and (b) in scenarios 3 and 4.

Table 3. Pearson's correlation coefficients and probabilities

	Identification of ethical dilemma	Ethical judgement	Ethical intentions
Scenario 1—Approving questionable expense report			
Perceived potential harm	0.055 (0.448)	−0.090 (0.215)	0.116 (0.112)
Perceived social pressure	0.078 (0.286)	**0.184 (.0011)**	**0.156 (0.032)**
Identification of ethical dilemma		−0.064 (0.383)	−0.033 (0.651)
Ethical judgement			0.077 (0.291)
Scenario 2—Manipulating company books			
Perceived potential harm	0.008 (0.913)	**0.312 (0)**	**0.366 (0)**
Perceived social pressure	**0.211 (0.004)**	**0.324 (0)**	0.121 (0.098)
Identification of ethical dilemma		0.122 (0.092)	−0.030 (0.686)
Ethical judgement			**0.402 (0)**
Scenario 3—Bypassing capital expenditure policy			
Perceived potential harm	**0.342 (0)**	**0.322 (0)**	**0.300 (0)**
Perceived social pressure	**0.299 (0)**	**0.264 (0)**	**0.396 (0)**
Identification of ethical dilemma		**0.251 (0.001)**	**0.287 (0)**
Ethical judgement			**0.495 (0)**
Scenario 4—Extending questionable credit			
Perceived potential harm	**0.300 (0)**	**0.590 (0)**	**0.469 (0)**
Perceived social pressure	**0.329 (0)**	**0.331 (0)**	**0.341 (0)**
Identification of ethical dilemma		**0.507 (0)**	**0.336 (0)**
Ethical judgement			**0.687 (0)**

Neither of the two factors of moral intensity was significantly related to identification of an ethical dilemma in scenario 1 but perceived social pressure was significantly related in scenario 2 and both factors were significantly related in scenarios 3 and 4 (Table 3). Further analysis was carried out and the relationship between the individual components of moral intensity and each of the decision-making steps were examined separately. Only the social consensus component was significant in scenario 2. For scenario 3, all individual components were significant other than proximity, which was marginally insignificant. Neither temporal immediacy nor proximity was significant in scenario 4.

For ethical judgement, perceived social pressure was significant in scenario 1 (social consensus component of this significant but not proximity) (Table 3). In the other three scenarios, both factors were significant. When the individual components of moral intensity were analysed for these scenarios, proximity was insignificant in scenarios 3 and 4 but all other components were significant. For ethical intentions, only perceived social pressure was significant for scenario 1 (social consensus component of this significant but not proximity). For scenario 2, perceived potential harm was significant and perceived social pressure marginally insignificant (social consensus component significant). Both factors were significant for the other two scenarios (though proximity component was insignificant in scenario 4). These bi-variate correlations provide initial partial support for hypotheses 2(a), 2(b), and 2(c). More comprehensive testing of the impact of moral intensity on ethical intentions, ethical identification and ethical judgement is carried out using multiple regression analysis.

Multiple Regression Analysis

Each of the hypotheses has been tested using univariate analysis in the previous sections. Given the relationships predicted between each of the variables (moral intensity is hypothesized to impact directly on each of the stages of ethical decision-making but each of the stages of decision-making are hypothesized to impact on each other), it is not possible to determine from the uni-variate analysis if moral intensity has a direct effect on ethical judgement or ethical intentions. To examine the direct impact of moral intensity, hierarchical ethical judgement regressions were run with ethical identification (entered in first step) and the two factors of moral intensity (entered in second step) as the explanatory variables and hierarchical ethical intention regressions were run with ethical identification (entered in first step), ethical judgement (entered in second step), and the two factors of moral intensity (entered in third step) as the explanatory variables (Table 4).

The significance of the F Change statistic in Table 4 indicates whether the added variables in each model are significant when the impact of the previously added variables is removed. For both the ethical intention and ethical judgement regressions, the F change statistic was significant when the moral intensity components were added for all cases. This indicates the moral intensity has a significant direct relationship with both ethical judgement and ethical intention. For the ethical judgement regressions, perceived potential harm was significantly related to ethical judgement in scenarios 2, 3 and 4 and perceived social pressure was significantly related to ethical judgement in scenarios 1, 2 and 3. For the ethical intention regressions, perceived social pressure was significantly related to ethical intentions in scenarios 1, 3 and 4. Perceived potential harm was marginally insignificant in scenario 1 and significant in scenario 2. Consistent with the correlation analysis ethical identification was only directly related to ethical judgement and ethical intention in scenarios 3 and 4 and ethical judgement was directly related to ethical intention in scenarios 2, 3 and 4.

Differences between Scenarios

Table 5 shows the mean and standard deviation for each variable on each scenario. Results of MANOVA tests shown in Table 5 reveal that the means of each of the variables are significantly different between scenarios providing support for H3.

All scenarios were seen to involve ethical dilemmas with students more likely to identify an ethical dilemma in scenarios 1 and 2. Students were most likely to form an ethical judgement in scenarios 2 and 3 and students were most likely to form an intention to act ethically in scenarios 2 and 3. Overall, the results show significant differences in the three stages of ethical decision-making in the context of different scenarios. Regarding the ethical intensity factors, in general scenarios 2 and 3 are perceived as more ethically intense than scenarios 1 and 4. Scenario 3 has the highest ranking for both factors and scenario 1 the lowest ranking for both factors.

Demographics

Gender

t tests were carried out to identify any gender effects in the responses to each statement. The only significant difference was in the social consensus statement in scenario 1 ($t = -2.353$, $P = 0.020$) where females perceived a significantly higher social consensus that the action was unethical compared to males. No other significant differences were found to exist between male and female students.

Table 4. Hierarchical regression results for ethical judgement and ethical intention regressions

	Scenario 1			Scenario 2			Scenario 3			Scenario 4		
	Coefficient	Std error	Sig. t	Coefficient	Std error	Sig. t	Coefficient	Std error	Sig. t	Coefficient	Std error	Sig. t
Dependent variable: Ethical evaluation												
Model 1												
Ethical identification	−0.075	0.095	0.306	0.114	0.087	0.120	0.245	0.077	**0.001**	1.667	0.341	**0**
Constant	4.505	0.565	**0**	3.958	0.522	**0**	3.317	0.426	**0**	0.501	0.067	**0**
Model summary	Adj. R sq. = 0, F = 1.052, Sig. F = 0.306			Adj. R sq. = 0.008, F = 2.436, Sig. F = 0.120			Adj. R sq. = .055, F = 11.649, Sig. F = 0.001			Adj. R sq. = 0.247, F = 61.620, Sig. F = 0		
Model 2												
Ethical identification	−0.085	0.094	0.238	0.047	0.081	0.487	0.107	0.080	0.159	0.337	0.061	**0**
Perceived potential harm	−0.071	0.028	0.328	0.308	0.022	**0**	0.249	0.025	**0.001**	0.463	0.019	**0**
Perceived social pressure	0.187	0.049	**0.010**	0.304	0.044	**0**	0.176	0.053	**0.016**	0.092	0.040	0.117
Constant	4.061	0.792	**0**	0.925	0.662	0.164	1.317	0.610	**0.032**	−0.626	0.415	0.133
Model summary	Adj. R sq. = 0.032, F = 3.041, Sig. F = 0.030, Sig. F change = 0.020			Adj. R sq. = 0.189, F = 15.407, Sig. F = 0, Sig. F change = 0			Adj. R sq. = 0.140, F = 10.911, Sig. F = 0, Sig. F change = 0			Adj. R sq. = 0.462, F = 53.863, Sig. F = 0, Sig. F change = 0		
Dependent variable: Ethical Intentions												
Model 1												
Ethical identification	−0.045	0.088	0.542	−0.040	0.096	0.591	0.281	0.076	**0**	0.329	0.074	**0**
Constant	4.343	0.525	**0**	4.429	0.571	**0**	2.865	0.424	**0**	2.220	0.378	**0**
Model summary	Adj. R sq. = −0.003, F = 0.373, Sig. F = 0.542			Adj. R sq. = 0.002, F = 0.290, Sig. F = 0.591			Adj. R sq. = 0.074, F = 15.601, Sig. F = 0			Adj. R sq. = 0.103, F = 22.287, Sig. F = 0		

(Table continued)

Table 4. Continued

	Scenario 1			Scenario 2			Scenario 3			Scenario 4		
	Coefficient	Std error	Sig. t	Coefficient	Std error	Sig. t	Coefficient	Std error	Sig. t	Coefficient	Std error	Sig. t
Model 2												
Ethical identification	-0.041	0.089	0.581	-0.085	0.089	0.215	0.172	0.071	**0.010**	-019	0.066	0.762
Ethical judgement	0.054	0.068	0.463	0.396	0.074	**0**	0.443	0.066	**0**	0.694	0.063	**0**
Constant	4.118	0.609	**0**	2.725	0.602	**0**	1.386	0.439	**0.002**	1.046	0.311	**0.001**
Model summary	Adj. R sq. = -0.006, F = 0.456, Sig. F = 0.634, Sig. F change = 0.463			Adj. R sq. = 0.147, F = 17.054, Sig. F = 0, Sig. F change = 0			Adj. R sq. = 0.256, F = 32.416, Sig. F = 0, Sig. F change = 0			Adj. R sq. = 0.463, F = 80.720, Sig. F = 0, Sig. F change = 0		
Model 3												
Ethical identification	-0.063	0.088	0.389	-0.083	0.087	0.216	0.081	0.072	0.231	-0.047	0.067	0.456
Ethical judgement	0.034	0.068	0.644	0.297	0.079	**0**	0.366	0.067	**0**	0.618	0.074	**0**
Perceived potential harm	0.137	0.026	**0.060**	0.278	0.024	**0**	0.100	0.023	0.141	0.079	0.022	0.231
Perceived social pressure	0.163	0.046	**0.028**	0.033	0.050	0.635	0.252	0.048	**0**	0.131	0.041	**0.025**
Constant	2.736	0.788	**0.001**	1.292	0.715	**0.072**	-0.060	0.554	0.914	0.309	0.418	0.460
Model summary	Adj. R sq. = 0.026, F = 2.25, Sig. F = 0.065, Sig. F change = 0.019			Adj. R sq. = 0.208, F = 13.247, Sig. F = 0, Sig. F change = 0			Adj. R sq. = 0.316, F = 22.162, Sig. F = 0, Sig. F change = 0			Adj. R sq. = 0.478, F = 43.323, Sig. F = 0, Sig. F change = 0		

Table 5. Differences in variables between scenarios

	S1: Approving questionable expense report	S2: Manipulating company books	S3: Bypassing capital expenditure Policy	S4: Extending questionable credit	F statistic (sig.)
IDENTIFYING DILEMMA mean	5.79	5.84	5.34	4.84	1402.525 (0.000)
Standard deviation	1.426	1.285	1.560	1.602	
ETHICAL JUDGEMENT mean	3.95	4.75	4.71	4.20	902.576 (0.000)
Standard deviation	1.869	1.553	1.677	1.668	
ETHICAL INTENTIONS mean	4.04	4.13	4.48	3.90	659.202 (0.000)
Standard deviation	1.736	1.686	1.680	1.692	
PERCEIVED POTENTIAL HARM	16.66	17.53	19.16	17.14	1251.224 (0.000)
Standard deviation	4.800	4.716	4.867	5.119	
PERCEIVED SOCIAL PRESSURE	7.72	8.75	9.01	8.20	1129.851 (0.000)
Standard deviation	2.743	2.350	2.277	2.409	

Accounting and Non-accounting Students

Table 6 sets out significant differences in responses between accounting and non-accounting students. For all except 4 statements higher mean scores were found for accounting students compared to non- accounting students though only the statements reported in Table 6 were significantly higher.

In three of the scenarios, accounting students were significantly more likely to identify an ethical dilemma than were non-accounting students. Ethical judgement and ethical intentions of accounting students were also significantly higher than those of non-accounting students for scenario 3. Accounting students perceived scenario 3 as being significantly more intense on both moral intensity factors regarding ethical intensity.

Discussion

This paper examined the impact of moral intensity on each of the first three stages of ethical decision-making and found that moral intensity was significantly directly related to ethical judgement and ethical intentions in all four scenarios and significantly directly related to identification of an ethical dilemma in three of the four scenarios. The study also investigated the relationship between the three stages of ethical decision-making and found a significant relationship between the three stages in two of the scenarios. Finally, the study examined the impact of the

Table 6. Statements with statistically significant differences across stream

Statement	Accounting mean	Non-accounting mean	t	Sig.
Ethical identification Scenario 1	6.03	5.49	2.528	0.013
Ethical identification Scenario 3	5.73	4.88	3.807	0
Ethical judgement Scenario 3	4.93	4.44	2.003	0.047
Ethical intentions Scenario 3	4.79	4.10	2.878	0.004
Perceived potential harm Scenario 3	19.84	18.32	2.142	0.033
Perceived social pressure Scenario 3	9.56	8.33	3.805	0
Ethical identification Scenario 4	5.09	4.54	2.372	0.019

nature of the scenario, gender and academic major on each of the variables and found that the nature of the scenarios had a significant impact on each of the variables. Gender was not found to be significant while academic major had an impact on only some of the variables.

Levels of Moral Intensity

All variables measured were significantly different between scenarios and consistent with Leitsch (2004) and Flory and Phillips (1992) scenario 3 (bypassing capital expenditure policy) was perceived as being the most ethically intense. The significant differences in moral intensity between scenarios suggest that individuals perceive some situations as being more morally intense supporting Jones's (1991) theory. The relationships between the three stages of ethical decision-making and ethical intensity were weakest for scenario 1 with only perceived social pressure being significantly related to ethical judgement and ethical intentions. Social consensus was the only significant component of this factor. Jones (1991) maintained that large differences in ethical intensity between scenarios are required to observe differences in the impact of moral intensity. Scenario 1 (approving questionable expense reports) had the lowest ranking for ethical intensity and it may be the case that the level was not sufficient to observe the impact of the other components of moral intensity.

Components of Moral Intensity

The two factor solution for moral intensity that emerged from the findings support the multi-dimensional nature of moral intensity (Jones, 1991). The loading of the components on these two factors was consistent with Singhapakdi *et al.* (1996) whose sample consisted of marketing professionals but inconsistent with Leitsch's (2006) study, which was based on undergraduate accounting students. Leitsch found that concentration of effect loaded as a separate factor and further research is needed to examine the reasons for the emergence of different factors.

In this study, perceived social pressure emerged as the factor of moral intensity most strongly related to the ethical decision-making process with social consensus the most significant component in this factor. This is consistent with previous research, which suggested that, when dealing with student groups, social consensus was the most important component but, when dealing with manager groups, magnitude of consequences emerged as the most important component (Barnett and Valentine, 2004). The importance of social consensus indicates that respondents' perceptions of society's attitudes to issues influence their decisions and is consistent with lower levels of cognitive moral development (Kohlberg, 1969; Rest, 1986). According to Kohlberg's model, at conventional levels of moral reasoning individuals are influenced by rules laid down by society, which reflect societal consensus on the ethicality of particular actions. Individuals are guided by perceived societal acceptance of an action and perceived societal acceptance of an action is inextricably linked to cultural environment on the individual. Perceived organizational consensus is likely to have a significant impact on perceived social consensus and this is discussed under 'Implications of the findings and future research' section. As individuals progress to post conventional levels of moral reasoning, general moral principles and the fairness of rules are used to guide actions. As Barnett (2001) pointed out, when respondents are students with an average age of around 20 it is to be expected that their beliefs about societal opinion would be a very important influence. Studies based on older respondents showing magnitude of consequences as the most important dimension may indicate higher levels of moral reasoning for these respondents (Barnett, 2001).

The only scenario for which perceived social pressure had virtually no influence on ethical intentions was scenario 2, which dealt with manipulating company books (though it was significantly related to ethical identification and ethical judgement in that scenario). Ethical identification and ethical judgement were highest for this case and it may be the case that certain characteristics of this ethical dilemma were so compelling that the presence of one diminishes the importance of others. In scenario 2, findings suggest that, when forming ethical intentions, perceived potential harm of the case was more influential than perceived social pressure.

Of the components of moral intensity, the relationships with the three stages of ethical decision-making were weakest for proximity. This is consistent with previous research such as Davis et al. (1998) who identified no relationship between proximity and ethical judgement and Singhapakdi et al. (1996) who found that, in general, proximity was not related to ethical intentions. As Jones (1991) pointed out, proximity is made up of four different variables (social, cultural, psychological, and physical proximity) which he combined for simplification. A more comprehensive measure of proximity may be needed to capture these four different variables. In addition, Jones (1991) maintained that a certain threshold level of some dimensions of moral intensity might be needed before any influence from the others can be observed. It may be the case that these scenarios failed to meet the threshold levels needed to observe the impact of proximity.

Influence of Demographics

Of the 36 statements in the study, only one revealed a significant difference in response between male and female students supporting some of the previous findings of no gender differences in ethical decision-making (Hegarty and Sims, 1978; Singhapakdi and Vitell, 1990; Serwinek, 1992; Sikula and Costa, 1994). The impact of the use of student samples on gender differences in previous studies has been questioned, as students are inexperienced in both life and the workplace (Loe et al., 2000). It may be the case that this inexperience has so significant an impact on both genders that it prevents any gender differences emerging.

Regarding differences between accounting and non-accounting students, in all four scenarios accounting students were more likely to identify an ethical dilemma compared to non-accounting students and differences were significant in 3 of the scenarios. One possible explanation for the greater ability of accounting students to identify ethical dilemmas may be recent accounting scandals, which have generated a significant ethical interest in the accounting domain. The only other differences between the two groups occurred for the two factors of moral intensity (i.e. ethical judgement and ethical intentions) in scenario 3 with accounting students exhibiting higher mean scores. Scenario 3 involved bypassing capital expenditure policy and, as suggested by Leitsch (2004), accounting students may look at the issue from an accounting standpoint and identify that the expenditure problems being experienced by the firm were only further compounded by the suggested unethical action in the scenario.

Strengths and Limitations of the Study

Strengths of the study include the use of previously tested scenarios and variables, reduction of social desirability bias using anonymous responses, high response rate from distribution of questionnaires in the classroom, and detailed and rigorous statistical testing. Limitations of the study arise from a narrow sample (taken only from one university), use of single item measures for each of the stages of ethical decision-making and each of the components of moral intensity, and the ordering of statements after each scenario which may have produced unintended order effects. In addition, respondents may have experienced difficulties in relating to scenarios due to a lack of work experience. However, it would be expected that their business courses would prepare them for responding to likely dilemmas in the workplace. A further limitation arose from the measurement of the variable 'identification of an ethical dilemma' as respondents' ability to recognize an ethical issue is likely to be heightened when specifically asked to consider the ethicality of an issue. Finally, the sample may be biased as it consisted of students who attended the particular lectures and non-attendees may have different ethical attitudes.

Implications of the Findings and Future Research

There are a number of implications for educators, the accounting profession and employers arising from the study. Findings show that individuals are likely to vary their intentions to act ethically or unethically based on the social consensus dimension of moral intensity. This finding may be related to the age and moral development of participants where younger individuals look to others for guidance on right and wrong. If this is the case, it is particularly important that organizations conduct training sessions to expose younger employees to ethical issues. Organizations such as accounting firms recruit a large number of employees directly from college and opportunities are needed where these individuals can discuss the consensus among members of the organization, profession and society regarding the ethicality of certain decisions that employees may make while on the job. Previous research showing quality- threatening behaviours at audit trainee levels in accounting firms (Sweeney and Pierce, 2004) and revealing a lack of ethical concern with the behaviours (Pierce and Sweeney, 2006) highlight the necessity of strong ethical guidance in these firms. An improvement in 'the tone at the top' of accounting firms has been recommended in the ethics literature (Pierce, 2007) and it is important that the firms develop and communicate a strong organizational consensus on what constitutes an ethical situation and what behaviour is expected from employees. A longitudinal study examining the influence of different components of moral intensity on ethical decision-making as accounting students progress from college through their professional training is needed in order to gain a better understanding of the relative importance of social consensus at different stages. Also, an examination of the impact of perceived organizational consensus (which is likely to be related to perceived organizational culture) on ethical decision-making should prove fruitful.

This study found a relationship between the three stages of ethical decision-making in two of the scenarios; codes of ethical conduct, which would increase the ability of employees to recognize an ethical dilemma and hence influence their judgement and intentions, are likely to be important in organizations. The Sarbanes Oxley (2002) act in the USA, which applies in Ireland to companies listed on the US stock exchange requires companies to adopt a code of ethics or disclose why they have not done so. It is likely that codes of ethical conduct will assume greater importance in all organizations. However, implementing codes of ethical conduct is only a partial solution as problems arise in accounting that cannot be easily resolved by reference to ethical codes of conduct (Hull *et al.*, 1999). Indeed, it has been argued in the ethics literature that creating rules for solving problems removes the scope or need for exercising judgement and can actually 'de-professionalize' the accountant (Pierce, 2007). Therefore, care is needed to ensure that codes of ethical conduct focus on broad principles that guide ethical decision-making and future research is needed to examine the impact of codes of conduct on ethical decision-making.

Educators in third level colleges have an extremely important role to play in ethical development as they are in a position to communicate the acceptability of behaviours to students and develop students' understanding of society's consensus on the ethicality of business issues before they commence employment. Concerns have been expressed regarding the limited ethical education of accounting students at university level (Pierce and O'Gorman, 2004) and, more generally, the overly technical nature of accounting education (McPhail, 2006). Indeed, McPhail (2006) pointed to the much-quoted evidence that exists suggesting a negative impact of conventional accounting education on students' ethical predispositions. Instilling in students a strong sense of ethics should increase their confidence in their own views and make them less reliant on social consensus as a guide for making ethical decisions. For accounting educators it is encouraging that accounting students in this study were significantly more likely to identify an ethical dilemma than other business students in three of the four scenarios but their ethical judgement and ethical intentions were only significantly higher for scenario 3 (bypassing capital expenditure policy). This suggests that accounting education may be effective in raising accounting students' awareness of what constitutes an ethical dilemma but this may not translate into improved ethical judgement and intentions. Further research is needed on other factors that may influence the relationship between the three stages of ethical decision-making.

The accounting profession is also positioned to influence trainees' ethicality through education and communication of the profession's view of ethical situations. The treatment of auditing in professional examinations has been criticised for its technical emphasis and the fact that it is '... rarely viewed as an activity which has social, organizational, and behavioural dimensions and for this reason is dangerously myopic' (Roslender, 1992, p. 185). Ethical guidelines are given little attention in professional examinations and time pressure has resulted in a professional education and training emphasis that is '... inconducive to the reflection and deep learning necessary for effective ethics instruction' (Hull et al., 1999, p. IX). Future research could examine trainee accountants' understanding of the professional ethical guidelines and their perceived influence on ethical decision-making.

In conclusion, this study examined three stages in the ethical decision-making process and it provides additional support for the role of moral intensity in making ethical decisions. The empirical analysis at least partially supported all of the hypotheses developed in the paper. Ethical identification was significantly related to ethical judgement and ethical intentions in two of the four scenarios and ethical judgement was significantly related to ethical intentions in three of the four scenarios. The two dimensions of moral intensity were differentially associated with stages of the ethical decision-making process with social consensus emerging as the most significant component of moral intensity. Last, the nature of the situation impacted on all the variables examined in the study.

Appendix

Scenario 1

Tom Waterman is a young management accountant at a large, diversified company. After some experience in accounting at headquarters, he has been transferred to one of the company's recently acquired divisions run by its previous owner and president, Howard Heller. Howard has been retained as vice-president of this new division, and Tom is his accountant. With a marketing background and a practice of calling his own shots, Howard seems to play by a different set of rules than those to which Tom is accustomed. So far it is working, as earnings are up and sales projections are high.

The main area of concern to Tom is Howard's expense reports. Howard's boss, the division president, approves the expense reports without review, and expects Tom to check the details and work out any discrepancies with Howard. After a series of large and questionable expense reports, Tom challenges Howard directly about charges to the company for typing that Howard's wife did at home. Although company policy prohibits such charges, Howard's boss again signed off the expense. Tom feels uncomfortable with this and tells Howard that he is considering taking the matter to the Board Audit Committee for review. Howard reacts sharply, reminding Tom that 'the Board will back me anyway' and that Tom's position in the company would be in jeopardy.

ACTION: **Tom decides not to report the expense charge to the Audit Committee.** Please evaluate this action of Tom by <u>circling the extent of your agreement</u> with each of the following statements:

Scenario 2

Anne Devereaux, company controller, is told by the chief financial officer that, in an executive committee meeting, the CEO told them that the company 'has to meet its earnings forecast, is in need of working capital and that's final'. Unfortunately, Anne does not see how additional working capital can be raised even through increased borrowing, since income is well below the forecast sent to the bank. Seth suggests that Anne review bad debt expense for possible reduction and holding sales open longer at the end of the month.

1. The situation above involves an ethical dilemma

| Strongly disagree | Disagree | Slightly disagree | Neither agree/disagree | Slightly agree | Agree | Strongly agree |

2. Tom should not do the proposed Action

| Strongly disagree | Disagree | Slightly disagree | Neither agree/ disagree | Slightly agree | Agree | Strongly agree |

3. If I were Tom, I would make the same decision

| Strongly disagree | Disagree | Slightly disagree | Neither agree/disagree | Slightly agree | Agree | Strongly agree |

4. The overall harm (if any) done as a result of Tom's Action would be very small

| Strongly disagree | Disagree | Slightly disagree | Neither agree/disagree | Slightly agree | Agree | Strongly agree |

5. Most people would agree that Tom's Action is wrong

| Strongly disagree | Disagree | Slightly disagree | Neither agree/disagree | Slightly agree | Agree | Strongly agree |

6. There is a very small likelihood that Tom's Action will actually cause any harm

| Strongly disagree | Disagree | Slightly disagree | Neither agree/disagree | Slightly agree | Agree | Strongly agree |

7. Tom's Action will not cause any harm in the immediate future

| Strongly disagree | Disagree | Slightly disagree | Neither agree/disagree | Slightly agree | Agree | Strongly agree |

8. If Tom is a personal friend of the 'Victim', the Action is wrong

| Strongly disagree | Disagree | Slightly disagree | Neither agree/disagree | Slightly agree | Agree | Strongly agree |

9. Tom's Action will harm very few people (if any)

| Strongly disagree | Disagree | Slightly disagree | Neither agree/disagree | Slightly agree | Agree | Strongly agree |

He also brushes off the management letter request from the outside auditors to write down the spare parts stock to reflect its 'net sales value'.

At home at the weekend, Anne discusses the situation with her husband, Larry, a senior manager of another company in town. 'They're asking me to manipulate the books', she says. 'On the one hand', she complains, 'I'm supposed to be the conscience of the company and on other, I'm supposed to be absolutely loyal'. Larry tells her that companies do this all the time and, when business picks up again, she will be covered. He reminds her how important her salary is to help maintain their comfortable lifestyle, and that she should not do anything drastic that might cause her to lose her job.

ACTION: **Anne decides to go along with the suggestions proposed by her boss.**

Scenario 3

Drew Isler, the plant's chief accountant, is having a friendly conversation with Leo Sullivan, operations manager and old college buddy, and Fred LaPlante, the sales manager. Leo tells Drew that the plant needs a new computer system to increase operating efficiency. Fred adds that with the increased efficiency and decreased late deliveries their plant will be the top plant next year.

However, Leo wants to bypass the company policy which requires that items greater than €5,000 receive prior Board approval and be capitalized. Leo would prefer to generate orders for each component part of the system, each being under the €5,000 limit, and thereby avoid the approval 'hassle'. Drew knows that this is clearly wrong from a company and an accounting standpoint, and he says so. Nevertheless, he eventually says that he will go along.

Six months later, the new computer system has not lived up to its expectations. Drew indicates to Fred that he is really worried about the problems with the computer, and that the auditors will disclose how the purchase was handled in the upcoming visit. Fred acknowledges the situation by saying that production and sales are down and his sales representatives are also upset. Leo wants to correct the problems by upgrading the system (and increasing the expenses), and urges Drew to 'hang in there'.

ACTION: **Feeling certain that the system will fail without the upgrade, Drew agrees to approve the additional expense.**

Scenario 4

Paul Tate is the assistant controller at Stern Electronics, a medium-sized manufacturer of electrical equipment. Paul is in his late fifties and plans to retire soon. His daughter has been accepted into medical school, and financial concerns are weighing heavily on his mind. Paul's boss is out of the office recuperating from health problems, and in his absence, Paul is making all decisions for the department.

Paul receives a telephone call from an old friend requesting a sizable amount of equipment on credit for his new business. Paul is sympathetic but aware of the risk of extending credit to a new company, especially under Stern's strict credit control policy for such transactions. When Paul mentions this conversation to Warren, the general manager, he is immediately interested. Warren notes that the company needs an additional €250,000 in sales to meet the quarterly budget and, thus ensure bonuses for management, including Paul.

ACTION: **Paul decides to make the sale to his friend's new business.**

References

Barnett, T. (2001) Dimensions of moral intensity and ethical decision-making: an empirical study, *Journal of Applied Social Psychology*, 31(5), pp. 1038–1057.

Barnett, T. and Brown, G. (1994) The ethical judgements of college students regarding business issues, *Journal of Education for Business*, 69, pp. 333–339.

Barnett, T. and Valentine, S. (2004) Issue contingencies and marketers' recognition of ethical issues, ethical judgements and behavioral intentions, *Journal of Business Research*, 57(4), pp. 338–346.

Borkowski, S. C. and Ugras, Y. J. (1998) Business students and ethics: a meta-analysis, *Journal of Business Ethics*, 17(X), pp. 1117–1127.

Brennan, N. (1998) *Accounting Research: A Practical Guide* (Dublin: Oak Tree Press).

Brown, R. and Hernstein, R. (1975) *Psychology* (Boston: Little Brown).

Browning, R. F. and Zabriskie, R. A. (1983) How ethical are industrial buyers?, *Industrial Marketing Management*, 12(4), pp. 219–224.

Carlson, D. S., Kacmar, K. M. and Wadsworth, L. L. (2002) The impact of moral intensity dimensions on ethical decision making: assessing the relevance of orientation, *Journal of Managerial Issues*, XIV(1), pp. 15–30.

Chia, A. and Mee, L. S. (2000) The effects of issue characteristics on the recognition of moral issues, *Journal of Business Ethics*, 27(3), pp. 255–269.

Clarke, P., Hill, N. and Stevens, K. (1996) Ethical reasoning abilities: accountancy practitioners in Ireland, *Irish Business and Administrative Research*, 17, pp. 94–109.

Cohen, J. R., Pant, L. W. and Sharp, D. J. (1998) The effect of gender and academic discipline diversity on the ethical evaluations, intentions and ethical orientation of potential public accounting recruits, *Accounting Horizons*, 12(3), pp. 250–270.

Cohen, J. R., Pant, L. W. and Sharp, D. J. (1996) Measuring the ethical awareness and ethical orientation of Canadian auditors, *Behavioral Research in Accounting*, 8(Suppl.), pp. 98–119.

Cohen, J. R., Pant, L. W. and Sharp, D. J. (2001) An examination of differences in ethical decision-making between Canadian business students and accounting professionals, *Journal of Business Ethics*, 30(4), pp. 319–336.

Cronbach, L. (1951) Coefficient alpha and the internal structure of tests, *Psychometrika*, 16(3), pp. 297–334.

Davis, M. A., Johnson, N. B. and Ohmer, D. G. (1998) Issue-contingent effects on ethical decision-making: a cross-cultural comparison, *Journal of Business Ethics*, 17(4), pp. 373–389.

Douglas, P., Davidson, R. and Schwartz, B. (2001) The effect of organizational culture and ethical orientation on accountants' ethical judgements, *Journal of Business Ethics*, 34(2), pp. 101–121.

Dubinsky, A. J. and Levy, M. (1985) Ethics in retailing perceptions of retail salespeople, *Journal of the Academy of Marketing Science*, 13(1), pp. 1–16.

Etherington, L. D. and Schulting, L. (1995) Ethical development of accountants: the case of Canadian certified management accountants, *Research on Accounting Ethics*, 1, pp. 235–251.

Fishbein, M. and Ajzen, I. (1975) *Belief, Attitude, Intention and Behavior: An Introduction to Theory and Research* (Reading, MA: Addison-Wesley).

Flannery, B. L. and May, D. R. (2000) Environmental ethical decision-making in the U.S. metal fishing industry, *Academy of Management Journal*, 43(4), pp. 642–662.

Flory, S. M. and Phillips, T. J. (1992) A multidimensional analysis of selected issues in accounting, *The Accounting Review*, 67(2), pp. 284–302.

Gibbs, J. C. (1979) Kohnberg's moral stage theory: a Piagetian revision, *Human development*, 22, pp. 89–112.

Gilligan, C. (1982) *In a Different Voice: Psychological Theory and Women's development* (Cambridge, Mass.: Harvard University Press).

Guertin, M. R. (1986) Beyond a unidimensional theory of moral development: An analysis of Jung's personality typology and Kohlberg's theory of moral stages comparing career military officer's wives and civilian women. PhD dissertation, George Washington University.

Habermas, J. (1979) Moral development and ego identity, in: J. Habermas, (Ed.) *Communication and the Evolution of Society*, pp. 69–94 (Boston: Beacon Press).

Harrington, S. J. (1997) A test of a person-issue contingent model of ethical decision-making in organizations, *Journal of Business Ethics*, 16(4), pp. 363–375.

Hegarty, W. H. and Sims, H. P. (1978) Some determinants of unethical decision behaviour: an experiment, *Journal of Applied Psychology*, 63(4), pp. 451–457.

Hull, A., Wright, M. and Ennew, C. (1999) *Professional Ethics and Accountancy Training* (London: ICAEW).

Jones, T. M. (1991) Ethical decision making by individuals in organizations: an issue contingent model, *Academy of Management Review*, 16(2), pp. 366–395.

Jones, T. M. and Huber, V. L. (1992) Issue-contingency in ethical decision-making. Paper presented at the 3rd annual conference of the International Association for Business and Society, Leuven, Belgium.

Jones, J., Massey, D. W. and Thorne, L. (2003) Auditors' ethical reasoning: Insights from past research and implications for the future, *Journal of Accounting Literature*, 22, pp. 45–103.

Kohlberg, L. (1969) Stage and sequence: the cognitive-developmental approach to socialization, in: D. A. Goslin (Ed.) *Handbook of Socialisation Theory and Research*, pp. 347–480 (Chicago: Rand McNally).

Leitsch, D. L. (2006) Using dimensions of moral intensity to predict ethical decision-making in accounting, *Accounting Education: an international journal*, 15(2), pp. 135–149.

Leitsch, D. L. (2004) Differences in the perceptions of moral intensity in the moral decision process: an empirical examination of accounting students, *Journal of Business Ethics*, 53(4), pp. 313–323.

Loe, T., Ferrell, L. and Mansfield, P. (2000) A review of empirical studies assessing ethical decision-making in business, *Journal of Business Ethics*, 25(3), pp. 185–204.

McPhail, K. (2006) *Ethics and the Individual Professional Accountant: A Literature Review* (Edinburgh: ICAS)

Marshall, B. and Dewe, P. (1997) An investigation of the components of moral intensity, *Journal of Business Ethics*, 16(5), pp. 521–530.

May, D. R. and Pauli, K. P. (2002) The role of moral intensity in ethical decision-making: a review and investigation of moral recognition, evaluation, and intention, *Business and Society*, 41(1), pp. 85–118.

Morris, S. and McDonald, R. A. (1995) The role of moral intensity in moral judgements: an empirical investigation, *Journal of Business Ethics*, 14(9), pp. 715–726.

Nisbett, R. and Ross, L. (1980) *Human Inference: Strategies and Shortcomings of Social Judgement* (Englewood Cliffs, NJ: Prentice-Hall).

Nunnally, J. C. (1967) *Psychometric Theory* (New York: McGraw-Hill).

Pallant, J. (2001) *SPSS Survival Manual: A Step-by-Step Guide to Data Analysis using SPSS for Windows (Version 10)* (Buckingham: Open University Press).

Pierce, A. (2007) *Ethics and the Professional Accounting Firm: A Literature Review* (Edinburgh: ICAS).

Pierce, A. and O'Gorman, D. (2004) Ethical training of professional accountants in Ireland: an exploratory study. Paper presented at the 27th annual congress of the European Accounting Association, Prague, 1–3 April 2004.

Pierce, B. and Sweeney, B. (2006) Perceived adverse consequences of quality threatening behaviour in audit firms, *International Journal of Auditing*, 10(1), pp. 19–39.

Ponemon, L. A. and Gabhart, D. (1993) *Ethical Reasoning in Accounting and Auditing*, Research Monograph Number 21, CGA-Canada Research Foundation.

Randall, D. and Fernandes, M. (1991) The social desirability response bias in ethics research, *Journal of Business Ethics*, 10(11), pp. 805–817.

Rest, J. R. (1979) *Development in Judging Moral Issues* (Minneapolis: University of Minnesota Press).

Rest, J. R. (1986) *Moral Development: Advances in Research and Theory* (New York: Praeger).

Robin, D. P., Reidenbach, R. E. and Forrest, P. J. (1996) The perceived importance of an ethical issue as an influence on the ethical decision-making of advertising managers, *Journal of Business Research*, 35(1), pp. 17–28.

Roslender, R. (1992) *Sociological Perspectives on Modern Accountancy* (London: Routledge).

Serwinek, P. (1992) Demographic and related differences in ethical views among small businesses, *Journal of Business Ethics*, 11(7), pp. 555–566.

Shafer, W. E., Morris, R. E. and Ketchland, A. A. (2001) Effects of personal values on auditors' ethical decisions, *Accounting, Auditing and Accountability Journal*, 14(3), pp. 254–277.

Shaub, M. K. (1994) An analysis of the association of traditional demographic variables with the moral reasoning of auditing students and auditors, *Journal of Accounting Education*, 12(1), pp. 1–26.

Sikula, A. and Costa, A. (1994) Are age and ethics related?, *The Journal of Psychology*, 128(6), pp. 659–665.

Silver, L. and Valentine, S. (2001) College students' perceptions of moral intensity in sales situations, *Journal of Education for Business*, 75(6), pp. 309–314.

Singer, M. S. and Singer, A. E. (1997) Observer judgements about moral agents' ethical decisions: the role of scope of justice and moral intensity, *Journal of Business Ethics*, 16(5), pp. 473–484.

Singhapakdi, A. and Vitell, S. J. (1990) Marketing ethics: Factors influencing perceptions of ethical problems and alternatives, *Journal of Macromarketing*, 12(1), pp. 4–18.

Singhapakdi, A., Vitell, S. J. and Kraft, K. L. (1996) Moral intensity and ethical decision-making of marketing professionals, *Journal of Business Research*, 36(3), pp. 245–255.

Snell, R. S. (1996) Complementing Kohlberg: mapping the ethical reasoning used by managers for their own dilemma cases, *Human Relations*, 49(1), pp. 23–49.

Sullivan, E. V. (1977) A study of Kohlberg's structure theory of moral development: a critique of liberal social science ideology, *Human development*, 20, pp. 352–376.

Sweeney, B. and Pierce, B. (2004) Management control in audit firms: a qualitative investigation, *Accounting, Auditing and Accountability Journal*, 17(5), pp. 779–812.

Thorne, L. (1999) An analysis of the association of demographic variables with the cognitive moral development of Canadian accounting students: an examination of the applicability of American-based findings to the Canadian context, *Journal of Accounting Education*, 17(2), pp. 157–174.

Trevino, L. K. (1986) Ethical decision-making in organizations: a person-situation interactionist model, *Academy of Management Review*, 11(3), pp. 601–617.

Valentine, S. L. and Silver, L. (2001) Assessing the dimensionality of the Singhapakdi, Vitell and Kraft measure of moral intensity, *Psychological Reports*, 88(1), pp. 291–294.

Van de Ven, A. H. and Ferry, D. L. (1980) *Measuring and Assessing Organizations* (New York: Wiley).

Weber, J. (1990) Managers' moral reasoning: assessing their responses to three moral dilemmas, *Human Relations*, 43, pp. 687–702.

White, R. D. Jr (1999) Are women more ethical? Recent findings on the effects of gender upon moral development, *Journal of Public Administration Research and Theory*, 3, pp. 459–471.

Wright, G. B., Cullinan, C. P. and Bline, D. M. (1997) The relationship between an individual's value and perceptions of moral intensity: an empirical study, *Behavioral Research in Accounting*, 9, pp. 26–41.

The Role of Cultural Factors in the Learning Style Preferences of Accounting Students: A Comparative Study between Japan and Australia

SATOSHI SUGAHARA* and GREGORY BOLAND**

*Hiroshima Shudo University, Japan, **University of Canberra, Australia*

ABSTRACT *The purpose of this study is to examine empirically the relationship between cultural factors and students' learning style preferences in the context of the current global convergence in accounting education. Kolb's Learning Style Inventory and Hofstede's Value Survey Model for Young People were administered to 130 undergraduate students studying accounting in Japanese and Australian universities. The findings of this comparative study report that differences in the particular learning styles of doing/watching (AE–RO) between the two nationality groups are significantly associated with individualism (IDV). The supplementary t-test also revealed the mean scores of AE–RO and IDV for Australian accounting students were significantly higher than those of Japanese students, which suggests that Japanese like to learn by watching due to their relatively collective approach to learning. In contrast, Australian students who tended to be more individualistic in their learning were more willing to learn by doing. The results will be of interest to accounting educators to assist them with the smooth introduction of the International Education Standards (IES) prescribed by the International Accounting Education Standards Board (IAESB) of the International Federation of Accountants (IFAC).*

KEY WORDS: Cultural dimensions, learning style preferences, international education standards for professional accountants (IES), International Accounting Education Standards Board (IAESB), International Federation of Accountants (IFAC)

Introduction

The recent call for common global accounting education has enhanced the establishment of high quality accounting education standards across the world. To help achieve this goal since 2003, the Education Committee of the International Federation of Accountants (IFAC) has been releasing the International Education Standards (IES) for the accounting profession. These are now issued under the authority of the International Accounting Education Standards Board (IAESB) which operates within IFAC. IFAC expects the accounting sector to use the IES as the benchmarks that will enable member bodies of IFAC to meet the expected demand in the education and development of their professional skills (IFAC, 2003). However, it has been recognized by researchers that the various cultural environments existing around the world could present many challenges to the success of the international convergence of accounting education. For example, Lindahl and Fanelli (2002) reported on some American authors' experiences when presenting accounting lectures in France. They found a tendency for students in France to demand the 'right' answers when analysing case studies. This was not the case for a similar cohort of US students. Another study by Lin, Xiong and Liu (2005) examined the perceptions of required accounting knowledge and skills among accounting practitioners, educators and students in China and compared these results to a similar previous study in the USA by Albrecht and Sack (2000). Lin *et al.* (2005) found lower ratings for written and oral communication skills by Chinese respondents and concluded that these differences were due to the influence of their oriental culture where humbleness and strict obedience of orders from supervisors were the norm. These examples indicate the diversity existing within the accounting environment where different nations may have different teaching/ learning emphases.

In response, IFAC allows its member bodies certain flexibility when incorporating teaching methods into their educational programs. It suggests that members can still comply with the IES requirements by using a variety of different learning methods so long as the outcomes are of equivalent standard (IFAC, 2003, para. 31). Notwithstanding this, the IES do not provide any specific guidelines to assist in choosing suitable teaching methods for the particular cultural environment in which each member body operates. As an example, even though the IES encourages students to engage in learning to learn (IFAC, 2003, para. 38d), Hofstede (1986) implied that learning to learn (or learning how to learn) tends to be more suitable for people from individualist societies, where the primary purpose of learning is thought to improve one's own understanding. In contrast, learning to learn tends to be unacceptable in collectivist societies where knowledge is seen as being more a commodity to be transferred from teacher to student (Auyeung and Sands, 1996). Other studies have also found that, in such societies, individual understanding by students is considered not as important because students expect preferential treatment by learning in a way specifically transferred from their teachers (Hofstede, 1986). Therefore, factors as simple as the teaching methods employed may inhibit the smooth introduction of the IES to the world's various cultural environments. If IFAC's goal for international convergence of accounting education is to be a success then specific guidelines on delivery methods for different cultures may be useful for member bodies.

In seeking a solution, a possible approach is to study students' learning styles. The frameworks for learning style theory in accounting literature have predominantly applied the Learning Style Inventory (LSI) developed by Kolb (1976; 1984). According to Kolb (1976; 1984), learning style theory is based on the Experiential Learning Model, where learning is defined as the process of knowledge creation through the transformation of experience. More importantly, Kolb's theory assumes that one's learning style preference can drive the actual skills or competencies that are acquired through the learning process (Boyatzis and Kolb, 1995; Yamazaki, 2005). In the accounting literature, some prior works have discussed cultural barriers and other obstacles that may affect accounting students' learning style preference (e.g. Auyeung and Sands, 1996; Desai and Taylor, 1998; Marriot, 2002; Loo, 2002) because it is normally assumed that a country's culture is one of the crucial factors that shapes its inhabitants' preferred mode of learning through their experiences in socialization (Hofstede, 1997). However, these frameworks have not been tested. Therefore, for the purpose of helping achieve the smooth harmonization of global accounting education, this current study empirically explores the role that cultural differences play on the learning style preferences of students who are majoring in accounting (referred to as accounting students) across two different cultures.

The remainder of this paper is structured as follows. The next section reviews prior literature in an attempt to address the underlying affects of learning style preferences that this study is investigating. Theories underpinning the associations between cultural factors and learning styles are then discussed, from where the research hypothesis and sub-hypotheses are developed. The methodology, statistical analyses and interpretation of the collected data follows. Summarizing comments from this cultural comparison are provided in the concluding remarks section, together with limitations of this study, in an attempt to assist with the smooth implementation of the IES.

Literature Review

Many previous studies have explored the role that cultural differences play in determining students' learning styles. A number of these studies applied various instruments to address the differences in learning styles across cultures. These include Biggs' (1987) Study Process Questionnaire (SPQ), Felder and Soloman's (1999) Index Learning Style (ILS), Vermunt's (1994; 1996) Inventory of Learning Styles (ILS), and Kolb's (1976; 1984) Learning Style Inventory (LSI). The outcomes from these studies have enabled researchers to provide more effective teaching methods for diversified multicultural classrooms. For example, De Vita (2001) applied Felder and Soloman's (1999) ILS to examine students' learning style profiles in a multicultural international business management class in a British university. The ILS is an inventory to assess subjects' learning styles in terms of the four dimensions of active/reflective; sensing/intuitive; visual/verbal; sequential/ global. De Vita (2001) identified how cultural conditions are reflected on the actual learning style preferences of domestic and international students, and found that international students tended to accept various dimensions of learning styles more flexibly than their domestic counterparts did. Similarly, Ramburuth and McCormick (2001) applied Biggs's (1987) SPQ to compare the learning behaviours of international Asian with domestic Australian students who were studying at an Australian university. In general, the study found no significant difference in students' overall approach to learning, but specifically found that Australian students tended to balance their study programme in an attempt to achieve minimum requirements while international students, being more deeply motivated, strived for higher academic results. Of particular interest, Ramburuth and McCormick (2001) found that one of the most influential factors affecting one's learning style is the culturally-based value relating to individualism/collectivism. Likewise, Levinsohn (2007) examined the cultural dichotomy of students' learning styles and supported previous studies that have found that intrinsic cultural factors such as Chinese Confucianism can affect one's learning. Levinsohn (2007) researched learning style differences between Chinese international students and New Zealand domestic students who studied electrical and electronics trade courses in a New Zealand university. The study used Vermunt's (1994; 1996) ILS and provided evidence that the cultural dichotomy of learning styles between the two nationality groups was due to students' learning motivation which was found to be driven by family, culture and other outside factors for the Chinese students. This cultural dichotomy existing between western and eastern countries, as mentioned in previous papers, is a crucial attribute for this current study because such a dichotomy presents a major challenge for accounting educators and professional bodies as they strive for a successful implementation of IES among countries with different cultures. This prior research has indicated that a consensus on the effects that culture has on students' learning style preferences has not yet been achieved.

Further accounting research by Desai and Taylor (1998) explored the learning styles of tertiary students studying accounting in an attempt to recommend better teaching methods in multicultural classrooms. They collected data from students studying at an Australian university and divided them into the three student groupings of Australian, Asian and Other. Using Kolb's LSI, the study found that a comparison of learning styles between domestic Australian and international Asian students were significantly influenced by the individualism/collectivism dimension. Other studies that applied Kolb's LSI, however, have reported conflicting results. Marriott (2002), for instance, conducted a longitudinal study using UK accounting students from various nationalities to explore whether or not learning style preferences shifted in accordance with the educational programme delivered. Marriot (2002) confirmed that a single dominant learning style preference existed over the period, regardless of a student's nationality grouping. Loo (2002) also used a similar set of multicultural respondents in Canadian universities to examine learning style patterns. The results also reported that one dominant profile of learning style preference existed for students regardless of nationality. These results may suggest that the impact of culture has been marginal, particularly among people engaging in the same subject or job such as accounting. This has also been supported in other prior study findings where occupational identities could prescribe national culture in business organizations (Hofstede, 2001; Donald and Jackling, 2007). More recently Donald and Jackling (2007) examined accounting students' learning approaches at an Australian university in an attempt to address a growing concern that the intake of overseas' students is causing significant changes to the classroom environment. They applied Biggs's (1987) SPQ to assess the learning approaches of local Australian and International Chinese students with their findings, similar to those of Ramburuth and McCormick (2001), showing no significant differences in the learning approaches between the two groups of accounting students. Both studies concluded that Chinese accounting students, studying in a western environment, have little trouble adapting and combining elements of different learning approaches to their studies.

Other research investigating cultural differences in learning styles have attempted to compare learning styles among students studying in different nations. Among these studies, Auyeung and Sands (1996) used accounting students studying in Australia, Hong Kong and Taiwan to investigate whether the cultural factor of individualism/collectivism is reflected in their learning styles. The study provided evidence that learning styles of accounting students in the three countries investigated are reflected in their individualism/collectivism cultural construct. Although this study by Auyeung and Sands (1996) has been regularly cited in more recent research, their analytical tests were not comprehensive. They simply focused on the single factor of individualism/collectivism, which is only one of several cultural dimensions. To address such impairment, Jaju, Kwak and Zinkhan (2002) used the four cultural dimensions from Hofstede's framework to examine cross-cultural differences in the learning styles of undergraduate business students. Using survey data from students studying business in the USA, Korea and India, their findings successfully provided empirical evidence that students' learning styles are statistically different across the four cultural dimensions. The Jaju *et al.* (2002) study was the first to integrate Kolb's learning model with Hofstede's cross-cultural framework. However, the study simply based their research hypotheses on Hofstede's cultural index scores that were originally computed in the 1970s using the data of IBM employees as the benchmark. Another limitation was that Jaju *et al.* (2002) only focused on undergraduate business students in the context of broader educational globalization, and not specifically on accounting students in relation to the smooth implementation of IES, which is where the focus of this current study lies. As discussed above, although the associations between cultural dimensions and learning styles have been well documented in prior literature, results have either been inconsistent (e.g. Auyeung and Sands, 1996; Desai and Taylor, 1998; Marriott, 2002; Loo, 2002) or do not deal directly with accounting education.

Recent globalization has also called upon new research to be undertaken into the global trends of learning style preferences. Some studies have pointed to a geographical shift of cultural traits (e.g. Yamamura, Stedham and Satoh, 2004; Hofstede, 2001), which may have a significant impact on students' learning styles in different parts of the world. For example, Barron and Arcodia (2002) explored possible links between one's ethnic origin and learning style preferences using Confucian Heritage Culture (CHC) on the part of students majoring in hospitality and tourism management in a large Australian university. The study used Honey and Mumford's (1992) Learning Styles Questionnaire (LSQ). Opposed with the initial expectation that CHC students would prefer learning by watching (reflector), the respondents in this study demonstrated a relatively active characteristic in their learning style, which mirrored western students. The study concluded that this anomaly may be explained by the fact that CHC students who study in western universities are very adaptable and will change their approaches to learning depending on their global academic environment. Following on from this prior study, Yamamura et al. (2004) also reported statistical evidence to show that peculiar traits of cultural dimensions for students from eastern countries have been westernized over time. Using a sample of graduate business students in Japan, the replicated study empirically explored the possible shift of Hofstede's (2001) five cultural dimensions, and discovered that the scores in 2002 were dramatically different to those found in Hofstede's 1970's study. For example, Yamamura and Stedham (2004) found that the score of individualism for these Japanese students more than doubled from 46 in 1972 (Hofstede, 2001) to 96 in 2002, and this latter score aligned very closely to the score of 86 for US students in the same year (Yamamura et al., 2004). The results of this study emphasizes the impact that recent shifts in cultural traits has on one's learning style preference—particularly in relation to students from eastern countries. To address the void in accounting education literature, further investigation as made in this current study uses more recent data in an attempt to understand possible new associations between culture and students' learning styles.

Theoretical Framework

As discussed in the above section, previous studies have applied many theories and frameworks to examine associations between the cultural impact and students' learning style preferences. For this current study two theoretical frameworks were used that underpinned the research hypotheses. These frameworks are based on Kolb's Learning Styles, which is discussed in subsection (1) below and Hofstede's Cultural Dimensions, which is discussed in subsection (2). The association between students' learning styles and cultural affects is explained in subsection (3).

1.   Kolb's Learning Style

Previous frameworks of learning style theory in accounting literature have predominantly applied the Learning Style Inventory (LSI) developed by Kolb (1976; 1984). The present study also used Kolb's framework to assure comparability with the many previous studies.

Kolb's learning style theory is based on the Experiential Learning Model. Based on the theory, Kolb claimed that a learner's cycle is developed over four stages. These stages are Concrete Experience (CE) where learning is enhanced by experiences or related people, Reflective Observation (RO) where learning is conducted by watching and reflecting, Abstract Conceptualization (AC) where learning is the process of logical and systematic thinking, and Active Experimentation (AE) where learning is incurred by doing (Kolb, 1984). Furthermore, these four stages divide the learning cycle into two bi-polar axes of AC–CE and AE-RO with the resulting quadrants reflecting four learning style preferences. The AC–CE axis measures the degree to which respondents prefer learning by thinking (AC) or by feeling (CE), while the AE–RO represents the degree to which respondents prefer learning by doing (AE) or by watching (RO). Each of the four quadrants is defined as a learning ability relating to Diverging, Assimilating, Converging or Accommodating. Kolb, Osland and Rubin (1995) claims that all four learning abilities are relevant, but each individual tends to prefer one or more over another. This is described as one's learning style preference. The four learning style preferences are described briefly as follows (Kolb *et al.*, 1995):

Diverging (diverger). People with this learning style preference are best at viewing concrete situations (CE) from many different points of view. Their approach to a situation is to observe (RO) rather than take action.

Assimilating (assimilator). People with this learning style preference are best at understanding a wide range of information (RO) and putting it into concise and logical form. Their approach is to focus on abstract ideas and concepts (AC) rather than learning from other people.

Converging (converger). People with this learning style preference are best at finding practical uses for ideas and theories (AC). They like to process each problem through active experimentation (AE), but they are often less good at dealing with social interpersonal issues.

Accommodating (accommodator). People with this learning style preference have the ability to learn primarily from 'hands-on experience' (CE). This approach is to act on 'gut' feelings (AE) rather than on logical analysis.

2. Hofstede's Cultural Dimensions

The primary purpose of this study was to investigate the role that cultural differences have on learning style preferences for accounting students in two different nations. Accordingly, an appropriate theory on cultural differences was sought in order to examine this relationship. In this respect Gray (1988) is one of the pioneers in accounting literature who addressed cultural difference in the process of classifying diversities of accounting standards and systems within nations. Gray's study was based on Hofstede's (1980; 1983) cross-cultural study, which found that a country's culture is assumed to be one of the crucial factors shaping its inhabitants' preferred modes of learning though their experiences of socialization (Hofstede, 1997). This current study also applies Hofstede's theory with the five cultural dimensions of Individualism (IDV), Masculinity (MAS), Power Distance (PDI), Uncertainty Avoidance (UAI) and Long-term Orientation (LTO) discussed below:

Individualism (IDV). This dimension describes the relationship between the individuality and the collectivity notion that prevails within a given society (Hofstede, 2001).

Masculinity (MAS). The masculinity dimension does not point to gender egalitarianism, but rather to assertiveness, competitiveness and higher ambitions (Hofstede, 2001).

Power distance (PDI). The basic issue within this dimension is that human inequality can occur in areas such as prestige, wealth and power. Different societies place different measures on the status consistency among these areas (Hofstede, 2001).

Uncertainty avoidance (UAI). This cultural dimension is based on uncertainty regarding one's future. Such uncertainty is basic to human life where one tries to cope through the domains of technology, law and religion (Hofstede, 2001).

Long-term orientation (LTO). This dimension is oriented toward the virtues of future rewards based on perseverance and thrift, resulting from the past and present such as respect for tradition, preservation of face and fulfilling social obligations. There is emphasis on practice and good behaviour as specified by the tradition in each cultural phase (Hofstede, 2001).

3. Association between Cultural Dimensions and Learning Styles

To examine empirical associations between cultural dimensions and learning styles, it is considered necessary to understand and develop the theoretical frameworks between Hofstede's five cultural dimensions and Kolb's four learning style elements. The current study divided this investigation into the five sections of Hofstede's cultural dimensions in an attempt to describe the theoretical association between these and learning styles.

Individualism (IDV) and learning styles. In classroom situations, the degree of IDV affects students' learning styles in terms of whether they are willing to share what appears to be the class consensus or to insist on one's own ideas (Hofstede, 1986). In low IDV (collectivism) societies, education tends to be treated as a means of improving one's status in order to maintain relationships with other people. On the other hand, students from a high IDV society focus on the contents of education itself rather than interpersonal relationships (Hofstede, 1986; Yamazaki, 2005). Therefore, learning styles of students in a low IDV society may be drawn from experiences with other people (CE) while students from a high IDV society probably prefer to concentrate on their own understanding (AC). Additionally, in a low IDV society, knowledge is seen as a commodity that is transferred from a teacher to students because they are regarded as a collective and so the individual understanding of the students is relatively unimportant (Auyeung and Sands, 1996). This attitude may draw the specific learning style that simply focuses on watching in the classroom (RO). In contrast, in high IDV societies, a teacher is viewed as a guide to assist students to achieve their best understanding (Auyeung and Sands, 1996). In such learning environments individual students will speak up in class in response to a general invitation from the teacher (AE) (Hofstede, 1986).

Masculinity (MAS) and learning styles. According to Manikutty, Anuradha and Hansen (2007), it is believed that students in a learning environment with high MAS tend to place great importance on tangible success and be rewarded fairly for good performance regardless of whether an intense or stressful climate exists. Students in low MAS societies however, tend to have characteristics like modesty, humbleness, nurturing and responsibility. They normally associate their achievement with the establishment of close human relationship rather than tangible success (Manikutty *et al.*, 2007). Literature confirms that high MAS encourages effective competition, which usually leads to individual success rather than mutual success with others (Hofstede, 1986). Learning styles are therefore likely to be characterized by thinking systematically and effectively (AC). Conversely, people from low MAS societies consider mutual relationships to be more important in such learning environments (CE). Their success is characterized by the harmonization of all interests in the group. In addition, students from high MAS societies endeavour to make themselves visible in anticipation of teacher rewards that use the best student (based on performance) as a benchmark (Hofstede, 1986). They may need to display skills and abilities to get things done (AE). In contrast, people from low MAS societies may show signs of fear and be scared of disturbing others by their actions (Manikutty *et al.*, 2007). They prefer to watch rather than actively participate in their learning (RO).

Power distance (PDI) and learning styles. A high PDI society expresses certain social hierarchies that are acceptable to the society. Teachers, for example, are ranked higher than their students in terms of knowledge and authority in this learning environment (Hofstede, 1986). In such a society, students would be conditioned to accept what the teacher says rather than thinking for themselves. They would be too shy or apprehensive to question the teacher or extend themselves to unfamiliar situations (Hofstede, 1986). In other words, students estimate their power distance through hands-on experience with others before taking their own actions (CE). Conversely, students in lower PDI societies are brought up in a classroom that encourages two-way mutual communication to inspire effective learning (Hofstede, 1986). This trait could be considered as learning by thinking or based on 'gut feeling' (AC). Since teachers are considered highly credible and are not questioned in high PDI societies (Hofstede, 1986), students are expected to be good listeners and accept what the teacher says and so their learning style mode may be characterized by learning by watching (RO). In contrast, students in low PDI societies allow for contradiction or criticism on what the teacher has delivered (Hofstede, 1986). They are expected to find their own solutions through mutual understanding and dialogue with their teacher and classmates and so this mode of learning may rely on learning by doing (AE).

Uncertainty avoidance (UAI) and learning styles. Students with a high UAI rely on information that teachers give them as a means of reducing their risks, while students with a low UAI are willing to challenge autonomous and unstructured learning as long as they are satisfied with their understanding (Manikutty *et al.*, 2007). Applying these theories, it is likely that students from high UAI societies may try to gather as much information on a topic as possible (RO) to ensure validity of what is being taught by their teachers (CE). Conversely, students from low UAI societies are oblivious to any deviation from a rigid syllabus. They prefer unstructured assignments or subjective assessment to supplement their actual understanding. Such students are expected to perform, and receive reward for, innovative approaches to problem-solving (Hofstede, 1986). Students in these societies enjoy being challenged and are not afraid to make mistakes. Accordingly, the traits from this dimension may link to the learning styles of thinking (AC) and doing (AE).

Long -term orientation (LTO) and learning styles. Students in societies with high LTO are considered as those who gather information necessary to acquire the skills for the long-term goal of finding a well-paid job (Manikutty *et al.*, 2007). In such societies, education will be a source of information (RO) aimed to establish long-lasting relationships (CE). On the other hand, students with low LTO tend to set specific short-term learning goals and so put their best effort forward to achieve these goals logically and systematically (Manikutty *et al.*, 2007). This approach may be related to the learning style of thinking (AC). To obtain quick and tangible success, they also tend to take risks and receive rewards before actually gathering all relevant information due to time constraints (Manikutty *et al.*, 2007). This latter cultural trait may be linked to the learning style of doing (AE).

Hypotheses Development

From the above literature review and theoretical frameworks discussed, the current study developed the following primary hypothesis to test the associations mentioned.

> H_0: Hofstede's five cultural dimensions have no significant impacts on Kolb's learning style preferences among tertiary accounting students.

Before examining this primary hypothesis, the key for success of this study lies in choosing two dichotomous countries as the appropriate sample and to test whether they are actually dichotomous or not. For this purpose, two data populations were chosen: one from the eastern country of Japan and the other from the western country of Australia. Being a Commonwealth country, Australia is based on Anglo-Saxon heritage while Japan is located in that part of Asia where Confucianism widely prevails and so affects its peoples' behaviours. Nevertheless, the quality of higher education in both of these countries is commonly regarded as being well advanced. The latest 2008 university rankings, released by *Times Higher Education* (http://www.timeshighereducation.co.uk), shows several universities from both Japan and Australia being among the top 200 institutes in the world. From an accounting education point of view, the accounting professional bodies from both countries are members of IFAC, and are expected to incorporate IES within each of their own education system. It must be stressed that the present study focuses on the cultural impact of one's learning style, whereas the previous study by Yamamura *et al.* (2004) focused on the prominent shift in cultural traits occurring in an eastern country. Since this shift may influence the research construct of the current study, it is necessary to investigate possible differences in learning style preferences and cultural dimensions between students from the countries studied before the primary analysis is carried out. To achieve this, three sub-hypotheses in null form were prepared and tested as follows:

> H_0-1: There are no significant differences in learning style preferences between Australian accounting students and Japanese accounting students.

> H_0-2: There are no significant differences in cultural dimensions between Australian accounting students and Japanese accounting students.

The final sub-hypothesis investigates the role that cultural dimensions have on learning style patterns for both Australian and Japanese accounting students. Since this third sub-hypothesis incorporates the above two variables the combined examination will place us in a more informed position to investigate the primary research question that concerns the impact Hofstede's five cultural dimensions has on Kolb's learning style preferences among tertiary accounting students. The final sub-hypothesis is therefore presented in null form as follows:

> H_0-3: Cultural dimensions for accounting students from both Australia and Japan have no significant impact on their learning style preferences.

Research Method

1. Data Collection

The data for this study was collected via a questionnaire given to students studying at universities in Japan and Australia. This survey focused on domestic undergraduate students who were majoring in accounting in business-related faculties or schools. This study only used students whose birthplace was either Japan or Australia. For this purpose, the questionnaires were initially distributed to all students who attended the courses regardless of their major or nationality. Following collection, only students who majored in accounting and were born and studied in either Japan or Australia were identified, extracted and used in this research. The data collection was anonymous with respondents' names or ID not required on the survey instrument. The questionnaires were distributed to students in class time with the responses being collected immediately upon completion.

There were 324 students at five universities in Japan and 286 students at two universities in Australia who were given the questionnaire. The surveys were administered in September 2006 in both Japan and Australia with additional samples being collected in February 2007 at the two Australian universities to improve the number of respondents. The numbers of usable responses from domestic accounting students were 69 for Japan and 61 for Australia with an effective response rate of 21.30% and 21.32% respectively. The remaining responses were discarded because of the subjects' major (non-accounting students), different nationality, birthplace (international students) or incompletion.

Table 1 reports the descriptive information of the data. To examine comparability between the two groups, this study applied a t-test to investigate the differences in age and Chi-square tests to investigate differences in gender and job experiences. The results of these preliminary analyses revealed significant differences in gender ($\chi^2 = 4.807$, Sig. $= 0.028$) and job experiences ($\chi^2 = 28.094$, Sig. $= 0$) between Japanese and Australian students. Such attributes left open questions of homogeneity among the student groups, thus this must not be ignored in our primary analysis.

2. Questionnaire Development

The Value Survey Module for Young People 1997 (VSMY97) developed by Hofstede was incorporated into the questionnaire to investigate the cultural dimensions. The VSMY97 was revised from the Value Survey Model 1994 (VSM94), which was originally developed for working people in order to identify the cultural dimension, particularly for younger

Table 1. Descriptive information

Country	Japan	Australia	Total
n	69	61	130
Age (t $= -1.538$, Sig. $= 0.127$)			
Max	65	44	65
Min	18	17	17
Average	21.31	22.98	22.10
Gender ($\chi^2 = 4.807$, Sig. $= 0.028$)			
Male	47 (68.1%)	30 (49.2%)	77 (59.2%)
Female	22 (31.9%)	31 (50.8%)	53 (40.8%)
Job experience ($\chi^2 = 28.094$, Sig. $= 0$)			
Without experience	42 (60.9%)	9 (14.8%)	51 (39.2%)
With experience	27 (39.1%)	52 (85.2%)	79 (60.8%)

people without job experiences. In the VSMY97, several expressions from the original questionnaire were rewritten for the purpose of adjusting the original questions that dealt simply with work and situations in general life. Our study used the VSMY97 because respondents included students who did not have any job experiences and accordingly the VSMY97 allowed us to collect cultural dimensions data regardless of respondents' work experiences. The authors obtained the VSMY97 English version and VSM94 Japanese version from Professor Geert Hofstede. Our study used the VSMY97 English version for the Australian subjects and the VSM94 Japanese version which was edited and modified to accommodate the VSMY97 version for the Japanese subjects. Hofstede's (2001) cultural dimensions model is the measuring instrument used to provide the degree of national culture in each respondent's environmental setting. Computing raw data using particular formulae allowed the five dimensions to be returned as an index on national culture which then assists in country-level comparisons (Hofstede, 2001).

Kolb's Learning Style Inventory (LSI) version 3.1 was incorporated into the questionnaire to address students' learning style preference. The LSI was initially developed in the 1970's by Kolb (1976) and revised in 1985 (Mainemelis, Boyatzis and Kolb, 2002). Originally the LSI had received criticism due to its poor reliability and validity as a reputable instrument (e.g. Allinson and Hayes, 1988; Stout and Ruble, 1994). As a result, Kolb and Kolb (2005) refined the LSI and recently released the new LSI as version 3.1 where the new normative sample is based on a larger, more diverse and representative data of LSI users. This current study applied the new LSI 3.1 to ensure reliability with more accuracy (Kolb and Kolb, 2005). The LSI asked respondents to respond to 12 short questions concerning their own learning situations. Each question had four options, which corresponded to the four learning style dimensions of Concrete Experiences (CE); Reflective Observations (RO); Abstract Conceptualization (AC) and Active Experimentation (AE). Students were required to rank the four options of each question. The score for each dimension was then calculated and plotted on the Learning Style Type Grid formed by the two bi-polar axes of AC–CE and AE–RO. The AC–CE axis measures the degree to which respondents prefer learning by experiences or by thinking, while the AE–RO measures the degree to which respondents prefer learning by doing or by watching. As mentioned, the questionnaire also collected background information on students including their age, gender, job experiences, nationality at birth and their major unit of study.

Results

1. Difference in Learning Style Preference between Japanese and Australian Students

First, hypothesis H_0-1 was examined to explore the difference in learning style preferences between the Japanese and Australian groups. The average scores for each of AC, CE, AE, RO, AC–CE and AE-RO were computed as shown in Table 2. Table 2(a) also reports the 'Norm' range, which represents the range of scores between the 40th and 60th percentiles for over 1400 samples collected by Kolb (Adler *et al.*, 2004; 2008). The simple comparison of obtained mean scores displayed several deviations from this 'Norm'. To ensure statistical credibility of such deviations, a normality test was conducted using the Shapiro-Wilk technique and investigated whether the data obtained for each component was of normal distribution or not. The result of this analysis reported significant *P*-values in Table 2(b) for Japanese students where normality for AC and AC–CE was rejected while the remaining factors were proven statistically to have normal distributions. Following this normality test, a t-test was carried out with the assistance of the non-parametric Wilcoxon–Mann-Whitney (WMW) test to assess whether or not there are

Table 2. Difference in learning style preferences between Japanese and Australian students

(a) Means and distributions

Country (n)	Norm[d]	Japan (69)				Australia (61)			
		Means	Range	SD	Distribution (40th–60th)	Means	Range	SD	Distribution (40th–60th)
AC	28–31	32.90	12–45	7.98	31–34	33.02	20–46	5.68	31–34
CE	24–26	28.29	17–40	5.68	27–30	25.66	14–43	6.49	24–27
AE	32–37	29.20	17–43	7.01	27–32	32.54	17–44	6.70	31–35
RO	28–31	29.61	17–43	6.38	27–32	28.79	18–41	5.83	27–31
AC–CE	2.5–9	4.61	−26–25	12.28	1–10	7.36	−14–29	10.37	4–12.2
AE-RO	2–8.5	−0.41	−30–19	11.77	−5–5	3.75	−22–23	10.80	0–7.2

(b) Normality test, t-test and Wilcoxon–Mann-Whitney test

	Normality test (Shapiro-Wilk)				t-test		Wilcoxson–Mann-Whitney test			
	Japan (69)		Australia (61)							
	W	P-value[e]	W	P-value[e]	t-value	P-value	U	W	Z	P-value
AC	0.964	0.04[b]	0.985	0.67	−0.096	0.924	2063.0	3954.0	−0.194	0.846
CE	0.977	0.24	0.962	0.06[c]	3.466	0.015[b]	1546.0	3437.0	−2.609	0.009[a]
AE	0.968	0.07[c]	0.965	0.08[c]	−2.765	0.007[a]	1544.5	3959.5	−2.616	0.009[a]
RO	0.980	0.36	0.974	0.23	0.763	0.447	1969.0	3860.0	−0.633	0.527
AC–CE	0.965	0.05[b]	0.964	0.07*	−1.371	0.173	1862.5	4277.5	−1.130	0.259
AE-RO	0.967	0.07[c]	0.972	0.18	−2.091	0.039[b]	1683.0	4098.0	−1.968	0.049[b]

[a]Significant difference at the 0.01 level.
[b]Significant difference at the 0.05 level.
[c]Significant difference at the 0.10 level.
[d]Normal distribution stands for 40th to 60th percentile referred by Adler et al. (2004).
[e]Significant p-value (<0.05) by Shapiro-Wilk test reject a normal distribution of each attribute.

any differences in learning style components between Japanese and Australian students. Table 2(b) also displays these results where the scores of AE–RO for Australian students were rated significantly higher than those of Japanese students. Conversely, the score of AC–CE did not show any significant differences. Additionally, it was found that the two components of CE and AE showed significant differences in each average score between Japanese and Australian students. Accordingly, the results for this t-test and Mann-Whitney test reject the hypothesis H_0-1 in terms of AE–RO, CE and AE.

The average score for the overall learning style preference for both the Japanese and Australian student groups were plotted on the Learning Style Type Grid in Figure 1. The cut-points were applied at +7 and +6 for the AC-CE scale and the AE-RO scale respectively in accordance with Kolb and Kolb (2005). As shown, the average learning styles, as reflected in the overall trends among each nationality group, were found to be in the first quadrant of Diverging for Japanese accounting students and the fourth quadrant of Assimilating, for Australian accounting students.

In response to the major criticisms of the LSI (Stout and Ruble, 1991a; 1991b; 1994), this current study responded by calculating Cronbach alphas to measure internal consistency, created a modified intercorrelation matrix for scale construct validity, and examined the internal factor structure by applying the Rotated Principle Component test. These are the same techniques as applied by Kayes (2005) to ensure the internal validity and reliability of the original LSI version 3.0 developed in 1999. The Cronbach alphas calculated to determine the internal consistency of the four elements constituting the two scales of the learning style inventory (LSI) are displayed in Table 3(a). These scores ranged from 0.674 to 0.776 for each of the four dimensions. It is normally suggested that an alpha score of more than 0.7 is theoretically acceptable in order to prove consistency (Smith and Kolb, 1986; Duff, 2004). The results found that the three elements of AC, AE and RO met this requirement while the alpha score for CE was less than the normative score, coming in at 0.674. This may be due to the smaller numbers in our sample compared with the previous study. Nevertheless the overall consistency of the learning modes in this current study is deemed acceptable. Second, the modified correlation matrix was developed in Table 3(a) to conduct a minimum test of discriminant construct validity. The results indicated that the correlations within each scale, ranging from −0.111 to −0.515, were greater than the score of difference in correlations between scales (alphas) that ranged from 0.674 to 0.776. Therefore, the dimensional scale scores were considered acceptable. Thirdly, the Principle Component Analysis was implemented with the Varimax rotation method to examine the

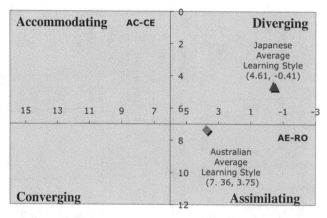

Figure 1. Difference in learning style preferences on the learning style type grid

Table 3. Internal validity and reliability for the LSI

Scale	AC	CE	AE	RO
(a) Internal consistency alphas and scale intercorrelations				
AC	0.776[c]	−0.513a[a]	−0.313[a]	−0.259[a]
CE	0.674[c]	−0.276[a]	−0.111	
AE	0.747[c]	−0.515[a]		
RO	0.705[c]			

Scale	Factor 1	Factor 2
(a) Results of principle component analysis		
AC	0.098	−0.916[b]
CE	0.141	0.814[b]
AE	−0.922[b]	0.083
RO	0.807[b]	0.125
Variance (%)	38.256	38.107
Eigenvalues	1.576	1.478

[a]Significance at the 0.01 level.
[b]Loaded components in each factor.
[c]Alphas are displayed in brackets.
Extracted method: Principal component analysis.
Rotation method: Varimax techniques with Kaiser normalization.
Factor loadings > 0.8 (absolute value).

internal factor structure. The result of this analysis returned the Factor 1 consisting of the AE–RO bipolar axis and the Factor 2 consisting of the AC–CE axis (see Table 3b). These two factors explain over 75% of the cumulative variance and are substantially consistent with the two bipolar dimensions of Kolb's theory. Consequently, the results of these supplementary analyses successfully confirmed sufficient validity and reliability for the LSI 3.1 version to be used in this current study.

2. Hofstede's Cultural Dimensions

Table 4 shows index scores of the four cultural dimensions for Japanese and Australian students. These index scores were calculated according to the instructions provided by Hofstede (2001). It was found that inequality signs for the four cultural dimensions of IDV, MAS, PDI and LTO were consistent with those from Hofstede (1980; 2001). Only the UAI deviated and produced the reverse sign of inequality from the results of Hofstede (1980; 2001).

Table 4. Index scores for dimensions of national culture

	Hofstede (1980; 2001)			The present study		
Country (n)	Japan	Australia	Inequality sign	Japan (69)	Australia (61)	Inequality sign
Individualism (IDV)	46	90	A > J	69.2	92.3	A > J
Masculinity (MAS)	95	61	J > A	77.0	28.9	J > A
Power distance (PDI)	54	36	J > A	21.9	−2.9	J > A
Uncertainty avoidance (UAI)	92	51	J > A	25.4	32.8	A > J[a]
Long-term orientation (LTO)	80	31	J > A	57.2	42.0	J > A

J = cultural index score for Japanese group; A = cultural index score for Australian group.
[a]Reversed inequality sign from the expected results of Hofstede (2001).

461

This study also used statistical testing to explore whether the score for cultural dimensions differ significantly between Japanese and Australian accounting students. Although Hofstede (2001) did not expect researchers to calculate cultural index scores at the individual level, this exploratory study examined and attempted to compute such scores to compare statistically any differences in factors among the two student groups. Initially, Shapiro-Wilk's normality test was applied and this statistical technique concluded that long-term orientation (LTO) for Japanese together with uncertainty avoidance (UAL) and LTO for Australian students did not have normal distributions (Table 5a). Following this the t-tests were conducted with an assistance of the non-parametric WMW test. The findings from these tests as displayed in Table 5(b) indicate that the scores for masculinity (MAS), power distance (PDI) and LTO for Japanese students were significantly higher than those for Australian students at the 0.01 level. In contrast, the score for individualism (IDV) for Japanese students was significant but lower than that for Australian students at the 0.01 level. Only UAI reported non-significant differences. Thus sub-hypothesis H_0-2 was rejected for all cultural dimensions except for UAI.

3. Multiple Regression Results

By applying multiple regressions using the stepwise method this study statistically investigated possible associations between Kolb's learning styles and Hofstede's (2001) five cultural dimensions. The scores for the two scales of AC–CE and AE–RO were treated separately as the dependent variables and both were regressed separately with the five cultural dimensions. The two attributes of gender (GEN) and students' job experience (JOB) were also incorporated into this regression model to determine potential differences in these two factors between Japanese and Australian students. In this regression model, each respondent's gender was anchored 1 for male; 0 for female, and their job experience was anchored 1 for job experience and 0 for no job experience.

Table 6(a,b) exhibit the results of our stepwise regressions for AC–CE and AE–RO, respectively. The analysis initially discovered significant relationships between the AE–RO axis and Uncertainty Avoidance (UAI) at the 0.01 level and with Individualism (IDV) at the 0.1 level. These associations with AE-RO were negative for the UAI but positive for the IDV. The F-statistic and adjusted R^2 were 6.899 and 0.086 respectively with a P-value of 0.001. The other five factors were excluded by the stepwise technique. These results gave assurance that our sub-hypothesis H_0-3 can be rejected in terms of the AE–RO regression. Furthermore, it was found that the AC–CE axis had a significant and negative association with the score for UAI at the 0.1 level. However, the P-value of this regression being 0.054, does not allow a rejection of H_0-3 in terms of AC–CE.

Interpretation

The multiple regression results for this study revealed significant associations between students' learning in the AE–RO style and the cultural dimensions of individualism (IDV) and uncertainty avoidance (UAI). The positive score for AE–RO indicate that students prefer to learn by doing while the negative score suggests that they like learning by watching. Among these results, the significant association between the AE–RO and IDV indicate that the more strongly students have IDV characteristics the more likely they prefer to learn by doing. This result is interesting because the supplementary t-tests also revealed the mean scores of AE–RO and IDV for Australian accounting students were significantly higher than those of Japanese students, which suggests statistically that Japanese like to learn by watching due to their relatively collective approach

Table 5. T-test results for five dimensions of national culture

(a) Means and distributions

	Japanese (69)			Shapiro-Wilk[b]		Australian (61)			Shapiro-Wilk[b]	
	Means	SD	Range	W	P-value	Means	SD	Range	W	P-value
IDV	70.00	54.03	−60–225	0.993	0.97	92.21	42.68	−20–185	0.977	0.33
MAS	77.10	104.42	−170–310	0.989	0.81	29.02	79.28	−170–240	0.978	0.36
PDI	21.59	47.85	−100–120	0.984	0.57	−2.87	53.89	−125–105	0.972	0.18
UAI	25.51	67.00	−120–210	0.990	0.87	32.87	75.66	−120–200	0.948	0.01[a]
LTO	57.10	27.92	0–120	0.945	0.00[a]	41.97	26.51	0–100	0.912	0.00[a]

(b) Normality test, T–test and Wilcoxon–Mann-Whitney test

	t-test		Wilcoxon–Mann-Whitney test				Inequality sign
	t-value	P-value	U	W	Z	P-value	
IDV	−2.615	0.010[a]	1546.5	3961.5	−2.608	0.009[a]	A > J
MAS	2.976	0.004[a]	1450.0	3341.0	−3.056	0.002[a]	J > A
PDI	2.722	0.007[a]	1540.5	3433.5	−2.633	0.008[a]	J > A
UAI	−0.584	0.560	2076.5	4491.5	−0.131	0.896	Non-sig.
LTO	3.168	0.002[a]	1473.0	3364.0	−3.018	0.003[a]	J > A

[a]Significant difference at the 0.01 level.
[b]Significant P-value (<0.05) by Shapiro-Wilk test reject a normal distribution of each attribute.
J = cultural index score for Japanese group, A = cultural index score for Australian group.

Table 6. Multiple regression results

(a) AC–CE

	Unstandardized coefficient		Standardized coefficients			
	B	Std error	Beta	t	Sig.	VIF
(Constant)	6.642	1.089		6.101	0	
UAI	−0.028	0.014	−0.171	−1.942	0.054[b]	1.000

$R = 0.171$, $R^2 = 0.029$, Adjusted $R^2 = 0.022$, F-statistics $= 3.773$, P-value $= 0.054$[b]

(b) AE–RO

	Unstandardized coefficient		Standardized coefficients			
	B	Std error	Beta	t	Sig.	VIF
(Constant)	0.129	1.882		0.068	0.946	
UAI	−0.045	0.014	−0.277	−3.252	0.001[a]	1.001
IDV	0.033	0.019	0.145	1.700	0.092[b]	1.001

$R = 0.316$, $R^2 = 0.100$, adjusted $R^2 = 0.086$, F-statistics $= 6.899$, P-value $= 0.001$[a]

[a]Significant at the 0.01 level.
[b]Significant at the 0.1 level

Note1. The variance inflation factors (VIF) for independent variables were calculated to examine any multicollinearity issues. The VIFs greater than 10 could generally indicate a serious multicollinearity problem. However, these scores in the analyses were sufficiently small enough to enable us to reject this concern.

Note 2. One of the important assumptions for linear regression analysis is that the residuals are normally distributed. In this respect, this research examined normality of the residuals. The results reported that the skewness (−0.388 for AC–CE and −0.448 for AE-RO) and kurtosis (-0.580 for AC-CE and 0.062 for AE-RO) were near 0, the test of normality with Kolmogorov-Smirnov technique were not significant (0.297 and 0.339 of p-values for AC-CE and AE-RO) and therefore failed to reject normality. The Q-Q plot for both residual sets looked normal.

Note 3. Durbin-Watson test (DW) was also conducted to examine whether there is serial correlation or not because such correlation can be the result of the impact of outliers. In this study, the scores of the DW test for both AE-RO and AC–CE regressions were 1.854 and 1.932, which were very near 2. Therefore, it is concluded that there is no statistical issue regarding outliers in this analysis.

to learning. In contrast, Australian students who tend to be more individualistic in their learning were more willing to learn by doing.

Compared to previous studies, the average score for AE–RO in this current study was similar to that of Auyeung and Sands (1996), who reported 3.66 and 4.03 for Australian accounting students from two Australian universities. In addition, the scores for AE–RO (−4.35 and −2.66) for Chinese students in Taiwan and Hong Kong in this prior study showed significantly lower scores to those of their Australian counterparts. This Chinese group is considered to come from a lower IDV society, as demonstrated by Hofstede (2001) who found the index of IDV for Taiwan and Hong Kong to be 17 and 25 respectively, which is lower than that for Australian students. Therefore, the results of this study supports Auyeung and Sands (1996) where accounting students in lower IDV countries such as Taiwan and Hong Kong tend to prefer learning by watching which is not the case in Australia. The present finding is also consistent with Desai and Taylor (1998), who reported that the learning style profile of IDV was higher for Australians and lower for Asian accounting students (Indonesian, Malaysian, Singaporean and Hong Kong Chinese). Since these prior studies did not actually test the empirical associations between the degree of individualism (IDV) and one's preference of learning by doing/watching, the present research can now successfully provide with statistical evidence, support to confirm this relationship.

The current study also found that the factor of uncertainty avoidance (UAI) had a significant relationship with the AE–RO axis. This result indicates that the stronger the UAI characteristics which students have, the more likely it is that they will prefer to learn by watching. Similarly, the more strongly students prefer taking risks, the more likely it is that they will prefer to learn by doing. However, this significant factor of UAI in the regression result for AE–RO showed non-significant differences between Australian and Japanese student groups via a t-test. The t-test result indicated that the UAI was no longer a factor that attributes to cultural dichotomy for either the western (Australian) or eastern (Japanese) groups, even though the UAI did have a significant impact on the AE–RO score. The initial expectation of an inequality sign from Hofstede (2001) reported that the score of UAI for Japanese was higher than that for Australians. However, the actual score in this study may have shifted as it did not confirm any significant difference. On reflection of this result, Hofstede (1980; 2001) anticipated the possibility of this cultural dimension shifting over time. The index score for cultural dimension from Hofstede's (2001) study is based on the survey conducted in the 1970s'. Therefore, this may explain why the index scores in the current study are different from those of previous studies. The results of this present study is supported by Yamamura *et al.* (2004), which proved empirically that the score of uncertain avoidance for Japanese students changed from 92 in 1972 (Hofstede, 2001) to 30 in 2002. Additionally, the score of uncertain avoidance for Japanese respondents in this current study was 25.4, which is consistent with the result of Yamamura *et al.* (2004). Given these outcomes, our research can verify that the individual characteristics of the UAI is very prominent in determining students' learning style preferences, but the same cannot be said when explaining cultural differences between Japanese and Australian students.

Concluding Remarks

The learning style pattern for Australian accounting students was found to be that of the *Assimilating* type, while for Japanese students it was found to be of the *Diverging* type. This study also found that the degree of individualism had significant impact on driving students' preference to learn by doing or by watching.

From a theoretical point of view, this latent association between students' individualism and learning by doing/watching preference also supports findings in some prior studies. In collectivist (i.e. less individualist) societies, neither the teacher nor any student ever wants to lose face by taking redundant actions in class because their learning purpose is to maintain consensus and improve one's status in such societies (Hofstede, 1986). Here, knowledge is seen as being a commodity to be transferred from a teacher to a student (Auyeung and Sands, 1996). Therefore, students like to attend class simply to absorb knowledge from watching what their teachers show them. The analyses of this current research successfully confirmed, through empirical analyses, this theoretical construct using Australian and Japanese dichotomous data sets.

The findings also enable accounting educators to reflect and facilitate on the most effective choice of teaching methods as prescribed by the IES. Although the IES encourages the use of a broad range of learner-centred teaching methods to master self-directed learning for post qualification (IFAC, 2003, para. 38), the findings of this study imply that the collective style of Japanese students may lead to their unwillingness to become active participants in the classroom. This is because they have a preference for learning by watching. Accounting educators must be sensitive to these students' needs when implementing teaching methods that may require their participation in front of a class. Such self-directed learning may also limit the amount of information that can be transferred from the teacher. For example, debating type activities or seminar presentations in the classroom may seem to be an effective way to enhance active and self-directed learning but the collectivist traits of Japanese students may inhibit and cause embarrassment for them in front of a group of fellow students and teachers (Auyeung and Sands, 1996; Hofstede, 1986). To alleviate these concerns, teachers may require extra training to equip them with special knowledge and teaching techniques that will enable the introduction of individualistic learning techniques in unthreatening environments.

Educators must also implement alternative teaching methods, such as self-directed learning, to help achieve more effective learning outcomes for students from collectivist societies. Since students in collectivist societies tend to treat education as a means of improving one's status in order to maintain relationships with other people (Hofstede, 1986), contributing to small group and e-learning activities may be preferable because they can achieve the benefits of self-directed learning without jeopardizing their relationships with others.

The finding of a significant linkage between individualism and learning by doing/ watching, also suggests that educators should refine some of their teaching methods to accommodate Japanese students' preference for learning by watching. Simple use of case studies or project work aimed to encourage self-directed learning may not be as effective for collective Japanese students because of their preference for learning by watching. One suggestion from the present finding is to combine student-centred teaching with formal lectures in an attempt to lessen such students' desire for learning by watching. Teachers can provide students with a short summarized lecture with reflective comments followed by student-centred teaching activities.

Finally, despite the regression model being statistically significant, the small adjusted R-squared score in the regression assumes that culture is not a primary factor in explaining a possible relationship with students' learning styles. This outcome suggests that it is not impossible to overcome any cultural differences in order for the IAESB to achieve a convergence in global accounting education.

There are some limitations with this paper. First, the current research applied only one of the various theories on students' learning style preferences. There are other recognised instruments that could have been used to measure learning styles in the literature, which this study failed to incorporate. Different perspectives on different learning style theories may draw different outcomes on the same issue. Therefore, there is still scope to address the same topic using different measures of learning styles. Second, this study only used a sample of students from the dichotomous countries of Japan and Australia. To enable the successful convergence in global accounting education, it is necessary to investigate the role of cultural dimensions on students' learning styles across a number of countries as there could still be many other ecological differences that affect learning. Apart from these limitations, this paper does contribute to a clearer understanding of the cultural affects on the learning style preferences of accounting students for the purpose of achieving global convergence in accounting education.

Acknowledgements

The authors are grateful for providing the research fund by the JSPS KAKENHI (19730319). The authors also wish to acknowledge Professor Richard M. S. Wilson (Editor of *Accounting Education: an international journal*), an Associate Editor and the two anonymous referees for their assistance in connection with the publication of this paper.

References

Adler, R. W., Whiting, R. H. and Wynn-Williams, K. (2004) Student-led and teacher-led case presentations: Empirical evidence about learning styles in an accounting course, *Accounting Education: an international journal*, 13(2), pp. 213–229.

Albrecht, W. S. and Sack, R. J. (2000) *Accounting Education: Charting the Course Through a Perilous Future* (Florida: American Accounting Association).

Allinson, C. W. and Hayes, J. (1988) The learning style questionnaire: An alternative to Kolb's inventory? *Journal of Management Studies*, 25(3), pp. 269–281.

Auyeung, P. and Sands, J. (1996) A cross-cultural study of the learning style of accounting students, *Accounting and Finance*, 36(2), pp. 261–274.

Barron, P. and Arcodia, C. (2002) Linking learning style preference and ethnicity: International students studying hospitality and tourism management in Australia, *Journal of Hospitality, Leisure, Sport & Tourism Education*, 1(2), pp. 15–27.

Biggs, J. B. (1987) *Study Process Questionnaire Manual* (Melbourne: Australian Council for Educational Research).

Boyatzis, R. E. and Kolb, D. A. (1995) From learning styles to learning skills: The Executive Skill Profile, *Journal of Managerial Psychology*, 10(5), pp. 3–17.

Desai, R. and Taylor, D. W. (1998) Learning styles of accounting students in multi-cultural cohorts, *Asian Review of Accounting*, 6(1), pp. 121–142.

De Vita, G. (2001) Learning styles, culture and inclusive instruction in the multicultural classroom: A business and management perspective, *Innovations in Education and Teaching International*, 38(2), pp. 165–174.

Donald, J. and Jackling, B. (2007) Approaches to learning: A cross-cultural study, *Asian Review of Accounting*, 15(2), pp. 100–121.

Duff, A. (2004) The role of cognitive learning styles in accounting education: Developing learning competencies, *Journal of Accounting Education*, 22(1), pp. 29–52.

Felder, R. M. and Soloman, B. A. (1999) *Index of Learning Styles*. Available at http://www.engr.ncsu.edu/learningstyles/ilsweb.html (accessed on 24 April 2008).

Gray, S. J. (1988) Toward a theory of cultural influence on the development of accounting system internationally, *Abacus*, 24(1), pp. 1–15.

Hofstede, G. (1980) *Culture's Consequences* (California: Sage Publications).

Hofstede, G. (1983) Dimensions of national cultures in fifty countries and three regions, in: J. B. Deregowski, S. Dziurawiec and R. C. Annis (Eds) *Expiscations in Cross-Cultural Psychology*, pp. 335–355 (Lisse, Netherland: Swets & Zeitlinger).

Hofstede, G. (1986) Cultural differences in teaching and learning, *International Journal of Intercultural Relations*, 10(3), pp. 310–320.

Hofstede, G. H. (1997) *Culture and Organization: Software of Mind* (New York: McGraw Hill).

Hofstede, G. (2001) *Culture's Consequences—2nd ed.* (California: Sage Publications).

Honey, P. and Mumford, A. (1992) *The Manual of Learning Styles* (Maidenhead, Berkshire: Peter Honey).

International Federation of Accountants (IFAC) (2003) *Introduction to International Education Standards* (New York: IFAC Education Committee).

Jaju, A., Kwak, H. and Zinkhan, G. M. (2002) Learning styles of undergraduate business students: A cross-cultural comparison between the US, India and Korea, *Marketing Education Review*, 12(2), pp. 49–60.

Kayes, D. C. (2005) Internal validity and reliability of Kolb's learning style inventory version 3 (1999), *Journal of Business and Psychology*, 20(2), pp. 249–257.

Kolb, D. A. (1976) *The Learning Style Inventory: Technical Manual* (Boston: McBer and Company).

Kolb, D. A. (1984) *Experiential Learning: Experience as the Source of Learning and Development* (New Jersey: Prentice-Hall).

Kolb, D. A., Osland, J. S. and Rubin, I. M. (1995) *Organizational Behavior* (6th ed.) (New Jersey: Prentice-Hall, Inc).

Kolb, D. A. and Kolb, A. Y. (2005) *The Kolb Learning Style Inventory—Version 3.1 2005 technical Specifications* (Boston: HeyGroup).

Levinsohn, K. R. (2007) Cultural differences and learning styles of Chinese and European trades students, *Institute for Learning Styles Journal*, 1(Fall), pp. 12–22.

Lin, Z. J., Xiong, X. and Liu, M. (2005) Knowledge base and skill development in accounting education: Evidence from China, *Journal of Accounting Education*, 23(3), pp. 149–169.

Lindahl, F. W. and Fanelli, R. (2002) Applying continuous improvement to teaching in another culture, *Journal of Accounting Education*, 20(4), pp. 285–295.

Loo, R. (2002) The distribution of learning styles and types for hard and soft business majors, *Educational Psychology*, 22(3), pp. 349–360.

Mainemelis, C., Boyatzis, R. E. and Kolb, D. A. (2002) Learning style and adaptive flexibility: Testing experiential learning theory, *Management Learning*, 33(1), pp. 5–33.

Manikutty, S., Anuradha, N. S. and Hansen, K. (2007) Does culture influence learning styles in higher education? *International Journal of Learning and Change*, 2(1), pp. 70–87.

Marriott, P. (2002) A longitudinal study of undergraduate accounting students' learning style preferences at two UK universities, *Accounting Education: an international journal*, 11(1), pp. 43–62.

Ramburuth, P. and McCormick, J. (2001) Learning diversity in higher education: A comparative study of Asian international and Australian students, *Higher Education*, 42(3), pp. 333–350.

Smith, D. M. and Kolb, D. A. (1986) *Learning Style Inventory: User's Guide* (Boston: McBer and Company).

Stout, D. E. and Ruble, T. L. (1991a) The Learning Style Inventory and accounting education research: a cautionary view and suggestions for future research, *Issues in Accounting Education*, 6(1), pp. 41–52.

Stout, D. E. and Ruble, T. L. (1991b) A reexamination of accounting student learning styles, *Journal of Accounting Education*, 9(2), pp. 341–354.

Stout, D. E. and Ruble, T. L. (1994) A reassessment of the Learning Style Inventory (LSI-1985) in accounting education research, *Journal of Accounting Education*, 12(2), pp. 89–104.

Vermunt, J. D. H. M. (1994) *Inventory of Learning Styles in Higher Education; Scoring Key for the Inventory of Learning Styles in Higher Education* (Tilburg: Tilburg University, Department of Educational Psychology).

Vermunt, J. D. (1996) Metacognitive, cognitive and affective aspects of learning styles and strategies: A phenomenographic analysis, *Higher Education*, 31(1), pp. 25–50.

Wynn-Williams, K., Whiting, R. H. and Adler, R. W. (2008) The influence of business case studies on learning style: An empirical investigation, *Accounting Education: an international journal*, 17(2), pp. 113–128.

Yamamura, J. and Stedham, Y. E. (2004) Globalization and Culture: An Exploratory Study (11 May 2004). Available at SSRN: http://ssrn.com/abstract=616261 (accessed on 25 April 2008).

Yamazaki, Y. (2005) Learning styles and typologies of cultural differences: A theoretical and empirical comparison, *International Journal of Intercultural Relations*, 29(5), pp. 521–548.

Understanding Student Plagiarism: An Empirical Study in Accounting Education

XIN GUO

University of the West of Scotland, UK

ABSTRACT   *The purpose of this paper is to: (i) identify factors concerning student plagiarism in accounting education; (ii) develop and empirically test a model of factors influencing students' plagiaristic behaviour; and (iii) make recommendations to accounting educators to reduce the incidence of student plagiarism. A questionnaire was administrated to 381 UK accounting students. Structural equation modelling was used to assist data analysis. Research results indicate four antecedents of student plagiarism labelled: (i) academic integration; (ii) cultural influences; (iii) moral capability; and (iv) gender. The surface learning approach taken by accounting students is found to be positively associated with their pressures such as fear of failure and time pressure. The paper concludes by suggesting that educators should adopt a supportive approach to motivating students to act in a consistent, ethical manner in their academic life.*

Introduction

The issue of student plagiarism has created significant concern within the UK higher education sector over the past decade. Although it is hardly new, many commentators (for example, Samuels and Bast, 2006; Selwyn, 2008) believe it is on the increase as a consequence of the availability of material on the Internet. Alongside concerns about plagiarism sit increased demands to improve the business and professional ethics of accountants (ICAS, 2007a; 2007b; IFAC, 2007) following high-profile corporate scandals such as Enron and Parmalat. In accounting education, plagiarism represents a breach of academic conduct of accounting students, many of whom will eventually become professional accountants and future business leaders.

The term 'plagiarism' is defined as 'the theft of words or ideas, beyond what would normally be regarded as general knowledge' (Park, 2003, p. 472). Samuels and Bast (2006) suggest that, legally, the plagiarist misappropriates another's work, while misrepresenting that he/she is the author of the plagiarized work.

Attempts to understand student plagiarism in higher education started from North America where an extensive literature has developed (for example, Ameen, Guffey and McMillan, 1996; Love and Simmons, 1998). After reviewing previous research on student plagiarism, Park (2003) identified seven essential themes:

   (i) the meaning and context of plagiarism;
  (ii) the nature of plagiarism;
 (iii) how students perceive plagiarism;
 (iv) how great a problem is student plagiarism;
  (v) what motivates students to cheat;
 (vi) the challenges posed by digital plagiarism; and
(vii) the demand for students' academic integrity.

A review of prior literature in accounting education identifies six relevant empirical studies. Ponemon (1993), after surveying 126 accounting students in the USA, reported that ethics interventions failed to improve accounting students' moral capability. Fresh evidence emerged to support a quadratic relationship where students with relatively low and high levels of ethical reasoning were most likely to engage in unethical behaviour.

Through sampling 386 accounting students in four universities in the USA, Ameen et al. (1996) measured students' perceptions of the severity of 22 forms of academic misconduct, identifying a range of positive and negative relationships between academic misconduct and environmental factors. For example, student misconduct was found to be positively related to cynicism, tolerance of cheating, and expectations that they themselves may cheat in the future, and to be negatively related to prior academic achievement—as measured by grade point average (GPA)—and expectations of punishment if being caught.

Extending this, Duff (1998) examined perceptions of 22 different types of academic misconduct including plagiarism by surveying 243 third-year accounting students in four universities in the UK. The most significant findings were that: (i) the perceived severity of behaviours was inversely related to the perceived frequency of occurrence; (ii) significant differences existed between institutions; (iii) fear of failure was the most common reason given by students for involvement in academic misconduct; and (iv) students aged over 25 years tended to rate academic misconduct as more serious than their younger peers.

Smith, Davy, Rosenberg and Haight (2002), after surveying 606 accounting students in the USA, reported that the primary influences on future academic misconduct were in-class deterrents, prior cheating, and the degree to which one neutralized prior cheating behaviour. Furthermore, Abdolmohammadi and Baker (2007) took a replication study of Ponemon (1993) and examined the relationship between accounting students' moral capability and their plagiaristic behaviour. After surveying 136 accounting students in the USA, they reported a significant inverse relationship between moral capability and plagiarism which was not consistent with the quadratic relationship reported by Ponemon (1993). More recently, Smith et al. (2007) investigated accounting students' perceptions of plagiarism by sampling 286 undergraduate accounting students in Malaysia, identifying four plagiarism-related factors: (i) lack of awareness; (ii) lack of understanding; (iii) lack of competence; and (iv) personal attitudes. They concluded that the incidence of plagiarism was positively related to academically weak, male students with negative attitudes towards their studies.

To summarize, first, previous empirical studies have discovered a variety of factors relating to student plagiarism such as moral capability, demographic variables, and environmental factors. However, it should be noticed that in each study only a limited number of plagiarism-related factors or their relationships with students' plagiaristic behaviour have been considered. In other words, no research has ever considered a comprehensive set of factors concerning plagiarism. Second, considering data analytic techniques used in pursuing the causes of student plagiarism, most of the previous studies tested linear relationships between constructs rather than the construct validity of hypothesized models by using structural equation modelling (SEM)—a more recently developed and accepted technique. Third, considering data collection, all the previous studies sampled undergraduate students; no research has ever used samples of postgraduate students (who are regarded as the major source of income in UK accounting departments in the twenty-first century). Collectively, the dearth of research is unexpected, given increased demands by the public to improve the business ethics of professional accountants and accounting students (IFAC, 2007). This paper therefore attempts to fill these research lacunae with an empirical study within the context of accounting education. Investigating student plagiarism in accounting education is relevant and significant to UK universities offering accounting programs, allowing them reasonably to allocate teaching resources to help students to fit in their academic life, incorporate cultural considerations in curriculum design, and ultimately motivate students to act in a consistent, ethical manner: a key role for accounting educators (Gray, Bebbington and McPhail, 1994).

In particular, this study introduces many factors which were omitted in the previous empirical studies into a hypothesized model, for example, accounting education—the research context itself. Accounting education and practice in the UK has historically been bonded to accounting professional bodies that set examinations and rules for all their members and students. Some commentators (for example, Ameen *et al.*, 1996 in the USA) suggest that pressure to obtain professional qualifications is a major factor that motivates accounting students to indulge in academic dishonesty. Others suggest that accounting students are inclined to adopt high levels of a surface approach to learning compared to students majoring in other subjects (Booth, Luckett and Mladenovic, 1999). The impact of these characteristics of accounting education on students' plagiaristic behaviour is examined in this paper, coupled with other factors such as new technology and cultural and educational backgrounds. A hypothesized model is proposed and empirically tested via SEM using data collected from 381 accounting students in the UK.

The objectives of the paper are three-fold; first, to identify factors that influence students' plagiaristic behaviour via literature review; second, to develop and empirically test a model of factors influencing students' plagiaristic behaviour; and third, to make recommendations for accounting educators to reduce the incidence of student plagiarism.

The remainder of this paper is structured as follows. The next section reviews the extant literature concerning factors relating to student plagiarism. These factors are introduced into a hypothesized conceptual model. Section three describes the conduct of questionnaire survey, respondents, and data analytic techniques used. Section four reports the results of hypothesis testing by structural equation modelling (SEM). The final section discusses and concludes the paper.

Literature Review: Factors Concerning Student Plagiarism

Nine primary factors concerning student plagiarism are identified in the extant literature which the author labels: (i) moral capability; (ii) awareness; (iii) academic integration;

(iv) pressures; (v) accounting education; (vi) new technology; (vii) institutional support; (viii) cultural influences; and (ix) demographic variables.

Moral Capability

Moral capability is one's ability to properly identify and respond in a moral situation. Kohlberg's (1981) moral developmental theory suggests that students' moral capability is related to their ethical behaviour. Empirical findings on the relationship between moral capability and unethical behaviour have been mixed (e.g. Ponemon, 1993; Abdol-mohammadi and Baker, 2007). Additionally, Duff's (1998) survey of 243 accounting students in the UK reported that the most commonly-cited reason for not plagiarizing was that 'it is immoral or dishonest'. Therefore, the following hypothesis is formulated:

H$_1$: Students with low levels of moral capability are more likely to plagiarize.

Awareness of Plagiarism

Two sublevel constructs concerning students' awareness of plagiarism are identified in the literature. First, Carroll (2002) argues that students' ambiguous knowledge of plagiarism often leads them to being accused of plagiarizing even when they have no intention to deceive. Without a good understanding of plagiarism, most students tend to ignore it and are reluctant to pursue what it really means (Love and Simmons, 1998). Many commentators (for example, Smith *et al.*, 2007; Yeo, 2007) have suggested that most university students do not fully understand what constitutes plagiarism, what penalties can result from its identification, and how to avoid plagiarism through proper referencing.

Second, lack of awareness of plagiarism being serious academic misconduct is another factor that contributes to student plagiarism. McCabe and Trevino (1996), surveying 6,096 college and university students in the USA, reported that 52% of them did not think that fabricating references was serious academic misconduct and 80% did not think that submitting coursework done by others was serious misconduct. Hayes and Introna (2005) reported that all the UK students participating in their focus groups believed it acceptable to copy a small amount of text from others without proper acknowledgement. In accounting education, Smith *et al.* (2007) found that the acknowledgement of authorship was not perceived to be essential by the Malaysian accounting students when they were surveyed. Therefore, the following hypothesis is formulated:

H$_2$: Students with low levels of awareness of plagiarism are more likely to plagiarize.

Academic Integration

Academic integration refers to how well students fit in to the overall academic environment and their academic life. For example, students who perceived themselves as well-integrated are inclined to have good attitudes towards learning and assessment (Kreger and Wrenn, 1990; Michie, Glachan and Bray, 2001). By contrast, disengaged students may feel bored about a particular module or a programme to the level where they become alienated from their institutions (Seemen, 1991; Davies, 2000), let alone learn to reference properly in order to avoid being caught plagiarizing. Ashworth, Bannister and Thorne (1997) identify that the main reasons for students experiencing alienation including: lack of contact with academic staff; the impact of large-class teaching; a widespread student dislike on the increased emphasis on group work as a method of assessment; and a belief that what they are doing is not considered significant in the eyes of their teachers. Carroll and Appleton (2001) suggest that students' perceptions of a certain module being taught poorly or of marginal importance can also contribute to their alien-ation from the education system and may consequently lead to plagiarism. Empirically, Caruana, Ramseshan and Ewing (2000) reported a negative relationship between academic integration and students' propensities to behave dishonestly by surveying 122 Australian business students. Therefore, the following hypothesis is formulated:

H_3: Students who are poorly integrated in to the academic environment are more likely to plagiarize.

Pressures

Four different types of student pressures are identified in the literature. First, pressure to succeed in one's studies forces many students to resort to plagiarism (Ameen *et al.*, 1996). Duff (1998) reported that 35% of the students in his sample rated 'fear of failure' as the most common reason for academic misconduct. Abdolmohammadi and Baker (2007) reported that accounting students were more likely to plagiarize at the end of a semester than at the beginning because of increased pressure of not failing in their studies.

Second, Bennett (2005), after surveying 249 UK business students, reported an inverse relationship between students' financial situation and minor degree of plagiarism. He explains that students with financial difficulties would normally spend more hours taking part-time employment and thus may experience greater temptations to take short-cuts in their academic work by plagiarizing. Although there is no empirical evidence reported within the context of accounting education, there is a possibility that Bennett's (2005) findings could be replicated by surveying accounting students.

Third, students who receive financial support from their families are under great pressure to succeed. This parental pressure is said to lead to fear of failure that could in turn motivate students to plagiarize (Haines, Diekhoff and LaBeff, 1986). This type of pressure also applies to those students funded by governments, funding councils, and com-panies. Empirically, Introna, Hayes, Blair and Wood (2003), after sampling 97 students undertaking postgraduate courses in the UK, reported that 40% of the students rated 'family pressure to achieve good grades' as 'very important'.

Fourth, lack of time is another factor that causes students to resort to plagiarism. Park (2003) suggests that there are many calls on students' time such as peer pressure for an active social life and family responsibilities. Additionally, students' poor time management skills and academic staff setting close deadlines for submitting a number of written assign-ments could create extraordinary time pressure for students (see Franklyn-Stokes and Newstead, 1995; Errey, 2002). Therefore, the following hypothesis is formulated:

H_4: Students under great pressures are more likely to plagiarize.

Accounting Education: The Surface Approach to Learning

Accounting education in the UK has historically been connected with a number of account-ing professional bodies that set examinations and rules for all their members and students [for example, the Institute of Chartered Accountants of Scotland (ICAS), the Institute of Chartered Accountants in England & Wales (ICAEW), the Association of Chartered Cer-tified Accountants (ACCA), and the Chartered Institute of Management Accountants (CIMA).] Accountancy degrees offered by UK universities are usually accredited by these professional bodies in response to stakeholders' demands to gain varying levels of exemptions from professional examinations.[1] In general, accounting students are more likely to take these professional examinations and pursue careers in accounting profession than students majoring in other subjects; and this could exert great pressure on accounting students which may induce them to cheat in order to achieve their professional accounting qualifications (Ameen et al., 1996). Empirically, Armstrong (1993), using a cognitive developmental approach, has identified 'a lower cognitive moral capability in accounting students than other undergraduates of similar age and education levels' (see Thorne, 2001, p. 105). Extending this, Beattie, Collins and McInnes (1996) suggest that the study of accounting is said to be partly mechanical and partly conceptual. Booth et al. (1999) and Eley (1992) both reported that accounting students were inclined to adopt lower deep and higher surface approaches to learning compared to students majoring in other subjects such as arts, education, and science. Many commentators (for example, Fleming, 1996; Ponemon, 1990) have suggested that it may be this surface approach to learning which leads to the decline in moral development in professional accountants since accounting graduates do not have to acquire the deep learning skills needed for complex moral reasoning. Collectively, the extant literature indicates that the surface approach to learning taken by accounting students may cultivate their habits of academic dishonesty and encourage them to indulge in plagiarism. Therefore, the following hypothesis is proposed:

H₅: The surface approach to learning taken by students in accounting education is positively related to their plagiaristic behaviour.

New Technology

The Internet has made it possible for students to find and save large amounts of information from diverse sources with little reading, effort, or originality (Park, 2003). Many commentators (for example, Auer and Krupar, 2001) have suggested that the rapid expansion of the Internet significantly facilitates the incidence of plagiarism. In accounting education, Duff (1998), after sampling 243 UK accounting students, reported that 17% of the students use essay banks to submit their coursework. More recently, after surveying 291 UK science students, Szabo and Underwood (2004) reported that 32% of the students admitted to using the copy and paste function to embed unacknowledged content from the Internet into their written assignments.

However, a variety of electronic detection systems have been developed to help educators to identify materials plagiarized from the Internet or other sources. One of the best known products is *Turnitin* that has been adopted by approximately 60% of UK institutions (Anderson, 2006). Most detection systems operate by using a range of search techniques, where the content of submitted coursework is checked against various sources such as web pages, previous documents, and electronic libraries (Evans, 2006). A significant implication of using detection systems is to impose a psychological impact on students (Hayes and Introna, 2005). In other words, fear of penalties that one could receive for plagiarism if being caught may mitigate students' engagement in plagiarism. Ameen et al. (1996) found that accounting students generally realized that academic misconduct could result in serious consequences and hence responded positively to institutional efforts to create a healthy environment of academic honesty. Considering the hypothesized relationship that may exist between new technology and students' plagiaristic behaviour and the uncertainty as to the direction given to these two potential opposing influences (i.e. the Internet and detection software), the following hypothesis is formulated:

H₆: New technology is a major factor influencing students' plagiaristic behaviour.

Institutional Support

Three sublevel constructs concerning institutional support are identified in the literature. First, prior research indicates that, although a majority of academic staff have the experience of detecting plagiarism, not all of the plagiarism cases have been treated seriously through formal institutional procedures (Bjorklund and Wenestam, 1999; Dordoy, 2002). The reasons for not engaging in the formal process by academic staff are said to include their reluctance to take on the extra workload of plagiarism enquiries and concerns that institutional regulations cannot be equally applied across different departments (Morgan, 1996). Others may feel sympathy for the possible impact of sanctions on students' future careers (Shapira, 1993; Keith-Spiegel, Tabachnick, Allen, Whitley and Washburn, 1998). In accounting education, Sierles, Hendrickx and Circle (1980) found that accounting students in the USA felt most educators did not want the aggravation of enforcing rules against cheating and plagiarism. Smith *et al.* (2007) reported that most Malaysian accounting students they surveyed had no fear of being caught plagiarizing as they believed their teachers would not and could not successfully detect plagiarism. Lack of enforcement by academic staff cultivates students' perceptions that the risk of being caught plagiarizing is minor and this encourages students' engagement in plagiarism.

Second, many accounting departments in UK universities have included ethics-related modules into their curriculum design (Ghaffari, Kyriacou and Brennan, 2008). It is anticipated that the inclusion of such modules will enhance accounting students' moral capabilities of recognizing and responding to ethical dilemmas that they may encounter in their future careers. Empirically, Shaub (1994) reported that accounting students who took an ethics course had higher cognitive moral capability than those who did not. Earley and Kelly (2004) reported that ethics educational interventions (such as lectures and case studies) had a positive impact on accounting students' moral development. Furthermore, to reduce the incidence of student plagiarism, many UK universities have offered courses in academic writing to enhance students' understanding of proper acknowledgement and awareness of plagiarism.

Thirdly, lack of guidance could leave students struggling with their academic workloads and making decisions that compromise their academic integrity. Stefani and Carroll (2001) contend that it is essential for academic staff to inform students clearly of expectations of their academic performance. Even with explicit guidance, many students still need special support. A critical issue that affects overseas students' capability of adjusting to the Western academic environment is the presence or lack of support networks, for example, language learning centres, spiritual needs, funding and immigration advice. Considering the hypothesized relationship that may exist between institutional support and students' plagiaristic behaviour and the uncertainty as to the direction given these potential opposing influences (i.e. guidance, enforcement, and curriculum design), the following hypothesis is formulated:

H_7: Institutional support is a major factor that influences students' plagiaristic behaviour.

Cultural Influences

The ways of teaching and learning in overseas countries are considered to vary from those in the UK (Hofstede, 1991). The differing cultural values may provide other explanations for misconduct behaviour including plagiarism among overseas students (Cordeiro, 1995; see Walker, 1998).

First, many overseas students are caught plagiarizing unwittingly because of little experience in written assignments. This is a particular issue for students from Asian countries where academic structures heavily depend on end-of-semester examinations rather than mid-term coursework (Carroll and Appleton, 2001). Empirical support is provided by Hayes and Introna (2005), who found that the Asian students participating in their study had little experience in writing coursework, perhaps only one essay and a couple of reports during their entire undergraduate education. Although these students were required to provide references in written assignments in their home countries, it was not as rigorous as in the UK.

Second, ambiguous knowledge of authorship could be another reason for overseas students frequently falling into plagiarism, since the concept that an author owns his/her text is not a prevalent one in some countries (Snowden, 2005). Moore (1997) reported that Asian students viewed text as containing general information rather than the views of a particular author. Such behaviour is due to a perception that an author's knowledge belongs to the realm of collective ownership rather than to an individual (Snowden, 2005). Howard (1995) suggests that overseas students heavily depend on the writing style of primary sources and described this source-dependent composition as 'patch writing'. Ironically but truly, plagiarism is even considered as highly acceptable academic conduct in some cultures where copying an authority's work is regarded as a form of respect (Pennycook, 1996; Devlin and Gray, 2007).

Finally, many overseas students find themselves struggling with written assignments because of their limited command of English. Although most of them need to produce satisfactory English language qualifications such as IELTS (International English Language Testing System) or TOEFL (Test of English as a Foreign Language) for admission to studying at UK universities, good scores in these examinations do not guarantee that they will cope with all the language demands in their studies. Wan (2001) suggests that many overseas students perform well in these examinations but have poor oral and writing skills. Schmitt (2006) estimates the average vocabulary of a university-level overseas student being around 5,000 words compared to 30,000–40,000 words of a native speaker. More importantly, many commentators (for example, Introna et al., 2003; Barrett and Cox, 2005) have suggested that some overseas students feel they cannot improve upon what is already written and prefer to use the original text rather than their own. As Watkins and Biggs (1996, p. 279) conclude: 'students who want to make a point particularly clearly see paraphrasing the source as a strange thing to do when the source itself makes the point better than they ever could reword it in an imperfectly mastered language'. Therefore, the following hypothesis is formulated:

H_8: Students' cultural and educational backgrounds are related to their plagiaristic behaviour.

Demographic Variables

First, male students are more inclined to cheat than are female students, evidenced by extensive literature (Ameen et al., 1996; Szabo and Underwood, 2004). In accounting education, prior research has shown that male students possess lower levels of cognitive moral capability, making them more likely to participate in academic dishonesty than their female peers (Etherington and Schulting, 1995). A recent study in Malaysia provided empirical evidence that male accounting students were more likely to engage in plagiarism than females (Smith et al., 2007).

Second, prior research has also suggested that age is a significant antecedent of plagiarizing, with younger students more likely to cheat than their older peers (Smith et al., 2002). Empirically, Franklyn-Stoke and Newstead (1995), after examining the relationship between age and academic dishonesty among 128 UK science students, reported that students aged over 25 years rated academic cheating as being more serious and less frequent than their younger peers. In accounting education, Duff's (1998) replication study of Franklyn-Stokes and Newstead (1995) reported findings that were consistent with those of Franklyn-Stokes and Newstead (1995).

Finally, mixed results have been found in the previous research on the relationship between students' academic performance and their plagiaristic behaviour. Crown and Spiller (1998), Emery (2004), and Haines *et al.*, (1986) all found that students with a higher grade point average (GPA) were less inclined to commit plagiarism. By contrast, Franklyn-Stokes and Newstead (1995) and Roberts, Anderson and Yanish (1997) found no such relationship in their studies. In accounting education, Smith *et al.* (2007) reported that undergraduate students exhibiting lower academic performance were more likely to engage in plagiarism than their better performing classmates. Love and Simmons (1998) explain that academically-weak students perhaps do not have the confidence to prepare good coursework at a technical or inter-personal level and hence may resort to plagiarism. Therefore, the following hypotheses are formulated:

H_{9a}: Male students are more likely to engage in plagiaristic behaviour than are female students.
H_{9b}: Younger students are more likely to plagiarize than are older students.
H_{9c}: Students with lower academic performance are more likely to engage in plagiarism than are those with higher academic performance.

To summarize, the literature review identified nine primary factors with a wide range of sublevel constructs relating to student plagiaristic behaviour. Figure 1 portrays these factors and their hypothesized relationships with plagiarism into a conceptual model to be further tested in the paper. The next section describes the conduct of questionnaire survey and the data analytic techniques used.

Methods

Questionnaire

An 81-item questionnaire was developed to capture accounting students' attitudes towards plagiarism, using closed-form questions only. The measurement items are derived from the scales of Franklyn-Stokes and Newstead (1995), Smith *et al.* (2007), and Entwistle and Tait (1995). Three focus groups were conducted with 13 accounting students in

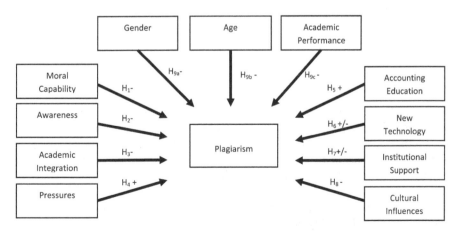

Figure 1. Hypothesized conceptual model

order to refine the questionnaire and contextualize the extant literature, allowing a better understanding of the intersection of student plagiarism, accounting education, new technology and cultural influences. Thirty-nine (out of 81) items were developed from or refined by the focus groups, covering all the primary factors proposed in the literature review. Given the limitation on the length of published papers, findings of the focus groups are reported in a separate paper available from the author. All the measurement items were presented in five-point Likert response format with the anchors 'strongly disagree' and 'strongly agree'. The questionnaire contained three sections and the items pertained to the hypothesized factors presented in the hypothesized model. Table 1 provides primary factors, sublevel constructs, examples of items used and their origins.

(i) Factors relating to student plagiarism. This section containing 65 items covers eight factors influencing students' plagiaristic behaviour: (i) awareness; (ii) moral capability; (iii) academic integration; (iv) pressures; (v) accounting education; (vi) institutional support; (vii) new technology; and (viii) cultural influences. The measurement items are derived from the scales of Franklyn-Stokes and Newstead (1995), Smith *et al.* (2007), and Entwistle and Tait (1995) and refined by the focus groups.

(ii) Extent of students' plagiaristic behaviour. This section (containing ten items) attempts to measure the extent of different types of plagiaristic behaviour which students exhibit in their writing practices. The items are derived from the scales of Franklyn-Stokes and Newstead (1995) and Roig and DeTommaso (1995), ranging from copying material without citation, paraphrasing, to fabricating references.

(iii) Demographic items relating to respondents. Section three contains demographic questions relating to age, gender, and self-evaluated academic performance.

Respondents

The questionnaire was administered to students enrolled in accounting-related programmes at both undergraduate and postgraduate levels at two universities in the UK, with the help of teaching staff. The students were assured of anonymity and confidentiality of the survey. As a result, a total of 381 useable responses were received; 80% of the enrolled students participated in the survey. Among the respondents, 44.1% were male students and 55.9% were females. The respondents aged under 21, between 22 and 24, and over 25 accounted for 52.3%, 28.3%, and 19.4% respectively. Chi-square tests indicated that no significant association existed between scores of students' plagiaristic behaviour and gender ($\chi2$ (22, $n = 381$) = 27.790, $P = 0.183$), and between scores of students' plagiaristic behaviour and age group ($\chi2$ (44, $n = 381$) = 45.306, $P = 0.417$).

Statistical Analysis

The statistical analysis proceeds in three parts. First, alpha coefficients are calculated for scores yielded by the questionnaire in terms of each hypothesized primary factor to estimate internal consistency reliability. Second, correlation coefficients are used as an exploratory investigation to ascertain if there are any significant relationships among the hypothesized constructs. Third, the hypothesized conceptual model is tested by structural equation modelling (SEM). Scale items were incorporated into multiple indicators (except for demographic properties such as age and gender) for each construct and this method would offer the ability of correcting for measurement error and allow confirmatory factor analysis of the hypothesized and alternative measurement models (e.g. see Fogarty,

Table 1. Factors and examples of items used in the questionnaire

Section	Factors	Sublevel constructs of items	Origin	Number	Examples of items
(i) Factors relating to plagiarism	Awareness	Knowledge, awareness	Scale of Smith *et al.* (2007); refined by focus groups	6	'I am aware that plagiarism is serious academic misconduct.'
	Moral capability	Moral capability	Scale of Franklyn-Stokes and Newstead (1995); refined by focus groups	2	'I feel plagiarism is immoral.'
	Pressures	Fear of failure, time pressure, financial pressure, and parental pressure	RASI—Scale of Entwistle and Tait (1995) and scale of Smith *et al.* (2007); refined by focus groups	12	'I often seem to panic if I get behind with my work.'
	Accounting education	Surface learning approach	RASI—Scale of Entwistle and Tait (1995); refined by focus groups	5	'I find I have to memorize a good deal of what I have to learn.'
	New technology	The Internet, and detection system	Scale of Smith *et al.* (2007); refined by focus groups	5	'I don't think detection software can identify it if I plagiarize.'
	Institutional support	Guidance, enforcement, and curriculum design	Scale of Smith *et al.* (2007); refined by focus groups	14	'I find the lecturers reluctant to take action against students who commit plagiarism.'
	Cultural influences	Experience, authorship and language capability	Items developed from focus groups; scale of Smith *et al.* (2007)	8	'Culturally, I feel it is not important to acknowledge the original author.'
	Academic integration	Academic integration, attitudes toward study, laziness, and academic confidence	RASI—Scale of Entwistle and Tait (1995); scale of Smith *et al.* (2007); refined by focus groups	13	'I know what I want to get out of this course and I am determined to achieve it.'
(ii) Extent of Plagiarism	Student plagiarism activities	Ten different types of plagiaristic behaviour, such as paraphrasing	Scale of Roig and DeTommaso (1995); and scale of Franklyn-Stokes and Newstead (1995)	10	'Paraphrased information from a secondary source, but did not cite the source in my reference section.'
(iii) Demographic items	Demographic variables	Gender, age, and academic performance		6	'Male or female'

Singh, Rhoads and Moore, 2000). The interrelationships between the constructs are also considered.

Confirmatory factor analysis (CFA) via AMOS 7.0 was undertaken to assess model fit to the data. AMOS is a statistical program to perform structural equation modeling, a form of multivariate analysis. Maximum likelihood estimation was used to conduct CFA using the covariance matrices of the scaled scores. To evaluate the fit of the models, normed fit index (NFI), comparative fit index (CFI), the standardized root mean square residual (SRMSR) were used in tandem with the root mean square error of approximation (RMSEA). The model fit standard of 0.6 is used for RMSEA and a cut-off value of 0.90 for NFI and CFI (e.g. see Fogarty et al., 2000). Although values of 0.05 or less are seen as being most desirable for SRMR (Sörbom and Jöreskog, 1982), Kline (1998) reports values of 0.1 or less as favourable. To perform the hypothesis testing, standardized path coefficients (i.e. regression weights) were calculated and statistical significance was undertaken ($\alpha = 0.05$).

Findings

Reliability

The internal consistency reliability of scores yielded by the constructs of the conceptual model is assessed—see Table 2. Alpha coefficients of the constructs ranged from 0.70 to 0.89. These values exceed the cut-off value of 0.70 suggested by Nunnally (1978) for instruments suitable for applied research in a variety of settings.

Correlations between all Constructs

The correlation coefficients between all the constructs in the conceptual model are calculated—see Table 3. Plagiarism is negatively associated with gender ($r = -0.17$), moral capability ($r = -0.30$), awareness ($r = -0.17$), institutional support ($r = -0.16$), cultural influences ($r = -0.36$), and academic integration ($r = -0.19$). These correlations are statistically significant ($\alpha = 0.05$) and broadly consistent with the hypotheses. Considering the interrelationships between these factors, many statistically significant correlations are notable. Specifically, accounting education is positively associated

Table 2. Internal consistency reliability estimates, means and standard deviations of constructs ($n = 381$)

Constructs	Reliability (alpha coefficient)	Mean	SD
Moral capability	0.89	3.91	0.93
Awareness of plagiarism	0.84	3.82	0.68
Pressures	0.75	3.52	0.49
Accounting education	0.70 (0.61)[a]	3.76	0.76
New technology	0.72 (0.63)[a]	3.38	0.68
Institutional support	0.79	3.85	0.46
Cultural influences	0.70 (0.64)[a]	3.49	0.73
Academic integration	0.72	3.50	0.41
Plagiarism[b]	0.81	1.41	0.43

[a]The alpha coefficients of Accounting Education, New Technology and Cultural Influences have improved to a conventionally acceptable level ($\alpha = 0.70$) after item attritions by examining item-to-total correlations.
[b]'Paraphrasing information from a secondary source' is rated as the most frequent plagiaristic behaviour.

Table 3. Correlations between constructs ($n = 381$)

	GEN	AGE	AP	MC	AWA	PRE	AE	NT	IS	CI	AI
AGE	0.07										
AP	0.08	-0.18^b									
MC	0.12^a	0.04	-0.07								
AWA	-0.03	0.00	-0.10^a	0.34^b							
PRE	0.15^b	-0.11^a	0.17^b	0.01	0.02						
AE	0.05	-0.05	0.18^b	-0.04	0.02	0.50^b					
NT	0.02	0.09	0.09	-0.02	0.01	0.21^b	0.22^b				
IS	0.02	0.06	-0.15^b	0.28^b	0.25^b	-0.14^b	-0.24^b	-0.10			
CI	0.05	0.05	-0.18^b	0.30^b	0.33^b	-0.10	-0.23^b	-0.11^a	0.38^b		
AI	-0.06	0.01	-0.19^b	0.25^b	0.28^b	-0.05	-0.13^a	0.24^b	0.32^b	-0.47^b	
P	-0.17^b	-0.01	0.09	-0.30^b	-0.17^b	-0.06	0.04	0.49	-0.16^b	-0.36^b	-0.19^b

GEN, gender; AGE, age; AP, academic performance; MC, moral capability; AWA, awareness; PRE, pressures; AE, accounting education; NT, new technology; IS, institutional support CI, cultural influences; AI, academic integration; P, plagiarism.

[a]Correlation is statistically significant ($P < 0.05$).

[b]Correlation is statistically significant ($P < 0.01$).

with pressures ($r = 0.50$); awareness of plagiarism is positively associated with student moral capability ($r = 0.34$); cultural influences is positively associated with awareness of plagiarism ($r = 0.33$); and academic integration is positively associated with institutional support ($r = 0.32$) and cultural influences ($r = -0.47$). These are important findings which are further tested by structural equation modelling (SEM).

Hypothesis Testing by SEM

SEM was used to test the hypothesized conceptual model, and CFA was conducted to assess the construct validity of the model. The first model (Model I) to be tested was the hypothesized conceptual model where all the sublevel constructs are related to plagiarism. Model I provided a less than satisfactory fit to the data ($\chi 2$ (3151) = 8756.083; NFI = 0.89; CFI = 0.91; RMSEA = 0.068; SRMR = 0.1215). Two alternative models were also tested for comparison purposes. The second model (Model II) discarded sublevel items that demonstrated low values of factoring loadings.[2] Model II also provided a less than satisfactory model fit to the data (χ^2 (2269) = 6444.068; NFI = 0.88; CFI = 0.90; RMSEA = 0.070; SRMR = 0.1232). Improving on Model II, the third model (Model III) released correlations between constructs by considering modification indices produced by CFA.[3] The fit indices generally supported Model III ($\chi 2$ (2250) = 5321.003; NFI = 0.94; CFI = 0.96; RMSEA = 0.060; SRMR = 0.1088). Consequently Model III was used in the subsequent hypothesis testing.[4] Standardized path coefficients and corresponding P-values are provided in Table 4.

First, the hypothesized relationships between the factors relating to plagiarism and the extent of plagiarism are tested. A negative relationship between moral capability and plagiarism is found as expected (standardized path coefficient = -0.23, $P < 0.05$), which supports Hypothesis 1. A statistically insignificant relationship between awareness and plagiarism is encountered (standardized path coefficient = -0.04, $P = 0.67$), so that Hypothesis 2 cannot be supported. Hypothesis 3 is supported as a statistically significant relationship is found between academic integration and plagiarism (standardized path coefficient = -0.22, $P < 0.05$). Non-statistically significant relationships are found between pressures and plagiarism (standardized path coefficient = -0.04, $P = 0.68$), between accounting education and plagiarism (standardized path coefficient = 0.08, $P = 0.37$), between new technology and plagiarism (standardized path coefficient = 0.02, $P = 0.70$), and between institutional support and plagiarism (standardized path coefficient = -0.01, $P = 0.94$), so that Hypotheses 4, 5, 6, and 7 cannot be supported. Cultural influences is negatively related to plagiarism (standardized path coefficient = -0.19, $P < 0.05$), which supports Hypothesis 8. Hypothesis 9a is supported on the basis of a significant negative relationship between gender and plagiarism (standardized path coefficient = -0.14, $P < 0.05$). Non-statistically significant relationships are found between age and plagiarism (standardized path coefficient = -0.03, $P = 0.54$) and between academic performance and plagiarism (standardized path coefficient = 0.01, $P = 0.94$), so that Hypotheses 9b and 9c cannot be supported.

Second, the interrelationships between the hypothesized factors are considered. Statistically significant correlations ($P < 0.05$) are provided in Table 4. As a result, awareness of plagiarism is positively associated with moral capability ($r = 0.35$), cultural influences ($r = 0.23$), and academic integration ($r = 0.27$). Institutional support is positively associated with awareness of plagiarism ($r = 0.31$) and academic integration ($r = 0.24$), and negatively associated with pressures ($r = -0.11$). Finally, pressures are positively related to accounting education ($r = 0.50$) and negatively related to age ($r = -0.13$).

Table 4. Results of hypothesis testing by SEM and CFA model fit statistics

Hypothesized relationships	Standardized path coefficient	P-value
H_1 MC → P (−)	−0.23	a
H_2 AWA → P (−)	−0.04	0.67
H_3 AI → P (−)	−0.22	a
H_4 PRE → P (+)	−0.04	0.68
H_5 AE → P (+)	0.08	0.37
H_6 NT → P (±)	0.02	0.70
H_7 IS → P (−)	−0.01	0.94
H_8 CI → P (−)	−0.19	a
H_{9a} GEN → P (−)	−0.14	a
H_{9b} AGE → P (−)	−0.03	0.54
H_{9c} AP → P (−)	0.01	0.94
Correlations between constructs	Correlation	P-value
AWA <−> MC	0.35	a
AWA <−> CI	0.23	a
AWA <−> AI	0.27	a
IS <−> AWA	0.31	a
IS <−> AI	0.24	a
IS <−> PRE	−0.11	a
PRE <−> AE	0.50	a
PRE <−> AGE	−0.13	a

CFA model fit statistics:
   Model I: $\chi2$ (3151) = 8756.083; NFI = 0.89; CFI = 0.91; RMSEA = 0.068; SRMR = 0.1215
   Model II: $\chi2$ (2269) = 6444.068; NFI = 0.88; CFI = 0.90; RMSEA = 0.070; SRMR = 0.1232
   Model III: $\chi2$ (2250) = 5321.003; NFI = 0.94; CFI = 0.96; RMSEA = 0.060; SRMR = 0.1088
GEN, gender; AGE, age; AP, academic performance; MC, moral capability; AWA, awareness; PRE, pressures; AE, accounting education; NT, new technology; IS, institutional support; CI, cultural influences; AI, academic integration; P, plagiarism.
[a]Standardized path coefficient or correlation is statistically significant ($P < 0.05$).

The results of SEM are summarized in Figure 2. Implications of these results are discussed in the next section.

Discussion and Implications

Discussion

This paper has developed and empirically tested a model of factors influencing student plagiarism within the context of accounting education. By reference to the prior research concerning student plagiarism, a hypothesized model was created by including a comprehensive set of plagiarism-related factors and associated sublevel constructs. The model was empirically tested by structural equation modelling using data collected from 381 accounting students in the UK.

The results provide sufficient evidence of four antecedents of students' plagiaristic behaviour in accounting education: (i) gender; (ii) academic integration; (iii) moral capability, and (iv) cultural influences. First, male students are more inclined to engage in plagiarism than are their female peers, a result consistent with those reported by Ameen *et al.* (1996) and Szabo and Underwood (2004). Second, students who perceived themselves to be poorly integrated into their academic life are more likely to engage in plagiaristic behaviour. These negative attitudes also include laziness and lack of academic

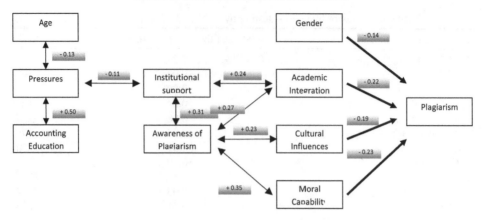

Figure 2. The final model. Standardized path coefficients are illustrated by bold, single arrows; correlations are illustrated by double arrows. All the path coefficients and correlations are statistically significant ($P < 0.05$).

confidence. Third, students with low levels of moral capability are likely to engage in plagiarism, as expected. Finally, ambiguous knowledge of authorship and limited command of English caused by various cultural backgrounds could trap overseas students into plagiarism.

More importantly, this paper advances our knowledge of student plagiarism by examining the inter-relationships between the hypothesized factors, especially those that failed to demonstrate adequate psychometric properties in hypothesis testing. Several important findings are found. Awareness, although failing to be related to plagiarism, is found to be positively associated with three antecedents of plagiarism (academic integration, moral capability, and cultural influences). Raising student awareness of plagiarism should remain a pivotal focus for accounting educators in preventing the incidence of plagiarism, and future research could usefully include these constructs in a more sophisticated model to demonstrate their relationships in a structural modelling context. Additionally, the results show that institutional support for students is negatively related to student pressures and positively related to awareness of plagiarism and academic integration; students aged over 25 feel under less pressure than their younger peers; and finally, this paper extends existing findings in that the surface learning approach taken by accounting students is significantly associated with their pressures ($r = 0.50$) such as fear of failure and time pressure.

New technology—a hypothesized factor with two sublevel constructs (the Internet and detection software)—is completely removed from the model as it failed to relate to any other factors. This result is unexpected and inconsistent with the extant literature highlighting that student plagiarism is on the increase as a consequence of the rapid expansion of the Internet. The removal of the factor and its associated constructs implies that we should reconsider exactly what impact new technology has on student plagiarism nowadays. The practical implications of the research findings are discussed in the next section.

Recommendations

Although many commentators have urged that UK higher education institutions (HEIs) should adopt a robust prevention approach to tackling academic dishonesty, this paper suggests that accounting educators should take a supportive approach to motivating students to act in a consistent, ethical manner. Recommendations to accounting educators to reduce the incidence of student plagiarism are provided as follows.

(i) Understand cultural influences.   Students' cultural backgrounds may cause problems for many overseas students when they study at UK HEIs. Academic and professional development provided by the HEIs ought to create an environment that deters plagiarism by encouraging recognition of cultural diversity. Special efforts ought to be made in helping students to understand and fit in to the existing academic environment and in ensuring that they are not being unfairly excluded from the provision of higher education. Summer schools or foundation courses, for example, should centre on these objectives.

(ii) Include ethics-related modules.   It is suggested that ethics-related modules should be included in the curriculum design in all UK accounting departments at both undergraduate and postgraduate levels. This type of educational intervention has attested to the positive impact on students' moral capability of recognising and responding to ethical dilemmas such as plagiarism and cheating (see Earley and Kelly, 2004). The intervention is also necessitated by increased demand by the public to improved professional ethics of accountants.

(iii) Integrate students into their academic life.   Establishing and maintaining a healthy supporting system for new and continuing students to become properly integrated into their academic life should remain a focus for university management. Constructive advice on career possibilities could be given to accounting students in the early stage of their studies. Additionally, accounting educators should make every effort to create an interactive environment that goes beyond the traditional lecture format, encouraging students to participate in an interactive, deep approach to learning.

(iv) Reconsider the impact of new technology on plagiarism.   The results indicate that the 'new technology' factor was lacking in psychometric properties and consequently was discarded. This unexpected finding, although being inconsistent with many empirical studies, actually warns us against exclusively blaming the rapid expansion of the Internet for the plague of student plagiarism and excessively relying on electronic detection systems in tackling plagiarism. Alternatively, the paper suggests that accounting educators should focus their efforts on the antecedents of plagiarism presented in the final model (academic integration, moral capability, and cultural influences) and adopt a supportive approach to motivating students to act in a consistent, ethical manner. Theoretically, incorporating these constructs into a more refined model is certainly called for.

(v) Another two comments on student plagiarism.   First, the results indicate that awareness of plagiarism is positively related to three antecedents of plagiarism; therefore, educating students in what constitutes plagiarism and raising students' awareness of its legal implications should be critical. Emphasis should be placed on paraphrasing, as 'paraphrasing information from a secondary source' was rated as the most frequent plagiaristic behaviour in the survey. Accounting educators should explicitly inform students of both the positive reasons for proper acknowledgement and the negative implications they must receive if being caught plagiarizing. Concrete examples should be given of those offenders failing in their studies or being expelled from institutions.

Second, some educators in practice have replaced written assignments with other assessment methods such as class tests to lessen opportunities for plagiarism; however, without proper guidance, this amendment could trigger other types of misconduct behaviour such as cheating. Written coursework should remain as one of the primary assessment methods, as through its preparation it allows students to acquire many employability skills.

Under such circumstances, accounting educators are recommended to: first, modify assessment tasks each time the course is taught and avoid setting close deadlines for several assignments (see Carroll and Appleton, 2001); and second, provide clear guidance and feedback on students' written assignments (for example, interim comments focusing on referencing could effectively reduce the incidence of plagiarism).

As a conclusion, the paper advances our knowledge of what causes accounting students to plagiarize by introducing a comprehensive set of factors into a conceptual model. Many constructs in accounting education, new technology, and cultural influences are empirically tested for the first time within the research context of accounting education. Several important inter-relationships are reported, for example, the surface approaches to learning taken by accounting students is positively associated with student pressures such as fear of failure and time pressure. Through hypothesis testing by SEM, this paper concludes that gender, academic integration, cultural influences, and moral capability are the four antecedents of plagiarism. The reflections of the research findings reinforces the extant literature and policies in reducing the incidence of student plagiarism, but also suggests university management and accounting educators should adopt a supportive approach to motivating students to act in a consistent, ethical manner in their academic life.

Finally, five directions are suggested for future research. First, this paper has presented a review of the prior research concerning factors relating to students' plagiaristic behaviour, providing sufficient details for replication purposes in the future. Second, the results indicate that accounting education (the surface approach to learning), although failing to relate to plagiarism, is positively associated with student pressures. In future research, it would be both interesting and necessary to examine whether the surface approach to learning would indulge accounting students in resorting to other academic misconduct such as freeloading or cheating. Thirdly, the results indicate that the 'new technology' factor is completely removed from the final model as no psychometric support is found in data analysis, a result being inconsistent with many previous empirical studies. This unexpected finding suggests that future research on reconsidering and revaluating the impact of new technology on student plagiarism is deemed necessary and can be recommended. Fourth, in the present paper, no comparative analysis between UK and overseas students has been undertaken. Future research is suggested to identify the differences that may exist between UK and overseas students' perceptions of plagiarism and other academic misconduct. Finally, this paper acknowledges the limitations of self-reporting by accounting students regarding their own plagiarism activities and academic performance (for example, some may not fully understand what constitutes plagiarism or what paraphrasing is when being surveyed). Future research could usefully consider using 'true' scores (for example, originality reports of students' written assignments produced by electronic detection software) in measuring the extent of student plagiarism.

Notes

[1] For example, the Institute of Chartered Accountants of Scotland (ICAS) provides up to five exemptions to accounting graduates from accredited universities.

[2] Exploratory factor analysis (EFA) was conducted and items with low values of factoring loadings of less than 0.5 were discarded from the model (Facteau, Dobbins, Russell, Ladd and Kudisch, 1995). As a result, 11 items were discarded including two items in Accounting Education, two items in New Technology, three items in Institutional Support, two items in Cultural Influences, and two items in Academic Integration.

[3] The release of correlations was made one by one since the deletion of one item may affect other parts of the model simultaneously (Segars and Grover, 1993).

[4] In Model III, 54.7% of variance (R^2) is explained by the predictors on plagiarism.

References

Abdolmohammadi, M. J. and Baker, C. R. (2007) The relationship between moral reasoning and plagiarism in accounting course: a replication study, *Issues in Accounting Education*, 22(1), pp. 45–55.

Ameen, E. C., Guffey, D. M. and McMillan, J. J. (1996) Gender differences in determining the ethical sensitivity of future accounting professionals, *Journal of Business Ethics*, 15(5), pp. 591–597.

Anderson, J. (2006) *Implementation of the University's Plagiarism Policy*. Available at: http://www.paisley.ac.uk/schoolsdepts/CAPD/signposts/downloads/PPIWG-Report.pdf (accessed 6 January 2011).

Armstrong, M. (1993) Ethics and professionalism in accounting education: a sample course, *Journal of Accounting Education*, 11(1), pp. 77–92.

Ashworth, P., Bannister, P. and Thorne, P. (1997) Guilty in whose eyes: university student perception of cheating and plagiarism, *Studies in Higher Education*, 22(2), pp. 187–203.

Auer, N. J. and Krupar, E. M. (2001) Mouse click plagiarism: the role of technology in plagiarism and the librarian's role in combating it, *Library Trends*, 49(3), pp. 415–433.

Barrett, R. and Cox, A. L. (2005) At least they're learning something: the hazy line between collaboration and collusion, *Assessment and Evaluation in Higher Education*, 30(2), pp. 107–122.

Beattie, V., Collins, B. and McInnes, B. (1997) Deep and surface learning: a simple or simplistic dichotomy? *Accounting Education: an international journal*, 6(1), pp. 1–12.

Bennett, R. (2005) Factors associated with student plagiarism in a post-1992 university, *Assessment and Evaluation in Higher Education*, 30(2), pp. 137–162.

Bjorklund, M. and Wenestam, C. (1999) *Academic Cheating: Frequency, Methods and Causes*. Proceedings of the 1999 European Conference on Educational Research, Lahti, Finland. Available at: http://www.leeds.ac.uk/educol/documents/00001364.htm (accessed 6 January 2011).

Booth, P., Luckett, P. and Mladenovic, R. (1999) The quality of learning in accounting education: the impact of approaches to learning on academic performance, *Accounting Education: an international journal*, 8(4), pp. 277–300.

Carroll, J. (2002) *A Handbook for Deterring Plagiarism in Higher Education* (Oxford: Oxford Centre for Staff and Learning Development).

Carroll, J. and Appleton, J. (2001) *Plagiarism: A Good Practice Guide*. Joint Information Systems Committee. Available at: http://www.jisc.ac.uk/pub01/brookes.pdf (accessed 1 February 2010).

Caruana, A., Ramaseshan, B. and Ewing, M. T. (2000) The effect of anomie on academic dishonesty amongst university students, *The International Journal of Educational Management*, 14(1), pp. 23–30.

Cordeiro, W. P. (1995) Should a school of business change its ethics to conform to the cultural diversity of its students? *Journal of Education for Business*, 71(1), pp. 27–29.

Crown, D. F. and Spiller, M. S. (1998) Learning from the literature on college cheating: a review of empirical research, *Journal of Business Ethics*, 17(2), pp. 683–700.

Davies, P. (2000) Computerized peer assessment, *Education and Training International*, 37(4), pp. 346–355.

Devlin, M. and Gray, K. (2007) In their own words: a qualitative study of the reasons Australian students plagiarize, *Higher Education Research and Development*, 26(2), pp. 181–198.

Dordoy, A. (2002) *Cheating and Plagiarism: Student and Staff Perceptions at Northumbria*. Proceedings from the first Northumbria conference 2002, Educating for the Future, Newcastle, July.

Duff, A. (1998) Staff and student perceptions of academic misconduct: a survey of Scottish academic staff and students, *Accounting Forum*, 21(3–4), pp. 283–305.

Earley, C. E. and Kelly, A. P. (2004) Note on ethics educational interventions in an undergraduate auditing course: is there an 'Enron effect'? *Issues in Accounting Education*, 19(1), pp. 53–72.

Eley, M. G. (1992) Differential adoption of study approaches within individual students, *Higher Education*, 23(3), pp. 231–254.

Emery, E. (2004) Dishonour Dode: Cheating Rampant Probe of AFA Test, Teen Survey Suggest Rise in Moral Lapses, *Denver Post*, 12 May.

Entwistle, N. and Tait, H. (1995) Approaches to studying and perceptions of the learning environment across disciplines, *New Directions for Teaching and Learning*, 64(4), pp. 93–103.

Errey, L. (2002) Plagiarism: something fishy or just a fish out of water? *Teaching Forum for Oxford Brookes University*, 50(3), pp. 17–20.

Etherington, L. and Schulting, L. (1995) Ethical development of accountants: the case of Canadian certified management accountants, *Research on Accounting Ethics*, 1(3), pp. 235–251.

Evans, R. (2006) Evaluating an electronic plagiarism detection service: the importance of trust and the difficulty of proving students don't cheat, *Active Learning in Higher Education*, 7(1), pp. 87–100.

Facteau, J. D., Dobbins, G. H., Russell, J. E. A., Ladd, R. T. and Kudisch, J. D. (1995) The influence of general perceptions of the training environment on pertaining motivation and perceived training transfer, *Journal of Management*, 21(1), pp. 1–25.

Fleming, A. I. M. (1996) Ethics and accounting education in the UK: a professional approach? *Accounting Education: an international journal*, 5(3), pp. 207–217.

Fogarty, J., Singh, J., Rhoads, G. and Moore, R. (2000) Antecedents and consequences of burnout in accounting: beyond the role stress model, *Behavioral Research in Accounting*, 12(1), pp. 31–67.

Franklyn-Stokes, A. and Newstead, S. (1995) Undergraduate cheating: who does what and why? *Studies in Higher Education*, 20(2), pp. 159–172.

Ghaffari, F., Kyriacou, O. and Brennan, R. (2008) Exploring the implementation of ethics in UK accounting programs, *Issues in Accounting Education*, 23(2), pp. 183–198.

Gray, R., Bebbington, J. and McPhail, K. (1994) Teaching ethics in accounting and the ethics of accounting teaching: educating for immorality and a possible case for social and environmental accounting education, *Accounting Education: an international journal*, 3(1), pp. 51–75.

Haines, V., Diekhoff, G., LaBeff, E. and Clark, R. (1986) College cheating: immaturity, lack of commitment and the neutralising attitude, *Research in Higher Education*, 25(4), pp. 342–354.

Hayes, N. and Introna, L. D. (2005) Cultural values, plagiarism, and fairness: when plagiarism gets in the way of learning, *Ethics and Behaviour*, 15(3), pp. 213–231.

Hofstede, G. (1991) *Culture and Organizations: Software of the Mind* (London: McGraw Hill).

Howard, R. M. (1995) Plagiarism, authorships, and the academic death penalty, *College English*, 57(7), pp. 788–806.

ICAS (2007a) *Clearly Ahead* (Edinburgh: ICAS).

ICAS (2007b) *IBE—Living Up to Our Values* (Edinburgh: ICAS).

IFAC (2007) *Approaches to Developing and Maintaining Professional Values, Ethics, and Attitudes* (IFAC: New York).

Introna, L. D., Hayes, N., Blair, L. and Wood, E. (2003) *Cultural Attitudes towards Plagiarism* (Report of the University of Lancaster).

Keith-Spiegel, P. C., Tabachnick, B. G., Allen, M., Whitley, B. E. J. and Washburn, J. (1998) Why professors ignore cheating: opinions of a national sample of psychology instructors, *Ethics and Behaviour*, 8(3), pp. 215–227.

Kline, R. B. (1998) *Principles and Practices of Structural Equation Modeling* (New York: Guilford).

Kohlberg, L. (1981) *The Philosophy of Moral Development* (San Francisco: Harper).

Kreger, L. and Wrenn, R. (1990) Perspectives and differences, *New Directions for Student Services*, 51(1), pp. 37–47.

Love, P. G. and Simmons, J. (1998) Factors influencing cheating and plagiarism among graduate students in a college of education, *College Student Journal*, 32(4), pp. 539–551.

McCabe, D. L. and Trevino, K. L. (1996) What we know about cheating in college, *Change*, 28(1), pp. 28–33.

Michie, F., Glachan, M. and Bray, D. (2001) An evaluation of factors influencing the self-concept, self-esteem and academic stress for direct and re-entry students in higher education, *Educational Psychology*, 21(40), pp. 455–472.

Moore, T. (1997) From test to note: cultural variation in summarization practices, *Prospect*, 12(3), pp. 54–63.

Morgan, K. (1996) *Plagiarism: Does It Matter?* Available at: http://www.canberrac.act.edu.au/plagiarism.htm (accessed 20 May 2009).

Nunnally, C. J. (1978) *Psychometric Methods* (New York: Harper and Row).

Park, C. (2003) In other (people's) words: plagiarism by university students—literature and lessons, *Assessment and Evaluation in Higher Education*, 28(5), pp. 471–488.

Pennycook, A. (1996) Borrowing others' words: text, ownership, memory and plagiarism, *TESOL Quarterly*, 30(2), pp. 210–230.

Ponemon, L. A. (1990) Ethical judgements in accounting: a cognitive development perspective, *Critical Perspectives on Accounting*, 1(2), pp. 191–215.

Ponemon, L. A. (1993) Can ethics be taught in Accounting? *Journal of Accounting Education*, 11(2), pp. 185–209.

Roberts, P., Anderson, J. and Yanish, P. (1997) *Academic Misconduct: Where Do We Start?* (Jackson, Wyoming: Northern Rocky Research Association).

Roig, M. and DeTommaso, L. (1995) Are college cheating and plagiarism related to academic procrastination? *Psychological Reports*, 77(2), pp. 691–698.

Samuels, L. B. and Bast, C. M. (2006) Strategies to help legal studies students avoid plagiarism, *Journal of Legal Studies Education*, 23(2), pp. 151–167.

Segars, A. H. and Grover, V. (1993) Re-examining perceived ease of use and usefulness: a confirmatory factor analysis, *MIS Quarterly*, 17(4), pp. 517–525.

Schmitt, D. (2006) *International Students, Plagiarism and Reality in a Spacetime Continuum: A Workshop*, in the conference program of the 2nd International Plagiarism Conference, Newcastle upon Tyne. Available at:

http://www.jiscpas.ac.uk/conference2006/documents/2006ConferenceProgramme.pdf (accessed 10 July 2009).

Seeman, M. (1991) Alienation and anomie, in: J. P. Robinson, P. R. Shaver and L. S. Wrightsman (Eds) *Measures of Personality and Social Psychological Attitudes*, pp. 291–372 (San Diego: Academic Press).

Selwyn, N. (2008) 'Not necessarily a bad thing …': A study of online plagiarism amongst undergraduate students, *Assessment and Evaluation in Higher Education*, iFirst Article, 33(5), pp. 1–17.

Shapira, G. (1993) Did she or did she not?, in: P. Schwartz and G. Webb (Eds) *Case Studies on Teaching in Higher Education*, pp. 29–35 (London: Kogan Page).

Shaub, M. K. (1994) An analysis of the association of traditional demographic variables with the moral reasoning of auditing students and auditors, *Journal of Accounting Education*, 12(1), pp. 1–26.

Sierles, F., Hendrickx, I. and Circle, S. (1980) Cheating in medical school, *Journal of Medical Education*, 55(2), pp. 124–125.

Smith, K. J., Davy, J. A., Rosenberg, D. L. and Haight, G. T. (2002) A structural modeling investigation of the influence of demographic and attitudinal factors and in-class deterrents on cheating behaviour among accounting majors, *Journal of Accounting Education*, 20(1), pp. 45–65.

Smith, M., Ghazali, N. and Minhad, F. S. N. (2007) Attitudes towards plagiarism among undergraduate accounting students: Malaysian evidence, *Asian Review of Accounting*, 15(2), pp. 122–146.

Snowden, C. (2005) Plagiarism and the culture of multilingual students in higher education abroad, *ELT Journal*, 59(2), pp. 226–233.

Sörbom, D. and Jöreskog, K. G. (1982) The use of structural equation models in evaluation research, in: C. Fornell (Ed.) *A Second Generation of Multivariate Analysis* (New York: Praeger).

Stefani, L. and Carroll, J. (2001) *Assessment: A Briefing on Plagiarism* (York: LTSN Generic Centre).

Szabo, A. and Underwood, J. (2004) Cybercheats: is information and communication technology fuelling academic dishonesty? *Active Learning in Higher Education*, 5(2), pp. 180–199.

Thorne, L. (2001) Refocusing ethics education in accounting: an examination of accounting students' tendency to use their cognitive moral capability, *Journal of Accounting Education*, 19(2), pp. 103–117.

Walker, J. (1998) Student plagiarism in universities: what are we doing about it? *Higher Education Research and Development*, 17(1), pp. 89–106.

Wan, G. (2001) The learning experiences of Chinese students in American universities: a cross cultural perspective, *College Student Journal*, 35(1), pp. 28–45.

Watkins, D. and Biggs, J. (1996) *The Chinese Learner, Cultural, Psychological and Contextual Influences* (Hong Kong: University of Hong Kong).

Yeo, S. (2007) First year science and engineering students' understanding of plagiarism, *Higher Education Research and Development*, 26(2), pp. 199–216.

Expanding the Horizons of Accounting Education: Incorporating Social and Critical Perspectives

GORDON BOYCE*, SUSAN GREER*, BILL BLAIR** and CINDY DAVIDS†

*La Trobe University, Australia; **Macquarie University, Australia; †Deakin University, Australia

ABSTRACT   This paper examines a case of accounting education change in the context of increased interest in ethical, social, and environmental accountability, presenting a reflexive case study of a new university accounting subject incorporating social and critical perspectives. Foundational pedagogical principles and key aspects of curriculum are outlined. The pedagogy draws on the integration of humanistic and formative education (principally based on Gramscian and Freirean approaches) and deep and elaborative learning. Two key aspects of curriculum and pedagogy are analysed. First, a curriculum based on a broad conception of accounting and accountability as power-laden social processes, drawing on a range of research literature. Second, the adoption of an authentic, supportive, and collegial team teaching approach. Students' feedback relating to identified issues is presented. The paper contributes to the renewal of the social and ethical worth of accounting education, concluding that deep accounting educational change encompasses both the content and practice of classroom activity and changes in the self-consciousness of staff and students.

KEY WORDS: Social accounting, critical accounting, team teaching, social construction, humanistic education, deep learning

1. Introduction

Calls for deep reform to accounting and accounting education have again become prominent in the post-Enron environment (e.g. Amernic and Craig, 2004; Boyce, 2004; Williams, 2004; Mayper, Pavur, Merino and Hoops, 2005; Humphrey, 2005; Ravenscroft and Williams, 2004; 2005; Horniachek, 2008). These renewed calls stand against a long-standing and high-profile 'official' accounting education reform agenda and numerous 'clarion calls' for reform over many years. Despite consistent and ongoing calls for reform, there has been little in the way of systemic change, and traditional approaches to accounting education continue to dominate (Merino 2006). The Bedford Committee (Bedford *et al.*, 1986) and the Accounting Education Change Commission (1990) in the USA, and the Mathews Committee in Australia (Review Committee of the Accounting Discipline in Higher Education 1990) directed attention to the need for a 'revolution in accounting education' (Bedford *et al.*, 1986), but to the extent that reform has happened, it has generally been reactive and driven by perceived changing needs of the profession and of the labour market more generally (c.f. Guthrie, 2010).

To some degree, the lack of durable progress in accounting education is reflective of business disciplines more broadly. For instance, following the Enron and WorldCom scandals, there was an initial flurry to infuse ethics and social responsibility into business school programmes in the USA, but 'as the Enron fervor died down, so did these efforts' and most of these reforms have been subsequently wound back (Middleton, 2010, p. 32). In accounting, there remains a perception that professional body accreditation necessitates the dominance of an expanding array of technical skills and highly-structured knowledge based around proliferating regulatory requirements (Gray and Collison, 2002, p. 817).

In this context, many debates over accounting education reform 'are rarely debates at all' (Gray and Collison, 2002, p. 827) because they fail to challenge the traditional tenets of the discipline and continue to prioritise the perceived technical needs of professional practice. Unsurprisingly, the desire to produce more rounded graduates with a much broader range of general skills has largely been sidelined (notwithstanding a number of successful individual efforts) and even moves to accept students from more diverse backgrounds into accounting studies have resulted in little practical change (Andon, Chong and Roebuck, 2010).

Questionable corporate ethical practices and major economic and financial scandals accentuate concerns that accounting education may serve to ethically 'cripple' our students (Tinker and Gray 2003, p. 728; see also Gray, Bebbington and McPhail, 1994; McPhail, 2001), in part because of '... a series of major structural impediments that make innovation more difficult', related both to the pressures under which universities operate and the perception that the traditional technical content still constitutes the *substance* of accounting. An observed general lack of progress led Owen (2005) to argue that accounting educators and students must both challenge the tenets of accounting and incorporate a broad set of values oriented around community and ethics. Despite this pressing need, Owen lamented the capture by business of the teaching agenda in accounting, with a curriculum that reflects a narrow set of interests substantially grounded in the elevation of private property rights and the vested interests of the accounting profession. There continues to be insufficient recognition of the depth of accounting's complicity in creating the environment from which corporate scandals have emerged (c.f. Leung and Cooper, 2003; Tinker and Carter, 2003; Doost and Fishman, 2004; Tinker, 2004; Williams, 2004; Ravenscroft and Williams, 2005; Young, 2005).

Although it is recognised that effective change requires a broad systemic reform effort, the focus of this paper is a localised effort at accounting education change in a large accounting and finance department in one Australian university. The paper outlines and analyses the first offering of a newly-developed subject designed to examine the socially-constructed nature of accounting and to engage with social and critical perspectives. We provide insight into the practice of social and critical accounting education not as an add-on or supplement to existing programmes, but as an alternative way to examine accounting in the higher education setting. This draws on the contemporary context of accounting's socio-political influence via interactions with a range of social, environ-mental, and political phenomena, which is as important as its economic functionality.

This paper is a reflexive case study which analyses how a group of academics have sought to enact accounting education reform at a local level, drawing on regular inter-actions and collective reflections of the teaching team during the development and first offering of the subject. Overall, the paper seeks to contribute to the renewal of accounting education and practice through an illustrative, exploratory case study (c.f. Scapens, 1990) of the expansion of student and staff horizons via social and critical accounting education. Although environmental accounting has had some exposure in the extant literature, there is little consideration of broader social and critical perspectives from an educational perspective.

To contextualise the work, the next section provides an outline of the context of accounting education in the 'noughties' decade (2001–2010), setting the scene faced by the teaching team, describing the background to the introduction of the subject, and its broad aims. Section 3 then outlines two underpinning pedagogical principles. The first drew broadly on a Gramscian approach to integrate the humanistic and formative elements of education. The second emphasised deep and elaborative learning approaches and out-comes to encourage students to make sense of their learning, to determine inter-relation-ships, and to apply underlying principles to their study of accounting in a social context. The blending of deep learning with Gramscian insights about formative and humanistic education is a unique element of the approach adopted.

Building on these underlying pedagogical principles, sections 4 and 5 examine broad practical elements of the curriculum and pedagogy applied. First is the curriculum design, including an underlying social constructionist perspective on accounting (which formed a thematic flow for the entire subject), and the use of research literature to fulfil the function normally occupied by a prescribed textbook. The second is the use of team teaching as the core teaching approach: a team of four staff collaborated on all aspects of the subject. Although team teaching has been mentioned in the accounting education literature, there is little evidence of its authentic application in a real-time classroom environment. We make an important case for the use of this approach.

Although the focus of our analysis is not on students' feedback as such, the students' understanding of 'social and critical perspectives on accounting' is important. Therefore, feedback obtained from students at the end of the semester is incorporated into each area of discussion in sections 4 and 5. We conclude with overall reflections and observations in section 6, including a reflective critical analysis of our work and an outline of the impli-cations of the project for integrating critical and social perspectives into accounting education.

2.   The Present Context of Accounting Education

In the contemporary global environment, a key role claimed for accounting and accounting education is in developing business accountability and responsibility in the *public interest* (see ACCA, 2005, for example).[1] The recognition of the economic, social, and ethical impacts of business and associated accounting activity within this environment presents new challenges for accounting education. Although there have been many efforts in recent years to address the ongoing accounting education reform agenda centred on the need for a broad knowledge base and the development of a wide range of critical and analytical skills (Bedford *et al.*, 1986; Accounting Education Change Commission, 1990; Review Committee of the Accounting Discipline in Higher Education, 1990; IFAC, 1994), the mainstream in accounting research and education continues to reflect a decontextualised, technicist and positivist approach (Humphrey, 2005; Ravenscroft and Williams, 2005; Merino, 2006).

More than a quarter of a century after the internationally-recognised Bedford Committee report and the subsequent formation of the Accounting Education Change Commission in the USA, there are renewed calls for action to meet the challenges facing accounting higher education (Guthrie, 2010). Humphrey suggests that '[s]erious academic attention [must] be devoted to the education of professional accountants' and that 'the pursuit of change needs to be handled in a sophisticated, and potentially incremental, fashion' (2005, pp. 347–348). Educators must be prepared to step outside the dominant managerial perspective to question and challenge the tenets of contemporary business (Ravenscroft and Williams, 2004; Owen, 2005). Stepping 'outside the circle' (Boyce, 2004) of conventional accounting can prepare students for action in the world within and beyond business, complementing technical proficiency in accounting with historical, social, political, and international knowledge of accounting and its effects. This necessarily includes the development of an understanding of 'the relation of accounting to the mundane activities, language, and interactions of daily life ... and how these relate to the larger social system' (Boyce, 2004, p. 581). The resultant blend of technical competence with an understanding of the socio-political significance as well as the cultural and social breadth of accounting not only produces well-rounded and versatile graduates, but also serves the economic interests of students. These are skills that are highly valued by employers and which can result in high salary prospects but which are often lacking in accounting graduates (see Tinker and Gray, 2003).

2.1. Beyond the 'Professional Accounting' Core Sequence

Academic control over key elements of teaching and learning is 'crucial to the long-term health of universities' (Aronowitz, 2000, p. 34) but the contemporary environment is characterised by systematic and sustained moves to diminish academic influence and to embed corporatist and managerialist approaches (Boyce, 2002; Parker, 2002; Saravana-muthu and Tinker, 2002; Christensen, 2004; Saravanamuthu and Filling, 2004). Despite the strength of these disempowering moves, opportunities for resistance remain (Anderson, 2006) and many aspects of the conduct of teaching remain in the hands of lecturers.

Academics retain considerable influence over setting course and subject structure, syllabus and curriculum design, selection of texts and materials, and implementation of teaching and assessment strategies including the setting and assessment of students' work (Boyce, 2004). The achievement of meaningful action in these areas, however, requires both individual and collective effort to:

> ... direct things that individuals can do to change, rather than reinforce, the status quo ... expose students to a wide range of material and perspectives ... Stimulate students and do not just replicate the approaches of conventional, standard accounting textbooks... Collectively, individual academics can also achieve much—working through formal and informal networks ... experimentation and the expression of new thoughts and ideas. (Humphrey, 2005, p. 348)

A number of university departments have developed specialist subjects and topics, especially in the area of environmental and/or sustainability accounting, with varying degrees of success (see Gibson, 1997; Bebbington, 1995; 1997; Grinnell and Hunt, 2000; Coulson and Thomson, 2006; Hazelton and Haigh, 2010; Kemp, 2010; Lodhia, 2010). The subject which we developed was intended to change the way learners and teachers looked at and experienced accounting rather than merely to add a new accounting subject.

2.2. Developing a New Subject

Against the background outlined above and a shared post-Enron recognition of the need to renew accounting education, a group of staff members in the Macquarie University (Sydney) Accounting and Finance Department[2] proposed a new third-year elective subject in 'Social and Critical Perspectives on Accounting'. This was a four credit-point, one-semester subject offered as part of a standard three-year 68-credit-point under-graduate degree.

Drawing on the academic discourse that challenges the idea that accounting (including research and education) can be abstracted from its social context (see Moore, 1991; Roslender and Dillard, 2003), the subject sought to redress the vocationally-oriented imbalance of traditional accounting education (and of many reform proposals). It drew on a body of research that incorporates socially-critical perspectives and explores the socio-historical knowledge of the functioning of accounting (see Preston, 1992; Boyce, 1999; 2002; 2004). The teaching team aimed to ensure that essential components of the subject were used in a way that made the *technical* content of accounting (mainly gained from prior studies and other subjects) relevant (Saravanamuthu, 2004). Thus, rather than merely adding to the stock of accounting knowledge within a broadly tra-ditional frame, the adoption of a social and critical perspective was intended to allow students to see a different perspective on accounting that could be applied across a broad spectrum.

This was the Department's first major attempt to address the realm of 'accounting studies' in its teaching program and to incorporate a critique of accounting itself. It was accepted that development of knowledge, understanding, and skills in this area was valu-able both for those students who seek future employment in accounting *and* for the large but often unrecognised group of students who wish to undertake major studies in account-ing but may not wish to complete a 'professional accounting' sequence leading to eligi-bility for membership of an organised accounting body.[3] The Department aimed to expand the horizons of academic learning with the introduction of this new subject.

Although accounting may contain many possibilities for emancipatory practice, it still tends to produce one-sided constructions of reality that serve narrow and particular social and economic interests (Tinker, 1985; Richardson, 1987; Tinker, 1991; Chua, 1996; Catchpowle, Cooper and Wright, 2004). Central to the aims of the subject was a consider-ation of how accounting is implicated in social power relations and how it interrelates with 'government', in a broad sense.

A secondary emphasis was the development of students' generic skills, especially higher-level critical thinking and analysis, and communication skills. This reflected a wider concern both in the institutional environment (a key element of the teaching and learning plan of the university) and the professional environment (a prominent part of accreditation requirements for university accounting degrees and accounting education reform blueprints—e.g. see Accounting Education Change Commission, 1990; ASCPA and ICAA, 1996). Thus, the aim of the teaching team was to develop critical skills beyond the notion of routinised or instrumental knowledge, developing the intellectual capacities of students in examining, pondering, wondering, theorising, criticising, and imagining alternatives in critical and creative ways (Aronowitz and Giroux, 1993).

In order to make the subject available to a wide student group, prerequisite prior studies were kept to a minimum: a clear pass in any first-year accounting subject and sufficient study credit points that meant students were in their third year of studies.[4] With this background, it was expected that students would be familiar with the conventional view of accounting as an *economic* phenomenon, and be capable of examining accounting as a *social, ethical, cultural*, and *political* phenomenon. It was hoped that students would develop the ability to articulate clearly a range of views, ideas, concepts, and perspectives about accounting and its effects as well as their own personal and collective positions on these issues. Taken together, these elements implied a critical consideration of the received notions of accounting with which students were already familiar (see Chua, 1998; Merino, 1998; Craig, Clarke and Amernic, 1999).

3. Foundational Pedagogical Principles

Gray and Collison (2002, pp. 812–813) identified 'widespread disquiet about the current state of accounting education in universities … by academics, professionals and employers alike …', suggesting that a major revision of accounting degrees was necessary if accounting was to retain the status of a profession. They identified three broad areas of concern in relation to accounting education:

(1) an over-emphasis on rote and shallow forms of learning;
(2) insufficient attention to the development of intellectual, ethical, reflective, and critical capacities in students; and
(3) inappropriate preparation for future employment.

   Gray and Collison suggested that this situation produced graduates who unquestioningly and unknowingly reproduce the given state of affairs without any critical engagement with the moral and social choices that underlie accounting practice. These criticisms were not new. From her overview of more than 100 years of accounting education reform, Merino (2006) found that a constancy of criticism of the overemphasis on technical knowledge within the accounting curriculum had failed to produce any meaningful change in the delivery of accounting courses.

   Whilst recognising that it is not possible to reform accounting education from within a single subject alone, we sought to develop a foundation from which to address each of the deficiencies identified by Gray and Collison. Our aim was to challenge traditional ways of thinking about the nature and role of accounting in society, and to illuminate its sociopolitical dimensions. The explicit adoption of a social and critical perspective meant that the values and assumptions underlying accounting would be problematised and that accounting itself would be viewed as an ethically, socially, environmentally, culturally, and politically charged practice, offering a basis from which the 'social obligation' of accountants and accounting subjects (Merino, 2006) could be recognised and recovered. These considerations were distilled into two key principles that provided a foundation for curriculum and pedagogy in the subject:

(1) the integration of humanistic and formative education; and
(2) teaching strategies to encourage deep and elaborative learning on the part of students.

3.1. *Integrating Humanistic and Formative Education*

In designing the subject and its individual elements, the teaching team drew on the Gramscian notion of a balanced humanistic and formative education that seeks to develop practical skills and knowledge through an examination and critique of actual life problems and circumstances. Gramsci (1971) recognised a fundamental distinction between being *informed* and being educated, advocating that the traditional distinction between classical humanistic education, on the one hand, and vocational or professional education, on the other hand, should be broken down. His suggested approach to education was 'formative, *while* being 'instructive'' (Giroux, 1988, p. 200, emphasis added), and provided an integrated preparation for manual/practical *and* intellectual/critical work (Gramsci, 1971, p. 27 et seq.; see also Boyce, 2004; 2008). Gramsci rejected adulation of the immediacy of human needs and 'mere factuality' in favour of a disciplined approach to learning important basic skills and knowledge within defined boundaries. He emphasised the need to concurrently develop '… the fundamental power to think and ability to find one's way in life' (Gramsci, 1971, p. 26).

In practical terms, the Gramscian approach produces a 'fusion between the academic and the technical', integrating theory and practice, consciousness and action (Mayo, 2008, p. 427). Although many of Gramsci's reflections on education were directed at secondary schooling, their application is especially relevant in the contemporary context of adult education (Giroux, 1988: Ch 15; Coben, 1998; Mayo, 1999; Borg, Buttigieg and Mayo, 2002; Mayo, 2008).

In the specific domain of accounting education, there is every reason to think that it is possible to combine the provision of "the wherewithal to undertake gainful and 'productive' employment" with the development of 'a civilized and just society [through] the development of well-read, thoughtful, scholarly individuals with a well-developed capacity for independent critical thought' (Gray and Collison, 2002, p. 799). The latter, though, necessarily requires a 'capacity to challenge all 'totalizing' tendencies and to resist [the] indoctrination and repression' (Gray and Collison, 2002, p. 808) that typifies contemporary accounting education (Ravenscroft and Williams, 2004). Gray and Collison emphasise that educators must make 'explicit choices' to encourage students to consider (and accept if they wish) 'fundamental challenges to the current state of received wisdom' (p. 809).

Building on the aim to integrate humanistic and formative education, in designing the subject the team took the view that accounting education—as education generally—should be conceived as preparing students for economic *and* social life. This approach stood in contrast to both traditional curricula and the mainstream accounting education reform agenda that have largely remained rooted in the assumption that university education is about preparation for working life. The vocational approach—traditional or reformist— is doubly flawed because it not only denies students wider educational opportunities but it is also based on a mistaken assumption that the future vocation of accounting students will centre on professional accounting careers, whereas it is now known that large numbers of accounting graduates face a quite different future in varied jobs and sometimes multiple careers (Tinker and Koutsoumadi, 1997, 1998; Cooper and Tinker, 1998; Boyce, 2004).

It is recognised that *education*—relating to the development of the whole person—as opposed to the lesser remit of vocationally-oriented *training* is difficult to achieve in accounting because professional body accreditation requirements may be regarded as naturally leading to a relatively narrow vocational approach. However, in looking beyond the 'professional accounting' core sequence in planning the subject curriculum, the approach adopted by the teaching team was broadly consistent with, and informed by, the view of education that seeks to balance humanistic, formative and vocational elements. Extension beyond preparation for the world of work is regarded as an *obligation* of educators as this approach aims to prepare students for both manual/practical and intellectual/theoretical work (see Gramsci, 1971, p. 27 et seq.). Viewing education as preparation for economic *and* social life results in a more rounded and socially focused problematisation of pervasive ideas of the times, and provides avenues for social and professional critique and for questioning received understandings of phenomena such as accounting and their social context (see Neimark, 1996; Craig *et al.*, 1999; Young, 2005; Mayper *et al.*, 2005). The associated provision of a space for active difference, debate, contestation and dissent becomes an important aspect of preparing students for full participation in democratic social and political life (see Newman, 1996; Craig *et al.*, 1999; Aronowitz, 2000; Gray and Collison, 2002; Boyce, 2004; Saravanamuthu, 2004). This broader perspective on education requires a deliberate mind-shift on the part of teachers and students who operate within an accounting education system that largely serves to 'indoctrinate, pacify and cripple ethically our students' (Tinker and Gray, 2003, p. 728).

This broad approach is not dissimilar to the model of accounting education envisaged by 'progressive' reformers whose calls have been heard for over a century. Merino's (2006) study of the history of accounting education reform movements in the USA, for example, shows how in the early twentieth century the Progressive educational reform movement 'emphasised flexibility, creativity, and critical thinking, coupled with an understanding of the social obligations of professions' and that 'Progressive accounting *practitioners* echoed this call' (Merino, 2006, p. 364, emphasis added). These reform calls fell on deaf ears as accounting educators and university administrators promoted technical education oriented towards professional examinations. Accounting textbooks narrowed in scope, curricula became more technically-oriented, and the narrowing effects of market discourse magnified over time. This evolution suppressed, but did not resolve, the tension between, on the one hand, the market forces and the self-interested behaviour they promote and, on the other, professionalism with its claims of concern for social impacts and advancing the public good (see also Parker, 2001; Giroux, 2003).

As noted earlier in the paper, the current accreditation requirements and educational frameworks of the contemporary accounting profession also echo much of the rhetoric of broader education, emphasising the importance of broad 'generic skills' including analytical and critical thinking skills, judgement and synthesis skills, personal and interpersonal skills, management and organisational skills, and the ability to apply these skills in a range of unique situations (see Bedford *et al.*, 1986; Accounting Education Change Commission, 1990; Review Committee of the Accounting Discipline in Higher Education, 1990; Boyce, Williams, Kelly and Yee, 2001; Parker, 2001; Howieson, 2003; Boyce, 2004; Merino, 2006). It is also consistent with (although not developed from) more recent developments such as *The Principles for Responsible Management Education* (UN Global Compact, 2007; 2008b):[5]

> Purpose: We will develop the capabilities of students to be future generators of sustainable value for business and society at large and to work for an inclusive and sustainable global economy.

> Values: We will incorporate into our academic activities and curricula the values of global social responsibility as portrayed in international initiatives such as the United Nations Global Compact.

> Method: We will create educational frameworks, materials, processes and environments that enable effective learning experiences for responsible leadership. (See UN Global Compact, 2007, Principles 1–3)

Although the meaning and application of the Principles is open to interpretation (and critique—see footnote 5), we interpreted them through a Gramscian framework where 'The entire function of educating and forming the new generations ceases to be private and becomes public ...' (Gramsci, 1971, p. 30). Thus, we saw the development of social and critical perspectives on accounting as working in opposition to current tendencies for education to move from a public to a private good where the discourse of the market and the corporate world dominates (Giroux, 2002; Merino, 2006), and the pervasiveness of consumer culture buttresses vocationalism in the preferences of students who may (initially at least) think non-vocational perspectives are 'irrelevant' (Hazelton and Haigh, 2010). To counter these tendencies, we recognised and encouraged an understanding that the pursuit of relevance for accounting and management education need *not*:

> ... overlook or reject traditions and moralities that emphasize education as an object of faith and beauty and its connection to humanity and human identities ... education and research can be ... organized to provide grace, meaning, delicacy, and elegance to human life, not because those attributes can be shown to yield competitive advantage but because they are basic elements of an educational faith. (Augier and March, 2007, pp. 141–142)

As Augier and March (2007, p. 143) imply, most problems in management (and, by extensions, accounting) relate to 'dilemmas of life and their human resolution'.

3.2. *Deep and Elaborative Learning*

The teaching team understood that teaching and learning in universities does influence both students' content knowledge and their values, beliefs, and priorities (see Boyce, 2002; Gentile and Samuelson 2003; Boyce 2008; Low, Davey and Hooper, 2008), but the nature and extent of that influence is contingent. The design and implementation of the curriculum required efforts to overcome the acknowledged traditional preferences of students who choose to study accounting that are manifested in shallow and surface learning approaches (Blundell and Booth 1988; Booth and Winzar, 1993; Gow, Kember and Cooper, 1994; Booth, Luckett and Mladenovic, 1999; Kovar, Ott and Fisher, 2003; Briggs, Copeland and Haynes, 2007; Andon *et al.*, 2010).

The twin overall learning objectives of the subject, *viz.* understanding accounting as socially-constructed and used in socially, ethically, culturally, and politically charged contexts; and developing higher-order generic and critical skills, required deep learning on the part of students. Deep learning is characterised by an inherent quest for sense- and meaning-making, contrasting with shallow learning approaches which are characterised by memorisation or reproduction of content (Marton and Säljö, 1976a; 1976b; Lucas, 1996; Boyce *et al.*, 2001). Successful deep learning strategies involve relating ideas to experience, distinguishing evidence from argument, identifying patterns and principles, understanding inter-relationships between different areas of knowledge, and applying principles to new situations, while shallow learning typically involves acquisition, rote memorisation, and reproduction of individual facts that are not incorporated into integrated knowledge sets (Lucas, 2001). Rote-learning-like strategies based around fact retention and methodical study *can* aid meaningful learning but only when they are enhanced with deep learning approaches that involve critical evaluation, conceptual organisation of material, the capacity to compare and contrast information studied, and elaborative approaches that translate new information into already-understood terminology, generating concrete examples from existing experience, and the application of new information to lived experience (see Schmeck, 1983; Boyce *et al.*, 2001).

It is important to recognise that different approaches to learning 'do not constitute a characteristic of the student but are, rather, a response to the student's perception of the context within which teaching and learning takes place' (Lucas, 2001, p. 162). Therefore, careful curriculum design and meaningfully constructed learning environments can change the way in which students approach their learning (Boyce *et al.*, 2001; English, Luckett and Mladenovic, 2004; Hall, Ramsay and Raven, 2004). Specifically, deep and

ACCOUNTING EDUCATION RESEARCH

elaborative learning approaches can be encouraged even if students are not predisposed to them (see Lucas, 1996; Boyce *et al.*, 2001; Lucas, 2001). The pedagogical focus must be on 'generating appropriate attitudes, including tolerance for uncertainty and ambiguity; willingness to deal with complexity and confusion, acceptance of conflicting information, [and the] courage to take risks ...' (Boyce *et al.*, 2001, p. 54).

Whilst these issues must be addressed at the program level (that is, across students' entire degree programs), the focus in the present study is on the area where there is the most immediate potential impact—the 'micro perspective' that focuses on actions and activities in specific classroom teaching and learning engagements (Boyce *et al.*, 2001, p. 43). Pedagogical practices and assessment strategies, taken holistically, can facilitate disciplinary understanding and improvement in a range of generic skills because they inherently involve 'active learning' which promotes the search for meaning and understanding, encourages greater student responsibility for learning, develops skills as well as knowledge, and looks beyond graduation to wider career and social settings (Lucas, 1997).

Figure 1 provides a diagrammatic summary of the above discussion in terms of the key influences on curriculum design, pedagogy, and assessment in the subject. Design, development and implementation sought to integrate humanistic, formative, and vocational elements of education, extending beyond the constrained goal of preparation for labour-market participation in particular kinds of accounting work. The overriding intention was to impart knowledge about the social functioning of accounting while inculcating a set of skills that is a precursor to future participation in democratic social and political life, in addition to economic life (see Newman, 1996; Craig *et al.*, 1999; Aronowitz, 2000; Gray and Collison, 2002; Boyce, 2004; 2008).

Building on the above considerations, the next two sections of the paper outline the broad elements of the pedagogy adopted (that is, the curriculum and the teaching approach):

(1) The curriculum centred on a broader conception of accounting and accountability which necessitated the employment of accounting and related research literature rather than the more conventional textbook as the primary materials.

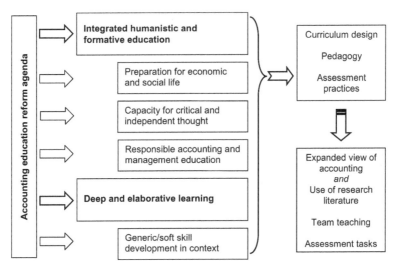

Figure 1. Curriculum and pedagogy

(2) The adoption of a team teaching approach whereby development *and delivery* of the weekly classroom agenda for learning and teaching was a product of genuinely collaborative interactions between members of the teaching team.[6]

Within each of these sections students' feedback relating to the application of the pedagogical element is discussed. This feedback was obtained via an anonymous qualitative instrument administered independently by a staff member from outside the Department in order to minimise the possible influence of teaching staff on students' responses. Completed feedback forms were collected and processed by the office of the Faculty Associate Dean (Learning and Teaching) and results were returned to the teaching team after the official release of students' results. The questions were designed to elicit the student's perspective, seeking qualitative written comments rather than typical Likert scales or yes/ no answers (the questions asked are reproduced in Appendix 1). Feedback was received from 20 out of the 25 enrolled students.

4. Curriculum and Pedagogy 1: Curriculum Design and Resources

To achieve the broad pedagogical goals of integrating humanistic and formative education and encouraging deep and elaborative forms of learning, it was important to ensure the provision of sufficient opportunities for active difference, debate, contestation and dissent. The specific aims were to overcome any sense of acquiescence and passivity on the part of students and to obviate any tendency that may have existed within the teaching team to take a 'knowledge transmission' approach to teaching.

These broad pedagogical objectives were made practical through the adoption of classroom approaches that were, philosophically, broadly Freirean (Freire, 1996; 1998). To ensure that accounting education (through this subject, at least) sought to prepare students for economic and social life, we accepted the need to raise students' awareness of the interaction between accounting and various real-world problems and issues that affected their individual and collective lives (broadly speaking, this was a process of 'conscientisation' in Freirean terms).

Freire's ideas have tended to be represented as advocating dialogic rather than banking approaches to accounting education (Boyce, 2004; Thomson and Bebbington 2004; 2005; Coulson and Thomson 2006; Bebbington, Brown, Frame and Thomson, 2007). The banking model is to some degree a reflection of the 'tunnel vision' characteristic of specialisation in a particular area (see Letterman and Dugan, 2004) and is characterised by the:

> ... act of depositing, in which the students are the depositories and the teacher is the depositor. Instead of communicating, the teacher issues communiqués and makes deposits which the students patiently receive, memorize, and repeat. (Freire, 1996, p. 53)

We adopted a broader approach which, whilst accepting the validity of dialogic approaches, drew inspiration from Freire's emphasis on the need to critique dehumanising tendencies in contemporary society and facilitate attempts to transcend and transform present social arrangements (McLaren and Leonard, 1993; Coben, 1998; Mayo, 1999; Glass, 2001). We were also cognisant of the practical limits of dialogue as critical pedagogy (Burbules, 2000), and therefore, recognised that 'a certain degree of instruction needs to be imparted to render any dialogical education an informed one ... striking a balance between spontaneity and conscious direction' (Mayo, 2008, p. 427).[7]

The translation of these commitments to the classroom situation produced an approach that was part didactic and part dialogic, with an infusion of polemical approaches designed to prompt discussion and debate.

4.1. *Expanded Conception of Accounting*

The teaching team adopted an expansive conception of accounting and its central role in creating and sustaining social reality (Hines, 1988) and in the operation of socio-political power (Tinker, 1980; Miller and O'Leary, 1987; Munro and Mouritsen, 1996). Noting Dillard and Tinker's (1996, p. 222) comment that '... a faculty member must critically, logically, analytically and continually explore all aspects of the subject matter including the theoretical base, historical and social context, technical content and societal implications', the teaching staff felt a responsibility to develop an educational praxis that challenged restricted mindsets.

4.1.1. Broad conception of accounting and accountability as social processes. Conventional approaches to accounting education take a conservative approach in delineating accounting in exclusively financial or economic terms, involving the identification, measurement (or calculation) and communication of economic information that re-presents what is taken to be an objective financial and economic reality. This approach is 'significantly and artificially constrained' (Gray, Owen and Adams, 1996, p. 11) and it serves an ideological function in downplaying the social and ecological impacts of both economic activity itself and the manner for which it is accounted (Boyce, 2000).

Students were introduced to accounting as a social process, with consequent duties involved in accountability relationships extending beyond financial reckoning to incorporate environmental, social, community, political, personal and ethical dimensions. Students were introduced to, and asked to critique, attempts to bring social, environmental, and other non-economic costs and benefits into the financial calculus of accounting (e.g. Gray, Bebbington and Walters, 1993; Schaltegger and Burritt, 2000; Bebbington and Gray, 2001). Gray *et al.*, (1994, p. 65) note that:

> ... *environmental* accounting provides a particularly good opportunity to explore the extent of accounting's implication in social issues ... and the moral imperatives that this implies for accounting's response in terms of pragmatics, ethics, public interest and professionalism ... (emphasis added)

Students were also asked to consider how technical processes of social and environmental accounting calculus could be constructed in particular ways to support vested interests (see Boyce, 2000). This led to a critique of the capacity for accounting and associated forms of expertise to shape the conduct of individuals and organisations, not through compulsion but through the power of ostensible truth and rationality, and its promised effectiveness (Miller and Rose, 1990; Robson, 1991).

Exemplars used in this subject related the theoretical and conceptual matters under consideration to real-world phenomena that would be (in all likelihood) familiar to students. This provided opportunities for students to draw on their own knowledge and experience—from within and without accounting—and to see accounting as being connected not just to the headline-grabbing prominent financial issues of the day, but also to the much more mundane aspects of economic and social life. In students' feedback (gathered in accordance with the procedures outlined earlier in the paper), we sought to discover if students had made this connection, by asking: *Did this unit develop your awareness of the role of accounting in society? If so how?* With the exception of one student who did not answer the question, *all* students answered in the affirmative (95%). Seventy-five per cent of respondents indicated that the subject content helped them see how accounting relates to current issues while 30% indicated it made them aware of a range of *non-financial* issues.[8] Additional explanatory comments from respondents showed how they came to see accounting as a broad and encompassing phenomenon. The following comments reflect the feedback received:

> Yes, it makes us understand [that] accounting is not only about numbers...

> After the course, I have understood that accounting affects different parts of the world (e.g. education, government and the relation to history).

> After studying the unit, I am aware of some concepts of accounting roles and not just financial terms.

> ... before taking this unit I thought of accounting as numbers and ethics only. However, this subject has made me aware that accounting has various perspectives related to political, ethical, social and globalisation.

These responses indicate a developing understanding of accounting as a social phenomenon and some integration of prior understanding of disciplinary knowledge with pre-existing social and personal understandings.

4.1.2. Accounting as socially-constructed. Through the adoption of a broad view of accounting and accountability, accountants came to be seen not as professionals who practise a specialist technical craft, but as part of social processes of reality construction which at least partly reflect the context. This was important because, even though conventional accounts of economy and society are partial and largely one-sided, such accounts are generally taken as 'real' by those who read and are affected by them (Hines, 1988).

Three key areas were considered in introducing the concept of social construction to students. The *first* area related to the role of social, cultural, and other human factors in the construction of knowledge (about accounting and other phenomena). Parts of Berger and Luckmann's classic work (1984) were used to introduce the general concept of social construction:

> It is important to keep in mind that the objectivity of the institutional world, however massive it may appear to the individual, is a humanly produced, constructed objectivity. The process by which the externalized products of human activity attain the character of objectivity is objectivation. The institutional world is objectivated human activity, and so is every single institution. In other words, despite the objectivity that marks the social world in human experience, it does not thereby acquire an ontological status apart from the human activity that produced it. The paradox [is] that man is capable of producing a world that he then experiences as something other than a human product... (Berger and Luckmann, 1984, p. 78)

Noting that accounting is a human construction led to the *second* area of consideration: the nature of some of the core assumptions that underlie accounting research, and the socio-political view of accounting that emerges from a questioning of these assumptions. For instance, the general privileging of capital and profit over labour and the environment was considered (drawing on Tinker, 1985; Tinker and Gray, 2003; Catchpowle *et al.*, 2004; Ravenscroft and Williams, 2004; Gray, 2006). Students could also see that, *because* social realities created through accounting are taken as being objectively and naturally real, they have seemingly intractable social effects.

The *third* element considered possible alternatives to numerical representation, drawing on Chua's (1996) work on accounting as a monolingual language in a multilingual world. This allowed students to see how the dominance of the 'empirical/calculative tradition' has resulted in an unnecessarily narrow view of what accounting is and what it could be:

Numbers do not intrinsically enslave, they do so when numbers which appear 'neutral' to one set of debates are taken to be neutral absolutely, their persuasive power is decontextualised (both culturally and historically), their limitations as modes of representing social life are downplayed and their dominance rules out all debates about the political ideals and values which quantification itself expresses ... (Chua, 1996, p. 154)

Although not seeking to ignore or downplay the importance of financial accountability, the broader view adopted allowed the students to consider the implications of the power of numbers and explore both alternative forms of numbers and different types of account (e.g. narratives—Haynes, 2006). In order to nurture a developing capacity for critical and independent thought, the manner in which narratives and discourses could themselves reinforce the social *status quo* was also considered (Neu and Taylor, 1996; Christensen, 2004).

The combination of these elements prompted a questioning of taken-for-granted assumptions. Students started to develop an understanding of the social and political significance of accounting beyond mere financial reporting, and considered how alternatives to dominant forms of accounting might be developed and used. In feedback obtained at the end of the course, a number of students highlighted the importance of the theme of social construction, including it in their list of 'most interesting' topics. Illustrating a capacity to think through the broader implications of social construction, one student, for example, emphasised the connection between:

... social constructionalism [sic] and globalisation and how socially constructed views are used to shape views and manipulate situations which can have an effect/impact on a global level.

Comments such as this provide an indication of the receptivity of students to the broad perspective on accounting which we adopted.

4.1.3. Accounting and social power. Boyce (2004, p. 572) observes that students are rarely given the opportunity to discover the power of accounting. Indeed, the subject of power is almost entirely omitted from mainstream accounting:

The impact, range, and power of US corporations are global. ... Yet the index of any accounting text can be scanned and one would be hard-pressed to find an entry under 'power.' There is a mindless acceptance of the status quo ... (Ravenscroft and Williams, 2004, p. 8)

By contrast, building on the expanded conception of accounting, we introduced students to the importance of accounting as a form of social power, starting with the idea that:

The world of the critical theorist is a battleground of hegemonic interests. In this world there are striking disparities in the distribution of power: some people have dominant power; others have far less power; most have no power at all. This is a world torn apart by dynamics of oppression, manipulation and coercion. (Crotty, 1998, p. 63)

We sought to critically consider where accounting fits into the picture outlined by Crotty: specifically, accounting and its related techniques of notation, computation, calculation, and evaluation as elements of the operation of power and rule in society (Miller and Rose, 1990). This analysis drew on research that ties social and economic injustices and the sustaining of the system that produces these injustices to the practice of accounting (e.g. Tinker, 1985, 1991; Arnold and Hammond, 1994; Chwastiak, 1998), Here, the ideological role in legitimating social and political arrangements is revealed (see Richardson, 1987; Cooper, 1995; Lehman, 1995; Neimark, 1996; Reiter, 1998).

The consideration of accounting as a constituent element in the 'fundamental relationship between political and economic forces in society' (Miller, 1994, p. 9) and the associated intrinsic role of accounting in relations of domination and exploitation formed a significant focus for some topics in the subject. At various points, students considered the pervasiveness of accounting's effects on: the type of world we inhabit; our social reality; our understanding of our choices and those of organisations; the way we manage and organise activities; and the way in which we administer our lives and those of others. (A list of topics and resources is provided in Appendix 2.)

Recognition of the distributive and hegemonic dimensions of accounting is, however, incomplete without acknowledging the significant role of accountants (and accounting education, and accounting educators) in this process. This material afforded the students with the opportunity to think about how accounting empowers those who use it; how it instils values, legitimises actions, masks discrimination and injustice and promotes the preferences of particular social orders (Baker and Bettner, 1997, p. 305).

4.1.3.1. *Students' feedback.* To obtain formal feedback on how students reflected on accounting as an element of social power, the end-of-semester feedback instrument asked: *Are the concepts and practices of accounting applied in [this subject] different to those taught in other accounting units you have studied? If so, how are they different?* Results showed that students found that the concepts and practices examined were very different to those previously studied (85% of respondents), with a range of comments including:

> ... More concepts and practices applied here gave us the opportunities to discover the uses of accounting in a broad way (either in a positive or a negative way)...

> Increased my awareness of accountings [sic] different roles and impacts on society, not just economic aspects and impacts. Opened/widened my knowledge on how accounting is and can be used by people in society to achieve their goals.

> This unit has drawn a lot of attention to me regarding current social issues and problems which [I] have never come across before. It gives a depth of understanding towards society and our living world...

In response to questions about the development of their awareness of the role of accounting in society, one student indicated that some of the material in the subject was 'too theoretical' and another said it was 'hard', but overwhelmingly students expressed in positive terms the 'challenging' nature of the material that facilitated the depth of under-standing referred to above. This feedback indicates that students found the struggle with the subject material to be a useful learning process, reflecting positively about the oppor-tunity to relate accounting-in-action to daily aspects of their own lives. Representative comments included:

> ... I like these topics because they are realistic. For example, I can jump from accounting the-ories and see how they apply in different forms.

> ... I learn [sic] more about what is 'real accounting'—its effect on society.

> It made me think back to the unit when I was watching documentaries and movies. It shows the complex picture of why they said what they said. There is always some background.

These comments reinforce our conclusion that students were both receptive to the broad socially-constructionist view of accounting, and, more importantly, could see—and experience—the connection between accounting and the wider social world.

4.2. *Research Literature*

The subject was structured around research literature in accounting and related areas, partly because of the absence of a suitable stand-alone textbook that reflected the expanded conception of accounting as being socially-constructed. In addition, textbooks often tend towards 'disciplinary insularity' (Patten and Williams, 1990) and may be dominated by illiberal, uncritical, economically rational and market-centred versions of accounting, centred on standard and standardised practices (Clarke *et al.*, 1999; Craig, Craig and Amernic, 1999).[9] It has also been suggested that reliance on textbooks is associated with a limited range of teaching methods that often reflect traditional teacher-centred didactic modes of 'instruction' based on formalised knowledge (Brown and Guilding, 1993b), providing few opportunities for student discussion, active learning, or liberal and socially critical modes of education (see Preston, 1992).

The main subject content for each week built on the core notion of social construction (drawing on Berger and Luckmann, 1984), plus two or three selected research articles (from a range of journals) for each week. The selection of suitable readings was not a straightforward task and it took considerable time and effort to assess potential articles for each topic, considering:

(1) the substantive content of the article, which needed to suit the course's aims and the specific topic in question;
(2) the 'background knowledge' required of any reader, given that most students had no prior exposure to the research literature in accounting; and
(3) the 'pitch' of the article, which had to be readable by a diverse student group (including a high proportion of students for whom English was a second language) with no prior understanding of sociological and related concepts.

The course content was not structured as a series of 'bite-sized chunks' that could be easily digested and regurgitated by students. A comprehensive outline and guide was provided for each topic, assisting students to focus their reading and to promote their analysis and critique of the materials. Questions posed in topic outlines provided a framework for broad-ranging discussions in which students could develop their own answers, build their own perspectives, and integrate their own experiences in relation to the range of problems encountered. Set 'answers' were not provided.

4.2.1. *Students' feedback.* For many of the students the presentation of different perspectives within the topics had been a challenging and enlightening experience because their prior accounting studies had been substantially technicist, uncritical and largely divorced from their own personal knowledge. Feedback responses made it clear that a proportion of students found the relatively heavy program of reading required in the subject to be quite onerous, but most attempted to 'keep up' and engage with the materials. The students' 'struggle' with the literature represented both their personal difficulties in grappling with complex arguments and discussion and what, on reflection, we have come to realise was a shortcoming in their prior accounting education.

In response to a question about how the unit could be improved, 15% of respondents suggested fewer readings; another 15% suggested 'easier' readings; while 10% of students suggested 'summaries' of readings should be provided. Nevertheless, most students clearly indicated that they had been extended in beneficial ways, and had come to appreciate both the expansion of their subject-knowledge and understanding on the one hand, and the development of a range of broadly-applicable skills, on the other hand. For example, students were asked: *What skills did you get by doing the assessment tasks in the unit?* Responses ranked improvement in writing skills as being the most significant (including technical skills such as structure, citation and referencing, for which detailed guidance was provided). Analytical, critical thinking, reading, and communication skills also featured prominently. Explanatory comments from students included:

> Writing 4500 words was a heck of a challenge. Interesting critical analysis on three or more papers was challenging as well.

> Definitely, try to write in a proper way, not just giving concepts but also critical analysis
> I learned a lot of [sic] essay writing, which I did not have to do for other units.

These comments suggest that social and critical perspectives provide an excellent forum for generic skill development.

5.0. Curriculum and Pedagogy 2: Team Teaching

From the beginning, the notion of a single 'expert' teacher was avoided (c.f. Coulson and Thomson, 2006) and the Department supported a team teaching approach which allowed every class to be facilitated by two teachers from a team of four assigned to the subject. This provided opportunities to draw on a synergistic mix of interests and expertise covering areas including environmental, social, critical, educational, indigenous, and criminological perspectives on accounting.

While team teaching may be approached in a number of ways, maximising the benefits of this approach requires *more* than just the coordination of classes, topics, and teaching activities. *Authentic* team teaching is characterised by greater collaboration and involvement between colleagues (McDaniel and Colarulli, 1997), resulting in some reduction in individual academic autonomy. However, the collective autonomy that comes to supplement individualistic approaches produces stronger and better-informed teaching and learning engagements and enhanced curricular coherence. This is, in part, because there are opportunities for teachers to learn and teach outside their own areas of specialist expertise.

We developed a teaching roster that provided for one staff member with particular expertise in each topic area to be accompanied by a second staff member who may or may not have had such expertise. Classes were organised into a one-hour interactive seminar each Thursday and a two-hour follow-up seminar each subsequent Tuesday. Some seminar time was used semi-didactically to introduce particular materials (e.g. summaries of papers or explanations of concepts and other material not included in assigned readings) but, even in this format, both lecturers contributed in a way which exposed students to differing perspectives, real-world examples, and related material from other areas. Students were also encouraged to participate actively by asking questions or offering explanations of their own understandings.[10]

5.1.1. *Benefits for Students.* The literature on team teaching suggests that there are several potential benefits of this approach for *students*. In particular, the opportunity to receive knowledge from several 'experts' and to be exposed to different perspectives on issues; and the development of critical-thinking skills, eventuating from the exposure of students to multiple perspectives and the relationship of these to a larger conceptual framework (Letterman and Dugan, 2004; Yanamandram and Noble, 2006).

The presentation of multiple perspectives in team teaching may disadvantage some students who experience frustration and confusion. However, this may be because a standard 'please the teacher' strategy (Harrigan and Vincenti, 2004) becomes unviable. The absence of a single 'correct' answer to problems and questions can also prove to be unsettling but, interestingly, only one student made mention of this in the feedback received.

5.1.2. *Students' feedback.*

Students positively responded to the diversity of perspectives presented. Asked: *Did you like the team approach to teaching in this unit? Why, why not?*, only one student responded negatively, stating that:

> The approach was different to what I am used to, at the time it felt like it was taking up too much time and not much was getting through.

While obviously disconcerted by this approach, the student conceded that the staff managed to 'put their message across'. All other respondents (95%) indicated that they found this approach interesting and worthwhile. The most common reason (cited by 40% of respondents) was that the teaching team provided different opinions and perspectives. The benefits of active discussion and interaction between staff and students were also clearly appreciated by students (30%). Some students also cited benefits in gaining 'expertise' from more than one lecturer. One student said the subject 'became frightening when the topic [was] challenging to take in', but team teaching 'allowed more interaction and more learning'. As summed up by another respondent:

> ... everybody feels free to participate and give ideas in the unit.

These comments, together with the feedback reported in section 4 of the paper, suggest that the expected benefits of team teaching outlined above were achieved.

5.1.3. *Benefits for staff.*

Staff reflections at the end of the teaching period indicated a number of benefits from participating in the team teaching process. First, collaboration between the team-members and the presence of two of the team in the class room reduced the risk of an individual team member engaging in a 'banking' model of education (discussed earlier in the paper). In the classroom, staff 'bounced' ideas off each other as well as the students, and the second teacher would often (politely) interject by asking questions, raising issues, providing elaborations, or contributing a different perspective. This meant that the material being presented did not come across as unquestionable, and a dynamic model of inquiry and questioning was actively exemplified (see Letterman and Dugan, 2004). Each team member reported that this process not only deepened his/her knowledge but also afforded a greater freedom to explore and to take risks within the classroom. Spin-off benefits for students flowed from the translation of this staff approach to a relaxed but dynamic classroom experience (Yanamandram and Noble, 2006). One student, for example, said in the final feedback that he/she:

> ... enjoyed the unit *because* it is the first time to [get] closer to the lecturer when we have classes like this. (Emphasis added.)

Active participation was facilitated by organising students into small discussion groups, assisted and guided by roving staff members, although it remained somewhat difficult to conduct interactive discussions at the level of the entire class, largely for reasons of students' cultural background and prior academic experience.

The collaborative model also obviated the normally isolated experience of teaching and facilitated a deepening of relationships between team members (Yanamandram and Noble,

2006). Each team member was committed not only to the subject as an important endeavour in his/her teaching activities, but also to the provision of a more challenging (and, therefore, rewarding) education experience for students (see Harrigan and Vincenti, 2004). All staff worked collaboratively in the development of syllabus materials, and all team members were prepared to submit their work to the critique of others and to offer constructive suggestions. The pooling of knowledge and resources (Letterman and Dugan, 2004), the constant interactions, and the willingness to contribute to others were important in deepening the relationships among the team members.

The spreading of teaching workload implicit in the above provided natural 'breathing spaces' within the teaching period, thus maintaining enthusiasm and energy. Overall, the combination of a team of staff with differing but complementary research expertise and an ongoing collegial process of mutual mentoring produced both an appreciation and practise of the social context of research and teaching. This resulted in a situation of educational praxis where teaching was informed by research in an ongoing, dynamic, active, and reflexive way.

6.0. Conclusions: Lessons Learned, Reflections and Implications

Despite decades of attempts to reform accounting education, the expanding array of technical and regulatory requirements continues to dominate (Humphrey, 2005), and has been magnified by the contemporary managerialist and corporatist turn within universities (Tinker and Gray, 2003; Merino, 2006). This state of affairs comes as no surprise to those who accept the view that '[i]t is not the consciousness of men that determines their being, but, on the contrary, their social being that determines their consciousness' (Marx, 1970). Just as accounting plays a role in the construction and maintenance of social institutions, in its traditional forms it shapes the conceptions that educators themselves generally hold and reproduce in their students.

At the conclusion of the semester's teaching, we distilled our critical reflections into several key factors central to the success of the subject. The *first* key factor related to the nature and content of the subject itself and its broader socio-political relevance. The social *and* critical orientation of the subject allowed a critique *of* accounting and imagination of alternative possibilities *for* accounting. In seeking to balance the humanistic and formative dimensions of education, we took inspiration from The *Principles for Responsible Management Education* (UN Global Compact, 2007; 2008b), connecting accounting with the aspiration for an 'inclusive and sustainable global economy'. At the same time, a broader social and environmental perspective opened up a critique of these very concepts. This was an essential inclusion, given our understanding of knowledge as socially, historically, and contextually grounded, and our commitment to a public perspective on 'educating and forming the new generations' (Gramsci, 1971, p. 30).

The *second* key factor was collegiality amongst the teaching team, which involved the devotion of considerable time and resources both to individual preparation and discussion of content, teaching strategy, and assessment modes and standards. A key challenge for the lecturer formally in charge of the course was to ensure that the team members were rostered so as to best utilise their strengths whilst complementing other team members and keeping a smooth flow to the succession of topics within the subject. The cooperation of the team did not amount to 'groupthink' in any sense, because there was significant productive challenge and critique to balance the support offered. This authentic experience of team teaching stands in contrast to the isolated and pressurised experience that teaching has become for many (Churchman, 2002; Parker, 2002). The fact that no staff member was left to fend for him or herself fostered a significant level of harmony within the team.

By utilising interdisciplinary strengths, the team teaching approach generated professional benefits for staff which had significant spin-off benefits for students. Our reflective assessment is that the outcomes rewarded the devotion of more resources in terms of staff time and effort, from both the Department and the individuals concerned. This stands as a reminder that aspirations to improve the quality of learning and teaching carry resource implications; quality is much more than a spare-time add-on.

A *third* factor integral to the course experience was the fact that the team members were enthused by the opportunity to experiment with an innovative approach to teaching. The prior teaching experiences (a combined total of more than 70 years) of all team members had often been characterised by very large cohorts of students (see footnote 2) with little variation in either the method of delivery or course content. Based on students' feedback and staff reflections, we conclude that social and critical perspectives are central to the development of capacities for critical thought which are vital for educated and engaged citizens. The relationship between course content and real-world, real-life issues was integral to the encouragement and nurturing of deep and elaborative learning. By drawing on lived experiences, the subject content was made meaningful.

We accept that a singular experience of innovation will not overcome the malaise that afflicts accounting education in many quarters (c.f. Albrecht and Sack 2000; Amernic and Craig, 2004). However, truly active learning can only exist if education is related to life (Gramsci, 1971). In accounting, this means that students must be given the opportunity to develop their abilities to articulate clearly different perspectives, views, ideas, and concepts. Ultimately, students must be equipped to develop their own personal and collective positions on accounting issues, and to discover possibilities for activating those positions through praxis.

Accounting education change must encompass the content and practice of classroom activity, but it also requires change to the self-consciousness of all actors involved. This paper shows how the development of social, critical, environmental and ethical perspectives in accounting education provides an opportunity for impact. These areas are often not given serious consideration by accounting departments, but this omission is to the detriment of a well-rounded education. Support for their development is required from Accounting Department Heads, accounting faculty, professional accounting bodies, and accreditation agencies.

As Mayper *et al.* (2005, p. 53) observe, '[w]e know that accounting impacts our everyday life, and our duty is to have our students deliberate about the impact of accounting on society'. Individual facts are not to be learnt merely for their 'immediate practical or professional end' (Gramsci, 1971, p. 37). The ultimate 'end' of accounting education—as with any process of education—is 'the interior development of personality, the formation of character ...' (Gramsci, 1971, p. 37). Whether as teachers or students, through accounting education we should be empowered to learn to *be* ourselves and to *know* ourselves consciously.

Acknowledgements

The authors are grateful for the feedback received from participants at the 6th Australasian CSEAR conference in Wellington, New Zealand; the Second Innovation in Accounting and Corporate Governance Education Conference in Hobart, Australia; the 19th International Congress on Social and Environmental Accounting Research in St Andrews, UK; and from the journal's reviewers.

Notes

[1]The force of this imperative remains, even though such calls for responsible business and accounting in the public interest may be based on very narrow conceptions of the public interest, and operate more at the rhetorical rather than the practical level (Davids and Boyce, 2005; Boyce, 2008; Dellaportas and Davenport, 2008).

[2]Macquarie University has one of the largest university accounting and finance departments in Australia. When the new elective subject was in its development phase in 2005, the Department taught 3,365 equivalent full-time undergraduate and postgraduate students studying in several different degrees, including programs recognised as satisfying the tertiary education entry qualifications for the major Australian professional accounting bodies. At the time the new subject was first offered in 2006, the Department's programmes were taught and managed by 55 full-time staff and over 100 part-time, casual, and adjunct staff. The four authors were all employed at Macquarie University at the time, and they formed the teaching team for the subject.

[3]The Department's experience showed that, although a large number of accounting graduates seek employment in the profession, a significant proportion either do not go on to undertake professional qualification programs and/or do not go on to employment in the accounting industry.

[4]Unfortunately, an apparent bureaucratic mishap led to the exclusion of this subject from published programmes. This resulted in a relatively small group of 25 students electing to take the subject (a larger number of students were enrolled initially, but 25 students kept their enrolments current past the 'census date' at which they become liable for student fees, contributions, and charges (four weeks into the semester). Most of the enrolled students had generally poor academic records reflected in a mean Grade Point Average of just 1.14 (a Grade Point Average of 2.0 represents a clear pass average). The teaching team was not deterred by the academic history of the students, instead viewing this as a challenge to ensure that the subject content was relevant to these students and presented in such a way as to provide them with opportunities that they may not have had previously.

[5]*The Principles for Responsible Management Education* were developed under the auspices of the United Nations Global Compact, which ostensibly seeks to 'align business operations and strategies everywhere with ten universally accepted principles in the areas of human rights, labour, environment and anti-corruption' (UN Global Compact 2008a, p. 2). The Principles are stated to be 'a global call to transform curricula, research and teaching methodologies on the basis of universally recognized values of sustainability, social responsibility and good corporate citizenship' (UN Global Compact 2008b, p. 2). We accept as valid many of the criticisms of the Global Compact, particularly its perpetuation of problematic market doctrines (c.f. Merino, 2006), its contentment with aspirational statements, its inherent voluntarism (these factors contrast the Global Compact with comparable initiatives that deal with corporate rights rather than responsibilities, such as World Trade Association rules and the aborted Multilateral Agreement on Investment), and the failure to produce significant (non-rhetorical) outcomes (see Bakan, 2004; Bailey, Harte and Sugden, 2000; Utting, 2007).

[6]Note that assessment strategies were considered as part of the overall learning and teaching in the subject, and were constructively aligned to the curricular elements discussed in this paper (see Lucas, 2001). Detailed consideration of specific assessment strategies is beyond the scope of this paper.

[7]Thus it *does* matter *what* you teach (c.f. Thomson and Bebbington, 2004).

[8]Some students' responses encompassed both areas.

[9]Ferguson, Collison, Power and Stevenson (2005) found that the interests of shareholders and management dominated accounting texts. Heavy reliance on prescribed textbooks constrains the conception of appropriate accounting knowledge and diminishes the educational space for critical analysis of extant theory and practice (Brown and Guilding, 1993a). Ferguson *et al.* (2005, p. 42) concluded that 'accounting academics must resist the single perspective presented in textbooks . . . and provide alternative perspectives' in order to develop critical thinkers and active independent learners.

[10]Since this approach worked well, at the end of the semester a decision was taken to increase class contact time for the next offering of the subject to four (2×2) hours per week, providing extra time for discussion, debate, and explanation.

References

ACCA (2005) *Global Insight into Responsible Business: ACCA's World-Class Research Programme* (London: Association of Chartered Certified Accountants).

Accounting Education Change Commission (1990) Objectives of Education for Accountants: Position Statement Number One, *Issues in Accounting Education*, 5(2), pp. 307–312.

Albrecht, W. S. and Sack, R. J. (2000) *Accounting Education: Charting the Course through a Perilous Future. Accounting Education Series, Number 16* (Sarasota: American Accounting Association).

Amernic, J. and Craig, R. (2004) Reform of accounting education in the post-Enron era: moving accounting 'out of the shadows', *Abacus*, 40(3), pp. 342–378.

Anderson, G. (2006) Carving out time and space in the managerial university, *Journal of Organizational Change Management*, 19(5), pp. 578–592.

Andon, P., Chong, K. M. and Roebuck, P. (2010) Personality preferences of accounting and non-accounting graduates seeking to enter the accounting profession, *Critical Perspectives on Accounting*, 21(4), pp. 253–265.

Annisette, M. (2004) The true nature of the World Bank, *Critical Perspectives on Accounting*, 15(3), pp. 303–323.

Arnold, P. and Hammond, T. (1994) The role of accounting in ideological conflict: lessons from the South African divestment movement, *Accounting, Organizations and Society*, 19(2), pp. 111–126.

Aronowitz, S. (2000) *The Knowledge Factory: Dismantling the Corporate University and Creating True Higher Learning* (Boston: Beacon Press).

Aronowitz, S. and Giroux, H. A. (1993) *Education Still Under Siege* (Westport, Connecticut: Bergin & Garvey).

ASCPA and ICAA (1996) *Guidelines for joint administration of accreditation of tertiary courses by the professional accounting bodies* (Melbourne and Sydney: Institute of Chartered Accountants in Australia and Australian Society of Certified Practising Accountants).

Augier, M. and March, J. G. (2007) The pursuit of relevance in management education, *California Management Review*, 49(3), pp. 129–146.

Bailey, D., Harte, G. and Sugden, R. (2000) Corporate disclosure and the deregulation of international investment, *Accounting, Auditing and Accountability Journal*, 13(2), pp. 197–218.

Bakan, J. (2004) *The Corporation: the Pathological Pursuit of Profit and Power* (New York: Free Press).

Baker, C. R. and Bettner, M. S. (1997) Interpretive and critical research in accounting: a commentary on its absence from mainstream accounting research, *Critical Perspectives on Accounting*, 8(4), pp. 293–310.

Bebbington, J. (1995) Teaching social and environmental accounting: a review essay, *Accounting Forum*, 19(2–3), pp. 263–264.

Bebbington, J. (1997) Engagement, education and sustainability: a review essay on environmental accounting, *Accounting, Auditing and Accountability Journal*, 10(3), pp. 365–381.

Bebbington, J., Brown, J., Frame, B. and Thomson, I. (2007) Theorizing engagement: the potential of a critical dialogic approach, *Accounting, Auditing and Accountability Journal*, 20(3), pp. 356–381.

Bebbington, J. and Gray, R. (2001) An account of sustainability: failure, success and a reconceptualization, *Critical Perspectives on Accounting*, 12(5), pp. 557–587.

Bedford, N., Batholemew, E. E., Bowsher, C. A., Brown, A. L., Davidson, S., Horngren, C. *et al.* (1986) Future accounting education: preparing for the profession (The special report of the American Accounting Association Committee on the Future Structure, Content, and Scope of Accounting Education), *Issues in Accounting Education*, 1(1), pp. 168–195.

Berger, P. and Luckmann, T. (1984) *The Social Construction of Reality: A Treatise in the Sociology of Knowledge* (Harmondsworth: Pelican).

Blundell, L. and Booth, P. (1988) Teaching innovative accounting topics: student reaction to a course in social accounting, *Accounting and Finance*, 28(1), pp. 75–85.

Booth, P., Luckett, P. and Mladenovic, R. (1999) The quality of learning in accounting education: The impact of approaches to learning on academic performance, *Accounting Education: an international journal*, 8(4), pp. 277–300.

Booth, P. and Winzar, H. (1993) Personality biases of accounting students: some implications for learning style preferences, *Accounting and Finance*, 33(2), pp. 109–120.

Borg, C., Buttigieg, J. and Mayo, P. (Eds) (2002) *Gramsci and Education. Culture and Politics Series* (Lanham, Maryland: Rowman & Littlefield).

Boyce, G. (1999) Computer-assisted teaching and learning in accounting: pedagogy or product? *Journal of Accounting Education*, 17(2–3), pp. 191–220.

Boyce, G. (2000) Public discourse and decision-making: exploring possibilities for financial, social, and environmental accounting, *Accounting, Auditing and Accountability Journal*, 13(1), pp. 27–64.

Boyce, G. (2002) Now and then: revolutions in higher learning, *Critical Perspectives on Accounting*, 13(5–6), pp. 575–601.

Boyce, G. (2004) Critical accounting education: teaching and learning outside the circle, *Critical Perspectives on Accounting*, 15(4–5), pp. 565–586.

Boyce, G. (2008) The social relevance of ethics education in a global(ising) era: from individual dilemmas to system crises, *Critical Perspectives on Accounting*, 19(2), pp. 255–290.

Boyce, G., Williams, S., Kelly, A. and Yee, H. (2001) Fostering deep and elaborative learning and generic (soft) skill development: the strategic use of case studies in accounting education, *Accounting Education: an international journal*, 10(1), pp. 37–60.

Briggs, S. P., Copeland, S. and Haynes, D. (2007) Accountants for the 21st century, where are you? A five-year study of accounting students' personality preferences, *Critical Perspectives on Accounting*, 18(5), pp. 511–537.

Brown, R. B. and Guilding, C. (1993a) Knowledge and the academic accountant: an empirical study, *Journal of Accounting Education*, 11(1), pp. 1–13.

Brown, R. B. and Guilding, C. (1993b) A survey of teaching methods employed in university business school accounting courses, *Accounting Education: an international journal*, 2(3), pp. 211–218.

Burbules, N. C. (2000) P.P. Trifonas (ed.), *The limits of dialogue as a critical pedagogy. Revolutionary Pedagogies: Cultural Politics, Instituting Education, and the Discourse of Theory*, pp. 251–273 (New York: RoutledgeFalmer).

Bush, B. and Maltby, J. (2004) Taxation in West Africa: transforming the colonial subject into the 'governable person', *Critical Perspectives on Accounting*, 15(1), pp. 5–34.

Catchpowle, L., Cooper, C. and Wright, A. (2004) Capitalism, states and accounting, *Critical Perspectives on Accounting*, 15(8), pp. 1037–1058.

Charles, E. (2006) Dirty money, *In the Black*, 76(2), pp. 32–36.

Chew, A. and Greer, S. (1997) Contrasting world views on accounting: accountability and aboriginal culture, *Accounting, Auditing and Accountability Journal*, 10(3), pp. 276–298.

Christensen, M. (2004) Accounting by words not numbers: the handmaiden of power in the academy, *Critical Perspectives on Accounting*, 15(4–5), pp. 485–512.

Chua, W. F. (1996) Teaching and learning only the language of numbers—monolingualism in a multilingual world, *Critical Perspectives on Accounting*, 7(2), pp. 129–156.

Chua, W. F. (1998) Historical allegories: let us have diversity, *Critical Perspectives on Accounting*, 9(6), pp. 617–628.

Churchman, D. (2002) Voices of the academy: academics' responses to the corporatizing of academia, *Critical Perspectives on Accounting*, 13(5–6), pp. 643–656.

Chwastiak, M. (1998) Star Wars at the bottom line: the accounting forum for defense contractors, *Accounting, Organizations and Society*, 23(4), pp. 343–360.

Clarke, F. L., Craig, R. J. and Amernic, J. H. (1999) Theatre and intolerance in financial accounting research, *Critical Perspectives on Accounting*, 10(1), pp. 65–88.

Coben, D. (1998) *Radical Heroes: Gramsci, Freire and the Politics of Adult Education* (New York: Garland).

Cooper, C. (1995) Ideology, hegemony and accounting discourse: a case study of the National Union of Journalists, *Critical Perspectives on Accounting*, 6(3), pp. 175–209.

Cooper, C., Neu, D. and Lehman, G. (2003) Globalization and its discontents: a concern about growth and globalization, *Accounting Forum*, 27(4), pp. 359–364.

Cooper, D. and Tinker, T. (1998) Accounting in a post-work era: editorial foreword, *Critical Perspectives on Accounting*, 9(1), pp. 1–3.

Coulson, A. B. and Thomson, I. (2006) Accounting and sustainability, encouraging a dialogical approach; integrating learning activities, delivery mechanisms and assessment strategies, *Accounting Education: an international journal*, 15(3), pp. 261–273.

Craig, R. J., Clarke, F. L. and Amernic, J. H. (1999) Scholarship in university business schools: Cardinal Newman, creeping corporatism and farewell to the 'disturber of the peace'? *Accounting, Auditing and Accountability Journal*, 12(5), pp. 510–524.

Crotty, M. (1998) *The Foundations of Social Research: Meaning and Perspective in the Research Process* (Sydney: Allen & Unwin).

Davids, C. and Boyce, G. (2005) D. Crowther, R. Jatana (Eds). *An Abrogation of Social and Ethical Responsibility: Conflicts of Interest in Professional Accounting. Social Responsibility in India*, pp. 6–14 (Leicester: Social Responsibility Research Network).

Dean, M. (1999) *Governmentality: Power and Rule in Modern Society* (London: Sage).

Dellaportas, S. and Davenport, L. (2008) Reflections on the public interest in accounting, *Critical Perspectives on Accounting*, 19(7), pp. 1080–1098.

Dillard, J. F. and Tinker, T. (1996) Commodifying business and accounting education: the implications of accreditation, *Critical Perspectives on Accounting*, 7(1–2), pp. 215–225.

Doost, R. K. and Fishman, T. (2004) Beyond Arthur Andersen: searching for answers, *Managerial Auditing Journal*, 19(5), pp. 623–639.

English, L., Luckett, P. and Mladenovic, R. (2004) Encouraging a deep approach to learning through curriculum design, *Accounting Education: an international journal*, 13(4), pp. 461–488.

Everett, J. (2003) Globalization and its new spaces for (alternative) accounting research, *Accounting Forum*, 27(4), pp. 400–424.

Ferguson, J., Collison, D., Power, D. and Stevenson, L. (2005) What are recommended accounting textbooks teaching students about corporate stakeholders? *British Accounting Review*, 37(1), pp. 23–46.

Financial Action Task Force (2005) *Money Laundering and Terrorist Financing Typologies* (Paris: OECD).

Freire, P. (1996) *Pedagogy of the Oppressed* (London: Penguin).

Freire, P. (1998) *Pedagogy of Freedom: Ethics, Democracy, and Civic Courage* (Lanham, Maryland: Rowman & Littlefield).

Gentile, M. C. and Samuelson, J. (2003) *The State of Affairs for Management Education and Social Responsibility* (New York: Aspen Institute).

Gibson, K. (1997) Courses on environmental accounting, *Accounting, Auditing and Accountability Journal*, 10(4), pp. 584–593.

Giroux, H. A. (1988) *Teachers as Intellectuals: Toward a Critical Pedagogy of Learning* (Granby, Massachusetts: Bergin and Garvey).

Giroux, H. A. (2002) C. Borg, J. Buttigieg and P. Mayo (Eds), *Rethinking Cultural Politics and Radical Pedagogy in the Work of Antonio Gramsci. Gramsci and Education*, pp. 41–66 (Lanham, Maryland: Rowman & Littlefield).

Giroux, H. A. (2003) Selling out higher education, *Policy Futures in Education*, 1(1), pp. 179–200.

Glass, R. D. (2001) On Paulo Freire's philosophy of praxis and the foundations of liberation education, *Educational Researcher*, 30(2), pp. 15–25.

Gow, L., Kember, D. and Cooper, B. (1994) The teaching context and approaches to study of accountancy students, *Issues in Accounting Education*, 9(1), pp. 118–130.

Graham, C. and Neu, D. (2003) Accounting for globalization, *Accounting Forum*, 27(4), pp. 449–471.

Gramsci, A. (1971) *Selections from the Prison Notebooks* (London: Lawrence and Wishart).

Gray, R. (2006) Social, environmental and sustainability reporting and organisational value creation? Whose value? Whose creation? *Accounting, Auditing and Accountability Journal*, 19(6), pp. 793–819.

Gray, R., Bebbington, J. and McPhail, K. (1994) Teaching ethics in accounting and the ethics of accounting teaching: educating for immorality and a possible case for social and environmental accounting education, *Accounting Education: an international journal*, 3(1), pp. 51–75.

Gray, R., Bebbington, J. and Walters, D. (1993) *Accounting for the Environment (The Greening of Accountancy, Part II)* (London: Paul Chapman).

Gray, R. and Collison, D. (2002) Can't see the wood for the trees, can't see the trees for the numbers? Accounting education, sustainability and the public interest, *Critical Perspectives on Accounting*, 13(5–6), pp. 797–836.

Gray, R., Owen, D. and Adams, C. (1996) *Accounting & Accountability: Changes and Challenges in Corporate Social and Environmental Reporting* (London: Prentice Hall).

Grinnell, D. J. and Hunt, H. G. (2000) Development of an integrated course in accounting: a focus on environmental issues, *Issues in Accounting Education*, 15(1), pp. 19–42.

Guthrie, J. (2010) *Time for Action: Challenges Facing Accounting Higher Education* (Sydney: Institute of Chartered Accountants in Australia).

Hall, M., Ramsay, A. and Raven, J. (2004) Changing the learning environment to promote deep learning approaches in first-year accounting students, *Accounting Education: an international journal*, 13(4), pp. 489–505.

Harrigan, A. and Vincenti, V. (2004) Developing higher-order thinking through an intercultural assignment: a scholarship of teaching inquiry project, *College Teaching*, 52(3), pp. 113–120.

Haynes, K. (2006) Linking narrative and identity construction: using autobiography in accounting research, *Critical Perspectives on Accounting*, 17(4), pp. 399–418.

Hazelton, J. and Haigh, M. (2010) Incorporating sustainability into accounting curricula: lessons learnt from an action research study, *Accounting Education: an international journal*, 19(1–2), pp. 159–178.

Hines, R. D. (1988) Financial accounting: in communicating reality, we construct reality, *Accounting, Organizations and Society*, 13(3), pp. 251–261.

Hines, R. D. (1989) The sociopolitical paradigm in financial accounting research, *Accounting, Auditing and Accountability Journal*, 2(1), pp. 52–76.

Hopwood, B., Mellor, M. and O'Brien, G. (2005) Sustainable development: mapping different approaches, *Sustainable Development*, 13(1), pp. 38–52.

Horniachek, D. (2008) Reflections on Amernic and Craig: a note, *Abacus*, 44(3), pp. 310–316.

Howieson, B. (2003) Accounting practice in the new millennium: is accounting education ready to meet the challenge? *British Accounting Review*, 35(2), pp. 69–103.

Humphrey, C. (2005) In the aftermath of crisis: reflections on the principles, values and significance of academic inquiry in accounting: Introduction, *European Accounting Review*, 14(2), pp. 341–351.

IFAC (1994) *2000 and Beyond: A Strategic Framework for Prequalification Education for the Accountancy Profession in the Year 2000 and Beyond* (New York: International Federation of Accountants).

Ivanitz, M. and McPhail, K. (2003) I. Holland and J. Fleming (Eds), *ATSIC: Autonomy or accountability? Government Reformed: Values and New Political Institutions*, pp. 185–201 (Burlington, Vermont: Ashgate).

Kemp, S. (2010) Enhancing graduate skills by incorporating sustainability into accounting education, *Journal of the Asia Pacific Centre for Environmental Accountability*, 16(1), pp. 3–14.

Kovar, S. E., Ott, R. L. and Fisher, D. G. (2003) Personality preferences of accounting students: a longitudinal case study, *Journal of Accounting Education*, 21(2), pp. 75–94.

Lehman, C. R. (1995) *Accounting's Changing Role in Social Conflict* (Princeton and London: Markus Wiener and Paul Chapman).

Letterman, M. R. and Dugan, K. B. (2004) Team teaching a cross-disciplinary honors course: preparation and development, *College Teaching*, 52(2), pp. 76–80.

Leung, P. and Cooper, B. J. (2003) The Mad Hatter's corporate tea party, *Managerial Auditing Journal*, 18(6–7), pp. 505–511.

Lodhia, S. (2010) Teaching a sustainability accounting course in an Australian university: insights for sustainability accounting education, *Journal of the Asia Pacific Centre for Environmental Accountability*, 16(1), pp. 15–22.

Low, M., Davey, H. and Hooper, K. (2008) Accounting scandals, ethical dilemmas and educational challenges, *Critical Perspectives on Accounting*, 19(2), pp. 222–254.

Lucas, U. (1996) Student approaches to learning—a literature guide, *Accounting Education: an international journal*, 5(1), pp. 87–98.

Lucas, U. (1997) Active learning and accounting educators, *Accounting Education: an international journal*, 6(3), pp. 189–190.

Lucas, U. (2001) Deep and surface approaches to learning within introductory accounting: a phenomenographic study, *Accounting Education: an international journal*, 10(2), pp. 161–184.

Marton, F. and Säljö, R. (1976a) On qualitative differences in learning: I—Outcome and process, *British Journal of Educational Psychology*, 46(1), pp. 4–11.

Marton, F. and Säljö, R. (1976b) On qualitative differences in learning—II. Outcome as a function of the learner's conception of the task, *British Journal of Educational Psychology*, 46(2), pp. 115–127.

Marx, K. (1970) *A Contribution to the Critique of Political Economy* (London: Lawrence and Wishart).

Mayo, P. (1999) *Gramsci, Freire and Adult Education: Possibilities for Transformative Action* (London and New York: Zed).

Mayo, P. (2008) Antonio Gramsci and his relevance for the education of adults, *Educational Philosophy and Theory*, 40(3), pp. 418–435.

Mayper, A. G., Pavur, R. J., Merino, B. D. and Hoops, W. (2005) The impact of accounting education on ethical values: an institutional perspective, *Accounting and the Public Interest*, 5, pp. 32–55.

McDaniel, E. A. and Colarulli, G. C. (1997) Collaborative teaching in the face of productivity concerns: the dispersed team model, *Innovative Higher Education*, 22(1), pp. 19–36.

McLaren, P. and Leonard, P. (Eds) (1993) *Paulo Freire: A critical encounter* (London: Routledge).

McPhail, K. (2001) The dialectic of accounting education: From role identity to ego identity, *Critical Perspectives on Accounting*, 12(4), pp. 471–499.

Merino, B. (2006) Financial scandals: another clarion call for educational reform—A historical perspective, *Issues in Accounting Education*, 21(4), pp. 363–381.

Merino, B. D. (1998) Critical theory and accounting history: challenges and opportunities, *Critical Perspectives on Accounting*, 9(6), pp. 603–616.

Middleton, D. (2010) Building a core of principles, *The Australian*, 12 May, p. 32.

Miller, P. (1994) A.G. Hopwood, P. Miller (Eds) *Accounting as Social and Institutional Practice: An Introduction. Accounting as Social and Institutional Practice* (Cambridge: Cambridge University Press).

Miller, P. and O'Leary, T. (1987) Accounting and the construction of the governable person, *Accounting, Organizations and Society*, 12(3), pp. 235–265.

Miller, P. and Rose, N. (1990) Governing economic life, *Economy and Society*, 19(1), pp. 1–31.

Moore, D. C. (1991) Accounting on trial: the critical legal studies movement and its lessons for radical accounting, *Accounting, Organizations and Society*, 16(8), pp. 763–791.

Munro, R. and Mouritsen, J. (Eds) (1996) *Accountability: Power, Ethos and the Technologies of Managing* (London: International Thompson Business Press).

Neimark, M. K. (1996) Caught in the squeeze: an essay on higher education in accounting, *Critical Perspectives on Accounting*, 7(1), pp. 1–11.

Neu, D. (2000) 'Presents' for the 'Indians': land, colonialism and accounting in Canada, *Accounting, Organizations and Society*, 25(2), pp. 163–184.

Neu, D. and Taylor, A. (1996) Accounting and the politics of divestment, *Critical Perspectives on Accounting*, 7(4), pp. 437–460.

Neu, D. and Therrien, R. (2003) *Accounting for Genocide: Canada's Bureaucratic Assault on Aboriginal People* (Black Point, Nova Scotia: Fernwood).

Newman, J. H. (1996) *The Idea of a University* (New Haven: Yale University Press).

O'Dwyer, B., Unerman, J. and Hession, E. (2005) User needs in sustainability reporting: perspectives of stakeholders in Ireland, *European Accounting Review*, 14(4), pp. 759–787.

Owen, D. (2005) CSR after Enron: a role for the academic accounting profession? *European Accounting Review*, 14(2), pp. 395–404.

Owen, D. L., Swift, T. A., Humphrey, C. and Bowerman, M. (2000) The new social audits: accountability, managerial capture or the agenda of social champions? *European Accounting Review*, 9(1), pp. 81–98.

Parker, L. D. (2001) Back to the future: the broadening accounting trajectory, *British Accounting Review*, 33(4), pp. 421–453.

Parker, L. D. (2002) It's been a pleasure doing business with you: a strategic analysis and critique of university change management, *Critical Perspectives on Accounting*, 13(5–6), pp. 603–619.

Patten, R. J and Williams, D. Z. (1990) There's trouble—right here in our accounting programs: the challenge to accounting educators, *Issues in Accounting Education*, 5(2), pp. 175–179.

Preston, N. (1992) Computing and teaching: a socially-critical view, *Journal of Computer Assisted Learning*, 8, pp. 49–56.

Ravenscroft, S. and Williams, P. F. (2004) Considering accounting education in the USA post-Enron, *Accounting Education: an international journal*, 13(Suppl. 1), pp. 7–23.

Ravenscroft, S. and Williams, P. F. (2005) Rules, rogues, and risk assessors: academic responses to Enron and other accounting scandals, *European Accounting Review*, 14(2), pp. 363–372.

Reiter, S. A. (1998) Economic imperialism and the crisis in financial accounting research, *Critical Perspectives on Accounting*, 9(2), pp. 143–171.

Review Committee of the Accounting Discipline in Higher Education (1990) Accounting in Higher Education: Report of the Review of the Accounting Discipline in Higher Education, Volume 1: Main Report and Recommendations (Canberra: Australian Government Publishing Service).

Richardson, A. J. (1987) Accounting as a legitimating institution, *Accounting, Organizations and Society*, 12(4), pp. 341–355.

Robson, K. (1991) On the arenas of accounting change: the process of translation, *Accounting, Organizations and Society*, 16(5–6), pp. 247–570.

Roslender, R. and Dillard, J. F. (2003) Reflections on the interdisciplinary perspectives on acounting project, *Critical Perspectives on Accounting*, 14(3), pp. 325–351.

Saravanamuthu, K. (2004) Gold-collarism in the academy: the dilemma in transforming bean-counters into knowledge consultants, *Critical Perspectives on Accounting*, 15(4–5), pp. 587–607.

Saravanamuthu, K. and Filling, S. (2004) A critical response to managerialism in the academy, *Critical Perspectives on Accounting*, 15(4–5), pp. 437–452.

Saravanamuthu, K. and Tinker, T. (2002) The university in the new corporate world, *Critical Perspectives on Accounting*, 13(5–6), pp. 545–554.

Scapens, R. W. (1990) Researching management accounting practice: the role of case study methods, *British Accounting Review*, 22(3), pp. 259–281.

Schaltegger, S. and Burritt, R. (2000) *Contemporary Environmental Accounting: Issues, Concepts and Practice* (Sheffield: Greenleaf).

Schmeck, R. R. (1983) Learning styles of college students. in R. Dillon and R. R. Schmeck (Eds.) *Individual Differences in Cognition*. Vol. 1, pp. 233–279 (New York: Academic Press).

Thomson, I. and Bebbington, J. (2004) It doesn't matter what you teach? *Critical Perspectives on Accounting*, 15(4–5), pp. 609–628.

Thomson, I. and Bebbington, J. (2005) Social and environmental reporting in the UK: a pedagogic evaluation, *Critical Perspectives on Accounting*, 16(5), pp. 507–533.

Tinker, A. M. (1980) Towards a political economy of accounting: an empirical illustration of the Cambridge Controversies, *Accounting, Organizations and Society*, 5(1), pp. 147–160.

Tinker, T. (1985) *Paper Prophets: A Social Critique of Accounting* (New York: Praeger).

Tinker, T. (1991) The accountant as partisan, *Accounting, Organizations and Society*, 16(3), pp. 297–310.

Tinker, T. (2004) 'The end of business schools?' More than meets the eye, *Social Text*, 22(2), pp. 67–80.

Tinker, T. and Carter, C. (2003) Spectres of accounting: contradictions or conflicts of interest? *Organization*, 10(3), pp. 577–582.

Tinker, T. and Gray, R. (2003) Beyond a critique of pure reason: from policy to politics to praxis in environmental and social research, *Accounting, Auditing and Accountability Journal*, 16(5), pp. 727–761.

Tinker, T. and Koutsoumadi, A. (1997) A mind is a wonderful thing to waste: 'think like a commodity', become a CPA, *Accounting, Auditing and Accountability Journal*, 10(3), pp. 454–467.

Tinker, T. and Koutsoumadi, A. (1998) The accounting workplace: a joyless future? *Accounting Forum*, 21(3–4), pp. 289–316.

Tregidga, H. and Milne, M. J. (2006) From sustainable management to sustainable development: a longitudinal analysis of a leading New Zealand environmental reporter, *Business Strategy and the Environment*, 15(4), pp. 219–241.

UN Global Compact (2007) *The Principles for Responsible Management Education* (New York: United Nations).

UN Global Compact (2008a) *Corporate Citizenship in the World Economy: United Nations Global Compact* (New York: United Nations).

UN Global Compact (2008b) *A Global Initiative—A Global Agenda: Principles for Responsible Management Education* (New York: United Nations).

Unerman, J. and Bennett, M. (2004) Increased stakeholder dialogue and the internet: towards greater corporate accountability or reinforcing capitalist hegemony? *Accounting, Organizations and Society*, 29(7), pp. 685–707.

Utting, P. (2007) CSR and equality, *Third World Quarterly*, 28(4), pp. 697–712.

Williams, P. F. (2004) You reap what you sow: the ethical discourse of professional accounting, *Critical Perspectives on Accounting*, 15(6–7), pp. 995–1001.

Wright, A. (2006) *Organised Crime* (Cullompton, Devon, UK: Willan).

Yanamandram, V. and Noble, G. (2006) Student experiences and perceptions of team-teaching in a large undergraduate class, *Journal of University Teaching and Learning Practice*, 3(1), pp. 49–66.

Young, J. (2005) Changing our questions: reflections on the corporate scandals, *Accounting and the Public Interest*, 5, pp. 1–13.

Appendix 1: Contents of Student Feedback Instrument

Learning Outcomes

(a)   Did you like the team approach to teaching in this unit? Why or why not?

(b)   Did this unit develop your awareness of the role of accounting in society? If so, how?

(c)   Are the concepts and practices of accounting applied in [this subject] different to those taught in other accounting units which you have studied? If so, how are they different?

Content of Unit

(d)   Which of the topics did you find the most interesting, and why?

Assessment Tasks

(e)   What skills did you get by doing the assessment tasks in this unit?

(f)   Did you find the feedback from the assessment tasks useful? Why or why not?

General

(g)   What changes can we make to improve the unit?

Appendix 2: Topic and Resource List

• Theories and Concepts for Social and Critical Perspectives on Accounting
  Berger and Luckmann (1984, ch 1); Hines (1988); Miller (1994); Crotty (1998, chs. 3, 6

and 7); Hines (1989); Chua (1996); Richardson (1987); Catchpowle, Cooper and Wright (2004).

- Sustainability Accounting, Environmental Accounting, Corporate Social Responsibility
Hopwood, Mellor and O'Brien (2005); Tregidga and Milne (2006); O'Dwyer, Unerman and Hession (2005); Owen, Swift, Humphrey and Bowerman (2000); Unerman and Bennett (2004).
- Accounting and Crime
Charles (2006); Financial Action Task Force (Financial Action Task Force 2005: Part I); Wright (2006, ch. 3).
- Accounting and Imperialism
Annisette (2004); Bush and Maltby (2004); Neu (2000).
- Accounting and Indigenous Peoples
Chew and Greer (1997); Ivanitz and McPhail (2003); Neu and Therrien (2003, ch. 8); Neu (2000).
- Accounting and Neoliberal Government(ality)
Dean (1999, ch. 1); Bush and Maltby (2004); Neu (2000).
- The Intersection between Globalisation and Accounting
Graham and Neu (2003); Boyce (2002); Cooper, Neu and Lehman (2003); Everett (2003); Boyce (2008).

Index

Note: Page numbers in **bold** type refer to figures
Page numbers in *italic* type refer to tables
Page numbers followed by 'n' refer to notes

sustainability 493–4
Sweeney, B.: and Costello, F. 425–47
Sydney University (Australia) 273, 277–9,
280n, 284, 297
Szabo, A.: and Underwood, J. 483

Tait, H.: and Entwistle, N.J. 76, 477–8
Tan, K.: and Choo, F. 39
Tanzania 113, 115–16, 119, 121, 123, 125–7
tax: laws 12
Taylor, D.W.: and Desai, R. 451
Teacher Learning and Development Unit
(TLDU) 389, 403
teachers: concept mapping used as 358; and
lecturers in East Africa 114, 126; meta
programmes results 257–62, 258, 263
teaching: approaches 38–41, 39, 50, 89, 92–4,
96–8, 130–8, 134, 159, 170, 173–4, 500,
509; boredom 40–1; case studies use 181–2;
and computing 38; consequentialism 47;
contexts 89–90, 92, 94–5, 493, 501; core 47;
development 74, 75, 130, 166–8, 173–4,
177; education and training 35; ethical
maturity 36, 38, 42–3, 45–6; ethical
reasoning 44–5, 44, 47, 50–2, 51; ethics 35–
59; failure within 36, 41, 164–7, 411, 494;
feedback from students 500, 504–5, 507,
516; grading 111–12, 470, 477; lack of
enforcement 475–6; learner centered
methods 155–6, 158, 159, 161, 163–5, 169–
70, 173–4; learning context 270; learning
orientations 39–40, 40; learning processes
271; meta programmes within 254, 264–5;
motivation and development 178; non
reflective practices 166–7; peer-assisted
learning 93, 96–7; perceptions 297–8, 298,
305, 306, 307–8; practitioners 23, 32, 35,
50, 61; prizes 165; problem-based learning
92–3, 95–6; promotion criteria 163–5, 170;
quality 304, 307–8, 312–13, 508–9;
reflection of performance 413; sabbatical
leave 166; support mechanisms 160, 162–6,
173; as team 506–9; technical 107;
techniques acquisition 35, 92, 97–8, 163;
theory 38; traditional techniques 86, 89;
unfamiliarity with resources 167–8, see also
assessment; examinations; tests; learning
team teaching 506–9
technology 229–30, 235n; and plagiarism 474,
477–8, 484–5, see also internet technology
Telfer, R.: and Biggs, J.B. 272
tertiary accounting education: obstacles to
learner-centred approaches 154–75
Test of English as a Foreign Language
(TOEFL) 475

tests 460; nonparametric 157–8; Test of
English as a Foreign Language (TOEFL)
475
textbooks: authors 338–40, 339, 341–2; as
cultural and political artifacts 332–49, 342
Thatcher, Margaret 260, 344
theory 340; learning and concept mapping
352–3, 362, 364
Thompson, J.B. 337
Thomson, A. 64
Thorne, P.: Bannister, P. and Ashworth, P. 472
Times Higher Education 456
Tinker, T. 7; and Dillard, J.F. 501
Tocher, K. 5
Tomkins, C.: and Groves, R.E.C. 8
training 35, 61, 68; of trainers (TOT) 113,
115–16, 118–19, 126
training programmes: East Africa 117–18,
121, 125–7; and ethics integration 330
Trevino, K.L.: and McCabe, D.L. 472
Trigwell, K.: and Prosser, M. 150, 298, 300
Tschudi, F.: and Hackner, E. 359
Tyson, T. 26

Uganda 113, 115–16, 119, 121, 123, 125–7
Umapathy, S. 308
uncertainty: student 182, 187, 188 90
undergraduate courses: degree 23–4, 28–9,
31–2, 35, 73, 82, 90, 163, 264, 339, 470;
financial accounting 386–424; senior 1, 105
undergraduates: accounting and business
students 425–47
Underwood, J.: and Szabo, A. 483
Underwood, S. 210
United Kingdom (UK): accounting bodies
60, 473; British Institute of Management
(BIM) 61; Chartered Association of
Certified Accountants (ACCA) 61–4;
Chartered Institute of Management
Accountants (CIMA) 61; Chartered
Institute of Public Finance and
Accountancy (CIPFA) 61; Council for
National Academic Awards (CNAA) 91;
East Africa imports from 113–29;
educational institutions 475; financial
statements 43; financial theory component
361; government 237; Indian society 15;
London School of Economics (LSE) 210,
237; management training 61; Nottingham
Trent University 80; plagiarism 472;
University of Hull 352
United Nations Educational Scientific and
Cultural Organization (UNESCO) 117,
334
United States of America (USA): accounting
studies within 24–5, 448–50; American
Accounting Association (AAA) 215, 224;

www.routledge.com/9780415699204

Personal Transferable Skills in Accounting Education

Edited by Kim Watty, Beverley Jackling and Richard M. S. Wilson

The development of generic skills (often referred to as 'soft skills') in accounting education has been a focus of discussion and debate for several decades. During this time employers and professional bodies have urged accounting educators to consider and develop curricula which provide for the development and assessment of these skills. In addition, there has been criticism of the quality of accounting graduates and their ability to operate effectively in a global economy. Embedding generic skills in the accounting curriculum has been acknowledged as an appropriate means of addressing the need to provide 'knowledge professionals' to meet the needs of a global business environment.

This book was originally published as a special issue of *Accounting Education: an international journal*.

January 2012: 246 x 174: 192pp
Hb: 978-0-415-69920-4
£80 / $125